Teacher's Edition

Realidades B

    realidades.com

Digital Edition

Peggy Palo Boyles
OKLAHOMA CITY, OK

Myriam Met
ROCKVILLE, MD

Richard S. Sayers
LONGMONT, CO

Carol Eubanks Wargin

PEARSON

Boston, Massachusetts | Chandler, Arizona
Glenview, Illinois | Upper Saddle River, New Jersey

WE DEDICATE THIS BOOK TO THE
MEMORY OF OUR ESTEEMED COLLEAGUE,
Carol Eubanks Wargin.

Front cover, left: Teen girl
Center left: La Boca neighborhood, Buenos Aires, Argentina
Center right: Boats at Xochimilco, Mexico City, Mexico
Right: Decorated ox cart, Sarchí, Costa Rica

Copyright © 2014 Pearson Education, Inc., or its affiliates. All Rights Reserved. Printed in the United States of America. This publication is protected by copyright, and permission should be obtained from the publisher prior to any prohibited reproduction, storage in a retrieval system, or transmission in any form or by any means, electronic, mechanical, photocopying, recording, or likewise. For information regarding permissions, write to Rights Management & Contracts, Pearson Education, Inc., One Lake Street, Upper Saddle River, New Jersey 07458.

Pearson, Prentice Hall, Pearson Prentice Hall, PresentationExpress, and eText™ are trademarks, in the U.S. and/or other countries, of Pearson Education, Inc., or its affiliates.

ExamView® is a registered trademark of eInstruction Corporation.

Pre-AP* is a registered trademark of the College Board. Use of the trademark implies no relationship, sponsorship, endorsement, sale, or promotion on the part of Pearson Education, Inc., or its affiliates.

PEARSON

ISBN-13: 978-0-13-319950-5
ISBN-10: 0-13-319950-9

3 4 5 6 7 8 9 10 V0UD 17 16 15 14

Professional Development Handbook

Realidades B

realidades.com

Digital Edition

Table of Contents

realidades.com Get started on **realidades.com**!

Now that you have purchased Realidades ©2014,
follow these steps to set up a new account:

a. Go to **realidades.com** and click "Register."
b. Select the account type you need.
c. Provide your School Code or use the search tool to find it.
d. Follow directions to complete registration.

**For Video Modules and other implementation
support, visit:**

my PearsonTraining.com

• Video Modules and PDFs for product training

Realidades, Research, and the Standards

Realidades is based on the belief that the purpose of learning Spanish is to communicate with the people who speak it and to understand their cultures. *Realidades* presents a fresh, exciting approach to Spanish by making language learning real for today's students.

. . . .

Topics covered:

▶ *Realidades* and Research-based Instruction

▶ Achieving the Standards with *Realidades*

REALIDADES and the Common Core State Standards

The *Common Core State Standards for English Language Arts and Literacy in History/Social Studies, Science, and Technology Subjects* define general, cross-disciplinary literacy expectations to ensure that all students are prepared for success in college or workforce training programs. These Standards contain four strands: Reading, Writing, Speaking and Listening, and Language.

Teachers using *REALIDADES* can be assured that they are supporting the Common Core Standards. Look for the National Standards for Language Learning correlations within a chapter as evidence of support:
- Reading: 1.2, 2.1, 2.2, 3.1, 3.2, 4.1, 4.2, 5.1
- Writing: 1.3, 2.1, 2.2, 3.1, 3.2, 4.1, 4.2, 5.1
- Speaking and Listening: 1.1, 1.3, 2.1, 2.2, 3.2, 4.1, 5.2

ⓒ You'll also find this icon next to Common Core activities in the *¡Adelante!* section.

Realidades and Research-based Instruction

Realidades reflects the most current research on how students learn languages and what teachers and materials need to do to help them become proficient language users. Let's take a look at some of the basic premises about language and language learning.

Communication

Communication is an authentic exchange of information for a real purpose between two or more people. By this we mean that people tell each other (through speech or writing) something the other person doesn't already know.

Communicating meaning has several aspects. Students need to listen to and read Spanish in order to interpret intended meanings. Students need to express meaning by conveying their own messages for a purpose and to a real audience. They also need to negotiate meaning through the natural give-and-take involved in understanding and making oneself understood. Research tells us that classroom activities must provide students practice in interpreting, expressing, and negotiating meaning through extensive and frequent peer interactions.

Throughout *Realidades,* students are engaged in understanding messages, in sending their own messages, and thus in communicating real ideas and real meanings for real purposes.

Comprehensible input

Research states that students learn best when they have ample opportunities to internalize meanings before they have to produce them. In other words, comprehension precedes production. The term "comprehensible input" suggests that learners acquire language by understanding what they hear and read. Students need many opportunities to match what they hear with visual cues (pictures, video, or teacher pantomime) or experiences (physical actions). Reading input should be supported by a close connection between text and visuals. All these strategies for comprehensible input help students associate meaning with forms.

In keeping with this research, *Realidades* begins each chapter of Levels 1–3 with a section called *A primera vista*. These four pages of language input give students opportunities to comprehend new language before producing it. The visualized presentation of vocabulary in context, the reading input in the *Videohistoria,* and the listening input in the *A primera vista* video segment provide a wide range of comprehensible input of new language that addresses all students and all learning styles.

Practice activities

Research tells us that students need extensive practice using new language to create and convey their own messages. The *Manos a la obra* section in Levels 1–3 provides a wide range of practice activities. New vocabulary and grammar are first practiced in skill-getting activities that provide concrete practice. This basic practice helps to develop accuracy in using the language and prepares students to transition into more communicative tasks. In the transitional activities that follow the basic practice, students work with a partner or in small groups with information- or opinion-gap activities that are characteristic of real-life communication. Students then continue on to more open-ended, personalized speaking or writing tasks.

> **"Communication is an authentic exchange of information for a real purpose between two or more people."**

Meaningful context in language learning

All effective learning is rooted in a meaningful context. We know from research that information is most likely to be retained when it is connected to other information in a meaningful way. Thus, language learning is most successful and retention more likely when we present new language organized into topics or by situations.

Realidades is organized into themes. All material in a chapter—vocabulary, grammar, culture—is rooted in a context and used meaningfully. Students engage in communicative tasks that are relevant to their lives. Students work with readings, realia, photography, and art that are authentic to the Spanish-speaking world. The video programs and Internet links show native speakers engaged in real-life situations and experiences.

Understanding grammar

Students learn grammar most effectively when it is presented and practiced in a meaningful context and when it connects to real communication needs. Students also benefit when shown how the patterns of grammar work.

In *Realidades,* new structures are foreshadowed through lexical presentation (grammar is presented as vocabulary) in the *Vocabulario en contexto* language input section in Levels 1–3. In addition, early vocabulary activities in the *Vocabulario en uso* section have students work with the grammar lexically. This allows students to see the grammar and work with it in a meaningful context before being formally presented with the rules or paradigms.

Grammar is formally presented with clear explanations and examples in the *Gramática* section in Levels 1–3. Comparisons between English and Spanish grammar are made whenever possible. Students then practice the grammar concepts in a variety of tasks that range from concrete activities that focus primarily on the structures to more open-ended tasks that focus on communication.

To further facilitate the learning of grammar, *Realidades* offers *GramActiva,* a multi-modality approach to grammar that includes grammar videos and hands-on grammar activities. By teaching and practicing grammar through different learning styles, more students will be able to learn grammar.

Building cultural perspectives

The *Standards for Foreign Language Learning* have expanded how culture is taught in today's classroom. We want students to understand the *why* (perspectives) of culture that determines the *what* (products and practices).

The approach to culture in *Realidades* not only teaches students the *what* but asks students to explore the *why*. Cultural products, practices, and comparisons are presented throughout *Realidades* in features such as *Arte y cultura, Fondo cultural, La cultura en vivo,* and *Perspectivas del mundo hispano,* and in *Realidades 3, Puente a la cultura.* Students read information about cultures that offer different perspectives and they are asked questions that encourage them to think and make observations about cultures.

Strategies for Success

Research shows that effective learners know how to help themselves become successful learners. One way they do this is by using specific problem-solving strategies.

Realidades teaches students strategies to be effective communicators whether listening, speaking, reading, or writing. Each reading selection in Levels 1–3 is supported by a reading strategy. Each performance-based task in Levels 1–3 includes a useful strategy that connects to a step-by-step approach that helps students plan, rehearse, and present or publish. Each also includes a rubric so students know how they might be evaluated.

We know more than ever about how foreign languages are learned. *Realidades* is based on solid research in second-language acquisition, on accepted theories about the teaching of culture, and on sound pedagogical practices that are common to all disciplines. We are sure that you and your students will find this an exciting, motivating, and enormously successful approach to learning Spanish.

Achieving the Standards with *Realidades*

The *Standards for Foreign Language Learning* provide an important and useful framework to guide the teaching and learning of foreign languages. This framework should result in a new generation of language learners prepared to meet the demand for competence in other languages that our nation will face in an increasingly interdependent world.

Realidades is written based upon the Standards. This means that instruction used in *Realidades* will help students develop the competencies delineated in the *Standards for Foreign Language Learning.* Teachers will find a correlation to the Standards at the beginning of each chapter and with the notes that accompany each activity (if appropriate) in the Teacher's Edition.

Goal 1: Communication

1.1 (Interpersonal): Each chapter provides a wide range of paired and group activities. Students speak with a partner, work in small groups, and interview classmates.

1.2 (Interpretive): *Realidades* builds the interpretive listening skill through the Audio Program. This program in Levels 1–3 supports activities in the Student Edition (input checks, dictations, listening comprehension, and test preparation) and the *Writing, Audio, & Video* section of the *Communication Workbook.* The Video Program also develops listening through the different language, grammar, and storyline mystery video segments.

Realidades provides extensive support for the interpretive reading skill. Students read throughout the chapter: comprehensible input, practice activities, realia, culture notes, and reading selections. Reading is seamlessly integrated with practice and anchored in real-life contexts. Whenever possible, readings are supported by focused strategies.

1.3 (Presentational): Each chapter in Levels 1–2 ends with a performance-based task: in the "A" chapters, a speaking task, in the "B" chapters a presentation writing task. Both presentations are supported by strategies and the speaking or writing process, step-by-step support to help students successfully complete the task.

Goal 2: Culture

2.1 (Practices and Perspectives) and **2.2** (Products and Perspectives): Each chapter in *Realidades* explores a cultural theme through a wide range of practices, products, and perspectives. Students see authentic culture through realia, art, photographs, popular sayings, tongue twisters, rhymes and songs, hands-on projects, readings, and authentic literature. In addition, the unique *Fondo cultural* readings in Levels 1–3 generally include a Standards-based critical thinking question.

Goal 3: Connections

3.1 (Cross-curricular Connections): *Realidades* integrates cross-curricular activities (*Conexiones*) within the *Manos a la obra section* in Levels 1–3. Students make connections to a variety of disciplines through activities that integrate the language of the chapter.

3.2 (Connections to Target Culture): *Realidades* exposes students to perspectives only available within the target culture through art, realia, pronunciation activities, and readings.

Goal 4: Comparisons

4.1 (Language Comparisons): *Realidades* enables students to see comparisons between languages in both the grammar explanations in the text and *GramActiva* videos, and in a unique section called *Exploración del lenguaje* in Levels 1–2. Students learn to look for language connections, to understand how language works, and to integrate these new skills as they continue in their study of Spanish.

4.2 (Cultural Comparisons): *Realidades* is rich in cultural comparisons. A unique feature called *Fondo cultural* in Levels 1–3 generally informs students about a cultural product or practice and is followed by a question that challenges students to think critically and make comparisons between cultures.

Goal 5: Communities

5.1 (Outside the Classroom): *Realidades* provides informative features called *El español en la comunidad* and *El español en el mundo del trabajo* in Levels 1–3. These sections help students see how to use Spanish beyond the classroom, in their communities, and in the world of work.

5.2 (Lifelong Learners): For a textbook to help students achieve this goal, it must motivate students to want to communicate and want to learn more about the culture. The core of *Realidades*—real language, real culture, real tasks—motivates students. The video programs and other technology support engage learners in ways that may encourage them to continue their exploration of the Spanish language and cultures.

Standards for Foreign Language Learning

Goal 1: Communicate in Languages Other Than English

- Standard 1.1: Students engage in conversation, provide and obtain information, express feelings and emotions, and exchange opinions.
- Standard 1.2: Students understand and interpret written and spoken language on a variety of topics.
- Standard 1.3: Students present information, concepts and ideas to an audience of listeners or readers on a variety of topics.

Goal 2: Gain Knowledge and Understanding of Other Cultures

- Standard 2.1: Students demonstrate an understanding of the relationship between the practices and perspectives of the culture studied.
- Standard 2.2: Students demonstrate an understanding of the relationship between the products and perspectives of the culture studied.

Goal 3: Connect with Other Disciplines and Acquire Information

- Standard 3.1: Students reinforce and further their knowledge of other disciplines through the foreign language.
- Standard 3.2: Students acquire information and recognize the distinctive viewpoints that are only available through the foreign language and its cultures.

Goal 4: Develop Insight into the Nature of Language and Culture

- Standard 4.1: Students demonstrate understanding of the nature of language through comparisons of the language studied and their own.
- Standard 4.2: Students demonstrate understanding of the concept of culture through comparisons of the cultures studied and their own.

Goal 5: Participate in Multilingual Communities at Home and Around the World

- Standard 5.1: Students use the language both within and beyond the school setting.
- Standard 5.2: Students show evidence of becoming life-long learners by using the language for personal enjoyment and enrichment.

Program Organization

Realidades is a communication-based six-level series with a full range of print and technology components that allow teachers to meet the needs of the different students in today's Spanish classroom.

Middle School

Realidades A and ***B*** are separate middle school books that meet the needs of the younger learners. Each Student Edition provides the same content of ***Realidades 1*** but has been adapted with new art, photographs, and activities that are age-appropriate for the younger learner. Students completing ***Realidades B*** will make a smooth transition into ***Realidades 2***.

High School

Each high school Student Edition provides the complete curriculum for one year of instruction. The spiraling of themes and extensive recycling of content allows for smooth articulation between levels. Students completing ***Realidades 3 and 4*** will have a solid foundation for advanced Spanish study.

Realidades A
• Introductory section ***Para empezar***
• Temas 1–4

Realidades B
• Review section ***Para empezar***
• Temas 5–9

Realidades 1
• Introductory section ***Para empezar***
• Temas 1–9

Realidades 2
• Review section ***Para empezar***
• Temas 1–9

Realidades 3
• Review section ***Para empezar***
• Capítulos 1–10

Realidades 4
• Capítulos 1–12

Chapter Organization

▶ Temas

Realidades B begins with an introductory section followed by nine units, called *Temas*.
Each *Tema* is divided into two chapters.

Tema	Capítulo	
Para empezar	1. Mis amigos y yo 2. La escuela 3. La comida 4. Los pasatiempos	
	A	**B**
5: Fiesta en familia	5A: *Una fiesta de cumpleaños*	5B: *¡Vamos a un restaurante!*
6: La casa	6A: *En mi dormitorio*	6B: *¿Cómo es tu casa?*
7: De compras	7A: *¿Cuánto cuesta?*	7B: *¡Qué regalo!*
8: Experiencias	8A: *De vacaciones*	8B: *Ayudando en la comunidad*
9: Medios de comunicación	9A: *El cine y la televisión*	9B: *La tecnología*

▶ Chapters

Each chapter in *Realidades* is built around a clear sequence of instruction.

Chapter Section	Pedagogical support
A primera vista • Vocabulario en contexto • Videohistoria	Provides comprehensible language input for the chapter's new vocabulary and grammar within an authentic context. Input includes words, dialogues, narration, visuals, audio, and video. Students' language production focuses on comprehension and limited production.
Manos a la obra • Vocabulario en uso • Gramática	Provides productive language practice with a variety of concrete, transitional, and open-ended activities. The activities develop all four language skills and focus on relevant language tasks. Many activities build off of authentic documents, *realia,* and photographs.
¡Adelante! • Lectura • La cultura en vivo / Perspectivas del mundo hispano • Presentación oral/escrita	Provides culminating theme-based activities that have students apply what they have learned. The section features a culturally-based reading, performance-based speaking or writing tasks, cultural activities, and the storyline mystery video *¿Eres tú, María?*
Repaso del capítulo • Vocabulario y gramática • Preparación para el examen	Provides complete support for the end-of-chapter assessment. One page summarizes what students need to know (vocabulary and grammar). The second page outlines the proficiency and culture sections of the test by describing the task, providing a practice task, and referring students to chapter activities for review.

▶ **Scope and Sequence** | **Articulation**

Realidades offers a completely articulated Scope and Sequence across all levels. The recursive themes allow for the recycling, review, and reteaching of vocabulary and grammar.

Realidades 1

Tema	Capítulo
Para empezar	• En la escuela: greetings; introductions; leave-takings; numbers; time; body parts • En la clase: classroom, dates, asking for help • El tiempo: weather, seasons

Tema	A	B
1: Mis amigos y yo	**1A ¿Qué te gusta hacer?** Vocabulary: activities and expressions for saying what you like and don't like to do Grammar: infinitives; making negative statements	**1B Y tú, ¿cómo eres?** Vocabulary: adjectives and vocabulary to ask about and describe someone's personality Grammar: adjectives; definite and indefinite articles; word order
2: La escuela	**2A Tu día en la escuela** Vocabulary: classroom items and furniture; parts of the classroom; prepositions of location Grammar: subject pronouns; the present tense of -ar verbs	**2B Tu sala de clases** Vocabulary: classroom items and furniture; parts of the classroom; prepositions of location Grammar: the verb estar; plurals of nouns and articles
3: La comida	**3A ¿Desayuno o almuerzo?** Vocabulary: foods; beverages; adverbs of frequency; expressions to show surprise Grammar: present tense of -er and -ir verbs; me gusta(n), me encanta(n)	**3B Para mantener la salud** Vocabulary: food; beverages; expressions to discuss health; expressions to discuss preferences, agreement, disagreement, and quantity; adjectives to describe food Grammar: the plural of adjectives; the verb ser
4: Los pasatiempos	**4A ¿Adónde vas?** Vocabulary: leisure activities; places; expressions to tell where and with whom you go; expressions to talk about when things are done Grammar: the verb ir; interrogative words	**4B ¿Quieres ir conmigo?** Vocabulary: leisure activities; feelings; expressions for extending, accepting, and declining invitations; expressions to tell when something happens Grammar: ir + a + infinitive; the verb jugar
5: Fiesta en familia	**5A Una fiesta de cumpleaños** Vocabulary: family and parties Grammar: the verb tener; possessive adjectives	**5B ¡Vamos a un restaurante!** Vocabulary: describing people and ordering a meal Grammar: the verb venir; the verbs ser and estar
6: La casa	**6A En mi dormitorio** Vocabulary: bedroom items; electronic equipment; colors; adjectives to describe things Grammar: comparisons and superlatives; stem-changing verbs: poder and dormir	**6B ¿Cómo es tu casa?** Vocabulary: rooms in a house and household chores Grammar: affirmative tú commands; the present progressive tense
7: De compras	**7A ¿Cuánto cuesta?** Vocabulary: clothing; shopping; numbers 200–1,000 Grammar: stem-changing verbs: pensar, querer, and preferir; demonstrative adjectives	**7B ¡Qué regalo!** Vocabulary: places to shop; gifts; accessories; buying and selling Grammar: preterite of -ar, -car, and -gar verbs; direct object pronouns lo, la, los, las
8: Experiencias	**8A De vacaciones** Vocabulary: vacation places; activities; modes of transportation Grammar: preterite of -er and -ir verbs; preterite of ir; the personal a	**8B Ayudando en la comunidad** Vocabulary: recycling and volunteer work; places in a community Grammar: the verb decir; indirect object pronouns; preterite of hacer and dar
9: Medios de comunicación	**9A El cine y la televisión** Vocabulary: television shows; movie genres; giving opinions Grammar: acabar de + infinitive; gustar and similar verbs	**9B La tecnología** Vocabulary: computers; communication; computer-related activities Grammar: the verbs pedir and servir; saber and conocer

Scope and Sequence

Realidades A and B provide the same Scope and Sequence as *Realidades 1*.

Realidades A covers the same content as the *Para empezar* section and *Temas* 1–4.

Tema	Capítulo
Para empezar	• En la escuela: greetings; introductions; leave-takings; numbers; time; body parts • En la clase: classroom, dates, asking for help • El tiempo: weather, seasons

A / **B**

Tema	Capítulo (A)	Capítulo (B)
1: Mis amigos y yo	**1A ¿Qué te gusta hacer?** Vocabulary: activities and expressions for saying what you like and don't like to do. Grammar: infinitives; making negative statements	**1B Y tú, ¿cómo eres?** Vocabulary: adjectives and vocabulary to ask about and describe someone's personality. Grammar: adjectives; definite and indefinite articles; word order
2: La escuela	**2A Tu día en la escuela** Vocabulary: classroom items and furniture; parts of the classroom; prepositions of location. Grammar: subject pronouns; the present tense of -ar verbs	**2B Tu sala de clases** Vocabulary: classroom items and furniture; parts of the classroom; prepositions of location. Grammar: the verb estar; plurals of nouns and articles
3: La comida	**3A ¿Desayuno o almuerzo?** Vocabulary: foods; beverages; adverbs of frequency; expressions to show surprise. Grammar: present tense of -er and -ir verbs; me gusta(n), me encanta(n)	**3B Para mantener la salud** Vocabulary: food; beverages; expressions to discuss health; expressions to discuss preferences, agreement, disagreement, and quantity; adjectives to describe food. Grammar: the plural of adjectives; the verb ser
4: Los pasatiempos	**4A ¿Adónde vas?** Vocabulary: leisure activities; places; expressions to tell where and with whom you go; expressions to talk about when things are done. Grammar: the verb ir; interrogative words	**4B ¿Quieres ir conmigo?** Vocabulary: leisure activities; feelings; expressions for extending, accepting, and declining invitations; expressions to tell when something happens. Grammar: ir + a + infinitive; the verb jugar

Realidades B provides a review section called *Para empezar* and continues with *Temas* 5–9.

Tema	Capítulo (A)	Capítulo (B)
5: Fiesta en familia	**5A Una fiesta de cumpleaños** Vocabulary: family and parties. Grammar: the verb tener; possessive adjectives	**5B ¡Vamos a un restaurante!** Vocabulary: describing people and ordering a meal. Grammar: the verb venir; the verbs ser and estar
6: La casa	**6A En mi dormitorio** Vocabulary: bedroom items; electronic equipment; colors; adjectives to describe things. Grammar: comparisons and superlatives; stem-changing verbs: poder and dormir	**6B ¿Cómo es tu casa?** Vocabulary: rooms in a house and household chores. Grammar: affirmative tú commands; the present progressive tense
7: De compras	**7A ¿Cuánto cuesta?** Vocabulary: clothing; shopping; numbers 200–1,000. Grammar: stem-changing verbs: pensar, querer, and preferir; demonstrative adjectives	**7B ¡Qué regalo!** Vocabulary: places to shop; gifts; accessories; buying and selling. Grammar: preterite of -ar, -car, and -gar verbs; direct object pronouns lo, la, los, las
8: Experiencias	**8A De vacaciones** Vocabulary: vacation places; activities; modes of transportation. Grammar: preterite of -er and -ir verbs; preterite of ir; the personal a	**8B Ayudando en la comunidad** Vocabulary: recycling and volunteer work; places in a community. Grammar: the verb decir; indirect object pronouns; preterite of hacer and dar
9: Medios de comunicación	**9A El cine y la televisión** Vocabulary: television shows; movie genres; giving opinions. Grammar: acabar de + infinitive; gustar and similar verbs	**9B La tecnología** Vocabulary: computers; communication; computer-related activities. Grammar: the verbs pedir and servir; saber and conocer

Realidades 2 uses a recursive Scope and Sequence that revisits the themes from *Realidades A, B,* or *1.* This natural recycling allows for important review and reteaching. In addition, students expand their vocabulary, grammar, and cultural understanding as they revisit each theme in greater depth.

Realidades 2

Tema	Capítulo	
Para empezar	**A.** ¿Cómo eres tú? *Repaso:* describing people; asking for information; nationalities; adjective agreement; the verb *ser*	
	B. ¿Qué haces? *Repaso:* leisure activities; seasons of the year; regular *-ar, -er,* and *-ir* verbs	
	A	**B**
1: Tu día escolar	**1A ¿Qué haces en la escuela?** Vocabulary: classroom items, activities, and rules Grammar: *(Repaso)* stem-changing verbs; affirmative and negative words	**1B ¿Qué haces después de las clases?** Vocabulary: extracurricular activities Grammar: making comparisons; *(Repaso)* the verbs *saber* and *conocer; hace* + time expressions
2: Un evento especial	**2A ¿Cómo te preparas?** Vocabulary: daily routines, getting ready for an event Grammar: reflexive verbs; *(Repaso)* the verbs *ser* and *estar;* possessive adjectives *mío, tuyo, suyo*	**2B ¿Qué ropa compraste?** Vocabulary: shopping vocabulary, prices, money Grammar: *(Repaso)* the preterite of regular verbs; demonstrative adjectives
3: Tú y tu comunidad	**3A ¿Qué hiciste ayer?** Vocabulary: running errands; locations in a downtown; items purchased Grammar: *(Repaso)* direct object pronouns; the irregular preterite of the verbs *ir, ser, hacer, tener, estar, poder*	**3B ¿Cómo se va . . . ?** Vocabulary: places in a city or town; driving terms; modes of transportation Grammar: *(Repaso)* direct object pronouns: *me, te, nos;* irregular affirmative *tú* commands; *(Repaso)* present progressive: irregular forms
4: Recuerdos del pasado	**4A Cuando éramos niños** Vocabulary: toys; play terms; describing children Grammar: the imperfect tense: regular verbs and irregular verbs; *(Repaso)* indirect object pronouns	**4B Celebrando los días festivos** Vocabulary: expressions describing etiquette; holiday and family celebrations Grammar: the imperfect tense: describing a situation; reciprocal actions
5: En las noticias	**5A Un acto heroico** Vocabulary: natural disasters; emergencies; rescues; heroes Grammar: the imperfect tense: other uses; the preterite of the verbs *oír, leer, creer,* and *destruir*	**5B Un accidente** Vocabulary: parts of the body; accidents; events in the emergency room Grammar: the irregular preterites: *venir, poner; decir, traer;* the imperfect progressive and preterite
6: La televisión y el cine	**6A ¿Viste el partido en la televisión?** Vocabulary: watching television programs; sporting events Grammar: the preterite of *-ir* stem-changing verbs; other reflexive verbs	**6B ¿Qué película has visto?** Vocabulary: movies; making a movie Grammar: verbs that use indirect objects; the present perfect
7: Buen provecho	**7A ¿Cómo se hace la paella?** Vocabulary: cooking expressions; food; appliances; following a recipe; giving directions in a kitchen Grammar: negative *tú* commands; the impersonal *se*	**7B ¿Te gusta comer al aire libre?** Vocabulary: camping and cookouts; food Grammar: *Usted* and *ustedes* commands; uses of *por*
8: Cómo ser un buen turista	**8A Un viaje en avión** Vocabulary: visiting an airport; planning a trip; traveling safely Grammar: the present subjunctive; irregular verbs in the subjunctive	**8B Quiero que disfrutes de tu viaje** Vocabulary: staying in a hotel; appropriate tourist behaviors; traveling in a foreign city Grammar: the present subjunctive with impersonal expressions; the present subjunctive of stem-changing verbs
9: ¿Cómo será el futuro?	**9A ¿Qué profesión tendrás?** Vocabulary: professions; making plans for the future; earning a living Grammar: the future tense; the future tense of irregular verbs	**9B ¿Qué haremos para mejorar el mundo?** Vocabulary: environment; environmental issues and solutions Grammar: the future tense: other irregular verbs; the present subjunctive with expressions of doubt

Realidades 3 offers ten thought-provoking thematic chapters that integrate rich vocabulary groups and a thorough presentation of grammar. Chapter activities combine communication, culture, and cross-curricular content with authentic literature and poetry.

Realidades 3

Capítulo	Each thematic chapter is divided into two sections. Each of these sections (1 and 2) present and practice vocabulary and grammar.	
Para empezar	1. Tu vida diaria *Repaso:* daily routines; school life; leisure activities; present tense verbs; reflective verbs 2. Días especiales *Repaso:* weekend activities; celebrations; special events; verbs like *gustar:* possessive adjectives	
	1	**2**
1: Un día inolvidable	**Vocabulary:** hiking objects, activities, and perils; weather **Grammar:** *(Repaso)* preterite verbs with the spelling change *i–y;* *(Repaso)* preterite of irregular verbs; *(Repaso)* preterite of verbs with the spelling change *e–i* and *o–u*	**Vocabulary:** getting ready for an athletic or academic competition; emotional responses to competition; awards and ceremonies **Grammar:** *(Repaso)* the imperfect; uses of the imperfect
2: ¿Cómo te expresas?	**Vocabulary:** describing art and sculpture; tools for painting; describing what influences art **Grammar:** *(Repaso)* the preterite vs. the imperfect; *estar* + participle	**Vocabulary:** musical instruments; describing dance; describing drama **Grammar:** *(Repaso) ser* and *estar;* verbs with special meanings in the preterite vs. the imperfect
3: ¿Qué haces para estar en forma?	**Vocabulary:** nutrition; illnesses and pains; medicine; habits for good health **Grammar:** *(Repaso)* affirmative *tú* commands; *(Repaso)* affirmative and negative commands with *Ud.* and *Uds.*	**Vocabulary:** exercises; getting and staying in shape; health advice **Grammar:** *(Repaso)* the subjunctive: regular verbs; *(Repaso)* the subjunctive: irregular verbs; *(Repaso)* the subjunctive with stem changing *-ar* and *-er* verbs
4: ¿Cómo te llevas con los demás?	**Vocabulary:** personality traits; interpersonal behavior; friendship **Grammar:** *(Repaso)* the subjunctive with verbs of emotion; *(Repaso)* the uses of *por* and *para*	**Vocabulary:** expressing and resolving interpersonal problems; interpersonal relationships **Grammar:** commands with *nosotros;* possessive pronouns
5: Trabajo y comunidad	**Vocabulary:** after-school work; describing a job **Grammar:** *(Repaso)* the present perfect; *(Repaso)* the past perfect	**Vocabulary:** volunteer activities; the benefits and importance of volunteer work **Grammar:** the present perfect subjunctive; demonstrative adjectives and pronouns
6: ¿Qué nos traerá en el futuro?	**Vocabulary:** jobs and professions; qualities of a good employee **Grammar:** *(Repaso)* the future; *(Repaso)* the future of probability	**Vocabulary:** technology; inventions; jobs in the future **Grammar:** the future perfect; *(Repaso)* the use of direct and indirect object pronouns
7: ¿Mito o realidad?	**Vocabulary:** archaeological terms and activities; describing archaeological sites **Grammar:** the present and past subjunctive in expressions of doubt	**Vocabulary:** myths and legends; ancient beliefs; pre-Columbian scientific discoveries **Grammar:** the subjunctive in adverbial clauses
8: Encuentro entre culturas	**Vocabulary:** architecture and history of Spain **Grammar:** the conditional	**Vocabulary:** Spain in the Americas; the encounter between Cortés and the Aztecs; family heritage **Grammar:** the past subjunctive; the past subjunctive with *si* clauses
9: Cuidemos nuestro planeta	**Vocabulary:** caring for the environment **Grammar:** present subjunctive with conjunctions (*mientras, tan pronto como,* etc.); relative pronouns *que, quien, lo que*	**Vocabulary:** environmental issues; endangered animals **Grammar:** present subjunctive with other conjunctions (*a menos que, sin que, para que,* etc.)
10: ¿Cuáles son tus derechos y responsabili-dades?	**Vocabulary:** rights and responsibilties **Grammar:** the passive voice: *ser* + past participle; the present vs. the past subjunctive	**Vocabulary:** government; the role of government; individual rights **Grammar:** the past perfect subjunctive; the conditional perfect

Program Organization

▶ Scope and Sequence

Realidades 4 offers twelve thought-provoking thematic chapters that integrate unique and thorough scope and sequence, careful progression of activities, and a wealth of authentic literature, songs, and paintings by renowned artists from the Spanish-speaking world.

Realidades 4

Capítulo	Each thematic chapter is divided into two sections. Each of these parts (1 and 2) present and practice vocabulary and grammar.	
	Primera parte	**Segunda parte**
1: Esas modas que van y vienen	Vocabulary: fashion trends and fads Grammar: the preterit tense; the imperfect tense	Vocabulary: the influence of fashion on cars Grammar: preterit vs. imperfect
2: La tecnología y el progreso	Vocabulary: environmental issues affecting your world Grammar: uses of *ser, estar,* and *haber;* the future tense	Vocabulary: professions and activities in the future Grammar: the subjunctive in noun clauses
3: Los derechos humanos	Vocabulary: human rights and foreign policy Grammar: indirect commands	Vocabulary: the work of charitable organizations Grammar: direct and indirect object pronouns and the personal *a; gustar* and similar verbs
4: El individuo y la personalidad	Vocabulary: personality and routines Grammar: reflexive constructions	Vocabulary: discussing personality Grammar: agreement, form, and position of adjectives; the past participle and the present perfect indicative and subjunctive
5: Las relaciones personales	Vocabulary: styles of communication and relationships with friends and family Grammar: subjunctive vs. indicative in adjective clauses	Vocabulary: feelings and qualities Grammar: the future perfect and the pluperfect tenses; comparisons with nouns, adjectives, verbs, and adverbs; superlatives
6: El mundo del espectáculo	Vocabulary: entertainers and shows Grammar: subjunctive vs. indicative in adverbial clauses	Vocabulary: music, musicians, and musical events Grammar: formal and informal commands; subjunctive with *ojalá, tal vez,* and *quizá(s)*
7: La diversidad humana	Vocabulary: equality of opportunity Grammar: review of the preterit and imperfect; *hacer* and *desde* in time expressions	Vocabulary: ethnic and gender diversity Grammar: *por* and *para;* verbs that require a preposition before an infinitive
8: Las artes culinarias y la nutrición	Vocabulary: foods and their preparation Grammar: the imperfect subjunctive	Vocabulary: foods and nutrition Grammar: the conditional and conditional perfect; the indicative or subjunctive in *si*-clauses
9: Nuestra compleja sociedad	Vocabulary: crime and personal safety Grammar: the pluperfect subjunctive	Vocabulary: social problems and personal excesses Grammar: uses of *se* with impersonal and passive constructions; indefinite and negative expressions
10: El empleo y la economía	Vocabulary: career choices and the interview process Grammar: indirect speech	Vocabulary: talking about finances Grammar: the relative pronouns *que, quien,* and *lo que* and the relative adjective *cuyo/a(s);* the relative pronouns *el / la cual* and *los / las cuales*
11: El tiempo libre	Vocabulary: outdoor activities and sports Grammar: sequence of tenses with the subjunctive	Vocabulary: what you do in your free time Grammar: uses of definite and indefinite articles; uses of the infinitive and the -ing (-*ndo*) form of the verb
12: Temas que no pasan de moda	Vocabulary: 21st Century advances and challenges Grammar: *se* for unplanned events	Vocabulary: how life will be in the future Grammar: the passive voice; diminutives and augmentatives

Integrating 21st Century Skills in the Spanish Classroom

Spanish teachers recognize the need for students to interact effectively with the many Spanish speakers in the United States and across the globe. Today's world languages curriculum and instruction are based upon the 5Cs (Communication, Cultures, Connections, Comparisons, and Communities) with the goal of building communicative proficiency and cultural understanding. World languages learners are 21st Century Learners.

However, as today's students enter into an increasingly global economy, it is important that they have a diverse range of skills to succeed. The Partnership for 21st Century Skills, a national organization that advocates for 21st century readiness for every student, has developed a Framework for 21st Century Learning. This document fuses the traditinoal 3Rs with what they call the 4Cs:

- Critical thinking and problem solving
- Communication
- Collaboration
- Creativity and innovation

World Languages 21st Century Skills Map

The American Council on the Teaching of Foreign Languages (ACTFL) has worked with the Partnership for 21st Century Skills to create a 21st Century Skills Map that describes the integration of World Languages and 21st Century Skills. This map provides concrete examples of how 21st Century Skills can be integrated into all world language classrooms.

By combining the 5Cs of the National Standards for Foreign Language Learning with the 4Cs from the Partnership for 21st Century Skills, world languages teachers now have a unique opportunity. As schools, districts, and states expand assessment and instruction to focus on 21st Century Skills, we can further prepare students for their future. The 4Cs can be seamlessly integrated on a daily basis within the world languages classroom.

Realidades and the 21st Century World Languages Classroom

Teachers using *Realidades* will easily be able to integrate 21st Century Skills into daily instruction due to the series' pedagogical framework, the alignment of assessment and instruction, and the integration of print and digital resources. In *Realidades*:

- Each chapter is built around thematic instruction based upon real-world tasks and authentic sources.
- Instruction is learner-centered; students take responsibility for the learning and creation of new content.
- Technology is integrated with instruction and assessment to support and enhance learning.
- Instruction and assessment are differentiated to meet the needs of individual learners.
- Assessment is focused on what students can do with the language; students know what they will be asked to do and how they will be assessed.
- Instruction and assessment of culture focuses on the relationship between the products, practices, and perspectives of the target culture as well as comparisons between cultures.
- Students explore opportunities to use the language outside of the classroom.

Realidades and the 4 Cs

Realidades provides a wide range of resources, activities, and assessments that support the 4Cs. At the beginning of each *Tema* in the Teacher's Edition for Levels 1–3, the "b" page contains a chart with recommended activities and assessments in each chapter that build the skills outlined on the 21st Century Skills Map for World Languages.

For further information about the Partnership for 21st Century Skills, please visit their Web site: www.p21.org.

Program Components

Realidades offers a wide range of program components to support the diverse students in today's Spanish classroom!
To provide more teaching and learning options, program components are available in three convenient formats: print, DVD, or online at **realidades.com**.

For the Student

Student Edition ETEXT, DVD, PRINT

- My eText on DVD and online contains embedded audio and video files plus flashcards.

Workbooks ONLINE, DVD, PRINT

Leveled Vocabulary and Grammar Workbook

PART 1: GUIDED WORKBOOK

- Vocabulary clip art and study sheets
- Step-by-step grammar activities
- Simplified reading, speaking, and writing activities

PART 2: CORE WORKBOOK

- Focused practice for vocabulary and grammar
- End-of-chapter Crossword Puzzle and Organizer

Communication Workbook with Test Preparation

PART 1: WRITING, AUDIO, AND VIDEO ACTIVITIES

- Additional writing practice
- Student response pages for the Audio Program and *A primera vista: Vocabulario en contexto* video segments

PART 2: TEST PREPARATION

- Thematic readings that prepare students for standardized assessments
- Reading Skills Study Sheets
- Integrated Performance Assessments (IPA)

Realidades para hispanohablantes Workbook

- All-Spanish companion worktext to Student Edition
- Grammar explanations in Spanish
- More practice for language mechanics, usage, vocabulary, grammar, reading, and writing

¿Eres tú, María? Video Workbook PRINT

- A variety of activities for language and culture

Readers PRINT

Lecturas

- Sixteen readings per level

Grammar Study Guide PRINT

- Laminated cards summarize grammar for Levels 1–2

realidades.com

Students have complete access to all these digital assets on their account:

Student Edition

- eText with embedded audio and video files plus flashcards

DK Bilingual Visual Dictionary

- Over 6,000 vocabulary items organized by topics

DK Reference Atlas

- Complete overview of Spanish-speaking world

Mapa global interactivo

- .kmz files and activities

Videos

Videocultura: Theme-based culture videos

Videohistoria: Video segments that present new vocabulary

GramActiva: Videos that teach grammar using context, humor, and graphics

Tutorials: Grammar videos with comparisons to English

Videomodelos: Videos that model interpersonal speaking tasks

¿Eres tú, María?: 10-episode mystery video (starts in *Capítulo* 5A)

Audio

- All audio for Student Edition and workbooks
- *Canciones de hip hop* (downloadable)

Animations

- Animated Grammar

Assignable content

- Auto-graded activities from eText, Instant Check, and workbooks
- Interactive auto-graded games for fun, end-of-chapter review
- Teacher-graded RealTalk! speaking activities
- Teacher-graded speaking, writing, and culture activities from eText and workbooks

Assignable assessments

- Quizzes
- Quizzes with Study Plans
- Chapter Tests
- Cumulative Tests
- Integrated Performance Assessments

For the Teacher

PLANNING AND INSTRUCTION

Interactive Teacher's Edition and Resources DVD

- Interactive Teacher's Editions (TE)
- Point-of-use links in TE to PDF file of resources
- PDF files of resources

Interactive Whiteboard Vocabulary and Grammar Activities ONLINE DVD

- Interactive practice activities for vocabulary and grammar
- Teaching suggestions, extensions, and answers
- Downloadable SMART Notebook Files
- Use with or without a SMART Interactive Whiteboard
- Over 6,000 images from DK Bilingual Visual Dictionary in Image Gallery
- DVD includes DK dictionary eText

PresentationExpress™ DVD

Presentation tool that includes:

- Vocabulary images and clip art
- Student Edition audio files
- DK Bilingual Visual Dictionary eText
- *GramActiva* videos
- Animated Verbs
- Transparencies

Transparencies (on PresentationExpress™ DVD) ONLINE DVD

- *Vocabulario en contexto*
- Answer Keys to Student Edition
- Maps, Graphs, Realia, and Rapid Review
- *Videohistoria*
- Answer Keys to Workbooks
- Fine Art Transparencies: 72 to be used across all levels with accompanying notes and activities

Video Programs ONLINE DVD

Video Program
- *Videohistoria:* Vocabulary presentation videos
- *GramActiva:* Engaging grammar explanations
- *¿Eres tú, María?:* Mystery video (starting in *Capítulo* 5A)

Videomodelos Video Program
- Videos model speaking tasks

Videocultura Video Program
- Theme-based culture videos

Audio Program ONLINE DVD

All audio is available on a single DVD organized by chapter using mp3 files or on **realidades.com**:

- *Vocabulario en contexto*
- Communication Workbook Audio activities
- Student Edition *Escuchar* activities
- *Videohistoria*
- *Pronunciación*
- Listening section of *Examen del capítulo*

Teacher's Resource Book ONLINE PRINT DVD

Includes by chapter:

- Theme Project
- School-to-Home Letter
- Chapter Resource List
- Input Script
- Audio and Video Script
- *Lecturas* Teacher's Guide
- Communicative Pair Activities
- Situation Cards
- *GramActiva* Blackline Masters
- Vocabulary Clip Art
- Answer Keys for Workbooks
- 21st Century Skills Rubric

Pre-AP* Resource Book ONLINE PRINT DVD

- Strategies for building Pre-AP® skills at all levels
- Activities to practice for AP® Spanish Language and Culture Examination

TPR Stories ONLINE PRINT DVD

- Complete support for integrating TPR Storytelling into instruction

ASSESSMENT AND REMEDIATION

Assessment Program ONLINE PRINT DVD

- Use for core assessment

realidades.com

- *Pruebas* for Vocabulary Recognition: auto-graded
- *Pruebas* with Study Plans for Vocabulary Production and Grammar: auto-graded with built-in remediation and retesting
- *Examen del capítulo*: auto- and teacher-graded
- RealTalk! Speaking Tasks: *Presentación oral, Examen del capítulo*, Integrated Performance Assessments

Alternate Assessment Program ONLINE PRINT DVD

- For students needing adapted assessment or retesting

Assessment Program: *Realidades para hispanohablantes* ONLINE PRINT DVD

- For heritage learners

Communication Workbook with Test Preparation ONLINE PRINT DVD

- Integrated Performance Assessments

ExamView® Assessment Suite CD-ROM

- Four editable test banks per chapter: two for core assessment, one for heritage learners, one for Pre-AP® learners
- Test banks available in **realidades.com** Question Library

Getting Started

Students get started in *Realidades B* with these colorful reference and introductory sections:

▶ **Mapas**

▶ **Getting Started on realidades.com**

▶ **Para empezar**

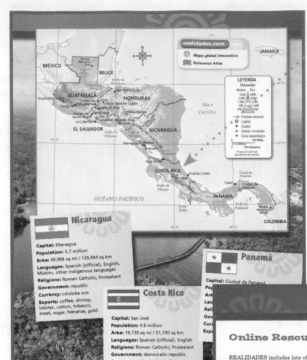

Mapas
Colorful atlas pages support geography skills.

Students can explore more online:
- 🌐 *Mapa global interactivo*
- 📖 Reference Atlas

Nicaragua

Capital: Managua
Population: 5.7 million
Area: 49,998 sq mi / 129,494 sq km
Languages: Spanish (official), English, Miskito, other indigenous languages
Religions: Roman Catholic, Protestant
Government: republic
Currency: córdoba oro
Exports: coffee, shrimp, lobster, cotton, tobacco, meat, sugar, bananas, gold

Costa Rica

Capital: San José
Population: 4.6 million
Area: 19,730 sq mi / 51,100 sq km
Languages: Spanish (official), English
Religions: Roman Catholic, Protestant
Government: democratic republic
Currency: colón de Costa Rica
Exports: coffee, bananas, sugar, textiles, electronic components

Panamá

Capital: Ciudad de Panamá

Online Resources with realidades.com

REALIDADES includes lots of online resources to help you learn Spanish! You can easily link to all of them when you log on to your Home Page within realidades.com. Your teacher will assign some activities, such as the ones in the workbooks. Others you can access on your own.

You'll find these resources highlighted on the pages of your print or online Student Edition with technology icons. Here's a list of the different icons used.

Bilingual Visual Dictionary Links to additional vocabulary words presented visually

Reference Atlas Quick links to the countries in the online atlas

Mapa global interactivo Links to GIS showing locations across the Spanish-speaking world

Videos

Videocultura Cultural overview of each theme

Videohistoria Vocabulary video to help present the new vocabulary

GramActiva Grammar explanations to help present the new grammar

Grammar Tutorials Clear explanations of grammar with comparison to English

Animated Verbs Animations that highlight verb conjugations

¿Eres tú, María? A 10-episode mystery video starting in *Capítulo 5A*

Modelo **Videomodelos** Video models of speaking activities

Audio Audio files for vocabulary, listening practice, and pronunciation

Canciones de hip hop Songs to help practice new vocabulary and grammar

Flashcards Practice for the new vocabulary

RealTalk! Speak-and-record tool for speaking activities

GramActiva Activity Extra practice for the *GramActiva* video

Más práctica **Online practice**

Instant Check Short activities that check your progress right away

Guided Workbook Step-by-step vocabulary and grammar practice

Core Workbook Vocabulary and grammar exercises

Communication Workbook Listening, video, and writing activities

Cultural Reading Activity Questions for the *Lectura* reading

Actividades Questions for the *Videomisterio*

Puzzles End-of-chapter games

vi

Getting Started on realidades.com

Students get a complete overview of online resources available on **realidades.com**.

Para empezar

This bridge section provides a thorough review of *Realidades A*.

Thorough Review

All four themes from *Realidades A* are reviewed.

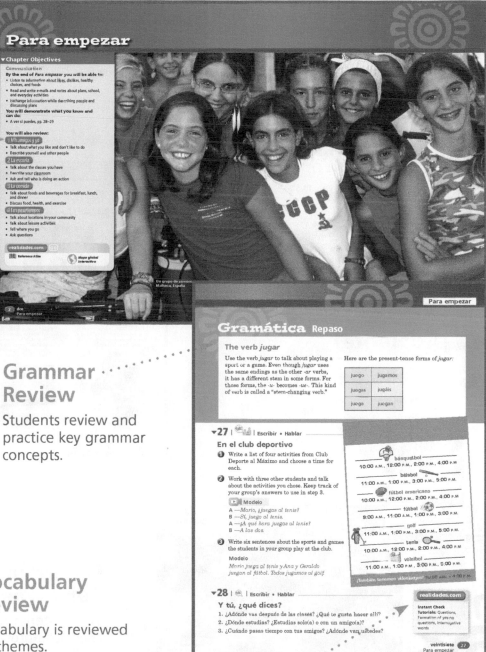

Grammar Review

Students review and practice key grammar concepts.

Vocabulary Review

Vocabulary is reviewed by themes.

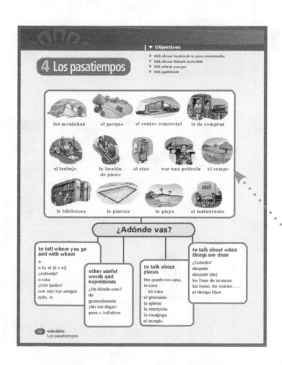

Students can go online for additional review activities.

Chapter Organization

Chapter Sequence

- ▶ Vocabulario en contexto
- ▶ Vocabulario en uso
- ▶ Gramática y vocabulario en uso
- ▶ ¡Adelante!
- ▶ Repaso del capítulo

A primera vista

Vocabulario en contexto

This six-page section gives students a "first look" at the new vocabulary and grammar through comprehensible input that integrates visuals and text with audio and video.

Visualized Vocabulary

New words are presented visually and in context.

Language Input

Input continues with visuals accompanied by narrative. All new vocabulary words and grammar are highlighted in blue.

Chapter opener *Capítulo 5A*

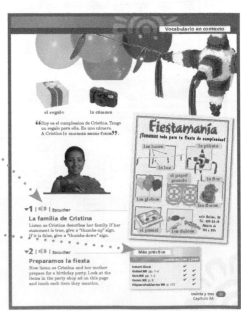

🔊 Listening Comprehension

Short listening activities check comprehension.

More Practice

Extra practice is available in the workbooks and online.

Reading and Language Input

The input of new vocabulary and grammar continues through a short, engaging reading written as a *videohistoria*. This story is based upon the accompanying *A primera vista* video segment.

Reading Strategies

Pre-reading strategies prepare students for reading the *Videohistoria*.

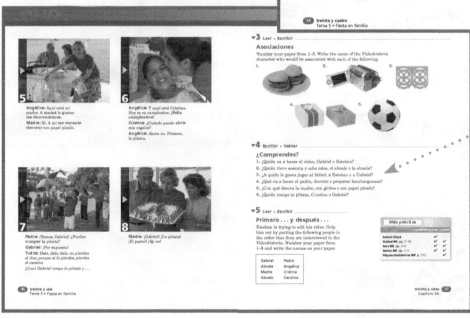

Reading Comprehension

Questions check students' comprehension of the story while practicing the new vocabulary and grammar.

▶ Videos and Language Input

The language, characters, and culture of the *Videohistoria* come to life in the *A primera vista* video segment. Each video segment is approximately 5 minutes in length. The videos were filmed in San Antonio, Mexico City, Costa Rica, and Spain (Madrid and Toledo). To help students with language input, each video is shown twice. The first time, key vocabulary is labeled on the screen. The second time, the words are not shown. Additional video activities can be found in the Writing, Audio & Video section of the Communication Workbook.

From the *A primera vista* video segment

Chapter Organization

Manos a la obra
Vocabulario en uso

Students "get to work" using the chapter's new vocabulary.

Integrated Culture

Cultural notes are embedded throughout the chapter.

Focused Practice

Students start with activities that focus on reading, listening, and basic writing.

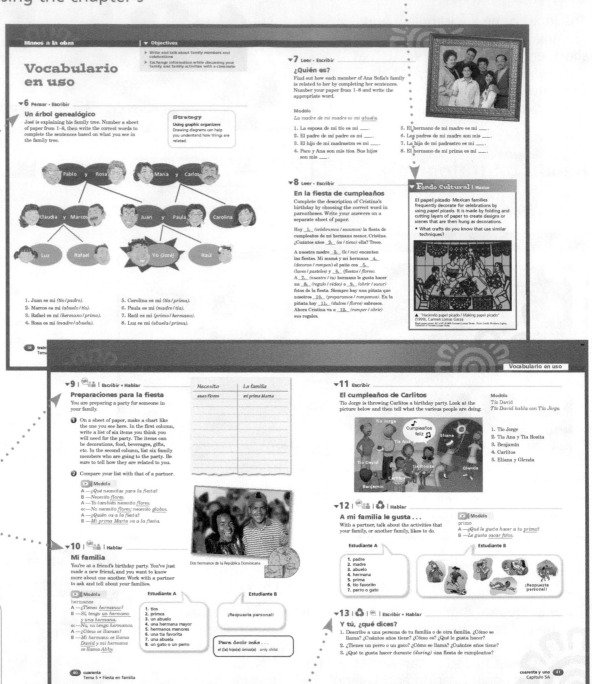

Paired Practice

Students transition to paired practice activities that focus on the new vocabulary.

Modelo Students can view videos that model the conversation.

Talk! Paired students can record their conversations online!

Personal Responses

The sequence of exercises culminates with personalized speaking and writing tasks.

Gramática y vocabulario en uso

Students practice and learn grammar using a variety of modalities.

Grammar Integrated with Communication

The complete grammar presentation features clear explanations and examples.

Language and Culture

Culture is woven together with language practice.

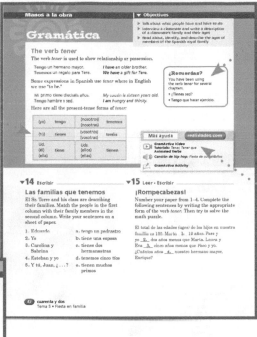

Review and Recycling

¿Recuerdas? notes help students remember what they've already learned about the grammar point.

Reinforce Grammar through Videos

Graphics and humor in the *GramActiva* video segments help students "see" how grammar works!

Connections to Other Disciplines

Cross-curricular activities are woven into the practice sequence.

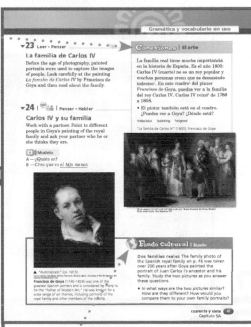

Hands-on Learning

Fun, interactive games help students learn new concepts.

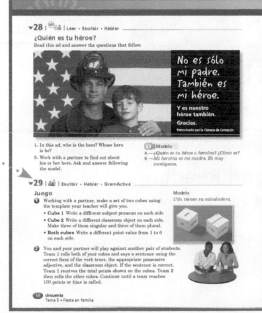

Interactive Geography

Students expand their geography skills using our online *Mapa global interactivo* activities.

Chapter Organization

¡Adelante!

Students apply their language skills with culminating activities that include culturally authentic readings, performance-based speaking and writing tasks, a mystery video, and a variety of cultural activities.

 Common Core: Reading

Reading Strategies

Reading strategies help students become better readers.

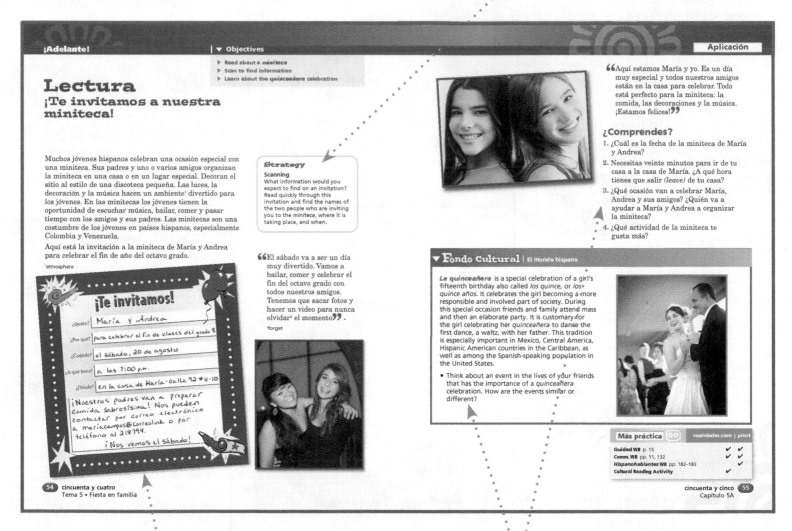

Real-world Readings

Students are able to connect to the cultural richness and diversity in the Spanish-speaking world.

Cultural Comparisons

Standards-based questions focus students on cultural perspectives and comparisons.

Page 1 (left panel)

¡Adelante!

La cultura en vivo

El papel picado

As you've seen in this chapter, *el papel picado* (cut-paper decorations) is a well-known Mexican craft. Tissue paper is cut into small patterns similar to making paper snowflakes. The cut paper is then hung on string to make a banner to use as decoration at many different celebrations. Here's how to make *papel picado* to decorate your classroom.

Una fiesta con música de mariachi

Materials

- colored tissue paper cut into 12" x 18" sheets
- scissors
- stapler
- string

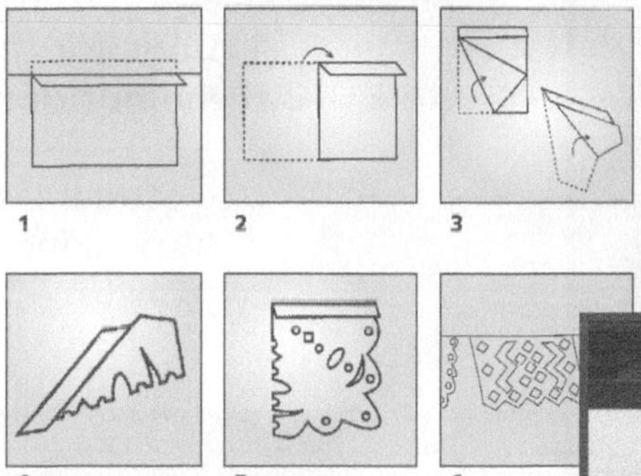

Directions

1 Spread the tissue paper flat. Fold down 1" on the 18" side for making a hanging flap.

2 Fold the paper in half on the 12" side and crease on the fold to make a sharp line.

3 Fold the paper twice diagonally.

4 Cut out designs along the folded edge. Experiment with snowflake or other geometric designs.

5 Cut a scalloped design on the outside edge.

6 Open the cutout and staple to a string to hang across a room to decorate for a *fiesta*.

56 cincuenta y seis
Tema 5 • Fiesta en familia

Hands-on Culture

La cultura en vivo offers a fun, hands-on experience with a wide range of cultural products and practices.

Page 2 (right panel)

Perspectivas del mundo hispano

A la hora de comer

Imagine that you had two hours for lunch every day. Or imagine that every time you ate a meal, you sat down at a table with a friend or family member and had a lengthy conversation. Now imagine that you didn't jump up from dinner as soon as you finished eating. What do these situations have in common?

Una familia en la República Dominicana

In many Spanish-speaking cultures, even ordinary mealtimes are considered social events, a time to spend enjoying food and company. People often take time after a meal to relax, to sit around the table and enjoy a good conversation or just to have a laugh. This custom, called the *sobremesa*, is more important in many cultures than getting to the next appointment or saving time and money by buying a quick meal.

Not surprisingly, most Spanish-speaking countries have very few drive-through restaurants. Since people rarely take food "to go," they might be surprised if you suggested grabbing a sandwich to eat in the car. In fact, many cars don't have cup holders.

Una familia chilena come al aire libre, Renaca, Chile

Check it out! Figure out how much time you and your family spend at breakfast, lunch, and dinner on days when you're not in school or at work. Compare your results with those of your classmates. Then complete the following statements about practices among families in your community.

Modelo
En mi comunidad, es común *(common)* comer el desayuno en quince minutos.

1. En mi comunidad, es común comer el desayuno en ___ minutos.
2. En mi comunidad, es común comer el almuerzo en ___ minutos.
3. En mi comunidad, es común comer la cena en ___ minutos.

Think about it! What does your research say about the importance of relaxing and enjoying a leisurely meal with friends and family? How does it compare with what happens during meals in Spanish-speaking countries? Consider the two different attitudes towards mealtime. What benefits might each one have?

86 ochenta y seis
Tema 5 • Fiesta en familia

Cultural Perspectives

Perspectivas del mundo hispano provides a thought-provoking overview of a product or practice (and its related perspectives) from the Spanish-speaking world.

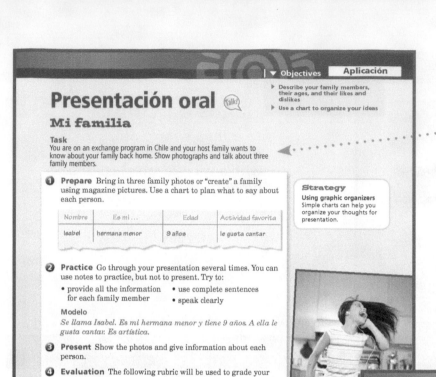

Presentación oral 🗨

Mi familia

Task
You are on an exchange program in Chile and your host family wants to know about your family back home. Show photographs and talk about three family members.

1 Prepare Bring in three family photos or "create" a family using magazine pictures. Use a chart to plan what to say about each person.

Nombre	Es mi...	Edad	Actividad favorita
Isabel	hermana menor	9 años	le gusta cantar

Strategy

Using graphic organizers
Simple charts can help you organize your thoughts for presentation.

2 Practice Go through your presentation several times. You can use notes to practice, but not to present. Try to:
- provide all the information for each family member
- use complete sentences
- speak clearly

Modelo
Se llama Isabel. Es mi hermana menor y tiene 9 años. A ella le gusta cantar. Es artística.

3 Present Show the photos and give information about each person.

4 Evaluation The following rubric will be used to grade your presentation.

Rubric	Score 1	Score 3	Score 5
How complete your preparation is	Your information is written down but without use of a chart.	You used the chart, but it is only partially completed.	You used the chart and provided all the information.
How much information you communicate	You bring in one photo and provide all the information.	You bring in two photos and provide all the information.	You bring in three photos and provide all the information.
How easily you are understood	You are extremely difficult to understand. Your teacher could only recognize isolated words and phrases.	You are understandable but have frequent errors in vocabulary and/or grammar that hinder your comprehensibility.	You are easily understood. Your teacher does not have to "decode" what you are trying to say.

cincuenta y si
Capítulo

Performance-based Speaking Tasks

Real-life speaking tasks are supported by strategies and a step-by-step process that helps all students to be successful. A rubric for this task appears at the bottom of the page.

🗨 Students can record their speaking using RealTalk!

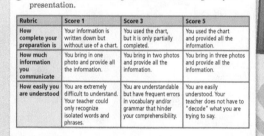

Performance-based Writing Tasks

Students become better writers with real-life tasks that are supported with the writing process and focused strategies. As with the speaking tasks, a rubric has been specially written for each *Presentación escrita*.

Students can submit writing tasks online for easy teacher grading!

| ▼ Objectives | Aplicación |

▶ Write a review of your favorite restaurant
▶ Use examples to persuade your reader

Presentación escrita

Un restaurante muy bueno

Task
Your school is creating a community guide for Spanish speakers. Your class is writing about restaurants. Write a review of your favorite restaurant.

1 Prewrite Think about the restaurant you like best. Copy the word web. Write the name of the restaurant in the middle circle. Write words and expressions associated with each category inside the appropriate circles.

2 Draft Write your review of the restaurant using information from the word web. Include information that might persuade others to try the restaurant.

3 Revise Read through your review and check for agreement, verb forms, and spelling. Share your review with a partner. Your partner should check the following:
- Did you provide information about all categories?
- Did you use the correct forms of the verbs?
- Do you have any errors in spelling or agreement?
- Is the review persuasive?

4 Publish Write a final copy of your review, making any necessary changes or additions. You may want to add illustrations and include your review in a booklet with your classmates' reviews or in your portfolio.

5 Evaluation The following rubric will be used to grade your review.

Strategy

Persuasion
Give specific information and concrete examples to persuade your readers to try a restaurant.

Rubric	Score 1	Score 3	Score 5
Completion of task	You provide information in three categories from the word web.	You provide information in four categories from the word web.	You provide information in five categories from the word web.
Use of new and previously learned vocabulary	You use very limited and repetitive vocabulary.	You use only recently acquired vocabulary.	You use both recently acquired and previously learned vocabulary.
Accurate spelling/use of grammar	You have many patterns of misspelling and misuse of grammar.	You have frequent patterns of misspelling and misuse of grammar.	You have very few patterns of misspelling and misuse of grammar.
Correct use of verbs	You have many repetitions of incorrect verb forms.	You have frequent repetitions of incorrect verb forms.	You have very few incorrect verb forms.

ochenta y siete 87
Capítulo 5B

Videomisterio ▶

▼ Objective
▶ Understand the expanding plot of a mystery video set in Spain

Madrid, España

¿Eres tú, María?
Episodio 1

Antes de ver el video
Personajes importantes

Lola Lago, detective

Doña Lupe, portera

Nota cultural In many apartment buildings in Spain, you will find a *portero* or *portera*. In exchange for a small salary and free apartment (in Spain, an apartment is called *un piso*), this person watches over the building and its residents, doing small chores such as taking messages and receiving packages. Because the *portero* or *portera* knows everyone in the building, he or she is often a good source of information about the residents.

Resumen del episodio

Estamos en el piso de Lola Lago, una detective que trabaja en Madrid, la capital de España. Es la una de la mañana. Desde¹ su balcón, ella ve a dos personas hablando enfrente de un edificio.² ¿Qué pasa? Más tarde, Lola encuentra³ algo muy importante en la calle.⁴ Al día siguiente,⁵ doña Lupe, la portera del edificio, entra en el piso de doña Gracia y . . .

¹From ²building ³finds ⁴street ⁵The next day

Palabras para comprender

investigar	to investigate
las llaves	keys
el periódico	newspaper
el piso	apartment; floor (of a building)

58 cincuenta y ocho
Tema 5 • Fiesta en familia

▶ **Motivate and Build Confidence with a Mystery Video**

In *Temas 5–9*, students join Lola Lago as she solves the mystery of *¿Eres tú, María?* This 10-episode "whodunit" is beautifully filmed in Madrid and is easily comprehensible to first-year students.

Video

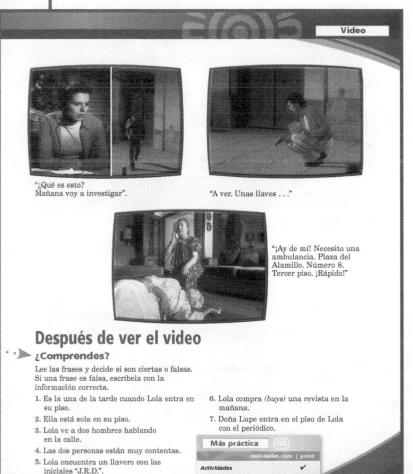

"¿Qué es esto? Mañana voy a investigar".

"A ver. Unas llaves . . ."

"¡Ay de mí! Necesito una ambulancia. Plaza del Alamillo. Número 8. Tercer piso. ¡Rápido!"

Comprehension Checks

A variety of questions check student comprehension of the video.

Después de ver el video
¿Comprendes?

Lee las frases y decide si son ciertas o falsas. Si una frase es falsa, escríbela con la información correcta.

1. Es la una de la tarde cuando Lola entra en su piso.
2. Ella está sola en su piso.
3. Lola ve a dos hombres hablando en la calle.
4. Las dos personas están muy contentas.
5. Lola encuentra un llavero con las iniciales "J.R.D.".
6. Lola compra (*buys*) una revista en la mañana.
7. Doña Lupe entra en el piso de Lola con el periódico.

Más práctica [GO]
realidades.com | print
Actividades ✓

cincuenta y nueve **59**
Capítulo 5A

Repaso del capítulo

These two pages provide complete review and preparation for the chapter test.

realidades.com

Instant Check

End-of-chapter activity provides extra practice.

Review Games

Online interactive games make review fun!

Additional Review

Flashcards, Tutorials, *GramActiva* Videos, Animated Verbs, and *Canciones de hip hop* for this chapter are available online.

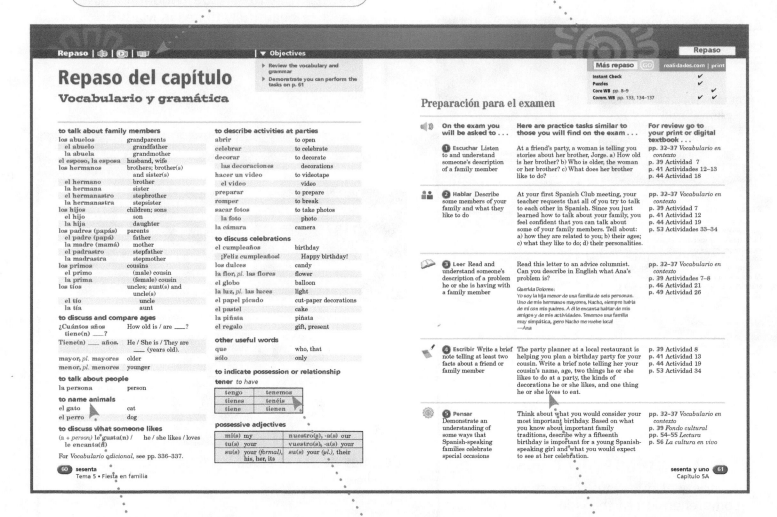

Repaso | ▼ **Objectives**
► Review the vocabulary and grammar
► Demonstrate you can perform the tasks on p. 61

Repaso del capítulo
Vocabulario y gramática

to talk about family members

los abuelos	grandparents
el abuelo	grandfather
la abuela	grandmother
el esposo, la esposa	husband, wife
los hermanos	brothers; brother(s) and sister(s)
el hermano	brother
la hermana	sister
el hermanastro	stepbrother
la hermanastra	stepsister
los hijos	children; sons
el hijo	son
la hija	daughter
los padres (papás)	parents
el padre (papá)	father
la madre (mamá)	mother
el padrastro	stepfather
la madrastra	stepmother
los primos	cousins
el primo	(male) cousin
la prima	(female) cousin
los tíos	uncles; aunt(s) and uncle(s)
el tío	uncle
la tía	aunt

to discuss and compare ages

¿Cuántos años tiene(n) ___?	How old is / are ___?
Tiene(n) ___ años.	He / She is / They are ___ (years old).
mayor, *pl.* mayores	older
menor, *pl.* menores	younger

to talk about people

| la persona | person |

to name animals

| el gato | cat |
| el perro | dog |

to discuss what someone likes

| (a + *person*) le gusta(n) / le encanta(n) | he / she likes / loves |

For *Vocabulario adicional*, see pp. 336–337.

60 sesenta
Tema 5 • Fiesta en familia

to describe activities at parties

abrir	to open
celebrar	to celebrate
decorar	to decorate
las decoraciones	decorations
hacer un video	to videotape
el video	video
preparar	to prepare
romper	to break
sacar fotos	to take photos
la foto	photo
la cámara	camera

to discuss celebrations

el cumpleaños	birthday
¡Feliz cumpleaños!	Happy birthday!
los dulces	candy
la flor, *pl.* las flores	flower
el globo	balloon
la luz, *pl.* las luces	light
el papel picado	cut-paper decorations
el pastel	cake
la piñata	piñata
el regalo	gift, present

other useful words

| que | who, that |
| sólo | only |

to indicate possession or relationship

tener *to have*

tengo	tenemos
tienes	tenéis
tiene	tienen

possessive adjectives

mi(s) my	nuestro(s), -a(s) our
tu(s) your	vuestro(s), -a(s) your
su(s) your (formal), his, her, its	su(s) your (pl.), their

Preparación para el examen

On the exam you will be asked to . . .	Here are practice tasks similar to those you will find on the exam . . .	For review go to your print or digital textbook . . .
Más repaso GO	realidades.com	print
	Instant Check	✓
	Puzzles	✓
	Core WB pp. 8–9	✓ ✓
	Comm. WB pp. 133, 134–137	✓ ✓
1 Escuchar Listen to and understand someone's description of a family member	At a friend's party, a woman is telling you stories about her brother, Jorge. a) How old is her brother? b) Who is older, the woman or her brother? c) What does her brother like to do?	pp. 32–37 *Vocabulario en contexto* p. 39 Actividad 7 p. 41 Actividades 12–13 p. 44 Actividad 18
2 Hablar Describe some members of your family and what they like to do	At your first Spanish Club meeting, your teacher requests that all of you try to talk to each other in Spanish. Since you just learned how to talk about your family, you feel confident that you can talk about some of your family members. Tell about: a) how they are related to you; b) their ages; c) what they like to do; d) their personalities.	pp. 32–37 *Vocabulario en contexto* p. 39 Actividad 7 p. 41 Actividad 12 p. 44 Actividad 19 p. 53 Actividades 33–34
3 Leer Read and understand someone's description of a problem he or she is having with a family member	Read this letter to an advice columnist. Can you describe in English what Ana's problem is? *Querida Dolores:* *Yo soy la hija menor de una familia de seis personas. Uno de mis hermanos mayores, Nacho, siempre habla de mí con mis padres. A él le encanta hablar de mis amigos y de mis actividades. Tenemos una familia muy simpática, ¡pero Nacho me vuelve loca!* *—Ana*	pp. 32–37 *Vocabulario en contexto* p. 39 Actividades 7–8 p. 46 Actividad 21 p. 49 Actividad 26
4 Escribir Write a brief note telling at least two facts about a friend or family member	The party planner at a local restaurant is helping you plan a birthday party for your cousin. Write a brief note telling her your cousin's name, age, two things he or she likes to do at a party, the kinds of decorations he or she likes, and one thing he or she loves to eat.	p. 39 Actividad 8 p. 41 Actividad 13 p. 44 Actividad 19 p. 53 Actividad 34
5 Pensar Demonstrate an understanding of some ways that Spanish-speaking families celebrate special occasions	Think about what you would consider your most important birthday. Based on what you know about important family traditions, describe why a fifteenth birthday is important for a young Spanish-speaking girl and what you would expect to see at her celebration.	pp. 32–37 *Vocabulario en contexto* p. 39 Actividad 7 pp. 54–55 *Lectura* p. 56 *La cultura en vivo*

sesenta y uno **61**
Capítulo 5A

Vocabulary List

Chapter vocabulary is listed as language functions and with English translations.

Grammar Summary

Chapter grammar is conveniently summarized.

Complete Test Preparation

This page prepares students for the proficiency and culture sections of the chapter test. Students are told how they will be tested, what the task might be like, and how to review.

End-of-Book Student Resources

Bilingual Visual Dictionary

Complete e-Text with over 6,000 additional visualized vocabulary words

Additional Thematic Vocabulary

Useful lists provide additional thematic vocabulary.

Grammar Summary and Charts

This quick reference guide helps students build a strong grammar foundation.

Expressions for Communication

This handy list can help students become better communicators.

End Glossaries

Helpful Spanish-English and English-Spanish glossaries are located at the end of the book.

Students can listen to pronunciation online.

Using the Teacher's Edition

realidades.com

Use the Lesson Plans, teacher resources, and program content to plan for instruction and assign activities.

▶ **Teaching the Theme**

▶ **Planning for Instruction**

▶ **Alignment with the Standards for Foreign Language Learning**

▶ **Complete Teaching Support**

Teaching the Theme

The Teacher's Edition provides complete planning support for teaching the themes.

Theme Support

Time-saving teaching ideas include bulletin board suggestions, games, and other activities.

21st Century Skills

This correlation highlights ways to integrate 21st Century Skills into instruction.

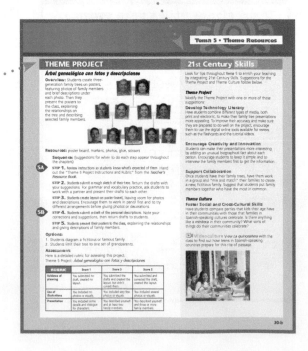

Theme Project

Each theme includes a project divided into manageable steps. The rubric is on the page as well as in the Teacher's Resource Book and in the Assessment Program.

Planning for Instruction

The Teacher's Edition provides four pages of planning support interleaved at the beginning of each chapter.

Chapter Overview

This section gives a quick overview of each chapter.

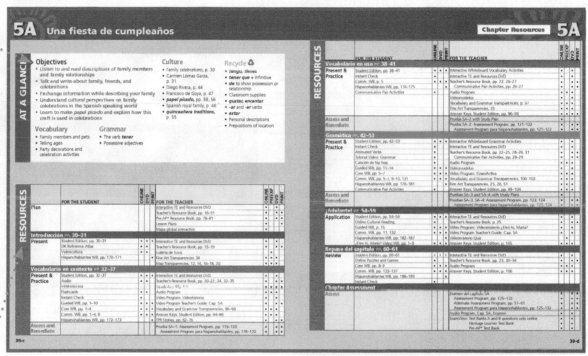

Program Resources

This section shows all the program resources available for this chapter. All resources are conveniently referenced at point of use in the chapter.

Lesson Plans

Lesson Plans are provided for each chapter.

Lesson plans are also available on **realidades.com**.

Alignment with the Standards for Foreign Language Learning

Realidades provides complete coverage of the Standards for Foreign Language Learning. Correlations to the standards are provided throughout the Teacher's Edition.

Standards Correlation

A complete correlation of chapter activities to the standards is provided at the beginning of each chapter.

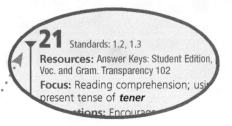

Standards Correlations per Activity

Teaching support includes references to the standards addressed in each activity.

You can also easily access the Standards on the Pearson Content link on **realidades.com**.

Complete Teaching Support

Complete support is provided for each activity.

Complete Teaching Support

Realidades provides teachers with complete instructional support in both print and technology formats.

Chapter Objectives

Each chapter provides a well-organized structure, clear student outcomes based upon the standards, and a variety of activities that develop all language skills.

> **Objectives**
> - Listen to and read about activities people like and don't like to do
> - Talk and write about what you and others like and don't like to do
> - Describe your favorite activities and ask others about theirs
> - Describe dances and music from the Spanish-speaking world and compare them to dances you know
> - Compare favorite activities of Spanish-speaking teens to those of teens in the United States

Assessment

Teachers are provided with multiple print and technology tools that measure student progress in listening, speaking, reading, and writing. The program also offers an Integrated Performance Assesssment for each chapter.

> **✔ASSESSMENT**
>
> Prueba 1A-2 with Study Plan (online only)
>
> **Quiz: Vocabulary Production**
> Prueba 1A-2: pp. 15–16

> **Más repaso** [GO]
>
> **Instant Check**
> **Puzzles**
> **Core WB** pp. 20–21
> **Comm. WB** pp. 117, 118–120

> **Presentación oral** [Talk?]
>
> **A mí me gusta mucho . . .**
>
> **Task**
> You are a new student at school and have been asked to tell the class a little bit about your likes and dislikes.

Differentiated Instruction

Realidades provides teaching suggestions to help all students learn Spanish. Each level also provides differentiated assessment.

> **DIFFERENTIATED INSTRUCTION**
>
> **Students with Learning Difficulties**
> Have students review the *Repaso del capítulo* and create flashcards for any words that they do not know. Pair them with a student who is more confident with the vocabulary to practice. Before the test, provide students with a practice test, so they can become comfortable with the format.
>
> **Heritage Language Learners**
> Have students write a few paragraphs telling about their perfect day: What activities are they going to do? Whom are they going to invite? What activities do they like the most? Encourage them to use as many vocabulary words from this chapter as they can.

> **DIFFERENTIATED ASSESSMENT**
>
> **CORE ASSESSMENT**
> - Assessment Program: Examen del capítulo 1A, pp. 19–25
> - Audio Program DVD: Cap. 1A, Track 23
> - ExamView: Chapter Test, Test Banks A and B
>
> **ADVANCED/PRE-AP***
> - ExamView: Pre-AP* Test Bank
> - Pre-AP* Resource Book, pp. 61–65
>
> **STUDENTS NEEDING EXTRA HELP**
> - Alternate Assessment Program: Examen del capítulo 1A
> - Audio Program DVD: Cap. 1A, Track 23
>
> **HERITAGE LEARNERS**
> - Assessment Program: Realidades para hispanohablantes: Examen del capítulo 1A
> - ExamView: Heritage Learner Test Bank

Instructional Planning and Support

Realidades provides complete planning and teaching support. The Teacher's Edition, the Interactive Teacher's Edition and Resources DVD, the PresentationEXPRESS™ DVD, **realidades.com**, and other program components provide time-saving teaching tools to help you teach all your students.

Assessment

Topics covered:

▶ **Assessing Student Progress**

▶ **Purposes of Assessment**

▶ **Forms of Assessment**

▶ ***Realidades* and the ACTFL Performance Guidelines**

▶ **Integrating Technology with Assessment**

▶ **Assessment Resources in *Realidades***

> 66 Performance assessment does not determine *who* is best but helps learners *do* their best. 99
> —*Challenge for a New Era; Nebraska K–12 Foreign Language Frameworks*

An assessment program in a second language classroom should be based on the premise that the main purpose of learning a language is to communicate in a meaningful and culturally appropriate way. As you begin to teach a unit of instruction, you might want to start by asking a few key questions: What do I expect my students to learn? What do I want them to be able to do? How can I assess what I am looking for in student performance?

Assessing Student Progress

The role of assessment in the world languages classroom is to provide both the teacher and students with a measure of progress toward achieving predetermined outcomes. It is an integral and ongoing part of the learning process. Here are key factors to consider as you develop curriculum that aligns assessment with instruction:

- Focus assessment on what students can do in the language (not just what they know).

- Performance tasks should be based upon real-world, authentic activities.

- Consider the principles of backward design to align assessment with instruction: determine outcomes, decide upon the evidence of transfer (performance tasks), and then create the learning activities.

- Give students multiple opportunities to show what they can do with the language that take into consideration cultures, learning styles, languages, and individual abilities.

- Use rubrics to evaluate performance tasks. This tool measures specific criteria against a defined scale. Provide the rubric to students in advance of the performance task.

- Provide students with anchors, or representative samples, of the performance task so that they can better understand the desired outcomes.

- Utilize both formative and summative assessments to provide ongoing feedback to students.

- Provide opportunities for students to self-evaluate and reflect upon their learning and progress.

Purposes of Assessment

The following chart outlines the various purposes for assessment:

Purposes of Assessment

Entry-level assessment	• Analyzes students' ability to communicate as a basis for placing students at an appropriate level in an established world languages program
Formative assessment	• Provides real-time feedback during the instructional process • Can take many different forms in the classroom • Helps the teacher and student determine the next steps to further learning • Takes place prior to the summative assessment
Summative assessment	• Documents and judges students' learning or success at a point in time such as the end of a unit, chapter, or course of study

Forms of Assessment

Achievement tests determine what students know by evaluating them on specific, previously learned material, such as the names of items of clothing or the conjugation of *-ar* verbs. Students are tested on discrete bits of information. Achievement tests are used to measure the incremental steps involved in learning a second language—for example, to cover what was taught in a specific chapter. Achievement may be quizzed or tested with some frequency as proof of regular progress for both student and teacher.

Performance-based speaking task in *Realidades B Capítulo 5A*

Performance-based assessment measures what students can do with this knowledge and how well they can perform in the language. These tests do not involve testing specific items; rather they are performance-based, checking how well students integrate what they have learned. Their characteristic open-endedness permits students to use what they know to receive or communicate a message, since the emphasis is on communication needs. Performance-based assessment addresses this question: How well and at what level can the student use the language to receive and express meaningful communication?

Performance-based writing task in *Realidades B Capítulo 5B*

Realidades and the ACTFL Performance Guidelines

The ACTFL Performance Guidelines for K–12 Learners describe the language proficiency of learners in Standards-based language programs such as *Realidades*. They are organized around three Modes of Communication: Interpersonal, Interpretive, and Presentational and provide for three Benchmark Levels: Novice, Intermediate, and Pre-Advanced.

Realidades has been carefully written to provide activities that develop and assess the Modes of Communication at levels appropriate to the students' proficiency. The last page in each chapter of Levels 1–3, called *Preparación para el examen*, provides an overview of the chapter outcomes and performance tasks organized around the three Modes. The Communication Workbook features an Integrated Performance Assessment (IPA) as an alternate assessment resource.

Assessment Resources in *Realidades*

Realidades offers a wide range of assessment resources found in various print and digital components. The chart on page T37 provides an overview.

Integrating Technology with Assessment

There are many opportunities to use the technology in *Realidades* to assess student performance. These include:

 RealTalk! Use the RealTalk tool in **realidades.com** to evaluate your students' interpersonal and presentation skills.

 Online Games Who says learning can't be fun? Each chapter within **realidades.com** offers three games that help students monitor their learning.

 Interactive Whiteboard Activities Get your students talking using the *¡Cuéntame!* and *Encuesta* Interactive Whiteboard Activities.

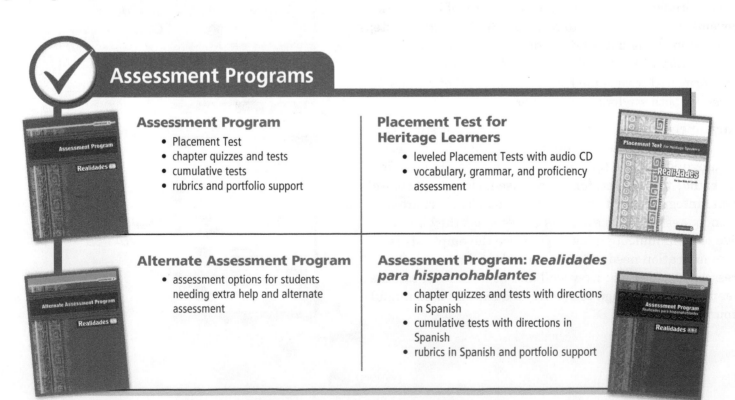

Assessment Programs

Assessment Program
- Placement Test
- chapter quizzes and tests
- cumulative tests
- rubrics and portfolio support

Placement Test for Heritage Learners
- leveled Placement Tests with audio CD
- vocabulary, grammar, and proficiency assessment

Alternate Assessment Program
- assessment options for students needing extra help and alternate assessment

Assessment Program: *Realidades para hispanohablantes*
- chapter quizzes and tests with directions in Spanish
- cumulative tests with directions in Spanish
- rubrics in Spanish and portfolio support

Assessment Resources in *Realidades*

▶ Assessment Resources	Self-Evaluation	Formative	Summative: Achievement	Summative: Performance
Student Edition				
Actividades (various)		X		X
Presentación oral				X
Presentación escrita				X
Preparación para el examen				X
realidades.com				
Actividades with 💬	X	X		X
Presentación oral with 💬				X
Instant Checks	X	X		
Online Games	X			
Chapter Quizzes with Study Plans		X		
Chapter Tests with 💬			X	X
Integrated Performance Assessments with 💬				X
Assessment Programs				
Placement Tests				
Chapter Quizzes		X		
Chapter Tests			X	X
Cumulative Tests			X	X
Rubrics				X
Chapter Checklist and Self-Assessment Worksheet	X			
Communication Workbook				
Audio and Writing Activities		X		
Practice Tests				X
Integrated Performance Assessments				X
Teacher Resource Book				
Communicative Pair Activities		X		
Situation Cards				X
Pre-AP® Resource Book				
Activities				X
Interactive Whiteboard Activities				
Vocabulary and Grammar		X		X
ExamView® Computer Test Generator				
Test Banks			X	

Differentiated Instruction

All students are capable of and can benefit from learning a second language. However, today's students bring into the classroom a wide range of needs, interests, motivations, home languages, and literacy levels. This diversity presents heightened challenges to both curriculum and instruction. It should be clearly acknowledged that individual needs of some students require additional specialized support. However, the goal of a comprehensive program remains the provision of teaching all students to develop proficiency in Spanish. All students should have access to a communicative and culturally rich program in addition to whatever specialized intervention may be required. *Realidades* has been developed especially to meet the diverse needs of students in Spanish classrooms.

Topics covered:

▶ **Success in Teaching All Students**

▶ **Effective Instructional Strategies**

▶ **Teaching Today's Students**

▶ **Teaching Spanish to Students with Learning Disabilities**

▶ **Accommodating Instruction**

▶ **Accommodations for Students with Special Needs**

▶ **Accommodation in *Realidades***

▶ **Teaching Heritage Learners**

▶ **Teaching Heritage Learners with *Realidades para hispanohablantes***

▶ **Teaching Heritage Learners with *Realidades B***

▶ **Teaching All Students: Summary**

Success in Teaching All Students

All students are able to access learning when teachers provide curriculum and instruction in ways that allow all learners in the classroom to participate and achieve the instructional and behavioral goals of general education, as well as those of the core curriculum. Success is achieved in classrooms that consistently and systematically integrate instructional strategies that are responsive to the needs of all learners with a special focus on students that need extra help—students with learning difficulties, heritage learners, and students who are eligible for and receiving special education services.

Effective Instructional Strategies

Here are general strategies that deliver effective instruction for all learners in the Spanish classroom.

- **Clarify the objectives for a chapter.** Students need to understand the outcomes for which they will be assessed.

- **Provide "thinking time" before students have to talk.** You may want to ask a question and then count to 10 before expecting a response. If a student is struggling, state that you want him/her to think about it, and indicate that you'll be back for the response in a minute. Move on to another student, and then return to the student for his/her response.

- **Write all assignments on the board.** Assignments given both verbally and visually are clearer to all students.

- **Use visuals throughout the lesson.** Present vocabulary visually. Use charts to present grammar. Use video that provides visual support (such as vocabulary words highlighted on the screen) and grammar videos that visualize grammar patterns. Use graphic organizers whenever possible. Connect communicative tasks to photos, art, and realia.

- **Assist in time management.** When requiring students to complete projects or long-term assignments, provide a calendar that breaks down requirements by due dates. Many students experience significant difficulties in self-managing the time needed to complete complex projects.

- **Build in opportunities for reteaching and practicing vocabulary words and grammar.** Students need many opportunities to learn new concepts and need to practice in a variety of formats.

- **Build vocabulary skills by teaching the patterns of language.** Teach the meaning of prefixes, suffixes, and the role of cognates. Point out connections between English, Spanish, and Latin.

- **Work with students based on their strengths rather than their weaknesses.** Allow students to experience success by using their strengths while working on areas of weakness.

- **Consider alternative means for demonstrating understanding.** Think beyond the common modes of reading and writing. Students could present information orally, create a poster or visual representation of work, record their ideas on an audio file, or act out their understanding.

- **Have students begin all work in class.** Prior to class dismissal, check to ensure that each student has a good start and understands what is expected.

> **" All students are capable of and can benefit from learning a second language. "**

- **Assign work using the Calendar on *realidades.com* or create a class Web page.** Homework assignments could be posted and easily accessed by parents and students outside of school hours.

Teaching Today's Students

The strategies presented on these pages provide an overview of instructional strategies that are effective with all learners. Today's students need instruction that enables them to see how learning is relevant, that helps them organize their time and learning, that provides focus on what is important (either within instructional materials or with classroom activities), that provides multiple opportunities to learn utilizing different modalities, and that assures students know what is expected of them whether in the classroom or for homework.

Teaching Spanish to Students with Learning Disabilities

There are many reasons why students may experience difficulties in learning a second language. In general, these difficulties may be characterized by the inability to spell or read well, problems with auditory discrimination and in understanding auditory input, and difficulty with abstract thinking. Research by Ganchow and Sparks (1991) indicates that difficulties with one's first language are a major factor in foreign language learning difficulties.

It is not always evident which students will experience difficulties with learning a second language. Many times these students are bright and outgoing. They may have experienced reading or spelling problems in elementary school, but they have learned to compensate over time. Ask students what problems they may have experienced with their first language, especially in the areas of reading and dictation.

Accommodating Instruction

Students with learning disabilities can develop a level of proficiency in a second language with some modifications to instruction and testing. These learners benefit from a highly structured approach that teaches new content in context and in incremental amounts. Teach, practice, and assess using multi-sensory strategies. Many students benefit when instruction combines seeing, hearing, saying, and writing. For example, a teacher would first show a visual of a word and say it aloud. This is followed by using the new word in context. The teacher then writes the word on the board. Students would say the word aloud with the teacher. They then write it down and say it aloud again. In subsequent days, many students benefit from frequent reviews of learned auditory materials.

Accommodations for Students with Special Needs

Here are suggestions for instruction for students with special needs. For additional support, see the *Realidades* Alternate Assessment Program.

Hearing impairments

- Help students comprehend oral information or instructions. Provide written directions/materials and/or visual cues to support what is presented orally. Face the students when speaking, repeat as needed, and speak clearly. Seat these students in the front of the classroom. Provide outlines of lectures or oral presentations. Have another student take notes and make copies of notes available to all students. Use the audio and video scripts of the *Realidades* Audio or Video Program. Utilize the close-captioned version of the Video Program.

- Allow students to refer to their textbooks or to other written materials during oral presentations.

- Limit background noises that may distract students. Avoid seating these students where they may hear extraneous noise.

- Change listening activities and assessments to reading/writing activities. In activities that require aural/oral skills, let students demonstrate skills through alternative responses such as writing.

- Provide access to the audio and video materials. Students can download all Student Edition audio material from **realidades.com.** The eText provides pronunciation support for all vocabulary, access to all Student Edition listening activities, and access to the vocabulary and grammar videos.

Visual perception problems

- Help students access information provided visually. Allow for preferred seating in the front of the class, including providing space for a guide dog, if necessary. Avoid seating students where they will be distracted by extraneous auditory or visual stimuli. Give students additional time to review visual input prior to an oral or written task. Highlight important information by providing key words, visuals, and simple outlines.

- Provide support for accessing printed information. Make sure the print is easy to read. The readings should be designed to maximize readability: easy-to-read font, layout, and design. Teach reading strategies that highlight the visual aspects of a selection: text organization, use of visuals, titles and headers, and the use of color. Provide copies of reading selections with additional support: underline key words/sentences/concepts or magnify the text in duplication.

- Teach, practice, and assess using multi-sensory strategies.

ADHD/ADD

- Provide additional support that enables students to focus. Present information in small "chunks." This includes new content, short instructions or directions, and shorter assignments, or break assignments into steps. Limit extraneous auditory and visual stimulation. Provide visual and written support for aural instructions or input. Repeat and explain (again) as needed. Provide outlines of oral presentations. Support readings with strategies similar to those for students with visual perception problems. Use graphic organizers.

- Verify that students "got it." Check that students are looking at you (eye contact) when providing oral instructions. Ask students to repeat what you just told them. Move closer to students to increase attention. Provide preferential seating that allows you to monitor students' focus and attention. Allow extra wait time when students are responding.

- Provide a variety of different learning activities that reach different learning styles. This will also allow for frequent changes of activities within a class. Provide for hands-on activities, vocabulary clip art, and grammar manipulatives.

- Use technology to provide interactive learning. These students will benefit from using the online resources at **realidades.com.**

- Be predictable. Establish a daily routine for managing the classroom and be consistent. Avoid surprises with these students.

- Help students organize themselves and their learning. Ask students to maintain notebooks that are organized by dividers. Provide study guides, summary sheets, and organizers for daily or weekly assignments.

Accommodation in *Realidades*

Realidades B provides a wide range of support for accommodating instruction.

Student Edition
- clean design and layout of pages
- visualized presentation of vocabulary
- step-by-step scaffolding of activities
- online vocabulary and grammar tutorials and extra practice at **realidades.com**

Teacher's Edition
- Differentiated Instruction article
- Differentiated Instruction suggestions

Leveled Vocabulary and Grammar Workbook: Guided Practice
- vocabulary clip art to create flashcards
- focused vocabulary practice
- simplified grammar instruction
- Answer Key in Teacher's Resource Book

Alternate Assessment Program
- additional suggestions for accommodating assessment
- for students needing extra help

Teaching Heritage Learners

A diverse background

Those who have a home language other than English bring a wider range of language abilities to the classroom. These abilities range from minimal functioning in the language to complete fluency and literacy. It is important for teachers to assess the language skills of the different heritage learners in the classroom. This diversity includes:

- Students who are able to understand the spoken language, but are unable to respond in the language beyond single-word answers.

- Students who are able to understand the language and communicate at a minimal level. These students may be able to read some items, but because of their limited vocabulary, they may not comprehend much information. They may write what they are able to sound out, but errors are evident.

- Students who can speak the language fluently but who have little to no experience with the language in its written form.

- Students who have come to the United States from non-English-speaking countries. They can understand and speak the language fluently; however, their reading and writing skills may be limited due to lack of a formal education in their country of origin.

- Fluent bilingual students who can understand, speak, read, and write another language very well and have possibly received formal instruction in that language in the United States or in another country.

Program goals

Heritage learners bring rich home language experiences to the classroom that can serve as a foundation for learning. Because of their language background, these students have the potential to be bilingual, biliterate, and bicultural. Heritage learners need to be exposed to a program that can improve and maintain the home language. Students need to study the grammar and focus on vocabulary development. Emphasis should be placed on building reading and writing skills. It is important that students develop a sensitivity to when standard and non-standard language should be employed and comfortably adjust their language accordingly. In addition, students should be exposed to the diverse cultures within the Spanish-speaking community while developing a sense of pride in their own heritage. Heritage learners need to reach a high level of proficiency and accuracy that will ensure success at the advanced level of language study and testing. These students should also be ready to transition into a focused study of Spanish in specific professional areas.

Focus on individual needs

Due to their diverse backgrounds, heritage learners differ greatly in language skills and may need individualized instruction. In many of today's classrooms, teachers encounter classes that contain a mixture of beginning-level students and heritage learners. These groups need different materials, different instructional approaches, and different objectives. Here are several strategies that may be helpful for heritage learners:

- Build upon their background knowledge. Develop instructional units around themes and topics that relate to their life experiences. Encourage students to use these experiences as the foundation for building language skills through vocabulary development, reading, and writing.

- Help students connect aural with written language. If students don't understand a word in a reading, have them read it aloud or ask a friend or teacher to read it aloud. Often they can recognize the word once they hear it. Allow for opportunities for students to follow along as a story is read aloud.

- Use strategies that are effective in a language arts classroom, such as building schema, teaching language-learning strategies, using graphic organizers, and incorporating pre- and post-reading tasks. Use the writing process to develop good writers.

- Encourage students to begin communicating, especially in writing. Have them write down their thoughts in the way they sound to them. Then have students work with the teacher or another student for corrections. Students can also look through textbooks and dictionaries to assist with error correction.
- Maintain high standards. Require students to focus on accuracy and proficient communication. Many heritage learners experience frustration with reading and writing in the home language when they have good aural/oral skills. Building language skills takes time.

Teaching Heritage Learners with *Realidades B*

Realidades B offers the ideal solution for heritage learners who begin Spanish instruction with a first-year textbook. It is recommended that teachers use *Realidades B* and the companion worktext, *Realidades para hispanohablantes,* with these students. This gives teachers three options: (1) the student textbook with English support; (2) the companion all-Spanish worktext; or (3) a combination of both.

Teaching All Students: Summary

The diverse needs of today's Spanish students pose a challenge to teachers, curriculum developers, and school administrators as they design programs to ensure that all students develop language proficiency. With *Realidades,* teachers have at their disposal a variety of materials and strategies to enable them to provide access to Spanish for all learners. Clearly, some students will require additional tutoring and specialized services to reach their full learning potential. However, the activities and materials that accompany *Realidades,* coupled with instructional strategies described within this article, constitute a viable framework for reaching and teaching all learners.

Teaching Heritage Learners with *Realidades para hispanohablantes*

Realidades B provides extensive support for teaching heritage learners.

Student Edition
- focused vocabulary and grammar
- integrated language and culture
- extensive reading and writing

Realidades para hispanohablantes
- all-Spanish companion worktext
- all-Spanish grammar explanations
- companion pages for each section of Student Edition
- increased emphasis on reading and writing
- accompanying Teacher's Guide

Assessment Program: *Realidades para hispanohablantes*
- direction lines in Spanish
- complete assessment support
- rubrics in Spanish

Placement Test
- leveled Placement Test with audio
- vocabulary, grammar, and proficiency assessment

Instructional Planning and Support

Today's Spanish classroom is a vibrant and interactive learning community, integrating language with culture. Teachers are planning for instruction that is communicative, motivating, and real for *all* students. They are incorporating a wide range of strategies, activities, and technology to achieve clearly defined teaching objectives. This section provides an overview of instructional strategies that will help teachers achieve these goals.

Topics covered:

▶ **Creating a Communicative Learning Community**

▶ **The Role of Grammar in a Communicative Classroom**

▶ **Pair and Group Activities in a Communicative Classroom**

▶ **Integrating Technology in the Classroom**

For more issues online, see
*my*PearsonTraining.com

Creating a Communicative Learning Community

A communicative classroom is built upon activities that enable students to use language in meaningful and purposeful ways. One of the challenges is to get students ready, willing, and able to communicate. Here are several strategies that can be built into communicative tasks to help all students be successful.

Teach and use learning strategies
Research states that successful language students use a wide range of learning strategies. In contrast, unsuccessful students employ fewer strategies and tend to give up quickly. Strategies are inherently student-centered and when employed by learners, allow them to become more independent and more successful. Learning strategies enable students to:

- Learn and recall information more efficiently
- Interpret and comprehend language when reading or writing
- Speak more effectively
- Write more effectively
- Take more risks and be more positive
- Work more cooperatively with others

Use activities based upon multiple intelligences

The Multiple Intelligences Theory tells us that students learn in different ways. If new material is presented in a variety of formats, more students will likely learn and be able to demonstrate proficiency with the new material. Howard Gardner in 1983 proposed the theory of Multiple Intelligences in his book *Frames of Mind*. This theory states that a person has many different ways of acquiring and demonstrating intelligence. Some people remember just about anything if learned to the tune of a jingle or chant, while someone else may be able to grasp an idea, concept, or grammatical point if presented as a graph, chart, or picture.

Gardner presents the notion that there is no "general intelligence," but rather that the mind is organized around distinct functional capacities, which he defines as "intelligences." Though each of the intelligences is developed independently of the others over the course of a lifetime, they usually work together and do not often appear in isolation. Gardner has identified and labeled eight main styles of acquiring and demonstrating knowledge; those eight intelligences are:

- Verbal/Linguistic
- Visual/Spatial
- Bodily/Kinesthetic
- Logical/Mathematical
- Interpersonal/Social
- Intrapersonal/Introspective
- Musical/Rhythmic
- Naturalist

In this Teacher's Edition, you will find frequent specific suggestions for accommodating and teaching to the Multiple Intelligences. This is not meant to be construed as a paradigm for labeling every student in your class. On the contrary, they are presented as tools to help more students access content while recognizing that they are intelligent in many ways and that their overall "intelligence" is based upon the sum of all their intelligences.

Activities that incorporate critical thinking tend to be more interesting for students as they are guided to think differently in ways such as:

- ⏛ use or apply
- ⏛ illustrate/sketch/diagram
- ⏛ compare and contrast
- ⏛ analyze
- ⏛ categorize
- ⏛ create
- ⏛ organize/prepare
- ⏛ evaluate
- ⏛ revise
- ⏛ value

Provide activities that require critical thinking

All students learn more effectively when activities help them make connections and see and use information in new and different ways. Critical thinking skills can be used as tools for learning and are easily integrated in a variety of tasks beginning in the first year of language study in both communication and culture activities.

Scaffold communicative tasks

Communicating in a second language is a complicated task. There are mental steps that take place as a student attempts to communicate a message. Activities that help students get through these mental steps allow students to be successful. This "scaffolded" support is provided throughout *Realidades*.

For example, in preparing for a speaking task, students think through what they might want to say using a chart. In writing, they might fill out a word web before attempting the first draft. By providing a scaffold that asks students to think, plan, process, and then communicate, more students will become effective communicators.

Scaffolded tasks

Step-by-step support builds success.

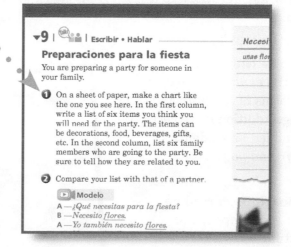

▾9 | Escribir • Hablar

Preparaciones para la fiesta
You are preparing a party for someone in your family.

❶ On a sheet of paper, make a chart like the one you see here. In the first column, write a list of six items you think you will need for the party. The items can be decorations, food, beverages, gifts, etc. In the second column, list six family members who are going to the party. Be sure to tell how they are related to you.

❷ Compare your list with that of a partner.

▶ Modelo
A —¿Qué necesitas para la fiesta?
B —Necesito flores.
A —Yo también necesito flores.

Necesi
unas flo

The Role of Grammar in a Communicative Classroom

In a proficiency-based curriculum, vocabulary and grammar are viewed as tools that students need in order to communicate, rather than as ends in themselves.

Input grammar in context

For students to internalize grammar, it needs to be presented in a meaningful context. For example, students can grasp the concept of the preterite more easily if it is presented within a topic, like shopping. As the teacher presents clothing and store vocabulary, she can tell the class what items of clothing she or another person bought, when it was purchased, and how much was paid. As the teacher points to a picture of a sweater on an overhead transparency or clip art or an actual sweater, she begins with comprehensible input that uses the *yo* form of the preterite: *Ayer, yo fui de compras y compré un suéter nuevo. Y pagué veinte dólares. No es mucho, ¿verdad?* Repetition of the input can continue with other articles of clothing, allowing students to easily deduce and internalize the meaning of *compré* and *pagué*. The teacher then begins to ask students questions using *compraste* and *pagaste* and makes summary comments about what is said in the class, drawing other students into the discussion as she introduces other preterite forms. As students begin to internalize these forms and the chapter vocabulary, they begin to make simple statements or ask questions to a partner about shopping for clothing.

Input grammar in small, manageable chunks

Present new grammar in manageable chunks that can be immediately practiced. In the example above, students can use a few preterite forms of *comprar* and *pagar* as they talk about shopping. Additional *-ar* verbs and other preterite forms can be added as students become comfortable using *comprar* and *pagar*.

Input grammar in readings

Grammar input can also take place through reading. As students read sentences, short paragraphs, and dialogues with supporting contextual and visual cues, they can understand new grammatical forms. Through carefully planned out questions asked by their teacher, students can be led to explain grammatical concepts.

Teach what is needed for the immediate communication objectives

Teach students the grammar needed to accomplish the communicative objective. This allows students to learn the concept in context and practice. For example, if you teach *pensar* or *querer* in connection with a theme, don't give students an additional list of all *ie* stem-changing verbs. Rather, teach additional *ie* verbs in later chapters as they connect to the themes.

Practice grammar in a variety of activities

Just as there are several ways to provide input, there are many useful methods for practicing grammar. This practice can involve hands-on activities and games that let students manipulate grammatical structures. Grammar practice is effectively integrated into communicative activities such as surveys, Venn diagrams, and paired and group activities. In addition, practice can involve activities on **realidades.com** where students can practice grammar again and again at their own pace.

Grammar and communication

Grammar can be successfully integrated in a communicative classroom with activities that deal with grammatical accuracy at different levels. When presented in meaningful contexts, in manageable chunks, and with presentation and practice that incorporate a variety of activities, students will develop increasing accuracy with grammar.

Pair and Group Activities in a Communicative Classroom

Benefits of group work

Effective group work develops a friendly and cooperative atmosphere by giving students a chance to get to know each other better. This sense of camaraderie leads to a more relaxed classroom in which students are more willing to talk and to participate. Group work also allows more opportunity for "student talk," thereby increasing the quantity of student practice in the target language.

Grouping options and techniques

The communicative activities in a Spanish classroom allow for a variety of grouping options.

The most common option is random grouping that includes pairing up two students or creating small groups of three to five students. Some possible ways to randomly group students include:

- Count off by going left to right or up and down in rows.
- Write on pieces of paper vocabulary words (English/Spanish), countries/capitals, opposites, colors, or categories that can be matched up, in a bag. Have students draw a piece of paper and find their partner(s).
- Order students along a continuum by birthday, height, phone numbers, etc.
- Place numbers or a deck of cards in a hat, bag, or box and have students draw.
- Turn to the student to the left or right, front or back.

Another grouping option is to place students by their ability level. Homogeneous grouping allows students of similar ability to work together. In this case, teachers assign tasks based upon the ability level of the group. Advanced students are given a more challenging task. Other students are given tasks that they can successfully complete. Heterogeneous grouping places students of varying abilities together. This allows for stronger students to help weaker students.

Grouping students by interest level is another option to consider. Students could group themselves for an activity or longer project based upon mutual interest.

Planning and facilitating an effective group activity

- Make sure that the task involves a true exchange of information.
- Think through the language functions and content information to make certain students can complete the task.
- Prepare all materials in advance and anticipate questions.
- Explain the task before the students break up into groups. Be sure to model the task if necessary.
- Determine in advance how students will be evaluated and share those criteria with the class.
- Allow adequate time for the task. Make sure at least three quarters of the students at different ability levels can complete it. Tell students how much time they have and stick to the plan.
- Encourage students to stay on task by walking around the class and monitoring the groups.
- Build into your grading system a way to include group participation and staying on task.
- Develop some sort of follow-up upon completion of the task.

Error correction

As students work in groups, they will be making mistakes. Here are strategies that can help students focus on accuracy while doing group work.

- Listen for common errors while monitoring the class. If the error is one of vocabulary usage or grammar, discuss the error with the class and do some focused practice once the task is completed. If the error is one of meaning (very common in beginning writing), have the class work together to determine how best to express the message.
- If you want to correct an individual student error, correct the student only after he or she has spoken. Restate the student's response using the correction in your restatement.

Integrating Technology in the Classroom

For the Teacher

Realidades provides many time-saving digital resources to help teachers plan, teach, assess, and remediate or enrich instruction.

	Teacher Resources	eText	realidades.com	DVD
Planning	• Interactive Teacher's Edition		•	Interactive Teacher's Edition and Resources DVD
	• Teacher Resources (PDF files)		•	Interactive Teacher's Edition and Resources DVD
	• Lesson Plans (links to PDF files)		•	
	• DK Bilingual Visual Dictionary (enrichment)	•	•	Interactive Whiteboard DVD
Chapter Opener	• *Videocultura* Videos		•	*Videocultura* Video Program
	• Fine Art and Map Transparencies		•	PresentationExpress™ DVD
Vocabulario en contexto	• Audio	•	•	Audio Program, PresentationExpress™ DVD
	• *Videohistoria* Videos	•	•	Video Program
	• Transparencies, Clip Art		•	PresentationExpress™ DVD
	• *Prueba:* Voc. Recognition Quiz		•	Teacher's Resources DVD
Vocabulario en uso	• Interactive Whiteboard Vocabulary Activities		•	Interactive Whiteboard DVD
	• *Videomodelos* Videos	•	•	*Videomodelos* Video Program
	• Audio	•	•	Audio Program
	• *Prueba:* Voc. Production Quiz with Study Plan		•	Interactive Teacher's Edition and Resources DVD
Gramática y vocabulario en uso	• Interactive Whiteboard Grammar Activities		•	Interactive Whiteboard DVD
	• *GramActiva* Videos	•	•	PresentationExpress™ DVD, Video Program
	• Tutorial Videos		•	
	• Animated Verbs	•	•	PresentationExpress™ DVD
	• *Videomodelos* Videos	•	•	*Videomodelos* Video Program
	• Audio	•	•	PresentationExpress™ DVD, Audio Program
	• Transparencies		•	PresentationExpress™ DVD
	• *Canciones de hip hop*		•	
	• *Prueba:* Grammar Quiz with Study Plan		•	Interactive Teacher's Edition and Resources DVD
¡Adelante!	• *¿Eres tú, María?* Videos			Video Program
Repaso del capítulo	• Integrated Performance Assessment		•	Interactive Teacher's Edition and Resources DVD
	• Situation Cards		•	Interactive Teacher's Edition and Resources DVD
	• *Examen del capítulo*		•	Interactive Teacher's Edition and Resources DVD
	• ExamView® Assessment Suite			ExamView® Assessment Suite CD-ROM

For the Student

Realidades is ready for today's digital learner! Through **realidades.com,** students can access a wide array of interactive online activities and multimedia resources. They can monitor their own progress, complete graded assignments and assessments, record speaking tasks, explore the Spanish-speaking world, and much more! Here is a list of the resources available for students on **realidades.com.**

	Student Resources	Auto-graded	Teacher-graded
Chapter Opener	*Mapa global interactivo*		•
	eText *Actividades*	•	•
	Videocultura and *Actividades*		•
	DK Reference Atlas		
Vocabulario en contexto	eText *Actividades*	•	•
	Flashcards		
	Videohistoria and *Actividades*	•	•
	Instant Check	•	
	Workbook activities	•	•
	Quiz	•	•
	Additional practice	•	
Vocabulario en uso	eText *Actividades*	•	•
	Videomodelos		
	RealTalk! speaking tasks		•
	Workbook activities	•	•
	Quiz with Study Plans	•	
	Communicative Pair Activities		•
Gramática y vocabulario en uso	eText *Actividades*	•	•
	GramActiva and *Actividad*	•	
	Tutorials, Animated Verbs		
	Canciones de hip hop		
	Instant Check	•	
	Workbook activities	•	•
	RealTalk! speaking tasks		•
	Quizzes with Study Plans	•	
	Additional practice	•	
¡Adelante!	eText *Actividades*	•	•
	Presentación oral		•
	Culture Reading Activity		•
	Workbook activities	•	•
	¿Eres tú, María? and *Actividades*	•	•
	DK Bilingual Visual Dictionary	•	
Repaso del capítulo	eText *Actividades*	•	•
	Games and Puzzles	•	
	Instant Check and Self-Test	•	
	Workbook activities	•	
	Situation Cards	•	•
	Integrated Performance Assessment	•	•
	Examen del capítulo		•

Bibliography

realidades.com

Go online for links to state and national professional organizations, regional conferences, Web sites of interest, and Listservs.

Assessment

Boyles, Peggy. "Assessing the Speaking Skill in the Classroom: New Solutions to an Ongoing Problem." *Northeast Conference Reports: Testing, Teaching, and Assessment,* ed. Charles R. Hancock. Lincolnwood, IL: National Textbook Company, 1994.

Cooper, Thomas C., Daniel J. Yanosky II, and Joseph M. Wisenbaker. "Foreign Language Learning and SAT Verbal Scores Revisited." *Foreign Language Annals,* Summer 2008.

James, W. "Formative Assessment: Why, What, and Whether," from *Transformative Assessment,* W. James. Popham, Chapter 1. ASCD Member Book, 2008.

Liskin-Gasparro, Judith. "Assessment: From Content Standards to Student Performance." *National Standards. A Catalyst for Reform,* ed. Robert Lafayette. Lincolnwood, IL: National Textbook Co., 1996.

National K–12 Foreign Language Resource Center. "National Assessment Summit Papers", *New Visions in Action,* Iowa State University, 2005.

New Visions in Action: National Assessment Summit Papers, ed. Marcia Harmon Rosenbusch, National K–12 Foreign Language Resource Center, Iowa State University, 2005.

Pettigrew, Frances and Ghislaine Tulou. "Performance Assessment for Language Students." *Language Learners of Tomorrow: Process and Promise,* ed. Margaret Ann Kassen. Lincolnwood, IL: National Textbook Co., 1999.

Tomlinson, Carol Ann. "Learning to Love Assessment." *Educational Leadership,* Jan. 2008.

Block Scheduling

Blaz, Deborah. *Teaching Foreign Languages on the Block.* Larchmont, NY: Eye on Education, 1998.

Canady, R. L., and M. D. Rettig. *Block Scheduling: A Catalyst for Change in High Schools.* Larchmont, NY: Eye on Education, 1995.

———. *Teaching on the Block: Strategies for Engaging Active Learners.* Larchmont, NY: Eye on Education, 1996.

Culture

Byram, Michael. *Teaching and Assessing Intercultural Competence.* Clevedon, U.K.: Multilingual Matters, 1997.

Fantini, Alvino. "Comparisons: towards the Development of Intercultural Competence." *Foreign Language Standards: Linking Theory, Research, and Practice,* ed. June Phillips. Lincolnwood, IL: National Textbook Co., 1999.

Galloway, Vicki. "Bridges and Boundaries: Growing the Cross-Cultural Mind." *Language Learners of Tomorrow: Process and Promise.* Lincolnwood, IL: National Textbook Co., 1999.

Heusvinkveld, Paula R., ed. *Pathways to Culture.* Yarmouth, ME: Intercultural Press, Inc. 1997.

Koning, Patricia. "Let's Go to the Movies." *The Language Editor,* Vol. 6, Issue 4 (2011): 32–36.

Curriculum and Instruction

ACTFL Performance Guidelines for K–12 Learners. Yonkers, NY: ACTFL, 1999.

"Challenge for a New Era." *Nebraska K–12 Foreign Language Frameworks.* Lincoln: Nebraska Department of Education, 1996.

Chamot, Anna U. "Reading and Writing Processes: Learning Strategies in Immersion Classrooms." *Language Learners of Tomorrow: Process and Promise,* ed. Margaret Ann Kassen. Lincolnwood, IL: National Textbook Company, 1999.

Davis, Robert. "Group Work is NOT Busy Work: Maximizing Success of Group Work in the L2 Classroom." *Foreign Language Annals,* Vol. 30 (1997): 265–279.

Ferguson, Susan. "Breathing Life Into Foreign Language Reading," *Educational Leadership,* Vol. 63 No. 2 (2005): 63–65.

Foreign Language Framework for California Public Schools Kindergarten Through Grade Twelve. Sacramento: California State Department of Education, 2002.

Guntermann, G., ed. *Teaching Spanish with the Five C's: A Blueprint for Success.* New York: Harcourt College Publishers, 2000.

Hall, Joan Kelly. "The Communication Standards." *Foreign Language Standards: Linking Theory, Research, and Practice,* ed. June Phillips. Lincolnwood, IL: National Textbook Co., 1999.

Jackson, Claire, et al. *Articulation & Achievement: Connecting Standards, Performance, and Assessment in Foreign Language.* New York: College Board of Publications, 1996.

Klee, Carol A. "Communication as an Organizing Principle in the National Standards: Sociolinguistic Aspects of Spanish Language Teaching." *Hispania.* Vol. 81 (2) (1998), pp. 339–351.

Krashen, Stephen. *Principles and Practice in Second Language Acquisition.* Oxford: Pergamon Press, 1982.

Met, Myriam, with J. Phillips. *Curriculum Handbook.* Association for Supervision and Curriculum Development, 1999.

———. "Making Connections." *Foreign Language Standards: Linking Theory, Research, and Practice,* ed. June Phillips. Lincolnwood, IL: National Textbook Co., 1999.

Moeller, Aleidine. "Optimizing Student Success: Focused Curriculum, Meaningful Assessment, and Effective Instruction," *The 2005 Report of the Central States Conference on the Teaching of Foreign Languages. The Year of Languages: Challenges, Changes, and Choices,* ed. Peggy Boyles and Paul Sandrock. Eau Claire, WI: Crown Prints. 2005.

National K–12 Foreign Language Resource Center. "A Guide to Aligning Curriculum with the Standards." Ames: Iowa State University, 1996.

———. *Bringing the Standards into the Classroom: A Teacher's Guide.* Ames: Iowa State University, 1997.

Patrick, Paula. "The Keys to the Classroom." *The ACTFL Guide for Professional Language Education.* ACTFL, 2007.

Standards for Foreign Language Learning in the 21st Century: Including Chinese, Classical Languages, French, German, Italian, Japanese, Portuguese, Russian, and Spanish. Lawrence, KS: Allen Press, 1999.

VanPatten, Bill and Wong, Wynne. "The Evidence is IN: Drills are OUT." *Foreign Language Annals,* Fall 2003.

Zaslow, Brandon. "Teaching Language for Proficiency: From Theory to Practice (An Instructional Framework)." Unpublished document. School of Education, University of California, Los Angeles, 2001.

Heritage Learners
Blanco, George. "El hispanohablante y la gramática." *Bilingual Research Journal* 18 (1995): 23–46.

Colombi, Cecilia M. and Francisco X. Alarcón, eds. *La enseñanza del español a hispanohablantes: Praxis y teoría.* Boston: Houghton Mifflin Co., 1997.

Rodríguez-Pino, Cecilia, and Daniel Villa. "A Student-Centered Spanish for Native Speakers Program: Theory, Curriculum Design, and Outcome Assessment." *Faces in a Crowd: The Individual Learner in Multisection Courses,* ed. Carol Klee. Boston: Heinle and Heinle, 1994.

Miller, Barbara L., and John B. Webb, eds. *Teaching Heritage Language Learners: Voices from the Classroom,* ACTFL Series. Princeton: Princeton University, 2000.

Methodology
Hadley, Alice Omaggio. *Teaching Language in Context,* 3rd ed. Boston: Heinle and Heinle, 2001.

Hall, Joan Kelly. *Methods for Teaching Foreign Languages: Creating a Community of Learners in the Classroom.* Upper Saddle River, NJ: Merrill Prentice Hall, 2001.

Hamilton, Heidi E., Crane, Cori, Bartoshesky, Abigal. "Doing Foreign Language: Bringing Concordia Language Villages into Language Classrooms." Pearson Education, Inc. 2005.

Lee, James, and Bill Van Patten. *Making Communicative Language Teaching Happen.* New York: McGraw Hill, 1995.

Oxford, Rebecca L. *Language Learning Strategies: What Every Teacher Should Know.* New York: Newbury House, 1990.

Shrum, Judith, and Eileen Glisan. *Teacher's Handbook: Contextualized Language Instruction.* Boston: Heinle and Heinle, 1994.

Multiple Intelligences
Armstrong, Thomas. *Multiple Intelligences in the Classroom.* Alexandria, VA: Association for Supervision and Curriculum Development, 1994.

Gardner, Howard. *Frames of Mind: The Theory of Multiple Intelligences.* New York, NY: Basic Books, 1983.

Lazear, David. *Seven Pathways of Learning: Teaching Students and Parents about Multiple Intelligences.* Tucson, AZ: Zephyr Press, 1994.

Middle School
Raven, Patrick T. and Jo Anne S. Wilson. "Middle-School Foreign Language: What Is It? What Should It Be?" *Visions and Reality in Foreign Language Teaching: Where We Are, Where We Are Going,* ed. William N. Hatfield. Lincolnwood, IL: National Textbook Co., 1993.

Verkler, Karen W. "Middle School Philosophy and Second Language Acquisition Theory: Working Together for Enhanced Proficiency." *Foreign Language Annals,* Vol. 27 (1994): 19–42.

Differentiated Instruction & Inclusion
Ganschow, Leonore, and Richard Sparks. "A Screening Instrument for the Identification of Foreign Language Learning Problems." *Foreign Language Annals,* Vol. 24 (1991): 383–398.

———, and James Javorsky, John Patton, Jane Pohlman, Richard Sparks. "Test Comparisons among Students Identified as High-Risk, Low-Risk, and Learning Disabled in High School Foreign Language Courses," *The Modern Language Journal,* Vol. 76 (1992): 142–159.

Sax Mabbott, Ann. "An Exploration of Reading Comprehension, Oral Reading Errors, and Written Errors by Subjects Labeled Learning Disabled." *Foreign Language Annals,* Vol. 27 (1994): 294–324.

Sheppard, Marie. "Proficiency as an Inclusive Orientation: Meeting the Challenge of Diversity." *Reflecting on Proficiency from the Classroom Perspective,* ed. June Phillips. Lincolnwood, IL: National Textbook Co., 1993.

Tomlinson, Carol Ann and McTighe, Jay. "Integrating Differentiated Instruction & Understanding by Design." ASCD Publication, 2006.

Treviño, María. "Inclusion in the languages other than English classroom." *LOTE CED Communiqué,* Issue 9. Austin, TX: 2003.

Technology
Moore, Zena T. "Technology and Teaching Culture: What Spanish Teachers Do. *Foreign Language Annals,* Vol. 39, No. 4, pp. 579–593.

Muyskens, Judith Ann., ed. *New Ways of Learning and Teaching: Focus on Technology and Foreign Language Education.* Boston: Heinle and Heinle, 1997.

21st Century Skills
Simplicio, Joseph S.C. *Educating the 21st Century Student.* Bloomington, IN: AuthorHouse, 2007.

Trilling, Bernie and Charles Fadel. *21st Century Skills: Learning for Life in Our Times.* San Francisco, CA: Jossey-Bass, 2009.

Understanding by Design
Wiggins, Grant and McTighe, Jay. *Understanding by Design,* 2nd edition. ASCD Publication, 2005.

Index of Cultural References

Index of Cultural References

Guatemala, 272–273
in the Spanish-speaking world, 148

I

Iguazú Falls, Argentina, 216
Inca empire, 240–241
indigenous cultures, xiv, xx, xxi, 44, 177–178, 185, 242, 261, 270
Bolivia and Peru (Quechua and Aymara), xx, xxi
folk art, Kuna Indian *molas*, 177–178
language and folk art, Paraguay, 185
languages, Mexico and Central America, 270
Mexico, xiv, 44
words incorporated into Spanish, 295
Internet use: *ciberspanglish*, 328–329
cybercafés, 313, 330
in Spain vs. the United States, 318
Interplast, 259
Iztaccíhuatl, Mexico, xv

K

Kahlo, Frida, 228
Kuna Indian clothing, 177–178

L

La Capilla de San Miguel, 85
Lake Titicaca, 241
languages, 184, 270, 295, 328
Las Tablas, Panama, 176
Latin Grammy awards, 108
Little Havana, Miami, Florida, 28, 208
Lomas Garza, Carmen, 31
Los Angeles, *calle Olvera*, 209
luminarias, outdoor lanterns, 118

M

Machu Picchu, Inca ruins, Peru, 240
Madrid, Spain, 59, 89, 206, 305, 313
Managua, Nicaragua, xvii
maps
Canary Islands, xxv
Caribbean, the, xix
Central America, xvii
Equatorial Guinea, xxv
Mexico, xv
Panama, 176
Peru, 240
South America, xxi, xxiii
Spain, xxv
United States, 1
Márquez, Gabriel García, 269
Mayas, xiv, xvi
McKinley, William, 201
meals and mealtimes, 86
metric weights, 81
metro (subway) in Mexico City, Mexico, 228
Mexico, xiv–xv
art and artists, 44, 228
celebrations, *Guelaguetza*, 205

Christmas decorations, 118
country facts, xii
flag (history), 103
folk art, 242
geography, xv
glass art, 261
homes, 92
indigenous languages, xiv, 270
indigenous life, 44, 242
map, xv
Mexico City, xiv, 62, 228
Oaxaca, xv, 270
papel picado, 39, 56
Playa del Carmen, 154
population, xiv
transportation in Mexico City, 228
Miami
Community service, 248, 264
Little Havana and calle Ocho, 28, 208
miniteca, dance party, 54
Miró, Joan, 155
Mobility Project, the, 269
molas, Panamanian clothing / folk art, 177–178

Monteverde, rain forest, Costa Rica, 259
Morro, El (fortress), San Juan, Puerto Rico, xviii
Museo del Oro, Bogotá, Colombia, 198
music, Latin Grammy Awards, 108
musical styles, *flamenco*, 270a

N

Naciones Unidas, Las, 273
names, 51
ñandutí, Paraguayan lace weavings, 185
Nazca Lines, Peru, 241
New York, 116th Street, 208
newspapers in Spain, 120
Nicaragua
country facts and map, xvii
national flag, 103
Tipitapa, 308
Nogués, Xavier, 63
Nobel prizes, 269
nonverbal language, 166, 227, 302

O

Oaxaca (Mexico), xv, 205, 270
ojo de Dios, weaving, 242
One Laptop Per Child, 309

P

País, El (Spanish newspaper), 120
Panama, xvii, 176–177
clothing, 176–177
country facts, xvii
homes, 149
maps, xvii, 176
national flag, 103
papel picado, Mexico, 39, 56
Paraguay
country facts and map, xxii–xxiii
folk art, 185
national flag, 103
Paraná River, South America, 226
pastel de tres leches, recipe, 30-a
Patagonia (Argentina), xxiii, 235
patios, 135, 148
Peace Corps, 249
penguins, Patagonia, 235
Peru, xx–xxi, 240–241, 273
country facts, xx
currency, 165
Inca empire, 240–241
maps, xxi, 240
national flag, 103
Nazca Lines, 241
peseros, 228
petroglyphs (wall art), 319
Picasso, Pablo, 309
piñatas, 33, 36
Plaza de España, Seville (Spain), 325
plazas in Spanish-speaking countries, 88, 89

Realidades B

 realidades.com

Digital Edition

Peggy Palo Boyles
OKLAHOMA CITY, OK

Myriam Met
ROCKVILLE, MD

Richard S. Sayers
LONGMONT, CO

Carol Eubanks Wargin

PEARSON

Boston, Massachusetts | Chandler, Arizona
Glenview, Illinois | Upper Saddle River, New Jersey

i

WE DEDICATE THIS BOOK TO THE
MEMORY OF OUR ESTEEMED COLLEAGUE,
Carol Eubanks Wargin.

Front cover, left: Teen girl
Center left: La Boca neighborhood, Buenos Aires, Argentina
Center right: Boats at Xochimilco, Mexico City, Mexico
Right: Decorated ox cart, Sarchí, Costa Rica

Acknowledgments appear on page 374, which constitutes an extension of this copyright page.

ISBN-13:   978-0-13-319964-2
ISBN-10:   0-13-319964-9

3 4 5 6 7 8 9 10   V092   17 16 15 14 13

PEARSON

Realidades B

realidades.com

Digital Edition

Realidades Authors

Peggy Palo Boyles

During her foreign language career of over thirty years, Peggy Palo Boyles has taught elementary, secondary, and university students in both private and public schools. She is currently an independent consultant who provides assistance to schools, districts, universities, state departments of education, and other organizations of foreign language education in the areas of curriculum, assessment, cultural instruction, professional development, and program evaluation. She is also a part-time instructor at Oklahoma State University. She was a member of the ACTFL Performance Guidelines for the K–12 Learners task force and served as a Senior Editor for the project. She currently serves on the Advisory Committee for the ACTFL Assessment for Performance and Proficiency of Languages (AAPPL). Peggy is a Past-President of the National Association of District Supervisors of Foreign Language (NADSFL) and was a recipient of ACTFL's K–12 Steiner Award for Leadership in K–12 Foreign Language Education. Peggy lives in Oklahoma City, OK with her husband, Del. Their son, Ryan, works at the University of Texas at Arlington.

Myriam Met

For most of her professional life, Myriam (Mimi) Met has worked in the public schools, first as a high school teacher in New York, then as K–12 supervisor of language programs in the Cincinnati Public Schools, and finally as a Coordinator of Foreign Language in Montgomery County (MD) Public Schools. She is currently a Senior Research Associate at the National Foreign Language Center, University of Maryland, where she works on K–12 language policy and infrastructure development. Mimi Met has served on the Advisory Board for the National Standards for Foreign Language Learning, on the Executive Council of ACTFL, and as President of the National Association of District Supervisors of Foreign Languages (NADSFL). She has been honored by ACTFL with the Steiner Award for Leadership in K–12 Foreign Language Education and the Papalia Award for Excellence in Teacher Education.

Richard S. Sayers

Rich Sayers has been an educator in world languages since 1978. He taught Spanish at Niwot High School in Longmont, CO for 18 years, where he taught levels 1 through AP Spanish. While at Niwot High School, Rich served as department chair, district foreign language coordinator, and board member of the Colorado Congress of Foreign Language Teachers. Rich has also served on the Board of the Southwest Conference on Language Teaching. In 1991, Rich was selected as one of the Disney Company's Foreign Language Teacher Honorees for the American Teacher Awards. Rich has served as a world languages consultant for Pearson since 1996. He is currently the Curriculum Specialist Manager for Pearson in the Mountain Region.

Carol Eubanks Wargin

Carol Eubanks Wargin taught Spanish for 20 years at Glen Crest Middle School, Glen Ellyn, IL, and also served as Foreign Languages department chair. In 1997, Ms. Wargin's presentation "From Text to Test: How to Land Where You Planned" was honored as the best presentation at the Illinois Conference on the Teaching of Foreign Languages (ICTFL) and at the Central States Conference on the Teaching of Foreign Languages (CSC). She was twice named Outstanding Young Educator by the Jaycees. Ms. Wargin passed away in 2004.

Contributing Writers

Eduardo Aparicio
Chicago, IL

Daniel J. Bender
New Trier High School
Winnetka, IL

Marie Deer
Bloomington, IN

Leslie M. Grahn
Howard County Public Schools
Ellicott City, MD

Thomasina Hannum
Albuquerque, NM

Nancy S. Hernández
World Languages Supervisor
Simsbury (CT) Public Schools

Patricia J. Kule
Fountain Valley School of Colorado
Colorado Springs, CO

Jacqueline Hall Minet
Upper Montclair, NJ

Alex Paredes
Simi Valley, CA

Martha Singer Semmer
Breckenridge, CO

Dee Dee
Drisdale Stafford
Putnam City Schools
Oklahoma City, OK

Christine S. Wells
Cheyenne Mountain Junior High School
Colorado Springs, CO

Michael Werner
University of Chicago
Chicago, IL

National Consultants

María R. Hubbard
Braintree, MA

Patrick T. Raven
Milwaukee, WI

¡Bienvenidos!

Welcome back to **Realidades!** You've already begun to understand, speak, read and write Spanish. You've also explored many different Spanish-speaking cultures. Because learning a language is a process in which you build on what you already know, it is important to practice what you've learned. Before you move on to **Realidades** Level B, you need to review the Spanish you learned in **Realidades** Level A. The *Para empezar* chapter will give you the practice you need to feel more comfortable. So, let's get started!

Tips for Reviewing

Here are some ways you can review.

- **Organize your information.** It's easier to remember a word if you think about the category it belongs to. The material you learned in Level A was organized into four *Temas:* friends, school, foods and beverages, and leisure activities. Brainstorm a list of words and expressions you remember that relate to each of these categories. How many can you think of?

- **Make flashcards.** A great way to refresh your memory is to review with flashcards. Put the Spanish word on one side and either an English word or a drawing on the other. Then pair up with a classmate to quiz one another on the words.

- **Look for meaning within the context of a sentence.** If you can't remember a word or phrase, try reading or listening to the entire sentence, and see if you can figure out its meaning based on what else is being said.

¡Bienvenidos! **v**

Online Resources with realidades.com

REALIDADES includes lots of online resources to help you learn Spanish! You can easily link to all of them when you log on to your Home Page within realidades.com. Your teacher will assign some activities, such as the ones in the workbooks. Others you can access on your own.

You'll find these resources highlighted on the pages of your print or online Student Edition with technology icons. Here's a list of the different icons used.

 Bilingual Visual Dictionary Links to additional vocabulary words presented visually

Reference Atlas Quick links to the countries in the online atlas

 Mapa global interactivo Links to GIS showing locations across the Spanish-speaking world

 Videos

Videocultura Cultural overview of each theme

Videohistoria Vocabulary video to help present the new vocabulary

GramActiva Grammar explanations to help present the new grammar

Grammar Tutorials Clear explanations of grammar with comparison to English

Animated Verbs Animations that highlight verb conjugations

¿Eres tú, María? A 10-episode mystery video starting in *Capítulo 5A*

▶️ Modelo *Videomodelos*
Video models of speaking activities

 Audio Audio files for vocabulary, listening practice, and pronunciation

 Canciones de hip hop Songs to help practice new vocabulary and grammar

 Flashcards Practice for the new vocabulary

 RealTalk! Speak-and-record tool for speaking activities

 GramActiva **Activity** Extra practice for the *GramActiva* video

 Más práctica GO **Online practice**

Instant Check Short activities that check your progress right away

Guided Workbook Step-by-step vocabulary and grammar practice

Core Workbook Vocabulary and grammar exercises

Communication Workbook Listening, video, and writing activities

Cultural Reading Activity Questions for the *Lectura* reading

Actividades Questions for the *Videomisterio*

Puzzles End-of-chapter games

Getting Started on realidades.com

At the beginning of the year, you'll want to get registered on realidades.com. Your teacher will help you get started. If you log on to realidades.com using a non-school computer, be sure to check out the System Requirements to make sure you are using compatible browsers and have the needed software.

realidades.com Home Page

After you register, you'll land on your realidades.com Home Page. Here you'll be able to access assignments, grades, and study resources. You'll also be able to communicate with your teacher.

 You'll find everything that's in the book online as eText.

RealTalk!

You'll be able to record many of your speaking activities using RealTalk! You can use the microphone in your computer or a headset with microphone. If you want, you can download and save your recording.

Mapa global interactivo

Build your geography skills and learn about more locations throughout the Spanish-speaking world. You can download .kmz files from realidades.com and link to sites using Google Earth™ or other geographic information systems.

Tabla de materias

Tema 5 Fiesta en familia

Tema 6 La casa

Tema 7 De compras

Tema 8 Experiencias

Tema 9 Medios de comunicación

México

Ciudad de Guanajuato, México

El Zócalo, México, D.F.

México

Capital: México, D.F.

Population: 113.7 million

Area: 761,606 sq mi / 1,972,550 sq km

Languages: Spanish (official), Nahuatl, various Mayan and other indigenous languages

Religions: Roman Catholic, Protestant

Government: federal republic

Currency: *peso mexicano*

Exports: manufactured products, oil and oil products, silver, coffee, cotton

ESTADOS UNIDOS

Tijuana

30° N

Ciudad Juárez

Chihuahua

Nuevo Laredo

Monterrey

Golfo de México

Trópico de Cáncer

20° N

Guadalajara

Querétaro

Mérida

Paracutín

Ciudad de México

Iztaccíhuatl

Veracruz

Península de Yucatán

Puebla

Popocatépetl

Oaxaca

ISTMO DE TEHUANTEPEC

BELICE

Acapulco

SIERRA MADRE DEL SUR

GUATEMALA

OCÉANO PACÍFICO

EL SALVADOR

Baja California

Golfo de California (Mar de Cortés)

SIERRA MADRE OCCIDENTAL

SIERRA MADRE ORIENTAL

Río Grande

Río Bravo del Norte

110° O

100° O

LEYENDA
Elevación

Metros	Pies
3,000	9,840
2,000	6,560
1,000	3,280
500	1,640
200	656

— Frontera nacional
✪ Capital
● Ciudad
▲ Volcán o montaña

0   200 Millas
0   200 Kilómetros

Proyección cónica conforme de Lambert

N O E S

realidades.com GO

🌐 *Mapa global interactivo*

DK Reference Atlas

Mapa global interactivo

Download the *Mapa global interactivo* files for Mexico and preview the activity. For this activity, you visit Mexico and the Baja Peninsula.

Sierra Tarahumara

México   xv

América Central

Guatemala

Capital: Ciudad de Guatemala

Population: 13.8 million

Area: 42,043 sq mi / 108,890 sq km

Languages: Spanish (official), Quiche, Cakchiquel, Kekchi, Mam, Garifuna, Xinca, and other indigenous languages

Religions: Roman Catholic, Protestant, traditional Mayan beliefs

Government: constitutional democratic republic

Currency: *quetzal*, U.S. dollar *(dólar)*

Exports: coffee, sugar, petroleum, clothing, textiles, bananas, vegetables

Honduras

Capital: Tegucigalpa

Population: 8.1 million

Area: 43,278 sq mi / 112,090 sq km

Languages: Spanish (official), indigenous languages

Religions: Roman Catholic, Protestant

Government: democratic, constitutional republic

Currency: *lempira*

Exports: coffee, bananas, shrimp, lobster, meat, zinc, wood

El Salvador

Capital: San Salvador

Population: 6.1 million

Area: 8,124 sq mi / 21,040 sq km

Languages: Spanish (official), Nahua

Religions: Roman Catholic, Protestant

Government: republic

Currency: U.S. dollar *(dólar)*

Exports: offshore assembly parts, equipment, coffee, sugar, shrimp, textiles, chemicals, electricity

El Canal de Panamá

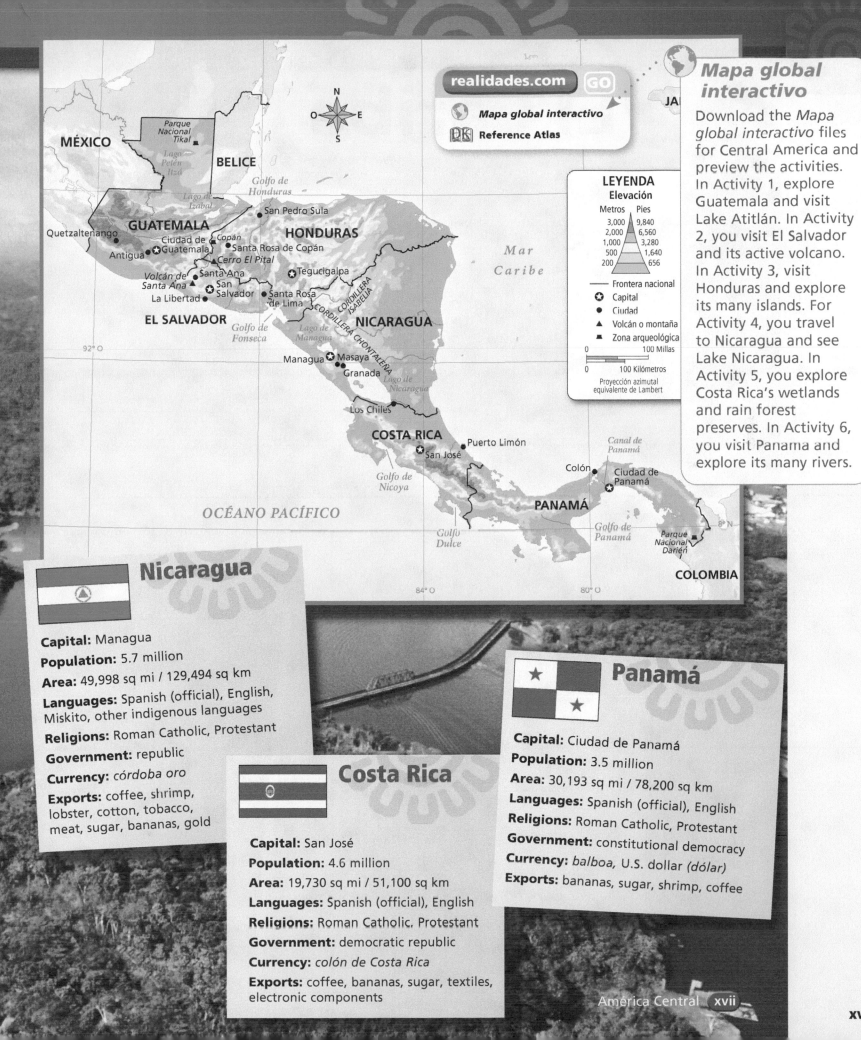

realidades.com **GO**

🌎 *Mapa global interactivo*

📖 Reference Atlas

Mapa global interactivo

Download the *Mapa global interactivo* files for Central America and preview the activities. In Activity 1, explore Guatemala and visit Lake Atitlán. In Activity 2, you visit El Salvador and its active volcano. In Activity 3, visit Honduras and explore its many islands. For Activity 4, you travel to Nicaragua and see Lake Nicaragua. In Activity 5, you explore Costa Rica's wetlands and rain forest preserves. In Activity 6, you visit Panama and explore its many rivers.

LEYENDA
Elevación

Metros	Pies
3,000	9,840
2,000	6,560
1,000	3,280
500	1,640
200	656

— Frontera nacional
✪ Capital
● Ciudad
▲ Volcán o montaña
■ Zona arqueológica

0   100 Millas
0   100 Kilómetros

Proyección azimutal
equivalente de Lambert

MÉXICO

Parque Nacional Tikal

Lago Petén Itzá

BELICE

Golfo de Honduras

Lago de Izabal

San Pedro Sula

GUATEMALA

Quetzaltenango

Ciudad de Guatemala ✪   Copán   **HONDURAS**

Antigua   ● Santa Rosa de Copán

Cerro El Pital ▲   Santa Ana

Volcán de Santa Ana ▲   San Salvador ✪   ● Tegucigalpa

La Libertad   ● Santa Rosa de Lima

EL SALVADOR

Golfo de Fonseca

CORDILLERA ISABELIA

CORDILLERA CHONTALEÑA

NICARAGUA

Mar Caribe

Lago de Managua

Managua ✪ ● Masaya

● Granada

Lago de Nicaragua

Los Chiles

COSTA RICA

✪ San José   ● Puerto Limón

Golfo de Nicoya

OCÉANO PACÍFICO

Golfo Dulce

Canal de Panamá

● Colón

Ciudad de Panamá ✪

PANAMÁ

Golfo de Panamá

Parque Nacional Darién ■

COLOMBIA

92° O   84° O   80° O   8° N

Nicaragua

Capital: Managua

Population: 5.7 million

Area: 49,998 sq mi / 129,494 sq km

Languages: Spanish (official), English, Miskito, other indigenous languages

Religions: Roman Catholic, Protestant

Government: republic

Currency: *córdoba oro*

Exports: coffee, shrimp, lobster, cotton, tobacco, meat, sugar, bananas, gold

Costa Rica

Capital: San José

Population: 4.6 million

Area: 19,730 sq mi / 51,100 sq km

Languages: Spanish (official), English

Religions: Roman Catholic, Protestant

Government: democratic republic

Currency: *colón de Costa Rica*

Exports: coffee, bananas, sugar, textiles, electronic components

Panamá

Capital: Ciudad de Panamá

Population: 3.5 million

Area: 30,193 sq mi / 78,200 sq km

Languages: Spanish (official), English

Religions: Roman Catholic, Protestant

Government: constitutional democracy

Currency: *balboa*, U.S. dollar (*dólar*)

Exports: bananas, sugar, shrimp, coffee

El Caribe

El Morro, San Juan,
Puerto Rico

Un arrecife de coral, República Dominicana

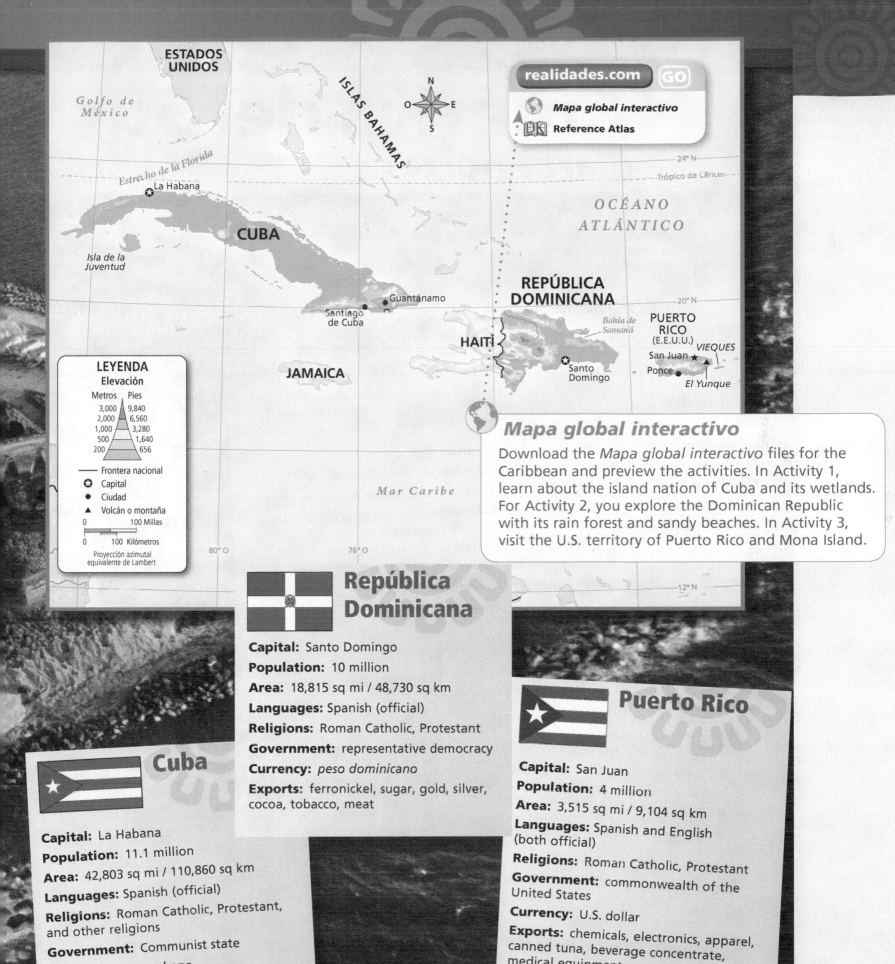

ESTADOS UNIDOS

Golfo de México

ISLAS BAHAMAS

Estrecho de la Florida

La Habana

CUBA

Isla de la Juventud

Guantánamo

Santiago de Cuba

JAMAICA

OCÉANO ATLÁNTICO

24° N

Trópico de Cáncer

REPÚBLICA DOMINICANA

20° N

Bahía de Samaná

PUERTO RICO (E.E.U.U.)

San Juan

Ponce

VIEQUES

El Yunque

HAITÍ

Santo Domingo

Mar Caribe

80° O

76° O

12° N

LEYENDA
Elevación

Metros	Pies
3,000	9,840
2,000	6,560
1,000	3,280
500	1,640
200	656

— Frontera nacional

✪ Capital

● Ciudad

▲ Volcán o montaña

0   100 Millas

0   100 Kilómetros

Proyección azimutal equivalente de Lambert

Mapa global interactivo

Download the *Mapa global interactivo* files for the Caribbean and preview the activities. In Activity 1, learn about the island nation of Cuba and its wetlands. For Activity 2, you explore the Dominican Republic with its rain forest and sandy beaches. In Activity 3, visit the U.S. territory of Puerto Rico and Mona Island.

República Dominicana

Capital: Santo Domingo

Population: 10 million

Area: 18,815 sq mi / 48,730 sq km

Languages: Spanish (official)

Religions: Roman Catholic, Protestant

Government: representative democracy

Currency: *peso dominicano*

Exports: ferronickel, sugar, gold, silver, cocoa, tobacco, meat

Cuba

Capital: La Habana

Population: 11.1 million

Area: 42,803 sq mi / 110,860 sq km

Languages: Spanish (official)

Religions: Roman Catholic, Protestant, and other religions

Government: Communist state

Currency: *peso cubano*

Exports: sugar, nickel, tobacco, shellfish, medical products, citrus, coffee

Puerto Rico

Capital: San Juan

Population: 4 million

Area: 3,515 sq mi / 9,104 sq km

Languages: Spanish and English (both official)

Religions: Roman Catholic, Protestant

Government: commonwealth of the United States

Currency: U.S. dollar

Exports: chemicals, electronics, apparel, canned tuna, beverage concentrate, medical equipment

América del Sur
(Parte norte)

Colombia

Capital: Bogotá

Population: 44.7 million

Area: 439,736 sq mi / 1,138,910 sq km

Languages: Spanish (official)

Religion: Roman Catholic

Government: republic

Currency: *peso colombiano*

Exports: textiles, petroleum, coal, coffee, gold, emeralds, bananas, flowers, pharmaceuticals, sugar

Ecuador

Capital: Quito

Population: 15 million

Area: 109,483 sq mi / 283,560 sq km

Languages: Spanish (official), Quechua, other indigenous languages

Religion: Roman Catholic

Government: republic

Currency: U.S. dollar (*dólar*)

Exports: oil, bananas, tuna, shrimp, cocoa, gold, tropical wood

Las ruinas de Machu Picchu, Perú

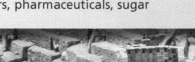

Perú

Capital: Lima

Population: 29.2 million

Area: 496,226 sq mi / 1,285,220 sq km

Languages: Spanish (official), Quechua, (official), Aymara, and other indigenous languages

Religion: Roman Catholic and other religions

Government: constitutional republic

Currency: *nuevo sol*

Exports: gold, zinc, copper, fish and fish products, textiles

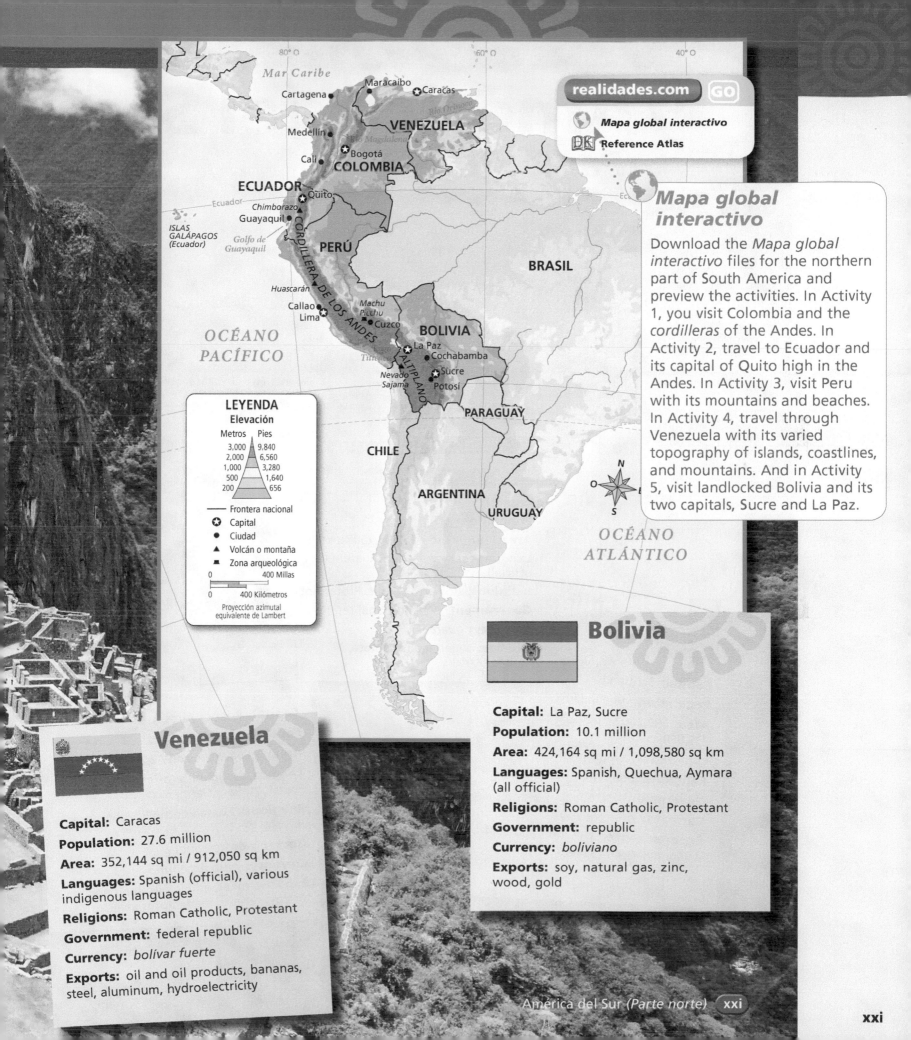

Mapa global interactivo

Download the *Mapa global interactivo* files for the northern part of South America and preview the activities. In Activity 1, you visit Colombia and the *cordilleras* of the Andes. In Activity 2, travel to Ecuador and its capital of Quito high in the Andes. In Activity 3, visit Peru with its mountains and beaches. In Activity 4, travel through Venezuela with its varied topography of islands, coastlines, and mountains. And in Activity 5, visit landlocked Bolivia and its two capitals, Sucre and La Paz.

realidades.com GO

Mapa global interactivo

Reference Atlas

LEYENDA
Elevación

Metros	Pies
3,000	9,840
2,000	6,560
1,000	3,280
500	1,640
200	656

— Frontera nacional
✪ Capital
● Ciudad
▲ Volcán o montaña
■ Zona arqueológica

0   400 Millas
0   400 Kilómetros

Proyección azimutal equivalente de Lambert

Venezuela

Capital: Caracas

Population: 27.6 million

Area: 352,144 sq mi / 912,050 sq km

Languages: Spanish (official), various indigenous languages

Religions: Roman Catholic, Protestant

Government: federal republic

Currency: *bolívar fuerte*

Exports: oil and oil products, bananas, steel, aluminum, hydroelectricity

Bolivia

Capital: La Paz, Sucre

Population: 10.1 million

Area: 424,164 sq mi / 1,098,580 sq km

Languages: Spanish, Quechua, Aymara (all official)

Religions: Roman Catholic, Protestant

Government: republic

Currency: *boliviano*

Exports: soy, natural gas, zinc, wood, gold

# América del Sur
(Parte sur)

Monte Fitz Roy, Patagonia, Argentina

 Paraguay

Capital: Asunción
Population: 6.5 million
Area: 157,047 sq mi / 406,750 sq km
Languages: Spanish and Guaraní (both official)
Religions: Roman Catholic, Protestant
Government: constitutional republic
Currency: *guaraní*
Exports: sugar, meat, tapioca, hydroelectricity

 **Chile**

Capital: Santiago
Population: 16.9 million
Area: 292,260 sq mi / 756,950 sq km
Languages: Spanish (official)
Religions: Roman Catholic, Protestant
Government: republic
Currency: *peso chileno*
Exports: copper, fish, iron, iodine, fruit, wood, paper and pulp, chemicals

 **Argentina**

Capital: Buenos Aires
Population: 41.8 million
Area: 1,068,302 sq mi / 2,766,890 sq km
Languages: Spanish (official), English, French, Italian, German
Religions: Roman Catholic, Protestant, Jewish
Government: republic
Currency: *peso argentino*
Exports: meat, edible oils, fuels and energy, cereals, feed, motor vehicles

VENEZUELA

Mar Caribe

COLOMBIA

Ecuador

ECUADOR

PERÚ

BRASIL

OCÉANO PACÍFICO

BOLIVIA

Río Paraguay

ALTIPLANO

CORDILLERA DE LOS ANDES

GRAN CHACO

PARAGUAY

Asunción ☆

Cataratas del Iguazú

Tróp

Ecuador

0°

LEYENDA
Elevación

Metros	Pies
3,000	9,840
2,000	6,560
1,000	3,280
500	1,640
200	656

—— Frontera nacional
☆ Capital
● Ciudad
▲ Volcán o montaña

0   400 Millas
0   400 Kilómetros

Proyección azimutal
equivalente de Lambert

CHILE

Río Paraná

ARGENTINA

Viña del Mar
Valparaíso ●
Santiago ● *Cerro Aconcagua* ▲

Rosario ●

URUGUAY

Buenos Aires ●

Montevideo ☆
Punta del Este ●

OCÉANO ATLÁNTICO

PAMPAS

Río de la Plata

Mar del Plata ●

40° S

PATAGONIA

Cerro de
San Valentín ▲

Torres del
Paine ▲

TIERRA DEL FUEGO

Estrecho de Magallanes

Cabo de Hornos

80° O   60° O   40° O

🌐 *Mapa global interactivo*

📖 **Reference Atlas**

Mapa global interactivo

Download the *Mapa global interactivo* files for the southern part of South America and preview the activities. In Activity 1, you visit Chile and the island of Chiloé. For Activity 2, you travel to Paraguay and explore the Paraná River. Activity 3 takes you to Argentina and its cosmopolitan capital city of Buenos Aires. In Activity 4, visit Uruguay and its beautiful capital city of Montevideo.

Uruguay

Capital: Montevideo

Population: 3.3 million

Area: 68,039 sq mi / 176,220 sq km

Languages: Spanish (official), Portuñol/Brazilero

Religions: Roman Catholic, Protestant, and other religions

Government: constitutional republic

Currency: *peso uruguayo*

Exports: foods, vehicles, meat, rice, timber

España
Guinea Ecuatorial

España

Capital: Madrid

Population: 46.8 million

Area: 194,897 sq mi / 504,782 sq km

Language: Castilian Spanish (official); Catalan, Galician, Basque (official regionally)

Religion: Roman Catholic

Government: parliamentary monarchy

Currency: *euro*

Exports: food, machinery, motor vehicles

El Alcázar de Segovia, Segovia, España

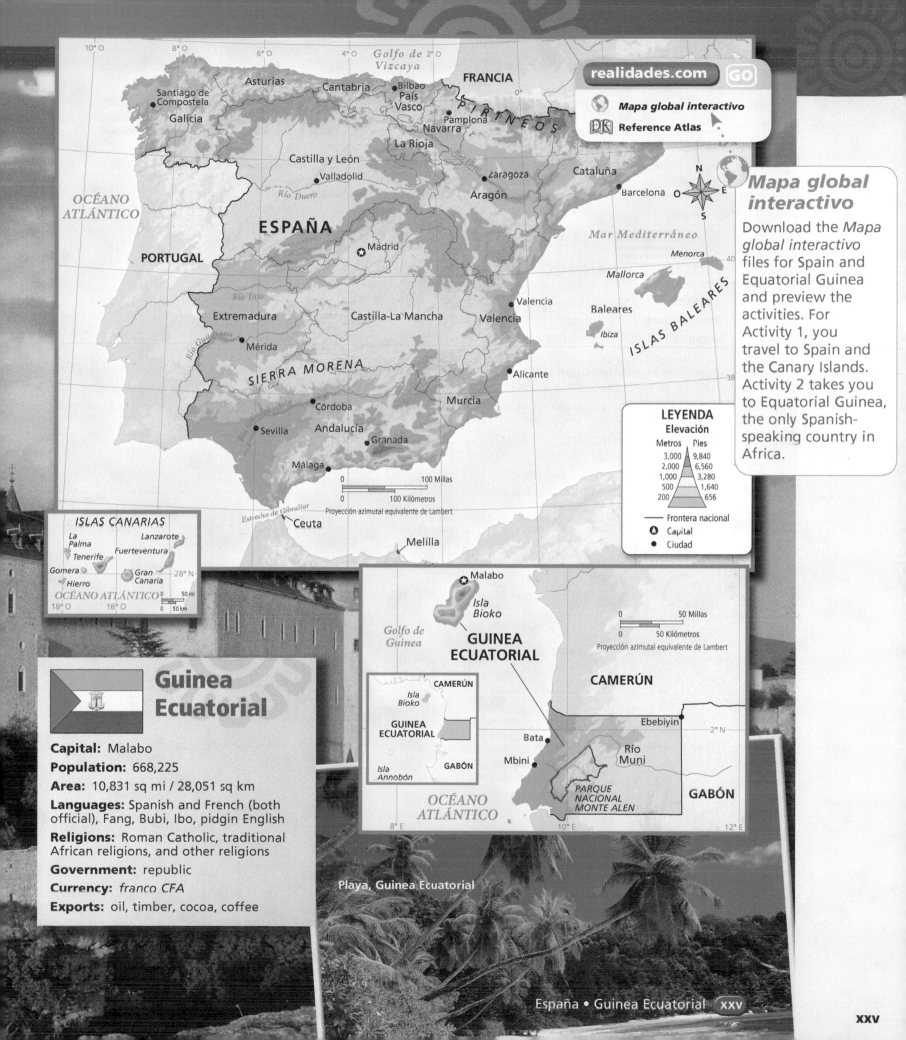

10° O   **8° O**   **6° O**   **4° O**   Golfo de Vizcaya   **2° O**   **FRANCIA**

Santiago de Compostela

Asturias   Cantabria   Bilbao   País Vasco

Galicia

PIRINEOS

Pamplona

Navarra

La Rioja

Castilla y León

Río Ebro

Zaragoza   Cataluña

Valladolid

Barcelona

OCÉANO ATLÁNTICO

Río Duero

Aragón

ESPAÑA

Madrid

Mar Mediterráneo

Menorca

PORTUGAL

Mallorca

Río Tajo

Valencia

Baleares

Extremadura

Castilla-La Mancha

Valencia

Ibiza

ISLAS BALEARES

Río Guadiana

Mérida

SIERRA MORENA

Alicante

Murcia

Río Guadalquivir

Córdoba

Sevilla   Andalucía

Granada

Málaga

0   100 Millas

0   100 Kilómetros

Proyección azimutal equivalente de Lambert

Estrecho de Gibraltar   Ceuta

Melilla

realidades.com **GO**

🌐 *Mapa global interactivo*

📖 Reference Atlas

N O E S

LEYENDA
Elevación

Metros	Pies
3,000	9,840
2,000	6,560
1,000	3,280
500	1,640
200	656

— Frontera nacional
⊗ Capital
• Ciudad

Mapa global interactivo

Download the *Mapa global interactivo* files for Spain and Equatorial Guinea and preview the activities. For Activity 1, you travel to Spain and the Canary Islands. Activity 2 takes you to Equatorial Guinea, the only Spanish-speaking country in Africa.

ISLAS CANARIAS

La Palma   Lanzarote

Tenerife   Fuerteventura

Gomera   Gran Canaria

Hierro

OCÉANO ATLÁNTICO   28° N

18° O   16° O   0   50 mi   0   50 km

Guinea Ecuatorial

Capital: Malabo

Population: 668,225

Area: 10,831 sq mi / 28,051 sq km

Languages: Spanish and French (both official), Fang, Bubi, Ibo, pidgin English

Religions: Roman Catholic, traditional African religions, and other religions

Government: republic

Currency: *franco CFA*

Exports: oil, timber, cocoa, coffee

Malabo

Isla Bioko

Golfo de Guinea

GUINEA ECUATORIAL

0   50 Millas

0   50 Kilómetros

Proyección azimutal equivalente de Lambert

CAMERÚN

CAMERÚN

Isla Bioko

GUINEA ECUATORIAL

Ebebiyin   2° N

Bata

Mbini

Río Muni

GABÓN

Isla Annobón

PARQUE NACIONAL MONTE ALEN

GABÓN

OCÉANO ATLÁNTICO

8° E   10° E   12° E

Playa, Guinea Ecuatorial

Estados Unidos

 **Estados Unidos**

Capital: Washington, D.C.

Population: 313.2 million

Area: 3,717,813 sq mi / 9,631,418 sq km

Languages: English, Spanish, other Indo-European languages, Asian and Pacific Islander languages, other languages

Religions: Protestant, Roman Catholic, Jewish, Muslim, and other religions

Government: federal republic

Currency: U.S. dollar

Exports: motor vehicles, aircraft, medicines, telecommunications equipment, electronics, chemicals, soybeans, fruit, wheat, corn

Las grandes llanuras

Caras estadounidenses

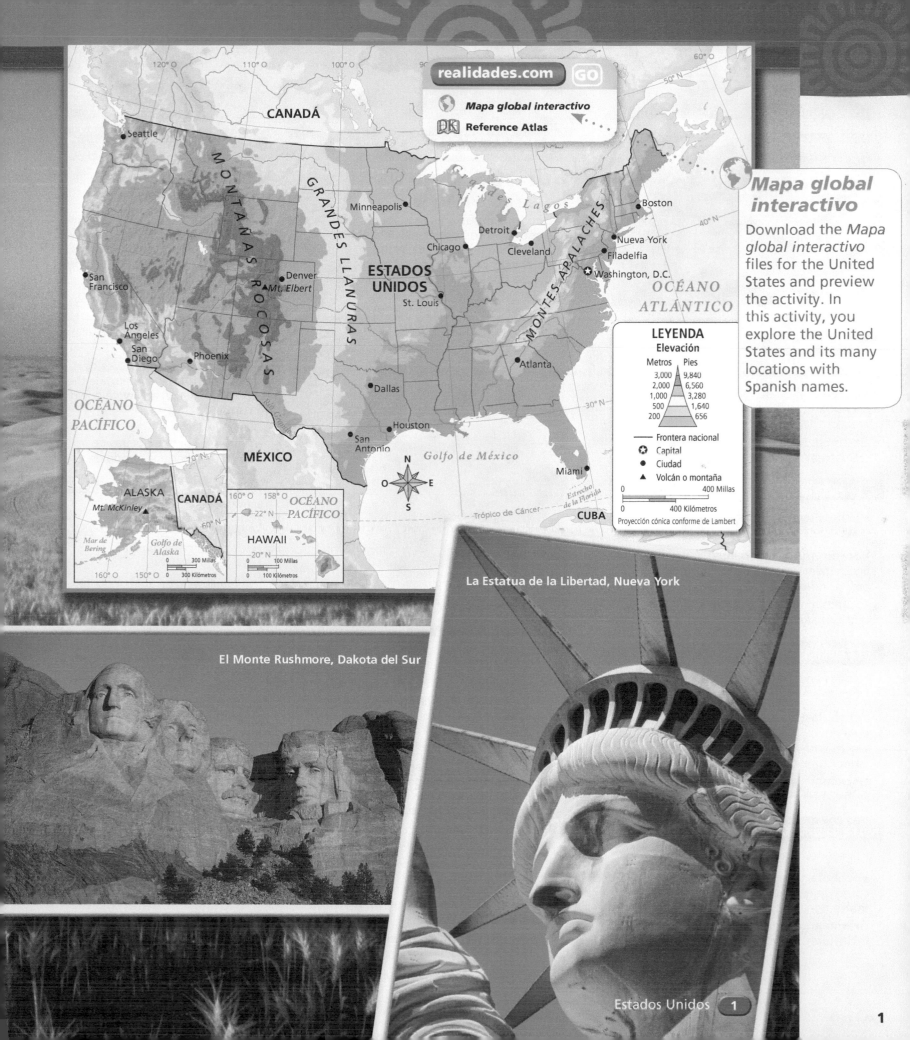

realidades.com **GO**

🌐 *Mapa global interactivo*

📖 Reference Atlas

CANADÁ

Seattle

MONTAÑAS ROCOSAS

GRANDES LLANURAS

Grandes Lagos

MONTES APALACHES

San Francisco

Denver
▲ Mt. Elbert

ESTADOS UNIDOS

Minneapolis

Detroit

Chicago

Cleveland

St. Louis

Boston

Nueva York

Filadelfia

✪ Washington, D.C.

Los Ángeles

San Diego

Phoenix

Dallas

Atlanta

OCÉANO ATLÁNTICO

OCÉANO PACÍFICO

Houston

San Antonio

MÉXICO

Golfo de México

Miami

LEYENDA
Elevación

Metros	Pies
3,000	9,840
2,000	6,560
1,000	3,280
500	1,640
200	656

— Frontera nacional
✪ Capital
● Ciudad
▲ Volcán o montaña

0 ——— 400 Millas
0 ——— 400 Kilómetros
Proyección cónica conforme de Lambert

ALASKA
CANADÁ
Mt. McKinley ▲

OCÉANO PACÍFICO

22° N

Mar de Bering

Golfo de Alaska

HAWAII
20° N

0 ——— 300 Millas
0 ——— 300 Kilómetros

0 ——— 100 Millas
0 ——— 100 Kilómetros

N
O — E
S

Trópico de Cáncer

Estrecho de la Florida

CUBA

Mapa global interactivo

Download the *Mapa global interactivo* files for the United States and preview the activity. In this activity, you explore the United States and its many locations with Spanish names.

La Estatua de la Libertad, Nueva York

El Monte Rushmore, Dakota del Sur

1 Mis amigos y yo

- Activities, descriptions

Vocabulary: what you and others like and do not like to do; what you and others are like

Grammar: infinitives; the verb *gustar;* adjectives

2 La escuela

- School-related items; classes and activities

Vocabulary: school-related items; classes and activities; items in the classroom; prepositions

Grammar: subject pronouns; the present tense of *-ar* verbs

3 La comida

- Foods and health

Vocabulary: breakfast, lunch, and dinner foods; dessert; health

Grammar: present tense of *-er* and *-ir* verbs; the plurals of adjectives

4 Los pasatiempos

- Locations and events in the community

Vocabulary: locations and events in the community; question words; adjectives that describe emotions; invitations

Grammar: asking questions; *ir + a +* infinitive; the verb *jugar*

THEME SUPPORT

Bulletin Boards

Theme: *Mis amigos y yo*

Ask students to cut out, copy, or download photos of common community or school activities; food items; and locations in schools or communities. Cluster photos to reflect the three categories just mentioned.

Hands-on Culture

The Spanish Yellow Pages

Teachers can usually obtain free copies of the Yellow Pages in Spanish by calling the telephone company.

1. Divide students into small groups (3–4 students). Ask each group to quickly scan the Yellow Pages for words they know and for advertisements that interest them.

2. Ask each group to find an advertisement for each of the following categories: restaurant / food; schools / education; community locations / events; entertainment.

3. Have each group write down the names of the advertisements they chose. They must then make a list of the cognates they find, the words they already know, and the words they can identify through context.

4. Students explain why they would choose to patronize the business or not.

5. Each group presents their findings to the class.

Game

¡Descripciones locas!

This game practices the skill of recognizing vocabulary words, answering questions and conjugating verbs. Play it to review the vocabulary and grammar presented in the *Para empezar* chapter.

Players: entire class, playing pairs

Materials: paper, pen or pencil

Rules:

1. Players have to ask for and provide the following information and write down their partners' responses:
   a. ¿Cómo te llamas?
   b. ¿Cómo es la persona detrás de ti?
   c. ¿Cómo es la persona al lado de ti?
   d. ¿Adónde vas para estudiar?
   e. ¿Qué hacen tú y tus amigos? (dos actividades)
   f. ¿Cuál de tus clases es difícil?
   g. ¿Cómo estás?
   h. ¿Es la clase mala o buena?
   i. ¿Qué te gusta comer?

2. Place the following paragraph on the board or prepare a copy to hand out to students after they have asked and answered their questions:
   Mi amigo(a) __a.__ es una persona muy __b.__ y yo soy __c.__. Nosotros pasamos todo el día en __d.__. Nosotros __e.__ allí. Mi clase favorita es la clase de __f.__. Mi profesor(a) está __g.__ porque soy muy __h.__ en la clase. Bueno, tengo hambre y voy a comer un sándwich de __i.__. ¿Te gustaría comer conmigo?

3. Players fill in the paragraph with their partners' responses, making all adjectives agree with the nouns they describe.

4. Players read their paragraphs to the class and the class votes on the silliest paragraph.

Variation: Each group creates its own paragraph and questions, then exchanges them with another group.

THEME PROJECT

Mi comunidad: Folleto de información

Overview: Students will create an illustrated tourist brochure describing their community. They should include short descriptions of one restaurant and its food choices; their school and its academic offerings; popular community events and locations; and descriptions of two interesting people in the community. Students present their brochure to the class, explaining why they chose each element.

Resources: colored pencils, crayons or markers, pens, construction paper, glue, magazines, photos, or electronic layout tools and online images

> **Sequence:** (suggestions for when to do each step are found throughout the chapter)
>
> **STEP 1.** Review instructions so students know what is expected of them. Hand out the "*Para empezar* Project Instructions and Rubric" from the *Teacher's Resource Book*.
>
> **STEP 2.** Students should submit a list of the places and people they chose to include in their brochure. Each location should be accompanied by a list of possible vocabulary words that students can include in their presentations. Return the lists with your suggestions.
>
> **STEP 3.** Students create layouts for the four sections to go in the brochure. Each section should contain a description of the location, event, or person the student chose.
>
> **STEP 4.** Students should submit a draft of the sections of their brochure. Note your corrections and suggestions, then return drafts to students. Students correct their drafts, then partner to describe their brochures.
>
> **STEP 5.** Students present their brochures to the class, explaining why they chose each item they included.

Options:

1. Students research and present an informational brochure about a Spanish-speaking community.
2. Students go out into the community to request photos or brochures from businesses or historical locations. They can then include these items in their brochures.

Assessment:

Here is a detailed rubric for assessing this project:

Para empezar: Mi comunidad: Folleto de información

RUBRIC	Score 1	Score 3	Score 5
Evidence of planning	You didn't submit a list and draft.	You submitted the list and draft, but didn't correct them.	You submitted and corrected your list and draft.
Use of illustrations	You didn't include any illustrations.	You included illustrations for most items.	You included illustrations for all items.
Presentation	You listed items included in the brochure but didn't adequately describe them or explain why they were chosen.	You described items in the brochure but did not adequately explain why they were chosen.	You described items in the brochure and explained why they were chosen.

21st Century Skills

Look for tips throughout *Para empezar* to enrich your teaching by integrating 21st Century Skills. Suggestions for the Theme Project and Theme Support follow below.

Theme Project

Modify the Theme Project with one or more of these suggestions:

Encourage Creativity and Innovation

Invite students to design a novel visitor's guide for tourists, combining audio, video, and online sources. The handout "Innovate" will help them develop, plan, and implement their groundbreaking guide.

Support Critical Thinking and Problem Solving

Have students focus on a specific group of people to reach with their brochure about the community. Who are they compiling this information for? Students like themselves? People coming from abroad? The handout "Make Decisions" can help them analyze their options.

Develop Media Literacy

Have students consider how they would advertise their tourist brochure. Describe elements of a successful advertising campaign, such as street signs or newspaper ads and radio, television, and Internet campaigns. Which advertising elements would work best to reach the audience they chose in the previous step, and why?

Theme Culture

Foster Social and Cross-Cultural Skills

Have students reflect on what they learned about their own community while creating their tourist brochure. What did they learn when choosing a specific group to address? Did they learn anything new about their own surroundings?

AT A GLANCE

Objectives

- Talk about what you like and don't like to do
- Describe yourself and other people
- Talk about the classes you have
- Describe your classroom
- Ask and tell who is doing an action
- Talk about foods and beverages for breakfast, lunch, and dinner
- Discuss food, health, and exercise
- Talk about locations in your community
- Talk about leisure activities
- Tell where you go
- Ask questions

Vocabulary

- Adjectives that tell what people are like
- Words to talk about family members and friends
- School subjects, related activities, supplies, and classroom items
- Words to identify location
- Breakfast and lunch foods
- Verbs for eating and drinking
- Places and leisure activities
- Telling what time something happens
- Extending, accepting, or declining invitations

Grammar

- Negatives
- Infinitives
- Agreement of adjectives
- Subject pronouns
- The present tense of *-ar* verbs
- The verb *estar*
- The verbs *gustar* and *encantar*
- The present tense of *-er* and *-ir* verbs
- The plurals of adjectives
- Asking questions
- *ir* + *a* + infinitive

RESOURCES

	FOR THE STUDENT	ONLINE	DVD	PRINT	FOR THE TEACHER	ONLINE	PREEXP	DVD	PRINT
Plan					Interactive TE and Resources DVD	•		•	
					Teacher's Resource Book, pp. 1–14	•		•	•
					Pre-AP* Resource Book, pp. 60–61	•		•	•
					Lesson Plans	•			•
Introducción PP. 2–3									
Present	Student Edition, pp. 2–3	•	•	•	Interactive TE and Resources DVD	•		•	
	DK Reference Atlas	•	•		Teacher's Resource Book, pp. 2–3	•		•	
					Galería de fotos			•	
Mis amigos y yo PP. 4–9									
Present & Practice	Student Edition, pp. 4–9	•	•	•	Interactive Whiteboard Vocabulary and Grammar Activities	•		•	
	Audio	•	•		Interactive TE and Resources DVD	•		•	
	Instant Check	•			Teacher's Resource Book, pp. 5–7	•		•	•
	Tutorial Video: Grammar	•			Communicative Pair Activities, pp. 6–7	•		•	•
	Communicative Pair Activities	•			Audio Program	•	•	•	
					Videomodelos	•		•	
					Vocabulary and Grammar Transparencies, 36	•	•	•	
					Answer Keys: Student Edition, pp. 88–89	•	•	•	
Assess and Remediate					Prueba P-1: Mis amigos y yo with Study Plan	•			

RESOURCES

La escuela PP. 10–15

Present & Practice

For the Student	ONLINE	DVD	PRINT	For the Teacher	ONLINE	PREEXP	DVD	PRINT
Student Edition, pp. 10–15	•	•	•	Interactive Whiteboard Vocabulary and Grammar Activities	•		•	
Audio	•	•		Interactive TE and Resources DVD	•		•	
Instant Check	•			Teacher's Resource Book, pp. 5, 8–9	•		•	•
Tutorial Video: Grammar	•			Communicative Pair Activities, pp. 8–9	•		•	•
Communicative Pair Activities	•			Audio Program	•	•	•	
				Videomodelos	•		•	
				Answer Keys: Student Edition, p. 90	•	•	•	•

Assess and Remediate

For the Student	ONLINE	DVD	PRINT	For the Teacher	ONLINE	PREEXP	DVD	PRINT
				Prueba P-2: La escuela with Study Plan	•			

La comida, PP. 16–21

Present & Practice

For the Student	ONLINE	DVD	PRINT	For the Teacher	ONLINE	PREEXP	DVD	PRINT
Student Edition, pp. 16–21	•	•	•	Interactive Whiteboard Vocabulary and Grammar Activities	•		•	
Audio	•	•		Interactive TE and Resources DVD	•		•	
Instant Check	•			Teacher's Resource Book, pp. 10–11	•		•	•
Tutorial Video: Grammar	•			Communicative Pair Activities, pp. 10–11	•		•	•
Communicative Pair Activities	•			Audio Program	•	•	•	
				Videomodelos	•		•	
				Answer Keys: Student Edition, p. 91	•	•	•	

Assess and Remediate

For the Student	ONLINE	DVD	PRINT	For the Teacher	ONLINE	PREEXP	DVD	PRINT
				Prueba P-3: La comida with Study Plan	•			

Los pasatiempos PP. 22–27

Present & Practice

For the Student	ONLINE	DVD	PRINT	For the Teacher	ONLINE	PREEXP	DVD	PRINT
Student Edition, pp. 22–27	•	•	•	Interactive Whiteboard Vocabulary and Grammar Activities	•		•	
Audio	•	•		Interactive TE and Resources DVD	•		•	
Instant Check	•			Teacher's Resource Book, pp. 5, 12–13	•		•	•
Tutorial Video: Grammar	•			Communicative Pair Activities, pp. 12–13	•		•	•
Communicative Pair Activities	•			Audio Program	•	•	•	
				Videomodelos	•		•	
				Answer Keys: Student Edition, p. 92	•	•	•	

Assess and Remediate

For the Student	ONLINE	DVD	PRINT	For the Teacher	ONLINE	PREEXP	DVD	PRINT
				Prueba P-4: Los pasatiempos with Study Plan	•			

A ver si puedes... PP. 28–29

Application

For the Student	ONLINE	DVD	PRINT	For the Teacher	ONLINE	PREEXP	DVD	PRINT
Student Edition, pp. 28–29	•	•	•	Interactive TE and Resources DVD	•		•	
Online Puzzles and Games	•			Teacher's Resource Book, p. 5	•		•	•
Instant Check	•			Audio Program	•	•	•	
				Answer Keys: Student Edition, p. 93	•	•	•	

REGULAR SCHEDULE (50 MINUTES)

DAY	Warm-up / Assess	Preview / Present / Practice / Communicate	Wrap-up / Homework Options
1	Introduction (10 min.)	Mis amigos y yo (35 min.) • Objectives • Presentation: ¿Qué te gusta hacer? • Presentation: Y tú, ¿cómo eres? • Interactive Whiteboard Vocabulary Activities • Actividad 1 • ¿Recuerdas?	Wrap-up and Homework Options (5 min.) • Clip Art Vocabulary
2	Warm-up (5 min.) • Homework check	Mis amigos y yo (40 min.) • Presentation: Infinitives • Interactive Whiteboard Grammar Activities • Actividades 2, 3	Wrap-up and Homework Options (5 min.)
3	Warm-up (5 min.) • Homework check	Mis amigos y yo (40 min.) • Presentation: Adjectives • Interactive Whiteboard Grammar Activities • Actividades 4, 5, 7 • ¿Recuerdas? • Communicative Pair Activities	Wrap-up and Homework Options (5 min.) • Actividad 6 • Prueba P-1: Mis amigos y yo with Study Plan
4	Warm-up (5 min.) • Homework check ✔Formative Assessment (10 min.) • Prueba P–1: Mis amigos y yo with Study Plan	La escuela (30 min.) • Presentation: El horario de clases; Tu día en la escuela • Presentation: Tu sala de clases • Interactive Whiteboard Vocabulary Activities • Actividades 8, 9	Wrap-up and Homework Options (5 min.)
5	Warm-up (5 min.) • Homework check • Review Prueba P-1: Mis amigos y yo with Study Plan	La escuela (40 min.) • Presentation: Subject pronouns • Presentation: Present tense of -ar verbs • Interactive Whiteboard Grammar Activities • Actividades 10, 11 • ¿Recuerdas?	Wrap-up and Homework Options (5 min.) • Actividad 12
6	Warm-up (5 min.) • Homework check	La escuela (40 min.) • Actividad 13 • Juego: Actividad 14 • Communicative Pair Activities	Wrap-up and Homework Options (5 min.) • Prueba P–2: La escuela with Study Plan
7	Warm-up (5 min.) • Homework check ✔Formative Assessment (10 min.) • Prueba P–2: La escuela with Study Plan	La comida (30 min.) • Presentation: En el desayuno; En el almuerzo • Presentation: En la cena; Para mantener la salud • Interactive Whiteboard Vocabulary Activities • Actividad 15 • ¿Recuerdas?	Wrap-up and Homework Options (5 min.)
8	Warm-up (5 min.) • Homework check • Review Prueba P-2: La escuela with Study Plan	La comida (40 min.) • Presentation: Present tense of -er and -ir verbs • Interactive Whiteboard Grammar Activities • Actividades 16, 17 • Communicative Pair Activities	Wrap-up and Homework Options (5 min.)

REGULAR SCHEDULE (50 MINUTES)

DAY			
9	**Warm-up (5 min.)** • Homework check	**La comida (40 min.)** • Presentation: The plurals of adjectives • Interactive Whiteboard Grammar Activities • *¿Recuerdas?* • *Actividades* 18, 19	**Wrap-up and Homework Options (5 min.)** • *Actividad 20* • *Prueba P–3: La comida with Study Plan*
10	**Warm-up (5 min.)** • Homework check ✔**Formative Assessment (10 min.)** • *Prueba P–3: La comida with Study Plan*	**Los pasatiempos (30 min.)** • Presentation: *¿Adónde vas?* • Presentation: *¿Quieres ir conmigo?* • Interactive Whiteboard Vocabulary Activities • *Actividades* 21, 22 • *¿Recuerdas?*	**Wrap-up and Homework Options (5 min.)**
11	**Warm-up (5 min.)** • Homework check • Review *Prueba P-3: La comida with Study Plan*	**Los pasatiempos (40 min.)** • Presentation: Asking questions • Interactive Whiteboard Grammar Activities • *Actividades* 23, 24	**Wrap-up and Homework Options (5 min.)**
12	**Warm-up (5 min.)** • Homework check	**Los pasatiempos (40 min.)** • Presentation: *Ir + a +* infinitive • Interactive Whiteboard Grammar Activities • *Actividades* 25, 26	**Wrap-up and Homework Options (5 min.)**
13	**Warm-up (5 min.)** • Homework check	**Los pasatiempos (40 min.)** • Presentation: The verb *jugar* • Interactive Whiteboard Grammar Activities • *Actividades* 27, 28 • Communicative Pair Activities	**Wrap-up and Homework Options (5 min.)** • *Prueba P–4: Los pasatiempos with Study Plan*
14	**Warm-up (5 min.)** • Homework check ✔**Formative Assessment (10 min.)** • *Prueba P-4: Los pasatiempos with Study Plan*	**A ver si puedes... (30 min.)** • *Escuchar: Actividades* 1, 2 • *Hablar: Actividades* 1, 2	**Wrap-up and Homework Options (5 min.)**
15	**Warm-up (5 min.)** • Homework check • Review *Prueba P-4: Los pasatiempos with Study Plan*	**A ver si puedes... (40 min.)** • *Leer: Actividad* 1 • *Escribir: Actividades* 1, 2	**Wrap-up and Homework Options (5 min.)**

Para empezar

Standards for *Para empezar*
• To achieve the goals of the Standards, students will:

Communication
1.1 Interpersonal
• Greet and introduce themselves to others
• Use correct leave-taking phrases
• Ask how others are
• Provide others with the correct numbers of or for things
• Ask and provide others the correct time
• Talk about classroom people and objects
• Ask for and provide others the date or day of the week
• Talk about the weather

1.2 Interpretive
• Read and listen to information about appropriate greetings, introductions, and leave-takings
• Read and listen to information about how to ask about how someone is
• Read and listen to information about classroom directions and commands
• Read and listen to information about numbers
• Read and listen to information about telling time
• Read and listen to information about parts of the body
• Read and listen to information about classroom people and objects
• Read and listen to information about the alphabet
• Read and listen to information about the calendar
• Read and listen to information about weather and seasons

1.3 Presentational
• Present information about appropriate greetings, introductions, and leave-takings
• Write the correct numbers of or for things
• Present information about people and things
• Present information about the Spanish alphabet
• Present information about dates and days of the week
• Present information about seasons and the weather

Culture
2.1 Practices and Perspectives
• Talk about *los sanfermines*

Connections
3.1 Cross-curricular
• Discuss the hieroglyphics of the Maya
• Discuss the Aztec calendar
• Discuss geography and climatology in the Southern Hemisphere
• Reinforce math and metric conversion skills

Comparisons
4.1 Language
• Explain the difference between *tú* and *usted*
• Discuss that nouns are either masculine or feminine
• Discuss some rules of punctuation and accent marks

4.2 Culture
• Compare customs of greetings and introductions
• Compare festivals in which animals play a role

▼ Chapter Objectives

Communication
By the end of *Para empezar* you will be able to:
• Listen to information about likes, dislikes, healthy choices, and foods
• Read and write e-mails and notes about plans, school, and everyday activities
• Exchange information while describing people and discussing plans

You will demonstrate what you know and can do:
• A ver si puedes, pp. 28–29

You will also review:

 Mis amigos y yo
• Talk about what you like and don't like to do
• Describe yourself and other people

 La escuela
• Talk about the classes you have
• Describe your classroom
• Ask and tell who is doing an action

 La comida
• Talk about foods and beverages for breakfast, lunch, and dinner
• Discuss food, health, and exercise

4 Los pasatiempos
• Talk about locations in your community
• Talk about leisure activities
• Tell where you go
• Ask questions

realidades.com (GO)

📖 **Reference Atlas**   🌐 **Mapa global interactivo**

Un grupo de jóvenes, Mallorca, España

ENRICH YOUR TEACHING

Using Backward Design
Have students preview the sample performance tasks on *A ver si puedes . . .*, p. 28, and connect them to the Chapter Objectives. Explain to students that by completing the sample tasks they can self-assess their learning progress.

tres 3
Para empezar

DIFFERENTIATED INSTRUCTION

Digital resources such as the *Interactive Whiteboard* activity banks, *Videomodelos*, additional *Online Activities*, *Study Plans*, automatically graded *Leveled Workbook*, animated *Grammar Tutorials*, *Flashcards*, and *Vocabulary and Grammar Videos* will help you reach students of different ability levels and learning styles.

STUDENTS NEEDING EXTRA HELP

Guided Practice Activities
- Flashcards, Vocabulary Check, pp. 1–10

HERITAGE LEARNERS

Realidades para hispanohablantes
- Chapter Opener, pp. x–1
- En la escuela, pp. 2–3
- En la clase, pp. 4–5
- El tiempo, pp. 6–7
- Repaso del capítulo, pp. 8–9

ADVANCED/PRE-AP*

Pre-AP* Resource Book,
- pp. 60–61

Chapter Opener
Core Instruction

Suggestions: Explain that, in *Para empezar*, students will review some of the material they learned in Level A to prepare them for the new material they will learn in Level B. Throughout this section, students will see vocabulary reminders in graphic organizer form, input exercises, and grammatical structures that ask them to review what they have learned. Suggest that they look back at portfolio pieces from the previous level to refresh their memories.

Teaching with Photos

Have students imagine that someone in the photo is their pen pal. Ask them to write an imaginary invitation to themselves from that student, talking about the activities they would be able to do at the school.

Teacher-to-Teacher

Students may be apprehensive at first and may seem to have forgotten much over the summer. Reassure them that their Spanish will come back quickly. If there were activities or songs from Level A that students particularly enjoyed, use them as a means of getting students excited and energized.

Culture Note

Ágora Portals International School in Calvià, Mallorca uses Spanish, Catalan, and English as languages of instruction. Students also gain proficiency in a "foreign" language—German, French, and Chinese are popular choices. In addition to math, science, and social studies, classes in music, art, and sports—including sailing—are offered. (The school is near the Puerto Portals marina.) Teachers and staff are often trilingual.

1 Mis amigos y yo

INTERACTIVE WHITEBOARD
Vocabulary Activities PE

Mis amigos y yo
Core Instruction

Standards: 1.2

Focus: Reviewing leisure activities and expressions for likes and dislikes

Suggestions: Use the Input Scripts from the *Teacher's Resource Book* for ideas on how to review this vocabulary. Throughout this unit, use transparencies from Level A to help you refresh students' memories. Place a transparency on the screen with the images hidden by removable adhesive notes. Say *Me gusta...* plus an activity name and pantomime the activity correctly or incorrectly. Students should respond: *A mí también me gusta...* and mimic your action only if you pantomime the correct activity. Reveal each image and word after students have responded. Say: *Y también me gusta...* until you have gone through the activities shown.

To review the expressions in the word boxes, conduct a talk-show interview with a volunteer. Ask *sí / no* questions and forced-response questions to make it easy for the student to respond. Say, for example: *A mí me gusta nadar y esquiar, pero me gusta más correr. ¿Qué te gusta más, correr, nadar o esquiar? A mí no me gusta nada bailar. ¿Te gusta bailar?*

After the interview, ask students questions about the interviewee's responses.

BELLRINGER REVIEW

Provide this Venn diagram on the board:

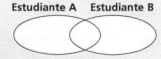

Estudiante A   Estudiante B

Have students work in pairs to describe their likes and dislikes, filling in one diagram for likes and one for dislikes.

Teacher-to-Teacher

To help students get to know each other, have them walk around the room and introduce themselves to three classmates, describe themselves, and talk about what they like to do after school.

bailar   escuchar música   nadar   escribir cuentos   montar en monopatín

correr   esquiar   dibujar   cantar   pasar tiempo con amigos

ver la tele   usar la computadora   hablar por teléfono   tocar la guitarra   leer revistas

¿Qué te gusta hacer?

to tell what you like to do
(A mí) me gusta ___.
(A mí) me gusta más ___.
(A mí) me gusta mucho ___.
A mí también
ir a la escuela
jugar videojuegos
montar en bicicleta
patinar
practicar deportes
trabajar

to say what you don't like to do
(A mí) no me gusta ___.
(A mí) no me gusta nada ___.
A mí tampoco.

to ask others what they like to do
¿Qué te gusta hacer?
¿Qué te gusta más?
¿Te gusta ___?
¿Y a ti?

other useful words and expressions
ni . . . ni	sí
o	también
pues	y

DIFFERENTIATED INSTRUCTION

Advanced Learners/Pre-AP*
Each student writes a "screen name" on his or her paper, a greeting, something he or she likes to do, and a question. You will be the Internet Service Provider. Collect the papers and redistribute them. Have students write responses. Repeat the process twice, then have students guess the identities.

Students with Learning Difficulties
Some students may need to have the material in these graphic organizers broken down into smaller pieces in order to successfully manage the information. You might copy the page and cut it apart into individual components. The students can practice reassembling the words in their correct categories.

realidades.com

Verb Conjugator

artístico, -a

desordenado, -a

impaciente

trabajador, -a

perezoso, -a

atrevido, -a

talentoso, -a

gracioso, -a

reservado, -a

estudioso, -a

sociable

deportista

Y tú, ¿cómo eres?

to talk about what you and others are like
bueno, -a
inteligente
ordenado, -a
paciente
serio, -a
simpático, -a

to tell people what someone likes or doesn't like
le gusta . . .
no le gusta . . .

to describe someone
soy
no soy
es

other useful words and expressions
a veces
muy
pero
según
según mi familia

to tell whom you are talking about
el chico
la chica
yo
él
ella

Mis amigos y yo
Core Instruction
Standards: 1.2

Focus: Reviewing adjectives to describe oneself and others

Suggestions: Place the transparency on the screen. Describe your students in another class period by telling about activities they like to do. Have students point to the image showing the personality trait of each person, based on what they like to do. Have students guess the identities of the people you describe.

Ask students if they always behave the same way around their family as they do around friends. Tell students about a trait your family thinks you have, which, according to your friends, you do not have: *Según mi familia, soy reservado(a), pero según mis amigos, soy muy sociable.* Ask individual students: *Según tu familia, ¿eres ordenado o desordenado? Y, ¿según tus amigos?* Ask about several traits.

Teacher-to-Teacher
Have students create a poster of themselves as seen through the eyes of someone who thinks very highly of them, for example, a younger brother or sister. Have them write descriptive adjectives around the image. Be sure the adjectives agree with the students' gender.

Pre-AP* Support

- **Learning Objective:** Interpretive: Audio
- **Activity:** Show Voc. and Gram. Transparency 36. Have students number 1–10 on a sheet of paper. As you point to an activity, say true/false sentences using "*Me gusta....*" expressions and the illustrated vocabulary. Have students write *C (Cierta)* or *F (Falsa)* to respond appropriately. (Ex. Point to the dancing scene and say *Me gusta nadar.*)
- ***Pre-AP* Resource Book:** Comprehensive guide to Pre-AP* vocabulary skill development, pp. 51–57

cinco **5**
Para empezar

ENRICH YOUR TEACHING

Culture Note
Students who enjoy singing, dancing, and guitar music will be interested in learning about the Spanish folk art of **flamenco. Flamenco** originated in the Andalusia region of Spain and was passed down through the years from artist to artist. **Flamenco** involves intricate guitar work, rapid dance movements, and syncopated rhythms produced by hand-clapping, foot-tapping, and castanets (**castañuelas**).

1 Standards: 1.2, 1.3

Resources: Answer Keys: Student Edition, p. 88

Focus: Reading comprehension of letter describing activities and likes and dislikes

Suggestions: Review the *¿Recuerdas?* with students. Ask students if they like a singer or musical group that you know is unpopular with people their age. If students are unfamiliar with the artists' music, sing them your worst rendition of it. Have them respond to your questions with *¡No, no me gusta nada!* Before students write their answers, read each item as a class and have students identify the key word or words that they should look for in the letter.

Answers:
1. falso; Yo soy de Santiago de los Caballeros en la República Dominicana.
2. cierto
3. falso; No soy muy talentoso.
4. falso; Me gusta leer libros de historia.
5. cierto
6. cierto

Extension: Have students write true and false statements about their own likes and dislikes, exchange papers with a partner, and guess if each other's statements are true or false.

BELLRINGER REVIEW

Distribute one set of Clip Art (see the LA TRB, *Capítulo* 1A) to pairs of students. Have one student read aloud the letter on p. 6 while the other arranges on his/her desktop the pictures presenting what Jaime likes to do, setting aside those not mentioned. Confirm their work.

Theme Project

Give students copies of the Theme Project outline and rubric from the *Teacher's Resource Book*. Explain the task to them, and have them perform Step 1. (For more information, see p. 2-b.)

¡Hola!

Me llamo Jaime Ordóñez Soriano. Soy de Santiago de los Caballeros en la República Dominicana. Yo soy deportista y un poco reservado. Me gusta leer libros de historia y montar en bicicleta. Mi amiga Clara es de Camagüey, Cuba. No es ni deportista ni reservada. Ella es muy talentosa, pero yo no. No me gusta ni tocar la guitarra ni dibujar. Tampoco me gusta bailar. Y tú, ¿cómo eres? ¿Qué te gusta hacer?

¿Recuerdas?

In Spanish, you might use one or more negatives after answering "no".

—¿Te gusta cantar?

—**No, no** me gusta **nada.**

If you want to say that you do not like either of two choices, use *ni . . . ni:*

• **No** me gusta **ni** nadar **ni** dibujar.

▼**1** Leer • Escribir

Hola, soy Jaime

Read the letter from your new pen pal, Jaime. Number your paper from 1–6 and for each of Jaime's statements, write *cierto* if it is true, or *falso* if it is false. Correct the false statements.

1. Yo soy de Camagüey.
2. Mi amiga Clara no es reservada.
3. Yo soy muy talentoso.
4. Me gusta leer revistas.
5. No me gusta ni bailar ni dibujar.
6. Me gusta montar en bicicleta.

6 seis
Mis amigos y yo

DIFFERENTIATED INSTRUCTION

Students with Special Needs

If students are not able to draw pictures for *Actividad* 2, allow them to choose pictures from the Clip Art images that represent their chosen activities. The Clip Art is available in the *Teacher's Resource Book*.

Multiple Intelligences

Intrapersonal/Introspective: Ask students if they believe that "birds of a feather flock together." (The Spanish equivalent is: *Cada quién con su cada cual.*) Have them write a paragraph comparing their traits and their likes and dislikes to those of their friends to prove or disprove the saying.

Gramática Repaso

Infinitives

Verbs are words that are most often used to name actions. The most basic form of a verb is called the **infinitive.** In English, you can spot infinitives because they usually have the word "to" in front of them. Spanish infinitives are only one word, and always end in *-ar, -er,* or *-ir:*

nadar, leer, escribir

The verb *gustar*

It's easy to talk about the things you like to do once you know the infinitive. Just add the infinitive to *te gusta* or *me gusta.*

¿Te gusta practicar deportes?

Sí, me gusta correr.

Gramática

Core Instruction

Standards: 4.1

INTERACTIVE WHITEBOARD
Grammar Activities PE

Suggestions: Divide students into groups. Have them study the activities on p. 4 for 30 seconds. Then give them two minutes to write as many **-ar** verbs as they can remember. The group with the most verbs will read their list while the other groups act out the verbs. Repeat the activity with **-er** and **-ir** verbs.

▼2 | | Dibujar • Hablar

¿Te gusta dibujar?

❶ On a sheet of paper, make simple sketches of three activities that you like to do, and three that you do not like to do.

❷ Work with a partner. Exchange your sketches and take turns asking each other whether or not you like doing each activity shown.

▶️ **Modelo**

A —¿Te gusta *bailar?*
B —No, no me gusta *bailar. ¿Y a ti?*
A —Sí, me gusta mucho *bailar con mis amigos.*
o:—A mí tampoco. Me gusta más *cantar.*

▼**2** Standards: 1.1

Focus: Drawing and discussing activities one likes and dislikes

Suggestions: Draw two sketches on the board, one of an activity you like and the other of an activity you dislike. Invite a student to do the same. Act out the model with the student, using the sketches you drew.

Answers will vary but may include:

hablar por teléfono, pasar tiempo con amigos, usar la computadora, escuchar música, bailar.

▼**3** |  | Escribir • Hablar

Y tú, ¿qué dices?

1. ¿Qué te gusta hacer en invierno? ¿Qué te gusta hacer en verano?
2. ¿Qué te gusta hacer más después de las clases?
3. ¿Qué no te gusta hacer los fines de semana?
4. ¿Qué revistas te gusta leer? ¿Qué libros?
5. ¿Con quién te gusta hablar por teléfono?

siete ⑦
Para empezar

▼**3** Standards: 1.1, 1.3

Focus: Answering personalized questions about preferences

Suggestions: Ask questions to make sure students remember the key words in each item before having them work independently. For example, ask: *¿Qué tiempo hace en el invierno? ¿Y en el verano?* (Pointing to a calendar) *¿En una semana, es martes antes de lunes o después de lunes? ¿Cuáles son los días del fin de semana?* (Holding up a magazine and then a book) *¿Es esto una revista o un libro?*

Answers will vary.

Extension: Have students write one more question. When finished, they should work with a partner to ask and answer questions.

ENRICH YOUR TEACHING

Culture Note

Direct attention to the boy's name in the letter on p. 6. In many Spanish-speaking cultures, a child has two surnames (**apellidos**): the first surname is the father's first surname and the second surname is the mother's first surname.

Teacher-to-Teacher

Is the librarian at your school a skateboard fanatic or is a Language Arts teacher writing the Great American Novel? Do some research and create a bulletin board titled **¿Quién soy?** with sentences describing activities that people at your school enjoy. Who can be the first to successsfully match the people at your school to their descriptions?

Gramática

Core Instruction

Standards: 4.1

INTERACTIVE WHITEBOARD

Grammar Activities PE

Suggestions: Prepare index cards with masculine and feminine forms of adjectives, as well as adjectives that could be either masculine or feminine. Review the *Gramática•Repaso*. Place the index cards face up on a table. Have a male and a female student stand at the table. When you say ¡*Adelante!* they will race to be the first one to pick up the cards that could be used to describe themselves.

4 Standards: 1.2

Resources: Teacher's Resource Book: Audio Script, p. 5; Audio Program DVD: Cap. PE, Track 1; Answer Keys: Student Edition, p. 88

Focus: Listening comprehension of personality traits

Suggestions: Review the listed activities and have students tell what personality traits people who like those activities might have.

Script and Answers:

1. Juanita es una chica estudiosa y trabajadora. *(estudiar)*
2. Carolina también es talentosa. Es muy artística. *(dibujar)*
3. Joaquín es inteligente y serio. *(leer)*
4. Alejandro es deportista y atrevido. *(montar en monopatín)*
5. Santiago es simpático, pero reservado. No es muy sociable. *(usar la computadora)*

5 Standards: 1.3

Resources: Answer Keys: Student Edition, p. 89

Focus: Practicing vocabulary and grammar about personality traits and activities

Suggestions: Read the adjectives and have students tell you the feminine forms.

Answers:

1. Gloria es atrevida.
2. Lola es sociable.
3. Felipe es gracioso.
4. Marisol es talentosa.
5. Juan es desordenado.
6. Carolina es perezosa.

Gramática Repaso

Adjectives

Words that describe people and things are called adjectives *(adjetivos)*.

In Spanish, most adjectives have both masculine and feminine forms. The masculine form usually ends in the letter -*o* and the feminine form usually ends in the letter -*a*.

Masculine adjectives are used to describe masculine nouns and feminine adjectives are used to describe feminine nouns.

> Paco es ordenado y simpático.
> Marta es ordenada y simpática.

Adjectives that end in -*e* describe both masculine and feminine nouns.

> Anita es inteligente y Pedro es inteligente.

When the masculine form of an adjective ends in -*or*, its feminine form ends in -*ora*.

> Juan Carlos es trabajador y Marilú es trabajadora también.

Some adjectives that end in -*a*, such as *deportista*, describe both masculine and feminine nouns. You will need to learn which adjectives follow this pattern.

> Tomás es deportista y Raquel es deportista.

▼4 | Escuchar

Los amigos de Jorge

Listen to Jorge describe his friends. Write the numbers 1–5 on a sheet of paper. For each of his statements, write the name of the activity you think his friends would prefer.

1. ver la tele o estudiar
2. correr o dibujar
3. leer o jugar videojuegos
4. montar en monopatín o escribir cuentos
5. hablar por teléfono o usar la computadora

▼5 Escribir

¿Cómo son los estudiantes?

Number your paper from 1–6. Use the words in the box below to write a sentence describing each of the following people.

atrevido	gracioso
talentoso	perezoso
sociable	trabajador
desordenado	

1.

Gloria

2.

Lola

3.

Felipe

4.

Marisol

5.
Juan

6.
Carolina

8 **ocho**
Mis amigos y yo

DIFFERENTIATED INSTRUCTION

Students with Learning Difficulties

If students find the scrambled sentences in *Actividad* 6 confusing, print them on strips of paper and cut them apart so students can manipulate and resequence the words. Give clues for identifying the subjects of the sentences.

Heritage Language Learners

Have students write a poem describing themselves, a family member, or a friend. In their poem, they should include both personality traits and activities the person likes and dislikes.

Practice and Communicate PE

▼**6** Leer • Escribir

En la clase de español de Jaime

Unscramble the following descriptions from your pen pal Jaime's letter in which he talks about people in his Spanish class. Write your paragraph on a sheet of paper.

¿Recuerdas?

In Spanish, adjectives usually come after the noun they describe. Notice how *artística* follows *chica* in this sentence:

• Margarita es **una chica artística.**

Me gusta mucho mi clase de español.

1. estudioso soy chico un yo.

2. Cruz una es profesora la paciente Sra. muy.

3. seria chica una es Ana.

4. no un Rafael chico es serio.

5. él un gracioso chico es.

Me gusta ir a la escuela y pasar tiempo con amigos.

▼**7** |  | Hablar

¿Cómo eres y qué te gusta hacer?

Working with a partner, find out what each other is like. Ask questions using the following adjectives and answer following the model.

▶ **Modelo**

A —¿Eres *talentoso(a)*?
B —*Sí, soy un(a) chico(a) talentoso(a). Me gusta mucho escribir cuentos.*
o: *Pues, no soy un(a) chico(a) muy talentoso(a). Me gusta más ver la tele.*

realidades.com

Instant Check
Verb Conjugator
Tutorial: Noun-adjective agreement

Estudiante A

artístico, -a
deportista
estudioso, -a
perezoso, -a
reservado, -a
talentoso, -a

¡Respuesta personal!

Estudiante B

¡Respuesta personal!

nueve **9**
Para empezar

▼**6** Standards: 1.2, 1.3

Resources: Answer Keys: Student Edition, p. 89
Focus: Reading; identifying word order
Suggestions: Review the *¿Recuerdas?* with students. Have sets of index cards with sentences similar to those in *Actividad* 6 written on them, one word per index card. Divide the class into groups. Give one set of the index cards to each group of students and have them unscramble the sentence. Then have students work independently to unscramble the *Actividad* 6 sentences.

Answers:

1. Yo soy un chico estudioso.
2. La Sra. Cruz es una profesora muy paciente.
3. Ana es una chica seria.
4. Rafael no es un chico serio.
5. Él es un chico gracioso.

Extension: Have students prepare banners with appreciative sentences on them to give to other teachers at your school. For example, *¡La Señora Robertson es una profesora muy simpática!* Students will write each word on a separate piece of paper and tape the pieces of paper to a long string. Have students present the banners to each teacher.

▼**7** Standards: 1.1

Focus: Using vocabulary and grammar to find out more about a classmate
Suggestions: Have students look at the list of adjectives and match each one to a pictured activity. Brainstorm with students other activities they might mention for each adjective when they are playing the Student B role.
Answers will vary.

Extension: Have Student A extend the conversation by asking a follow-up question: B —*Sí, soy un(a) chico(a) talentoso(a). Me gusta mucho escribir cuentos.* A —*¿Te gusta dibujar también?*

Additional Resource
• Teacher's Resource Book: Communicative Pair Activity BLM, pp. 6–7

✓**ASSESSMENT**

Prueba P–1: Mis amigos y yo with Study Plan (online only)

ENRICH YOUR TEACHING

Culture Note
Tell students about the Hispanic Heritage Awards Foundation which honors Americans of Latino heritage for their talents and achievements in music, film, literature, and politics. Mention that the Foundation has an annual Youth Awards ceremony in which qualifying high school seniors receive educational grants for their academic achievements.

21st Century Skills

Flexibility and Adaptability Remind students of the digital tools available in **realidades.com**, such as the tutorial on noun-adjective agreement. Agreement is often a new concept for English speakers, and this demonstration can help prepare students for a new way of thinking.

La escuela

Core Instruction

Standards: 1.2

Focus: Reviewing vocabulary used to talk about one's school schedule

Suggestions: Place the transparency on the overhead and cover the images and the school subjects with adhesive notes. With an erasable marker, write dashes under each class hour with one dash for every letter in the Spanish name for the subject. Divide the class into groups. Give a clue about the first subject: For example, *Me gusta esta clase porque me gustan las computadoras.* If students cannot guess the word **tecnología,** have them play Hangman to figure it out. They will guess letters, one group guessing a letter at a time, until they are able to guess the whole word. Write the letters they guess on the appropriate dashes. Once they guess the subject, reveal the image and the subject and repeat with the rest of the subjects.

Bring in school supplies and ask: *¿Qué necesitas para la clase de (matemáticas)?* Have a student pick out the items that are required and tell you: *Necesito (el libro, una calculadora y un lápiz).* You can also use the objects to practice **¿Quién?** by asking *¿Quién tiene (un diccionario)?* Students respond by holding up the appropriate item.

Students love to give their opinions about their classes. Once you have reviewed the various subjects, begin to make commentary about the other disciplines using the adjectives shown. When it comes to **español,** of course it is the **clase favorita.**

BELLRINGER REVIEW

Have students explain when they have these *clases: español, inglés, matemáticas.*

Theme Project

Students can perform Step 2 at this point. Be sure they understand your suggestions. (For more information, see p. 2-b.)

2 La escuela

▼ Objectives
▶ Talk about the classes you have
▶ Describe your classroom
▶ Ask and tell who is doing an action

INTERACTIVE WHITEBOARD
Vocabulary Activities PE

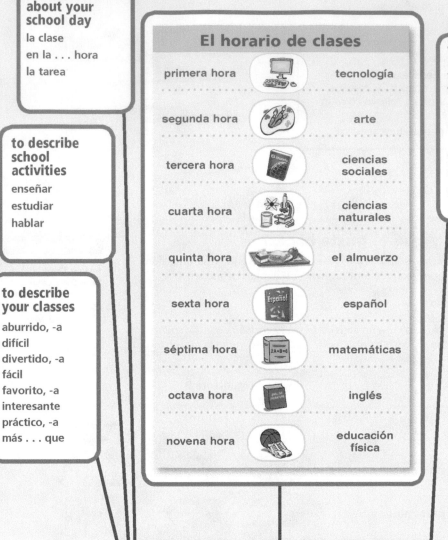

to talk about your school day
la clase
en la . . . hora
la tarea

to describe school activities
enseñar
estudiar
hablar

to describe your classes
aburrido, -a
difícil
divertido, -a
fácil
favorito, -a
interesante
práctico, -a
más . . . que

El horario de clases

primera hora		tecnología
segunda hora		arte
tercera hora		ciencias sociales
cuarta hora		ciencias naturales
quinta hora		el almuerzo
sexta hora		español
séptima hora		matemáticas
octava hora		inglés
novena hora		educación física

to talk about things you need for school
la calculadora
la carpeta de argollas
el diccionario
necesito
necesitas

other useful words and expressions
a ver . . .
para . . .
¿Quién?
mucho, -a

Tu día en la escuela

10 diez
La escuela

DIFFERENTIATED INSTRUCTION

Heritage Language Learners
If students have attended school in a Spanish-speaking country, have them write a letter to a student in that country who is moving to the United States. Have students compare school life in the Spanish-speaking country and in the United States and describe their school schedules.

Multiple Intelligences
Verbal/Linguistic: Tell students that all the teachers at your school will be attending a teachers' conference in Hawaii next week. Due to a substitute teacher shortage, the students will be the teachers. In groups have them decide what classes they will teach and which they will not and present a reason for teaching or not teaching each class.

el reloj

la bandera

el cartel

la puerta

las ventanas

el sacapuntas

la papelera

la computadora

el escritorio

la silla

Tu sala de clases

to identify gender and quantity of nouns
los, las
unos, unas

to talk about classroom items
el escritorio
la mochila
la pantalla
el ratón
el teclado

to indicate possession
de
mi
tu

to indicate location
al lado de la/del
allí
aquí
debajo de la/del
delante de la/del
detrás de la/del
¿Dónde?
en
encima de la/del

to identify (description, quantity)
Es un(a)
Hay
¿Qué es esto?

La escuela
Core Instruction
Standards: 1.2

Focus: Reviewing classroom objects and location expressions

Suggestions: Use real objects in the classroom to ask and answer *¿Qué es esto? Es un(a)....* Then attach possessives to the objects: *¿Es mi silla, o la silla de Jared?* Be sure to use plurals to review the plural articles.

Review location expressions by asking what is above, under, in front of, behind, beside, and on various objects: *¿Qué hay al lado de la puerta?* Then place the transparency on the overhead. Have students study the location of classroom objects on the transparency for 30 seconds. Shut off the projector and ask true / false questions about the location of items on the transparency.

Next, assign groups of students a number and give them a pad of adhesive notes. Tell them to write their group number and the names of classroom objects on individual notes. Instruct them to place the notes on the correct items around the classroom. If your class is small, this could be a timed assignment to see which group can attach all their notes to the correct objects and return to their seats first. When students have returned to their seats, they must use prepositions to correctly identify the locations of the various objects.

If you have a computer in your classroom, use it to review the computer terms shown. Combine these with questions about location of the various components on the computer table.

Teacher-to-Teacher
Play *¿Quién quiere ganar un millón de dólares?* Prepare sets of multiple-choice questions about the vocabulary on these pages. Make the questions of increasing difficulty and assign each one a dollar amount leading up to $1 million. The goal is to win the most money.

ENRICH YOUR TEACHING

Culture Note
The emblem on the Mexican flag is derived from the legend of how the Aztecs founded their capital, Tenochtitlán ("Place of the Prickly Pear Cactus"). The Aztecs were told by the god Huitzilopochtli to seek an eagle eating a snake on a cactus. This would be the sign that they should build their capital in that location. After wandering for many years, they saw the omen the god had described on an island at Lake Texcoco. In 1325 they built their city there, on the site that later became Mexico City.

Horario

Estudiante: Gabriela del Mar Romero
1ª hora: inglés
2ª hora: matemáticas
3ª hora: tecnología
4ª hora: arte
5ª hora: educación física
6ª hora: almuerzo
7ª hora: ciencias naturales
8ª hora: español
9ª hora: ciencias sociales

8 Standards: 1.2

Resources: Teacher's Resource Book: Audio Script, p. 5; Audio Program DVD: Cap. PE, Track 2; Answer Keys: Student Edition, p. 90

Focus: Listening comprehension of a school schedule

Suggestions: Before you play the audio recording, have students guess what items Gabriela might need for each class. Pause after each statement to allow students time to respond.

Script and Answers:

1. Bueno, necesito mi calculadora y lápiz. *(segunda hora/matemáticas)*
2. Necesito papel para dibujar. *(cuarta hora/arte)*
3. Para escribir cuentos necesito un bolígrafo, papel y un diccionario de inglés. *(primera hora/inglés)*
4. ¡Ay, sí! Mi sándwich ... necesito mi sándwich. *(sexta hora/almuerzo)*
5. También necesito mi diccionario de español. *(octava hora/español)*

Extension: Tell students that Gabriela forgot to bring two items she needs for two different classes. Have pairs of students role-play a conversation between Gabriela and her mother or father. Gabriela will tell what she needs and for what classes. The parent doesn't hear Gabriela well because the battery in the cell phone is getting low. The parent asks questions to verify what Gabriela needs.

▼ 8 | Escuchar

¿Para qué clase?

Look at the schedule above as you listen to Gabriela get ready for school. Write the numbers 1–5 on a sheet of paper. For each statement that you hear, write the class period that Gabriela is gathering items for.

▼ 9 | Escribir • Hablar

¿Cómo es tu horario?

1. Using Gabriela's schedule as a model, write your own schedule on a sheet of paper.

2. With a partner, use your schedules to talk about your classes.

▶ **Modelo**
A —*Para ti, ¿qué clase es más fácil?*
B —*Para mí, la clase de arte es más fácil. Me gusta mucho dibujar.*
A —*¿En qué hora es la clase?*
B —*Es en la segunda hora.*

Estudiante A

fácil   interesante
aburrida   práctica
difícil   divertida

Estudiante B

¡Respuesta personal!

9 Standards: 1.1, 1.3

Focus: Asking and giving information about school schedules

Suggestions: Point out that Student B must give a reason why he or she thinks a class is easy, hard, boring, fun, and so forth. As a class, brainstorm explanations Student B might give.

Answers will vary.

Extension: Tell pairs of students to use the model conversation in *Actividad* 9 to create a class schedule that they would both like to have.

Additional Resource

• Teacher's Resource Book: Communicative Pair Activity BLM, pp. 8–9

 doce
La escuela

DIFFERENTIATED INSTRUCTION

Heritage Language Learners

Have students imagine that they are applying for a job as a teacher. Tell them to write an application essay. They will tell which school subject or subjects they want to teach, and describe why they believe they would make a good teacher.

Multiple Intelligences

Interpersonal/Social: Tell students that they are going to start their own private school. Have groups of students work together to write the school curriculum, then prepare a brochure or TV commercial to advertise their school.

Gramática Repaso

Subject pronouns

The subject of a sentence tells who is doing the action. You can also use subject pronouns, which replace people's names.

Eduardo toca muy bien la guitarra.
Él toca muy bien la guitarra.

Laura y yo practicamos muchos deportes.
Nosotros practicamos muchos deportes.

Here are the subject pronouns in Spanish:

yo	I	nosotros nosotras	we (masc., masc./fem.) we (fem.)
tú	you (familiar)	vosotros vosotras	you (masc., masc./fem.) you (fem.)
usted (Ud.)	you (formal)	ustedes (Uds.)	you (formal)
él ella	he she	ellos ellas	they (masc., masc./fem.) they (fem.)

Present tense of -ar verbs

You will want to use verbs in ways other than in the infinitive form. To create the present-tense form of most -ar verbs, you first drop the -ar ending, leaving the stem. Then you add new endings to the stem. These verb endings tell you who is doing the action.

Here are the present-tense forms of the verb *hablar*:

(yo)	hablo	(nosotros) (nosotras)	hablamos
(tú)	hablas	(vosotros) (vosotras)	habláis
Ud. (él) (ella)	habla	Uds. (ellos) (ellas)	hablan

▼10 Escribir

Las actividades de mis amigos

Use the words in the box to write sentences about what you and your friends do.

1. yo
2. mi mejor (best) amigo(a)
3. mi profesor(a)
4. los estudiantes en mi clase de español
5. mis amigos y yo

estudiar	montar en monopatín
usar la computadora	escuchar música
patinar	trabajar
nadar	bailar

Practice and Communicate PE

Gramática

Core Instruction

Standards: 4.1

INTERACTIVE WHITEBOARD
Grammar Activities PE

Suggestions: As a class, come up with hand gestures to represent each personal pronoun (point to yourself for **yo**, point at an imaginary person in front of you for **tú**, a gesture with one hand to indicate short hair for **él**, long hair for **ella**, and so forth). Practice saying the pronoun and having students do the gestures, then do the gestures and have students say the pronouns. Finally, review the **-ar** verbs by calling out a verb and giving a pronoun hand gesture. Students should say the correct verb form.

BELLRINGER REVIEW

Using a calendar, review frequency expressions that students might use in *Actividad* 10: **todos los días, a veces, nunca,** etc.

▼10 Standards: 1.3

Focus: Using **-ar** verbs in personalized context; expressions of frequency

Suggestions: Pantomime the verbs and use the hand gestures for personal pronouns from the *Gramática•Repaso*. Have students tell you the verb form of the verb you are pantomiming. Then have students complete the activity.

Answers will vary.

Extension: Have students exchange papers with a partner. Tell them to extend their partner's sentences using the words **y, pero,** and **con,** plus another phrase.

ENRICH YOUR TEACHING

Culture Note

Tell students that Spanish belongs to the family of languages known as Romance languages. They are called this not because they sound romantic, but because they all evolved from Latin, which was spread across Europe by the Roman Empire. This is why there are many similar words in Spanish, French, Italian, and other Romance languages. Write the following French verbs on the chalkboard and have students match them to the Spanish verbs in the *Actividad* 10 word box: *écouter (de la musique), travailler, monter, nager, patiner, étudier.*

13

▼**11** Standards: 1.1

Focus: Asking and telling about weekend activities

Suggestions: Point out that when Student B replies negatively to a question, he or she must then tell an activity that their friends do.

Answers will vary.

BELLRINGER REVIEW

Have several students at a time stand at the chalkboard. Call out different times of day and have them draw clocks depicting those times.

▼**12** Standards: 1.3

Resources: Answer Keys: Student Edition, p. 90

Focus: Reviewing forms of *estar*, leisure activities and time

Suggestions: Review the *¿Recuerdas?* Then place students around the room and ask: *¿Dónde está April? ¿Dónde están Sara y Lupita?* Brainstorm with students place words they know that they can use when answering.

Answers: may vary, but the verbs will be:

1. está
2. está
3. estoy
4. están
5. estamos

Extension: Have students write where they are each hour of the day on a typical school day. Then have students ask each other where they are at different times of the day.

Theme Project

Students can perform Step 3 at this point. (For more information, see p. 2-b.)

▼**11** | 🗣️👥 | **Hablar**

¿Qué hacen los fines de semana?

With a partner, take turns asking about what you and your friends do on the weekends.

▶️ **Modelo**

A —*¿Estudias tú los sábados?*
B —*Sí, yo estudio los sábados.*
A —*¿Y tus amigos?*
B —*Sí, mis amigos y yo estudiamos mucho.*
o: *No, ellos no estudian, pero usan la computadora.*

Estudiante A

¡Respuesta personal!

Estudiante B

¡Respuesta personal!

▼**12** **Escribir**

¿Generalmente dónde están?

Number your paper from 1–5. For each of the times below, write a sentence to tell where you and the people you know generally are.

Modelo

el domingo a las ocho de la mañana: *(nombre)* y *(nombre)*
El domingo a las ocho de la mañana, Joaquín y Sarita están en la iglesia.

1. el lunes a las diez de la mañana: tu mejor amigo(a) *(nombre)*
2. el miércoles al mediodía: la profesora *(nombre)*
3. el sábado a las ocho de la noche: tú
4. el viernes a la una de la tarde: los profesores *(nombre)* y *(nombre)*
5. el domingo a las once de la mañana: tu amigo(a) *(nombre)* y tú

> **¿Recuerdas?**
>
> *Estar* is irregular because the *yo* form doesn't follow a regular pattern, and because *estás, está,* and *están* require accent marks. *Estar* is used to tell how someone feels or where something is located.
>
> • **Estoy** en la escuela.

14 catorce
La escuela

DIFFERENTIATED INSTRUCTION

Students with Special Needs

To help students with visual impairments perform *Actividad* 13, pair them with seeing students and position actual items on a table in the classroom just as they are shown in the picture. The visually impaired student can locate the objects by touch.

Multiple Intelligences

Verbal/Linguistic: Have students role-play a cell phone conversation between two friends. In the conversation, each person should ask where the person is right now and what he or she is doing.

▼13 | Hablar

¿Qué hay y dónde está?

With a partner, take turns asking if various items are in the following picture, and where each item is located.

la pantalla
el ratón
el teclado
la mesa

▶ **Modelo**

A —¿Hay una computadora?
B —Sí, hay una computadora.
A —Pues, ¿dónde está?
B —Está encima de la mesa.

¿Recuerdas?

When the preposition *de* is followed by the masculine definite article *el,* the contraction *del* must be used.

• La computadora está encima **del** escritorio.

▼14 | Escribir • Hablar

Juego

Make a list of five items you can see in your classroom for which you know the names in Spanish. With a partner, describe where each item is, and your partner will guess which item you are talking about.

▶ **Modelo**

A —Está al lado de la puerta, debajo del sacapuntas.
B —¿Es la papelera?
A —¡Claro que sí!
o: —No, está cerca de la papelera, pero no es la papelera.

realidades.com

Instant Check
Verb Conjugator
Tutorials: Subject pronouns, Verbs, *-ar* verbs
Animated Verbs

quince **15**
Para empezar

ENRICH YOUR TEACHING

Teacher-to-Teacher

There are many Spanish-language Web sites for young people with information about popular music, movies, and TV shows, as well as games, advice columns, and educational features. Research some sites that might interest your students. Screen sites for inappropriate content before recommending them.

21st Century Skills

Technology Literacy Have students use the digital technology within **realidades.com** to access and manage the audio files and activities that support grammar-learning and review.

---

13 Standards: 1.1

Focus: Practicing classroom object vocabulary and prepositions of location

Suggestions: Have students flip a coin. The winners of the coin toss get to decide if they will play the Student A role first or second. Tell them to keep track of which objects they have discussed and not to repeat them.

Answers will vary.

Extension: Have pairs of students each draw a classroom with five objects in it. They will take turns guessing the objects in each other's drawing. The first one to guess all the items in the other's drawing wins.

BELLRINGER REVIEW

Give students a location expression and have them tell you its opposite: *encima de / debajo de, cerca de / lejos de,* and so on.

14 Standards: 1.1, 1.3

Focus: Describing the location of classroom objects

Suggestions: Have pairs of students do the activity in front of the rest of the class while you time them. Have other pairs try to beat their time.

Answers will vary.

Extension: Have students repeat the activity, this time describing the location of five countries or U.S. states. Provide maps, atlases, or globes for students' reference.

Multiple Intelligences

Visual/Spatial: Give groups of students a shoebox and assign them a school subject. Tell them to decorate the interior of the box to make it look like a classroom for their school subject. Use the boxes to practice location expressions.

✓ASSESSMENT

Prueba P–2: La escuela with Study Plan (online only)

15

INTERACTIVE WHITEBOARD
Vocabulary Activities PE

La comida
Core Instruction
Standards: 1.2

Focus: Reviewing food vocabulary

Suggestions: Review the following categories of vocabulary in a few groups: breakfast items, lunch / dinner items, beverages, and expressions for asking and telling about food choices. Use the transparencies from *Tema 3* in Level A. Have students pretend they are on a game show where they must guess the name of an item in order to win it. Bring in packages that represent the various foods or mount pictures on poster board and arrange them at the front of the room. Divide students into teams. Give clues to each food item using as many of the words on these two pages as possible. Have one of the teams try to name the item. If they answer correctly, they get to collect the item. If they guess incorrectly, the other team gets to guess. The team with the most items at the end wins.

Review the expressions in the boxes by asking students if they like the foods shown on the transparency. Have them respond *¡Sí, por supuesto!* when they like an item and *¡No! ¡Qué asco!* when they do not. If they say they like an item, follow up with a question about how often they eat or drink it.

BELLRINGER REVIEW

Refer to the foods pictured on pp. 16–17. Have students label two columns— *Bueno(a) para la salud; Malo(a) para la salud*—and write the words for ten of the food items under the appropriate column.

▼ **Objectives**

▶ Talk about foods and beverages for breakfast, lunch, and dinner

▶ Discuss food, health, and exercise

3 La comida

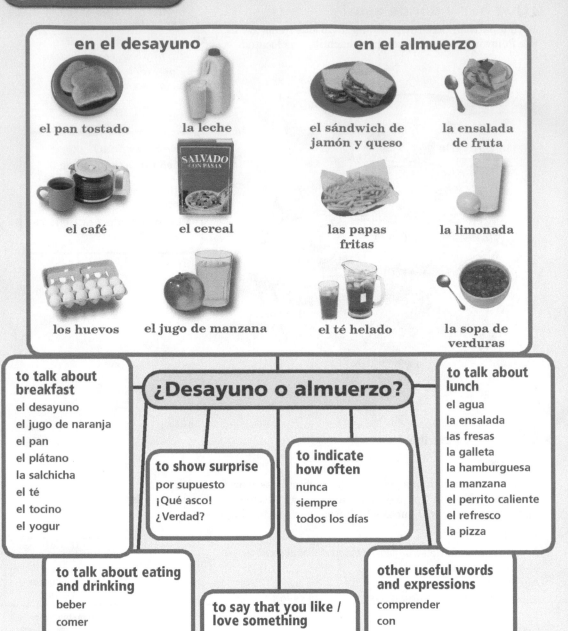

en el desayuno

el pan tostado
la leche
el café
el cereal
los huevos
el jugo de manzana

en el almuerzo

el sándwich de jamón y queso
la ensalada de fruta
las papas fritas
la limonada
el té helado
la sopa de verduras

¿Desayuno o almuerzo?

to talk about breakfast
el desayuno
el jugo de naranja
el pan
el plátano
la salchicha
el té
el tocino
el yogur

to show surprise
por supuesto
¡Qué asco!
¿Verdad?

to indicate how often
nunca
siempre
todos los días

to talk about lunch
el agua
la ensalada
las fresas
la galleta
la hamburguesa
la manzana
el perrito caliente
el refresco
la pizza

to talk about eating and drinking
beber
comer
la comida
compartir

to say that you like / love something
Me / te encanta(n) ____ .
Me / te gusta(n) ____ .

other useful words and expressions
comprender
con
¿Cuál?
más o menos
sin

16 dieciséis
La comida

DIFFERENTIATED INSTRUCTION

Multiple Intelligences
Musical/Rhythmic: Tell students they are the owners of a new restaurant. They must come up with a clever jingle for their radio commercial. Students can make up their own melody or write their jingle to the tune of a well-known Spanish-language song, such as *"De colores,"* or an English-language song, such as "Row, Row, Row Your Boat."

Advanced Learners/Pre-AP*
Have students create crossword puzzles with the food vocabulary. They can use a combination of written or picture clues. Provide copies of the Clip Art from the *Teacher's Resource Book*. Check their work, then have others solve the puzzles.

realidades.com

Verb Conjugator

en la cena

el bistec

la cebolla

las judías verdes

los guisantes

la lechuga

las uvas

el pollo

el arroz

los espaguetis

los tomates

las papas

el pescado

la carne

la mantequilla

las zanahorias

Para mantener la salud

to talk about being hungry and thirsty
Tengo hambre.
Tengo sed.

to indicate agreement and disagreement
Creo que . . .
Creo que sí / no.
(No) estoy de acuerdo.

to talk about dessert
el helado
los pasteles

to discuss health
caminar
hacer ejercicio
  (yo) hago
  (tú) haces
levantar pesas
para la salud
para mantener la salud

to describe something horrible
malo, -a
sabroso, -a

other useful words and expressions
algo
cada día
muchos, -as
¿Por qué?
porque
todos, -as
(yo) prefiero
(tú) prefieres

diecisiete **17**
Para empezar

La comida
Core Instruction

Standards: 1.2

Focus: Reviewing food vocabulary and expressions

Suggestions: Place the transparency on the overhead. Tell students: *Tengo hambre, pero quiero comer comida que es buena para la salud.* Point to each item and ask if you can eat it: *¿Puedo comer el bistec? ¿Es bueno para la salud?* Have students respond: *Creo que sí / no.* When students tell you *Creo que no,* review other expressions from the word boxes by arguing in favor of the unhealthy foods. Ask them why you can't eat the items; tell them that they are tasty and that you prefer them; bargain with students telling them the kinds of exercise you will do to make up for eating the item. In the end, agree that the students are right and that you should not eat the unhealthy foods, at least not every day.

ENRICH YOUR TEACHING

Culture Note
Tell students that in Mexico special festivals called **ferias** are held to celebrate the seasonal harvests of foods in different regions. Some of the foods used to celebrate these festivals include corn, rice, chilis, pineapples, coffee, and the nopal cactus, which is made into salads, stew, and even ice cream.

Teacher-to-Teacher
Have students role-play a scene between two teenagers who try to order hot dogs, French fries, and ice cream from an extremely health-conscious waiter who tries to get them to order healthful foods instead.

15 Standards: 1.1

Focus: Discussing food and drink items

Suggestions: Review the ¿Recuerdas? Then hold up Clip Art images of singular and plural food items. Students will tell you they like the items, using **me gusta(n)** or **me encanta(n).** Then have volunteers read the model. You might have students write down two food items and a drink item for each meal before they do the activity with their partner.

Answers will vary but they may include the food item from the menu "Café Miami."

Extension: Hand pairs of students a folded piece of paper with a dollar amount showing their "meal allowance." Have them repeat the activity, this time writing down the dollar amounts of the foods they like at each meal. Afterwards, have them add up their food items and see how close they came to their allowance. The pair of students that comes closest without going over the amount wins.

Teacher-to-Teacher

Find a copy of Dr. Seuss's *Green Eggs and Ham* (perhaps a Spanish translation) and read a portion of it to students. Have pairs of students create a skit modeled on the story. Student A will ask if Student B likes a food item for breakfast. Student B will say he or she does not like that food item for breakfast. Student A will ask if Student B likes that same item for lunch. Student B will say he doesn't like the item for lunch or for breakfast! Student A will continue asking about the same item, adding different twists to the question.

Café Miami

Menú del día

El desayuno

cereal con plátanos	$3.75
huevos con tocino y pan tostado	$4.50
huevos con salchichas y pan tostado	$4.50
ensalada de frutas	$4.25
con yogur	$5.00

El almuerzo

sándwiches con papas fritas	$5.25
de jamón	$5.75
de jamón y queso	$5.75
perrito caliente con papas fritas	$6.25
hamburguesa con papas fritas	$3.50
pizza	$4.75
ensalada	$5.25
sopa de verduras con ensalada y pan	

La cena

bistec con papas y judías verdes	$11.25
pollo con arroz y zanahorias	$9.25
pescado con arroz y guisantes	$12.00
espaguetis con salsa de tomate y queso	$8.50

ensalada de lechuga y tomate incluida con todas las cenas

El postre

pasteles del día	$3.75
helado	$3.00

Bebidas

refrescos	$1.25
té helado	$1.00
limonada	$2.00
jugo de naranja	$2.50
jugo de manzana	$2.00
té o café	$1.50
leche	$1.25

15 **Hablar**

¿Qué te gusta comer?

With a partner, look at the menu above to talk about what you like to eat and drink for breakfast, lunch, and dinner.

▶ **Modelo**

A —¿Qué te gusta comer en el desayuno?
B —Me gusta el tocino y me encantan los huevos.
A —¿Y para beber?
B —Pues, me gusta mucho el jugo de naranja.

¿Recuerdas?

Use *me gusta* and *me encanta* to talk about a singular noun.

• Me encanta el café, pero no me gusta la leche.

Use *me gustan* and *me encantan* to talk about a plural noun.

• Me gustan los plátanos, y me encantan las uvas.

18 dieciocho
La comida

DIFFERENTIATED INSTRUCTION

Heritage Language Learners

Ask students who have lived in or visited other countries if the items on this menu are typically served at restaurants in their heritage country. Have them describe food items that are typically found in restaurants there. They can create their own menu with those items.

Gramática Repaso

Present tense of -er and -ir verbs

To create the present-tense forms of -er and -ir verbs, drop the endings from the infinitives, and add the appropriate verb endings to the stem.

Here are the present-tense forms of regular -er verbs:

como	comemos
comes	coméis
come	comen

Here are the present-tense forms of regular -ir verbs:

comparto	compartimos
compartes	compartís
comparte	comparten

▼16 Escribir

¿Qué hacen para mantener la salud?

Write sentences to say what the following people do or don't do to stay healthy, based on what you see in the drawings.

Modelo
Tú bebes leche.
tú

1.
Juan/correr

2.
Laura y Ana/comer

3.
Pedro y yo/beber

4.
Manuela y Rosa/compartir

5.
Roberto/comer

6. **¡Respuesta personal!**
yo

▼17 |(Talk!) 👥| Hablar

¿Qué bebes y qué comes?

With a partner, talk about what you eat and drink for breakfast, lunch, and dinner.

▶ **Modelo**
A —¿Comes salchichas en el desayuno?
B —Sí, me encantan. Como salchichas en el desayuno los domingos.

Estudiante A

las papas fritas	los pasteles	el café
el cereal	el pollo	los refrescos
la ensalada	el pescado	la leche

Estudiante B

me gusta(n)
me encanta(n)
no me gusta(n) nada
¡Qué asco!

ENRICH YOUR TEACHING

Culture Note

Chili peppers are important in Mexican cuisine. There are many varieties and their heat varies greatly, from innocent bell peppers to extremely hot **habaneros.** The best way to take away the heat after a run-in with a **jalapeño** is to drink milk. The proteins in milk break down the capsaicin that gives the pepper its heat.

Teacher-to-Teacher

Have students create a poster showing, on the left side, things that one should not eat, drink, or do to stay healthy and, on the right side, things that one should eat, drink, and do to stay healthy.

Practice and Communicate `PE`

Gramática

Core Instruction

Standards: 4.1

INTERACTIVE WHITEBOARD
Grammar Activities PE

Review the verb charts with students using the transparencies and the *GramActiva* Video from *Capítulo* 3A. Bring carrots to class and use them to review the forms of **comer** and **compartir.** Munch on a carrot and say: *Como una zanahoria.* Hand one to a student and say: *Julia, tú comes una zanahoria.* Ask: *¿Qué come Julia?* Break a carrot in two and repeat the process with **compartir.** If students are going to actually eat the food be absolutely certain that they do not have food allergies!

▼16 Standards: 1.3

Resources: Answer Keys: Student Edition, p. 91

Focus: Using -er and -ir verbs to discuss activities one does to maintain one's health

Suggestions: Have students identify the items in which they will need to use the negative **no** in their response.

Answers
1. Juan corre.
2. Laura y Ana no comen helado.
3. Pedro y yo bebemos jugo de naranja.
4. Manuela y Rosa comparten un sándwich.
5. Roberto come una ensalada.
6. Answers will vary.

▼17 Standards: 1.1

Focus: Asking and responding to questions about food and meals

Suggestions: Have two volunteers read the model. Then have two other volunteers model a conversation using **beber** instead of **comer.** Remind Student B to tell how often they eat an item or to say they never eat that item.

Answers will vary.

Additional Resource

• Teacher's Resource Book: Communicative Pair Activity BLM, pp. 10–11

Gramática

Core Instruction

Standards: 4.1

INTERACTIVE WHITEBOARD

Grammar Activities PE

Suggestions: Perform "The Amazing Rubber Pencil Trick" for students. Grab a long pencil in the middle with your thumb and middle finger. Hold the pencil loosely and horizontally in front of you. Now wag the pencil up and down quickly in the air. With a little practice, you can make the pencil appear to flop in the air as if made of rubber. While performing the trick, say: *¡Soy talentoso(a)!* Teach a student the trick and say: *¡Eres talentoso(a)!* Tell the class *¡Somos talentosos(as)!* Teach another student the trick and say: *¡Son talentosos(as)!* Then review the grammar. Use the transparencies and the *GramActiva* Video to reinforce the concepts.

BELLRINGER REVIEW

Pantomime the personality traits listed in the word box for *Actividad* 18 and have students guess the traits.

▼18 Standards: 1.3

Focus: Writing sentences using *ser* and adjectives

Suggestions: Point to the images and ask students to tell you the form of *ser* they will use for each one. Have them work independently to write their sentences.

Answers will vary but may include:

1. Juanita y yo somos perezosos.
2. Ana y María son generosas.
3. Joaquín y Luis son atrevidos.
4. Claudia y Marisa son deportistas.
5. Los estudiantes en mi clase de arte son talentosos.
6. Natalia y Angelito son trabajadores.

Theme Project

Students can perform Step 4 at this point. Be sure they understand your corrections and suggestions. (For more information, see p. 2-b.)

Gramática Repaso

The plurals of adjectives

Just as adjectives agree with nouns depending on whether they are masculine or feminine, they also agree according to whether the nouns are singular or plural. To make adjectives plural, just add -*s* after the vowel at the end of the adjective. If the adjective ends in a consonant, add -*es*.

> La manzana es buena para la salud. Las manzanas son buenas para la salud.

El pastel aquí es popular. Los pasteles del Café Nuñoz son populares.

When an adjective describes a group including both masculine and feminine nouns, use the masculine plural form.

> Las zanahorias y los tomates son buenos para la salud.

> **¿Recuerdas?**
>
> *Ser*, which means "to be," is an irregular verb. Use *ser* to describe what a person or thing is like. Here are the present-tense forms:
>
> | soy | somos |
> |-----|-------|
> | eres | sois |
> | es | son |

▼18 | ♻ | Escribir

¿Cómo son los estudiantes?

Using the words from the list below, write sentences to describe Alejo and his friends.

deportista	atrevido
talentoso	trabajador
perezoso	estudioso
generoso	

Clara y Paula

Modelo
Clara y Paula son estudiosas. Estudian mucho.

1.

Juanita y yo

2.

Ana y María

3.

Joaquín y Luis

4.

Claudia y Marisa

5.

los estudiantes en mi clase de arte

6.

Natalia y Angelito

20 veinte
La comida

DIFFERENTIATED INSTRUCTION

Heritage Language Learners

Have students write their own version of a well-known fairy tale such as "Cinderella," "The Three Little Pigs," or a folk tale from their heritage country. Tell them to describe each character's personality, paying close attention to adjective agreement.

Multiple Intelligences

Intrapersonal/Introspective: Have students write a paragraph defining what makes a good friend. Write: *Para mí, un(a) buen(a) amigo(a) debe ser…* on the chalkboard to get students started. Have them illustrate their paragraphs and post them in the room.

▼**19** | 👥 | Pensar • Escribir • Hablar

¿Qué comemos para mantener la salud?

1 On a separate sheet of paper, copy this food pyramid and fill in at least two items for each category.

2 Work with a partner. For each category on the food pyramid, take turns asking and answering questions about what you prefer to eat or drink and why you like those items.

▶ **Modelo**

A —*¿Qué frutas prefieres comer?*
B —*Me gustan mucho las fresas y las manzanas.*
A —*Y, ¿por qué?*
B —*Porque son muy sabrosas y son buenas para la salud. Yo soy deportista y necesito mantener la salud.*

las verduras
la cebolla · los guisantes
las frutas
las papas · las uvas
el pan · los cereales

MiPlato
Choose **MyPlate**.gov
Frutas · Granos · Productos Lácteos · Vegetales · Proteína

las grasas
la mantequilla · la leche
la carne
el pollo · el bistec · el pescado
los espaguetis · el arroz

▼**20** | 🗨 | Escribir • Hablar

Y tú, ¿qué dices?

1. ¿Qué prefieres comer en el desayuno? ¿En el almuerzo?
2. ¿Qué frutas son buenas para la salud? ¿Qué verduras?
3. ¿Qué comida que es buena para la salud te gusta comer?
4. ¿Qué comida que es mala para la salud te gusta comer?
5. ¿Qué actividades te gusta hacer para mantener la salud?

realidades.com

Instant Check
Verb Conjugator
Tutorials: *-er* verbs, *-ir* verbs
Animated Verbs

veintiuno **21**
Para empezar

ENRICH YOUR TEACHING

Culture Note
Before the Spanish conquistadors brought over cows and goats from Europe, people in what is now Mexico did not eat cheese. Since that time, cheese-making has become an important tradition throughout Mexico. The key cheese-making regions in Mexico are Chihuahua, Oaxaca, Chiapas, and Querétaro.

21st Century Skills

Critical Thinking and Problem Solving
Encourage students to compare concepts they are learning about the MyPlate.gov food groups, with the older "food pyramid" that used to be familiar. What are the differences? Why do they think one was substituted for the other?

BELLRINGER REVIEW
Name a food item and a MyPlate.gov category. Have students raise their hand if the item matches the food category.

▼**19** Standards: 1.1, 1.3
Focus: Asking and responding to questions about healthful foods
Suggestions: Review the model with students. Then brainstorm ideas for things Student B can say when asked about *Las grasas* (*Pues, no son muy buenas para la salud, pero son muy sabrosas,* and *No como el helado y los pasteles cada día*).
Answers will vary.
Extension: Have students draw two overlapping circles to create a Venn diagram. On the left side they will write the foods that they prefer, which their partner does not. On the right side, they will write the foods their partner prefers, which they do not. In the middle section where the circles overlap, they will write the foods they both prefer.

▼**20** Standards: 1.1, 1.3
Focus: Writing about healthful and unhealthful foods
Suggestions: Have students suggest how a complete-sentence response will begin. For items 3 and 4 suggest that they simply use *Me gusta comer....*
Answers will vary.

Teacher-to-Teacher
Spanish-language versions of the MyPlate guide are readily available from government agencies and on the Internet. Obtain copies and make them available to students for reference.

✓ASSESSMENT
Prueba P–3: La comida with Study Plan (online only)

INTERACTIVE WHITEBOARD
Vocabulary Activities PE

Los pasatiempos

Core Instruction

Standards: 1.2

Focus: Reviewing leisure activities and places in the community

Suggestions: Place the transparency on the overhead. Review the various locations by asking: *¿Adónde vas?* Place two covered coffee cans with marbles inside on a table at the front of the room. Have two students stand at the table. Tell them that you will point to a location on the transparency and make three statements about activities you are going to do there. One of the statements will be illogical *(Voy a las montañas para ver una película.)* When they hear the illogical statement, they must try to be the first one to shake their coffee can and say *¡No me digas!* The first person to do so stays and the other person sits down. Repeat with a new student challenger.

Then ask questions to help students review the expressions in the word boxes. Ask questions that provide students a choice of two answers: *¿Adónde vas para estudiar, a casa o a la biblioteca? ¿Con quién te gusta ir al centro comercial, con tus amigos o tu hermanito? ¿Qué te gusta hacer después de las clases, estudiar o ver la tele?*

| ▼ Objectives

▶ Talk about locations in your community
▶ Talk about leisure activities
▶ Tell where you go
▶ Ask questions

4 Los pasatiempos

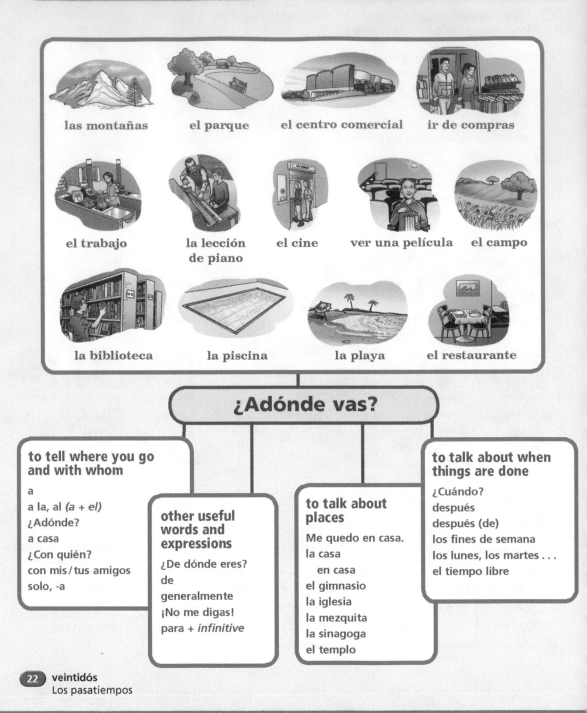

las montañas   el parque   el centro comercial   ir de compras

el trabajo   la lección de piano   el cine   ver una película   el campo

la biblioteca   la piscina   la playa   el restaurante

¿Adónde vas?

to tell where you go and with whom
a
a la, al *(a + el)*
¿Adónde?
a casa
¿Con quién?
con mis / tus amigos
solo, -a

other useful words and expressions
¿De dónde eres?
de
generalmente
¡No me digas!
para + *infinitive*

to talk about places
Me quedo en casa.
la casa
  en casa
el gimnasio
la iglesia
la mezquita
la sinagoga
el templo

to talk about when things are done
¿Cuándo?
después
después (de)
los fines de semana
los lunes, los martes . . .
el tiempo libre

22 veintidós
Los pasatiempos

DIFFERENTIATED INSTRUCTION

Students with Learning Difficulties
Use the Clip Art from the *Teacher's Resource Book* to make copies of the various pictures shown. Have students sort the pictures according to places and activities. Have them label each place with **Voy a...** and each activity with **Me gusta....**

Advanced Learners/Pre-AP*
Have students write a multiple-choice self-quiz titled *¿Eres una persona activa?* that will reveal how a person likes to spend his or her leisure time. Have students exchange their self-quizzes with a partner and complete each other's quiz.

Language Input **PE**

el baile el concierto la fiesta el partido ir de pesca

jugar al
básquetbol

jugar al
fútbol
americano

jugar al
vóleibol

jugar al tenis

jugar al golf

jugar al béisbol

jugar al
fútbol

¿Quieres ir conmigo?

to tell what time something happens

¿A qué hora?
a la una
a las ocho
de la mañana
de la noche
de la tarde
este fin de semana
esta noche
esta tarde

to describe how someone feels

cansado, -a
contento, -a
enfermo, -a
mal
ocupado, -a
triste

to extend, accept, or decline invitations

conmigo
contigo
(yo) puedo
(tú) puedes
¡Ay! ¡Qué pena!
¡Genial!
lo siento

¡Oye!
¡Qué buena idea!
(yo) quiero
(tú) quieres
¿Te gustaría?
Me gustaría
Tengo que ____.

other useful words and expressions

demasiado
entonces
un poco (de)
ir + a + *infinitive*
(yo) sé
(tú) sabes

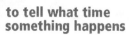

Verb Conjugator

veintitrés **23**
Para empezar

Los pasatiempos

Core Instruction

Standards: 1.2

Focus: Reviewing leisure activities; invitations

Suggestions: Place the transparency on the screen. Point to the activities and invite students to do them with you both at reasonable times of day (*¿Quieres jugar al tenis esta tarde a las cuatro?*) and at unreasonable times of day (*¿Quieres ir de pesca conmigo a las once de la noche?*). Students will accept reasonable invitations with *¡Genial!* or *¡Buena idea!* and come up with an excuse for unreasonable invitations. Then give a toy "cell phone" or a chalkboard eraser to a student at one end of the classroom and another to a student at the other end. Have one of the students "call" the other student on her "cell phone" and invite the student to do an activity. The student will either accept or make up an excuse to decline. After their conversation, they will hand the toys or erasers to two other students, who will repeat the activity.

Teacher-to-Teacher

On the Internet, you can find examples of party invitations in Spanish produced by major greeting card companies. You may also be able to find these in greeting card displays. Bring in examples and have students fill them in. Deliver the invitations to other students, then have them "call up" to accept or decline.

ENRICH YOUR TEACHING

Culture Note

Legendary golfer Lee Trevino was born in Dallas, Texas, in 1939. He became a professional golfer in 1960. One of his achievements was winning $1 million for making a hole-in-one during a golf tournament in Michigan. Other famous golfers of Spanish-language heritage are Chi Chi Rodríguez and Lorena Ochoa.

21st Century Skills

Collaboration Have students work with a partner to create a list of five questions about leisure time activities. Then have them ask the questions to an exchange student at school, or another native Spanish speaker. Have students share the responses with the class.

21
Standards: 1.2

Resources: Teacher's Resource Book: Audio Script, p. 5; Audio Program DVD: Cap. PE, Track 3; Answer Keys: Student Edition, p. 92

Focus: Listening comprehension of locations in the community

Suggestions: Direct students' attention to the *¿Recuerdas?* Make statements about activities you and other people are going to do. Have students guess the places where you or they are going. As students listen to the activity, circulate around the room to make sure students are pointing to the correct locations.

Script and Answers:

1. Me gusta mucho hablar con amigos. Quiero beber un café con Susana y Joaquín. *(café)*
2. ¡Uf! Tengo que estudiar y necesito un libro de arte y uno de la historia de España. *(biblioteca)*
3. Prefiero levantar pesas y hacer ejercicio después de las clases. *(gimnasio)*
4. Cuando hace sol, generalmente camino una hora. No me gusta estar en el gimnasio. *(parque)*
5. Necesito ir de compras. Quiero comprar un disco compacto nuevo. *(centro comercial)*
6. Estoy aburrida. ¿Por qué no vamos a ver una película? *(cine)*

22
Standards: 1.2, 1.3

Resources: Answer Keys: Student Edition, p. 92

Focus: Using *ir*

Suggestions: Have students tell you the pronoun they could replace each subject with and then point to the corresponding form of *ir* in the *¿Recuerdas?*

Answers:

1. voy   2. vamos   3. va   4. van   5. vas

Extension: Write the paragraph on the chalkboard with blanks for the *ir* verb forms and blanks for other words as well. Write the missing words on index cards. Have pairs of students race to see who can tape the words in the correct spaces in the least amount of time.

▼21 | Escuchar

¿Adónde va Carmen?

Listen to Carmen describe her plans for the week. As you hear each statement she makes, point to the place on the map where she is going.

¿Recuerdas?

To say where someone is going, use the verb *ir.* Here are the present-tense forms:

voy	vamos
vas	vais
va	van

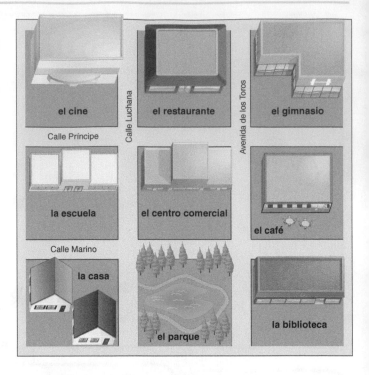

el cine · el restaurante · el gimnasio
Calle Príncipe · Calle Luchana · Avenida de los Toros
la escuela · el centro comercial · el café
Calle Marino
la casa · el parque · la biblioteca

▼22 Leer • Escribir

Los fines de semana de Arturo

Read Arturo's description of his weekends. Number your paper from 1–5, and write the appropriate form of the verb *ir*.

Me encantan los fines de semana. A veces me quedo en casa, pero generalmente __1.__ al parque para correr. Los sábados por la noche, mis amigos y yo __2.__ al cine. Me gustan mucho las películas. Mi mejor amigo, Jonatán, siempre __3.__ conmigo. Muchos de mis amigos son estudiosos y __4.__ a la biblioteca los sábados. ¿Y tú? ¿Adónde __5.__ este fin de semana?

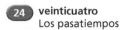

24 veinticuatro
Los pasatiempos

DIFFERENTIATED INSTRUCTION

Heritage Language Learners

Have students interview a friend or family member about their favorite activities and places. Students should prepare a list of questions using as many of the interrogatives as possible. Check for spelling, especially the written accents. Have them conduct the interview and write up their findings.

Advanced Learners

Have students write five sentence starters such as: *Cuando quiero nadar…, Cuando quiero estar solo(a)…, Cuando quiero ir de compras….* Have them exchange sentence starters with a partner and finish each other's sentences, telling the places they go in each situation.

Gramática Repaso

Asking questions

In Spanish, when you ask a question with an interrogative word (*who, what, where,* etc.), you put the verb before the subject.

¿Qué bebe María en el café?

¿Por qué estudian Juan y Flor en la biblioteca?

Here are some interrogative words you know:

¿Qué?   ¿Adónde?
¿Cómo?   ¿De dónde?
¿Quién(es)?   ¿Cuál?
¿Con quién(es)? ¿Por qué?
¿Dónde?   ¿Cuándo?
¿Cuántos(as)?

▼**23** Leer • Escribir

¡Qué chica curiosa!

Isabel is curious and can't stop asking questions. Number your paper from 1–5 and for each question, write the letter that corresponds to what she asks.

1. ¿Qué hay en tu mochila?
2. ¿Con quién vas al cine?
3. ¿Por qué van Julio y Rosibel a la biblioteca?
4. ¿Dónde está el cine?
5. ¿Quién va al parque?

a. Clara, Lucía y yo vamos al parque.
b. El cine está al lado del restaurante.
c. Hay una carpeta y dos libros porque yo voy a la escuela.
d. Porque ellos necesitan estudiar.
e. Voy al cine con mis amigos.

▼**24** Escribir • Hablar

¿Adónde vas los fines de semana?

❶ Use the map in Actividad 21 to make a list of three places you go to and the reasons why you go there.

❷ Exchange your list with a partner, and write two questions about each activity that you see on the list.

Modelo
¿Cuándo vas a la biblioteca para estudiar?

❸ With your partner, use your questions to talk about where you go.

▶ **Modelo**
A —*¿Cuándo vas a la biblioteca para estudiar?*
B —*Voy a la biblioteca los lunes después de las clases.*
A —*¿Y con quién vas?*
B —*Generalmente yo voy con mis amigos.*

Gramática

Core Instruction
Standards: 4.1

 INTERACTIVE WHITEBOARD
Grammar Activities PE

Suggestions: Review the *Gramática• Repaso*. Then tell students to imagine that an exchange student from Spain is coming to visit. As a class, brainstorm questions students would like to ask him or her.

▼**23** Standards: 1.2, 1.3
Resources: Answer Keys: Student Edition, p. 92
Focus: Reading comprehension of questions and responses
Suggestions: Have students cover the responses on the right. Read each question and have students predict the kinds of information that will be in the response.
Answers:

1. c   2. e   3. d   4. b   5. a

Extension: Have students write three questions to ask a classmate, using Isabel's questions as a model.

▼**24** Standards: 1.1, 1.3
Focus: Asking and responding to questions
Suggestions: Look at the map in *Actividad* 21 together and brainstorm reasons why students would go to each place.
Answers will vary.
Extension: Have students write sentences about three places they do not go and the reasons why *(No voy al café porque no me gusta beber café.)*.

Additional Resource
• Teacher's Resource Book: Communicative Pair Activity BLM, pp. 12–13

ENRICH YOUR TEACHING

Teacher-to-Teacher
Bring to class interviews from Spanish-language magazines. Entertainment, sports, and teen magazines are good sources for these. (Be sure to look carefully through the magazines to be sure there is no inappropriate content.) Give students photocopies of the interviews or make a transparency and have students highlight all the interrogative words they can find. Have students guess what is being asked based on the person being interviewed and on cognates and contextual clues.

25

Gramática

Core Instruction

Standards: 4.1

INTERACTIVE WHITEBOARD

Grammar Activities PE

Suggestions: Use the *GramActiva* Video from *Capítulo* 4A of Level A to review *ir* and ways to ask questions. Pass out Clip Art images of the sports on p. 23. Tell students that you are going to give them a college sports scholarship to play the sport shown on the paper they received. Have students group themselves by sport by asking each other: *¿Qué vas a jugar?* Once they are standing in groups, ask students questions about what sport they are going to play and what students in other groups are going to play.

▼25 Standards: 1.3

Focus: Using *ir* + *a* + **infinitive** to tell what people are going to do

Suggestions: Review the model with students. Then point out the article *el* used with *sábado.* Tell students to be sure to use *el* + day of the week when they write their responses to items 1 and 4.

Answers will vary but may include:

1. Yo voy a ...
2. Mi amigo(a) *(nombre)* va a ...
3. Mi profesor(a) va a ...
4. Mis amigos y yo vamos a ...
5. Los estudiantes en la clase de español van a ...

▼26 Standards: 1.1, 1.3

Focus: Asking questions about people's plans using *ir* + *a* + **infinitive**

Suggestions: Make a chart on the chalkboard showing your own plans and when and with whom you are going to do them. Have students practice by asking you questions.

Answers will vary.

Theme Project

Students can perform Step 5 at this point. Record their presentations for inclusion in their portfolio. (For more information, see p. 2-b.)

Gramática Repaso

Ir + *a* + infinitive

Just as you use "to be going" + an infinitive in English to say what you are going to do, in Spanish you use a form of the verb *ir* + *a* + an infinitive to express the same thing.

Voy a correr hoy.

¿Tú vas a jugar al golf esta tarde?

▼25 Escribir

¿Qué van a hacer tú y tus amigos?

On a sheet of paper, write sentences that tell what the following people are going to do at different times.

Modelo

mi amigo(a) *(nombre)* / sábado por la mañana
Mi amiga Eliana va a ver la tele el sábado por la mañana.

1. yo / lunes por la tarde
2. mi amigo(a) *(nombre)* / mañana por la noche
3. mi profesor(a) de español / después de las clases
4. mis amigos y yo / sábado por la noche
5. los estudiantes en la clase de español / mañana en la clase

▼26 | 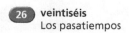 | Escribir • Hablar

¿Qué vas a hacer?

Make a chart like this one to describe five things you're going to do, when you are going to do them, and with whom. Then ask your partner what his or her plans are. Use the following words to talk about when you're going to do these things: *esta tarde, esta noche, mañana, el lunes . . . , el fin de semana.*

¿Qué?	¿Cuándo?	¿Con quién?
tocar la guitarra	esta tarde	mis amigos

 Modelo

A —*¿Qué vas a hacer esta tarde?*
B —*Esta tarde mis amigos y yo vamos a tocar la guitarra.*

26 veintiséis
Los pasatiempos

DIFFERENTIATED INSTRUCTION

Students with Special Needs

If students have physical impairments that prevent them from playing sports, allow them to do *Actividad* 27 by replacing *Club Deporte al Máximo* with *Centro de actividades* and have them substitute activities they do.

Advanced Learners

Tell students they have won a weekend with their favorite athlete or allow them to make up one. Have them write their schedule for that weekend, telling all the activities they and their sports idol are going to do.

Gramática *Repaso*

The verb *jugar*

Use the verb *jugar* to talk about playing a sport or a game. Even though *jugar* uses the same endings as the other *-ar* verbs, it has a different stem in some forms. For those forms, the *-u-* becomes *-ue-*. This kind of verb is called a "stem-changing verb."

Here are the present-tense forms of *jugar*:

juego	jugamos
juegas	jugáis
juega	juegan

▼**27** | **Escribir • Hablar**

En el club deportivo

❶ Write a list of four activities from Club Deporte al Máximo and choose a time for each.

❷ Work with three other students and talk about the activities you chose. Keep track of your group's answers to use in step 3.

> ▶ **Modelo**
>
> A —*Mario, ¿juegas al tenis?*
> B —*Sí, juego al tenis.*
> A —*¿A qué hora juegas al tenis?*
> B —*A las dos.*

❸ Write six sentences about the sports and games the students in your group play at the club.

> **Modelo**
>
> *Mario juega al tenis y Ana y Geraldo juegan al fútbol. Todos jugamos al golf.*

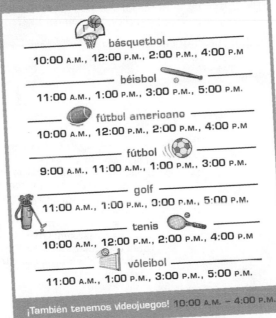

básquetbol
10:00 A.M., 12:00 P.M., 2:00 P.M., 4:00 P.M

béisbol
11:00 A.M., 1:00 P.M., 3:00 P.M., 5:00 P.M.

fútbol americano
10:00 A.M., 12:00 P.M., 2:00 P.M., 4:00 P.M

fútbol
9:00 A.M., 11:00 A.M., 1:00 P.M., 3:00 P.M.

golf
11:00 A.M., 1:00 P.M., 3:00 P.M., 5:00 P.M.

tenis
10:00 A.M., 12:00 P.M., 2:00 P.M., 4:00 P.M

vóleibol
11:00 A.M., 1:00 P.M., 3:00 P.M., 5:00 P.M.

¡También tenemos videojuegos! 10:00 A.M. – 4:00 P.M.

▼**28** | **Escribir • Hablar**

Y tú, ¿qué dices?

1. ¿Adónde vas después de las clases? ¿Qué te gusta hacer allí?
2. ¿Dónde estudias? ¿Estudias solo(a) o con un amigo(a)?
3. ¿Cuándo pasas tiempo con tus amigos? ¿Adónde van ustedes?

> **realidades.com**
>
> **Instant Check**
> **Tutorials:** Questions, Formation of yes-no questions, Interrogative words

veintisiete **27**
Para empezar

ENRICH YOUR TEACHING

Culture Note

Among Cuban Americans, a popular leisure time activity is playing dominoes. In Miami, Florida, the domino culture flourishes at Máximo Gómez Domino Park in the Calle Ocho district.

21st Century Skills

Technology Literacy Have students search the Internet using the keywords *Club deportivo* and *Actividades de verano*. Have them look at images of club activities in different Web sites, and scan the summer activities schedules. Which activities seem to be more popular?

Gramática

Core Instruction

Standards: 4.1

 INTERACTIVE WHITEBOARD
Grammar Activities PE

Suggestions: Bring a soccer ball to class. Call out a subject pronoun and toss the ball to a student. That student will give the form of *jugar* for that subject pronoun and toss the ball to another student as he or she calls out a different subject pronoun.

▼**27** Standards: 1.1, 1.3

Focus: Using forms of *jugar* to discuss activities

Suggestions: Sit down and join each group for a few minutes to help get the conversation going and also to make sure all students are participating.

Answers will vary.

▼**28** Standards: 1.1, 1.3

Focus: Writing personal answers to questions about activities

Suggestions: Let students know if you want them to answer in complete sentences. Have the class suggest sentence starters for the responses.

Answers will vary.

Teacher-to-Teacher

Have students write a letter or e-mail to another student. In their letters, they should ask at least two questions to find out activities the other person likes to do. Then students may write a letter in response.

✓ASSESSMENT

Prueba P–4: Los pasatiempos with Study Plan (online only)

Review Activities

Standards: 1.1, 1.2, 1.3

Resources: Teacher's Resource Book: Audio Script, p. 5; Situation Cards, p. 14; Audio Program DVD: Cap. PE, Tracks 4–5; Answer Keys: Student Edition, p. 93

Focus: Performing various language tasks to demonstrate preparedness

Escuchar

Activity 1:

Suggestions: Have students suggest adjectives that might describe an athlete, activities an athlete might enjoy, and the things an athlete might do and not do to stay healthy.

Script:

Interviewer: Lupita, ¿qué hace Ud. para mantener la salud?

Athlete: Yo soy una chica seria y trabajadora. Cada día, a las seis y media de la mañana, levanto pesas por treinta minutos, corro por una hora y juego al tenis por dos horas. Nunca como pasteles ni papas fritas porque son malos para la salud.

Interviewer: ¿Qué hace Ud. cuando no juega al tenis?

Athlete: Pues, no tengo mucho tiempo libre, pero me gusta pasar tiempo con mis amigos. Me encanta ir al parque o a las montañas. No me gusta nada estar en casa ni mirar la tele.

Answers:
a. She's serious and hardworking.
b. She likes to spend time with friends and to go to the park or the mountains. (Also accept lifting weights, running, and playing tennis.)
c. She doesn't like to stay home or to watch TV.
d. She lifts weights, runs, plays tennis, and doesn't eat pastries or French fries.

Activity 2:

Suggestions: Before beginning, have students list what they eat for breakfast. Tell them to circle any foods on their list that the first student mentions. Tell them to draw a box around any foods on their list that the second student mentions.

Script:

Marco: Siempre como huevos, tocino y pan tostado en el desayuno y me gusta beber leche. No me gusta ni el té ni el café. Es importante comer un buen desayuno.

Elena: ¡Qué asco! ¡Un desayuno grande! Nunca como huevos. Todos los días como yogur de fresas o pan tostado, con un jugo de naranja, ¡claro! A veces bebo té pero sólo a veces.

Answers will vary.

▼ **Objective**
▶ Demonstrate you can perform the tasks on pp. 28–29

A ver si puedes . . .

Now that you've completed *Para empezar*, you should be able to complete these practice tasks . . .

Escuchar

 1 Listen to an interview with a professional tennis player. a) What is she like? b) What are two things she likes doing? c) What is one thing she dislikes doing? d) What does she do to stay healthy?

2 Listen as two students describe what they typically eat and drink for breakfast. Which one is most like the kind of breakfast you eat? Which foods mentioned do you not like?

Hablar

1 You are trying to find out the name of someone in your class. You ask the students sitting next to you, but they don't understand whom you are talking about. Describe what the person you are trying to identify is like and tell where he or she is in the classroom. Give at least three statements to describe his or her location in relation to various classroom objects.

2 Your best friend calls to find out where you are going and what you are going to do this weekend. Mention at least three places you plan to go and three things you plan to do. For example, you might say *Voy a hacer ejercicio en el gimnasio a las 4:30.*

DIFFERENTIATED INSTRUCTION

Students with Learning Difficulties

You may want to provide copies of written support materials for the various performance tasks. Allow students to use their notes or to look back in the book to find support for their responses. Also remind them of the resources available for review at the end of the book.

Multiple Intelligences

Interpersonal/Social: Have students plan a party. They need to come up with invitations, a menu, and a list of the activities that will be available. Various "committees" could be given each of these tasks, and then the work can be put together.

 ## Leer

1. You are checking your e-mail and receive several responses to invitations that you sent out last week for a party at your house. Read them to see why some people declined the invitation.

a) Me gustaría, pero no puedo. Tengo que trabajar el sábado.

b) ¡Genial! ¡Una fiesta! Ay, pero no puedo, voy de pesca.

c) ¿A las seis? No puedo. Juego un partido de fútbol a las siete.

Escribir

1. A school in Uruguay wants to exchange e-mails with your school. Tell your e-pal your name and describe your class schedule. Include a description of your favorite class.

2. Your family is going to host an exchange student from Madrid, Spain. His name is Alejandro and he is going to spend the summer with you. Write him a note to find out more about him and to tell him about you. Ask him with whom he spends time on weekends and where he goes. Tell him about the places you and your friends go in your community and how you spend your free time.

realidades.com

Instant Check

veintinueve **29**
Para empezar

Hablar
Activity 1:

Suggestions: Model the activity for students before they work with their partners.
Answers will vary.

Activity 2:

Suggestions: Have partners work together to write a dialogue for this activity. Suggest that Student B provide only one piece of information at a time so that Student A can practice asking for more information.
Answers will vary.

Leer
Activity 1:

Suggestions: Assign names to the e-mail senders: a) Arturo; b) Bernardo; c) Carlos. After students have read the e-mail responses, ask questions to check students' comprehension: *¿Quién va a trabajar? ¿Qué va a hacer Bernardo? ¿A qué hora juega Carlos al fútbol?*

Answers:
a. has to work
b. going fishing
c. playing in a soccer game at 7:00

Escribir
Activity 1:

Suggestions: Prepare several e-pal messages and distribute them to groups of students to use as models for their own messages.

Answers will vary.

Activity 2:

Suggestions: Brainstorm the kinds of questions students might ask to find out more about Alejandro. For example, they might want to find out what Alejandro likes to eat for breakfast, lunch, and dinner.

Answers will vary.

ENRICH YOUR TEACHING

Culture Note
Although *piñatas* are associated with Mexican culture, they are believed to have originated in China as a New Year's Eve ritual performed to bring good luck. Marco Polo is thought to have introduced the *piñata* to Italy. From Italy, the tradition spread to Spain and from Spain to the Americas, through the Spanish explorers and conquistadors.

Teacher-to-Teacher
Have students research a *feria* day celebrated in Mexico or another Spanish-speaking country. Have them find out the history and traditions of the *feria* and of the region where it is celebrated and have them present their findings to the class. Have students vote on a *feria* day they would like to celebrate in class.

5A Una fiesta de cumpleaños

- **Family relationships and celebrations**
Vocabulary: family and parties
Grammar: the verb *tener;* possessive adjectives
Cultural Perspectives: the importance of family; the *quinceañera* tradition

5B ¡Vamos a un restaurante!

- **Personal descriptions and eating out**
Vocabulary: describing people and ordering a meal
Grammar: the verb *venir;* the verbs *ser* and *estar*
Cultural Perspectives: family celebrations; dining in restaurants; family mealtimes

THEME SUPPORT

Bulletin Boards

Theme: *Fiestas de familia*

Ask students to cut out, copy, or download photos of family celebrations and meals from many cultures. Cluster photos into categories of celebrations—weddings, baptisms, birthdays, bar and bat mitzvahs, graduations, and so on—so that similarities and differences are evident.

Hands-on Culture

Recipe: *Pastel de tres leches*

This dish is popular throughout the Spanish-speaking world for family celebrations.

Ingredients:
4 eggs
2 c. flour
¾ c. oil
1 T. baking powder
1 c. milk
1 c. sugar

1. Mix all the ingredients together well.
2. Grease and flour a 9" x 11" cake pan. Pour the batter into the pan.
3. Bake at 400 degrees Fahrenheit for about 30 minutes.
4. Immediately after taking the cake out of the oven, prick it all over with a fork. Next, pour the following mixture evenly over the top of the cake:

   1 can sweetened condensed milk
   1 can evaporated milk
   1 small carton half and half

5. After the cake cools, ice it with whipped cream.

Game

¿Han visto a mi amigo?

Play this game in *Capítulo* 5B, after students have learned vocabulary for physical descriptions.

Players: 15 to 20

Materials: scarf for blindfold

Rules:

1. Players stand in line. The first player in line is designated the Leader. The Leader wears a blindfold. The following exchange takes place:
   Leader: *¿Han visto a mi amigo?*
   Others: *No, señor / señorita.*
   Leader: *¿Saben dónde está mi amigo?*
   Others: *Sí, señor / señorita.*

2. The Leader then takes eight slow steps forward. While he or she is doing this, the others switch places quickly. The player who ends up directly behind the Leader must remain quiet.
   Others: *¿Quién está detrás de ti?*

3. The Leader guesses who is standing directly behind him or her. The Leader is allowed to ask three questions before guessing a name. For example:
   Leader: *¿Es chico o chica?*
   Others: *Es chica.*
   Leader: *¿Es alta?*
   Others: *No, es baja.*
   Leader: *¿Tiene pelo negro?*
   Others: *No, tiene pelo rubio.*
   Leader: *¿Es Emily?*

4. If the Leader guesses correctly, he or she gets another turn. If not, another player becomes the Leader and the game begins again.

Variation: Each of the other players holds an object that the Leader asks questions about and then guesses.

THEME PROJECT

Árbol genealógico con fotos y descripciones

Overview: Students create three-generation family trees on posters, featuring photos of family members and brief descriptions under each photo. Then they present the posters to the class, explaining the relationships on the tree and describing selected family members.

Resources: poster board, markers, photos, glue, scissors

Sequence: (suggestions for when to do each step appear throughout the chapters)

5A **STEP 1.** Review instructions so students know what's expected of them. Hand out the "Theme 5 Project Instructions and Rubric" from the *Teacher's Resource Book*.

STEP 2. Students submit a rough sketch of their tree. Return the drafts with your suggestions. For grammar and vocabulary practice, ask students to work with a partner and present their drafts to each other.

STEP 3. Students create layout on poster board, leaving room for photos and descriptions. Encourage them to work in pencil first and to try different arrangements before gluing photos or decorations.

5B **STEP 4.** Students submit a draft of the personal descriptions. Note your corrections and suggestions, then return drafts to students.

STEP 5. Students present their posters to the class, explaining the relationships and giving descriptions of family members.

Options:
1. Students diagram a fictitious or famous family.
2. Students limit their tree to one set of grandparents.

Assessment:
Here is a detailed rubric for assessing this project:
Theme 5 Project: *Árbol genealógico con fotos y descripciones*

RUBRIC	Score 1	Score 3	Score 5
Evidence of planning	You submitted no draft, created no layout.	You submitted the drafts and created the layout, but didn't correct them.	You submitted and corrected the draft, created the layout.
Use of illustrations	You included no photos or visuals.	You included very few photos or visuals.	You included several photos or visuals.
Presentation	You included some details and dialogue for characters.	You described yourself and at least two family members.	You described yourself and three or more family members.

21st Century Skills

Look for tips throughout *Tema 5* to enrich your teaching by integrating 21st Century Skills. Suggestions for the Theme Project and Theme Culture follow below.

Theme Project

Modify the Theme Project with one or more of these suggestions:

Develop Technology Literacy

Have students combine different types of media, both print and electronic, to make their family tree presentations more appealing. To improve their accuracy and make sure they are prepared to do well on the project, encourage them to use the digital online tools available for review, such as the flashcards and the tutorial videos.

Encourage Creativity and Innovation

Students can make their presentations more interesting by adding an unusual biographical fact about each person. Encourage students to keep it simple and to interview the family members first to get the information.

Support Collaboration

Once students have their family trees, have them work in a group and "mix and match" their families to create a new, fictitious family. Suggest that students put family members together who have the most in common.

Theme Culture

Foster Social and Cross-Cultural Skills

Have students compare parties that kids their age have in their communities with those that families in Spanish-speaking cultures celebrate. Is there anything like a *miniteca* in their community? What sorts of things do their communities celebrate?

▶ **Videocultura** View *La quinceañera* with the class to find out how teens in Spanish-speaking countries prepare for this rite of passage.

AT A GLANCE

Objectives

- Listen to and read descriptions of family members and family relationships
- Talk and write about family, friends, and celebrations
- Exchange information while describing your family
- Understand cultural perspectives on family celebrations in the Spanish-speaking world
- Learn to make *papel picado* and explain how this craft is used in celebrations

Vocabulary

- Family members and pets
- Telling ages
- Party decorations and celebration activities

Grammar

- The verb *tener*
- Possessive adjectives

Culture

- Family celebrations, p. 30
- Carmen Lomas Garza, p. 31
- Diego Rivera, p. 44
- Francisco de Goya, p. 47
- *papel picado,* pp. 39, 56
- Spanish royal family, p. 46
- *quinceañera traditions,* p. 55

Recycle ♻

- *tengo, tienes*
- *tener que* + infinitive
- *de* to show possession or relationship
- Classroom supplies
- *gustar, encantar*
- *-ar* and *-er* verbs
- *estar*
- Personal descriptions
- Prepositions of location

RESOURCES

FOR THE STUDENT	ONLINE	DVD	PRINT	FOR THE TEACHER	ONLINE	PREEXP	DVD	PRINT
Plan				Interactive TE and Resources DVD	•		•	
				Teacher's Resource Book, pp. 16–51	•		•	•
				Pre-AP* Resource Book, pp. 78–81	•		•	•
				Lesson Plans	•			•
				Mapa global interactivo	•			
Introducción PP. 30–31								
Present Student Edition, pp. 30–31	•	•	•	Interactive TE and Resources DVD	•		•	
DK Reference Atlas	•	•		Teacher's Resource Book, pp. 15–19	•		•	•
Videocultura	•	•		Galería de fotos		•		
Hispanohablantes WB, pp. 170–171			•	Fine Art Transparencies, 34	•	•	•	
				Map Transparencies, 12, 14, 16–18, 20	•	•	•	
Vocabulario en contexto PP. 32–37								
Present & Practice Student Edition, pp. 32–37	•	•	•	Interactive TE and Resources DVD	•		•	
Audio	•	•		Teacher's Resource Book, pp. 20–22, 24, 32–35	•		•	•
Videohistoria	•	•		Vocabulary Clip Art	•	•	•	•
Flashcards	•	•		Audio Program	•	•	•	
Instant Check	•			Video Program: Videohistoria	•		•	
Guided WB, pp. 1–10	•	•	•	Video Program Teacher's Guide: Cap. 5A	•		•	•
Core WB, pp. 1–4	•	•	•	Vocabulary and Grammar Transparencies, 96–99	•	•	•	
Comm. WB, pp. 1–4, 8	•	•	•	Answer Keys: Student Edition, pp. 94–96	•		•	
Hispanohablantes WB, pp. 172–173			•	TPR Stories, pp. 62–76	•		•	
Assess and Remediate				Prueba 5A–1: Assessment Program, pp. 119–120	•		•	•
				Assessment Program para hispanohablantes, pp. 119–120	•		•	•

FOR THE STUDENT	ONLINE	DVD	PRINT	FOR THE TEACHER	ONLINE	PREEXP	DVD	PRINT
Vocabulario en uso PP. 38–41								
Present & Practice								
Student Edition, pp. 38–41	•	•	•	Interactive Whiteboard Vocabulary Activities	•		•	
Instant Check	•			Interactive TE and Resources DVD	•		•	
Comm. WB, p. 5	•	•	•	Teacher's Resource Book, pp. 22, 26–27	•		•	•
Hispanohablantes WB, pp. 174–175			•	Communicative Pair Activities, pp. 26–27	•		•	•
Communicative Pair Activities	•			Audio Program	•	•	•	
				Videomodelos	•		•	
				Vocabulary and Grammar Transparencies, p. 97	•	•	•	
				Fine Art Transparencies, 35	•	•	•	
				Answer Keys: Student Edition, pp. 96–99	•	•	•	•
Assess and Remediate				Prueba 5A–2 with Study Plan	•			
				Prueba 5A–2: Assessment Program, pp. 121–122	•		•	•
				Assessment Program para hispanohablantes, pp. 121–122	•		•	•
Gramática PP. 42–53								
Present & Practice								
Student Edition, pp. 42–53	•	•	•	Interactive Whiteboard Grammar Activities	•		•	
Instant Check	•			Interactive TE and Resources DVD	•		•	
Animated Verbs	•			Teacher's Resource Book, pp. 22–25, 28–29, 31	•		•	•
Tutorial Video: Grammar	•			Communicative Pair Activities, pp. 28–29	•		•	•
Canción de hip hop	•			Audio Program	•	•	•	
Guided WB, pp. 11–14	•	•	•	Videomodelos	•		•	
Core WB, pp. 5–7	•	•	•	Video Program: GramActiva	•		•	
Comm. WB, pp. 5–7, 9–10, 131	•	•	•	Vocabulary and Grammar Transparencies, 100–103	•	•	•	
Hispanohablantes WB, pp. 176–181			•	Fine Art Transparencies, 25, 26, 51	•	•	•	
Communicative Pair Activities	•			Answer Keys: Student Edition, pp. 99–104	•	•	•	
Assess and Remediate				Pruebas 5A–3 and 5A–4 with Study Plans	•			
				Pruebas 5A–3, 5A–4: Assessment Program, pp. 123, 124	•		•	•
				Assessment Program para hispanohablantes, pp. 123, 124	•		•	•
¡Adelante! PP. 54–59								
Application								
Student Edition, pp. 54–59	•	•	•	Interactive TE and Resources DVD	•		•	
Online Cultural Reading	•			Teacher's Resource Book, p. 25	•		•	•
Guided WB, p. 15	•	•	•	Video Program: Videomisterio ¿Eres tú, María?	•		•	
Comm. WB, pp. 11, 132	•	•	•	Video Program Teacher's Guide: Cap. 5A	•		•	
Hispanohablantes WB, pp. 182–187			•	Videomisterio Quiz			•	
¿Eres tú, María? Video WB, pp. 1–9	•	•	•	Answer Keys: Student Edition, p. 105	•		•	
Repaso del capítulo PP. 60–61								
Review								
Student Edition, pp. 60–61	•	•	•	Interactive TE and Resources DVD	•		•	
Online Puzzles and Games	•			Teacher's Resource Book, pp. 23, 30–34	•		•	•
Core WB, pp. 8–9	•	•	•	Audio Program	•	•	•	
Comm. WB, pp. 133–137	•	•	•	Answer Keys: Student Edition, p. 106	•		•	
Hispanohablantes WB, pp. 188–189			•					
Instant Check	•							
Chapter Assessment								
Assess				Examen del capítulo 5A	•		•	•
				Assessment Program, pp. 125–132	•		•	•
				Alternate Assessment Program, pp. 57–61	•		•	•
				Assessment Program para hispanohablantes, pp. 125–132	•		•	•
				Audio Program, Cap. 5A, Examen	•		•	
				ExamView: Test Banks A and B questions only online	•		•	
				Heritage Learner Test Bank	•		•	
				Pre-AP* Test Bank	•		•	

REGULAR SCHEDULE (50 MINUTES)

DAY	Warm-up / Assess	Preview / Present / Practice / Communicate	Wrap-up / Homework Options
1	Return Examen del capítulo (10 min.)	**Vocabulario en contexto** (35 min.) • Objectives • Presentation • *Actividades* 1, 2 • Arte y cultura • Videocultura: *La quinceañera*	**Wrap-up and Homework Options** (5 min.) • Core Practice • Vocabulary Clip Art
2	**Warm-up** (5 min.) • Homework check	**Vocabulario en contexto** (40 min.) • Review: *Vocabulario en contexto* • Presentation: *Videohistoria ¡Feliz cumpleaños!* • View: Video *¡Feliz cumpleaños!* • Video Activities • *Actividades* 3, 4, 5	**Wrap-up and Homework Options** (5 min.) • *Prueba* 5A-1: Vocabulary recognition • Core Practice
3	**Warm-up** (5 min.) • Homework check ✔**Formative Assessment** (10 min.) • *Prueba* 5A-1: Vocabulary recognition	**Vocabulario en uso** (30 min.) • Objectives • Interactive Whiteboard Vocabulary Activities • *Actividades* 6, 7 • *Fondo cultural*	**Wrap-up and Homework Options** (5 min.) • *Actividad* 8
4	**Warm-up** (10 min.) • Homework check • Return *Prueba* 5A-1: Vocabulary recognition	**Vocabulario en uso** (35 min.) • Review: *Vocabulario* • *Actividades* 9, 10, 11, 12 • Communicative Pair Activities	**Wrap-up and Homework Options** (5 min.) • *Actividad* 13
5	**Warm-up** (10 min.) • Homework check	**Gramática y vocabulario en uso** (35 min.) • Presentation: The verb *tener* • *GramActiva* Video • Interactive Whiteboard Grammar Activities • *Actividades* 14, 16, 17	**Wrap-up and Homework Options** (5 min.) • *Actividad* 15
6	**Warm-up** (5 min.) • Homework check	**Gramática y vocabulario en uso** (40 min.) • Review: The verb *tener* • *Fondo cultural* • *Actividades* 18, 19 • *Pronunciación*	**Wrap-up and Homework Options** (5 min.) • *Actividad* 20
7	**Warm-up** (5 min.) • Homework check	**Gramática y vocabulario en uso** (40 min.) • *Actividades* 21, 22, 24 • *Conexiones: Actividad* 23 • *Fondos culturales* • Communicative Pair Activities	**Wrap-up and Homework Options** (5 min.) • Core Practice • *Prueba* 5A-3 with Study Plan: The verb *tener*
8	**Warm-up** (5 min.) • Homework check ✔**Formative Assessment** (10 min.) • *Prueba* 5A-3 with Study Plan: The verb *tener*	**Gramática y vocabulario en uso** (30 min.) • Presentation: Possessive adjectives • *GramActiva* Video • Interactive Whiteboard Grammar Activities • *Actividades* 25, 27	**Wrap-up and Homework Options** (5 min.) • *Actividad* 26 • *Prueba* 5A-2 with Study Plan: Vocabulary production

REGULAR SCHEDULE (50 MINUTES)

DAY	Warm-up / Assess	Preview / Present / Practice / Communicate	Wrap-up / Homework Options
9	**Warm-up** (5 min.) • Homework check • Return *Prueba 5A-3* with Study Plan: The verb *tener* ✔**Formative Assessment** (10 min.) • *Prueba 5A-2* with Study Plan: Vocabulary production	**Gramática y vocabulario en uso** (30 min.) • *Actividades 28, 30* • *Juego: Actividad 29* • *El español en la comunidad*	**Wrap-up and Homework Options** (5 min.) • Core Practice • *Prueba 5A-4* with Study Plan: Possessive adjectives
10	**Warm-up** (5 min.) • Homework check • Return *Prueba 5A-2* with Study Plan: Vocabulary production ✔**Formative Assessment** (10 min.) • *Prueba 5A-4* with Study Plan: Possessive adjectives	**Gramática y vocabulario en uso** (30 min.) • *Exploración del lenguaje* • *Actividades 32, 33, 34*	**Wrap-up and Homework Options** (5 min.) • *Actividad 31*
11	**Warm-up** (5 min.) • Homework check • Return *Prueba 5A-4* with Study Plan: Possessive adjectives	**¡Adelante!** (40 min.) • *Presentación oral:* Prepare • *Lectura* • *Fondo cultural*	**Wrap-up and Homework Options** (5 min.) • *Presentación oral:* Prepare
12	**Warm-up** (5 min.) • Homework check	**¡Adelante!** (40 min.) • *Presentación oral:* Practice • *La cultura en vivo*	**Wrap-up and Homework Options** (5 min.)
13	**Warm-up** (5 min.) • Homework check	**¡Adelante!** (40 min.) • *Presentación oral:* Present	**Wrap-up and Homework Options** (5 min.) • Writing Activities • Core Practice Organizer
14	**Warm-up** (5 min.) • Homework check • Core Practice Organizer	**¡Adelante!** (20 min.) • *Videomisterio* **Repaso** (20 min.) • *Vocabulario y gramática* • *Preparación para el examen*	**Wrap-up and Homework Options** (5 min.) • Instant Check • *Examen del capítulo*
15	**Warm-up** (5 min.) • Answer questions ✔**Summative Assessment** (45 min.) • *Examen del capítulo*		

Capítulo 5A Una fiesta de cumpleaños

Standards for *Capítulo* 5A

• To achieve the goals of the Standards, students will:

Communication

1.1 *Interpersonal*
• Talk about families and celebrations
• Talk about classes and school materials
• Talk about favorite activities and preferences
• Talk about the royal family of Spain
• Talk about personal heroes

1.2 *Interpretive*
• Read and listen to information about family celebrations
• Read a picture-based story
• Listen to and watch a video about a birthday party
• Read about the royal families of Carlos IV, Juan Carlos I
• Read about the family of Carlos IV
• Read a child's birthday card
• Read about a *quinceañera;* read an invitation to a *miniteca*
• Watch and listen to a video mystery
• Read a public service announcement

1.3 *Presentational*
• Present information about families and celebrations
• Write about how family members are related
• Present information about party supplies
• Present information about a *miniteca*

Culture

2.1 *Practices and Perspectives*
• Understand Hispanic names and naming conventions
• Learn about celebration traditions like the *piñata*
• Learn about a *miniteca;* read about the traditional party, the *quinceañera*

2.2 *Products and Perspectives*
• Learn about Carmen Lomas Garza and her painting
• Learn about *papel picado*
• Learn about the royal family of Spain; learn about Francisco de Goya and his painting; learn about the family of Carlos IV
• Learn about Diego Rivera and his portrayal of indigenous people through painting

Connections

3.1 *Cross-curricular*
• Learn about important artists: Lomas Garza, Goya, Rivera
• Learn about the royal family of Spain

3.2 *Target Culture*
• Read a version of the fairy tale *"Cenicienta"*

Comparisons

4.1 *Language*
• Learn new vocabulary through the recognition of cognates
• Compare the uses of *tener* idioms with English
• Compare the use of possessive adjectives
• Understand the use of diminutives in Spanish

4.2 *Culture*
• Compare family celebrations
• Compare crafts
• Compare the role of families
• Compare pictorial representations of families

Communities

5.1 *Beyond the School*
• Identify Hispanic surnames in a local phonebook

5.2 *Lifelong Learner*
• View a video mystery series

▼ Chapter Objectives

Communication

By the end of this chapter you will be able to:
• Listen to and read descriptions of family members and family relationships
• Talk and write about family, friends, and celebrations
• Exchange information while describing your family

Culture

You will also be able to:
• Understand cultural perspectives on family celebrations in the Spanish-speaking world
• Learn to make *papel picado* and explain how this craft is used in celebrations

You will demonstrate what you know and can do:
• Presentación oral, p. 57
• Preparación para el examen, p. 61

You will use:

Vocabulary
• Family members and pets
• Telling ages
• Party decorations and celebration activities

Grammar
• The verb *tener*
• Possessive adjectives

Exploración del mundo hispano

Country Connection
Family Celebrations

Texas
España
México
República Dominicana

realidades.com GO

DK Reference Atlas

▶ Videocultura y actividad

🌐 Mapa global interactivo

30 treinta
Tema 5 • Fiesta en familia

ENRICH YOUR TEACHING

Using Backward Design
Have students preview the sample performance tasks on *Preparación para el examen*, p. 61, and connect them to the Chapter Objectives. Explain to students that by completing the sample tasks they can self-assess their learning progress.

Mapa global interactivo
Download the *Mapa global interactivo* files for Chapter 5A and preview the activities. Activity 1 looks at Mexico and the countries of Central America, the region known as Mesoamerica. Use Activity 2 to explore the Palacio Real and its surroundings in Madrid, Spain.

Una familia mexicanoamericana celebrando un cumpleaños

Arte y cultura | Estados Unidos

Carmen Lomas Garza (1948–) is best known for her paintings that show Mexican American family life in her native South Texas in the 1950s.

• What do you see in the painting that would make this family celebration similar to or different from family parties that you're familiar with?

▼ "Barbacoa para cumpleaños / Birthday Party Barbecue" (1993), Carmen Lomas Garza

Alkyds on canvas, 36 x 48 inches. ©1993 Carmen Lomas Garza (reg. 1994). Photo credit: M. Lee Fatherree. Collection of Federal Reserve Bank of Dallas.

treinta y uno **31**
Capítulo 5A

Chapter Opener
Core Instruction

Resources: Map Transparencies 12, 14, 16–18, 20

Suggestions: Have students predict what specific content words will be taught for each objective. Ask students to describe parties and family get-togethers they attend. Explain that strong family ties and allegiances are central to the social structures of many Spanish-speaking countries. Remember that for some students the family is a sensitive subject. When possible, offer an alternative to focusing on a student's own family by using a fictional family (from books, TV, etc.) or that of a famous person.

▶ **Videocultura** View *La quinceañera* with the class to find out how teens in Spanish-speaking countries prepare for this rite of passage.

Arte y cultura

Standards: 2.2, 3.1, 4.2

Resources: Fine Art Transparencies, p. 34

Suggestions: Emphasize that Lomas Garza based this painting on childhood memories and experiences in a close-knit Mexican American community. Discuss the childlike style of the painting. Point out that this style is the artist's intent, and imitates a traditional Mexican art style.

Answers will vary.

▶ TEACHING WITH ART

Resources: Fine Art Transparencies, p. 34

Suggestions: To guide discussion of the painting, ask: Who is present in the painting? What are the decorations like? What story does the picture tell?

DIFFERENTIATED INSTRUCTION

Digital resources such as the *Interactive Whiteboard* activity banks, *Videomodelos*, additional *Online Activities*, *Study Plans*, automatically graded *Leveled Workbook*, animated *Grammar Tutorials*, *Flashcards*, and *Vocabulary and Grammar Videos* will help you reach students of different ability levels and learning styles.

STUDENTS NEEDING EXTRA HELP
Guided Practice Activities
• Flashcards, pp. 1–6
• Vocabulary Check, pp. 7–10
• Grammar Support, pp. 11–15

HERITAGE LEARNERS
Realidades para hispanohablantes
• Chapter Opener, pp. 170–171
• A primera vista, p. 172
• Videohistoria, p. 173
• Manos a la obra, pp. 174–181
• ¡Adelante!, pp. 182–187
• Repaso del capítulo, pp. 188–189

ADVANCED/PRE-AP*
Pre-AP* Resource Book,
• pp. 78–81
Communications Workbook
• Integrated Performance Assessment, p. 133

Read, listen to, and understand information about
▸ families
▸ parties and celebrations

BELLRINGER REVIEW

Review numbers with students by having students say each of the ages listed under the family members.

Vocabulario en contexto

Core Instruction

Standards: 1.2

Resources: Teacher's Resource Book: Input Script, p. 20, Clip Art pp. 32–35, Audio Script, p. 21; Voc. and Gram. Transparencies 96–97; TPR Stories Book, pp. 62–76; Audio Program DVD: Cap. 5A, Tracks 6–7

Focus: Presenting visualized vocabulary for family members, celebrations, and parties

Suggestions: Use the transparencies to present the vocabulary in three sections: the family tree, Cristina's introduction to her family, and the party-room scene.

Ask questions that require limited verbal response, such as: *¿Es Esteban el padre de Cristina? ¿Te gusta comer dulces?*

If students are unfamiliar with the structure of the family tree, emphasize that the youngest members are at the bottom, then parents in the middle, and grandparents at the top. Explain the structure of the tree; for example, people who are connected with a horizontal blue line are brothers and sisters.

For sample presentation scripts, use the Input Script from the *Teacher's Resource Book* or use the *TPR Stories Book*.

Vocabulario en contexto

mis abuelos

Ricardo
mi abuelo, 68

Ana María
mi abuela, 61

Más vocabulario

el padrastro   stepfather
la madrastra   stepmother
el hermanastro   stepbrother
la hermanastra   stepsister

mis padres

mis tíos

María
mi madre, 39

José Antonio
mi padre, 42

Josefina
mi tía, 38

Andrés
mi tío, 42

Capitán
mi perro

Michi
mi gato

mis hermanos

mis primos

Angélica
mi hermana, 16

Cristina
yo, 13

Esteban
mi hermano, 15

Carolina
mi prima, 17

Gabriel
mi primo, 13

❝¡Hola! Me llamo Cristina. Hoy es mi **cumpleaños**. Toda mi familia va a **preparar** una fiesta para **celebrar**. ¡Va a ser muy divertido!❞

❝Aquí está mi familia. Tengo dos hermanos: mi hermana **mayor**, Angélica, **que tiene 16 años**, y mi hermano, Esteban, que tiene 15 años. Y aquí están mis primos: Carolina tiene 17 años. **Su hermano menor** Gabriel, tiene **sólo 13 años**❞.

❝Mira a las personas de las fotos. Es la familia de mi tía Josefina. Mi tío Andrés es **el esposo** de Josefina. Ellos tienen dos **hijos: su hijo** Gabriel y su **hija Carolina**❞.

DIFFERENTIATED INSTRUCTION

Heritage Language Learners

Ask students if they call their mother, father, grandmother, or grandfather different names from those listed in the vocabulary (for example: *abuelita* or *papi*).

Students with Learning Difficulties

If students are struggling with the organization of the family tree, suggest that they review p. 60 for a more concise list of the vocabulary words and their meanings. Review the family tree prior to starting *Actividad* 1.

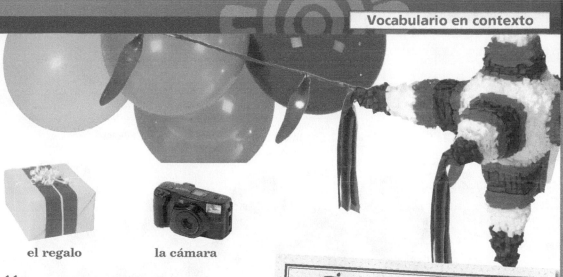

el regalo   la cámara

66 Hoy es el cumpleaños de Cristina. Tengo un regalo para ella. Es una cámara. A Cristina le encanta sacar fotos 99.

▼1 | 🔊 | Escuchar

La familia de Cristina

Listen as Cristina describes her family. If her statement is true, give a "thumbs-up" sign. If it is false, give a "thumbs-down" sign.

▼2 | 🔊 | Escuchar

Preparamos la fiesta

Now listen as Cristina and her mother prepare for a birthday party. Look at the items in the party shop ad on this page and touch each item they mention.

Fiestamanía

¡Tenemos todo para tu fiesta de cumpleaños!

las luces

la luz

la piñata

el papel picado

la flor

los globos

las flores

el pastel

los dulces

calle Bolívar, 23
Tel. 455-23-19
Abierto de
10h a 20h

Más práctica	GO

realidades.com | print

Instant Check	✔	
Guided WB pp. 1–6	✔	✔
Core WB pp. 1–2	✔	✔
Comm. WB p. 8	✔	✔
Hispanohablantes WB p. 172	✔	

treinta y tres **33**
Capítulo 5A

---

1 Standards: 1.2

Resources: Teacher's Resource Book: Audio Script, p. 21; Audio Program DVD: Cap. 5A, Track 8; Answer Keys: Student Edition, p. 94

Focus: Listening comprehension about family members' ages and names

Suggestions: Review the words *menor* and *mayor.* Then play the audio or read the script. You may wish to allow students to hear the entire script once before asking them to respond.

🔊 **Script and Answers:**

1. Mi hermano se llama Esteban. *(up)*
2. Mi tío tiene cuarenta y dos años. *(up)*
3. Mi hermana menor se llama Ana Isabel. *(down)*
4. Mi madre tiene treinta y ocho años. *(down)*
5. Mi perro se llama Michi. *(down)*
6. Mi primo se llama Esteban. *(down)*
7. Mi abuela es mayor que mi abuelo. *(down)*
8. Mi perro se llama Capitán. *(up)*

Common Errors: Students confuse similar words that differentiate gender, such as *primo* and *prima.* Remind them that words ending in *a* are usually feminine and words ending in *o* are usually masculine.

2 Standards: 1.2

Resources: Teacher's Resource Book: Audio Script, p. 21; Audio Program DVD: Cap. 5A, Track 9; Answer Keys: Student Edition, p. 94

Focus: Listening comprehension about preparing for a party

Suggestions: Play the audio or read the script. Pause the reading between each statement to monitor students during the activity. Listen to the script again to review the answers.

🔊 **Script and Answers:**

1. Necesitamos muchos globos, ¿no? *(balloons)*
2. A Angélica le encantan las flores. *(flowers)*
3. A los chicos les encanta la piñata, ¿no? *(piñata)*
4. Hay globos y luces en la fiesta de cumpleaños, ¿no? *(balloons and lights)*
5. Ya tenemos dulces, ¿verdad? *(candies)*
6. No me gusta el papel picado de plástico. *(cut-paper decorations)*
7. Y en el pastel vamos a escribir "¡Feliz cumpleaños!" *(cake)*

ENRICH YOUR TEACHING

Culture Note

Paper flowers are popular party decorations in Mexico. The flowers are made from tissue paper (*papel de china*) that is folded and bound together with wire. While some paper flowers require a great deal of skill to fold, cut, and shape, there are simple techniques that children can use to create these decorations.

Teacher-to-Teacher

Bring in physical examples of vocabulary items such as balloons, or use the Clip Art to make large flashcards of them. Replay or reread the script for *Actividad* 2. Hold up the items or photos at random. Students should identify the objects correctly by saying *sí* or *no.*

5A Language Input

Videohistoria 🔊

Core Instruction

Standards: 1.2, 2.1

Resources: Voc. and Gram. Transparencies 98–99; Audio Program DVD: Cap. 5A, Track 10

Focus: Presenting additional vocabulary; extending presentation of vocabulary and grammar in the context of the story; previewing the language video

Suggestions:

Pre-reading: Direct students' attention to the *Strategy.* Have them look at all the pictures and point out the details that will help them with the story line. Using the transparencies, go panel by panel and ask students to predict what will happen.

BELLRINGER REVIEW

Have students write two sentences telling how old four of their family members or friends are. (Ex. *Mi primo James tiene quince años.*)

¡Feliz cumpleaños!

¿Qué pasa en la fiesta de Cristina? Lee la historia.

Texas · Carolina · Angélica · Gabriel · Esteban · Cristina

Antes de leer

Strategy **Using visuals** Look at the pictures as you read to help you get the details of the story.

• What does the family do to get ready for the party?

1. Think about parties that you or your friends have had. Who was invited? What were you celebrating?

2. What do you or your friends do to prepare for parties that you give?

3. What activities are common at birthday parties that you go to? What are some similarities and differences between what you are used to and what you see in the *Videohistoria* photos?

 34 treinta y cuatro
Tema 5 • Fiesta en familia

DIFFERENTIATED INSTRUCTION

Multiple Intelligences

Musical/Rhythmic: Have students use the Internet or library resources to look for Spanish folk songs like the *piñata* song. Have them bring in the lyrics, and if you are familiar with the tune, have all students sing along. Suggest that students find out the occasions on which the song is sung. Remind them that they do not need to focus on the meaning of the lyrics in their research, but it may be helpful.

Esteban: Vamos a **hacer un video.** Uno . . . dos . . . tres . . . ¡Acción!

Angélica: Hola, me llamo Angélica. Hoy es el cumpleaños de **nuestra** hermana, Cristina. Todos están aquí para celebrar.

Angélica: Aquí están mis abuelos. ¿Y cuántos años tienen Uds.?

Abuelo: Pues, yo tengo sesenta y ocho años y tu abuela . . .

Abuela: Por favor, Ricardo. Angélica, ¡qué pregunta!

Angélica: Aquí está Gabriel, mi primo menor. Le gusta mucho el fútbol. Y aquí está mi prima. ¿Cómo te llamas?

Carolina: Pero, Angélica, tú sabes mi nombre.

Angélica: Sí, pero es para el video. Por favor . . .

Angélica: **Él es nuestro** padre. ¿Qué haces, **papá?**

Padre: Voy a preparar unas hamburguesas y después voy a sacar fotos de la fiesta.

treinta y cinco **35**
Capítulo 5A

Suggestions:

Reading: Have student volunteers play the roles of the characters or use the audio. Using transparencies and non-verbal clues, help students understand the new words in blue type. Ask students comprehension questions.

Post-reading: Complete *Actividad* 3 to check comprehension.

Pre-AP* Support

- **Learning Objective:** Presentational Writing and Speaking
- **Activity:** As a post-viewing activity, have groups of students rewrite the first three frames of the video, changing the names, the family members, and other details of the scene. Then have students act their new versions of the scene in front of the class.
- *Pre-AP* Resource Book:* Comprehensive guide to Pre-AP* vocabulary skill development, pp. 51–57

ENRICH YOUR TEACHING

Culture Note

Piñatas are crafts that serve as both party decorations and entertainment. Although other materials are now common, traditionally *piñatas* are made from a clay pot (*olla de barro*), with papier-mâché attached to complete the desired shape. Curled strips and streamers of tissue paper are then glued on the outside. The breaking of the *piñata* is a ritual, with a song urging the blindfolded child to hit the *piñata* and bring down the shower of candies, fruit, or small toys that it contains.

Video ▶️

Core Instruction

Standards: 1.2, 2.1

Resources: Teacher's Resource Book: Video Script, p. 24; Video Program: Cap. 5A; Video Program Teacher's Guide: Cap. 5A

Focus: Hearing and seeing new party-related vocabulary in context; listening comprehension

Suggestions:

Pre-viewing: Remind students that they should use prior experience to help them understand the video. Have them think of birthday parties they have attended and how people react when they are recorded on video. Tell them that when they see the images for the new vocabulary words in the video, they should try to listen for these words in the conversation. Before students watch the video, go through each panel and have students identify at least one new word that they should listen for in the video.

Viewing: Show the video once without pausing, then go back and show it again, stopping along the way to check for comprehension. Write difficult words on the board. Show the segment a final time without pausing.

Post-viewing: Complete the Video Activities in the *Communication Workbook*.

Additional Resources

• Communication Wbk.: Audio Act. 5, p. 4
• Teacher's Resource Book: Audio Script, pp. 21–22
• Audio Program DVD: Cap. 5A, Track 11

5

Angélica: Aquí está mi madre. A mamá le gustan las decoraciones.

Madre: Sí. A mí me encanta decorar con papel picado.

6

Angélica: Y aquí está Cristina. Hoy es su cumpleaños. ¡Feliz cumpleaños!

Cristina: ¿Cuándo puedo abrir mis regalos?

Angélica: Ahora no. Primero, la piñata.

7

Padre: ¡Vamos, Gabriel! ¿Puedes romper la piñata?

Gabriel: ¡Por supuesto!

Todos: *Dale, dale, dale, no pierdas el tino, porque si lo pierdes, pierdes el camino.*

¡Crac! *Gabriel rompe la piñata y . . .*

8

Madre: ¡Gabriel! ¡La piñata! ¡El pastel! ¡Ay, no!

 36 treinta y seis
Tema 5 • Fiesta en familia

DIFFERENTIATED INSTRUCTION

Advanced Learners

Have groups of students select sentences from each panel to tell a story. Have them copy their sentences onto paper, one sentence per line, and cut the sentences apart. Place the strips in envelopes. Randomly distribute the envelopes and have students put the sentences in order.

Students with Special Needs

Provide hearing-impaired students with a copy of the Video Script (see *Teacher's Resource Book: Cap.* 5A, Video Script) or use the closed captioning on the video.

3 Leer · Escribir

Asociaciones

Number your paper from 1–5. Write the name of the *Videohistoria* character who would be associated with each of the following.

1.

2.

3.

4.

5.

4 Escribir · Hablar

¿Comprendes?

1. ¿Quién va a hacer el video, Gabriel o Esteban?
2. ¿Quién tiene sesenta y ocho años, el abuelo o la abuela?
3. ¿A quién le gusta jugar al fútbol, a Esteban o a Gabriel?
4. ¿Qué va a hacer el padre, decorar o preparar hamburguesas?
5. ¿Con qué decora la madre, con globos o con papel picado?
6. ¿Quién rompe la piñata, Cristina o Gabriel?

5 Leer · Escribir

Primero . . . y después . . .

Esteban is trying to edit his video. Help him out by putting the following people in the order that they are interviewed in the *Videohistoria*. Number your paper from 1–8 and write the names on your paper.

Gabriel	Padre
Abuela	Angélica
Madre	Cristina
Abuelo	Carolina

Más práctica (GO)

realidades.com | print

Instant Check	✔	
Guided WB pp. 7–10	✔	✔
Core WB pp. 3–4	✔	✔
Comm. WB pp. 1–3	✔	✔
Hispanohablantes WB p. 173		✔

treinta y siete **37**
Capítulo 5A

ENRICH YOUR TEACHING

Multiple Intelligences

Visual/Spatial: Have students bring in a photo of a recent family celebration or a magazine cutout of people at a party. In small groups, have them ask and answer questions such as: *¿Qué celebran? ¿Quién está en la fiesta? ¿Qué hacen?*

---

3 Standards: 1.2

Resources: Answer Keys: Student Edition, p. 95

Focus: Recalling vocabulary words and searching for them within a reading

Suggestions: Have students make a list of characters from the *Videohistoria*.

Answers:

1. Padre / José Antonio   4. Cristina
2. Esteban y Angélica   5. Gabriel
3. Madre / María

4 Standards: 1.1, 1.3

Resources: Answer Keys: Student Edition, p. 95

Focus: Reading for understanding

Suggestions: Point out that each question is asking for students to identify one of two possible responses. When reviewing the responses, have them say in which panel they found the information.

Answers:

1. Esteban va a hacer el video.
2. El abuelo (de Cristina) tiene sesenta y ocho años.
3. A Gabriel le gusta el fútbol.
4. El padre va a preparar hamburguesas.
5. La madre decora con papel picado.
6. Gabriel rompe la piñata.

5 Standards: 1.2

Resources: Answer Keys: Student Edition, p. 96

Focus: Reading and sequencing information

Suggestions: You may want to create sets of laminated cards with each character's name on a card. Distribute a set to small groups of students and have them sequence the cards.

Answers:

1. Angélica	3. Abuela	5. Carolina	7. Madre
2. Abuelo	4. Gabriel	6. Padre	8. Cristina

✓ASSESSMENT

Quiz: Vocabulary Recognition
• Prueba 5A-1: pp. 119–120

▶ Write and talk about family members and celebrations
▶ Exchange information while discussing your family and family activities with a classmate

Vocabulario en uso

▼**6** Pensar • Escribir

Un árbol genealógico

José is explaining his family tree. Number a sheet of paper from 1–8, then write the correct words to complete the sentences based on what you see in the family tree.

Strategy

Using graphic organizers
Drawing diagrams can help you understand how things are related.

INTERACTIVE WHITEBOARD
Vocabulary Activities 5A

6 Standards: 1.3

Resources: Answer Keys: Student Edition, p. 96
Focus: Interpreting a diagram; reading family vocabulary

Suggestions: Introduce yourself as *José* and introduce the members of your family. Have volunteers answer a few questions about the relationships in your family before students do the activity. For example: *¿Quién es mi hermano?* Answer: *Raúl*

Answers:

1. padre	5. tía
2. tío	6. madre
3. primo	7. hermano
4. abuela	8. prima

Extension: Use the transparency of the family tree in *Actividad* 6 or draw a family tree of your own on the board. Describe the relationship of a family member to the other members of the family and have students determine who the person is from your clues. For example: *Soy la hija de Carlos y María y la tía de José y Raúl. ¿Quién soy?* Answer: *Carolina*

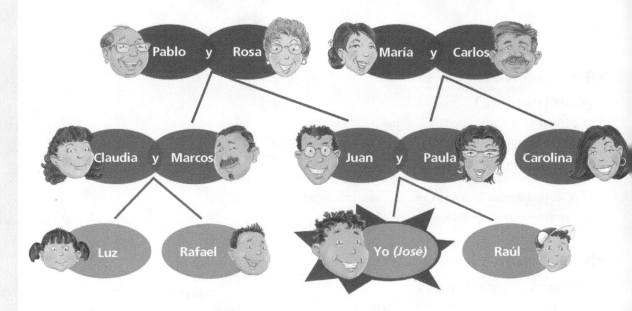

1. Juan es mi *(tío / padre)*.
2. Marcos es mi *(abuelo / tío)*.
3. Rafael es mi *(hermano / primo)*.
4. Rosa es mi *(madre / abuela)*.
5. Carolina es mi *(tía / prima)*.
6. Paula es mi *(madre / tía)*.
7. Raúl es mi *(primo / hermano)*.
8. Luz es mi *(abuela / prima)*.

38 treinta y ocho
Tema 5 • Fiesta en familia

DIFFERENTIATED INSTRUCTION

Heritage Language Learners

Have students illustrate their own family trees and write a paragraph explaining their diagram. Ask students to include descriptions of their family members, including what they like to do. Display students' work in the classroom.

Multiple Intelligences

Logical/Mathematical: Have students create a crossword puzzle using family vocabulary. Students should describe a relationship and have the vocabulary word be the missing clue. For example: *Soy la hermana de tu madre.* Answer: *tía*

7 Leer · Escribir

¿Quién es?

Find out how each member of Ana Sofía's family is related to her by completing her sentences. Number your paper from 1–8 and write the appropriate word.

Modelo
La madre de mi madre es mi abuela.

1. La esposa de mi tío es mi ___.
2. El padre de mi padre es mi ___.
3. El hijo de mi madrastra es mi ___.
4. Paco y Ana son mis tíos. Sus hijos son mis ___.
5. El hermano de mi madre es mi ___.
6. Los padres de mi madre son mis ___.
7. La hija de mi padrastro es mi ___.
8. El hermano de mi prima es mi ___.

8 Leer · Escribir

En la fiesta de cumpleaños

Complete the description of Cristina's birthday by choosing the correct word in parentheses. Write your answers on a separate sheet of paper.

Hoy __1.__ (celebramos / sacamos) la fiesta de cumpleaños de mi hermana menor, Cristina. ¿Cuántos años __2.__ (es / tiene) ella? Trece.

A nuestra madre __3.__ (le / me) encantan las fiestas. Mi mamá y mi hermana __4.__ (decoran / rompen) el patio con __5.__ (luces / pasteles) y __6.__ (fiestas / flores). A __7.__ (nuestro / tu) hermano le gusta hacer un __8.__ (regalo / video) o __9.__ (abrir / sacar) fotos de la fiesta. Siempre hay una piñata que nosotros __10.__ (preparamos / rompemos). En la piñata hay __11.__ (dulces / flores) sabrosos. Ahora Cristina va a __12.__ (romper / abrir) sus regalos.

▼ Fondo Cultural | México

El papel picado Mexican families frequently decorate for celebrations by using *papel picado*. It is made by folding and cutting layers of paper to create designs or scenes that are then hung as decorations.

• What crafts do you know that use similar techniques?

▲ "Haciendo papel picado / Making papel picado" (1999), Carmen Lomas Garza
Black paper cutout, 22" x 30". ©1998 Carment Lomas Garza. Photo Credit: Northern Lights, Collection of Carmen Lomas Garza.

treinta y nueve 39
Capítulo 5A

9
Standards: 1.1, 1.3
Resources: Voc. and Gram. Transparency 97
Focus: Party items; family members
Suggestions: Display the transparency for students to use as a word bank. Remind them that a fictional family may be used.
Answers will vary.

10
Standards: 1.1
Resources: Answer Keys: Student Edition, p. 98
Focus: Using vocabulary orally in a personalized context
Suggestions: Have students sketch their family tree and then reverse roles.
Answers:
Student A:
1. ¿Tienes tíos? ¿Cómo se llaman?
2. ¿Tienes primos? ¿Cómo se llaman?
3. ¿Tienes un abuelo? ¿Cómo se llama?
4. ¿Tienes una hermana mayor? ¿Cómo se llama?
5. ¿Tienes hermanos menores? ¿Cómo se llaman?
6. ¿Tienes una tía favorita? ¿Cómo se llama?
7. ¿Tienes una abuela? ¿Cómo se llama?
8. ¿Tienes un gato o un perro? ¿Cómo se llama(n)?
Student B answers will vary.

Common Errors: Remind students to use *se llama* when talking about one person and *se llaman* for more than one person.

11
Standards: 1.3
Resources: Answer Keys: Student Edition, p. 98
Focus: Writing about party activities
Suggestions: Guide students by asking: *¿Quién habla con Tío Jorge?*
Answers:
1. Tío Jorge come pastel. *or* Tío Jorge habla con Tío David.
2. Tía Ana y Tía Rosita cantan "Cumpleaños feliz" a Carlitos. *or* Tía Ana y Tía Rosita beben café.
3. Benjamín saca fotos.
4. Carlitos abre regalos.
5. Eliana y Glenda rompen la piñata.

---

9 | Escribir • Hablar

Preparaciones para la fiesta
You are preparing a party for someone in your family.

1 On a sheet of paper, make a chart like the one you see here. In the first column, write a list of six items you think you will need for the party. The items can be decorations, food, beverages, gifts, etc. In the second column, list six family members who are going to the party. Be sure to tell how they are related to you.

2 Compare your list with that of a partner.

Necesito	La familia
unas flores	mi prima Marta

▶ **Modelo**
A —¿Qué necesitas para la fiesta?
B —Necesito <u>flores</u>.
A —Yo también necesito <u>flores</u>.
o:—No necesito <u>flores</u>; necesito <u>globos</u>.
A —¿Quién va a la fiesta?
B —<u>Mi prima Marta</u> va a la fiesta.

10 | Hablar

Mi familia
You're at a friend's birthday party. You've just made a new friend, and you want to know more about one another. Work with a partner to ask and tell about your families.

Dos hermanos de la República Dominicana

▶ **Modelo**
hermanos
A —¿Tienes <u>hermanos</u>?
B —Sí, tengo <u>un hermano y una hermana</u>.
o:—No, no tengo <u>hermanos</u>.
A —¿Cómo se llaman?
B —Mi hermano se llama <u>David</u> y mi hermana se llama <u>Abby</u>.

Estudiante A
1. tíos
2. primos
3. un abuelo
4. una hermana mayor
5. hermanos menores
6. una tía favorita
7. una abuela
8. un gato o un perro

Estudiante B
¡Respuesta personal!

Para decir más . . .
el (la) hijo(a) único(a)   only child

40 cuarenta
Tema 5 • Fiesta en familia

DIFFERENTIATED INSTRUCTION

Advanced Learners/Pre-AP*
Have students plan a party in which every attendee has to bring something. Show students how to make a simple invitation with entries as follows: *La fecha: _____, La hora: _____; El lugar: _____ (la casa de Martina, el Restaurante Blanco).* Then have students make an entry for: *Por favor, necesitamos: _____ y _____,* and have them list items that people should bring. They should list two food items and two decoration items that they are asking this guest to bring. They can also use party-related illustrations to make the invitation attractive.

▼11 Escribir

El cumpleaños de Carlitos

Tío Jorge is throwing Carlitos a birthday party. Look at the picture below and then tell what the various people are doing.

Modelo
Tío David
Tío David habla con Tío Jorge.

1. Tío Jorge
2. Tía Ana y Tía Rosita
3. Benjamín
4. Carlitos
5. Eliana y Glenda

▼12 | 🗣️👥 | ♻️ | Hablar

A mi familia le gusta ...

With a partner, talk about the activities that your family, or another family, likes to do.

▶ **Modelo**
primo
A —¿Qué le gusta hacer a tu *primo*?
B —Le gusta *sacar fotos*.

Estudiante A

1. padre
2. madre
3. abuelo
4. hermana
5. prima
6. tío favorito
7. perro o gato

Estudiante B

¡Respuesta personal!

▼13 | ♻️ | 🗣️ | Escribir • Hablar

Y tú, ¿qué dices?

1. Describe a una persona de tu familia o de otra familia. ¿Cómo se llama? ¿Cuántos años tiene? ¿Cómo es? ¿Qué le gusta hacer?
2. ¿Tienes un perro o un gato? ¿Cómo se llama? ¿Cuántos años tiene?
3. ¿Qué te gusta hacer durante *(during)* una fiesta de cumpleaños?

cuarenta y uno **41**
Capítulo 5A

12 Standards: 1.1

Resources: Answer Keys: Student Edition, p. 99
Focus: Using family vocabulary orally in a personal context
Recycle: Leisure activities vocabulary
Suggestions: Brainstorm other "leisure activities" with students, and write them on the board for the *¡Respuesta personal!* Remind students to reverse roles.

Answers:
Student A:
1. ¿Qué le gusta hacer a tu padre?
2. ¿... a tu madre?
3. ¿... a tu abuelo?
4. ¿... a tu hermana?
5. ¿... a tu prima?
6. ¿... a tu tío favorito?
7. ¿... a tu perro o gato?

Student B:
Answers will vary.

Common Errors: Students may use *¿Qué gusta?* Remind them that they need to use the indirect object pronoun *le.*

13 Standards: 1.3

Focus: Using vocabulary in a personalized context orally and in writing
Recycle: Describing someone
Suggestions: Have students discuss the questions with a partner or a small group before reviewing them as a class.
Answers will vary.

Additional Resources

• Communication Wbk.: Audio Act. 6, p.5
• Teacher's Resource Book: Audio Script, p. 22, Communicative Pair Activity BLM, pp. 26–27
• Audio Program DVD: Cap. 5A, Track 12

ENRICH YOUR TEACHING

Culture Note

In many Spanish-speaking countries, people would almost never consider missing an important family event such as a baptism, wedding, or birthday. The attendees of parties for such events span several generations, from babies to grandparents. Good friends are also included in family events.

21st Century Skills

Creativity and Innovation Students can recycle vocabulary and grammar concepts by using a combination of print and visuals to create a chart on which they match each family member or friend with a color that represents a personality trait.

✓ASSESSMENT

Prueba 5A-2 with Study Plan (online only

Quiz: Vocabulary Production
• Prueba 5A-2: pp. 121–122

41

Gramática

Core Instruction

Standards: 4.1

Resources: Voc. and Gram. Transparency 100; Teacher's Resource Book: Video Script, pp. 24–25; Video Program: Cap. 5A

INTERACTIVE WHITEBOARD

Grammar Activities 5A

Suggestions: Direct attention to the *¿Recuerdas?* Use the transparency to reinforce the verb forms. Ask simple questions: *¿Quién tiene un hermano?* After students answer in the **yo** form, verify using the **tú** form (*¿De veras? ¿Tú tienes dos hermanos?*), and have another student reinforce it in the **Ud. / él / ella** form. Use the *GramActiva* Video as a follow-up.

▼14 Standards: 1.3

Resources: Answer Keys: Student Edition, p. 99

Focus: Correctly using present-tense forms of **tener,** according to the subject

Suggestions: Ask what subject pronoun would replace the proper noun(s).

Answers:

1. b. Eduardo tiene una esposa.
2. a. Yo tengo un padrastro.
3. e. Carolina y Sabrina tienen muchos primos.
4. d. Esteban y yo tenemos cinco tíos.
5. c. Y tú, Juan, ¿tienes dos hermanastras?

▼15 Standards: 1.2, 1.3

Resources: Answer Keys: Student Edition, p. 100

Focus: Using present-tense forms of **tener**

Suggestions: After students complete the sentences, have volunteers read them aloud as another student writes the ages on the board. Then subtract to get Enrique's age. Emphasize that **tenemos** is the only form of these four that doesn't include **ie.**

Answers:

1. tiene
2. tenemos
3. tienen
4. tiene
   Enrique tiene 23 años.
   (19+17+17+12+12 = 77; 100–77=23)

Gramática

▶ Talk about what people have and have to do
▶ Interview a classmate and write a description of a classmate's family and their ages
▶ Read about, identify, and describe the ages of members of the Spanish royal family

The verb *tener*

The verb *tener* is used to show relationship or possession.

Tengo un hermano mayor.	*I have* an older brother.
Tenemos un regalo para Tere.	*We have* a gift for Tere.

Some expressions in Spanish use *tener* where in English we use "to be."

Mi primo **tiene** dieciséis años.	*My cousin is* sixteen years old.
Tengo hambre y sed.	*I am* hungry and thirsty.

¿Recuerdas?

You have been using the verb *tener* for several chapters.

- ¿**Tienes** sed?
- **Tengo** que hacer ejercicio.

Here are all the present-tense forms of *tener:*

(yo)	tengo	(nosotros) (nosotras)	tenemos
(tú)	tienes	(vosotros) (vosotras)	tenéis
Ud. (él) (ella)	tiene	Uds. (ellos) (ellas)	tienen

Más ayuda   **realidades.com**

 GramActiva Video
Tutorials: *Tener, Tener que*
Animated Verbs

 Canción de hip hop: *Fiesta de cumpleaños*

 GramActiva Activity

▼14 Escribir

Las familias que tenemos

El Sr. Torre and his class are describing their families. Match the people in the first column with their family members in the second column. Write your sentences on a sheet of paper.

1. Eduardo
2. Yo
3. Carolina y Sabrina
4. Esteban y yo
5. Y tú, Juan, ¿ . . . ?

a. tengo un padrastro
b. tiene una esposa
c. tienes dos hermanastras
d. tenemos cinco tíos
e. tienen muchos primos

▼15 Leer • Escribir

¡Rompecabezas!

Number your paper from 1–4. Complete the following sentences by writing the appropriate form of the verb *tener.* Then try to solve the math puzzle.

El total de las edades *(ages)* de los hijos en nuestra familia es 100. Marta __1.__ 19 años. Paco y yo __2.__ dos años menos que Marta. Laura y Eva __3.__ cinco años menos que Paco y yo. ¿Cuántos años __4.__ nuestro hermano mayor, Enrique?

 cuarenta y dos
Tema 5 • Fiesta en familia

DIFFERENTIATED INSTRUCTION

Multiple Intelligences

Logical/Mathematical: Have students work in small groups and create their own *rompecabezas.* They can follow the model and use different numbers and equations. Have students give their *rompecabezas* to another group to solve the problem.

Students with Learning Difficulties

Make photocopies of *Actividad* 15 to distribute. Have students circle the numerals and the words for numbers that they see. By highlighting the numbers, they may have an easier time solving the puzzle as they read it.

▼16 | Hablar

¿Cuántos años tienen?

Look at the photos of Guillermo and his family and friends. Describe them by saying how old everyone is. Then interview three of your classmates to find out how old they are.

Modelo
El padre de Guillermo tiene cincuenta y dos años.

mi padre /52

1.

mi madre /43

2.

mis primos /20

3.

yo /13

4.

mis amigos y yo /13

5.

mi abuela /72

6.

Y tú, /¿cuántos . . . ?

▼17 | Hablar

¿Qué hay para la fiesta?

You are organizing a birthday party. With a partner, ask and answer questions about what people have for the party.

Ana

▶ **Modelo**
A —¿Qué tiene Ana?
B —Ana tiene la piñata.

1. David

2. Yolanda

3. tu abuela

4. tú

5. Uds.

6. Juan y Marcos

cuarenta y tres **43**
Capítulo 5A

16 Standards: 1.1

Resources: Answer Keys: Student Edition, p.100
Focus: Asking and telling someone's age
Suggestions: Remind students that they are writing sentences in the *Ud./él/ella* form, about Guillermo and his family. Tell them that the only exception is in item 6, when they should use the *yo* form of the verb to give their own age.

Answers:

1. La madre de Guillermo tiene cuarenta y tres años.
2. Los primos de Guillermo tienen veinte años.
3. Guillermo tiene trece años.
4. Los amigos y Guillermo tienen trece años.
5. La abuela de Guillermo tiene setenta y dos años.
6. Yo tengo ... años.

Extension: Have students create a sketch of their own family members, including their names and ages. Have them exchange their sketches with a partner and give the ages of their partner's family.

17 Standards: 1.1

Resources: Answer Keys: Student Edition, p.101
Focus: Practicing forms of *tener* and vocabulary
Suggestions: To review the pictured vocabulary before beginning, ask questions such as *¿En qué número hay dulces?* Have student volunteers act out the model. Remind students to switch roles during the activity so each person has the opportunity to ask and answer questions.

Answers:

1. —¿Qué tiene David?
   —David tiene los dulces.
2. —¿Qué tiene Yolanda?
   —Yolanda tiene el pastel.
3. —¿Qué tiene tu abuela?
   —Mi abuela tiene las luces.
4. —¿Qué tienes tú?
   —Tengo los regalos.
5. —¿Qué tienen Uds.?
   —Tenemos los globos.
6. —¿Qué tienen Juan y Marcos?
   —Tienen las flores.

Extension: Have students ask and answer questions about the contents of their backpacks using *tener.*

ENRICH YOUR TEACHING

Teacher-to-Teacher

Have students create a family photo album using real pictures, magazine cutouts, or illustrations. Make sure students include pictures of their families at birthday celebrations so they use all the appropriate vocabulary. Once students have completed the albums, give them accompanying activities. Include pair-work, presentations, and written questions with the activities. Keep the photo albums in the classroom to share with parents and guardians during conferences and open houses.

18 Standards: 1.1, 1.2, 1.3

Focus: Using family vocabulary and grammar in a personalized context

Recycle: Saying one's name; expressing likes; talking about activities

Suggestions: Remind students that they will need this information to complete *Actividad* 19. Point out item 4, and explain that the question *¿Cómo son?* should be answered with a description of the person's physical traits and personality. If a student is an only child, the interviewer can ask how many cousins, aunts, and uncles their partner has.

Answers will vary.

19 Standards: 1.3

Focus: Writing a paragraph based on an interview; *tener;* family vocabulary

Suggestions: Remind students that they will be using the information from *Actividad* 18 to prepare their paragraphs. Encourage students to be creative and to depart from the model. Students can trade papers and check each other's work for grammar and spelling.

Answers will vary.

Fondo cultural

Standards: 2.1, 2.2, 3.1

Resources: Fine Art Transparencies, p. 51

🌐 **Mapa global interactivo, Actividad 1**
Look at Mexico and the countries of Central America, the region known as Mesoamerica.

Suggestions: Have students describe the way the woman is working (her physical stance). How might the way she's working tell you something about her life?

Answers will vary but may include that because her work looks so physically challenging, she may have a difficult life.

▼**18** | 🗣️👥 | ♻️ | Hablar • Escribir

Entrevista

Interview a partner. Find out the answers to the following questions. Your partner may answer based on his or her own family or on a TV family. Write your partner's answers so that you can report your interview to the class.

1. ¿Cómo te llamas y cuántos años tienes? ¿Qué te gusta hacer?
2. ¿Cuántos hermanos mayores o menores tienes?
3. ¿Cómo se llaman tus hermanos(as) y cuántos años tienen?
4. ¿Cómo son tus hermanos(as)?
5. ¿Qué le gusta hacer a uno(a) de tus hermanos(as)?
6. ¿Tienes perros o gatos? ¿Cómo se llama(n)?

> **Nota**
> To say that a person likes or loves something, use *le gusta(n)* or *le encanta(n)*. When you include the name of the person or the pronoun, be sure to add *a:*
> • **A Pedro le gustan** los dulces.
> • **A ella le encanta** sacar fotos.

▼**19** Escribir • Hablar

¡Reportaje!

Based on your notes from Actividad 18, write a report of your interview. Your teacher may ask you to read your report to the class.

Modelo

> Anita tiene 13 años y le encanta escuchar música. Anita tiene tres hermanos: un hermano mayor y dos hermanos menores. Son simpáticos y deportistas. Su hermano mayor, Pedro, tiene 16 años. Sus hermanos menores se llaman Lisa y José. Ellos tienen sólo once y ocho años. A José le gusta jugar al básquetbol. Anita no tiene ni perros ni gatos.

🌐 Fondo Cultural | México

Diego Rivera (1886–1957) This painting by Mexican muralist Diego Rivera shows a woman grinding maize on a *metate,* a utensil used for grinding grain. This is one of many paintings in which Rivera portrays the daily life of the indigenous peoples of Mexico.

• Through paintings, an artist conveys feelings to the viewer. What do you think Rivera wants you to feel about this woman and her task?

"La molendera" (1924), Diego Rivera ▶

Oil on canvas, 35 7/16 x 46 1/16 in. Museo Nacional de Arte Moderno, Instituto Nacional de Bellas Artes, Mexico City, D.F., Mexico. © Banco de Mexico Diego Rivera & Frida Kahlo Museums Trust. Av. Cinco de Mayo n.° 2. Col. Centro, Del. Cuauhtemoc 06059, México, D.F. Reproduction authorized by the *Instituto Nacional de Bellas Artes y Literatura.* Courtesy of Art Resource, NY.

DIFFERENTIATED INSTRUCTION

Heritage Language Learners
Have students name a food item that is a staple of the diet in their heritage countries, as tortillas are in Mexico. If possible, have students bring in the recipes and have volunteers prepare the dishes to share with the class.

Advanced Learners
Explain that Diego Rivera made his art accessible to all by painting murals. Using long sheets of rolled paper, have students create murals that depict any of the cultural products, practices, or perspectives discussed in *Realidades*. Post the murals in the classroom.

▼ Pronunciación | 🔊 | 💬

The letters *p, t,* and *q*

In English, the consonants *p, t, q,* and the hard *c* sound are pronounced with a little puff of air.

Hold a tissue loosely in front of your mouth as you say these English words. You will notice that the tissue moves.

pan	papa	too	tea
comb	case	park	take

Now say these Spanish words with the tissue in front of your mouth. Try to say the consonants so that there is no puff of air and the tissue does not move.

pan	papá	tú	tía
cómo	queso	parque	taco

Try it out! Listen to this nursery rhyme. Listen particularly for the *p, t,* and *q* sounds. Then repeat the rhyme.

> **Tortillitas para mamá**
> **Tortillitas para papá**
> **Las quemaditas,¹ para mamá**
> **Las bonitas,² para papá**

¹the burned ones   ²the pretty ones

▼20 Escribir • Hablar

Preparaciones para una fiesta de cumpleaños

Contesta las preguntas.

Cuando una familia celebra un cumpleaños, ¿quién tiene que . . .

1. . . . decorar la casa? ¿Con qué?
2. . . . preparar la comida y las bebidas?
3. . . . comprar los regalos?
4. . . . hacer el pastel?
5. . . . hacer el video o sacar fotos?

> **¿Recuerdas?**
> Remember that *tener que* + infinitive means "to have to" (do something).
> • Sofía **tiene que decorar** el pastel.

Celebrando un cumpleaños con una piñata

cuarenta y cinco 45
Capítulo 5A

Pronunciación
Core Instruction
Standards: 4.1

Resources: Teacher's Resource Book: Audio Script, p. 22; Audio Program DVD: Cap. 5A, Tracks 13–14

Suggestions: Bring in a box of tissues so students can perform the "experiment."

When you model the English consonants, exaggerate the puff of air and pass around tissues so students can see the tissue move when saying the English words. Then have students say the Spanish words with you, without the puff and without moving the tissue.

Allow students to listen to the nursery rhyme a few times before repeating it. Use the tissues again to check the pronunciation.

▼20 Standards: 1.1, 1.3

Focus: Using vocabulary and ***tener que* + infinitive**

Suggestions: Direct students' attention to the *¿Recuerdas?* and have them practice answering using ***tener que* + infinitive.** You may want to prepare them for the activity by asking: *¿Qué tienes que hacer para preparar una fiesta?*

Encourage students to speak about more than one person doing something: *Mi madre y mi tía tienen que preparar la comida y las bebidas.*

Answers will vary.

ENRICH YOUR TEACHING

Culture Note
Rivera's painting highlights the **tortilla,** one of the staples of the traditional Mexican diet, along with **chiles,** tomatoes, and beans. The **tortilla** can accompany any meal and is most commonly made of cornmeal (though in the north, **tortillas** are made of wheat flour). Once upon a time, a woman's first task each morning would be to make the day's **tortillas** for the family. Nowadays, although families value handmade **tortillas,** they are more likely to purchase them from a **tortillería.**

Teacher-to-Teacher
In small groups, have students describe the scene using their vocabulary. Start them off with *En la fiesta, hay ...* and have them create two or three original sentences to be shared with the class. Once the responses have been discussed, ask students to compare the people and activities pictured with what might go on at their own birthday parties.

21 Standards: 1.2, 1.3

Resources: Answer Keys: Student Edition, p. 102
Voc. and Gram. Transparency 102

Focus: Reading comprehension; using the present tense of *tener*

Suggestions: Encourage students to read the entire paragraph before filling in the blanks. Upon completion of the paragraph, have students determine its meaning. Brainstorm unfamiliar words, write them on the board, and have students guess their meanings by using contextual cues as you review the story.

Answers:

1. tenemos	4. tienen	7. Tienes
2. Tengo	5. tiene	
3. tiene	6. tienen	

Extension: Have students use the transparency to create an imaginary family tree as preparation for the Theme Project.

22 Standards: 1.1, 1.2

Resources: Answer Keys: Student Edition, p. 102
Focus: Speaking using family vocabulary

Suggestions: Point out the relationship of the silhouette figures to the photo above.

As a point of reference, have students find the sentence that tells who is on the right and the left sides of the photo.

Answers: to silhouette numbers:

1. el rey Juan Carlos I	7. Leonor
2. Jaime	8. la reina Sofía
3. Elena	9. la infanta Cristina
4. la princesa Letizia	10. Iñaki
5. Sofía de Borbón y Ortiz	11. Irene
6. el príncipe Felipe	

Fondo cultural

Standards: 3.1

Suggestions: Remind students that monarchies are governments with kings and/or queens, and that they are less common today than they were in the past. You may wish to refer them to history books to help them answer the question.

Answers will vary but may include England and Jordan.

46

▼21 Leer · Escribir

La familia de Sofía

Look carefully at the photograph of Sofía's family, the royal family of Spain, as they celebrate her special day. As Sofía describes this family photo, complete the story with the appropriate forms of the verb *tener*.

Me llamo Sofía de Borbón y Ortiz. Mi cumpleaños es el 29 de abril. Nosotros __1.__ muchas fiestas en mi familia. En la foto celebramos un día muy especial para mí. Es el día de mi bautizo. (Yo) __2.__ una hermana mayor que se llama Leonor. Ella __3.__ dos años. Mis tíos, la infanta[1] Elena y su esposo Jaime están en el fondo,[2] a la izquierda de la foto. Ellos __4.__ dos hijos. En el fondo a la derecha están mis tíos Cristina e Iñaki con su hija Irene que __5.__ sólo cuatro meses más que mi hermana. Yo estoy en los brazos de mi mamá, la princesa Letizia. Mi padre, el príncipe Felipe, está al lado de ella con mi hermana. Mis abuelos, el rey Juan Carlos I y la reina Sofía, __6.__ 69 años. Ellos están a los dos lados de mis padres. Ellos son los reyes[3] de España. ¿ __7.__ tú tíos y primos?

[1] In the Spanish royal family, *una infanta* is a princess (*una princesa*) who is not heir to the throne.
[2] background
[3] Note that *el rey + la reina = los reyes*

La familia de Juan Carlos I, rey de España

▼ Fondo Cultural

La Familia Real *(royal)* **de España** Juan Carlos I and Sofía have been king and queen of Spain since 1975.

- What other countries can you name that are ruled by a monarchy?

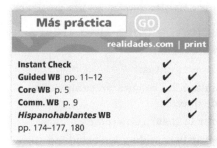

Más práctica	GO
	realidades.com	print

Instant Check	✔	
Guided WB pp. 11–12	✔	✔
Core WB p. 5	✔	✔
Comm. WB p. 9	✔	✔
Hispanohablantes WB pp. 174–177, 180		✔

▼22 | Talk! | Leer · Hablar · Pensar

¿Quiénes son los miembros de la Familia Real?

Work with a partner to identify the members of the royal family. Use the photograph and answers from Actividad 21 to help.

▶ Modelo

A —*Creo que el número uno es el abuelo de Sofía. Se llama Juan Carlos I.*
B —*Estoy de acuerdo.*
o:—*No estoy de acuerdo.*

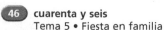

(46) cuarenta y seis
Tema 5 • Fiesta en familia

DIFFERENTIATED INSTRUCTION

Multiple Intelligences

Verbal/Linguistic: Provide groups of students with photos of families unknown to them. Then have them create a "royal family" to describe, assigning different titles to the people in the picture. Tell them that they must make up the country that this fictional family rules.

Students with Learning Difficulties

Reading comprehension can be better attained by activating students' prior knowledge. However, since students will most likely have little background on the Spanish royal family and the art of Francisco de Goya, provide it before they begin. Prepare a short list of key concepts for both readings and distribute it to students.

▼23 Leer · Pensar

La familia de Carlos IV

Before the age of photography, painted portraits were used to capture the images of people. Look carefully at the painting *La familia de Carlos IV* by Francisco de Goya and then read about the family.

▼24 | | Pensar · Hablar

Carlos IV y su familia

Work with a partner. Point to different people in Goya's painting of the royal family and ask your partner who he or she thinks they are.

▶ **Modelo**
A —*¿Quién es?*
B —*Creo que es el hijo menor.*

▲ "Autorretrato" (ca. 1815)
Oil on canvas. Academia de San Fernando, Madrid, Spain. Courtesy of The Bridgeman Art Library International Ltd.
Francisco de Goya (1746–1828) was one of the greatest Spanish painters and is considered by many to be the "Father of Modern Art." He was known for a wide range of art themes, including portraits of the royal family and other members of the nobility.

Conexiones | El arte

La familia real tiene mucha importancia en la historia de España. Es el año 1800: Carlos IV (cuarto) no es un rey popular y muchas personas creen que es demasiado indeciso¹. En este cuadro² del pintor Francisco de Goya, puedes ver a la familia del rey Carlos IV. Carlos IV reinó³ de 1788 a 1808.

• El pintor también está en el cuadro. ¿Puedes ver a Goya? ¿Dónde está?

¹indecisive ²painting ³reigned

"La familia de Carlos IV" (1800), Francisco de Goya

Oil on canvas. 110 1/4" x 132 1/4" (280 x 336 cm). Museo Nacional del Prado, Madrid.
Photo credit: Scala / Art Resource, NY.

Fondo Cultural | España

Dos familias reales The family photo of the Spanish royal family on p. 46 was taken over 200 years after Goya painted the portrait of Juan Carlos I's ancestor and his family. Study the two pictures as you answer these questions.

• In what ways are the two pictures similar? How are they different? How would you compare them to your own family portraits?

cuarenta y siete **47**
Capítulo 5A

ENRICH YOUR TEACHING

Culture Note
In 1975, upon the death of General Francisco Franco, King Juan Carlos acceded to the throne of Spain as a constitutional monarch. Although the king technically is the head of government, decisions and laws are made by a representative body, the **Cortes.** King Juan Carlos will be succeeded by his son, Felipe, Prince of Asturias.

21st Century Skills
Critical Thinking and Problem Solving When students compare the two versions of the royal family, have them use a Venn diagram to show what is unique about each version (of the family) and what might be common to both.

▼23 Standards: 1.2, 2.2, 3.1
Resources: Answer Keys: Student Edition, p. 104. Fine Art Transparencies, p. 26
Focus: Reading comprehension; looking at art
Suggestions: As students read the passage, have them identify the cognates. Upon completion, ask a volunteer to summarize the main idea of the reading.
Answers: Goya está a la izquierda.

▼24 Standards: 1.1
Focus: Using family vocabulary; looking at art
Suggestions: Remind students that they do not have to name the people, but practice using the family vocabulary and make good guesses as to relationships.
You can have Student A respond to Student B's *Creo que ...* with *Estoy de acuerdo.* or *No estoy de acuerdo.*
Answers will vary.

Fondo cultural
Standards: 3.1, 4.2
Resources: Fine Art Transparencies, p. 25
🌐 **Mapa global interactivo, Actividad 2** Explore the Palacio Real and its surroundings in Madrid, Spain.
Suggestions: To find differences and similarities, have students compare the number, age, clothing, and poses of the people in the painting and in the photo.
Answers will vary.

Additional Resources
• Communication Wbk.: Audio Act. 7, p. 5
• Teacher's Resource Book: Audio Script, pp. 22–23
• Audio Program DVD: Cap. 5A, Track 15

☑ASSESSMENT
Prueba 5A-3 with Study Plan (online only)
Quiz: The verb *tener*
• Prueba 5A-3: p. 123

Gramática

Core Instruction

Standards: 4.1

Resources: Voc. and Gram. Transparency 101; Teacher's Resource Book: Video Script, p. 25; Video Program: Cap. 5A

INTERACTIVE WHITEBOARD

Grammar Activities 5A

Suggestions: Direct attention to the *¿Recuerdas?*. Point out that they have already been using some of these words: **mi hermano, tu cumpleaños.**

Use the textbook and transparencies to present possessive adjectives. Use the *GramActiva* Video to reinforce your grammar explanation.

Point out that possessive adjectives must match the noun in number and gender and provide a few examples on the board. Underline the endings of the possessive adjectives and nouns to emphasize agreement with the object owned.

25 Standards: 1.3

Resources: Answer Keys: Student Edition, p. 102

Focus: Reading comprehension; using possessive adjectives

Suggestions: Tell students to first identify the subject of the sentence. If necessary, have them say the subject pronoun for the subject, and use the pronoun to determine the correct possessive adjective. For the sentences that have the same subjects, refer students to the gender and number of the item that is possessed.

Answers:

1. b   2. f   3. c   4. e   5. d   6. a

BELLRINGER REVIEW

Have students refer to page 32 and tell the class the relationship of one of the people pictured. (Ex. *José Antonio es el padre de Esteban.*)

▼ Objectives
▶ Identify to whom something belongs
▶ Read and write about family relationships
▶ Read and listen to a description of a birthday card
▶ Survey and interview classmates to write about birthday celebrations

Gramática

Possessive adjectives

You use possessive adjectives to tell what belongs to someone or to show relationships. In English, the possessive adjectives are *my, your, his, her, its, our,* and *their*.

Here are the possessive adjectives in Spanish:

mi(s)	nuestro(s) nuestra(s)
tu(s)	vuestro(s) vuestra(s)
su(s)	su(s)

¿Recuerdas?

You know that *de* shows possession or relationship and is the equivalent of *-'s* and *-s':*

• el regalo **de** Ana
• los primos **de** mis amigos

Javier y yo, con **nuestra** abuela

Mis padres, con **su** regalo

Like other adjectives, possessive adjectives agree in number with the nouns that follow them. Only *nuestro* and *vuestro* have different masculine and feminine endings.

mi cámara   mis cámaras

nuestro abuelo   nuestros abuelos

nuestra hija   nuestras hijas

Su and *sus* can have many different meanings: *his, her, its, your,* or *their*. To be more specific, you can use *de* + noun or pronoun.

sus flores = las flores de ella

sus regalos = los regalos de Javier y Carlos

Más ayuda   **realidades.com**

 GramActiva Video
Tutorials: Possessive Adjectives, Possessive Adjectives (Long Form), Possessive with *de* + pronoun

GramActiva Activity

▼25 Escribir

Muchos primos

Felipe's class is talking about their cousins. Number your paper from 1–6. Find out the names of everyone's cousins by matching the sentences in the first column with the sentences in the second column.

1. Yo tengo un primo.
2. Karin y yo tenemos dos primos.
3. Nosotros tenemos una prima.
4. También tengo tres primas.
5. Javier y Clara tienen un primo.
6. Ud. tiene dos primas.

a. Sus primas se llaman María y Ana.
b. Mi primo se llama Roberto.
c. Nuestra prima se llama Nelia.
d. Su primo se llama Gilberto.
e. Mis primas se llaman Micaela, Sara y Cristina.
f. Nuestros primos se llaman Luisa y Carlos.

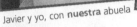

48 **cuarenta y ocho**
Tema 5 • Fiesta en familia

DIFFERENTIATED INSTRUCTION

Heritage Language Learners

Closely monitor the agreement of adjectives and verbs in students' written exercises. It is common for some heritage language learners who have not had extensive formal writing practice in Spanish to spell phonetically. If it is common to drop certain sounds when speaking, they may tend to drop the letters in their writing.

Advanced Learners

Brainstorm names of popular families from television shows or movies. Have students prepare a paragraph with information about one of the families, including the names of the members, their relationships to each other, their physical and personality traits, any pets they may have, etc.

▼26 Leer • Escribir

La Cenicienta y su familia

Complete the following story about *La Cenicienta* with the appropriate word or possessive adjective. Write your answers on a sheet of paper. *La Cenicienta* is a character from a well-known story. Who is she?

Cenicienta tiene una madrastra y dos hermanastras muy perezosas. **1.** *(Sus / Tus)* hermanastras se llaman Griselda y Anastasia. **2.** *(Nuestra / Su)* madrastra y **3.** *(su / sus)* hermanastras siempre dicen: "¡Cenicienta! Tenemos hambre. ¿Dónde está **4.** *(mi / nuestra)* comida?" Cada mañana Griselda le dice: "Quiero **5.** *(mi / su)* desayuno.

¿Dónde está?" Una noche Cenicienta va al baile del príncipe. Él le pregunta a Cenicienta: "¿Cómo te llamas? ¿Quiénes son **6.** *(tu / tus)* padres?" Las hermanastras **7.** *(de / su)* Cenicienta ven al príncipe cuando baila con Cenicienta. Ellas dicen: "¡ **8.** *(Nuestra / Su)* hermanastra baila con el príncipe! ¡Qué ridículo!"

▼27 | Hablar

¿Dónde están las decoraciones?

You and your friend are looking for some things for a school party. Ask and answer questions about where you can find the decorations and other items you need.

▶ Modelo
A —¿Dónde están <u>las luces de Renaldo?</u>
B —Sus luces están <u>en la oficina.</u>

Estudiante A
1. tus flores
2. los regalos de Uds.
3. mi piñata
4. el papel picado de Lupe
5. los globos de Marta y Tere
6. mis luces

Estudiante B
en la sala de clases
debajo de la mesa
allí
en la oficina
al lado de la silla
detrás de la puerta
en el escritorio

¡Respuesta personal!

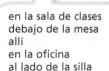

cuarenta y nueve **49**
Capítulo 5A

ENRICH YOUR TEACHING

Teacher-to-Teacher
Put students in groups to make their own *piñatas*. Begin by blowing up balloons and covering them with papier-mâché. Then have students form any necessary extensions using papier-mâché. Allow them to dry overnight, and then have students paint them however they like. When the paint dries, cut a hole at the top of each *piñata* and fill it with candy. Celebrate the completion of the lesson with a *piñata*-breaking party. Use extreme caution to avoid injuries.

26 Standards: 1.2, 3.2
Resources: Answer Keys: Student Edition, p. 103
Focus: Reading comprehension; using possessive adjectives
Suggestions: Have students read the story silently. Encourage them to use prior knowledge about the story to help with comprehension. Have students use the diagram on the opposite page to check adjective agreement for gender and plural endings.

Answers:
1. Sus   4. nuestra   7. de
2. Su   5. mi   8. Nuestra
3. sus   6. tus

Common Errors: Remind students that possessive adjectives agree with the item possessed, not the person possessing something.

27 Standards: 1.1
Resources: Answer Keys: Student Edition, p. 103
Focus: Using possessive adjectives in a conversation
Suggestions: Point out that for items 1, 3, and 6, students must change the first-person possessive adjective to the second-person possessive adjective or vice versa. Remind students that Student B can choose any of the locations when answering.

Answers will include:
1. —¿Dónde están tus flores?
   —Mis flores están …
2. —¿Dónde están los regalos de Uds.?
   —Nuestros regalos están …
3. —¿Dónde está mi piñata?
   —Tu piñata está …
4. —¿Dónde está el papel picado de Lupe?
   —Su papel picado está …
5. —¿Dónde están los globos de Marta y Tere?
   —Sus globos están …
6. —¿Dónde están mis luces?
   —Tus luces están …

Theme Project
Give students copies of the Theme Project outline and rubric from the *Teacher's Resource Book*. Explain the task to them, and have them perform Step 1. (For more information, see p. 30-b.)

28 Standards: 1.1, 1.2, 1.3

Focus: Reading comprehension; using possessive adjectives.

Suggestions: Ask students to give examples of people they consider heroes before beginning. Encourage them to use these examples when answering item 2.

Answers will vary but may include:
1. El padre es el héroe de su hijo.
2. —¿Quién es tu héroe o heroína?
   —Mi héroe es … / Mi heroína es …

29 Standards: 1.1, 1.3

Resources: Teacher's Resource Book: GramActiva BLM, p. 31

Focus: Using possessive adjectives and the forms of *tener*

Suggestions: Have students write on the template before making it into a cube. Remind students to use the form of *tener* for the subject pronoun they roll. Have students keep score on a sheet of scrap paper. To be more time efficient, set an egg timer and tell students that the team with the most points when it goes off is the winner. Have students save the cubes for future use and review.

Answers will vary.

Common Errors: Remind students to conjugate *tener* even when focusing on possessive adjectives.

▼**28** 💬👥 | **Leer • Escribir • Hablar**

¿Quién es tu héroe?

Read this ad and answer the questions that follow.

No es sólo mi padre. También es mi héroe.

Y es nuestro héroe también.

Gracias.

Patrocinado por la Cámara de Comercio

1. In this ad, who is the hero? Whose hero is he?
2. Work with a partner to find out about his or her hero. Ask and answer following the model.

▶ **Modelo**
A —*¿Quién es tu héroe o heroína? ¿Cómo es?*
B —*Mi heroína es mi madre. Es muy inteligente.*

▼**29** 👥 | **Escribir • Hablar • GramActiva**

Juego

Modelo
Uds. tienen su calculadora.

① Working with a partner, make a set of two cubes using the template your teacher will give you.

• **Cube 1** Write a different subject pronoun on each side.
• **Cube 2** Write a different classroom object on each side. Make three of them singular and three of them plural.
• **Both cubes** Write a different point value from 1 to 6 on each side.

② You and your partner will play against another pair of students. Team 1 rolls both of your cubes and says a sentence using the correct form of the verb tener, the appropriate possessive adjective, and the classroom object. If the sentence is correct, Team 1 receives the total points shown on the cubes. Team 2 then rolls the other cubes. Continue until a team reaches 100 points or time is called.

50 cincuenta
Tema 5 • Fiesta en familia

DIFFERENTIATED INSTRUCTION

Advanced Learners
Ask students to make a small poster of their hero, including a photo. They can choose a family member, a public figure, an athlete, or other individual. Have them tell the person's name and age and list several characteristics that explain why he or she is a hero.

Students with Special Needs
For *Actividad* 29, prepare an extra set of dice for students who may have difficulties with fine motor skills. You may want to limit the total points to 50.

El español en la comunidad

The five most common last names in the United States, in order, are Smith, Johnson, Williams, Brown, and Jones. The five most common last names in the United States for people of Spanish-speaking heritage, in order, are García, Martínez, Rodríguez, López, and Hernández.

- Look up these names in your school directory or local phone listings. Count the number of entries for each. Do the numbers in your community match the statement made above? Can you identify two other Hispanic last names that are common in your community or that you are familiar with?

▼**30** | **Escribir · Hablar**

¿Qué tienen que comprar para sus profesores?

You and your classmates are celebrating *el Día de los profesores*. What gifts do each of you need to buy, and for whom?

❶ Write the names of five teachers and the classes that they teach. Beside each name, write one item that you think is a good gift for that teacher.

❷ Interview a partner to find out what gifts they have to buy and for whom.

> **▶ Modelo**
>
> A —¿Qué tienes que comprar para tus profesores?
> B —Tengo que comprar una calculadora para la Sra. Cantos, mi profesora de matemáticas, y un diccionario para el Sr. Aldea, mi profesor de español.

❸ Write a paragraph to describe what gifts your partner has to buy and for whom.

> **Modelo**
>
> Ana tiene que comprar una calculadora para la Sra. Cantos, su profesora de matemáticas. También tiene que comprar un diccionario para el Sr. Aldea, su profesor de español.

> **Para decir más ...**
>
> comprar   to buy

> **¿Recuerdas?**
>
> You have already been using vocabulary for classroom supplies.

Más práctica	
realidades.com	print
Instant Check	✔
Guided WB pp. 13–14	✔ ✔
Core WB pp. 6–7	✔ ✔
Comm. WB pp. 6–7, 10, 131	✔ ✔
Hispanohablantes WB pp. 178–179, 181	✔

cincuenta y uno **51**
Capítulo 5A

Practice and Communicate 5A

El español en la comunidad

Core Instruction

Standards: 4,2, 5.1

Focus: Learning about Spanish-heritage last names

Suggestions: When students look up other last names in the local phone book, have them keep track of how many of each they find. Have students read their lists to the class. Keep a tally at the board of the most popular names in your area. Ask students to note any alternate spellings of some of the most common names and to count them.

▼**30** Standards: 1.1, 1.3

Focus: Using possessive adjectives in personal contexts, with classroom vocabulary and **tener**

Recycle: Classroom vocabulary

Suggestions: Have students brainstorm a list of classroom supplies. In part 2, have students create a chart to keep track of who will buy what. For part 3, encourage students to write one sentence with **nosotros** for something they both buy for a certain teacher.

Answers will vary.

Additional Resources

- Communication Wbk.: Audio Act. 8–9, pp. 6–7
- Teacher's Resource Book: Audio Script, p. 23, Communicative Pair Activity BLM, pp. 28–29
- Audio Program DVD: Cap. 5A, Tracks 17–18

ENRICH YOUR TEACHING

Culture Note

In many Spanish-speaking countries, a person's full name often includes two last names—the **apellido paterno**, or father's last name, followed by the **apellido materno**, or mother's last name. Have students determine what their last name would be if this naming system were used in the United States.

21st Century Skills

Communication Remind students of the various tools available in **realidades.com**, such as the eText with embedded audio files, and the computer corrected activities. Using these tools on a regular basis will help students develop fluency at a faster rate.

✔ ASSESSMENT

Prueba 5A-4 with Study Plan (online only)

Quiz: Possessive Adjectives
- Prueba 5A-4: p. 124

Exploración del lenguaje
Core Instruction

Standards: 4.1

Resources: Answer Keys: Student Edition, p. 104

Suggestions: Discuss the concept of diminutives and point out that in English diminutives are formed by adding -y or -ie to names: Bobby, Jenny, kitty, doggie. If students have chosen Spanish names, have them guess what the diminutive might be.

Answers: little grandmother, kitty, little Miguel, little daughter; Anita, Juanita, Evita, Lolita

▼31 Standards: 1.2

Resources: Voc. and Gram. Transparency 103; Answer Keys: Student Edition, p. 104

Focus: Reading for understanding

Suggestions: Before beginning, have students review the names of the items pictured. Then, ask them to identify the diminutives where applicable. Remind students that they do not need to understand every word to comprehend the meaning of the message.

Answers:

The birthday card is for a child. Diminutives: globitos, pastelito, regalitos, perritos, contentitos, añitos. Objects: luces, flores, globos, pastel, perro, piñata, regalos, papel picado

▼32 Standards: 1.2

Resources: Teacher's Resource Book: Audio Script p. 23; Audio Program DVD: Cap. 5A, Track 16; Answer Keys: Student Edition, p. 104

Focus: Listening for understanding

Suggestions: Play the audio or read the script. Allow students to listen a second time, giving time to determine the answer. Finally, allow them to listen a third time to check their work.

🔊 **Script and Answers:**

1. La fiesta es en un restaurante. (*F*)
2. Usan globos para decorar. (*C*)
3. Hay muchos perritos en la fiesta. (*C*)
4. Van a comer pastel en la fiesta de cumpleaños. (*C*)
5. Van a abrir regalos en la fiesta. (*C*)
6. Hay un gato en la fiesta. (*F*)

▼ Exploración del lenguaje

Diminutives

In Spanish you can add the suffix *-ito(a)* to a word to give it the meaning of "small" or "little." It can also be used to show affection. Words with this suffix are called diminutives (*diminutivos*).

abuelo → abuel**ito**

perros → perr**itos**

hermana → herman**ita**

Now that you know what the suffix *-ito(a)* means, can you figure out the meanings of these words?

abuelita   gatito   Miguelito   hijita

Some very popular names are diminutives. What do you think the diminutives of these names are?

Ana   Juana   Eva   Lola

▼31 Leer · Pensar

¡Feliz cumpleaños!

Read the birthday card. Who is it for? Find the diminutives. What words in the poem do you understand? How many objects can you name in Spanish in the picture?

▼32 🔊 Leer · Escuchar

La fiesta de cumpleaños

On a sheet of paper, write the numbers from 1–6. Read the birthday card and listen to the statements. If a statement is true (*cierto*) write *C*; if it is false (*falso*) write *F*.

Hay luces, y flores, y lindos globitos, un pastelito sabroso, y muchos regalitos,

y una piñata, y seis perritos que cantan y bailan, muy contentitos,

porque hoy cumples... ¡6 añitos!

Felipe

DIFFERENTIATED INSTRUCTION

Advanced Learners

Have students create a birthday card in Spanish. You can help by bringing in a few Spanish-language cards for wording.

Heritage Language Learners

When presenting the *Exploración del lenguaje*, ask students to list additional examples of diminutives. Do they or their family members speak commonly using diminutives? Whom would they most often address or describe using diminutives?

▼33 | 👥 | ♻ | Hablar · Escribir

Un cumpleaños divertido

❶ Find out from your classmates what they consider to be a great birthday. Make a chart like the one below on a sheet of paper and complete the first row about yourself.

❷ Then survey four classmates to find out what their preferences are and record the information in the chart.

Modelo

¿En qué mes es tu cumpleaños?
¿Cuál es tu actividad y lugar (place) favorito?
¿Cuáles son tus comidas favoritas?

	Mes del cumpleaños	Actividad y lugar favorito	Comidas favoritas
yo	julio	comer/un restaurante	pastel y helado
Miguel	enero	abrir regalos/en casa	pizza y ensalada
Anita	julio	bailar/un baile	hamburguesas y helado

❸ Write a paragraph describing the person you interviewed whose idea of a great birthday celebration is most like your own. Describe the similarities, but also mention differences.

Modelo

Nuestro cumpleaños es en julio. Nuestra comida favorita es el helado. A ella le gustan las hamburguesas pero a mí me gusta el pastel. Mi lugar favorito para mi cumpleaños es un restaurante porque me gusta comer. Su lugar favorito es un baile porque le gusta bailar.

▼34 | ♻ | Escuchar · Hablar

¿Quién es esta persona?

Use your completed chart from Actividad 33 and describe a classmate to the class. Do not give that person's name. The class will try to guess whom you are describing.

Modelo

Su cumpleaños es en enero. Para su cumpleaños le gusta abrir regalos en casa. Sus comidas favoritas en su cumpleaños son pizza y ensalada. ¿Quién es?

Un chico con su mejor amigo

cincuenta y tres 53
Capítulo 5A

---

33 Standards: 1.1, 1.3

Focus: Using party vocabulary in a personalized context

Recycle: Months; activities; places; food and drink vocabulary

Suggestions: As you read the directions, pause to discuss with students how they celebrate their birthdays. How do these activities vary based on when the birthday is? You can either have students work in groups of five or give students time to go around the room and interview four others. For Step 3, write the model on a transparency and highlight the parts that may be replaced.

Answers will vary.

34 Standards: 1.2, 1.3

Focus: Using party vocabulary in a personalized context

Recycle: Likes; food vocabulary

Suggestions: As students read their descriptions, encourage others to refer to their charts and guess which student in the group is being described.

Answers will vary.

Pre-AP* Support

• **Learning Objective:** Interpersonal Speaking
• **Activity 33:** Students practice informal speaking skills as they ask and answer survey questions.

Theme Project

Students can perform Step 2 at this point. Be sure students understand your corrections and suggestions. (For more information, see p. 30-b.)

ENRICH YOUR TEACHING

Culture Note

In Mexico, the use of the diminutive is so common that not to use it when talking of one's grandparents, for example, would seem to show a lack of affection. Friends often refer to each other using the diminutive form, even as adults.

21st Century Skills

Collaboration Have students work in small groups to set up a chart similar to the one on this page for family members of the group. Determine through this chart what the family members have in common. (For example: three fathers like pizza, two mothers were born in May, etc.) Make sure all students in the group participate.

53

ⓒ Common Core: Reading

Lectura

Core Instruction

Standards: 1.2, 1.3, 3.1

Focus: Reading comprehension of a birthday invitation

Suggestions:

Pre-reading: Using the suggestion provided in the *Strategy*, have students scan the invitation and look for names and dates.

Reading: Present the reading in three parts—the title and introductory paragraph, the invitation, and the quotations. Have students read each part silently before having a volunteer read them aloud. Pause every few sentences to check comprehension.

Post-reading: Ask a volunteer to summarize each section of the reading. Use the *¿Comprendes?* questions to check comprehension. Talk about how a *miniteca* compares with student parties in the United States. Where do teenagers go to dance in the United States? Do they dance at parties like at a *miniteca?*

BELLRINGER REVIEW

Have students write three things they might expect to find at a school or birthday party.

Pre-AP* Support

- **Learning Objective:** Interpretive: Print and Audio
- **Activity:** Have students look at the invitation for twenty seconds and then close their books. Read teacher-made false statements about the invitation and ask volunteers to correct your statements.
- *Pre-AP* Resource Book:* Comprehensive guide to Pre-AP* reading skill development, pp. 19–26

Lectura
¡Te invitamos a nuestra miniteca!

▶ Read about a *miniteca*
▶ Scan to find information
▶ Learn about the *quinceañera* celebration

Muchos jóvenes hispanos celebran una ocasión especial con una miniteca. Sus padres y uno o varios amigos organizan la miniteca en una casa o en un lugar especial. Decoran el sitio al estilo de una discoteca pequeña. Las luces, la decoración y la música hacen un ambiente[1] divertido para los jóvenes. En las minitecas los jóvenes tienen la oportunidad de escuchar música, bailar, comer y pasar tiempo con los amigos y sus padres. Las minitecas son una costumbre de los jóvenes en países hispanos, especialmente Colombia y Venezuela.

Aquí está la invitación a la miniteca de María y Andrea para celebrar el fin de año del octavo grado.

[1]atmosphere

Strategy

Scanning
What information would you expect to find on an invitation? Read quickly through this invitation and find the names of the two people who are inviting you to the *miniteca*, where it is taking place, and when.

❝El sábado va a ser un día muy divertido. Vamos a bailar, comer y celebrar el fin del octavo grado con todos nuestros amigos. Tenemos que sacar fotos y hacer un video para nunca olvidar[2] el momento❞ .

[2]forget

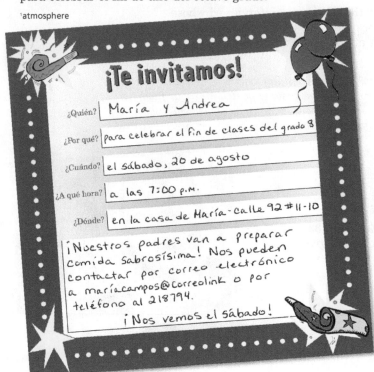

¡Te invitamos!

¿Quién?	María y Andrea
¿Por qué?	para celebrar el fin de clases del grado 8
¿Cuándo?	el sábado, 20 de agosto
¿A qué hora?	a las 7:00 p.m.
¿Dónde?	en la casa de María-Calle 92 #11-10

¡Nuestros padres van a preparar comida sabrosísima! Nos pueden contactar por correo electrónico a maríacampos@correolink o por teléfono al 218794.

¡Nos vemos el sábado!

54 cincuenta y cuatro
Tema 5 • Fiesta en familia

DIFFERENTIATED INSTRUCTION

Multiple Intelligences
Verbal/Linguistic: Have students write a description of their ideal celebration. Suggest that they begin their paragraph with a sentence such as *Me gustaría una celebración con…* After students complete the paragraphs, have them share their ideas with the class and compare what they say with the description of the *miniteca.*

Heritage Language Learners
If students have been to a *miniteca,* ask them to describe it. Who was there? What food was served? What did people do during the celebration? How can they describe the gifts and decorations? Have them write their description in a paragraph. If possible, have them bring in pictures to accompany their paragraphs.

"Aquí estamos María y yo. Es un día muy especial y todos nuestros amigos están en la casa para celebrar. Todo está perfecto para la miniteca: la comida, las decoraciones y la música. ¡Estamos felices!**"**

¿Comprendes?

1. ¿Cuál es la fecha de la miniteca de María y Andrea?

2. Necesitas veinte minutos para ir de tu casa a la casa de María. ¿A qué hora tienes que salir *(leave)* de tu casa?

3. ¿Qué ocasión van a celebrar María, Andrea y sus amigos? ¿Quién va a ayudar a María y Andrea a organizar la miniteca?

4. ¿Qué actividad de la miniteca te gusta más?

▼ Fondo Cultural | El mundo hispano

La quinceañera is a special celebration of a girl's fifteenth birthday also called *los quince,* or *los quince años.* It celebrates the girl becoming a more responsible and involved part of society. During this special occasion friends and family attend mass and then an elaborate party. It is customary for the girl celebrating her *quinceañera* to dance the first dance, a waltz, with her father. This tradition is especially important in Mexico, Central America, Hispanic American countries in the Caribbean, as well as among the Spanish-speaking population in the United States.

- Think about an event in the lives of your friends that has the importance of a *quinceañera* celebration. How are the events similar or different?

Más práctica GO	realidades.com | print
Guided WB p. 15	✔ ✔
Comm. WB pp. 11, 132	✔ ✔
Hispanohablantes WB pp. 182–183	✔ ✔
Cultural Reading Activity	✔

cincuenta y cinco **55**
Capítulo 5A

La cultura en vivo

Core Instruction

Standards: 2.1

Focus: Reading about and making *papel picado*

Suggestions: Have students describe party decorations they are familiar with. Elicit that decorations are usually bright, lively, and evoke a celebratory feeling.
They help set the mood. Explain that making *papel picado* is similar to making snowflakes, which students may have done in elementary school. Point to the picture at the bottom of the page, but note that not all *papel picado* looks alike. These are just examples.

Prepare the materials in advance. Pre-cut the paper to one size for all students. Have a variety of bright colors. Demonstrate the process by making a sample. Keep it simple, so the project moves quickly. Walk students through the steps. Remind them not to cut the hanging flap. Also they should not cut any folded edge completely. Some of it must remain intact to hold the paper together.

Paper punches come in a variety of sizes and shapes. They work well to make interior holes, stars, and other shapes.

To incorporate language use in this activity, you may want to give students words such as *cortar, doblar, abrir, colgar,* or *grapar.*

Additional Resources

Student Resource: Realidades para hispanohablantes, p. 186

¡Adelante!

La cultura en vivo

El papel picado

As you've seen in this chapter, *el papel picado* (cut-paper decorations) is a well-known Mexican craft. Tissue paper is cut into small patterns similar to making paper snowflakes. The cut paper is then hung on string to make a banner to use as decoration at many different celebrations. Here's how to make *papel picado* to decorate your classroom.

Una fiesta con música de mariachi

Materials

- colored tissue paper cut into 12" x 18" sheets
- scissors
- stapler
- string

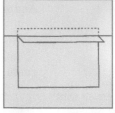  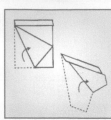

1 **2** **3**

Directions

1 Spread the tissue paper flat. Fold down 1" on the 18" side for making a hanging flap.

2 Fold the paper in half on the 12" side and crease on the fold to make a sharp line.

3 Fold the paper twice diagonally.

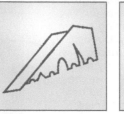 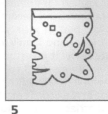 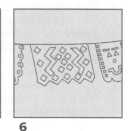

4 **5** **6**

4 Cut out designs along the folded edge. Experiment with snowflake or other geometric designs.

5 Cut a scalloped design on the outside edge.

6 Open the cutout and staple to a string to hang across a room to decorate for a *fiesta.*

DIFFERENTIATED INSTRUCTION

Multiple Intelligences

Visual/Spatial: Some students may be able to produce intricate patterns. Encourage creativity. If they begin by cutting out a symmetrical shape and folding that, they may obtain interesting results. Remind them to include the hanging flap.

Students with Special Needs

Some students may become frustrated with the level of detail necessary to make **papel picado.** Emphasize that the designs can be simple and do not need to be intricate to be festive. Provide assistance as needed.

Presentación oral

Mi familia

Task
You are on an exchange program in Chile and your host family wants to know about your family back home. Show photographs and talk about three family members.

① **Prepare** Bring in three family photos or "create" a family using magazine pictures. Use a chart to plan what to say about each person.

Nombre	Es mi ...	Edad	Actividad favorita
Isabel	hermana menor	9 años	le gusta cantar

Strategy

Using graphic organizers Simple charts can help you organize your thoughts for presentation.

② **Practice** Go through your presentation several times. You can use notes to practice, but not to present. Try to:

- provide all the information for each family member
- use complete sentences
- speak clearly

Modelo
Se llama Isabel. Es mi hermana menor y tiene 9 años. A ella le gusta cantar. Es artística.

③ **Present** Show the photos and give information about each person.

④ **Evaluation** The following rubric will be used to grade your presentation.

Rubric	Score 1	Score 3	Score 5
How complete your preparation is	Your information is written down but without use of a chart.	You used the chart, but it is only partially completed.	You used the chart and provided all the information.
How much information you communicate	You bring in one photo and provide all the information.	You bring in two photos and provide all the information.	You bring in three photos and provide all the information.
How easily you are understood	You are extremely difficult to understand. Your teacher could only recognize isolated words and phrases.	You are understandable but have frequent errors in vocabulary and/or grammar that hinder your comprehensibility.	You are easily understood. Your teacher does not have to "decode" what you are trying to say.

Presentación oral

Core Instruction

Standards: 1.3

Suggestions: Review the task and the four-step approach with students. Point out that their presentations must include the information listed in the chart; however, if they would like to add more information, they should not feel limited by the chart. They may wish to add a column called *¿Cómo es?*

Review the rubric with the class before they begin. If possible, have students record the presentation. Hearing it two or three times may help you grade it more accurately.

Pre-AP* Support

- **Learning Objective:** Presentational Speaking
- **Activity:** Remind students to focus on the presentational speaking skills used in this task such as fluency, pronunciation, and comprehensibility.
- *Pre-AP* Resource Book:* Comprehensive guide to Pre-AP* speaking skill development, pp. 39–50

Portfolio

Make video or audio recordings of student presentations in class, or assign the RealTalk activity so they can record their presentations online. Include the recording in their portfolios.

Additional Resources

Student Resources: Realidades para hispanohablantes, p. 187; Guided Practice: Presentación oral, p. 16

ENRICH YOUR TEACHING

21st Century Skills

Communication After they give their presentations, have students come up with new categories to add to their charts, such as favorite color, favorite food, birthday month, and one thing each family member does *not* like to do. Ask students to integrate the new information into their charts.

✓ ASSESSMENT

Presentación oral
- Assessment Program: Rubrics, p. T31
  Go over the descriptions of the different levels of performance. After assessing students, help individuals understand how their performance could be improved.

5A Video

Videomisterio ▶

Core Instruction

Standards: 1.2, 1.3, 5.2

Resources: Teacher's Resource Book: Video Script, p. 25; Video Program: Cap. 5A; Video Program Teacher's Guide: Cap. 5A

Focus: Introducing the events and vocabulary of this episode; scanning and reading the episode summary

Personajes importantes:

Lola Lago, detective

Doña Lupe, portera

Doña Gracia, vecina

María, sobrina de doña Gracia (una vecina)

Gabriel, empleado del kiosco (*newspaper stand attendant*)

Synopsis: Viewers meet Lola Lago, who finds some keys and sees the letters *J. R. D.* with the number eight as she leaves her apartment in a hurry at one in the morning. She buys a copy of the newspaper for doña Gracia, a neighbor, and hands it to doña Lupe, the building supervisor (*la portera*). But when doña Lupe brings it to doña Gracia, doña Lupe discovers that doña Gracia is unconscious, so she calls an ambulance.

Suggestions:

Pre-viewing: Point out to students that *Episodio* 1 takes place in Madrid, Spain. Review the *Nota* with the class. You may want to ask if there is a profession in the United States similar to the *portero(a)* in Spain. Point out the *Palabras para comprender* to the class, and provide examples in context. Remind students that these words are used only to help them understand the episode; otherwise, they are not responsible for that vocabulary.

Visual scanning: Direct students' attention to the first photo and ask who is standing by the sign (Lola Lago) and what **Detectives privados** means. Then have students look at the second photo of doña Lupe. What is she holding in her hand? (a broom) To what other Spanish word is **portera** related? (*puerta*) Before students read the *Resumen del episodio*, have them scan the text and find three cognate words. (*capital, balcón, personas, importantes, entra*) Then ask them to read the *Resumen del episodio* carefully and ask questions about what will happen in this episode.

¿Eres tú, María?

Madrid, España

Episodio 1

Antes de ver el video

Personajes importantes

Lola Lago, detective

Doña Lupe, portera

Nota cultural In many apartment buildings in Spain, you will find a *portero* or *portera*. In exchange for a small salary and free apartment (in Spain, an apartment is called *un piso*), this person watches over the building and its residents, doing small chores such as taking messages and receiving packages. Because the *portero* or *portera* knows everyone in the building, he or she is often a good source of information about the residents.

Resumen del episodio

Estamos en el piso de Lola Lago, una detective que trabaja en Madrid, la capital de España. Es la una de la mañana. Desde[1] su balcón, ella ve a dos personas hablando enfrente de un edificio.[2] ¿Qué pasa? Más tarde, Lola encuentra[3] algo muy importante en la calle.[4] Al día siguiente,[5] doña Lupe, la portera del edificio, entra en el piso de doña Gracia y . . .

[1]From   [2]building   [3]finds   [4]street   [5]The next day

Palabras para comprender

investigar	to investigate
las llaves	keys
el periódico	newspaper
el piso	apartment; floor (*of a building*)

DIFFERENTIATED INSTRUCTION

Heritage Language Learners

Have students write their own version of the story with the same characters, but with different outcomes. Have students incorporate the vocabulary from the chapter into their story. Have them focus on correct spelling and language accuracy. Students may wish to do a storyboard with captions and present their story to the class.

Students with Learning Difficulties

Pause the video when necessary to have students make note of the clues. Have students use their list of clues to answer the *¿Comprendes?* questions and to predict the outcome of the *Episodio*.

"¿Qué es esto?
Mañana voy a investigar".

"A ver. Unas llaves . . ."

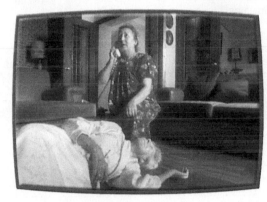

"¡Ay de mí! Necesito una
ambulancia. Plaza del
Alamillo. Número 8.
Tercer piso. ¡Rápido!"

Después de ver el video

¿Comprendes?

Lee las frases y decide si son ciertas o falsas.
Si una frase es falsa, escríbela con la
información correcta.

1. Es la una de la tarde cuando Lola entra en
   su piso.

2. Ella está sola en su piso.

3. Lola ve a dos hombres hablando
   en la calle.

4. Las dos personas están muy contentas.

5. Lola encuentra un llavero con las
   iniciales "J.R.D.".

6. Lola compra (buys) una revista en la
   mañana.

7. Doña Lupe entra en el piso de Lola
   con el periódico.

Más práctica	GO
realidades.com	print
Actividades	✔

cincuenta y nueve 59
Capítulo 5A

Viewing: Play *Episodio* 1 to the class.
Pause the video periodically to check for
comprehension. If there is time after
viewing the full episode, select some key
moments that you feel are important to
the story, such as the greeting exchange
between Lola and Gabriel at the
newsstand.

Post-viewing: Have students compare
what actually happened in the video with
the predictions that they made before
watching the video. Discuss how they
were different and similar.

▼**¿Comprendes?** Standards: 1.1, 1.2, 1.3

Resources: Answer Keys: Student Edition, p. 105

Focus: Verifying comprehension

Suggestions: Have students write the
statements on slips of colored paper (for
example, number 1 is on yellow paper,
number 2 is on red paper). Have students
arrange the papers accordingly. To check
comprehension, you simply have to look at
the order of the colors on students' desks.

Answers:

1. falsa: Es la una de la mañana cuando Lola entra
   en su piso.
2. cierta
3. falsa: Lola ve a una mujer y un hombre hablando
   en la calle.
4. falsa: Las dos personas no están muy contentas.
5. cierta
6. falsa: Lola compra un periódico en la mañana.
7. cierta

Theme Project

Students can perform Step 3 at this point.
(For more information, see p. 30-b.)

Additional Resources

• *¿Eres tú, María?* Video Workbook, Episode 1
• *¿Eres tú, María?* Teacher's Video Guide: Answer Key

ENRICH YOUR TEACHING

Culture Note

Tell students that almost all **madrileños,** or
people who live in Madrid, rent or own
apartments. Even on the outskirts of the city,
free-standing homes are relatively uncommon.

Teacher-to-Teacher

Pass out strips of paper with lines from the
video written on them. Have students read the
lines and have the rest of the class members
guess who said or would say the line in the
video.

5A Review

Repaso del capítulo
Vocabulario y gramática

Review Activities

To talk about family members and possessive adjectives: Have students draw fictional family trees and use the vocabulary to describe who each person is. Students can take turns asking how old each relative is and what they like: *Mi hermano menor tiene doce años y le gusta comer hamburguesas.*

To describe activities at parties: Have students work in pairs and plan a party. Have them create a chart and write what activities they will do, what food they will serve, and how they will decorate. Have them use their charts to discuss their plans with another pair.

To discuss and compare ages, talk about people, likes, and talk about animals: Have students work in groups of four or five and prepare a list with the names and the age of each member of the group. Have students list two or three activities that each member likes to do and does not like to do, and if they have an animal at home *(Clara tiene X años. Le gusta comer en restaurantes y decorar las fiestas. Ella tiene/no tiene un gato.)*

Tener: Have students write subject pronouns on note cards and shuffle them, face down. Student A picks a card and says the pronoun and Student B says or writes the appropriate form of **tener.** Students can roll their subject pronoun cubes for this as well.

Portfolio

Invite students to review the activities they completed in this chapter, including written reports, posters, or other visuals, and recordings of oral presentations or other projects. Have them select one or two items that they feel best demonstrate their achievements in Spanish to include in their portfolios.

Additional Resources

Student Resources: Realidades para hispanohablantes, p. 188

Teacher Resources:
- Teacher's Resource Book: Situation Cards, p. 30, Clip Art, pp. 31–34
- Assessment Program: Chapter Checklist and Self-Assessment Worksheet, pp. T56–T57

---

to talk about family members

los abuelos	grandparents
el abuelo	grandfather
la abuela	grandmother
el esposo, la esposa	husband, wife
los hermanos	brothers; brother(s) and sister(s)
el hermano	brother
la hermana	sister
el hermanastro	stepbrother
la hermanastra	stepsister
los hijos	children; sons
el hijo	son
la hija	daughter
los padres (papás)	parents
el padre (papá)	father
la madre (mamá)	mother
el padrastro	stepfather
la madrastra	stepmother
los primos	cousins
el primo	(male) cousin
la prima	(female) cousin
los tíos	uncles; aunt(s) and uncle(s)
el tío	uncle
la tía	aunt

to discuss and compare ages

¿Cuántos años tiene(n) ____?	How old is / are ____?
Tiene(n) ____ años.	He / She is / They are ____ (years old).
mayor, *pl.* mayores	older
menor, *pl.* menores	younger

to talk about people

la persona	person

to name animals

el gato	cat
el perro	dog

to discuss what someone likes

(a + *person*) le gusta(n) / le encanta(n)	he / she likes / loves

For *Vocabulario adicional,* see pp. 336–337.

to describe activities at parties

abrir	to open
celebrar	to celebrate
decorar	to decorate
las decoraciones	decorations
hacer un video	to videotape
el video	video
preparar	to prepare
romper	to break
sacar fotos	to take photos
la foto	photo
la cámara	camera

to discuss celebrations

el cumpleaños	birthday
¡Feliz cumpleaños!	Happy birthday!
los dulces	candy
la flor, *pl.* las flores	flower
el globo	balloon
la luz, *pl.* las luces	light
el papel picado	cut-paper decorations
el pastel	cake
la piñata	piñata
el regalo	gift, present

other useful words

que	who, that
sólo	only

to indicate possession or relationship

tener *to have*

tengo	tenemos
tienes	tenéis
tiene	tienen

possessive adjectives

mi(s) my		nuestro(s), -a(s) our
tu(s) your		vuestro(s), -a(s) your
su(s) your (*formal*), his, her, its		su(s) your (*pl.*), their

---

DIFFERENTIATED INSTRUCTION

Heritage Language Learners

Have students write a few paragraphs telling about their perfect birthday celebration: Where are they going to have it? Whom are they going to invite? What food are they going to eat? What kind of music are they going to play? What other activities do they enjoy with the guests? Encourage them to use as many vocabulary words from this chapter as they can and to share their work with the class.

Más repaso (GO) realidades.com | print

Instant Check	✔	
Puzzles	✔	
Core WB pp. 8–9		✔
Comm. WB pp. 133, 134–137	✔	✔

Preparación para el examen

On the exam you will be asked to . . .	Here are practice tasks similar to those you will find on the exam . . .	For review go to your print or digital textbook . . .
1 Escuchar Listen to and understand someone's description of a family member	At a friend's party, a woman is telling you stories about her brother, Jorge. a) How old is her brother? b) Who is older, the woman or her brother? c) What does her brother like to do?	pp. 32–37 *Vocabulario en contexto* p. 39 Actividad 7 p. 41 Actividades 12–13 p. 44 Actividad 18
2 Hablar Describe some members of your family and what they like to do	At your first Spanish Club meeting, your teacher requests that all of you try to talk to each other in Spanish. Since you just learned how to talk about your family, you feel confident that you can talk about some of your family members. Tell about: a) how they are related to you; b) their ages; c) what they like to do; d) their personalities.	pp. 32–37 *Vocabulario en contexto* p. 39 Actividad 7 p. 41 Actividad 12 p. 44 Actividad 19 p. 53 Actividades 33–34
3 Leer Read and understand someone's description of a problem he or she is having with a family member	Read this letter to an advice columnist. Can you describe in English what Ana's problem is? *Querida Dolores:* *Yo soy la hija menor de una familia de seis personas. Uno de mis hermanos mayores, Nacho, siempre habla de mí con mis padres. A él le encanta hablar de mis amigos y de mis actividades. Tenemos una familia muy simpática, ¡pero Nacho me vuelve loca!* *—Ana*	pp. 32–37 *Vocabulario en contexto* p. 39 Actividades 7–8 p. 46 Actividad 21 p. 49 Actividad 26
4 Escribir Write a brief note telling at least two facts about a friend or family member	The party planner at a local restaurant is helping you plan a birthday party for your cousin. Write a brief note telling her your cousin's name, age, two things he or she likes to do at a party, the kinds of decorations he or she likes, and one thing he or she loves to eat.	p. 39 Actividad 8 p. 41 Actividad 13 p. 44 Actividad 19 p. 53 Actividad 34
5 Pensar Demonstrate an understanding of some ways that Spanish-speaking families celebrate special occasions	Think about what you would consider your most important birthday. Based on what you know about important family traditions, describe why a fifteenth birthday is important for a young Spanish-speaking girl and what you would expect to see at her celebration.	pp. 32–37 *Vocabulario en contexto* p. 39 *Fondo cultural* pp. 54–55 *Lectura* p. 56 *La cultura en vivo*

Performance Tasks

Standards: 1.1, 1.2, 1.3, 2.1, 2.2

Student Resource: Realidades para hispanohablantes, p. 189

Teacher Resources: Teacher's Resource Book: Audio Script, p. 23; Audio Program DVD: Cap. 5A, Track 20; Answer Keys: Student Edition, p. 106

1. Escuchar

Suggestions: Use the audio or read the script.

Script:
Pues, en mi familia, yo soy la hija reservada y trabajadora. Mi hermano mayor, Jorge, es muy sociable. Tiene treinta y ocho años. A él le gusta hacer videos. Es muy talentoso.

Answers: a) He is 38 years old.
b) Her brother is older.   c) He likes to make videos.

2. Hablar

Suggestions: Remind students to use a graphic organizer, such as a family tree.

Answers will vary.

3. Leer

Suggestions: Have students use context and prior knowledge to determine Ana's problem. Have them comprehend the last line—*¡Nacho me vuelve loca!* (Nacho drives me crazy!)

Answers:
Ana's older brother Nacho always talks to their parents about Ana, her friends, and what they do.

4. Escribir

Suggestions: Students may want to use a graphic organizer before they begin writing their notes.

Answers will vary.

5. Pensar

Suggestions: Have students reread *Vocabulario en contexto, Fondo cultural, Lectura,* and *La cultura en vivo* and look at the photos throughout the chapter. Reflect with them on the questions asked here.

Answers will vary.

DIFFERENTIATED ASSESSMENT

CORE ASSESSMENT
- **Assessment Program:** Examen del capítulo 5A, pp. 125–132
- **Audio Program DVD:** Cap. 5A, Track 21
- **ExamView:** Chapter Test, Test Banks A and B

ADVANCED/PRE-AP*
- **ExamView:** Pre-AP* Test Bank
- **Pre-AP* Resource Book,** pp. 78–81

STUDENTS NEEDING EXTRA HELP
- **Alternate Assessment Program:** Examen del capítulo 5A
- **Audio Program DVD:** Cap. 5A, Track 21

HERITAGE LEARNERS
- **Assessment Program: Realidades para hispanohablantes:** Examen del capítulo 5A
- **ExamView: Heritage Learner Test Bank**

AT A GLANCE

Objectives

- Listen to, read, and write information about restaurant meals and service
- Write about plans for a celebration
- Exchange information while describing family members
- Understand cultural perspectives on meals and mealtimes in the Spanish-speaking world
- Explain aspects of the Hispanic history and culture of Santa Fe, New Mexico

Vocabulary

- Describing people and things
- Food and table settings
- Eating out
- Expressing needs

Grammar

- The verb *venir*
- The verbs *ser* and *estar*

Culture

- Extended families, p. 63
- Getting a server's attention, p. 72
- *arroz con leche*, p. 81
- *menú del día*, p. 82
- Santa Fe, p. 85
- Cultural perspectives on mealtimes, p. 86

Recycle ♻

- Family members
- Adjective agreement
- The verb *estar*
- The verb *ser*
- The verb *tener*
- Prepositions of location
- Foods

RESOURCES

FOR THE STUDENT	ONLINE	DVD	PRINT	FOR THE TEACHER	ONLINE	PREEXP	DVD	PRINT
Plan				Interactive TE and Resources DVD	•		•	
				Teacher's Resource Book, pp. 52–84	•		•	•
				Pre-AP* Resource Book, p. 78–81	•		•	•
				Lesson Plans	•		•	
				Mapa global interactivo	•			

Introducción PP. 62–63

FOR THE STUDENT	ONLINE	DVD	PRINT	FOR THE TEACHER	ONLINE	PREEXP	DVD	PRINT
Present Student Edition, pp. 62–63	•	•	•	Interactive TE and Resources DVD	•		•	
DK Reference Atlas	•	•		Teacher's Resource Book, pp. 52–53	•		•	•
Videocultura	•	•		Galería de fotos		•		
Hispanohablantes WB, pp. 190–191			•	Fine Art Transparencies, 60	•	•	•	
				Map Transparencies, 12–13, 15–18, 20	•	•	•	

Vocabulario en contexto PP. 64–69

FOR THE STUDENT	ONLINE	DVD	PRINT	FOR THE TEACHER	ONLINE	PREEXP	DVD	PRINT
Present & Practice Student Edition, pp. 64–69	•	•	•	Interactive TE and Resources DVD	•		•	
Audio	•	•		Teacher's Resource Book, pp. 54–56, 58, 66–68	•		•	•
Videohistoria	•	•		Vocabulary Clip Art	•	•	•	•
Flashcards	•	•		Audio Program	•	•	•	
Instant Check	•			Video Program: Videohistoria	•		•	
Guided WB, pp. 17–26	•	•	•	Video Program Teacher's Guide: Cap. 5B	•		•	
Core WB, pp. 10–13	•	•	•	Vocabulary and Grammar Transparencies, 104–107	•	•	•	
Comm. WB, pp. 12–15, 18	•	•	•	Answer Keys: Student Edition, pp. 107–108	•	•	•	
Hispanohablantes WB, pp. 192–193			•	TPR Stories, pp. 62–76	•		•	•
Assess and Remediate				Prueba 5B–1: Assessment Program, pp. 133–134	•		•	•
				Assessment Program para hispanohablantes, pp. 133–134	•		•	•

RESOURCES

Vocabulario en uso PP. 70–75

FOR THE STUDENT	ONLINE	DVD	PRINT	FOR THE TEACHER	ONLINE	PREEXP	DVD	PRINT
Present & Practice								
Student Edition, pp. 70–75	•	•	•	Interactive Whiteboard Vocabulary Activities	•		•	
Instant Check	•			Interactive TE and Resources DVD	•		•	
Comm. WB, pp. 15–16	•	•	•	Teacher's Resource Book, pp. 55–56, 60–61, 65	•		•	•
Hispanohablantes WB, pp. 194–195			•	Communicative Pair Activities, pp. 60–61	•		•	•
Communicative Pair Activities	•			Audio Program	•	•	•	
				Videomodelos	•		•	
				Vocabulary and Grammar Transparencies, 83	•	•	•	
				Answer Keys: Student Edition, pp. 109–111	•	•	•	
Assess and Remediate				Prueba 5B–2 with Study Plan	•			
				Prueba 5B–2: Assessment Program, pp. 135–136	•		•	•
				Assessment Program para hispanohablantes, pp. 135–136	•		•	•

Gramática PP. 76–83

FOR THE STUDENT	ONLINE	DVD	PRINT	FOR THE TEACHER	ONLINE	PREEXP	DVD	PRINT
Present & Practice								
Student Edition, pp. 76–83	•	•	•	Interactive Whiteboard Grammar Activities	•		•	
Instant Check	•			Interactive TE and Resources DVD	•		•	
Animated Verbs	•			Teacher's Resource Book, pp. 56–59, 62–63	•		•	•
Tutorial Video: Grammar	•			Communicative Pair Activities, pp. 62–63	•		•	•
Canción de hip hop	•			Audio Program	•	•	•	
Guided WB, pp. 27–30	•	•	•	Videomodelos	•		•	
Core WB, pp. 14–16	•	•	•	Video Program: GramActiva	•		•	
Comm. WB, pp. 16–17, 19–20, 138	•	•	•	Vocabulary and Grammar Transparencies, 108–109, 111	•	•	•	
Hispanohablantes WB, pp. 196–201			•	Answer Keys: Student Edition, pp. 111–113	•	•	•	
Communicative Pair Activities	•							
Assess and Remediate				Pruebas 5B–3 and 5B–4 with Study Plans	•			
				Pruebas 5B–3, 5B–4: Assessment Program, pp. 137, 138	•		•	•
				Assessment Program para hispanohablantes, pp. 137, 138	•		•	•

¡Adelante! PP. 84–89

FOR THE STUDENT	ONLINE	DVD	PRINT	FOR THE TEACHER	ONLINE	PREEXP	DVD	PRINT
Application								
Student Edition, pp. 84–89	•	•	•	Interactive TE and Resources DVD	•		•	
Online Cultural Reading	•			Teacher's Resource Book, p. 59	•		•	•
Guided WB, pp. 31–32	•	•	•	Video Program: Videomisterio ¿Eres tú, María?	•		•	
Comm. WB, pp. 21, 139	•	•	•	Video Program Teacher's Guide: Cap. 5B	•		•	
Hispanohablantes WB, pp. 202–207			•	Videomisterio Quiz		•		
¿Eres tú, María? Video WB, pp. 10–19	•	•	•	Answer Keys: Student Edition, p. 114	•	•	•	

Repaso del capítulo PP. 90–91

FOR THE STUDENT	ONLINE	DVD	PRINT	FOR THE TEACHER	ONLINE	PREEXP	DVD	PRINT
Review								
Student Edition, pp. 90–91	•	•	•	Interactive TE and Resources DVD	•		•	
Online Puzzles and Games	•			Teacher's Resource Book, pp. 57, 64, 66–68	•		•	•
Core WB, pp. 17–18	•	•	•	Audio Program	•	•	•	
Comm. WB, pp. 140–143	•	•	•	Answer Keys: Student Edition, p. 115	•	•	•	
Hispanohablantes WB, pp. 208–209			•					
Instant Check	•							

Chapter Assessment

FOR THE STUDENT	ONLINE	DVD	PRINT	FOR THE TEACHER	ONLINE	PREEXP	DVD	PRINT
Assess				Examen del capítulo 5B	•	•	•	•
				Assessment Program, pp. 139–145	•	•	•	•
				Alternate Assessment Program, pp. 62–66	•	•	•	•
				Assessment Program para hispanohablantes, pp. 139–145	•	•	•	•
				Audio Program, Cap. 5B, Examen	•	•	•	
				ExamView: Test Banks A and B questions only online	•	•		
				Heritage Learner Test Bank	•	•		
				Pre-AP* Test Bank	•	•		

REGULAR SCHEDULE (50 MINUTES)

DAY	Warm-up / Assess	Preview / Present / Practice / Communicate	Wrap-up / Homework Options
1	**Return Examen del capítulo (10 min.)**	**Vocabulario en contexto (35 min.)** • Objectives • Presentation • *Actividades* 1, 2 • Arte y cultura • Videocultura: *La quinceañera*	**Wrap-up and Homework Options (5 min.)** • Core Practice • Vocabulary Clip Art
2	**Warm-up (5 min.)** • Homework check	**Vocabulario en contexto (40 min.)** • Review: *Vocabulario en contexto* • Presentation: *Videohistoria En el restaurante Casa Río* • View: Video *En el restaurante Casa Río* • Video Activities • *Actividades* 3, 4, 5	**Wrap-up and Homework Options (5 min.)** • *Prueba* 5B-1: Vocabulary recognition • Core Practice
3	**Warm-up (5 min.)** • Homework check ✔**Formative Assessment (10 min.)** • *Prueba* 5B-1: Vocabulary recognition	**Vocabulario en uso (30 min.)** • Objectives • Interactive Whiteboard Vocabulary Activities • *Actividades* 6, 7, 9	**Wrap-up and Homework Options (5 min.)** • *Actividad* 8
4	**Warm-up (5 min.)** • Homework check • Return *Prueba* 5B-1: Vocabulary recognition	**Vocabulario en uso (40 min.)** • *Actividades* 11, 12 • *Fondo cultural* • Communicative Pair Activities	**Wrap-up and Homework Options (5 min.)** • *Actividad* 10
5	**Warm-up (5 min.)** • Homework check	**Vocabulario en uso (40 min.)** • *Actividades* 14, 15 • *Juego: Actividad* 13	**Wrap-up and Homework Options (5 min.)** • *Actividad* 14
6	**Warm-up (5 min.)** • Homework check	**Gramática y vocabulario en uso (40 min.)** • *Exploración del lenguaje* • Presentation: The verb *venir* • Interactive Whiteboard Grammar Activities • *Actividades* 16, 17	**Wrap-up and Homework Options (5 min.)** • *Actividad* 17
7	**Warm-up (5 min.)** • Homework check	**Gramática y vocabulario en uso (40 min.)** • Review: The verb *venir* • *Actividades* 18, 19, 20 • *Pronunciación* • Communicative Pair Activities	**Wrap-up and Homework Options (5 min.)** • Core Practice • *Prueba* 5B-3 with Study Plan: The verb *venir*
8	**Warm-up (5 min.)** • Homework check ✔**Formative Assessment (10 min.)** • *Prueba* 5B-3 with Study Plan: The verb *venir*	**Gramática y vocabulario en uso (30 min.)** • Presentation: The verbs *ser* and *estar* • *GramActiva* Video • Interactive Whiteboard Grammar Activities • *Actividades* 21, 23	**Wrap-up and Homework Options (5 min.)** • *Actividad* 22 • *Prueba* 5B-2 with Study Plan: Vocabulary production

REGULAR SCHEDULE (50 MINUTES)

DAY	Warm-up / Assess	Preview / Present / Practice / Communicate	Wrap-up / Homework Options
9	**Warm-up (5 min.)** • Homework check • Return Prueba 5B-3 with Study Plan: The verb *venir* ✔**Formative Assessment (10 min.)** • *Prueba* 5B-2 with Study Plan: Vocabulary production	**Gramática y vocabulario en uso (30 min.)** • *Actividad* 24 • *Conexiones: Actividad* 25 • *Fondo cultural*	**Wrap-up and Homework Options (5 min.)** • *Actividad* 26 • *Prueba* 5B-4 with Study Plan: The verbs *ser* and *estar*
10	**Warm-up (5 min.)** • Homework check • Return *Prueba* 5B-2 with Study Plan: Vocabulary production ✔**Formative Assessment (10 min.)** • *Prueba* 5B-4 with Study Plan: The verbs *ser* and *estar*	**Gramática y vocabulario en uso (30 min.)** • *Actividades* 27, 28, 29 • *El español en el mundo del trabajo*	**Wrap-up and Homework Options (5 min.)** • Core Practice
11	**Warm-up (5 min.)** • Homework check • Return *Prueba* 5B-4 with Study Plan: The verbs *ser* and *estar*	**¡Adelante! (40 min.)** • *Presentación escrita:* Prewrite • *Lectura* • *Fondo cultural*	**Wrap-up and Homework Options (5 min.)** • *¿Comprendes?*
12	**Warm-up (5 min.)** • Homework check	**¡Adelante! (40 min.)** • *Presentación escrita:* Draft, revise • *Perspectivas del mundo hispano*	**Wrap-up and Homework Options (5 min.)** • *Presentación escrita:* Publish
13	**Warm-up (5 min.)** • Homework check	**¡Adelante! (40 min.)** • *Presentación escrita:* Present	**Wrap-up and Homework Options (5 min.)** • Writing Activities • Core Practice Organizer
14	**Warm-up (5 min.)** • Homework check • Core Practice Organizer	**¡Adelante! (20 min.)** • *Videomisterio* **Repaso (20 min.)** • *Vocabulario y gramática* • *Preparación para el examen*	**Wrap-up and Homework Options (5 min.)** • Instant Check • *Examen del capítulo*
15	**Warm-up (5 min.)** • Answer questions ✔**Summative Assessment (45 min.)** • *Examen del capítulo*		

Standards for *Capítulo* 5B

- To achieve the goals of the Standards, students will:

Communication

1.1 Interpersonal
- Talk about family members and others descriptively
- Talk about table settings, meal customs in Spanish-speaking cultures
- Talk about foods and beverages

1.2 Interpretive
- Read and listen to descriptions of family members
- Read and listen to information about restaurants, table settings, meal customs in Spanish-speaking cultures
- Read a picture-based story
- Listen to and watch a video about restaurant service
- Read a restaurant review
- Read a recipe for *arroz con leche*
- Read a letter about a trip to Santa Fe

1.3 Presentational
- Present descriptions of people
- Write analogies to compare people and things
- Present information about food and beverages
- Present information about time and spatial relationships
- Present a skit between a server and customers
- Present information about Santa Fe

Culture

2.1 Practices and Perspectives
- Understand that extended families tend to be close-knit in Spanish-speaking countries
- Understand etiquette for summoning a server
- Understand typical restaurant offerings in Spanish-speaking countries
- Learn about the mealtime custom of *sobremesa* in Spanish-speaking countries
- Learn about the communal function of *plazas*

2.2 Products and Perspectives
- Learn about Xavier Nogués and his painting
- Learn about the communal function of *plazas*

Connections

3.1 Cross-curricular
- Learn about important artists and their work: Nogués
- Learn a recipe for *arroz con leche*
- Reinforce math and metric conversion skills
- Learn historical facts about Santa Fe

Comparisons

4.1 Language
- Understand the use of adjectives ending in *-ísimo*
- Learn new vocabulary through the recognition of cognates
- Understand the use of the verb *venir*
- Learn the pronunciation of the letters *b* and *v*
- The the differences between the verbs *ser* and *estar*

4.2 Culture
- Compare relationships with extended families
- Compare techniques for getting a server's attention
- Compare menu selections
- Compare local historical sites with those of Santa Fe

Communities

5.1 Beyond the School
- Learn of the need of Spanish-speaking employees at the United States Department of Agriculture

5.2 Lifelong Learner
- View a video mystery series

▼ Chapter Objectives

Communication

By the end of this chapter you will be able to:

- Listen to, read, and write information about restaurant meals and service
- Write about plans for a celebration
- Exchange information while describing family members

Culture

You will also be able to:

- Understand cultural perspectives on meals and mealtimes in the Spanish-speaking world
- Explain aspects of the Hispanic history and culture of Santa Fe, New Mexico

You will demonstrate what you know and can do:

- Presentación escrita, p. 87
- Preparación para el examen, p. 91

You will use:

Vocabulary
- Describing people and things
- Food and table settings
- Eating out
- Expressing needs

Grammar
- The verb *venir*
- The verbs *ser* and *estar*

Exploración del mundo hispano

Country Connection
Eating in a Restaurant with Your Family

Nuevo México · Texas · España
México · República Dominicana
Costa Rica · Colombia
Paraguay
Chile · Argentina

realidades.com GO

🖵 Reference Atlas
▶ Videocultura y actividad
🌐 Mapa global interactivo

ENRICH YOUR TEACHING

Using Backward Design

Have students preview the sample performance tasks on *Preparación para el examen*, p. 91, and connect them to the Chapter Objectives. Explain to students that by completing the sample tasks they can self-assess their learning progress.

Mapa global interactivo

Download the *Mapa global interactivo* files for Chapter 5B and preview the activity. For this activity, you visit Santa Fe, New Mexico and travel the Camino Real.

Una cena entre familia,
Ciudad de México

Arte y cultura | El mundo hispano

Extended families tend to be close-knit in Spanish-speaking cultures. Parents, children, grandparents, aunts, uncles, and cousins get together often for meals, and not just on special occasions. It is not uncommon for three generations to live under one roof or in the same neighborhood.

• How do extended families in Spanish-speaking cultures compare with your family and those of your friends?

• How does the painting "Tarde de domingo" reflect the idea of extended families? Compare this to how you and your family spend weekends.

"Tarde de domingo" (1923), Xavier Nogués
Nogués, Xavier. Tarde de Domingo - Sunday afternoon, 1923. Canvas, 60 × 75 cm,
Museo de Arte Moderno, Barcelona, Spain.

sesenta y tres 63
Capítulo 5B

Chapter Opener

Core Instruction

Resources: Map Transparencies 12–13, 15–18, 20

Suggestions: Explain that students will learn to describe people and things and to talk about eating in a restaurant. Brainstorm words and phrases used in ordering food. The *GramActiva* Videos will help students learn to use the verbs *venir, ser,* and *estar.*

▶ **Videocultura** View *La quinceañera* with the class to find out how teens in Spanish-speaking countries prepare for this rite of passage.

Arte y cultura

Standards: 2.1, 3.1, 4.2

Resources: Fine Art Transparencies, p. 60

Suggestions: Ask volunteers to talk about their extended families. Discuss how some family members in the United States may live hundreds of miles apart. Use Transparency 20, the map of the United States and have students point out where members of their families live.

Answers will vary, but may mention the fact that in the painting, several generations seem to be involved in activities together.

TEACHING WITH ART

▶ **Resources:** Fine Art Transparencies, p. 60

Suggestion: Explain to students that the cultural movement the painting represents emphasized values like imagination and tradition in art. Have students describe aspects of the painting that appear to reflect those values.

Culture Note

Xavier Nogués was born in Barcelona and was famous for his paintings, engravings, humorous drawings, and cartoons. He was part of an early 20th century Catalonian cultural movement called (in Spanish) *Novecentismo,* or "1900-ism." *Novecentismo* was marked by a return to ideas of order and beauty in art and was a reaction against the *Modernismo* of the time.

DIFFERENTIATED INSTRUCTION

Digital resources such as the *Interactive Whiteboard* activity banks, *Videomodelos,* additional *Online Activities, Study Plans,* automatically graded *Leveled Workbook,* animated *Grammar Tutorials, Flashcards,* and *Vocabulary and Grammar Videos* will help you reach students of different ability levels and learning styles.

STUDENTS NEEDING EXTRA HELP

Guided Practice Activities
• Flashcards, pp. 17–22
• Vocabulary Check, pp. 23–26
• Grammar Support, pp. 27–30

HERITAGE LEARNERS

Realidades para hispanohablantes
• Chapter Opener, pp. 190–191
• A primera vista, p. 192
• Videohistoria, p. 193
• Manos a la obra, pp. 194–201
• ¡Adelante!, pp. 202–207
• Repaso del capítulo, pp. 208–209

ADVANCED/PRE-AP*

Pre-AP* Resource Book,
• pp. 78–81

Communications Workbook
• Integrated Performance Assessment, p. 140

Vocabulario en contexto

Core Instruction

Standards: 1.2

Resources: Teacher's Resource Book: Input Script, p. 54, Clip Art, pp. 66–68, Audio Script, p. 55; Voc. and Gram. Transparencies 104–105; TPR Stories Book, pp. 62–76; Audio Program DVD: Cap. 5B, Tracks 1–2

Focus: Presenting new vocabulary about family; describing people

Suggestions: Use the story in the *TPR Stories Book* to present the new vocabulary and grammar, or use the *Input Script* from the *Teacher's Resource Book*.

Present the vocabulary in two sets: words to describe people, and restaurant vocabulary/table settings. Say each word on the transparencies but wait to point to each picture until students point to the correct picture in the book. Describe people shown on the transparencies and have volunteers come up and point to the correct picture. For example: *la chica pelirroja, el hombre viejo con pelo canoso, el chico joven con pelo rubio.*

Bring in dishes, glasses, or plasticware. Place the objects on a desk and have students select the object after you say the vocabulary word.

BELLRINGER REVIEW

Show Fine Art Transparency 60. Have students write three descriptive sentences about the transparency to share with the class.

A primera vista | 🔊 | 📖 | ▼ **Objectives**

Read, listen to, and understand information about
▶ descriptions of family members
▶ restaurant vocabulary
▶ table settings

Vocabulario en contexto

—Abuelito, ¿quiénes son las personas en la foto?

—La mujer es tu abuela y el hombre, soy yo. Y aquí está tu papá. Tiene sólo seis años.

el hombre   la mujer

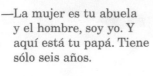

el pelo castaño

alto

baja

pelirroja   el pelo largo

el pelo corto

el pelo rubio

el pelo negro

viejo

el pelo canoso

joven

—¿Quién es **el joven** alto y **guapo**?

—Es tu primo Rafael.

—¿Y **la joven** baja al lado de primo Rafael?

—Es su amiga, Sara. Y estas **otras** personas son amigos también.

64 sesenta y cuatro
Tema 5 • Fiesta en familia

DIFFERENTIATED INSTRUCTION

Heritage Language Learners

Using the vocabulary on this page, have students talk about three members of their extended family, such as: *Mi abuela tiene el pelo canoso. Mi tía Rosa es joven.*

Students with Learning Difficulties

Encourage students to break their vocabulary list into small groups of related words. Students can then study categories such as physical characteristics, hair colors, or table settings.

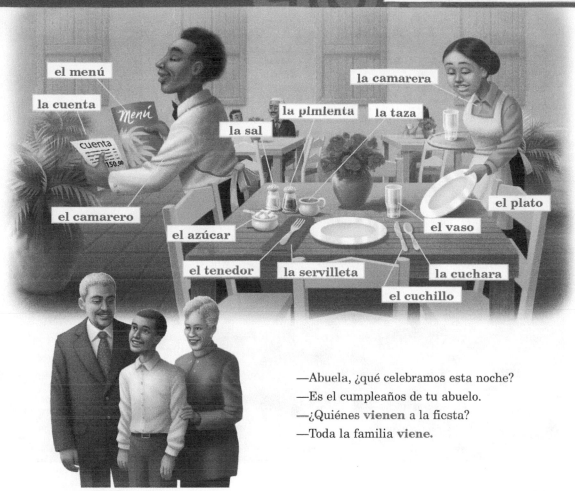

el menú
la cuenta
la camarera
la pimienta
la taza
la sal
el camarero
el plato
el azúcar
el vaso
el tenedor
la servilleta
la cuchara
el cuchillo

—Abuela, ¿qué celebramos esta noche?
—Es el cumpleaños de tu abuelo.
—¿Quiénes **vienen** a la ficsta?
—Toda la familia **viene**.

1 | 🔊 | Escuchar

¿Quiénes vienen?

Paquito is showing the family album to a friend. Point to the different pictures as he describes the people in the photographs.

2 | 🔊 | Escuchar

¿Qué necesitas para . . . ?

You will hear seven statements about the table setting. If a statement is correct, indicate *cierto* by raising one hand. If a statement is incorrect, indicate *falso* by raising two hands.

Más práctica		
realidades.com	print		
Instant Check	✔	
Guided WB pp. 17–22	✔	✔
Core WB pp. 10–11	✔	✔
Comm. WB p. 18	✔	✔
Hispanohablantes WB p. 192		✔

---

1 Standards: 1.2

Resources: Teacher's Resource Book: Audio Script, p. 55; Audio Program DVD: Cap. 5B, Track 3; Answer Keys: Student Edition, p. 107

Focus: Listening comprehension of new vocabulary about family members

Suggestions: Before the activity, read the picture captions with students so they are familiar with the characters. All statements are from the perspective of the little boy.

🔊 **Script and Answers:**

1. Mi padre está con mis abuelos. *(top)*
2. Mi primo es alto. *(left)*
3. En la foto, mi abuela tiene el pelo negro. *(top)*
4. El chico con el pelo rubio es amigo de mi padre. *(right)*
5. En la foto, mi padre es joven. Tiene seis años. *(top)*
6. La chica baja se llama Sara. *(left)*
7. El chico guapo es mi tío Rafael. *(left)*
8. La chica pelirroja es amiga de mi padre. *(right)*

2 Standards: 1.2

Resources: Teacher's Resource Book: Audio Script, p. 55; Audio Program DVD: Cap. 5B, Track 4; Answer Keys: Student Edition, p. 107

Focus: Listening comprehension of new vocabulary about table settings

Suggestions: Before playing the audio or reading the *script* to the class, introduce the artwork by calling out food items and asking students to name the utensil they would use for that item.

🔊 **Script and Answers:**

1. El plato está debajo del azúcar. *(falso)*
2. El cuchillo está al lado del plato. *(cierto)*
3. La sal está, pero la pimienta no está. *(falso)*
4. El tenedor está encima de la servilleta. *(cierto)*
5. El vaso está encima de la taza. *(falso)*
6. El menú no está en la mesa. *(cierto)*
7. La cuchara está al lado del cuchillo. *(cierto)*

ENRICH YOUR TEACHING

Teacher-to-Teacher

Have students bring in pictures of families from magazines. Have them label the family members and write a physical description of each person. Have them share their descriptions in small groups.

21st Century Skills

Initiative and Self-Direction Remind students of the various study tools available in **realidades.com** to help them monitor their own understanding and learning needs, such as the eText with embedded audio files, and the flashcards.

Videohistoria 🔊

Core Instruction

Standards: 1.2

Resources: Voc. and Gram. Transparencies 106–107; Audio Program DVD: Cap. 5B, Track 5; Answer Keys: Student Edition, p. 108

Focus: Presenting additional contextualized vocabulary and grammar; previewing the video

Suggestions:

Pre-reading: Have students scan the *Videohistoria* for three expressions the waiter uses. Point out to the students that since the video takes place in Texas, where there are many people of Mexican descent, the video characters use the word **mesero** instead of **camarero.**

Discuss the *Antes de leer* questions.

Answers:
1. unsure of himself; nervous
2. enchiladas, hamburgers
3. Yes, they are smiling.

En el restaurante Casa Río

La familia de Angélica come la cena en este restaurante. Lee lo que pasa durante la comida.

Antes de leer

Strategy **Scanning** You can use scanning to help you get an idea of what you might find in a reading. Think about what a waiter might say to you when you order in a restaurant.

- Look quickly through the dialogue and find three expressions that the waiter uses.

Before you read the *Videohistoria,* use the photos to help you answer the following questions.

1. How do you think the waiter is feeling when he first comes to the table?

2. What are some different foods available at this restaurant?

3. Are the members of the family enjoying their food? Why or why not?

DIFFERENTIATED INSTRUCTION

Multiple Intelligences
Verbal/Linguistic: Have students write an original conversation using the vocabulary presented in the video. Help them focus on spelling and vocabulary. Students can work on this skit throughout the chapter.

Heritage Language Learners
Have students work together to create a menu, in Spanish, offering a variety of foods from Spanish-speaking countries. Encourage students to include their favorites. Help students focus on spelling.

Luis: Bienvenidos al restaurante Casa Río. Soy Luis, su mesero. Hoy es mi primer día de trabajo. Estoy un poco nervioso. El menú está en la mesa.

> **También se dice . . .**
>
> **el/la camarero, -a = el/la mesero, -a** *(México, Puerto Rico);*
> **el/la mozo, -a** *(Argentina, Puerto Rico, Bolivia)*

Luis: ¿Qué va a pedir Ud. de bebida?

Papá: ¡Uy! Tengo calor. Para mí, un té helado.

Mamá: Y yo tengo frío. Para mí, café.

Luis: Y ahora . . . , ¿qué desean Uds. de plato principal?

Angélica: Quisiera el arroz con pollo.

Esteban: Para mí, una hamburguesa con papas fritas.

Luis: ¿Y qué desea Ud.?

Cristina: ¿Me trae las fajitas de pollo, por favor?

Luis: ¡Muy bien!

sesenta y siete 67
Capítulo 5B

Suggestions:

Reading: Read the captions with students or play the audio. Using the transparencies and nonverbal clues, help students understand the new words in blue type.

Post-reading: Complete *Actividades* 3–5 to check comprehension.

Teacher-to-Teacher

Whenever you have an opportunity, explain to students that different Spanish words are used in various parts of the Spanish-speaking world. ***Camarero(a)*** is used in most Spanish-speaking countries. Other words for "server" or "waiter" are ***mesero(a), mozo(a),*** or ***joven.*** When in doubt, it is fine to say ***caballero, señor,*** or ***señorita.***

Pre-AP* Support

- **Learning Objective:** Interpersonal Speaking
- **Activity:** Have students create a short dialogue based upon Scenes 1-2 in the video. One student will assume the role of the waiter, who will greet the client, and take his or her order. The other student will be the client. In the new scene, the client is undecided about what he or she wants to drink, and changes the order several times.
- ***Pre-AP* Resource Book:** Comprehensive guide to Pre-AP* vocabulary skill development, pp. 51–57

ENRICH YOUR TEACHING

Culture Note

An ***enchilada*** is typically a corn tortilla rolled around meat and cheese, covered in chili sauce, and topped with chopped onions, cheese, or sour cream. This is similar to ***papadzules,*** a traditional Mayan dish that is still strongly associated with the Yucatan region.

Papadzules are corn tortillas dipped in pumpkin seed sauce, rolled around chopped boiled egg, and smothered in tomato sauce. The ancient Maya reserved ***papadzules,*** which means "food of the nobles," for special occasions and royalty.

Video ▶

Core Instruction

Standards: 1.2

Resources: Teacher's Resource Book: Video Script, p. 58; Video Program: Cap. 5B; Video Program Teacher's Guide: Cap. 5B

Focus: Comprehending a story about ordering food in a restaurant

Suggestions:

Pre-viewing: Ask students if they have ever gone to a restaurant and had a server who was inexperienced.

Viewing: Show the video once without pausing. Show it again, stopping to check for comprehension. Ask students if Luis shows signs of nervousness.

Post-viewing: Complete the Video Activities in the *Communication Workbook*.

3 Standards: 1.2

Resources: Answer Keys: Student Edition, p. 108

Focus: Verifying understanding of the *Videohistoria*

Suggestions: Before beginning the activity, have students scan each sentence for key words that will help them understand it. When reviewing, ask that students point out where they found the information for the answer.

Answers:

1. mesero   4. mesero
2. cliente   5. cliente
3. mesero   6. mesero

Extension: Prepare additional *mesero / cliente* sentences and continue the activity.

Esteban: Señor, me faltan un cuchillo y un tenedor.
Luis: ¡Ah, sí! En un momento le traigo un cuchillo y un tenedor.

Luis: ¿Y para quién son las enchiladas?
Angélica: Creo que son para el señor de pelo castaño.
Luis: ¡Oh! ¡Gracias!
Angélica: De nada.

Luis: ¿Necesitan algo más? ¿Y cómo está la comida?
Mamá: La comida aquí es deliciosa. ¡Qué rica!

Luis: Ahora, ¿desean postre?
Mamá: Y otro café, por favor.
Papá: Para mí, nada. Pero quisiera un café, yo también. Ahora tengo sueño.

 68 sesenta y ocho
Tema 5 • Fiesta en familia

DIFFERENTIATED INSTRUCTION

Advanced Learners

Give students copies of the Video Script. Have them practice the script to later present to the class. You might have them practice saying each sentence along with the video, trying to mimic it exactly.

Heritage Language Learners

Ask students to write about a personal or invented family outing to a favorite restaurant. The students should include the name of the restaurant, who goes, and the foods and beverages ordered. Encourage students to include any funny or interesting events that occur during the meal.

▼3 Leer • Escribir

¿Mesero o cliente?

Read each of the following sentences from the *Videohistoria*. Number your paper from 1–6. If the sentence is something the waiter says, write *mesero* and if it is something one of the customers says, write *cliente*.

1. Bienvenidos al restaurante Casa Río.
2. ¿Me trae las fajitas de pollo, por favor?
3. ¿Necesitan algo más?
4. ¿Qué desean Uds. de plato principal?
5. Señor, me faltan un cuchillo y un tenedor.
6. ¿Y para quién son las enchiladas?

▼4 Leer • Escribir

¿Qué piden?

Help Luis by making a list of the food and drinks that Angélica's family orders. Copy this bill on your own paper and complete it based on the *Videohistoria*.

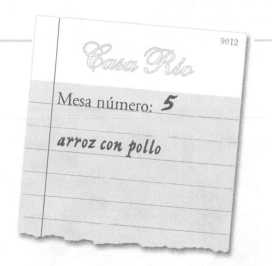

9012

Casa Río

Mesa número: **5**

arroz con pollo

▼5 Escribir • Hablar

¿Comprendes?

1. ¿Cómo se llama el restaurante?
2. ¿Cómo se llama el camarero?
3. ¿Por qué está nervioso el camarero?
4. ¿Quiénes quieren café?
5. ¿Quién tiene sueño?
6. Según la mamá, ¿cómo es la comida?

Más práctica

realidades.com | print

Instant Check	✔	
Guided WB pp. 23–26	✔	✔
Core WB pp. 12–13	✔	✔
Comm. WB pp. 12–14, 15	✔	✔
Hispanohablantes WB p. 193		✔

ENRICH YOUR TEACHING

Teacher-to-Teacher

Have students create their own menus by using the vocabulary from *Tema 3* in *Realidades* A. Using the *Videohistoria* as a model, have them write a dialogue between a server in a restaurant and a client. You may want to brainstorm a list of words to describe food and drinks. Then have half of the class pretend to be happy with their meals and the other half of the class pretend to be disappointed.

▼4 Standards: 1.2, 1.3

Resources: Answer Keys: Student Edition, p. 108

Focus: Writing vocabulary words

Suggestions: Space permitting, have students make two columns, one for food, the other for beverages. Classifying the foods and beverages will help students remember the words.

Answers:

Foods: arroz con pollo, hamburguesa con papas fritas, las fajitas de pollo, postre
Beverages: té helado, café

▼5 Standards: 1.1, 1.3

Resources: Answer Keys: Student Edition, p. 108

Focus: Reading for understanding

Suggestions: Before beginning the activity, brainstorm a list of question words. For each word, have students say what they need to look for to answer the question. For example, if the question begins with **quién,** they need to look for a person. To review, have students point out where they found the information for each answer.

Answers:

1. Casa Río
2. Luis
3. porque es su primer día de trabajo
4. Mamá y Papá
5. Papá
6. La comida es deliciosa.

Extension: Have students write at least one more question for *Actividad* 5 for which they find the answer in the *Videohistoria*. Then ask each student to read aloud the question(s) he or she wrote and have the rest of the class find the answer.

Additional Resources

- Communication Wbk.: Audio Act. 5, p. 15
- Teacher's Resource Book: Audio Script, pp. 55–56
- Audio Program DVD: Cap. 5B, Track 7

✓ ASSESSMENT

Quiz: Vocabulary Recognition
- Prueba 5B-1: pp. 133–134

▶ Listen to and write descriptions of people
▶ Read and understand a conversation in a restaurant
▶ Explain what you like to order in a restaurant
▶ Play a guessing game about table settings
▶ Write recommendations based on a restaurant review

INTERACTIVE WHITEBOARD
Vocabulary Activities 5B

6 Standards: 1.3

Resources: Answer Keys: Student Edition, p. 109

Focus: Writing descriptions of people

Suggestions: Brainstorm a list of adjectives that can be used to describe people. Focus on age, height, and hair color.

Answers:
1. El Sr. Ortega es viejo y tiene pelo canoso.
2. La señora Ortega es vieja y tiene pelo canoso.
3. Milagros es guapa y tiene pelo castaño.
4. Luz es pelirroja y tiene pelo largo.
5. Eduardo es rubio y alto.
6. Daniela es joven y baja.

BELLRINGER REVIEW

Show Voc. and Gram. Transparency 83, (frame 2). Have students give names to the students pictured and write one true statement and one false statement about them using descriptive words found on p. 64. Ask a partner to respond with **"Es cierto"** or **"Es falso."**

7 Standards: 1.2

Resources: Teacher's Resource Book: Audio Script, p. 55; Audio Program DVD: Cap. 5B, Track 6; Answer Keys: Student Edition, p. 109

Focus: Listening to descriptions of people

Suggestions: Before playing the audio or reading the script, have students look at the pictures, concentrating on hair color, height, and age of each person. Point out to students that there are six pictures, but only five descriptions.

◀)) Script and Answers:

1. Es muy guapo. Tiene el pelo negro. Le encanta hablar por teléfono. ¿Cuántos años tiene? Creo que tiene 20 años. Es joven. *(Alejandro)*
2. Tiene el pelo canoso. Ni es alto ni bajo. Tiene 65 años pero le encanta montar en bicicleta. ¡Qué gracioso es! *(Jorge)*
3. La joven es baja. Le gusta mucho esquiar. Sólo tiene 14 años. Es rubia y tiene el pelo largo. *(Rosalía)*
4. ¡Qué seria es ella! Tiene el pelo castaño y corto. Le encanta leer. Creo que tiene 60 años. *(María Elena)*
5. Es pelirroja y muy guapa. Tiene 18 años. Le gusta mucho dibujar. *(Lucía)*

Extension: Bring in photos and ask students to describe the people.

Vocabulario en uso

▼ 6 Escribir

Las personas en el restaurante

Look at the scene of the restaurant below. Number your paper from 1–6 and write a sentence to describe the following people.

Modelo
Daniela
Daniela es joven y tiene pelo negro.

1. el Sr. Ortega
2. la Sra. Ortega
3. Milagros
4. Luz
5. Eduardo
6. el Sr. Ramos

70 setenta
Tema 5 • Fiesta en familia

DIFFERENTIATED INSTRUCTION

Advanced Learners/Pre-AP*

Have students find five pictures of people in your school. They can be members of the volleyball team, the Spanish Club, or the football team, or they may just be of friends. Using the vocabulary introduced in this lesson, have students write captions for each picture.

Heritage Language Learners

Ask students to write a short paragraph describing three people. Suggestions include a favorite musician, artist, author, sports figure, or someone they see in the community, on a bus, or at the grocery store, etc. Check each description for proper spelling and grammar.

▼7 | ◀)) | Escuchar

¿Quiénes son?

You will hear descriptions of the people in the drawings below. Number your paper from 1–5, and write the name of the person who is being described.

> **También se dice . . .**
>
> **pelirrojo, -a** = colorado, -a *(Argentina);*
>   colorín, colorina *(Chile)*
>
> **el pelo** = el cabello *(muchos países)*
>
> **rubio, -a** = güero, -a *(México)*

Eduardo, 15   **Rosalía, 14**   **Lucía, 18**   **Alejandro, 20**   **María Elena, 60**   **Jorge, 65**

▼8 Escribir

Descripciones

Choose four people from the drawings above and write three sentences to describe each person.

Modelo

El joven muy alto es Eduardo. Tiene 15 años. Tiene el pelo castaño. Le gusta jugar al tenis.

> **¿Recuerdas?**
>
> Adjectives agree in number and gender with the nouns they modify.

▼9 | ♲ | Leer • Escribir

Las asociaciones

Number your paper from 1–7. Complete the following paragraph with the appropriate word from the list.

Yo soy un __1.__ y trabajo en el restaurante todos los viernes. Tengo el pelo __2.__ y soy bajo. Los viernes Carlitos y el Sr. Mendoza vienen a comer en el restaurante. El chico es __3.__ pero su abuelo es viejo. Al Sr. Mendoza le gusta pedir un plato de bistec con papas fritas y una __4.__ de café. Siempre necesita __5.__ para las papas y __6.__ para el café. A Carlitos le gusta pedir arroz con pollo de plato principal, y helado con fresas de __7.__ .

postre	sal
taza	camarero
corto	joven
baja	azúcar

setenta y uno **71**
Capítulo 5B

Practice and Communicate   5B

▼8 Standards: 1.1, 1.2, 1.3

Focus: Using vocabulary for descriptions

Suggestions: Brainstorm a list of two feminine nouns and two masculine nouns. Have students suggest an adjective to describe each word on the list. Then write the plural of each word and have students make the adjectives agree.

Answers will vary.

Common Errors: Remind students to make adjectives agree with nouns. Point out that in *Ellas tienen el pelo rubio,* **rubio** agrees with **pelo** and not with **ellas,** but in *Ellas son rubias,* **rubias** agrees with **ellas.**

▼9 Standards: 1.2, 1.3

Resources: Answer Keys: Student Edition, p. 110

Focus: Using new vocabulary in context

Recycle: *tener, ser, gustar*

Suggestions: Remind students to read each sentence completely before trying to fill in the missing word. Discuss clues that might help students, such as the meaning of the rest of the sentence or an article like *un.*

Answers:
1. camarero
2. corto
3. joven
4. taza
5. sal
6. azúcar
7. postre

ENRICH YOUR TEACHING

Teacher-to-Teacher

Go around the room and describe different students. Have students respond with *cierto* or *falso* according to the information you give about students. For example: *Ella es alta, ¿cierto o falso?*

21st Century Skills

Technology Literacy Have students use the digital technology within **realidades.com** to access and manage the audio files, videos, and activities that support learning the new vocabulary.

10 Standards: 1.3

Resources: Answer Keys: Student Edition, p. 110

Focus: Using vocabulary for utensils

Suggestions: Point out that the light outlines with the question marks above them represent the missing items students are to request.

Answers:
1. ¿Me trae una taza, por favor?
2. ¿Me trae un tenedor, por favor?
3. ¿Me trae un cuchillo, por favor?
4. ¿Me trae un vaso, por favor?
5. ¿Me trae un plato, por favor?
6. ¿Me trae una cuchara, por favor?

Fondo cultural

Standards: 2.1, 4.2

Suggestions: Point out that it is always a good idea to use the *Ud.* form of the verb when talking to a server as well as to use polite expressions such as *con permiso* and *por favor.*

Answers will vary but may include eye contact or polite expressions, such as "excuse me," to get someone's attention.

Pre-AP* Support

- **Learning Objective:** Interpretive: Print and Audio
- **Activity:** Have students look at the two photos on pp. 72 and 73. Ask them to write one descriptive sentence about each. Then, have volunteers read their sentences to the class so that class members can indicate which scene is being described.
- **Pre-AP* Resource Book:** Comprehensive guide to Pre-AP* communication skill development, pp. 10–57

▼10 Escribir

¿Me trae . . . ?

You ordered the following items in a restaurant, but your waiter has not brought you all the utensils you need for eating them. Ask him for the missing items.

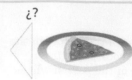

Modelo
¿Me trae una servilleta?

1.

2.

3.

4.

5.

6.

▼Fondo Cultural | Costa Rica | Colombia

En el restaurante Getting a server's attention at a restaurant in a Spanish-speaking country sometimes differs from how it is done in other cultures. For example, in Costa Rica people often make a *pfft* sound to get a server's attention, while in Colombia people may raise or clap their hands. Be careful in using this sort of attention-getting device—it may seem rude when done by someone from outside the culture!

- How do you get a server's attention in a restaurant? Compare this to what is acceptable in some Spanish-speaking countries.

Un restaurante en la Argentina

72 setenta y dos
Tema 5 • Fiesta en familia

DIFFERENTIATED INSTRUCTION

Advanced Learners

Have students work in groups to play a memory game. The first person asks the waiter to bring one item. The next student asks for the same item and adds one more. The third asks for the first two items plus an additional one, and so on.

Heritage Language Learners

Ask students to share with the class their knowledge of polite ways to get the attention of a waiter in their heritage country. Planning this activity in advance will allow students time to ask at home if they do not know the information.

▼11 | 🗣️👥 | Leer · Hablar

En el restaurante

With a partner, read the conversation between a waiter and two young people. Match what the waiter says with the logical response from the customers to recreate the conversation.

Un restaurante en la Argentina

El camarero

1. Buenas noches. ¿Qué desean de bebida?
2. ¿Qué desea pedir de plato principal?
3. ¡Ay, señor! Le falta el cuchillo, ¿no?
4. ¿Le gusta la sopa?
5. Señorita, ¿qué desea Ud. de postre?
6. Señor, ¿le traigo otra bebida?
7. ¿Desean Uds. algo más?
8. Gracias por venir a nuestro restaurante.

Los jóvenes

a. Sí, está deliciosa. Umm. ¡Qué rica!
b. No, sólo la cuenta, por favor.
c. Quisiera el arroz con pollo, por favor.
d. De nada. Hasta luego.
e. Un helado, por favor.
f. Sí. ¿Me trae uno, por favor?
g. Para mí, un refresco y, para la señorita, un té helado.
h. Sí, por favor. Tengo mucha sed.

▼12 | ♻️ | Escribir · Hablar

¿Qué te gusta pedir?

Write a sentence telling what you like to order in each of the following situations.

Modelo
Cuando tengo hambre, me gusta pedir pizza en un restaurante.

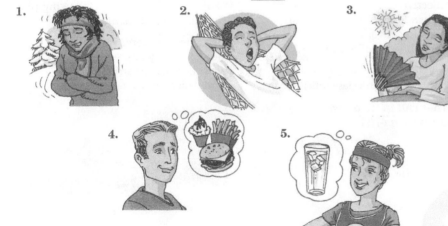

1.
2.
3.
4.
5.

setenta y tres **73**
Capítulo 5B

ENRICH YOUR TEACHING

Culture Note

Many restaurants in the Spanish-speaking world combine fine dining with a distinctive cultural performance. For example, in cities like Buenos Aires and Mendoza (both in Argentina), visitors and locals are given an opportunity to experience the *tango* while enjoying typical cuisine. During the meal, *tango* music is performed while several dancers demonstrate Argentina's national dance.

13 Standards: 1.1

Resources: Teacher's Resource Book: GramActiva BLM, p. 65

Focus: Using *faltar* to talk about missing items

Suggestions: After having students review the *Nota,* arrange pictures of table items on your desk, leaving out two items. Ask students: *¿Qué me faltan?* After students answer correctly, place the missing items back on the desk. Then remove one item and ask: *¿Qué me falta?*

Answers will vary.

Exploración del lenguaje
Core Instruction

Standards: 4.1

Resources: Answer Keys: Student Edition, p. 110

Suggestions: Remind students that since they are adding *-ísimo* to adjectives, the ending must agree in number and gender with the noun it is describing. Point out to students that *-ísimo* always has an accent mark.

Answers:
1. perezosísimo
2. interesantísimos
3. aburridísima
4. simpatiquísimas

▼ **13** | 👥 | **Hablar**

Juego

❶ Work in groups of three or four. Your teacher will give you copies of pictures of various table items. Cut or tear the pictures apart to make cards.

❷ Arrange the pictures in a table setting on a desk. While the other players have their backs turned, hide one or more of the cards. Then ask: *¿Qué me falta?* The first player to say correctly *Te falta(n)...* and name the missing item(s) receives a point.

❸ Put the hidden items back on the desk and continue playing until all players have had a chance to hide items. The player with the most points is the winner.

> **Nota**
> When one item is missing, use *me/te falta.* When more than one item is missing, use *me/te faltan.*

▼ **Exploración del lenguaje**

Adjectives ending in *-ísimo*

Muy + an adjective can be expressed in another way by adding the correct form of *-ísimo* to the adjective. The *-ísimo* ending conveys the idea of "extremely."

> un chico muy guapo = un chico guap**ísimo**
> una clase muy difícil = una clase dificil**ísima**

Adjectives that end in *-co or -ca* have a spelling change to *-qu-*. The *-o* or *-a* is dropped.

> unos pasteles muy ri**co**s
> = unos pasteles ri**qu**ísimos

Try it out! Rework the following phrases using the correct *-ísimo* form.

> un perro muy perezoso = ¿ ?
> dos libros muy interesantes = ¿ ?
> una clase muy aburrida = ¿ ?
> unas chicas muy simpáticas = ¿ ?

-ísimo
-ísima

DIFFERENTIATED INSTRUCTION

Heritage Language Learners
Have students create a radio ad for a restaurant specializing in food from their heritage countries. The ad should include a description of the food, the hours of operation, and the location of the restaurant. You might want to have students record the ad and play it for the class. Emphasize that they must speak clearly.

Students with Learning Difficulties
You may want to have students do the second part of *Actividad* 15 first as a written activity. They can then use the answers to help them form complex sentences.

▼14 | ♻ | Leer • Pensar • Escribir

Café Buen Libro

Read the review of the *Café Buen Libro*. Then, based on what the people listed below are looking for, decide whether or not you would recommend that they go to this café. Number your paper from 1–6 and write *sí* if you recommend the café to that person, or *no* if you do not.

Café Buen Libro
Nuevo León, 28

✓✓ ++ $ ☺☺

Es un café tranquilo con un ambiente* intelectual donde puedes pasar el tiempo en la compañía de un buen amigo o un buen libro. Los precios son muy razonables. Puedes comer un sándwich, una ensalada, un postre riquísimo o simplemente beber un café. También tienen lo último en libros, videos y música. Un "plus" es la presentación de grupos musicales los fines de semana.

Ambiente
aburrido ✓
tranquilo ✓✓
fantástico ✓✓✓
Comida y bebida
regular +
buena ++
excelente +++
Precios
barato $
medio $$
caro $$$
Servicio
regular ☺
bueno ☺☺
superior ☺☺☺

*atmosphere

1. **Carmen:** "Quisiera comer un bistec sabroso".
2. **Marta:** "Me encanta escuchar música".
3. **Diego:** "Tengo muchísima hambre y poco tiempo".
4. **Lupe:** "Me gusta pasar tiempo con otras personas interesantes y graciosas".
5. **Ana:** "No tengo mucho dinero (*money*) ahora".
6. Y a ti, ¿te gustaría ir al Café Buen Libro? ¿Por qué?

▼15 | (Talk!) | ♻ | Escribir • Hablar

¿Quién viene a la fiesta?

❶ Imagine you are planning a party and can invite any three people you want. They can be famous people who live today, people who lived long ago, or people you know personally. On a sheet of paper, write their names and why you want to invite each one.

Modelo
Albert Einstein viene a la fiesta porque es inteligente y talentoso.

❷ Now, work with a partner to talk about who is coming to the party. Take turns asking and answering each other's questions.

▶ **Modelo**
A —*¿Quién viene a la fiesta?*
B —*Albert Einstein viene.*
A —*¿Por qué?*
B —*Porque él es inteligente y talentoso.*

setenta y cinco **75**
Capítulo 5B

---

14 Standards: 1.2, 1.3, 4.1
Resources: Answer Keys: Student Edition, p. 111
Focus: Reading, writing, and speaking about a place to eat
Recycle: Foods; saying what you like
Suggestions: Have students look at the picture and give their opinions on what they think the restaurant is like. Review the symbols to the right of the text. How does the critic rate *Café Buen Libro?* Remind students to use cognates to help them understand the reading.
Answers:

| 1. no | 3. no | 5. sí |
| 2. sí | 4. sí | 6. Answers will vary. |

Extension: Have students choose a restaurant that they have been to and write a brief review. Encourage students to create their own rating system.

15 Standards: 1.1, 1.3
Focus: Practicing the verb **venir** and describing people
Recycle: Describing people
Suggestions: Before starting the activity, have students make a list of adjectives to describe people. Remind them that they can use more than one adjective to describe a person.

Answers will vary.

Additional Resources

• Communication Wbk.: Audio Act. 6, pp. 15–16
• Teacher's Resource Book: Audio Script, p. 56, Communicative Pair Activity BLMs, pp. 60–61
• Audio Program DVD: Cap. 5B, Track 8

✓ ASSESSMENT

Prueba 5B-2 with Study Plan (online only)

Quiz: Vocabulary Production
• Prueba 5B-2: pp. 135–136

ENRICH YOUR TEACHING

Culture Note

La Guía del Ocio is a guide to what's going on in major cities in Spain. It comes out every week and lists current films, plays, shows, and musical events. It also includes a listing of most restaurants and cafés with brief descriptions for each. It is extremely useful for tourists looking to make the most of their stay.

21st Century Skills

Media Literacy Have students working in small groups research Web sites in specific Spanish-speaking cities to find restaurants they would like to visit. They should present their selected restaurants to the class and explain why they chose them.

Gramática

Core Instruction

Standards: 4.1

Resources: Voc. and Gram. Transparency 108; Teacher's Resource Book: Video Script, p. 58; Video Program: Cap. 5B

INTERACTIVE WHITEBOARD

Grammar Activities 5B

Suggestions: After presenting the forms of *venir* to the class, ask volunteers to put the forms of *tener* and *venir* on the board. Have students compare them. Use the transparency to reinforce the verb.

▼16 Standards: 1.2, 1.3

Resources: Answer Keys: Student Edition, p. 111
Focus: Using the verb *venir*
Suggestions: Have students first read through the entire note for meaning.
Answers:

1. vengo	3. viene	5. vienen
2. venimos	4. vienen	6. viene

▼17 Standards: 1.2, 1.3

Resources: Teacher's Resource Book: Audio Script, p. 56; Audio Program DVD: Cap. 5B, Track 9
Focus: Listening to and writing family descriptions
Recycle: Describing people; names of family members
Suggestions: Play the audio or read the script several times. The first time, have students take brief notes. Have them listen again, write the full descriptions, and complete their drawings. Ask them to listen a final time to check for accuracy.

Script and Answers:

1. Mi amigo Roberto viene. Él es altísimo y muy artístico.
2. La hermana de Roberto viene. Ella es muy alta, rubia y guapa.
3. Dos primos de Roberto vienen. Tienen el pelo corto. Uno es ordenado y el otro primo es desordenado.
4. El hermano de Roberto viene también. Él es bajo y tiene el pelo negro y largo.

Gramática

▼ Objectives
▶ Read about and discuss celebrations and preparations
▶ Listen to a description of a family

The verb *venir*

Use *venir* to say that someone is coming to a place or an event.

¿A qué hora vienes a mi casa?
When are you coming to my house?

Siempre vengo a esta playa.
I always come to this beach.

Here are all the present-tense forms:

(yo)	vengo	(nosotros) (nosotras)	venimos
(tú)	vienes	(vosotros) (vosotras)	venís
Ud. (él) (ella)	viene	Uds. (ellos) (ellas)	vienen

Más ayuda **realidades.com**

 GramActiva Video
Tutorial: Irregular verbs
Animated Verbs

GramActiva Activity

▼16 | Leer • Escribir

¿Cómo vienen?

Your friend Antonio has invited you and some friends to his family's house for a party this weekend. Number your paper from 1–6 and complete his note with the appropriate forms of the verb *venir* to explain how and when everyone is coming.

¡Hola a todos!

La cena es este fin de semana. Yo __1.__ en bicicleta con mi amiga Marta. Nosotros __2.__ a las dos porque ella trabaja hasta la una. Mi abuela __3.__ en tren¹ con mis tíos. Ellos __4.__ a las once para ayudar² con la cena. Mis hermanitos también __5.__ en tren con mis tíos. Mi hermana mayor Cecilia __6.__ en autobús más tarde.

¡Nos vemos el sábado!

¹train ²to help

▼17 | Escuchar • Escribir • Dibujar

Escucha, escribe y dibuja

Roberto, a friend of Antonio, is also going to Antonio's party with his family. You will hear a description of Roberto's family. On a sheet of paper, write the four descriptions you hear and then draw a picture of the family. Compare your drawing with a partner's.

76 setenta y seis
Tema 5 • Fiesta en familia

DIFFERENTIATED INSTRUCTION

Advanced Learners

Have students write a letter to a friend describing a family party. Students should tell at what time different members of the family are coming and what each person is going to bring.

Students with Special Needs

For *Actividad* 17, if students are unable to draw the picture, provide them with copies of three or four different pictures, and have them choose the one that matches the description.

▼18 | ♻ | Escribir

¿A qué hora vienen?

There is a party at your school on Saturday night. On a separate sheet of paper, write sentences telling when the following people will come to the party.

Tomás

Modelo
Tomás viene a la fiesta a las siete y media.

 1. **Mariana y Carmen**

 2. **yo**

 3. **Verónica**

 4. **tú**

 5. **José**

6. **los chicos**

18 Standards: 1.3
Resources: Answer Keys: Student Edition, p. 112
Focus: Telling when people will arrive
Recycle: Telling time
Suggestions: Point out what will change with each substitution.
Answers:
1. Mariana y Carmen vienen a la fiesta a las ocho menos cuarto (las siete y cuarenta y cinco).
2. Yo vengo … a las siete.
3. Veronica viene … a las ocho y cuarto.
4. Tú vienes … a las ocho.
5. José viene … a las nueve y media.
6. Los chicos vienen … a las nueve menos cuarto (las ocho y cuarenta y cinco).

▼19 | 🗣 | ♻ | Hablar

¿Qué traen a tu casa?

You are at a friend's house. Talk about what different people bring when they come over to visit.

 Modelo

A —*Cuando tus tíos vienen a tu casa, ¿traen algo?*
B —*Sí, generalmente traen el postre.*
o: —*No, generalmente no traen nada.*

Nota
Traer, "to bring," follows the pattern of *-er* verbs except for the irregular *yo* form: *traigo.*
• Mañana **traigo** pasteles para todos.
• Y tú, ¿**traes** bebidas?

Estudiante A
1. tu(s) abuelo(s)
2. tu mejor amigo(a)
3. tus amigos
4. tus tíos
5. tus primos
6. los amigos de tus padres

Estudiante B
el plato principal
el postre
un regalo
flores
nada

¡Respuesta personal!

19 Standards: 1.1
Resources: Answer Keys: Student Edition, p. 112
Focus: Using the verb ***traer*** in conversation
Recycle: Foods; family members
Suggestions: Brainstorm items that one might bring to another's home.
Answers will vary, but verb forms are:
1. tu abuelo viene / trae; tus abuelos vienen / traen
2. tu mejor amigo(a) viene / trae
3. tus amigos vienen / traen
4. tus tíos vienen / traen
5. tus primos vienen / traen
6. los amigos de tus padres vienen / traen

▼20 | ♻ | Escribir · Hablar

¿Quiénes vienen?

You are talking with friends at a school party. Answer the following questions.

1. ¿Quiénes vienen a la fiesta? ¿A qué hora vienen?
2. ¿Vienen todos los profesores a la fiesta? ¿Qué traen ellos?
3. ¿Traen los estudiantes pizza o sándwiches? ¿Frutas o pasteles?
4. ¿Quién trae las decoraciones? ¿Qué traes tú?

Más práctica (GO)

realidades.com | print

Instant Check	✔	
Guided WB pp. 27–28	✔	✔
Core WB p. 14	✔	✔
Comm. WB pp. 16, 19	✔	✔
Hispanohablantes **WB** pp. 194–197		✔

setenta y siete **77**
Capítulo 5B

20 Standards: 1.1, 1.3
Focus: Using ***venir*** and ***traer***
Recycle: Telling time; foods
Suggestions: Have students read all of the questions before they begin.
Answers will vary.

ENRICH YOUR TEACHING

Culture Note

In most Spanish-speaking countries, people are generally more relaxed about arriving on time to a social event. Guests are not expected to arrive at the designated time, but just a bit later. However, in a business setting, punctuality is expected.

21st Century Skills

Initiative and Self-Direction Have students use the many tools available in **realidades.com** to support grammar learning, such as the online text with audio and the *GramActiva video*, as well as the online games. Have students track the different tools they use and how effective each is, so they can establish over time what type of learners they are. This will help them in all areas of learning.

Additional Resources
• Communication Wbk.: Audio Act. 7, p. 16
• Teacher's Resource Book: Audio Script, pp. 56–57
• Audio Program DVD: Cap. 5B, Track 10

✔ ASSESSMENT
Prueba 5B-3 with Study Plan (online only)
Quiz: The verb *venir*
• Prueba 5B-3: p. 137

Gramática

Core Instruction

Standards: 4.1

Resources: Voc. and Gram. Transparency 109; Teacher's Resource Book: Video Script, pp. 58–59; Video Program: Cap. 5B

INTERACTIVE WHITEBOARD

Grammar Activities 5B

Suggestions: Write several sample sentences on the board, leaving out *ser* or *estar.* Have students tell you which verb to use and the reason for their decision. Ask volunteers for sample sentences. Use the transparency to reinforce *ser* and *estar.* Use the *GramActiva* Video as a follow-up to your presentation.

21 Standards: 1.3

Focus: Using *ser* and *estar* in context

Suggestions: Remind students that *estar* is used for conditions that can change. *Ser* is used for characteristics that do not usually change. Students may benefit from adding the phrases "lasts a short time" and "lasts forever" in parentheses, as column heads.

Answers will vary, but the usual verb-adjective combinations are:

estar: cansado(a), contento(a), enfermo(a), nervioso(a), ocupado(a)

ser: alto(a), bajo(a), desordenado(a), guapo (a), moreno(a), ordenado(a), pelirrojo(a), popular, reservado(a), rubio(a), trabajador(a)

▼ Objectives

▶ Discuss and describe people and foods
▶ Read an interview and a recipe
▶ Exchange information while ordering and discussing food in a restaurant

Gramática

The verbs *ser* and *estar*

You know that both *ser* and *estar* mean "to be." Their uses, however, are different.

(yo)	soy	(nosotros) (nosotras)	somos
(tú)	eres	(vosotros) (vosotras)	sois
Ud. (él) (ella)	es	Uds. (ellos) (ellas)	son

(yo)	estoy	(nosotros) (nosotras)	estamos
(tú)	estás	(vosotros) (vosotras)	estáis
Ud. (él) (ella)	está	Uds. (ellos) (ellas)	están

Use *ser* to talk about characteristics that generally do not change. *Ser* is used for descriptions that are not about conditions or location. For example:

• who a person is or what a person is like
• what something is or what something is like
• where a person or thing is from

Teresa **es** mi prima. **Es** muy graciosa.

Los tacos **son** mi comida favorita. **Son** riquísimos.

Mis tíos **son** de México. **Son** muy simpáticos.

Use *estar* to talk about conditions that tend to change. For example:

• how a person feels
• where a person or thing is

¿Dónde **está** Mariana? No **está** aquí.

No puede venir hoy porque **está** muy enferma.

Más ayuda **realidades.com**

▶ *GramActiva* Video
Tutorial: *Ser* and *estar*
Animated Verbs

🔊 *Canción de hip hop:* Camarero

✎ *GramActiva Activity*

▼ 21 Escribir

Mi amigo(a) y yo

❶ Copy this chart on a sheet of paper. Fill in the chart correctly by choosing words from the box at right that best describe what one of your friends is like and how he or she is feeling.

Mi amigo(a) está	Mi amigo(a) es
cansado(a)	trabajador(a)

❷ Choose words from the list that describe you and write sentences to tell how you are feeling and what you are like.

Modelo

Yo soy trabajador. Estoy muy cansado.

alto, -a	ocupado, -a
bajo, -a	ordenado, -a
contento, -a	pelirrojo, -a
cansado, -a	popular
desordenado, -a	reservado, -a
enfermo, -a	rubio, -a

¡Respuesta personal!

DIFFERENTIATED INSTRUCTION

Advanced Learners

Have students bring in photos of their family members or friends and describe them to the class using *ser* and *estar.* They should include information on where each person is from, what the person is like, and where he or she is. Encourage volunteers to present their photos to the class.

Students with Special Needs

If you have a visually impaired student, pair him or her with another student who can give a description of the picture in *Actividad* 22. Have students continue working together to complete the activity.

▼**22** | ♻ | Leer • Escribir

En el restaurante mexicano

Read the following descriptions of people in a restaurant in San Antonio, Texas. Based on the picture below, write sentences telling where the people are in the restaurant.

Modelo

El Sr. Ramos no es joven. Es muy gracioso. Está contento hoy porque está en el restaurante con su familia.

El Sr. Ramos está al lado de la mujer con pelo castaño y delante de los dos chicos jóvenes.

1. Miguelito es joven. Tiene cinco años. Su hermana está enferma pero él está de buena salud. Sus padres son muy graciosos.
2. Ana, Diana y Sabrina son hermanas. Son jóvenes y muy deportistas. Están tristes y aburridas hoy porque llueve y no pueden jugar al fútbol.

3. El Sr. Soriano es serio y muy inteligente. Quisiera comer con su familia pero su esposa y sus dos hijos están en Nueva York y él está en San Antonio para el trabajo.
4. Esteban es muy trabajador. Es alto y rubio. Tiene treinta años. No es serio pero ahora está muy ocupado.
5. Elena es joven y muy talentosa. Tiene pelo largo. Está nerviosa hoy porque tiene un concierto muy importante.

▼**23** | ♻ | Leer • Escribir

Entrevista con una chef

Number your paper 1–10. Complete the following interview with Chef Ortiz with the appropriate form of the verb *ser* or *estar*.

— Bienvenida, Chef Ortiz. ¿Cómo __1.__ Ud. hoy?

— __2.__ muy bien, gracias.

— Ud. trabaja aquí en Asunción ahora pero, ¿de dónde __3.__ Ud. originalmente?

— Mi familia y yo __4.__ del campo.

— Y ¿cuál __5.__ su trabajo aquí?

— Yo __6.__ directora de los chefs en el famoso restaurante La Capital.

— La Capital __7.__ un restaurante muy popular aquí. ¿Dónde __8.__ el restaurante?

— Al lado de la catedral.

— Los platos en su restaurante __9.__ muy típicos de Paraguay, ¿no?

— Sí, y según los clientes, la comida en nuestro restaurante __10.__ deliciosa.

Paraguay

¡Qué rico!

setenta y nueve **79**
Capítulo 5B

22 Standards: 1.2, 1.3

Focus: Writing where people are

Recycle: Location words: *al lado de, delante de, a la derecha/izquierda*

Suggestions: Have students read all five paragraphs before beginning to write. Answer any vocabulary questions they have. Encourage them to use key words to help them find the person.

Answers will vary but may include:

1. Miguelito está al lado de su papá.
2. Ana, Diana y Sabrina están a la derecha.
3. El Sr. Soriano está al lado de la ventana.
4. Esteban está detrás de la familia Ramos.
5. Elena está al lado de su amigo.

BELLRINGER REVIEW

Have students name and describe one of the characters in the illustration.

23 Standards: 1.2, 1.3

Resources: Answer Keys: Student Edition, p. 113

Focus: Reading about a chef and using present-tense forms of *estar* and *ser*

Recycle: Locations; food vocabulary

Suggestions: Remind students that after choosing the correct verb, they have to conjugate it correctly according to the subject. Review the answers with the class by having one volunteer play the role of the interviewer and another the role of Chef Ortiz.

Answers:

1. está	5. es	9. son
2. Estoy	6. soy	10. es
3. es	7. es	
4. somos	8. está	

Theme Project

Students can perform Step 4 at this point. Be sure they understand your corrections and suggestions. (For more information, see p. 30-b.)

ENRICH YOUR TEACHING

Culture Note

In many restaurants in Paraguay, you can find *sopa paraguaya,* a traditional soup. It is said that a cook for the famous military leader Mariscal Francisco Solano López (1826–1870) created the dish when the balls of corn flour in the leader's soup fell apart. The cook made another dish, *sopa paraguaya,* from the corn flour in the soup.

Teacher-to-Teacher

For practice with *estar,* have students use pictures from magazines or other sources to write questions about where people are and how they feel. Students may write the answers on the back of the pictures and play a game in two teams to see who gets the most correct answers.

24 Standards: 1.1

Focus: Talking about where people are and what they are like using **estar** and **ser**

Recycle: Names of family members

Suggestions: Say the rhyme with the class, and then ask volunteers when they would use **ser**. Focus on where a person is from and what a person is like. Remind students that adjectives agree in number and gender with the nouns they describe.

Answers will vary.

Pronunciación
Core Instruction
Standards: 4.1

Resources: Teacher's Resource Book: Audio Script, p. 57; Audio Program DVD: Cap. 5B, Track 11

Suggestions: Have students pronounce the consonants **b** and **v** and the example words. Check for correct pronunciation.

Play or read the tongue twister (**trabalenguas**) aloud and let students practice it individually. Then ask volunteers to say it to the class.

▼ 24 | Talk! 👥 | ♻ | Hablar

¿Y las otras personas?

You were supposed to meet your friend and his or her family at a café, but only your friend is there. Ask your partner questions to find out what the members of his or her family are like and why they are not at the café.

Strategy
Using rhymes
To remember the uses of *estar*, memorize this rhyme:

For how you feel
And where you are,
Always use the verb *estar*.

📹 **Modelo**
A —¿Por qué no está tú primo?
B —Porque está en la escuela.
A —¿Cómo es?
B —Mi primo es inteligente y trabajador.

Estudiante A

abuelo, -a	primo, -a
padre	hermano, -a
madre	amigo, -a
tío, -a	

¡Respuesta personal!

Estudiante B

la escuela	artístico, -a
casa	estudioso, -a
el trabajo	inteligente
la lección	perezoso, -a
la biblioteca	trabajador, -a
ocupado, -a	

¡Respuesta personal!

▼ **Pronunciación** | 🔊 | Talk!

The letters b and v

In Spanish, *b* and *v* are pronounced the same. At the beginning of a word or phrase, *b* and *v* sound like the *b* in *boy*. Listen to and say these words:

voy	vienen	viejo
bolígrafo	bien	video

In most other positions *b* and *v* have a softer "b" sound. The lips barely touch as the *b* or *v* sound is pronounced. Listen to and say these words:

abuelo	joven	globo
divertido	huevos	Alberto

Try it out! Listen to and say this *trabalenguas*:

> **Cabral clava un clavo.**
> **¿Qué clavo clava Cabral?**

DIFFERENTIATED INSTRUCTION

Advanced Learners
Have students write an e-mail to a friend explaining that they cannot get together because a family member is coming. Suggest they say what time it is and where they are, and encourage them to describe the family member.

Heritage Language Learners
Students may have problems spelling words with **b** and **v**. To help students improve their spelling, have them add words with **b** and **v** to the list provided in *Pronunciación* and make simple crossword puzzles, along with the clues. Then, have students exchange puzzles and solve them.

▼**25** Leer • Pensar

Un postre delicioso

Your grandmother has given you her recipe for *arroz con leche* and you want to try it out. But the ingredients are given in *gramos* and *litros* and you don't know what the customary measure equivalents are. Study the conversion chart, convert the measurements given in the recipe, and answer the questions.

Conexiones | Las matemáticas

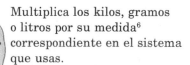

ARROZ CON LECHE
Para 8

300 gramos de arroz	un poco de vainilla
3 litros de leche	canela[1]
400 gramos de azúcar	

Pon el arroz en remojo[2] con la leche una hora y media. Luego cocina a fuego lento[3] una hora más o menos. Añade[4] el azúcar y la vainilla y cocina unos 5 minutos más. Pon el arroz en el refrigerador y esparce[5] un poco de canela encima.

Multiplica los kilos, gramos o litros por su medida[6] correspondiente en el sistema que usas.

1 kilo (kg) = 2.2 libras *(pounds)*
1 gramo (g) = 0.035 onzas *(ounces)*
1 litro (l) = 1.057 cuartos *(quarts)*

Calcula las onzas o los cuartos que hay en 300 gramos de arroz, tres litros de leche y 400 gramos de azúcar.

• ¿Cuántas libras hay en dos kilos de pollo?

[1]cinnamon   [2]soak   [3]cook slowly   [4]Add   [5]sprinkle   [6]measurement

El español en el mundo del trabajo

How can you combine an interest in nutrition and health with skills in Spanish? Here's one example. The U.S. Department of Agriculture provides the public with a wide range of nutritional information through print materials and Web sites. Much of this information is available in Spanish. There is a need for federal employees who are knowledgeable to translate and work with the Spanish-speaking community on issues related to nutrition.

• What other jobs can you think of that would combine communication skills with a knowledge of nutrition?

El edificio de USDA en Washington, D.C.

ochenta y uno **81**
Capítulo 5B

Practice and Communicate **5B**

▼**25** Standards: 1.2, 3.1

Resources: Answer Keys: Student Edition, p. 113
Focus: Using math

Suggestions: Before reading, brainstorm a list of measurements that might be used in a recipe. Ask students what metric measurements they are familiar with and which of those could be used to make a dessert. Explain to them that they are going to learn how to make *arroz con leche,* a typical dessert served in many Spanish-speaking countries. You may want to allow students to use a calculator to make their conversions. Remind students to use a comma instead of a period for a decimal.

Answers:
300 gramos de arroz = 10,5 onzas
3 litros de leche = 3,2 cuartos
400 gramos de azúcar = 14 onzas
2 kilos de pollo = 4,4 libras

El español en el mundo del trabajo

Core Instruction

Standards: 5.1

Suggestions: Brainstorm a list of professions that require knowledge of nutrition. Then ask students how Spanish would be useful in each.

Teacher-to-Teacher
Find other tongue twisters to use in transitions between activities and for practicing pronunciation. Short songs are also a good way to improve pronunciation and intonation.

ENRICH YOUR TEACHING

Culture Note
Bread pudding is a popular dessert in the United States. It has many of the same ingredients as rice pudding, and it is easy to make. A recipe can be found in many general cookbooks or online.

21st Century Skills

Creativity and Innovation After working with the *GramActiva* video, the *Canción de hip-hop: Camarero*, and the *ser-estar* tutorial, have students work with a partner or small group to create either a poem, a song, or a short story using *ser* and *estar*. Have students perform their piece for the class. The members of the class select the most creative piece as the winner.

26 Standards: 1.1, 1.3

Focus: Describing food in context

Recycle: Names of foods; *ser, estar*

Suggestions: Point out that in Step 2, Student A plays the role of the customer and Student B is the waiter. In Step 3, Student A is the waiter, and Student B is the customer. Review the *Nota* before students begin. Remind students to make adjectives agree with nouns.

Answers will vary.

Fondo cultural

Standards: 2.1, 4.2

Suggestions: Have students bring in a *menú del día* from a restaurant in their community that serves food from a Spanish-speaking country, or have them download one from the Internet.

Answers will vary but may include that pre-set menus don't give the widest selection, but they are usually less expensive and faster than ordering *a la carte*.

27 Standards: 1.1, 1.3

Resources: Voc. and Gram. Transparency 111

Focus: Asking questions in a restaurant

Recycle: Writing questions; food vocabulary

Suggestions: Have students read the menu and identify any new words. Ask them to guess the meaning of those words using context clues or cognates. Point out the use of commas in place of decimal points when writing numbers in Spanish. Explain to students that **estar** is used when talking about how a food or beverage tastes. Encourage students to ask about a variety of soups, salads, vegetables, main dishes, and desserts.

Answers will vary.

Theme Project

Students can perform Step 5 at this point. Record their presentations for inclusion in their portfolio. (For more information, see p. 30-b.)

82

▼**26** | 😃👥 | ♻️ | Escribir • Hablar

Conversación en el restaurante

1 Write a list of five food items and three drinks that you might order in a restaurant.

2 Exchange lists with your partner. Take turns playing the waiter and the customer. Use your lists as a menu and ask what the various items are like. The server will answer using words from the list.

bueno (para la salud)	sabroso
malo (para la salud)	delicioso
rico	horrible
riquísimo	¡Qué asco!

▶️ **Modelo**

A —¿Cómo está *el pollo*?

B —*El pollo* está *riquísimo y es bueno para la salud*.

Nota

To describe what a food item is like in general, use *ser*. To describe how a food item tastes at a particular time, use *estar*.

3 Now that the items have been served, ask and answer about how they taste.

▶️ **Modelo**

A —¿Cómo está *el pollo*?

B —*¡Qué asco! Está horrible*.

▼**Fondo Cultural** | El mundo hispano

El menú del día In many Spanish-speaking countries, restaurants and cafés often offer *un menú del día* or, as they are called in some parts of Mexico, *una comida corrida*. These menus usually offer one to three choices for each course at a reasonable fixed price.

• Do any restaurants that you know offer something similar to *el menú del día*? What would be the advantages and disadvantages of ordering from *un menú del día*?

DIFFERENTIATED INSTRUCTION

Heritage Language Learners

Ask students to choose a traditional dish from their heritage country and have them write a short paragraph describing the dish. Ask for volunteers to read their paragraphs to the class and have the class explain why they would or would not like the dish.

Advanced Learners

Have students write a conversation between customers and a waiter at a restaurant. Students may want to present their skits to the class.

▼27 | ♻ | Escribir

El menú del día

Use the *menú del día* from the *Restaurante Hidalgo* to write five questions that a waiter or waitress might ask and five questions that a customer might ask. Don't forget to use the formal *Ud.* in your questions.

Modelo

el (la) camarero(a)	el (la) cliente
¿Qué desea pedir de plato principal?	¿Cómo está el bistec?

Restaurante Hidalgo

⇒⇒⇒ Menú del día ⇒⇒⇒

$20,00

SOPAS Y ENSALADAS
Ensalada de tomate y cebolla
Sopa de verduras
Sopa Hidalgo

VERDURAS
Papas fritas
Papas al horno
Guisantes con jamón

PLATOS PRINCIPALES
Bistec
Pescado
Arroz con pollo

POSTRES
Pastel de chocolate
Helado de mango o papaya
Frutas frescas

▼28 | 🗣👥 | ♻ | Hablar

En el restaurante

Get together with a partner and use the questions that you wrote in Actividad 27 to play the roles of a server and customer at the Restaurante Hidalgo. Don't forget to use the formal *Ud.* in your conversation.

▶ Modelo

A —¿Qué desea pedir de plato principal?
B —No sé. ¿Cómo está el bistec?
A —Está muy sabroso.
B —¡Genial! Quisiera el bistec, por favor.

> **También se dice . . .**
> el menú = la carta (*México, España*)

▼29 | 🗣 | Escribir • Hablar

Y tú, ¿qué dices?

1. ¿Cuál es tu restaurante favorito?
2. ¿Dónde está el restaurante?
3. ¿Cómo son los camareros allí?
4. ¿Cuál es el plato principal que te gusta comer allí? ¿Cómo es?
5. ¿Te gusta pedir postre cuando comes allí? ¿Cómo es?

> **Más práctica** **GO**
> realidades.com | print
>
> | | | |
> |---|---|---|
> | Instant Check | ✔ | |
> | Guided WB pp. 29–30 | ✔ | ✔ |
> | Core WB pp. 15–16 | ✔ | ✔ |
> | Comm. WB pp. 16–17, 20, 138 | ✔ | ✔ |
> | *Hispanohablantes* WB pp. 197–201 | | ✔ |

ENRICH YOUR TEACHING

Teacher-to-Teacher

For practice using *ser,* students can prepare pictures and statements. They can use pictures of food and write descriptions of it, or pictures of people and write sentences describing what they are like.

21st Century Skills

Information Literacy Have students research Web sites from the United States and from some Spanish-speaking countries that deal with nutritional guidelines. Have them compare the information and identify similarities and differences.

▼28 Standards: 1.1

Focus: Ordering in a restaurant

Recycle: Food vocabulary; questions

Suggestions: Have students refer to the questions from *Actividad* 27, but encourage them not to read them word for word. Ask for volunteers to repeat their dialogues for the class.

Answers will vary.

▼29 Standards: 1.1, 1.3

Focus: Describing a favorite restaurant; using **ser** and **estar**

Suggestions: Encourage students to answer in complete sentences. Many of the words they will need are in the question.

Answers will vary.

Common Errors: Students often omit the verb in the sentence when forming a response. Remind them that each sentence must have a verb.

Extension: Have students make up one more question and answer it. They could describe a favorite waiter or waitress.

Pre-AP* Support

• **Learning Objective:** Interpersonal Writing

• **Activity 29:** Have students turn their responses into a short e-mail to a friend, inviting him or her to have lunch at their favorite restaurant. Ask them to include at least one question for their friend in their message.

• *Pre-AP* Resource Book:* Comprehensive guide to Pre-AP* writing skill development, pp. 27–38

Additional Resources

• Communication Wbk.: Audio Act. 8–9, pp. 16–17
• Teacher's Resource Book: Audio Script, p. 57, Communicative Pair Activity BLM, pp. 62–63
• Audio Program DVD: Cap. 5B, Tracks 12–13

✔ASSESSMENT

Prueba 5B-4 with Study Plan (online only)

Quiz: The verbs ser and estar
• Prueba 5B-4: p. 138

83

Lectura

Core Instruction

Standards: 1.2, 1.3, 3.1

Focus: Reading comprehension of a letter from relatives about a visit to Santa Fe

Mapa global interactivo, Actividad Visit Santa Fe, New Mexico and travel the Camino Real.

Suggestions:

Pre-reading: After students have written the three pieces of information suggested in the *Strategy,* have them look at the menu, photos, and captions that accompany the reading. Then ask them what kind of information they expected to find in the letter.

Reading: Have students read the letter without interruption. Remind them to use cognates to help them understand the reading. When they come across words they don't know, they should look for context clues. Point out the footnotes at the bottom of the page.

Post-reading: Have students make a list of the activities that Alicia and Pedro are planning for their friends. Ask students which activities they would like to participate in and which ones they would avoid.

Extension: Have students write a letter about a special place or a unique restaurant in their community that would be interesting to visit.

Teacher-to-Teacher

Have students create and display a Spanish version of the daily or weekly menu from the school cafeteria. You might want to have them make labels for the different dishes in the cafeteria.

Pre-AP* Support

- **Learning Objective:** Interpretive: Print and Audio
- **Activity:** Have students read each line of the letter, one sentence at a time. After each sentence, ask that they look up and then read aloud to them a teacher-made, short answer about that one line. Continue through the letter in this way.
- **Pre-AP* Resource Book:** Comprehensive guide to Pre-AP* reading skill development, pp. 19–26

¡Adelante!

Lectura

Una visita a Santa Fe
Nuevo México

Lee esta carta que escriben Alicia y Pedro. Ellos hablan de una visita que hacen sus primos a Santa Fe. ¿Qué cosas interesantes van a hacer? ¿Qué van a visitar?

Strategy

Skimming
Before you read this letter, make a list of three pieces of information you might expect to find. Quickly skim the letter. What information did you find that was on your list?

Queridos Rosario y Luis:

¡Esperamos[1] su visita en agosto! Aquí en Santa Fe vamos a hacer muchas cosas. ¿Saben que es una ciudad[2] con más de 400 años de historia y cultura? Vamos a visitar museos y tiendas, y vamos a comer comida típica. ¡Los cinco días van a pasar rápidamente![3]

Tenemos planes para pasar una noche muy especial en honor de su visita. Vamos a comer en un "restaurante" histórico que se llama Rancho de las Golondrinas[4]. Está a diez millas de nuestra casa, al sur de Santa Fe. El Rancho, en realidad, no es un restaurante; es una casa española.

Durante los días de su visita, el Rancho va a celebrar "un fandango", un baile histórico y típico, con una cena tradicional. Toda la comida es riquísima, pero nuestro plato favorito es el chile con carne y queso. Después de comer, vamos a bailar. ¡No sabemos bailar pero va a ser muy divertido! Mandamos[5] el menú con la carta.

¡Nos vemos en agosto!

Sus primos de Nuevo México,

Alicia y Pedro

Un paraje[6] en El Camino Real[7] desde la Ciudad de México hasta Santa Fe, es del año 1710. Ahora es un museo.

[1]We're looking forward to [2]city [3]quickly [4]Swallows [5]We're sending [6]a stopping place [7]the Royal Highway

---

DIFFERENTIATED INSTRUCTION

Multiple Intelligences

Verbal/Linguistic: Have students write a letter to invite a relative or friend to visit them. Have them suggest activities, places to visit, and good restaurants.

Heritage Language Learners

Ask students who are familiar with their heritage country to describe what they would recommend a tourist do on vacation there. Have other students write a letter to real or fictitious family members or friends inviting them to visit the United States and telling what is planned for the visit.

Menú del Fandango

Sopas
Sopa de arroz
Garbanzos con chile

Plato principal
Pollo relleno⁸
Chile con carne y queso

Postre
Bizcochitos⁹
Pudín de arroz con leche

Bebidas
Chocolate mexicano
Ponche
Café

⁸Stuffed chicken   ⁹Cookies

¿Comprendes?

1. ¿Cuáles son cuatro actividades que van a hacer durante la visita? ¿Cuál te gustaría hacer en Santa Fe?
2. ¿Por qué es importante Santa Fe?
3. ¿Por qué quieren ir Alicia y Pedro al Rancho de las Golondrinas?
4. Si no te gusta nada la comida picante *(spicy)*, ¿qué debes pedir del menú?
5. ¿Por qué es importante La Capilla de San Miguel?

Más práctica	GO	
realidades.com | print		
Guided WB p. 31	✔	✔
Comm. WB pp. 21, 139	✔	✔
Hispanohablantes WB pp. 202–203		✔
Cultural Reading Activity		✔

La Capilla de San Miguel, la iglesia más vieja de Santa Fe, del año 1626

El Palacio de los Gobernadores, construido en 1610, es el edificio *(building)* público más viejo de los Estados Unidos que todavía se usa. Ahora es un museo de historia.

▼ Fondo Cultural | Los Estados Unidos

¡A pensar! Santa Fe was established thirteen years before the Plymouth Colony was settled by the *Mayflower* Pilgrims. It has been a seat of government for Spain, Mexico, the Confederacy, and the United States.

- Find out when the oldest building in your community was built. How does it differ in age from the *Palacio de los Gobernadores* in Santa Fe?

ochenta y cinco 85
Capítulo 5B

ENRICH YOUR TEACHING

Perspectivas del mundo hispano

Core Instruction

Standards: 1.2, 2.1, 4.2

Focus: Reading about mealtime and the *sobremesa*

Suggestions: Present the idea of spending a couple of hours every day conversing with family and close friends. Call attention to the photos. Elicit from students that one photo shows friends and the other shows family spending time conversing after a meal. Explain that this is a common practice in Spanish-speaking countries and that it is considered an important and valuable time. Mealtime is a social event. Tell students that close friends, but not acquaintances, might well be included in a home meal and the conversation that follows. Have students read the text. Discuss how fast-food and eating "on the go" conflict with the general attitude toward mealtime and the **sobremesa.** Emphasize that mealtime in Spanish-speaking countries is a social time when the family relaxes and talks. Ask students to consider how their lives would be different if they were to do this. Ask where people get the time to spend two hours at lunch every day.

Answers will vary.

Teaching with Photos

To incorporate language use, have students describe people in the photos, or have them imagine the conversations suggested by the photos.

Teacher-to-Teacher

Careers: *Tema* 5 has focused on family, food, celebrations, and restaurants. Have students work in small groups to talk about a career in restaurant management. Have them write a list of words and expressions they have learned that might be useful for managing a restaurant. Ask groups to share their lists.

Additional Resources

Student Resource: Realidades para hispanohablantes, p. 206

Perspectivas del mundo hispano

A la hora de comer

Imagine that you had two hours for lunch every day. Or imagine that every time you ate a meal, you sat down at a table with a friend or family member and had a lengthy conversation. Now imagine that you didn't jump up from dinner as soon as you finished eating. What do these situations have in common?

Una familia en la República Dominicana

In many Spanish-speaking cultures, even ordinary mealtimes are considered social events, a time to spend enjoying food and company. People often take time after a meal to relax, to sit around the table and enjoy a good conversation or just to have a laugh. This custom, called the *sobremesa,* is more important in many cultures than getting to the next appointment or saving time and money by buying a quick meal.

Una familia chilena come al aire libre, Renaca, Chile

Not surprisingly, most Spanish-speaking countries have very few drive-through restaurants. Since people rarely take food "to go," they might be surprised if you suggested grabbing a sandwich to eat in the car. In fact, many cars don't have cup holders.

Check it out! Figure out how much time you and your family spend at breakfast, lunch, and dinner on days when you're not in school or at work. Compare your results with those of your classmates. Then complete the following statements about practices among families in your community.

Modelo
En mi comunidad, es común (*common*) comer el desayuno en <u>quince minutos</u>.

1. En mi comunidad, es común comer el desayuno en ___ minutos.
2. En mi comunidad, es común comer el almuerzo en ___ minutos.
3. En mi comunidad, es común comer la cena en ___ minutos.

Think about it! What does your research say about the importance of relaxing and enjoying a leisurely meal with friends and family? How does it compare with what happens during meals in Spanish-speaking countries? Consider the two different attitudes towards mealtime. What benefits might each one have?

 86 ochenta y seis
Tema 5 • Fiesta en familia

DIFFERENTIATED INSTRUCTION

Heritage Language Learners

Some students may practice a type of **sobremesa** in their families, or they may have experienced it. If so, allow them to share their experiences with the class. If not, have them ask family or friends about the tradition in their heritage country.

Presentación escrita

Un restaurante muy bueno

| ▼ Objectives | Aplicación |
▶ Write a review of your favorite restaurant
▶ Use examples to persuade your reader

Writing 5B

Task
Your school is creating a community guide for Spanish speakers. Your class is writing about restaurants. Write a review of your favorite restaurant.

❶ **Prewrite** Think about the restaurant you like best. Copy the word web. Write the name of the restaurant in the middle circle. Write words and expressions associated with each category inside the appropriate circles.

❷ **Draft** Write your review of the restaurant using information from the word web. Include information that might persuade others to try the restaurant.

❸ **Revise** Read through your review and check for agreement, verb forms, and spelling. Share your review with a partner. Your partner should check the following:
- Did you provide information about all categories?
- Did you use the correct forms of the verbs?
- Do you have any errors in spelling or agreement?
- Is the review persuasive?

❹ **Publish** Write a final copy of your review, making any necessary changes or additions. You may want to add illustrations and include your review in a booklet with your classmates' reviews or in your portfolio.

❺ **Evaluation** The following rubric will be used to grade your review.

Rubric	Score 1	Score 3	Score 5
Completion of task	You provide information in three categories from the word web.	You provide information in four categories from the word web.	You provide information in five categories from the word web.
Use of new and previously learned vocabulary	You use very limited and repetitive vocabulary.	You use only recently acquired vocabulary.	You use both recently acquired and previously learned vocabulary.
Accurate spelling/use of grammar	You have many patterns of misspelling and misuse of grammar.	You have frequent patterns of misspelling and misuse of grammar.	You have very few patterns of misspelling and misuse of grammar.
Correct use of verbs	You have many repetitions of incorrect verb forms.	You have frequent repetitions of incorrect verb forms.	You have very few incorrect verb forms.

Servicio — Platos principales — (Nombre del restaurante) — Otras comidas y bebidas — Postres — Descripción general

Strategy

Persuasion
Give specific information and concrete examples to persuade your readers to try a restaurant.

ochenta y siete **87**
Capítulo 5B

Presentación escrita

Persuasive
Standards: 1.3

Focus: Writing about restaurants in a personalized context; using language for persuasion

Suggestions: Review the task and the five-step approach with students. Point out the *Strategy* and the word web. Remind students that their review should include service, main dishes, beverages, desserts, and atmosphere.

Have students use the restaurant review on p. 75 as a model.

Provide time for a class discussion of the word web, comments, and questions.

Review the rubric with the class to explain how you will grade the reviews.

Pre-AP* Support

- **Learning Objective:** Presentational Writing
- **Activity:** Looking at the word web you created for this exercise, think about this restaurant's strong points. Then write a brief advertisement for this restaurant. Be sure to play up its strong points!
- **Pre-AP* Resource Book:** Comprehensive guide to Pre-AP* writing skill development, pp. 27–38

Portfolio
Have students include their written presentations in their portfolios.

Additional Resources
Student Resources: Realidades para hispanohablantes, p. 207; Guided Practice: Presentación escrita, p. 32

ENRICH YOUR TEACHING

Teacher-to-Teacher
e-amigos: Have students send e-mails to their *e-amigos* to ask about their favorite restaurant. Encourage them to use the word webs they created in the *Presentación escrita*. Ask them to print out or e-mail you their exchanges.

21st Century Skills

Responsibility and Leadership As part of the effort to develop the community guide for the Spanish-speaking residents, have students interview members of the community about the kinds of foods they prefer and then make sure that as many preferences as possible are included in the guide, so that the entire community is represented.

✓ ASSESSMENT

Presentación escrita
- Assessment Program: Rubrics, p. T31
  Go over the descriptions of the different levels of performance. After assessing students, help individuals understand how their performance could be improved.

5B Video

Videomisterio 📹

Core Instruction

Standards: 1.2, 1.3, 2.1, 5.2

Resources: Teacher's Resource Book: Video Script, p. 59, Video Program: Cap. 5B; Video Program Teacher's Guide: Cap. 5B

Focus: Preparing to view the video

Personajes importantes:

Inspector Gil, inspector de policía
Inspector Peña, inspector de policía
Doña Gracia Salazar, la víctima del crimen
Lola Lago, detective
Doña Lupe Aguirre, portera

Synopsis: The ambulance arrives for the victim, doña Gracia. Everyone is wondering where doña Gracia's niece María is. Inspector Gil asks questions of Lola Lago, who saw two people hurriedly leave doña Gracia's apartment building the night before. He asks her to call if she has any more information.

Suggestions:

Pre-viewing: Review with students the events of the previous episode. Lola Lago, while watering her plants late at night, sees two people hurriedly leaving the building across the street. After they leave, she finds a keychain that one of them dropped. It is labeled with the letters *J.R.D.* and the number eight. The next morning, doña Lupe, the caretaker, enters doña Gracia Salazar's apartment, and discovers her unconscious on the floor.

Review the *Nota cultural* with the class. You may want to ask students if they have ever been in a square similar to the ***plazas*** in Spain. Point out the *Palabras para comprender,* giving examples in context and writing the sentences on the board. Remind students that these words are only used to help them understand the episode and that they are not responsible for this vocabulary.

¿Eres tú, María? Episodio 2

Antes de ver el video

Personajes importantes

Inspector Gil, inspector de policía

Inspector Peña, inspector de policía

Doña Gracia Salazar, la víctima del crimen

Resumen del episodio

En este episodio, la ambulancia llega¹ y lleva² a doña Gracia Salazar al hospital. También llegan dos inspectores de policía. Le hablan a doña Lupe, la portera, sobre el incidente en el piso de doña Gracia. Lola se presenta³ a los dos hombres y les dice⁴ lo que sabe del incidente.

¹arrives ²takes away ³introduces herself ⁴tells them

88 ochenta y ocho
Tema 5 • Fiesta en familia

Nota cultural In the cities and towns of Spain and many Spanish-speaking countries, you will find *plazas,* open squares that are surrounded by buildings. The *plazas* are the social center of the community or neighborhood. They may contain benches, trees and flowers, statues, and fountains. In the evening, neighbors will spend time in the *plaza* sharing details about families, daily events, politics, and many other topics.

Palabras para comprender

vive *(vivir)*	she lives *(to live)*
la sobrina	niece
esperar	to wait
anoche	last night
vi *(ver)*	I saw *(to see)*
una barba	beard
¿Quién era?	Who was she?
ayudar	to help
saber	to know

DIFFERENTIATED INSTRUCTION

Heritage Language Learners

Ask students to use the vocabulary from *Palabras para comprender* to write about what happened in this episode. Also, ask any student who has lived in or visited their heritage country to comment on the *Nota cultural.* What do ***plazas*** look like? What activities take place in ***plazas***? Encourage them to bring in photos to share with the class.

"Es doña Gracia Salazar. Vive en el tercer piso con su sobrina, María".

"Anoche a la una de la mañana, vi a un hombre y a una mujer".

—¿Ud. es detective pero no tiene una descripción exacta ni del hombre ni de la mujer?

—A la una de la mañana es imposible ver mucho, ¿no?

Después de ver el video

¿Comprendes?

A. ¿Quién...?

1. ¿Quién es la víctima?
2. ¿Quiénes viven en el tercer piso?
3. ¿Quién es la sobrina?
4. ¿Quién es doña Lupe?
5. ¿Quiénes llegan para investigar el crimen?
6. ¿Quién espera en la plaza?
7. ¿Quién dice que es imposible ver mucho a la una de la mañana?
8. ¿Quién quiere ayudar a los inspectores?

B. Escoge una de las fotos de esta página y escribe tres frases para describir la foto.

Más práctica GO

realidades.com | print

Actividades ✔

ENRICH YOUR TEACHING

Culture Note

There are many squares (*plazas*) in the city of Madrid, the capital of Spain. One of the most famous squares is *La Puerta del Sol*, in the center of the city. Have students research *plazas* in Spain. Ask students to look for pictures of *plazas* so that they can compare them to the description in the *Nota*.

21st Century Skills

Initiative and Self-Direction Encourage students to develop their own process for understanding the video, depending on the kind of learner they are. As they work through the pre-viewing, viewing, and post-viewing tasks, they can identify and further develop the types of activities that are most effective for them.

Visual scanning: Point to the first two photos and ask who the people are (Inspector Gil and Inspector Peña) and what they might be doing in this episode. Then point to the third photo, of doña Gracia, the victim. Where are they taking her? Before students read the *Resumen del episodio*, have them scan the text and find cognates (**ambulancia, hospital, policia, incidente**). Ask them to read the *Resumen del episodio* carefully and ask questions about what will happen.

Viewing: Play *Episodio* 2 to the class. If there is time after viewing the full episode, select some key moments that you wish to highlight, such as when Inspector Gil questions Lola Lago.

Post-viewing: Have the class study the photos at the top of the page and ask volunteers to tell what is happening in the episode at the time of each picture. Write the vocabulary presented with this episode on the board to help students create sentences for each picture. Dramatize the quotation below the photos.

▼ **¿Comprendes?** Standards: 1.1, 1.2, 1.3

Resources: Answer Keys: Student Edition, p. 114

Focus: Verifying comprehension

Suggestions: Have students work in pairs. Allow them to look at the video again for answers, but encourage them to answer the questions from memory.

Answers:

Part A:
1. Doña Gracia Salazar es la víctima del crimen.
2. Doña Gracia Salazar y su sobrina María viven en el tercer piso.
3. María es la sobrina.
4. Doña Lupe Aguirre es la portera.
5. El Inspector Gil y el Inspector Peña llegan para investigar el crimen.
6. Lola espera en la plaza.
7. Lola Lago
8. Lola Lago quiere ayudar a los inspectores.

Part B:
Answers will vary but may include: Doña Gracia es la víctima del crimen. Ella vive en el tercer piso. Ella lee el periódico usualmente.

Additional Resources

• *¿Eres tú, María?* Video Workbook, Episode 2
• *¿Eres tú, María?* Teacher's Video Guide: Answer Key

Review Activities

To describe people: Have students bring in photos or pictures from a magazine. Student A will describe a person and Student B will identify the person being described. Have students reverse roles.

To describe how someone is feeling: Ask students to write three sentences to describe situations when someone would be warm, cold, or sleepy. Then have students get together in pairs and try to guess how their partner is feeling. For example, Student A says: *Son las diez de la noche y estudias en la biblioteca.* Student B says: *Tengo sueño.*

To describe table settings: Have students write a sentence describing what each item is used for without naming the object. Then have them work in pairs and guess the name of the object described.

To talk about eating out: Students work in pairs to practice a conversation between a waiter and a client in a restaurant.

Venir, ser, and estar: Have students play tic-tac-toe to practice conjugating the verbs. Have them set up a game board for each verb and write a different subject pronoun in the corner of each box. They should then take turns filling in the boxes with the correct form of the verb, as in tic-tac-toe. If the verb form is incorrect, the other person takes over the box by writing the correct conjugation.

Portfolio

Invite students to review the activities they completed in this chapter, including written reports, posters, or other visuals, and recordings of oral presentations or other projects. Have them select items that they feel best demonstrate their achievements in Spanish to include in their portfolios.

Additional Resources

Student Resources: Realidades para hispanohablantes, p. 208

Teacher Resources:
- Teacher's Resource Book: Situation Cards, p. 64, Clip Art, pp. 66–68
- Assessment Program: Chapter Checklist and Self-Assessment Worksheet, pp. T56–T57

Repaso | ▼ **Objectives**

Repaso del capítulo
Vocabulario y gramática

▶ Review the vocabulary and grammar
▶ Demonstrate you can perform the tasks on p. 91

to talk about people

el hombre	man
la mujer	woman
el joven	young man
la joven	young woman

to describe people and things

alto, -a	tall
bajo, -a	short *(stature)*
corto, -a	short *(length)*
guapo, -a	good-looking
joven	young
largo, -a	long
viejo, -a	old
el pelo	hair
canoso	gray
castaño	brown (chestnut)
negro	black
rubio	blond
pelirrojo, -a	red-haired

to describe how someone is feeling

tener calor	to be warm
tener frío	to be cold
tener sueño	to be sleepy

to talk about food

delicioso, -a	delicious
desear	to want
pedir *(e → i)*	to order
el plato principal	main dish
de plato principal	as a main dish
el postre	dessert
de postre	for dessert
rico, -a	rich, tasty

For *Vocabulario adicional,* see pp. 336–337.

to describe table settings

el azúcar	sugar
la cuchara	spoon
el cuchillo	knife
la pimienta	pepper
el plato	plate, dish
la sal	salt
la servilleta	napkin
la taza	cup
el tenedor	fork
el vaso	glass

to talk about eating out

el camarero, la camarera	waiter, waitress
la cuenta	bill
el menú	menu

to express needs

Me falta(n) . . .	I need . . .
Quisiera	I would like
traer	to bring
Le traigo . . .	I will bring you . . .
¿Me trae . . . ?	Will you bring me . . . ?
yo traigo	I bring

other useful words and expressions

ahora	now
¿Algo más?	Anything else?
De nada	You're welcome
otro, -a	other, another
¡Qué + *adjective!*	How . . . !

venir *to come*

vengo	venimos
vienes	venís
viene	vienen

DIFFERENTIATED INSTRUCTION

Students with Learning Difficulties

Have students review the *Repaso del capítulo* and create flashcards for any words that they do not know. Pair them with a student who is more confident with the vocabulary to practice. Before the test, provide students with a practice test, so they can become comfortable with the format.

Heritage Language Learners

Have students write a few paragraphs telling about their perfect birthday celebration: Where are they going to have it? Whom are they going to invite? What food are they going to eat? What kind of music are they going to play? Encourage them to use as many vocabulary words from this chapter as they can.

Preparación para el examen

Más repaso GO | realidades.com | print

Instant Check	✔
Puzzles	✔
Core WB pp. 17–18	✔ ✔
Comm. WB pp. 140, 141–143	✔ ✔

On the exam you will be asked to . . .	Here are practice tasks similar to those you will find on the exam . . .	For review go to your print or digital textbook . . .
1 Escuchar Listen and understand as people complain to room service that something is missing from their order	As you listen to complaints about room service, see if you can tell if there is a) missing silverware; b) missing food; c) missing condiments; d) all of the above.	pp. 64–69 *Vocabulario en contexto* p. 65 Actividad 2 p. 73 Actividad 11 p. 74 Actividad 13 p. 82 Actividad 26 p. 83 Actividad 27
2 Hablar Describe physical characteristics of family members to another person	Your aunt and uncle are going to celebrate their anniversary with you in a restaurant, but they're late. You describe them to the waiter so that he can recognize them when they arrive. Mention at least two physical characteristics about each person, such as hair color, height, or age.	pp. 64–69 *Vocabulario en contexto* p. 70 Actividad 6 p. 71 Actividad 7 p. 76 Actividad 17
3 Leer Read and understand a letter about an upcoming visit with a relative	As you read part of a letter about an upcoming trip to Santa Fe, can you determine what the writers are most looking forward to in the trip? What questions do they have about it? *Queridos Alicia y Pedro:* *Nosotros también esperamos impacientemente nuestra visita a Santa Fe en el verano. Me encanta la idea de visitar una ciudad con mucha historia. Nuestra ciudad también es muy histórica. ¿Cuál es una comida típica del Rancho de las Golondrinas?*	p. 75 Actividad 14 pp. 84–85 *Lectura*
4 Escribir Write a short report telling whether people are coming to an event and what they are bringing with them	You and your classmates decide to bring either a main dish, dessert, eating utensils, glassware, plates, or condiments for the Spanish Club party. Write a note to the club president indicating who is coming and what they are bringing. For example: *Ryan viene y trae las servilletas.*	p. 76 Actividad 16 p. 77 Actividades 19–20 p. 87 *Presentación escrita*
5 Pensar Demonstrate an understanding of cultural perspectives regarding meals	Think about how you spend lunch or dinner time during the school week. What would be at least three things that would be different at mealtime if you were an exchange student in a Spanish-speaking country? What is a *sobremesa*?	p. 72 *Fondo cultural* p. 82 *Fondo cultural* p. 86 *Perspectivas del mundo hispano*

Performance Tasks

Standards: 1.1, 1.2, 1.3, 2.1, 4.2

Student Resource: Realidades para hispanohablantes, p. 209

Teacher Resources:

Teacher's Resource Book: Audio Script, p. 57; Audio Program DVD: Cap. 5B, Track 15; Answer Keys: Student Edition, p. 115

1. Escuchar

Suggestions: Play the audio or read the *script*.

Script:

Soy el señor Chávez. Me faltan sal y pimienta. Por favor, necesito sal para la hamburguesa y pimienta para las papas fritas.

Answers: c) missing condiments: Sr. Chávez is not missing silverware or food. He is missing salt and pepper.

2. Hablar

Suggestions: Remind students that adjectives must agree in number and gender with the person or thing they are describing.

Answers will vary.

3. Leer

Suggestions: Before beginning, have students skim the *Lectura* about Santa Fe on p. 84.

Answers: They are looking forward to visiting the historical part of the city. They have questions about the meals served at the restaurant.

4. Escribir

Suggestions: Brainstorm a list of items that students would bring to a Spanish Club party. Review the forms of **venir** and **traer**.

Answers will vary.

5. Pensar

Suggestions: Have students discuss what time they usually eat breakfast, lunch, and dinner. Refer students to the *Perspectivas del mundo hispano* on p. 86 to review.

Answers will vary.

DIFFERENTIATED ASSESSMENT

CORE ASSESSMENT

- **Assessment Program:** Examen del capítulo 5B, pp. 139–145
- **Audio Program DVD:** Cap. 5B, Track 16
- **ExamView:** Chapter Test, Test Banks A and B

ADVANCED/PRE-AP*

- **ExamView Pre-AP* Test Bank**
- **Pre-AP* Resource Book,** pp. 78–81

STUDENTS NEEDING EXTRA HELP

- **Alternate Assessment Program:** Examen del capítulo 5B
- **Audio Program DVD:** Cap. 5B, Track 16

HERITAGE LEARNERS

- **Assessment Program: Realidades para hispanohablantes:** Examen del capítulo 5B
- **ExamView Heritage Learner Test Bank**

6 La casa

6A En mi dormitorio

- **A teen's bedroom**

Vocabulary: bedroom items; electronic equipment; colors; adjectives to describe things

Grammar: comparisons and superlatives; stem-changing verbs: *poder* and *dormir*

Cultural Perspectives: typical teen's bedroom

6B ¿Cómo es tu casa?

- **Houses and household chores**

Vocabulary: rooms in a house and household chores

Grammar: affirmative *tú* commands; the present progressive tense

Cultural Perspectives: rooms in a house and chores

THEME SUPPORT

Bulletin Boards

Theme: *La casa*

Ask students to cut out, copy, or download photos of the exteriors of houses and apartment buildings from around the world and the interiors of the different rooms in a house. Cluster photos according to rooms; then place the photos of the exteriors of houses in a ring around the clusters.

Hands-on Culture

Craft: *Flores de papel*

Tissue paper flowers are a popular decoration in many Spanish-speaking homes.

Materials for one flower:
  4 6" × 12" sheets of brightly
  colored tissue paper
  1 green pipe cleaner
  scissors

1. Stack the four sheets of tissue paper.
2. Starting at a long end of the sheets, fold the papers back and forth like a fan. When you finish, you should have a 12"-long closed fan, about 1" wide.
3. Round the ends of the closed fan by cutting off the corners.
4. Place the middle of the pipe cleaner around the middle of the closed fan and twist it to squeeze the paper. Pull both ends of the pipe cleaner down to create a stem.
5. Fan out the paper on both sides of the pipe cleaner. Gently pull each sheet of paper up to create flower petals. Rearrange and straighten the petals to your liking.
6. Twist the two ends of the pipe cleaner together to create a sturdy stem.

Game

Casa de obstáculos

Play this game in *Capítulo* 6B, after students have learned affirmative *tú* commands. You may need to print out the irregular form of the affirmative *tú* command for the verb *ir: ve.*

Players: the whole class

Materials: scarf for blindfold

Rules:

1. Designate different areas in the classroom as rooms in a house, and then rearrange desks, chairs, and tables to create an obstacle course.
2. Teach and write on the board the following words to help students give directions: *párate* (stop), and *derecho* (straight ahead).
3. Divide the class into two teams. Ask for a volunteer from each team to be the Searcher. Blindfold both volunteers and place them somewhere on the obstacle course.
4. Give each team a list of rooms and an activity to perform in each room.
5. On your cue, teams give their Searchers commands that will take them to the first room on the team's list. Once in the correct room, teams tell their Searchers what to do there. Searchers mime the activity they are told to do.
   Team members: *Ve derecho, párate, ve a la derecha, párate, ahora ve a la izquierda, párate. Estás en el comedor. Pon la mesa.*
6. The winner is the team whose Searcher first completes the obstacle course.

Variation: Team members take turns being the Searcher, switching out after the action is performed in a room.

THEME PROJECT

La casa de mis sueños

Overview: Students create a plan for their dream house on poster board or electronically, labeling each floor and room. They can use photos or drawings to furnish one bedroom in the house. Then, students write a short paragraph describing their dream house and bedroom and give an oral presentation, taking students on a tour of their house and bedroom.

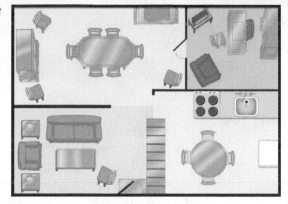

Resources: poster board, magazines, markers, glue, crayons, colored pencils, scissors, or electronic layout tools and online images

Sequence: (suggestions for when to do each step appear throughout the chapters)

 6A

STEP 1. Review instructions so students know what is expected of them. Hand out the "Theme 6 Project Instructions and Rubric" from the *Teacher's Resource Book.*

STEP 2. Students submit a rough sketch of their house plan and bedroom layout. Return the drafts with your suggestions. For grammar and vocabulary practice, ask students to partner to compare sketches.

STEP 3. Students create their house plan on poster board and do the layout of their bedroom. Encourage them to try different arrangements in the bedroom before finalizing their plans.

6B

STEP 4. Students submit a draft of the description of their house. Note your corrections and suggestions; then return drafts to students.

STEP 5. Students present their house plans to the class, taking the class on a room-by-room tour and then describing their bedroom in detail.

Options:

1. Students limit the plan to their ideal bedroom, label each item in it, and describe it in a paragraph.
2. Students create a house plan of their actual house or apartment.

Assessment:

Here is a detailed rubric for assessing this project:

Theme 6 Project: *La casa de mis sueños*

RUBRIC	Score 1	Score 3	Score 5
Evidence of planning	You didn't submit a sketch and draft.	You submitted the sketch and draft, but didn't correct them.	You submitted and corrected your sketch and draft.
Use of illustrations	You didn't include cutouts or drawings.	Your sketch is complete, but few labels and cutouts or drawings are included.	Several cutouts or drawings are included in your sketch.
Presentation	You list rooms in the house and items in the bedroom.	You describe the house and a few items in the bedroom.	You describe the house and most of the items in the bedroom in some detail.

21st Century Skills

Look for tips throughout *Tema 6* to enrich your teaching by integrating 21st Century Skills. Suggestions for the Theme Project and Theme Culture follow below.

Theme Project

Modify the Theme Project with one or more of these suggestions:

Encourage Technology Literacy

As an alternative, have students make an electronic version of their dream house, combining audio, video, and online sources. Have the students set up an online contest on the class Web site, so that class members can vote for the best dream house.

Develop Collaboration

Have students do Internet research to compare typical houses in Spanish-speaking countries to houses in the U.S., considering features such as outside color, materials, shape, and size. Have them compile, compare, and present the results to the class.

Support Critical Thinking and Problem Solving

Have students read the handout "Compare and Contrast," and then compare houses in different countries, discussing possible reasons for differences and similarities they find, and identifying any possible influences of one country on another.

Theme Culture

Promote Social and Cross-Cultural Skills

Have students working in groups prepare questions and interview native speakers of Spanish to find out what they have in their rooms and why their rooms are important to them. Students then compare the responses to their own.

▶ Videocultura View *La casa* with the class to learn how people in various Spanish-speaking countries live.

6A En mi dormitorio

AT A GLANCE

Objectives

- Listen to and read descriptions of bedrooms and colors
- Talk and write about your room
- Survey classmates about their bedrooms and compare theirs to your room
- Make a *luminaria* and understand the history and significance of this tradition

Vocabulary

- Bedroom items
- Electronic equipment
- Colors
- Comparisons

Grammar

- Making comparisons
- The superlative
- Stem-changing verbs: *poder* and *dormir*

Culture

- Salvador Dalí, p. 93
- Flags of the Spanish-speaking world, p. 103
- The Mexican flag, p. 103
- Latin Grammy Awards, p. 108
- *la siesta,* p. 112
- Electronic devices in the Spanish-speaking world, p. 117
- *las luminarias,* p. 118

Recycle ♻

- *estar* to express location
- *ser* to describe physical characteristics
- *más...que* to compare things
- *puedes, puedo*
- Adjective agreement
- Possessive adjectives

RESOURCES

FOR THE STUDENT	ONLINE	DVD	PRINT	FOR THE TEACHER	ONLINE	PREEXP	DVD	PRINT
Plan				Interactive TE and Resources DVD	•		•	
				Teacher's Resource Book, pp. 86–121	•		•	•
				Pre-AP* Resource Book, pp. 82–85	•		•	•
				Mapa global interactivo	•			
				Lesson Plans	•			•

Introducción PP. 92–93

Present Student Edition, pp. 92–93	•	•	•	Interactive TE and Resources DVD	•		•	
DK Reference Atlas	•	•		Teacher's Resource Book, pp. 86–89	•		•	•
Videocultura	•	•		Galería de fotos		•		
Hispanohablantes WB, pp. 210–211			•	Fine Art Transparencies, 14	•	•	•	
				Map Transparencies, 12, 15–18, 20	•	•	•	

Vocabulario en contexto PP. 94–99

Present & Practice Student Edition, pp. 94–99	•	•	•	Interactive TE and Resources DVD	•		•	
Audio	•	•		Teacher's Resource Book, pp. 90–92, 95, 104–105	•		•	
Videohistoria	•	•		Vocabulary Clip Art	•	•	•	•
Flashcards	•	•		Audio Program	•	•		
Instant Check	•			Video Program: Videohistoria	•		•	
Guided WB, pp. 33–42	•	•	•	Video Program Teacher's Guide: Cap. 6A	•		•	
Core WB, pp. 19–22	•	•	•	Vocabulary and Grammar Transparencies, 112–115	•		•	
Comm. WB, pp. 22–25, 29	•	•	•	Answer Keys: Student Edition, pp. 116–117	•			
Hispanohablantes WB, pp. 212–213			•	TPR Stories, pp. 77–91	•		•	•
Assess and Remediate				Prueba 6A–1: Assessment Program, pp. 147–148	•		•	•
				Assessment Program para hispanohablantes, pp. 147–148	•		•	•

RESOURCES

	FOR THE STUDENT	ONLINE	DVD	PRINT	FOR THE TEACHER	ONLINE	PREEXP	DVD	PRINT
Vocabulario en uso PP. **100–105**									
Present & Practice	Student Edition, pp. 100–105	•	•	•	Interactive Whiteboard Vocabulary Activities	•		•	
	Instant Check	•			Interactive TE and Resources DVD	•		•	
	Comm. WB, p. 26	•	•	•	Teacher's Resource Book, pp. 91–92, 98–99	•		•	•
	Hispanohablantes WB, pp. 214–215			•	Communicative Pair Activities, pp. 98–99	•		•	•
	Communicative Pair Activities	•			Audio Program	•	•	•	
					Videomodelos	•		•	
					Vocabulary and Grammar Transparencies, 118	•	•	•	
					Answer Keys: Student Edition, pp. 117–118	•	•	•	
Assess and Remediate					Prueba 6A–2 with Study Plan	•			
					Prueba 6A–2: Assessment Program, pp. 149–150	•		•	•
					Assessment Program para hispanohablantes, pp. 149–150	•		•	•
Gramática PP. **106–115**									
Present & Practice	Student Edition, pp. 106–115	•	•	•	Interactive Whiteboard Grammar Activities	•		•	
	Instant Check	•			Interactive TE and Resources DVD	•		•	
	Animated Verbs	•			Teacher's Resource Book, pp. 92–93, 95–96, 100–101	•		•	•
	Tutorial Video: Grammar	•			Communicative Pair Activities, pp. 100–101	•		•	•
	Canción de hip hop	•			Audio Program	•	•	•	
	Guided WB, pp. 43–46	•	•	•	Videomodelos	•		•	
	Core WB, pp. 23–25	•	•	•	Video Program: GramActiva	•		•	
	Comm. WB, pp. 26–28, 30–32, 144	•	•	•	Vocabulary and Grammar Transparencies, 116–117	•	•	•	
	Hispanohablantes WB, pp. 216–221			•	Answer Keys: Student Edition, pp. 118–121	•	•	•	
	Communicative Pair Activities	•							
Assess and Remediate					Pruebas 6A–3 to 6A–5 with Study Plans	•			
					Pruebas 6A–3 to 6A–5: Assessment Program, pp. 151–153	•		•	•
					Assessment Program para hispanohablantes, pp. 151–153	•		•	•
¡Adelante! PP. **116–121**									
Application	Student Edition, pp. 116–121	•	•	•	Interactive TE and Resources DVD	•		•	
	Online Cultural Reading	•			Teacher's Resource Book, pp. 96–97, 103	•		•	•
	Guided WB, pp. 47–48	•	•	•	Video Program: Videomisterio ¿Eres tú, María?	•		•	
	Comm. WB, p. 145	•	•	•	Video Program Teacher's Guide: Cap. 6A	•		•	
	Hispanohablantes WB, pp. 222–227			•	Videomisterio Quiz		•		
	¿Eres tú, María? Video WB, pp. 20–26	•	•	•	Answer Keys: Student Edition, p. 122	•	•	•	
Repaso del capítulo PP. **122–123**									
Review	Student Edition, pp. 122–123	•	•	•	Interactive TE and Resources DVD	•		•	
	Online Puzzles and Games	•			Teacher's Resource Book, pp. 93, 102, 104–105	•		•	•
	Core WB, pp. 26–27	•	•	•	Audio Program	•	•	•	
	Comm. WB, pp. 146–149	•	•	•	Answer Keys: Student Edition, p. 122	•	•	•	
	Hispanohablantes WB, pp. 228–229			•					
	Instant Check	•							
Chapter Assessment									
Assess					Examen del capítulo 6A	•		•	•
					Assessment Program, pp. 154–161	•		•	•
					Alternate Assessment Program, pp. 67–72	•		•	•
					Assessment Program para hispanohablantes, pp. 154–161	•		•	•
					Audio Program, Cap. 6A, Examen	•		•	
					ExamView: Test Banks A and B questions only online	•		•	
					Heritage Learner Test Bank	•		•	
					Pre-AP* Test Bank	•		•	

REGULAR SCHEDULE (50 MINUTES)

DAY	Warm-up / Assess	Preview / Present / Practice / Communicate	Wrap-up / Homework Options
1	Return Examen del capítulo (10 min.)	Vocabulario en contexto (35 min.) • Objectives • Presentation • *Actividades* 1, 2 • Arte y cultura • Videocultura: *La casa*	Wrap-up and Homework Options (5 min.) • Core Practice • Vocabulary Clip Art
2	Warm-up (5 min.) • Homework check	Vocabulario en contexto (40 min.) • Review: *Vocabulario en contexto* • Presentation: *Videohistoria El cuarto de Ignacio* • View: Video *El cuarto de Ignacio* • Video Activities • *Actividades* 3, 4	Wrap-up and Homework Options (5 min.) • *Prueba* 6A-1: Vocabulary recognition • Core Practice
3	Warm-up (5 min.) • Homework check ✔Formative Assessment (10 min.) • *Prueba* 6A-1: Vocabulary recognition	Vocabulario en uso (30 min.) • Objectives • Interactive Whiteboard Vocabulary Activities • *Actividades* 5, 6, 8 • *Juego: Actividad* 9 • *Fondo cultural*	Wrap-up and Homework Options (5 min.) • *Actividad* 7
4	Warm-up (10 min.) • Homework check • Return *Prueba* 6A-1: Vocabulary recognition	Vocabulario en uso (35 min.) • Review: *Vocabulario* • *Actividades* 11, 12 • *Fondo cultural*	Wrap-up and Homework Options (5 min.) • *Actividad* 10
5	Warm-up (5 min.) • Homework check	Vocabulario en uso (40 min.) • Review: Adjective agreement • *Actividades* 13, 14, 16 • *Conexiones: Actividad* 15 • Communicative Pair Activities	Wrap-up and Homework Options (5 min.) • *Actividad* 17
6	Warm-up (5 min.) • Homework check	Gramática y vocabulario en uso (40 min.) • Presentation: Making comparisons • *GramActiva* Video • Interactive Whiteboard Grammar Activities • *Actividades* 18, 19	Wrap-up and Homework Options (5 min.) • *Actividad* 20
7	Warm-up (5 min.) • Homework check	Gramática y vocabulario en uso (40 min.) • *Actividades* 21, 22, 23 • *Pronunciación* • *Fondo cultural* • Communicative Pair Activities	Wrap-up and Homework Options (5 min.) • Core Practice
8	Warm-up (5 min.) • Homework check	Gramática y vocabulario en uso (40 min.) • Presentation: The superlative • *GramActiva* Video • Interactive Whiteboard Grammar Activities • *Actividades* 24, 25, 26, 27	Wrap-up and Homework Options (5 min.) • *Actividad* 28 • Core Practice • *Prueba* 6A-3 with Study Plan: Making comparisons and the superlative

REGULAR SCHEDULE (50 MINUTES)

DAY	Warm-up / Assess	Preview / Present / Practice / Communicate	Wrap-up / Homework Options
9	**Warm-up (5 min.)** • Homework check ✔**Formative Assessment (10 min.)** • *Prueba* 6A-3 with Study Plan: Making comparisons and the superlative	**Gramática y vocabulario en uso (30 min.)** • Presentation: Stem-changing verbs: ***poder*** and ***dormir*** • *GramActiva* Video • Interactive Whiteboard Grammar Activities • *Actividades* 30, 31, 32 • *Fondo cultural*	**Wrap-up and Homework Options (5 min.)** • *Actividad* 29 • *Prueba* 6A-2 with Study Plan: Vocabulary production
10	**Warm-up (5 min.)** • Homework check • Return *Prueba* 6A-3 with Study Plan: Making comparisons and the superlative ✔**Formative Assessment (10 min.)** • *Prueba* 6A-2 with Study Plan: Vocabulary production	**Gramática y vocabulario en uso (30 min.)** • *Exploración del lenguaje* • *Actividades* 34, 35 • *El español en la comunidad*	**Wrap-up and Homework Options (5 min.)** • *Actividad* 33 • *Prueba* 6A-4 with Study Plan: Stem-changing verbs: ***poder*** and ***dormir***
11	**Warm-up (5 min.)** • Homework check • Return *Prueba* 6A-2 with Study Plan: Vocabulary production ✔**Formative Assessment (10 min.)** • *Prueba* 6A-4 with Study Plan: Stem-changing verbs: ***poder*** and ***dormir***	**¡Adelante! (30 min.)** • *Presentación oral:* Prepare • *Lectura* • *Fondo cultural*	**Wrap-up and Homework Options (5 min.)** • *Presentación oral:* Prepare • *¿Comprendes?*
12	**Warm-up (5 min.)** • Homework check • Return *Prueba* 6A-4 with Study Plan: Stem-changing verbs: ***poder*** and ***dormir***	**¡Adelante! (40 min.)** • *Presentación oral:* Practice • *La cultura en vivo*	**Wrap-up and Homework Options (5 min.)**
13	**Warm-up (5 min.)** • Homework check	**¡Adelante! (40 min.)** • *Presentación oral:* Present	**Wrap-up and Homework Options (5 min.)** • Writing Activities • Core Practice Organizer
14	**Warm-up (5 min.)** • Homework check • Core Practice Organizer	**¡Adelante! (20 min.)** • *Videomisterio* **Repaso (20 min.)** • *Vocabulario y gramática* • *Preparación para el examen*	**Wrap-up and Homework Options (5 min.)** • Instant Check • *Examen del capítulo*
15	**Warm-up (5 min.)** • Answer questions ✔**Summative Assessment (45 min.)** • *Examen del capítulo*		

Standards for *Capítulo* 6A

• To achieve the goals of the Standards, students will:

Communication

1.1 Interpersonal
• Talk about: bedroom and home furnishings and arrangement; lifestyle and entertainment preferences; the distribution of home electronics; colors and color association; flag colors and symbolism; the importance of sleep

1.2 Interpretive
• Listen to: descriptions of bedrooms and bedroom furnishings; information about colors vocabulary;
• Read a picture-based story
• Listen to and watch a video about bedroom neatness; information about students' personal preferences; the verbs *poder* and *dormir* in conversation

1.3 Presentational
• Present information about: entertainment preferences; items in the home
• Present a description of: a bedroom; people and things

Culture

2.1 Practices and Perspectives
• Learn about: the Latin Grammy awards; *la siesta;* the *luminarias* of Santa Fe

2.2 Products and Perspectives
• Learn about: Salvador Dalí and his painting; the Latin Grammy awards; Spanish-style architecture
• Learn a well-known riddle from Mexico
• Learn: colors and symbols of Spanish-speaking countries' flags; a Spanish *trabalenguas*

Connections

3.1 Cross-curricular
• Learn about Salvador Dalí
• Reinforce math skills
• Learn about interpretations of colors in psychology

Comparisons

4.1 Language
• Understand: comparisons in Spanish; superlatives in Spanish; the stem-changing verbs *poder* and *dormir;* the pronunciation of the letters *r* and *rr*
• Learn new vocabulary through the recognition of cognates
• Learn to build vocabulary through the use of root words

4.2 Culture
• Compare: symbolism of Mexico's flag to United States' flags; the pros and cons of importing *la siesta* to the United States; the use of light to celebrate events
• Identify the influence of Spanish architecture in the United States
• Identify pros and cons of the technological global community

Communities

5.2 Lifelong Learner
• Identify Latin recording artists whose music they enjoy
• View a video mystery series
• Visit the Web site of a prominent newspaper in Spain

Capítulo

6A En mi dormitorio

▼ Chapter Objectives

Communication

By the end of this chapter you will be able to:
• Listen to and read descriptions of bedrooms and colors
• Talk and write about your room
• Survey classmates about their bedrooms and compare theirs to your room

Culture

You will also be able to:
• Make a *luminaria* and understand the history and significance of this tradition

You will demonstrate what you know and can do:
• Presentación oral, p. 119
• Preparación para el examen, p. 123

You will use:

Vocabulary	Grammar
• Bedroom items	• Making comparisons
• Electronic equipment	• The superlative
• Colors	• Stem-changing verbs: *poder* and *dormir*
• Comparisons	

Exploración del mundo hispano

Country Connection
Homes and Traditions

Nuevo México
México
España

realidades.com GO

 Reference Atlas

▶ **Videocultura y actividad**

🌐 **Mapa global interactivo**

Dormitorio de una casa mexicana

ENRICH YOUR TEACHING

Using Backward Design

Have students preview the sample performance tasks on *Preparación para el examen*, p. 123, and connect them to the Chapter Objectives. Explain to students that by completing the sample tasks they can self-assess their learning progress.

Mapa global interactivo

Download the *Mapa global interactivo* files for Chapter 6A and preview the activity. In this activity, you will look at the tradition of *luminarias* on both sides of the Rio Grande.

Arte y cultura | España

Salvador Dalí (1904–1989) was a painter born in Figueras, Spain. This is one of his most famous paintings, made when he was only 20. Here he has painted his sister, who appears only from the back.

• Why do you think that Dalí painted her looking out the window rather than facing the viewer?

"Muchacha en la ventana" (1925), Salvador Dalí ▶

Museo Español de Arte Contemporáneo, Madrid, Spain.
The Bridgeman Art Library International Ltd. © 2003 Salvador Dalí,
Gala-Salvador Dalí Foundation/Artists Rights Society (ARS), NY.

noventa y tres 93
Capítulo 6A

Chapter Opener

Core Instruction

Resources: Map Transparencies 12, 15–18, 20

Suggestions: Explain that students will learn to talk about items in their bedrooms. Brainstorm a list of objects students may have in their rooms, including electronic equipment. Point out that students will learn to describe objects using adjectives for color, size, and appearance. Tell students that they will learn more stem-changing verbs and how to compare various items.

▶ **Videocultura** View *La casa* with the class to learn how people in various Spanish-speaking countries live.

Arte y cultura

Standards: 2.2, 3.1

Resources: Fine Art Transparencies, p. 14

Suggestions: If possible, bring in reproductions of Dalí's later work to compare with "*Muchacha en la ventana*." Discuss the differences in style. Which are more realistic, and which are more abstract or surreal? If possible, show both a realistic and a surrealistic picture by Dalí, asking students if they can define the word "surreal" based on the painting. Which style do they prefer? Can they say why?

Answers will vary.

▶ **TEACHING WITH ART**

Resources: Fine Art Transparencies, p. 14

Teacher-to-Teacher

Have an artistic student draw a mural of a bedroom on a large piece of butcher paper. Include the vocabulary items found in the vocabulary section.

DIFFERENTIATED INSTRUCTION

Digital resources such as the *Interactive Whiteboard* activity banks, *Videomodelos*, additional *Online Activities*, *Study Plans*, automatically graded *Leveled Workbook*, animated *Grammar Tutorials*, *Flashcards*, and *Vocabulary and Grammar Videos* will help you reach students of different ability levels and learning styles.

STUDENTS NEEDING EXTRA HELP

Guided Practice Activities
• Flashcards, pp. 33–38
• Vocabulary Check, pp. 39–42
• Grammar Support, pp. 43–46

HERITAGE LEARNERS

Realidades para hispanohablantes
• Chapter Opener, pp. 210–211
• A primera vista, p. 212
• Videohistoria, p. 213
• Manos a la obra, pp. 214–221
• ¡Adelante!, pp. 222–227
• Repaso del capítulo, pp. 228–229

ADVANCED/PRE-AP*

Pre-AP* Resource Book,
• pp. 82–85
Communications Workbook
• Integrated Performance Assessment, p. 146

93

6A Language Input

A primera vista | 🔊 | 📖 |

▼ Objectives
Read, listen to, and understand information about
▶ bedroom items
▶ electronic equipment
▶ colors

Vocabulario en contexto

Core Instruction
Standards: 1.2

Resources: Teacher's Resource Book: Input Script, p. 90, Clip Art, pp. 104–105, Audio Script, p. 91; Voc. and Gram. Transparencies 112–113; TPR Stories Book, pp. 77–91; Audio Program DVD: Cap. 6A, Tracks 1–2

Focus: Presenting new vocabulary for bedroom items, electronic equipment, and colors

Suggestions: Use the story in the *TPR Stories Book* to present the new vocabulary and grammar or use the Input Script from the *Teacher's Resource Book*. Present the vocabulary in four sets: parts of the house itself (wall, floor, window, closet), furniture, electronic equipment, and colors. Instead of using the transparencies, bring in old catalogs for students to look through, and ask them to point to the items as you say them. Ask questions about the vocabulary that require limited verbal response, such as *¿Te gustaría tener / Tienes un cartel en tu dormitorio?* or *¿De qué color es (item)?*

BELLRINGER REVIEW
Show Voc. and Gram. Transparency 58. Have students write two sentences telling the location of the two items on the table.

Vocabulario en contexto

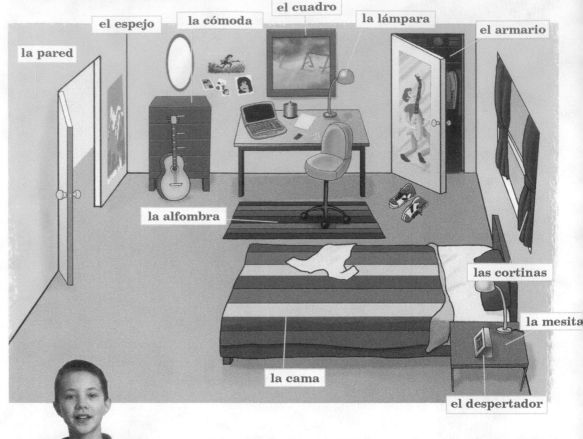

el cuadro · el espejo · la cómoda · la lámpara · el armario · la pared · la alfombra · las cortinas · la mesita · la cama · el despertador

> ❝ Tengo **un dormitorio pequeño.** Las paredes son azules. Tengo carteles de mis grupos musicales favoritos en las paredes. Generalmente, mi dormitorio está muy desordenado, pero hoy está ordenado. No comparto el dormitorio con otra persona—es mi **propio** dormitorio.
>
> En mi dormitorio tengo todas mis **posesiones más importantes:** mi guitarra, mis discos compactos, mis fotos, mi computadora. ¿Por qué me gusta mucho mi dormitorio? ¡Está encima del garaje! ¡Es **el mejor** dormitorio para tocar y escuchar música! ❞

94 noventa y cuatro
Tema 6 • La casa

DIFFERENTIATED INSTRUCTION

Multiple Intelligences
Verbal/Linguistic: Ask students to create a cloze passage to describe a bedroom and to provide a word bank with words that would fit logically in only one blank. Photocopy and distribute their passages, asking the rest of the class to fill in the blanks using the word bank.

Students with Special Needs
Take into consideration that some students may be colorblind. Be sure to use both words and colors when asking students to identify colors. Be careful to verify when asking students to describe colors of concrete objects.

el televisor*

el lector DVD

el estante

el disco compacto

el video

el equipo de sonido

—¿Te gusta el disco compacto de Mano Negra?

—¡Por supuesto! Me encanta su música. Pero es **menos** interesante **que** la música de Mecano.

—A mis padres les encanta escuchar música. Me gustaría tener mi propio equipo de sonido.

*El televisor refers to the actual appliance. La televisión (tele) is the programming that is watched.

los colores

amarillo, -a

negro, -a

azul

anaranjado, -a

blanco, -a

gris

marrón

rojo, -a

verde

morado, -a

rosado, -a

▼**1** 🔊 **|Escuchar**

Las posesiones

Listen as Marcos describes his bedroom. Look at the picture and touch each item as he mentions it.

▼**2** 🔊 **|Escuchar**

Los colores

As you hear a color named, point to an item on these pages that is that color.

Más práctica (GO)	realidades.com | print
Instant Check	✔
Guided WB pp. 33–38	✔ ✔
Core WB pp. 19–20	✔ ✔
Comm. WB p. 29	✔ ✔
Hispanohablantes **WB** p. 212	✔

noventa y cinco **95**
Capítulo 6A

1 Standards: 1.2

Resources: Teacher's Resource Book: Audio Script, p. 91; Audio Program DVD: Cap. 6A, Track 3; Answer Keys: Student Edition, p. 116

Focus: Listening comprehension: bedroom items

Suggestions: Play the audio or read the script aloud. Let students listen more than once. Monitor the activity, making sure that students are pointing to the correct objects.

🔊 **Script and Answers:**

Mi cuarto es pequeño. Las paredes son de color azul. *(the wall)*
La cama está al lado de la ventana. *(the bed; the window)*
Tengo un cuadro grande y unos carteles en las paredes. *(the painting; posters)*
El espejo está encima de la cómoda. *(the mirror; the dresser)*
Y tengo una mesita con lámpara al lado de la cama. *(the night stand, the lamp)*
Tengo una alfombra y unas cortinas. *(the rug, the curtains)*
Y, claro, ¡tengo despertador! *(the alarm clock)*

2 Standards: 1.2

Resources: Teacher's Resource Book: Audio Script, p. 91; Audio Program DVD: Cap. 6A, Track 4

Focus: Listening comprehension: colors

Suggestions: Play the audio or read the script aloud. As a variation, have students point to something in the classroom that is the color mentioned.

🔊 **Script:**

Yo veo algo amarillo.   Yo veo algo morado.
Yo veo algo anaranjado.   Yo veo algo negro.
Yo veo algo azul.   Yo veo algo rojo.
Yo veo algo blanco.   Yo veo algo rosado.
Yo veo algo gris.   Yo veo algo verde.
Yo veo algo marrón.
Answers will vary.

ENRICH YOUR TEACHING

Culture Note

Compared with many Spanish-speaking countries, the colors on the outside of homes in the United States are conservative. It is not uncommon to see neighborhoods of brightly colored houses in both rural and urban areas of Central and South America.

Teacher-to-Teacher

Reinforce listening activities by personalizing them. After students role-play the people in the Audio Activities, have them create their own listening activities to do with a partner or with the class. Record students' activities and reuse them throughout the lesson.

6A Language Input

Videohistoria 🔊

Core Instruction

Standards: 1.2

Resources: Voc. and Gram. Transparencies 114–115; Audio Program DVD: Cap. 6A, Track 5

Focus: Presenting additional vocabulary and grammar in context

Suggestions:

Pre-reading: Direct attention to the *Antes de leer* questions. Ask students to share their feelings about others "organizing" their things. Have them look at the photos to predict how the mother and Ignacio feel in panel 4 and then in panel 8.

El cuarto de Ignacio

¡El cuarto de Ignacio está muy desordenado!

España

Ignacio   Mamá

También se dice...
el dormitorio = el cuarto *(España)*

Antes de leer

Strategy **Using prior experience** Have you ever had someone go in and change things around in your room? How did you feel?

- Look at the photos and guess how Ignacio feels about his mother moving things around in his room.

1. Scan the reading for words that are familiar to you. What things has Mamá moved around, based on the words you have picked out?

2. Look at photo 8 and make a prediction about how Ignacio and his mother feel at the end of the story.

96 noventa y seis
Tema 6 • La casa

DIFFERENTIATED INSTRUCTION

Heritage Language Learners

Have students write a short paragraph about what their bedrooms are like. Are they tidy or messy? Who cleans them? Who is allowed in? Students can refer to the *Videohistoria* for words to include in their paragraphs. When necessary, talk to students individually about spelling or grammatical errors they may have made.

Advanced Learners

Have students write a short paragraph describing their idea of a tidy bedroom. Tell them to begin their paragraph with an introductory sentence, such as: *Para mí, un dormitorio está ordenado cuando....* Remind them to use both new and old vocabulary, the verb ***estar,*** and prepositions of location.

Mamá: Mira este cuarto . . . ¡qué **feo**! ¡Está muy **desordenado**! Ignacio, ¿cómo puedes hacer esto?

Mamá: ¿De qué color es esta camiseta? ¿**Gris**? ¿**Blanca**? Y esta camiseta de muchos colores, ¿qué es? ¡Ay, tengo que trabajar mucho en este cuarto!

Mamá: ¿Qué **podemos** hacer con este cuarto? El **cuadro** va en la pared y la lámpara va en la **mesita**. ¡Ay, ay, ay!

Ignacio: ¡Mamá! ¡Mi cuarto! ¡Mis **cosas**! ¿Dónde están?

Reading: Ask students to role-play the characters of Mamá and Ignacio, or play the audio. Using the transparencies and nonverbal clues, help students understand the new words in blue type.

Post-reading: Complete *Actividades* 3 and 4 on p. 99 to check comprehension.

Pre-AP* Support

- **Learning Objective:** Presentational Writing and Speaking
- **Activity:** As a post-viewing activity, have pairs of students write and act out a new scene for the video. Have them imagine a friend comes to visit Ignacio and is surprised by his newly organized room. Ignacio describes the changes to his room and expresses his satisfaction (or dissatisfaction) with the new order of things.
- *Pre-AP* Resource Book:* Comprehensive guide to Pre-AP* vocabulary skill development, pp. 51–57

ENRICH YOUR TEACHING

Teacher-to-Teacher

Bring in crayons and children's color-by-number books to use in a listening activity. Make copies of one image, distribute it to the class, and give students some crayons. Describe each part of the image, for example: *Las flores son amarillas.* Have students check their work by comparing their final product to one that you have already completed.

21st Century Skills

Communication After students have reviewed the *Videohistoria* in **realidades.com** and role-played the video with a partner, have them create a similar but personalized skit explaining where things are in their room, what someone did to change the order, and how they reacted.

Video

Core Instruction

Standards: 1.2

Resources: Teacher's Resource Book: Video Script, p. 95; Video Program: Cap. 6A; Video Program Teacher's Guide: Cap. 6A

Focus: Listening comprehension of vocabulary in the context of a story about a mother's reorganization of her son's bedroom

Suggestions:

Pre-viewing: Review the *Strategy*. Tell students to listen for intonation to determine how Ignacio feels.

Viewing: Show the video without pausing. Show it again, pausing along the way to check comprehension. Write difficult words on the board. Show the segment a final time without pausing.

Post-viewing: Complete the Video Activities in the *Communication Workbook.*

5

Mamá: Tu cuarto está mucho más **bonito.** Los libros **grandes** están aquí, y **a la izquierda** están las revistas. Y los discos compactos están **a la derecha de** los libros. Es mejor, ¿no crees?

6

Ignacio: Mamá, no es el **mismo cuarto. Para ti,** está **mejor que** antes, pero **para mí,** está **peor.** Tengo todas mis posesiones más importantes aquí y ahora no sé dónde están.

7

Mamá: Pero Ignacio, ¿cómo puedes **dormir** con todas las cosas encima de la cama?

Ignacio: Mamá, siempre **duermo** bien.

Mamá: ¡Ay! Está bien. Nunca más voy a organizar tu cuarto.

8

Ignacio: ¡Eres la mejor mamá! Muchas gracias.

Mamá: De nada, Ignacio.

98 noventa y ocho
Tema 6 • La casa

DIFFERENTIATED INSTRUCTION

Students with Learning Difficulties

Reproduce some of the direction lines from later chapters in the book onto one worksheet. Distribute it to the class as a model of how students will see the words in the *Nota* in subsequent chapters. You may want to form groups of students with varying abilities to practice comprehension of the direction lines.

▼3 Leer · Escribir

Según mamá

Escribe los números del 1 al 5 en una hoja de papel. Escribe frases para describir dónde debe estar cada uno de estos objetos, según Mamá.

1.

2.  3.

4. 5.

a. Debe estar en la pared.

b. Deben estar a la derecha de los libros.

c. Deben estar a la izquierda de los libros.

d. Debe estar en la mesa.

e. Deben estar al lado de las revistas.

▼4 Leer

¿Mamá o Ignacio?

Read the following sentences and decide if Mamá or Ignacio would say each one. Write the name of the person on your paper.

1. Creo que el cuarto es muy feo cuando está desordenado.

2. Tengo una camiseta blanca y otra camiseta de muchos colores.

3. Voy a organizar el cuarto.

4. No estoy contento cuando veo el cuarto ordenado.

5. Para mí, el cuarto es peor cuando está desordenado.

6. Ahora que el cuarto está más ordenado, no sé dónde están mis cosas.

7. Nunca más voy a organizar el cuarto de mi hijo.

8. Puedo dormir con todas las cosas encima de la cama.

Nota

Use reading strategies such as looking for cognates and understanding words from context when you read direction lines in Spanish. Here are some typical words you will see:

completa	*complete*	**mira**	*look*
contesta	*answer*	**pregunta**	*ask*
dibuja	*draw*	**trabaja**	*work*
escoge	*choose*	**una frase**	*a sentence*
escribe	*write*	**una hoja de papel**	*a piece of paper*
escucha	*listen*		
lee	*read*	**una palabra**	*a word*
habla	*speak*	**una respuesta**	*an answer*

Más práctica (GO)

realidades.com | print

Instant Check	✔	
Guided WB pp. 39–42	✔	✔
Core WB pp. 21–22	✔	✔
Comm. WB pp. 22–25	✔	✔
Hispanohablantes **WB** pp. 213–215		✔

3 Standards: 1.2, 1.3

Resources: Answer Keys: Student Edition, p. 116

Focus: Verifying comprehension of the *Videohistoria*

Suggestions: Challenge students to write as many answers as they can without referring back to the story.

Answers:

1. d 4. c
2. a 5. b
3. e

4 Standards: 1.2

Resources: Answer Keys: Student Edition, p. 117

Focus: Verifying comprehension of the *Videohistoria*

Suggestions: Make photocopies of p. 96 to distribute to students. Have students cut out the images of Mamá and Ignacio, and hold up the appropriate image as you read the sentences.

Answers:

1. Mamá
2. Ignacio
3. Mamá
4. Ignacio
5. Mamá
6. Ignacio
7. Mamá
8. Ignacio

Additional Resources

• Communication Wbk.: Audio Act. 5, p. 25
• Teacher's Resource Book: Audio Script, pp. 91–92
• Audio Program DVD: Cap. 6A, Track 7

ENRICH YOUR TEACHING

Teacher-to-Teacher

If possible, bring in some of the items from the vocabulary list to create a "bedroom" in the corner of the classroom. Use boxes and markers to make the furniture and electronics, but bring in curtains, old sheets and pillows, rugs, books, cases, and an alarm clock. (Be sure to provide students with the necessary vocabulary for items they don't know.) Have students re-enact the *Videohistoria* with the props, and use the bedroom throughout the chapter as a visual aid.

✓ASSESSMENT

Quiz: Vocabulary Recognition
• Prueba 6A-1: pp. 147–148

▼ Objectives

▶ Listen to a description of a room and label a room diagram
▶ Draw and describe your own room
▶ Exchange information while describing rooms and playing a game

Vocabulario en uso

BELLRINGER REVIEW

To review adjectives, show students five images from magazines, and have them describe what they see.

---

5 Standards: 1.3

Resources: Answer Keys: Student Edition, p. 117

Focus: Learning vocabulary through word associations

Suggestions: Before students begin, write a few words on the board and have students provide their opposites: *mayor / menor, calor / frío, delicioso / horrible.*

Answers:
1. feo
2. desordenado
3. izquierda
4. blanco
5. pequeño
6. mejor

---

6 Standards: 1.2, 1.3

Resources: Teacher's Resource Book: Audio Script, p. 91; Audio Program DVD: Cap. 6A, Track 6; Answer Keys: Student Edition, p. 117

Focus: Listening comprehension

Recycle: Prepositions of location

Suggestions: Students are drawing and will need longer pauses, but tell them not to be too detailed. Let them listen again to check their answers.

🔊 Script and Answers:

1. Hay una mesita a la derecha de la cama.
2. Hay una lámpara encima de la mesita.
3. Hay una cómoda a la izquierda de la ventana.
4. Hay un espejo sobre la cómoda.
5. Mi escritorio está en la pared que está delante de la cama.
6. Hay una computadora encima del escritorio.
7. Hay una silla enfrente del escritorio.
8. Hay una alfombra grande entre el escritorio y la cama.

▼5 Escribir

Palabras opuestas

Completa las frases con el opuesto (*opposite*) de las palabras subrayadas (*underlined*).

1. El cuadro no es bonito, es ___.
2. Mi dormitorio no está ordenado, está ___.
3. La mesita no está a la derecha de la cama, está a la ___.
4. Mi despertador no es negro, es ___.
5. Mi dormitorio no es grande, es ___.
6. Para mí, estudiar es peor que ver la tele, no es ___.

Strategy

Making word associations
Learning vocabulary as opposites helps you make quick associations to other words.

▼6 | ♻ | 🔊 | Escuchar · Dibujar · Escribir

Escucha, dibuja y escribe

Copy this drawing on a sheet of paper. You will hear Celia describing her room. As she mentions objects, draw them in the correct places in the room. Then label each object in Spanish.

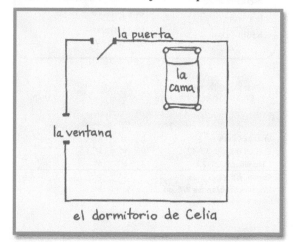

el dormitorio de Celia

También se dice . . .

el dormitorio = la habitación, la alcoba (España); la pieza (Argentina, Chile); la recámara (México)

bonito = lindo (México); mono (España)

marrón = de color café, castaño, de color chocolate (México, América del Sur)

la cómoda = el gavetero, el buró (México, otros países)

el armario = el guardarropa, el ropero (México, otros países)

pequeño = chico (México, otros países)

100 cien
Tema 6 • La casa

DIFFERENTIATED INSTRUCTION

Heritage Language Learners
Have students share other words they may know to describe a bedroom or objects in a bedroom.

Students with Special Needs
If students have trouble drawing the picture for *Actividad* 6, provide them with three or four illustrations, and have them choose the correct one as they listen. Remind them to use the drawing for the next three activities.

▼7 | ♻ | Dibujar · Escribir

Mi dormitorio

❶ Dibuja tu propio dormitorio o tu dormitorio ideal. Escribe los nombres de ocho cosas en el dibujo.

❷ Escribe siete frases para describir o *(either)* tu dormitorio o el dormitorio de Celia de la Actividad 6.

Modelo

El espejo está al lado de la cama.
Las cortinas en el dormitorio son largas.

> **¿Recuerdas?**
>
> Use *estar* to tell the location of items.
>
> Use *ser* to tell what items are like.

▼8 | 🗣👥 | ♻ | Hablar

¿Qué dormitorio es?

Trabaja con otro(a) estudiante. Muestra *(Show)* los dibujos de tu dormitorio y del dormitorio de Celia a tu compañero(a). Lee una de las frases que escribiste *(that you wrote)* en la Actividad 7. Tu compañero(a) tiene que identificar qué dormitorio describes.

▶ Modelo

A —*El espejo está al lado de la cama.*
B —*Es tu propio dormitorio.*
o: —*Es el dormitorio de Celia.*

> **Strategy**
>
> **Labeling**
> Put Spanish labels on the items in your bedroom so that you will see them every day. This will help you learn new words quickly.

▼9 | 👥 | ♻ | Escuchar · Hablar

Juego

Trabajen con un grupo de tres personas. Necesitan una moneda *(coin)* y uno de los dibujos de la Actividad 7. Una persona describe dónde está la moneda en el dormitorio. Los otros dos tratan de colocar *(try to place)* la moneda en el cuarto correctamente. La primera persona que coloca la moneda correctamente recibe un punto.

Modelo

La moneda está debajo de la cama.

ciento uno **101**
Capítulo 6A

Practice and Communicate 6A

Practice and Communicate 6A

▼7 Standards: 1.3

Focus: Using vocabulary in a personalized context

Recycle: Prepositions of location; ***estar***

Suggestions: Call attention to the *¿Recuerdas?* Tell students to keep drawings simple and remind them that they will be used for *Actividades* 8–9.

Answers will vary.

▼8 Standards: 1.1, 1.2

Focus: Practicing vocabulary and grammar about bedrooms in context

Recycle: Prepositions of location

Suggestions: Remind students to provide additional clues if their drawings have elements identical to those in Celia's bedroom.

Answers will vary.

▼9 Standards: 1.1, 1.2

Focus: Using vocabulary in a game

Recycle: Prepositions of location

Suggestions: Students will need to listen to the sentence before placing the coins.

Answers will vary.

Teacher-to-Teacher

Have students practice giving and understanding instructions. Ask each student to copy the floor plan from Actividad 6 twice. Have them draw in six pieces of furniture on one plan. This will be their model as they work with a partner. Put students in pairs. One student tells the partner to draw the furniture in the blank plan using his or her model as a guide. Have them compare drawings for accuracy. Then switch roles.

ENRICH YOUR TEACHING

Teacher-to-Teacher

Have students create and play a concentration game with opposites. Provide them with index cards and have them write one word per card, making sure that each word they write is paired with an opposite. Students should shuffle the cards and place them face down on the desk. Pairs of students can take turns looking for opposites, and the student with the most opposite pairs wins.

▼**10** Standards: 1.1, 1.2, 2.2

Resources: Answer Keys: Student Edition, p. 118

Focus: Reading comprehension

Suggestions: Remind students that the word order may be different from what they are used to since this is a poem.

Answers: un televisor

▼**11** Standards: 1.1, 1.2

Focus: Speaking and writing about things found in one's bedroom

Recycle: Prepositions of location

Suggestions: Remind students that when they write the results of their survey, they should not mention names. If students are uncomfortable talking about their family's possessions, give them pictures of rooms from magazines and suggest that they base their answers on what they see in the pictures.

Answers will vary but might include:

1. ¿Tienes tu propio lector de DVD?
2. ¿Tienes tu propia computadora?
3. ¿Tienes tu propio televisor?
4. ¿Tienes tu propio despertador digital?
5. ¿Tienes tus propios videos?

▼**10** | 👥 | Leer • Pensar • Hablar

¿Quién soy yo?

Aquí tienes una adivinanza (riddle) popular en las escuelas primarias en México. Trabaja con otro(a) estudiante para resolver la adivinanza.

> **Cine no soy,**
> **Radio tampoco.**
> **Tengo pantalla**
> **Y me creen poco.**
>
> **¿Quién soy yo?**

▼**11** | 🗣👥 | 👥 | ♻ | Hablar • Escribir

Tus propias cosas

1 Habla con otro(a) estudiante sobre las cosas que tienes en tu dormitorio. Pregunta y contesta según el modelo. Escribe las respuestas en una hoja de papel.

▶ Modelo

A —¿Tienes tu propio equipo de sonido?
B —Sí, tengo mi propio equipo de sonido. ¿Y tú?
A —No, pero puedo usar el equipo de sonido de mi familia.

Estudiante A

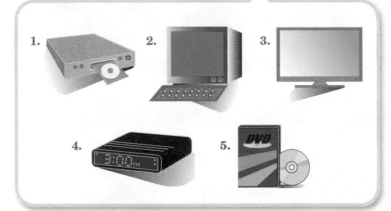

1. 2. 3. 4. 5.

Estudiante B

Sí, tengo mi propio(a) . . .
No, pero comparto . . .
  con . . .
No, pero puedo usar . . .
  de mi familia.
No, no tengo . . .
(No) me gustaría . . .

¡Respuesta personal!

2 Trabajen con otra pareja. Sumen (Add together) los resultados del paso (step) 1. Escriban frases para presentar los resultados a la clase. Compartan los resultados del grupo de ustedes con los otros grupos y sumen los resultados de toda la clase.

Modelo

Once estudiantes tienen computadoras en sus casas.

DIFFERENTIATED INSTRUCTION

Heritage Language Learners

Encourage students to share other riddles they know, perhaps some family favorites. Such riddle sharing will help all students build vocabulary.

Multiple Intelligences

Verbal/Linguistic: Have students continue the *¿Quién soy yo?* game by writing new riddles. Encourage them to create riddles that contain wordplay as well as the simpler type.

▼12 | 👥 | ♻ | Hablar

Las banderas

Working with a partner, describe the colors of the following flags from different Spanish-speaking countries. Your partner will name all countries whose flag it could be.

Mi familia es de Puerto Rico.

▶ **Modelo**

A —*La bandera tiene los colores rojo, amarillo y verde.*
B —*¿Es la bandera de Bolivia?*
A —*Sí.*

Argentina

Bolivia

Chile

Colombia

Costa Rica

Cuba

Ecuador

El Salvador

España

Guatemala

Guinea Ecuatorial

Honduras

Nicaragua

Panamá

Paraguay

Perú

Puerto Rico

República Dominicana

Uruguay

Venezuela

▼ Fondo Cultural | México

La bandera mexicana has a fascinating history. According to tradition, the Aztecs were to build their capital city, Tenochtitlán, where they found an eagle perched on a cactus and devouring a serpent. This image is what you see on the Mexican flag today.

• What flags can you identify in the United States that also contain a symbol with historical significance?

La bandera de México

ciento tres **103**
Capítulo 6A

13 Standards: 1.1

Focus: Using colors to describe items found in a bedroom

Recycle: *Tener; ser*

Suggestions: Direct students' attention to the *¿Recuerdas?* before beginning. Remind students that they have two options for answering. If they do not have the items on the list, have them name another item in their room to describe.

Answers will vary.

14 Standards: 1.1, 1.3

Focus: Using colors and adjectives in a personalized context

Suggestions: As an alternative to writing the colors, provide students with crayons or colored pencils, and have them recopy the words on their paper in the colors that they chose. Have students work in pairs to compare their answers, saying for example: *Para mí, "contento" es amarillo.*

Answers will vary.

15 Standards: 1.2, 1.3, 3.1, 4.1

Resources: Answer Keys: Student Edition, p. 118

Focus: Reading about the significance of colors in various cultures

Recycle: Cultural perspectives

Suggestions: Read the selection aloud with the class. Remind students to watch for cognates. Pause after each paragraph for students to provide an example that supports or negates what is being said in the reading.

Answers:
yellow traffic light—atención, precaución
green recycling symbol—buena salud, las plantas, tranquilidad
blue uniform—protección, autoridad
red roses—energía, pasión

▼13 **Hablar**

¿De qué color es . . . ?

Trabaja con otro(a) estudiante y habla de tu dormitorio. Describe el color de cada palabra en la lista.

▶ **Modelo**

A —*¿De qué color es la alfombra en tu dormitorio?*
B —*La alfombra es amarilla.*
o: *No tengo alfombra en mi dormitorio.*

¿Recuerdas?

Remember, when colors describe an object, they are adjectives. Adjectives agree with the noun they describe in both number and gender. If a color ends in a consonant, add *-es* regardless of gender.

• Las cortinas son rojas.
• Las cortinas son azules.

cama	equipo de sonido
paredes	cortinas
lámparas	alfombra
cómoda	

¡Respuesta personal!

▼14 **Pensar • Escribir**

¿De qué color es tu día?

¿Cuáles son los colores que asocias con estas palabras? Escribe los colores.

Modelo
regular   *gris*

1. contento
2. triste
3. calor
4. frío
5. artístico

6. sociable
7. horrible
8. gracioso
9. reservado
10. aburrido

Y para ti, ¿cuál es el color de tu personalidad?

104 ciento cuatro
Tema 6 • La casa

DIFFERENTIATED INSTRUCTION

Heritage Language Learners
Have students choose a color and write a poem about what that color makes them think of. Provide students with sample poetic genres, such as haikus, limericks, or sonnets, to use as an example. Have students write a final copy of their poem on a sheet of paper in the color that they chose.

Multiple Intelligences
Visual/Spatial: Have students create an "art museum" of Spanish-speaking artists, such as Dalí, Miró, and Picasso. Have them make cardboard frames and put them around colored images of the art, downloaded and printed from the Internet. Tell students to label the images with the name of the artist, the title of the painting, and the colors used.

▼15 | Leer • Pensar • Escribir

¿Qué significan los colores?

En la psicología, hay un estudio de los significados *(meanings)* de diferentes colores en diferentes culturas. Lee las descripciones aquí para contestar las preguntas.

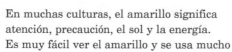 **Conexiones** | Las ciencias sociales

En muchas culturas, el verde significa buena salud, la primavera, las plantas y tranquilidad. Es un color de la paz[1].

El blanco, en las culturas de las Américas, significa generalmente inocencia y paz. En ciertas culturas asiáticas, el blanco significa la muerte[2].

El color que expresa energía, pasión y acción en muchas culturas diferentes es el rojo.

En muchas culturas, el amarillo significa atención, precaución, el sol y la energía. Es muy fácil ver el amarillo y se usa mucho para los taxis.

Un color que expresa protección, autoridad, confianza[3] y armonía es el azul. Vemos este color mucho en los uniformes de la policía y los militares.

[1]peace [2]death [3]confidence

Find words or expressions in the reading to explain the following uses of color:

- yellow traffic light
- green recycling symbol
- blue police uniform
- red roses for Valentine's day

 ▼16 Escribir • Hablar

Una bandera para ti

Imagina que vas a diseñar *(design)* una bandera para una organización, un club o un equipo *(team)*. ¿Qué colores vas a usar? ¿Por qué?

 ▼17 | | Escribir • Hablar

Y tú, ¿qué dices?

1. ¿Cuáles son tus colores favoritos? ¿Qué posesiones tienes en tu dormitorio de estos colores?
2. Escribe una lista de cinco cosas que están en tu dormitorio y el color de cada cosa. Por ejemplo: *Tengo una lámpara anaranjada.*

16 Standards: 1.1, 1.3

Focus: Identifying colors in a personalized context

Suggestions: Remind students to consider what the club or team stands for. Have them use the information in *Actividad* 15 to help them determine which colors are appropriate.

Answers will vary.

17 Standards: 1.1, 1.2, 1.3

Focus: Writing and speaking about favorite colors

Suggestions: You may want to have students write the answers to the questions in paragraph form, giving it the title *En mi dormitorio...*

Answers will vary.

Additional Resources

- Communication Wbk.: Audio Act. 6, p. 26
- Teacher's Resource Book: Audio Script, p. 92, Communicative Pair Activity BLM, pp. 98–99
- Audio Program DVD: Cap. 6A, Track 8

ENRICH YOUR TEACHING

Culture Note

The people of Argentina have a special name for the light, bright shade of blue in their national flag. They call it **celeste,** which means "of the sky", because they say that the color is as blue and as clear as the sky.

Teacher-to-Teacher

Using the colors of the rainbow, have students choose a favorite color, and then paint a rainbow on a large sheet of rolled paper. On each stripe, write the names of the students who chose the color. Ask them to write statements about something they own of that color. Glue their statements around the rainbow. For example: *Nosotros tenemos libros de español anaranjados.*

✓ASSESSMENT

Prueba 6A-2 with Study Plan (online only)

Quiz: Vocabulary Production
- Prueba 6A-2: pp. 149–150

105

Gramática

Core Instruction

Standards: 4.1

Resources: Voc. and Gram. Transparency 116; Teacher's Resource Book: Video Script, p. 95; Video Program: Cap. 6A

INTERACTIVE WHITEBOARD
Grammar Activities 6A

Suggestions: Direct students' attention to the *¿Recuerdas?*, and ask volunteers to give you an example of a comparison using *más...que.* Bring in photos and objects for students to compare. Use the visuals to guide students through the *Gramática* presentation. Ask students to respond to the comparisons that you make by saying *Estoy de acuerdo* or *No estoy de acuerdo.* Use the *GramActiva* video to reinforce your presentation.

▼18 Standards: 1.1, 1.3

Focus: Comparing people

Suggestions: You may wish to provide context for the activity by choosing a well-known television show or book and having the class compare the characters.

Answers will vary.

Pre-AP* Support

- **Learning Objective:** Interpretive: Audio
- **Activity:** Have students write five sentences similar to those found in *Actividad* 18 about classmates or other well-known students or teachers in your school. Ask that they make some of their sentences false. Collect these sentences and randomly read several to the class as a *Cierta* or *Falsa* activity.
- **Pre-AP* Resource Book:** Comprehensive guide to Pre-AP* communication skill development, pp. 10–57

Gramática

▶ Listen to a description of two different bedrooms
▶ Write about, discuss, and compare different music
▶ Exchange information while comparing opinions with a classmate

Making comparisons

Just as you can use *más . . . que* to compare two things, you can also use **menos . . . que** (*less . . . than*).

El disco compacto de Los Toros es **menos** popular **que** el disco compacto de Los Lobos.

*The CD by Los Toros is **less** popular **than** the CD by Los Lobos.*

The adjectives *bueno(a), malo(a), viejo(a),* and *joven* and the adverbs *bien* and *mal* have their own comparative forms. *Más* and *menos* are not used with these comparative adjectives and adverbs.

Adjective	Adverb	Comparative	
bueno, -a	bien	mejor (que)	*better than*
malo, -a	mal	peor (que)	*worse than*
viejo, -a		mayor (que)	*older than*
joven		menor (que)	*younger than*

Mejor, peor, mayor, and *menor* have plural forms that end in *-es.*

Los videos de Shakira son **mejores** que los videos de Juanes.

¿Recuerdas?

You have learned to use *más . . . que* to compare two things.

- La clase de inglés es **más** interesante **que** la clase de matemáticas.

Más ayuda **realidades.com**

▶ *GramActiva* **Video Tutorials:** Comparing things that are equal, Comparing things that are not equal

✎ *GramActiva* **Activity**

▼18 Escribir • Hablar

Las personas en mis fotos

Your friend wants to know about the people in the photos that you have in your room. On a separate sheet of paper, write sentences about people you know by completing the sentences with the names of friends or family members.

1. ___ es más alto(a) que ___.
2. ___ es menos deportista que ___.
3. ___ es mayor que ___.
4. ___ es menor que ___.
5. ___ es más deportista que ___.
6. ___ es menos serio(a) que ___.
7. ___ es más artístico(a) que ___.
8. ___ es menos atrevido(a) que ___.

DIFFERENTIATED INSTRUCTION

Students with Learning Difficulties

To help students prepare for *Actividad* 20, have them brainstorm ideas for decorating their own bedrooms. They should use each of the words in bold type.

Heritage Language Learners

Have students write sentences comparing their bedroom to the bedroom of a sibling or a friend. Review their work for correct spelling and grammar.

▼19 🔊 | Escuchar · Escribir

Dos dormitorios

En una hoja de papel, escribe los números del 1 al 6. Escucha las seis comparaciones de los dormitorios de Paco y Kiko. Escribe *C* (cierto) o *F* (falso).

El dormitorio de Paco

El dormitorio de Kiko

▼20 Leer · Escribir

Quiero decorar mi propio dormitorio

Lee el correo electrónico de Alicia sobre su idea del dormitorio perfecto. En una hoja de papel, escribe los números del 1 al 6. ¿Cuál es tu opinión? Indica para cada frase si estás de acuerdo con ella o no. Si no estás de acuerdo, ¿por qué no?

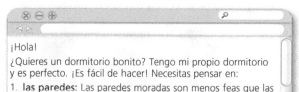

¡Hola!

¿Quieres un dormitorio bonito? Tengo mi propio dormitorio y es perfecto. ¡Es fácil de hacer! Necesitas pensar en:

1. **las paredes:** Las paredes moradas son menos feas que las paredes blancas.

2. **las cortinas:** Las cortinas anaranjadas son mejores que las cortinas azules.

3. **la alfombra:** Una alfombra roja es menos seria que una alfombra gris.

4. **la cómoda:** Una cómoda bonita es más importante que un estante bonito.

5. **los carteles:** Los carteles de actores son más interesantes que los carteles de deportes.

6. **el televisor:** Un televisor con videocasetera es más popular que un televisor con lector DVD. Tengo buenas ideas, ¿no estás de acuerdo?

Hasta luego,
Alicia

Modelo

el equipo de sonido: Los equipos de sonido grandes son mejores que los equipos de sonido pequeños.

Sí, estoy de acuerdo. Para mí, los equipos de sonido grandes son mejores que los equipos de sonido pequeños.

o: —*No estoy de acuerdo. Para mí, los equipos de sonido pequeños son mejores que los equipos de sonido grandes.*

o: —*No estoy de acuerdo. Para mí, los equipos de sonido grandes son peores que los equipos de sonido pequeños.*

ciento siete **107**
Capítulo 6A

---

19 Standards: 1.2, 1.3

Resources: Teacher's Resource Book: Audio Script, p. 92; Audio Program DVD: Cap. 6A, Track 9; Answer Keys: Student Edition, p. 118

Focus: Listening comprehension

Suggestions: Give students time to study the illustrations of the bedrooms before beginning the activity. Play the audio or read the script aloud. Allow students to listen more than once.

🔊 **Script and Answers:**

1. **Los dos cuartos están muy ordenados.** *(F)*
2. **Al lado de la cama hay una mesita.** *(C)*
3. **Encima de la mesita hay una lámpara pequeña.** *(C)*
4. **En el centro del cuarto hay una alfombra grande.** *(F)*
5. **A la izquierda de la alfombra está la cómoda.** *(F)*
6. **Paco y Kiko tienen equipos de sonido.** *(C)*

Extension: Have students use their drawings from *Actividad* 7 and compare their bedroom with that of a partner. Ask them to share their comparisons with the class and have the class indicate whether they agree or not.

BELLRINGER REVIEW

Ask students to look at the two illustrations on p. 107 and write down the Spanish words for three items that are found in both bedrooms.

20 Standards: 1.2, 1.3

Focus: Reading and responding to an e-mail message

Suggestions: Remind students that they need to write a sentence to respond to each statement.

Answers will vary.

Extension: Have students draw and color the bedroom they described.

ENRICH YOUR TEACHING

Teacher-to-Teacher

If possible, record a segment of a home improvement show where a bedroom is transformed or bring in "before" and "after" photos from a decorating magazine. Show the students the room before the changes. Have them brainstorm adjectives to describe the room. Show them the room after the transformation and have them write a new description. Ask students to work with a partner, compile their descriptions, and write a short paragraph expressing their opinions on the changes. Make sure they use expressions for making comparisons when talking about both rooms.

21 Standards: 1.1, 1.2, 1.3

Focus: Using comparatives to give personal opinions

Recycle: Adjectives

Suggestions: Have students give examples of different types of music. Remind them that adjectives must agree with nouns, and have them look at the definite articles for the words in *Para decir más...* to identify their gender.

Answers will vary.

Extension: Have students further discuss music preferences by using the adjectives to compare their favorite artists.

Fondo cultural

Standards: 2.1, 2.2, 5.2

Suggestions: Ask students if they are familiar with Latin music groups. Have them brainstorm the names of some Latin recording artists. If possible, play some recordings of Grammy-winning artists in class.

Theme Project

Give students copies of the Theme Project outline and rubric from the *Teacher's Resource Book*. Explain the task to them, and have them perform Step 1. (For more information, see p. 92-b.)

▼**21** | 😊👥 | ♻ | **Escribir • Hablar**

¡Viva la música!

❶ Escribe cinco frases con comparaciones de los varios tipos de música que ves aquí. Usa estos *(these)* adjetivos en la forma correcta con *más . . . que* o *menos . . . que.*

aburrido, -a	interesante
bonito, -a	serio, -a
divertido, -a	triste
feo, -a	popular
importante	

Para decir más . . .

el blues	el jazz
la música clásica	la música rap
la música folklórica	la salsa
la música hip-hop	la música reggae
la música rock	

Modelo
Para mí, la salsa es más divertida que la música rap.

❷ Lee tus comparaciones a otro(a) estudiante para ver si Uds. están de acuerdo.

 Modelo

A —*Para mí, la salsa es más divertida que la música rap.*

B —*Sí, estoy de acuerdo, pero la salsa es menos popular que la música rap.*

Grandes éxitos

▼**Fondo Cultural** | El mundo hispano

El Grammy latino Latin Grammy awards recognize the talents of Spanish and Portuguese speaking artists from around the world every year. In recent years, Latin Grammy winners include Alejandro Sanz, Juan Luis Guerra, Nelly Furtado, Camila, Rubén Blades, Café Tacuba, Juanes, and Marc Anthony.

• Who are some Latin recording artists you enjoy and what is their music like?

El grupo mexicano Camila, con sus premios Grammy

DIFFERENTIATED INSTRUCTION

Heritage Language Learners
Invite students to tell about recording artists popular in their heritage country who are not yet well known in the United States. Have students bring in recordings by some of these artists to share with the class.

Heritage Language Learners
As you work on the pronunciation of the **rr** sound, be aware that heritage language learners will pronounce this phoneme differently, depending on where they are from. In Mexico and the Caribbean, the **rr** is very strong, while in Central America, it is less pronounced.

▼ Pronunciación | 🔊 | 💬

The letters *r* and *rr*

Except at the beginning of a word or after *l* or *n*, the sound of the letter *r* is similar to the *dd* in the English word *ladder*. Listen to and say these words:

derecha	quiero	amarillo	bandera
pero	puerta	alfombra	morado

The sound of the letter *rr* is similar to saying "batter, batter, batter" over and over again very quickly. Listen to and say these words:

perro	correr	guitarra	marrón
aburrido	arroz	pelirrojo	horrible

When *r* is the first letter of a word or comes after *l* or *n*, it is pronounced like the *rr*.

Roberto	Rita	Ricardo	rojo	regalo
rubio	radio	reloj	romper	Enrique

Try it out! Listen to and say this *trabalenguas*:

Erre con erre cigarro, erre con erre barril. Rápido corren los carros cargados de azúcar del ferrocarril.

Pronunciación
Core Instruction

Standards: 4.1

Resources: Teacher's Resource Book: Audio Script, p. 92; Audio Program DVD: Cap. 6A, Track 10

Suggestions: Read the *Pronunciación* with students or use the audio. Model the two distinct sounds, exaggerating them somewhat for clarity. Have students repeat the words after you.

▼22 | 💬 | ♻ | Escribir · Hablar

¿Cómo se comparan los dos?

With a partner, choose two people or things for each category below. On your own sheet of paper compare the two. Your partner will do the same. Then take turns reading your comparisons and giving your opinions.

1. actividades   3. clases   5. libros o revistas
2. deportes   4. comidas   6. personas famosas

▶ **Modelo**

A —*Para mí, ir al cine es mejor que ver un video.*

B —*Estoy de acuerdo. Ir al cine es mejor que ver un video.*

o:—*No estoy de acuerdo. Ver un video es más divertido que ir al cine.*

▼22 Standards: 1.1, 1.3

Focus: Using comparatives to express opinions

Recycle: Activities and food vocabulary

Suggestions: Explain that students will write about two people or things for each category. Have partners complete their lists before each one begins writing their comparisons.

Answers will vary.

▼23 | 💬 | Escribir · Hablar

Y tú, ¿qué dices?

1. ¿Cómo es tu dormitorio? ¿Está más o menos ordenado que los dormitorios de tus amigos?

2. Describe a tu mejor amigo(a). ¿Es más serio(a) que tú? ¿Quién es más deportista?

3. ¿Cómo son tus clases? ¿Son menos aburridas que las clases de tus amigos? Explica.

4. ¿Cómo es la comida en la escuela? ¿Es mejor que la comida en un restaurante?

5. Compara tus dos grupos musicales favoritos.

Más práctica

realidades.com | print

Instant Check	✔	
Guided WB p. 43	✔	✔
Core WB p. 23	✔	✔
Comm. WB pp. 26, 30	✔	✔
***Hispanohablantes* WB** pp. 216–217, 219, 221		✔

ciento nueve **109**
Capítulo 6A

▼23 Standards: 1.1, 1.3

Focus: Making comparisons

Suggestions: Group students to discuss each question and then have groups present their discussions to the class.

Answers will vary.

Additional Resources

- Communication Wbk.: Audio Act. 7, p. 26
- Teacher's Resource Book: Audio Script, pp. 92–93
- Audio Program DVD: Cap. 6A, Track 11

ENRICH YOUR TEACHING

Culture Note

In recent years, Latin American music has become popular throughout the world, and in 2011 the Latin Grammy Awards were broadcast in more than 100 countries, including the United States. These awards feature traditional Central and South American musicians as well as Spanish-speaking pop stars. With talent from across the world, competition is high.

21st Century Skills

Initiative and Self-Direction Remind students that they have many tools that will help them understand and practice the grammar concepts in this program. Direct them to the eText activities, and the online tutorials, which make it possible for students to monitor their own progress and learning needs.

✔ ASSESSMENT

Prueba 6A-3 with Study Plan (online only)

Quiz: Making Comparisons
- Prueba 6A-3: p. 151

▼ Objectives
▶ Discuss and write about the best and worst in entertainment
▶ Exchange information about bedrooms and colors

Gramática

Core Instruction

Standards: 4.1

Resources: Teacher's Resource Book: Video Script, pp. 95–96; Video Program: Cap. 6A

INTERACTIVE WHITEBOARD
Grammar Activities 6A

Suggestions: Before introducing the grammar point, give students a list of categories (classes, musicians, or sports). Have students name the best and worst in their opinion. Use these opinions as a springboard to a discussion in Spanish.

▼ 24 Standards: 1.3

Focus: Understanding superlative expressions

Suggestions: Remind students that they are to complete the sentences with words that express their opinion. As students share their opinions with the class, have others give a "thumbs-up" or "thumbs-down" sign to show agreement or disagreement.

Answers will vary.

▼ 25 Standards: 1.1

Resources: Answer Keys: Student Edition, p. 119

Focus: Using superlatives to describe items in a house

Recycle: Objects and adjectives

Suggestions: Have students brainstorm their preferences on a sheet of paper before having them work in pairs.

Answers will vary; questions are:
1. —Para ti, ¿cuál es la posesión más importante?
2. ... el mejor disco compacto?
3. ... el video más interesante?
4. ... la foto más bonita?
5. ... el videojuego más divertido?

Gramática

The superlative

To say that someone or something is the "most" or "least," use:

definite article **(el, la, los, las)** + noun + **más / menos** + adjective

La foto de mi familia es **la posesión más importante** para mí.

To say that someone or something is the "best" or the "worst," use:

definite article + **mejor(es) / peor(es)** + noun

Rojo y azul son **los mejores colores** para mi dormitorio.

Más ayuda | **realidades.com**

▶ *GramActiva* **Video Tutorial:** Superlatives

✎ *GramActiva* **Activity**

▼ 24 Escribir

Espejo, espejo de la pared . . .

Imagine you have a magic mirror on the wall in your room. How would it complete these sentences? Write the sentences on a separate sheet of paper.

1. La persona más inteligente es___.
2. El peor actor es___.
3. Las clases más interesantes son___.
4. El videojuego menos divertido es___.
5. Los mejores discos compactos son___.
6. El color menos bonito es___.

▼ 25 Hablar

Las casas de los ricos y famosos

Una persona del programa de televisión "Las casas de los ricos y famosos" está en tu casa. Habla con él/ella sobre las cosas especiales en tu casa. Pregunta y contesta según el modelo.

1. posesión / importante
2. disco compacto / mejor
3. video / interesante
4. foto / bonita
5. videojuego / divertido

▶ **Modelo**
cuadro / bonito
A —*Para ti, ¿cuál es el cuadro más bonito?*
B —*Para mí, el cuadro más bonito es el cuadro de las flores rojas y amarillas.*

DIFFERENTIATED INSTRUCTION

Multiple Intelligences

Bodily/Kinesthetic: Have students prepare a comical skit based on *Actividad* 24. Ask students to prepare four questions using the superlative. Provide students with a mirror to act out their skit. Have one student stand behind the mirror, while the other student asks the questions.

Heritage Language Learners

Have students use superlatives to write a paragraph about their heritage country. If students have made flags earlier in the chapter, post their corrected paragraph with the flag.

▼**26** Escribir

No me gustan mucho

Do you like some things better than others in your room?
Describe the things that you like the least in your room.
For each object below use one of the adjectives in the word box.

Modelo
El cartel menos bonito en mi dormitorio es el cartel de los gatos.
o: *El cartel más feo en mi dormitorio es el cartel de los gatos.*

bonito, -a	feo, -a
interesante	aburrido, -a
importante	mejor
divertido, -a	peor

1. los discos compactos
2. los cuadros
3. el libro
4. el video
5. la foto
6. la posesión

▼**27**  Hablar

¡No seas tan negativo(a)!

Using the information from Actividad 26, tell your partner about the worst things in your room. Your partner will try to get you to be more positive by asking you about the best things in your room.

▶ Modelo

A —*El cartel menos bonito en mi dormitorio es el cartel de los gatos.*
B —*¿Cuál es el cartel más bonito en tu dormitorio?*
A —*El cartel más bonito es el cartel de los perros.*

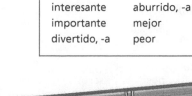

▼**28**  Escribir · Hablar

Y tú, ¿qué dices?

1. ¿Cuál es la película más graciosa? ¿Y cuál es la película más seria?
2. Según tus amigos y tú, ¿cuál es el grupo musical más popular? ¿Y cuál es el grupo musical menos popular?
3. ¿Quién es tu amigo(a) menos reservado(a)? ¿Y quién es tu amigo(a) menos atrevido(a)?
4. ¿Para ti, cuál es el mejor mes del año? ¿Y cuál es el peor mes del año? ¿Por qué?

Más práctica	GO

realidades.com | print

Instant Check	✔	
Guided WB p. 44	✔	✔
Core WB p. 24	✔	✔
Comm. WB pp. 27, 31, 144	✔	✔
Hispanohablantes **WB** p. 217		✔

ciento once **111**
Capítulo 6A

ENRICH YOUR TEACHING

Teacher-to-Teacher
Have students work in groups to prepare a television show in which they explore the home of a rich, famous person. Tell students to bring in props to decorate a "bedroom" in the classroom or auditorium, and describe it to their classmates. Remind them to point out the best and worst items in the room. As an alternative, students can do the activity individually at home. If possible, record the performances, and spend time in class viewing the videos.

26 Standards: 1.3
Focus: Using superlatives to write about the least-liked items in the bedroom
Suggestions: Remind students that they can use either *más* or *menos* in their descriptions of items in their bedroom, but that they should express the negative. You may need to provide students with vocabulary for number 6.
Answers will vary.

27 Standards: 1.1
Focus: Talking about favorite and least-favorite items in the bedroom
Suggestions: Have students list the items that they will include in their answers before they begin working with their partner.
Answers will vary.

28 Standards: 1.1, 1.2, 1.3
Focus: Giving opinions
Suggestions: Since each question has a different theme, divide students into small groups to discuss one question. Then, have a whole-class discussion where students share their opinions and invite others to respond.
Answers will vary.

Additional Resources
- Communication Wbk: Audio Act. 8, p. 27
- Teacher's Resource Book: Audio Script, p. 93
- Audio Program DVD: Cap. 6A, Track 12

✔ASSESSMENT
Prueba 6A-4 with Study Plan (online only)
Quiz: The superlative
- Prueba 6A-4: p. 152

Gramática

Core Instruction

Standards: 4.1

Resources: Voc. and Gram. Transparency 117; Teacher's Resource Book: Video Script, p. 96; Video Program: Cap. 6A

INTERACTIVE WHITEBOARD

Grammar Activities 6A

Suggestions: Remind students that they already know some stem-changing verbs, such as **tener, querer, preferir,** and **jugar.** Use the *GramActiva* video and/or the transparency either as an initial introduction to the structure or as a follow-up after your own grammar explanation.

▼ 29 Standards: 1.2, 1.3, 3.1

Resources: Answer Keys: Student Edition, p. 119
Focus: Completing sentences using **dormir**
Suggestions: Remind students that there are two parts to this activity—filling in the correct verb forms and determining how many hours each person sleeps.

Answers:

1. dormimos	4. dormimos
2. duerme	5. dormimos
3. duerme	6. duermen

Tomás duerme seis horas.
Catalina duerme diez horas.
Guillermo duerme ocho horas.
Paco duerme nueve horas.
Laura duerme nueve horas.
Yo duermo ocho horas.

Fondo cultural

Standards: 1.2, 2.1, 4.2
Suggestions: Point out to students that a **siesta** in the middle of the working day usually results in later hours. It is not uncommon, in large cities, for workers who take the **siesta** to stay at work until at least 8:00 P.M.
Answers will vary.

| ▼ Objectives

▶ Listen to, write, and discuss rules
▶ Read, write, and talk about sleep habits
▶ Describe objects to play a guessing game
▶ Design a dream bedroom for a classmate

Gramática

Stem-changing verbs: *poder* and *dormir*

Like *jugar*, *poder* and *dormir* are stem-changing verbs. They have a change from *o→ue* in all forms except *nosotros* and *vosotros*. Here are the present-tense forms:

(yo)	pued**o**	(nosotros) (nosotras)	pod**emos**
(tú)	pued**es**	(vosotros) (vosotras)	pod**éis**
Ud. (él) (ella)	pued**e**	Uds. (ellos) (ellas)	pued**en**

(yo)	duerm**o**	(nosotros) (nosotras)	dorm**imos**
(tú)	duerm**es**	(vosotros) (vosotras)	dorm**ís**
Ud. (él) (ella)	duerm**e**	Uds. (ellos) (ellas)	duerm**en**

Más ayuda **realidades.com**

 GramActiva Video
Animated Verbs

 Canción de hip hop: *¡No podemos dormir!*

 GramActiva Activity

¿Recuerdas?

You use *puedo* and *puedes* to say what you can or cannot do.

• ¿**Puedes** ir a la fiesta conmigo? No, no **puedo**.

▼ 29 Leer • Escribir • Pensar

Rompecabezas

¿Cuántas horas duermen las personas en esta familia? Escribe la forma apropiada del verbo *dormir* para cada frase. Después contesta la pregunta.

¡Mis hermanos y yo __1.__ 50 horas al día! Es mucho, ¿no? Tomás, mi hermano mayor, __2.__ menos, seis horas al día. Catalina __3.__ más horas que todos—cuatro horas más que Tomás. Guillermo y yo __4.__ el mismo número de horas. Juntos (*Together*) nosotros __5.__ el mismo número de horas que Tomás y Catalina. Paco y Laura __6.__ el mismo número de horas.

¿Cuántas horas duerme cada persona (Tomás, Catalina, Guillermo, Paco, Laura y yo)?

(112) **ciento doce**
Tema 6 • La casa

▼ Fondo Cultural | El mundo hispano

La siesta, an afternoon nap after the large midday meal, is a custom that has been observed in Spain and other Spanish-speaking countries for many centuries. However, with modern-day pressures and in larger cities, many people no longer take off work for *la siesta.*

• What would be some advantages and disadvantages of a *siesta* in your daily life?

En España, muchas tiendas se cierran entre las 14:00 y las 16:30 horas.

DIFFERENTIATED INSTRUCTION

Advanced Learners/Pre-AP*

Have students draw a cartoon using comparisons and the verb **poder.** The characters of their cartoon should describe what they are able to do and who does it better. If students are not willing or able to draw an entire cartoon, have them cut pictures out of celebrity magazines to include. Encourage humor and creativity.

▼30 | 🔊 | **Escuchar • Escribir • Hablar**

El Campamento Nadadivertido

It's the first day at your summer camp, el Campamento Nadadivertido. Your friend never listens to anything. Listen to the camp rules and answer your friend's questions.

1. ¿Podemos usar el equipo de sonido en la tarde?
2. ¿Quiénes no pueden ir a los dormitorios de los chicos?
3. ¿Podemos ver la televisión o videos en los dormitorios?
4. ¿Cuándo podemos escuchar discos compactos?
5. ¿Podemos beber refrescos en la cama?
6. ¿Podemos dormir hasta *(until)* las nueve?

> **Nota**
>
> When the forms of *poder* are followed by another verb, the second verb is in the infinitive form.
> • No **puedo dormir** bien cuando tengo calor.

▼31 | 😀 | ♻ | **Escribir • Hablar**

Las reglas

You are baby-sitting two children and you don't know the rules of the house. First, write five questions to ask the children. Then, working in groups of three, use the verbs in the box below to ask and answer questions according to the model.

comer	ir
beber	jugar
ver	escuchar

▶ **Modelo**

A —¿Uds. pueden comer helado después de las siete?

B —No, nunca podemos comer helado después de las siete.

o:—¡Claro! Siempre podemos comer helado después de las siete.

▼32 | 😀 | ♻ | **Hablar**

¡Podemos hacer muchas cosas!

Trabaja con otro(a) estudiante para decir qué pueden hacer diferentes personas con las posesiones que tienen.

▶ **Modelo**

Marcos / sacar fotos

A —¿Marcos puede sacar fotos?

B —¡Claro que sí! Tiene una cámara muy buena.

o:—No. No tiene una cámara.

Estudiante A

1. Uds. / ver películas en casa
2. Raquel / hacer la tarea de álgebra
3. tu papá (o tu mamá) / usar el Internet
4. tú / escuchar discos compactos
5. Guille y Patricio / jugar videojuegos

Estudiante B

ciento trece **113**
Capítulo 6A

ENRICH YOUR TEACHING

Culture Note

Though the *siesta* tradition is disappearing from Mexico's large cities, it is still observed in many smaller places, especially coastal towns and other areas where the weather is hot. It makes sense to many people to take an afternoon break after eating the main meal of the day.

21st Century Skills

Technology Literacy Have students create an online survey for the class to find out about the sleeping habits of their classmates. Have them compile the results and select "winners": who sleeps the most in a week, who the least, who gets up the earliest on the weekend, who sleeps the longest, etc. Have them post the results of the "sleep contest" on the class Web site.

---

30 Standards: 1.1, 1.2, 1.3

Resources: Teacher's Resource Book: Audio Script, p. 93; Audio Program DVD: Cap. 6A, Track 13; Answer Keys: Student Edition, p. 120

Focus: Listening comprehension

Suggestions: Allow students time to review the questions before they listen.

🔊 **Script and Answers:**

1. Regla número uno: No pueden usar el equipo de sonido después de las ocho. (Sí, pero no después de las ocho.)
2. Regla número dos: Las chicas no pueden estar en los dormitorios de los chicos. (las chicas)
3. Regla número tres: No pueden tener televisores ni lectores DVD en el campamento. (No, no podemos tener televisores en el campamento.)
4. Regla número cuatro: Pueden escuchar discos compactos, pero sólo los domingos. (sólo los domingos)
5. Regla número cinco: No pueden ni comer ni beber en las camas. (No, no podemos beber en las camas.)
6. Regla número seis: No pueden dormir después de las siete. (No, sólo hasta las siete.)

31 Standards: 1.1, 1.3

Focus: Asking and answering questions about rules

Recycle: Leisure activities

Suggestions: Before beginning, discuss with students some of the rules parents leave with baby-sitters.

Answers will vary.

32 Standards: 1.1, 1.3

Resources: Answer Keys: Student Edition, p. 121

Focus: Using *poder* to discuss use of electronic equipment

Recycle: *Tener* and leisure activities

Suggestions: Point out to students that all of the necessary equipment for the activities is pictured.

Answers will vary; questions are:

1. ¿Uds. pueden ver películas en casa?
2. ¿Raquel puede hacer la tarea de álgebra?
3. ¿Tu papá puede usar el Internet?
4. ¿Tú puedes escuchar discos compactos?
5. ¿Guille y Patricio pueden jugar videojuegos?

▼33 Standards: 1.1, 1.2, 1.3, 4.1

Resources: Answer Keys: Student Edition, p. 121

Focus: Reading comprehension

Suggestions: Have students scan the article and predict what it will be about. Point out that question 3 has a different structure from the other questions and give students guidelines for writing their answers.

Answers:
1. **El problema es que muchos adultos no duermen lo suficiente.**
2. **68%**
3. **sí; no; no; sí**
4. **Answers will vary.**

BELLRINGER REVIEW

Ask students to copy these sentences from the board and complete them with the correct form of *poder*:

1. *Yo no _____ patinar en el/la _____.*
2. *Mi amigo y yo no _____ beber limonada en el/la _____.*

Share with the class.

Exploración del lenguaje
Core Instruction

Standards: 4.1

Resources: Answer Keys: Student Edition, p. 121

Suggestions: Have the class brainstorm other words and roots they have learned. Keep a list posted that students can add to.

Answers:
beb ...*bebida*
televis ...*televisor*
green fields (verdant ...*verde*)
a blue sky (azure ...*azul*)
a gray-haired man (grizzled ...*gris*)

Theme Project
Students can perform Step 2 at this point. Be sure students understand your suggestions. (For more information, see p. 92-b.)

114

▼33 Leer • Escribir • Hablar

¿Duermes bien?

Lee este artículo de una revista y contesta las preguntas.

1. Según el artículo, ¿cuál es el problema?
2. ¿Qué porcentaje de las personas duerme menos de ocho horas diarias durante la semana?
3. ¿El artículo presenta estas ideas? Contesta *sí* o *no*.

   Las personas que duermen poco . . .
   . . . generalmente están más cansadas.
   . . . trabajan mejor.
   . . . juegan mucho y hacen ejercicio.
   . . . son menos sociables.

4. Y tú, durante los fines de semana, ¿cuántas horas duermes en la noche?

¿Cuántas horas duermes por noche?

Un nuevo estudio indica que muchos adultos no duermen ni[1] seis horas por noche, y afecta mucho a su calidad de vida.[2]

Durante la semana:
8 ó más — Menos de 6
15%
30%
6 a 6.9
24%
29%
7 a 7.9

Los fines de semana:
8 ó más — Menos de 6
10%
6 a 6.9
12%
52%
22%
7 a 7.9

Las personas que duermen menos de seis horas por noche:

- Tienen más estrés y fatiga
- Están más tristes y menos alertas
- Hacen peor su trabajo
- Sufren más lesiones[3]
- Tienen más problemas de relaciones interpersonales
- Comen más de lo usual
- Tienen menos energía

[1]not even [2]quality of life [3]injuries

▼ Exploración del lenguaje

Using root words

You can build your vocabulary, both in Spanish and in English, if you recognize the root of a word and know its meaning.

For example, because you know the root of one word, *comer*, you can more easily learn another word, *la comida*.

Try it out! Because you know the root of *beber*, you can easily remember *la __?__*. And since you know *ver la televisión*, you can easily recognize *el __?__*.

Once you learn another language, your mastery of your own language can increase. In part, this is because you begin to use the words from your second language to help you understand words in English that are new to you.

Try it out! Since you know *verde, azul,* and *gris,* what do you think these words mean?

verdant fields   *azure* sky   a *grizzled* old man

114 **ciento catorce**
Tema 6 • La casa

DIFFERENTIATED INSTRUCTION

Students with Learning Difficulties
If necessary, provide students with varied or more detailed graphs for *Actividad* 33. Practice graph-reading skills before having students answer the questions.

Advanced Learners
Have students take a survey of sleeping habits in the class and prepare a pie graph similar to the ones in *Actividad* 33 to show the results.

▼**34** | | | Escribir • Hablar

Juego

Work with a partner to write a description of three items. Then get together with another group and read your descriptions. The other group will try to guess which items you are describing. The group to guess the items in the least amount of time wins.

▶ **Modelo**

A —*Es una cosa que toca música. Puede ser grande o pequeño. Está en muchas casas. ¿Qué es?*

B —*Es un equipo de sonido.*

Strategy

Circumlocution
When you don't know or can't remember the word for something, you can describe it. You can tell what it is used for, what size it is, what color it is, where it is often found, and so on.

▼**35** | | | Escribir • Hablar • Dibujar

Y tú, ¿qué preguntas?

1 Write five questions that you could ask someone to get a better idea of what his or her perfect room would be like. You can ask what your partner is like and what his or her favorite activities, colors, and interests are.

2 Ask your questions and write your partner's responses.

3 Draw the perfect room for your partner based on the responses to your questions. Show the drawing to your partner and tell why you think the room is perfect.

Modelo

El dormitorio es especial para ti porque tus colores favoritos son azul y rojo. Hay muchas fotos en las paredes porque siempre sacas fotos de tus amigos. Hay muchos videos y revistas en la cama. Te gusta escuchar la música. En el estante, están tus discos compactos.

El español en la comunidad

In many U.S. communities, you can see the influence of Spanish-style architecture. Spanish-style buildings often have tile roofs, stucco exteriors, and interior courtyards or patios.

- Identify houses, buildings, or neighborhoods in your community that feature this style. Draw or take a picture of one example.

Más práctica	GO

realidades.com | print

Instant Check	✔	
Guided WB pp. 45–46	✔	✔
Core WB p. 25	✔	✔
Comm. WB pp. 28, 32	✔	✔
Hispanohablantes **WB** pp. 218, 220–221		✔

ciento quince **115**
Capítulo 6A

---

34 Standards: 1.1, 1.2, 1.3

Focus: Writing descriptions of new vocabulary

Recycle: Adjectives

Suggestions: Give an example of circumlocution as in the *Strategy*. Remind students to start with *Es una cosa que…* and to describe size, color, and function.

Answers will vary.

35 Standards: 1.1, 1.2, 1.3

Focus: Asking questions about preferences and interpreting answers through drawing

Recycle: Adjectives; *gustar*

Suggestions: If students are not comfortable drawing, encourage them to use old magazines and catalogues to make a collage of their partner's bedroom.

Answers will vary.

Pre-AP* Support

- **Learning Objective:** Interpersonal Speaking
- **Activity 35:** Students practice informal speaking skills as they ask questions and use the information they learn.

El español en la comunidad

Core Instruction

Standards: 2.2, 4.2

Suggestions: Bring in a picture to share with students.

Additional Resources

- Communication Wbk.: Audio Act. 9, p. 28
- Teacher's Resource Book: Audio Script, p. 93, Communicative Pair Activity BLM, pp. 100–101
- Audio Program DVD: Cap. 6A, Track 14

✔ASSESSMENT

Prueba 6A-5 with Study Plan (online only)

Quiz: Stem-changing verbs: *poder* **and** *dormir*

- Prueba 6A-5: p. 153

ENRICH YOUR TEACHING

Teacher-to-Teacher

Have students play a circumlocution game. Using words from all of the chapters that students have studied so far, make a stack of cards with one vocabulary word on each one. Students will work in pairs and take turns explaining the words to their partners without saying the words on the cards. For example, if the word is *libro,* the student should say *Es una cosa que lees*. If the partner guesses the word before a 20-second time limit, he or she gets one point. The person with the most points wins.

Lectura

Core Instruction

Standards: 1.1, 1.2, 1.3, 4.1

Focus: Reading comprehension; understanding cultural perspectives

Suggestions:

Pre-reading: Explain to students that they will be reading a letter to an advice columnist. Use their background knowledge to discuss what kinds of issues people typically send to these columnists. Direct students' attention to the *Strategy,* and find the words in the context of the story.

Reading: Have students read the passage silently before a volunteer reads it aloud. Students will probably create a mental image of the room. Pause between readings to have students share their images with the class.

Post-reading: Have students describe in their own words what is happening between the sisters, and why one of them is asking for advice. Briefly discuss problems students may have with sharing a room with siblings.

Pre-AP* Support

- **Learning Objective:** Interpersonal Writing
- **Activity:** After students have read just the letter from Rosario to Magdalena, ask them to write a short e-mail offering their own advice to Rosario. Then, have students read the response from Magdalena to Rosario on p. 117, and compare their recommendations to her own.
- *Pre-AP* Resource Book:* Comprehensive guide to Pre-AP* reading skill development, pp. 19–26

Teacher-to-Teacher

Have students practice giving and understanding instructions. Bring in ten items a student might have in a bedroom such as clothes, books, and posters. Show the items to the class. In teams of three, have students write instructions that tell someone where to place six of the items within the classroom. Example: Put the poster next to the desk. Have one team come to the front of the room and ask another team to read their instructions aloud one at a time. One member of the team in front of the class completes the first instruction. The next member completes the second, etc.

▼ **Objectives**
▸ Read a letter and a response in an advice column
▸ Look for cognates to understand what you read
▸ Explore differences in technology use in the Spanish-speaking world

Lectura
El desastre en mi dormitorio

Lee esta carta *(letter)* a Querida Magdalena. Ella da soluciones para los problemas de los jóvenes en una revista.

Strategy

Using cognates
As you read the letter and response, look for cognates to help you better understand Rosario's problem. Try to guess the meaning of some of the cognates: *el desorden, la situación, recomendar, considerar.*

¿Qué debo hacer?

Con tu amiga Magdalena

❝**Querida Magdalena:**
Mi problema tiene un nombre; es mi hermana Marta. Compartimos el mismo dormitorio y estoy desesperada. Todo en mi lado del dormitorio está en orden. Pero su lado es un desastre. Ella es la reina del desorden. Le encanta comer en el dormitorio. Hay pizza debajo de la cama. Hay botellas de agua en la mesita. Hay postre en el escritorio. Es horrible. Siempre deja[1] ropa,[2] videos y todas sus posesiones en el suelo,[3] en la mesita, en la cama. ¡No hay ni un libro en el estante!

Y ella no usa su propio equipo de sonido—¡no! Usa mi equipo y sin pedir[4] permiso. Y escucha música a toda hora (y a un volumen muy alto) y iyo no puedo dormir!

Las paredes en su lado del dormitorio son negras. Es el peor color y es feísimo. Mi color favorito es el amarillo, claro. Es más bonito que el negro, ¿no?

Estoy cansada de compartir el dormitorio con ella y su desorden.
¿Qué debo hacer?❞

Rosario Molino
Montevideo, Uruguay

[1]leaves [2]clothing [3]floor [4]asking for

Mi problema tiene un nombre; es mi hermana, Marta.

DIFFERENTIATED INSTRUCTION

Students with Learning Difficulties
Brainstorm with students what Rosario might say in a letter complaining about her sister and what Magdalena might give for advice. Carefully read the passage with students, emphasizing cognates. You may need to provide them with a copy of the *¿Comprendes?* questions with key words and phrases underlined.

Advanced Learners
Ask students to write a letter to Magdalena with the opposite problem. Have students take the role of a messy person sharing a room with a brother or sister who could be considered too neat. Encourage them to be creative and write an original letter or use the one in the book as a model.

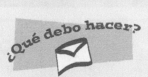

¿Qué debo hacer?

¡Es difícil compartir un dormitorio con otra persona!

Querida Rosario:

¡Qué problema! Es difícil compartir un dormitorio con otra persona, especialmente si la persona es tu hermana. Uds. son muy diferentes, ¿no? Tú eres más ordenada que ella. Ella cree que el color negro es el más bonito.

Necesitas hablar con tu hermana delante de tus padres. Tienes que explicar[5] la situación y recomendar unas soluciones. Es necesario encontrar[6] un punto intermedio.[7] Si la situación no es mejor después de unas semanas, tienes que considerar la posibilidad de separar el dormitorio con una cortina. ¡Pero no debe ser una cortina ni negra ni amarilla!

Tu amiga,
Magdalena

[5]explain [6]find [7]middle ground

¿Comprendes?

Lee las frases y decide quién dice *(says)* la frase. ¿Es Rosario, Marta o su madre?

1. "Pero me gusta comer en la cama y escuchar música".

2. "Soy una persona muy simpática y el color amarillo representa mi personalidad".

3. "Estoy muy ocupada y no tengo tiempo para un dormitorio perfecto".

4. "Uds. tienen que respetar las posesiones de la otra".

5. "Mi color favorito es el negro. No me gustan los colores amarillo, anaranjado o azul".

6. "Ella debe pedir permiso para escuchar mis discos compactos".

7. "Tu hermana no es ordenada como tú. Tienes que ser más paciente".

Y tú, ¿qué dices?

¿Eres desordenado(a) como *(like)* Marta o eres ordenado(a) como Rosario? ¿En qué? Incluye dos ejemplos en tu respuesta.

▼ Fondo Cultural | El mundo hispano

Los aparatos electrónicos Throughout the Spanish-speaking world you will find the latest electronic devices, and a demand for instant communication and electronic media. However, access to technologies such as Internet varies by country, and home computers are not as common as in the United States.

• Why do you think geographical location would be a factor in Internet access in Spanish-speaking countries? What reasons might influence home computer use?

Más práctica	GO
realidades.com	print

Guided WB p. 47	✔	✔
Comm. WB p. 145	✔	✔
***Hispanohablantes* WB** pp. 222–223		✔
Cultural Reading Activity	✔	

ciento diecisiete **117**
Capítulo 6A

▼ ¿Comprendes? Standards: 1.2, 1.3

Resources: Answer Keys: Student Edition, p. 122
Focus: Reading comprehension
Suggestions: Have students close their books. Divide the room into two teams. Put the names **Rosario, Marta,** and ***su madre*** on the board. Read the lines dramatically and have students call out who said them. The team with the most correct answers wins.

Answers:
1. Marta	5. Marta
2. Rosario	6. Rosario
3. Marta	7. su madre
4. su madre	

▼ Y tú, ¿qué dices? Standards: 1.2, 1.3

Focus: Stating opinions about neatness in a personalized context
Suggestions: Model how to respond by comparing yourself with Rosario or Marta, giving examples of why. *Soy como Rosario. Pongo mis cosas en orden....*
Answers will vary.

Fondo cultural

Standards: 4.2
Suggestions: Write the question at the top of a transparency and draw two columns: *advantages* and *disadvantages*. Have students form small groups and discuss the impact technology has had on the culture of the United States. Then ask them to reflect on how it might conceivably impact other cultures.
Answers will vary.

BELLRINGER REVIEW

Have students tell a partner one problem they have with their bedroom. (Ej. *Mi dormitorio es muy pequeño.*)

For Further Reading

Student Resource: Realidades para hispanohablantes: Lectura 2, pp. 224–225

ENRICH YOUR TEACHING

Teacher-to-Teacher

Have students write a letter asking for advice about a topic of interest to them. Then divide the class into pairs and exchange the letters. After each student reads the request for advice, have them give the person one or two pieces of advice using ***poder.*** If possible, bring to class some examples from Spanish-language newspapers or magazines of advice about issues suitable for teens.

La cultura en vivo

Core Instruction

Standards: 2.1, 2.2, 3.1

Focus: Reading about and making *luminarias*

🌐 **Mapa global interactivo, Actividad**
Look at the tradition of *luminarias* on both sides of the Rio Grande River.

Suggestions: If students are not familiar with them, introduce the concept of *luminarias,* lights used for special occasions to welcome people. Although once reserved for going to church, the tradition now extends to welcoming, visitors to one's home. Direct students' attention to the text. Explain that today *luminarias* are more of a symbol than a practicality since most places have street lights, whereas in the early days of this tradition these probably were the only way to light a path.

Direct students to the *Try it out!* section. Help them make their own *luminarias* to display in the classroom.

Prepare supplies in advance. You may wish to make a template out of cardboard for the star as shown in the drawing. Have a completed *luminaria* ready so students have a model to work from. Students may have difficulties cutting out the design without cutting the shorter sides of the bag. Help them avoid this error.

Direct attention to the *Think about it!* section and have students discuss the questions.

Answers will vary.

Additional Resources

Student Resource: Realidades para hispanohablantes, p. 226

Pre-AP* Support

- **Learning Objective:** Presentational Speaking (Cultural Comparisons)
- **Background:** This task prepares students for the Spoken Presentational Communication tasks that focus on cultural comparisons in the exam.
- **Activity:** Have students prepare a two-minute (maximum) presentation on the following topic: The use of lights and light-based decorations to signal holidays or special occasions can be found in different cultures. Think about the tradition of the *luminarias.* Then, think of an example of a similar use of light or special occasion decoration from your own culture. Explain the similarities and differences between the two.

¡Adelante!

La cultura en vivo
Las luminarias 🌐

To celebrate Christmas in Mexico and the southwest United States, countless bags, tons of sand, and candles are transformed into flickering outdoor lanterns called *luminarias*. They are lined up along window ledges, walkways, and roofs and are lit to welcome visitors.

Luminarias en Nuevo México

This tradition dates back more than 300 years, when villagers along the Río Grande built bonfires to light and warm their way to church on Christmas Eve. The *luminarias* used today go back to the 1820s, when traders introduced brown paper into the region and candles were set in sand in the bottom of the paper bags.

Try it out! Here's how you can make your own *luminarias.*

Materials

- 12" paper lunch bags
- sand
- small flashlights
- scissors

Figure 1   **Figure 2**   **Figure 3**

Directions

1. Trace a pattern on the side of the bag, leaving at least 4 inches at the top and 3 inches at the bottom. You may want to use the pattern in Fig. 1 or create your own.

2. Cut out the design, cutting through both sides of the bag. *(Fig. 1)*

3. Open the bag and fold down a 2" cuff around the top. *(Fig. 2)*

4. Fill the bag $\frac{1}{4}$ full of sand.

5. Place a flashlight in the sand. *(Fig. 3)*

6. Place the completed *luminarias* along your walkway, turn on the small flashlights, and enjoy these symbols of hope and joy for any special occasion.

Variations

1. Use white or brightly colored bags.

2. Paste white or pastel tissue paper behind the cut-out design.

3. Cut a scalloped edge along the top of the bag instead of folding down the cuff.

4. Instead of sand, use soil, cat litter, or gravel to hold the flashlight in place.

Think about it! What kind of decorations do you use for special events? How is light used in different cultures to celebrate events?

DIFFERENTIATED INSTRUCTION

Multiple Intelligences
Visual/Spatial: Have students who finish early help those who may be having difficulties. They can also prepare for a class celebration that will display the *luminarias* by setting up the finished ones to light the way for visitors.

Heritage Language Learners
Ask students who are familiar with *luminarias* to share their personal experiences with the class. They should include what the occasion was and any particular celebrations that took place.

Presentación oral

La personalidad de un dormitorio

Task
You are studying how a bedroom reflects the personality of its owner(s). Use a photo or drawing of a bedroom and explain what its contents and colors tell about the owner's personality.

1 Prepare Bring in a photo, magazine picture, or drawing of a bedroom. Use this word web to think through what you want to say about the room and the personality of its owner. Then answer the questions.

• En tu opinión, ¿cómo es la persona que vive *(lives)* en el dormitorio? ¿Qué le gusta hacer?

¿De qué color es?

¿Qué hay en el dormitorio?

El dormitorio

¿Qué cosas hay en las paredes?

¿Cómo es el dormitorio?

Strategy

Using graphic organizers
A word web can help you organize your thoughts for a presentation.

2 Practice Go through your presentation several times. You can use your notes to practice, but not to present. Try to:

• support your statements with examples
• use complete sentences
• speak clearly

3 Present Show your picture and give the information about the bedroom and the personality behind it.

4 Evaluation The following rubric will be used to grade your presentation.

Rubric	Score 1	Score 3	Score 5
Completeness of presentation	You describe the room, but have no visual.	You describe the room with a visual, but give no opinion.	You describe the room with a visual, and give your opinion.
Amount of information you communicate	You include two categories from the word web.	You include three categories from the word web.	You include all four categories from the word web.
How easily you are understood	You are extremely difficult to understand. Your teacher could only recognize isolated words and phrases.	You are understandable, but have frequent errors in vocabulary and/or grammar that hinder your comprehensibility.	You are easily understood. Your teacher does not have to "decode" what you are trying to say.

ciento diecinueve 119
Capítulo 6A

Presentación oral

Core Instruction
Standards: 1.3

Resources: Voc. and Gram. Transparency 119; Teacher's Resource Book: GramActiva BLM, p. 103

Focus: Speaking using vocabulary related to bedrooms

Suggestions: Review the task and steps with students. After reading the *Strategy,* model use of the graphic organizer. You may wish to provide students with a word web to fill in. Encourage them to articulate and to make eye contact during the presentation. Review the assessment rubric with the class to explain how you will grade the performance.

Pre-AP* Support

• **Learning Objective:** Presentational Speaking
• **Activity:** Remind students to focus on the presentational speaking skills used in this task such as fluency, pronunciation, and comprehensibility.
• *Pre-AP* Resource Book:* Comprehensive guide to Pre-AP* speaking skill development, pp. 39–50

Portfolio
Make video or audio recordings of student presentations in class, or assign the RealTalk activity so they can record their presentations online. Include the recording in their portfolios.

Additional Resources
Student Resources: Realidades para hispanohablantes, p. 227; Guided Practice: Presentación oral, p. 48

ENRICH YOUR TEACHING

21st Century Skills

Initiative and Self-Direction Have partners go through the practice steps and the rubric and evaluate each other's presentation. The partner should make sure that all the points listed in the practice step and in Score 5 of the rubric are being met as much as possible. Students should demonstrate improvement of their presentation based on partner feedback.

✓ASSESSMENT

Presentación oral
• Assessment Program: Rubrics, p. T31
Go over the descriptions of the different levels of performance. After assessing students, help individuals understand how their performance could be improved.

6A Video

Videomisterio ▶

Core Instruction

Standards: 1.2, 1.3, 4.1, 5.2

Resources: Teacher's Resource Program: Video Script, pp. 96–97; Video Program: Cap. 6A; Video Program Teacher's Guide: Cap. 6A

Focus: Introducing the events and characters of this episode

Personajes importantes:

Lola Lago, detective
Paco, colega de Lola
Margarita, la secretaria de la oficina de Lola
Doña Lupe Aguirre, portera
Pedro Requena, nieto de doña Gracia Requena

Synopsis: Lola tells Paco about the incident on Sunday at her apartment building, but Paco is only interested in knowing if there is a case and a paying client. Lola believes that this case could lead to a client and she questions doña Lupe, who found doña Gracia on the floor. There are three mysteries at hand: (1) What caused doña Gracia's incident? (2) Where is her niece, María? (3) Where are doña Gracia's jewels? María, a professional model, spent three months in the hospital after a car accident. Doña Gracia's only other relative is her grandson, Pedro Requena, who lives in Italy. His father did not get along with doña Gracia's husband.

Suggestions:

Pre-viewing: Review with students the events of *Episodio* 2. The ambulance arrives for the victim, doña Gracia. Everyone is wondering where doña Gracia's niece, María, is. Inspector Gil questions Lola Lago, who saw two people leave doña Gracia's apartment the night before. Inspector Gil asks Lola to call if she has any further information.

Visual scanning: Direct students' attention to the first two photos and ask who they are (Paco and Margarita), and what relationship they have to Lola (they work in the same office). Before students read the *Resumen del episodio,* have them scan the text and find three cognates (*importante, incidente, escena, describe, historia, familia*). Then ask them to read the *Resumen* carefully. Ask students questions about what will happen in this episode.

¿Eres tú, María? Episodio 3

Antes de ver el video

Personajes importantes

Paco, quien trabaja en la oficina de Lola y la ayuda con las investigaciones

Margarita, la secretaria de la oficina

Nota cultural *El País* is probably Spain's most widely read and influential newspaper. You can consult an electronic version of *El País* on the Internet.

Resumen del episodio

Este episodio es muy importante. Lola le explica a Paco lo que pasó[1] en el incidente del domingo pasado.[2] En otra escena, Lola habla con doña Lupe quien le describe el incidente en el piso de doña Gracia. También doña Lupe le explica a Lola la historia de la familia de doña Gracia. ¿Por qué cree que María va a recibir toda la fortuna de doña Gracia?

[1] what happened   [2] last Sunday

Palabras para comprender

dinero	money
periodista	newspaper reporter
¿Qué pasó . . . ?	What happened . . . ?
No ve casi nada.	She can hardly see anything.
abro	I open
muerta	dead
busco	I'm looking for
¿Robaron . . . ?	Did they steal . . . ?
las joyas	jewels
accidente de coche	car accident
Pasó antes de venir a vivir con doña Gracia.	It happened before she came to live with doña Gracia.
Pasó tres meses . . .	She spent three months . . .
el nieto	grandson
No viene aquí nunca.	He never comes here.
No conoce a su abuela.	He doesn't know his grandmother.

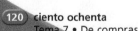

120 **ciento ochenta**
Tema 7 • De compras

DIFFERENTIATED INSTRUCTION

Students with Learning Difficulties

Photocopy the family tree pictured on p.121, so that students can write notes on it. Suggest that underneath the image of each person they write information that will help them better understand that person's role.

Heritage Language Learners

Have students read a daily edition of *El País* on the Internet. Ask them to summarize one news story for the rest of the class.

La familia Requena

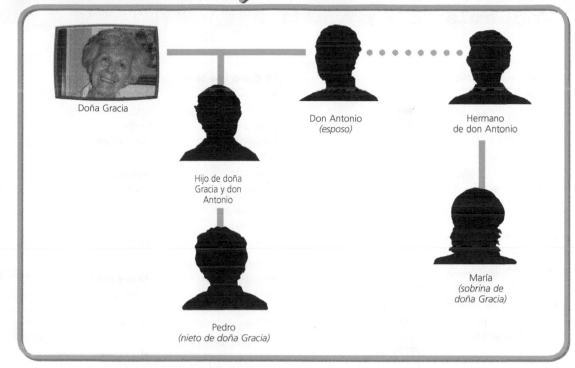

Doña Gracia

Don Antonio
(esposo)

Hermano
de don Antonio

Hijo de doña
Gracia y don
Antonio

María
*(sobrina de
doña Gracia)*

Pedro
(nieto de doña Gracia)

Después de ver el video

¿Comprendes?

Completa cada frase con la palabra apropiada
del recuadro.

1. Según Paco, si no hay cliente, si no hay ___,
   entonces no hay nada.

2. Lola dice que trabaja para *El País*, un periódico
   importante en España, y es ___.

3. María es la ___ de Lorenzo Requena y la ___ de doña Gracia.

4. Doña Gracia es muy rica. Tiene una fortuna en dinero,
   ___ y arte.

5. Antes de venir a vivir con doña Gracia, a María le pasó un
   grave ___.

6. Pedro, el nieto de doña Gracia, vive en Italia y su abuela
   no lo ___.

7. Según doña Lupe, María va a recibir la ___ de doña Gracia.

periodista	joyas
hija	conoce
fortuna	dinero
accidente de coche	sobrina

Más práctica GO

realidades.com | print

Actividades ✔

Post-viewing: Have the class study the
family tree at the top of the page and ask
who can tell what the last names *(apellidos)*
are of each person in the chart. You may
need to explain that in Spanish, people
most often use two last names: the father's
followed by the mother's maiden name.
One example will come up in *Episodio* 4.
(Dr. Sánchez Mata) When women marry,
they keep their maiden name and add *de*
plus their husband's last name: *Doña Gracia
Salazar de Requena.*

Write the vocabulary presented with this
episode on the board to help students
create sentences for each important scene
where a character is introduced. Direct
attention to the *¿Comprendes?*

▼ **¿Comprendes?** Standards: 1.2, 1.3

Resources: Answer Keys: Student Edition, p. 122

Focus: Demonstrating comprehension;
reviewing the plot

Suggestions: Ask students to read and
answer the questions. Then, in pairs, have
them write their responses and work
together to ensure that they both have
the correct answers.

Answers:
1. dinero
2. periodista
3. nieta; sobrina
4. joyas
5. accidente de coche
6. conoce
7. fortuna

Theme Project

Students can perform Step 3 at this point.
(For more information, see p. 92-b.)

Additional Resources

• *¿Eres tú, María?* Video Workbook, Episode 3
• *¿Eres tú, María?* Teacher's Video Guide: Answer Key

ENRICH YOUR TEACHING

Culture Note

Not unlike other countries, Spain has both local
and national newspapers. Many of the well-
known papers are geared towards a political
view. Two of the best-known papers in Spain
are *El País* and *El Mundo.*

21st Century Skills

Technology Literacy Have students find Web
sites to further explore the news media in
Spain. They should decide which topics interest
them and find Web sites that supply that
information. Have them work in small groups to
evaluate and organize the information, then
present it to the class.

Review Activities

To talk about things in a bedroom: Ask students to draw the shape of their bedrooms. Have them write the words from this list in the places where the items are located in their rooms. Then have them describe their rooms to their partners, using colors and other adjectives.

To talk about electronic equipment: Ask each student to put this list in the order of each item's importance to them. Or have them put the list in the order in which they would like to buy items they do not own.

To indicate location: Have the class divide into pairs and use these phrases to describe the location of objects in their drawings of their rooms. Have students ask their partners to guess the object they are talking about. Model an example for the class: *Está a la derecha de la cama y a la izquierda de las cortinas.*

Stem-changing verbs: poder and dormir: *Student A* will be the "child" asking if he or she can do some activity (*¿Puedo ir al cine?*). *Student B* will be the "parent," telling *Student A* that he or she cannot do the activity, but suggesting another one. Students then reverse roles.

Portfolio

Invite students to review the activities they completed in this chapter, including written reports, posters, or other visuals, and recordings of oral presentations or other projects. Have them select one or two items that they feel best demonstrate their achievements in Spanish to include in their portfolios. Have them include this with the Chapter Checklist and Self-Assessment Worksheet.

Additional Resources

Student Resources: Realidades para hispanohablantes, p. 228

Teacher Resources:
- Teacher's Resource Book: Situation Cards, p. 102, Clip Art, pp. 104–105
- Assessment Program: Chapter Checklist and Self-Assessment Worksheet, pp. T56–T57

Repaso del capítulo
Vocabulario y gramática

to talk about things in a bedroom

la alfombra	rug
el armario	closet
la cama	bed
la cómoda	dresser
las cortinas	curtains
el cuadro	painting
el despertador	alarm clock
el dormitorio	bedroom
el espejo	mirror
el estante	shelf, bookshelf
la lámpara	lamp
la mesita	night table
la pared	wall

to talk about electronic equipment

el disco compacto	compact disc
el equipo de sonido	sound (stereo) system
el lector DVD	DVD player
el televisor	television set
el video	video

to talk about colors

¿De qué color . . . ?	What color . . . ?
los colores	colors
amarillo, -a	yellow
anaranjado, -a	orange
azul	blue
blanco, -a	white
gris	gray
marrón	brown
morado, -a	purple
negro, -a	black
rojo, -a	red
rosado, -a	pink
verde	green

to describe something

bonito, -a	pretty
feo, -a	ugly
grande	large
importante	important
mismo, -a	same
pequeño, -a	small
propio, -a	own

to indicate location

a la derecha (de)	to the right (of)
a la izquierda (de)	to the left (of)

to compare and contrast

mejor(es) que	better than
el / la mejor; los / las mejores	the best
menos . . . que	less, fewer . . . than
peor(es) que	worse than
el / la peor; los / las peores	the worst

other useful words and expressions

la cosa	thing
para mí	in my opinion, for me
para ti	in your opinion, for you
la posesión	possession

stem-changing verbs: *dormir* and *poder*

duermo	dormimos
duermes	dormís
duerme	duermen

puedo	podemos
puedes	podéis
puede	pueden

For *Vocabulario adicional,* see pp. 336–337.

 122 ciento veintidós
Tema 6 • La casa

DIFFERENTIATED INSTRUCTION

Students with Learning Difficulties

Have students review the *Repaso del capítulo* and create flashcards for any words that they do not know. Pair them with a student who is more confident with the vocabulary to practice. Before the test, provide students with a practice test, so they can become comfortable with the format.

Heritage Language Learners

Have students write a few paragraphs telling about their perfect birthday celebration: Where are they going to have it? Whom are they going to invite? What food are they going to eat? What kind of music are they going to play? Encourage them to use as many vocabulary words from this chapter as they can.

Más repaso GO   realidades.com | print

Instant Check	✔	
Puzzles	✔	
Core WB pp. 26–27	✔	✔
Comm. WB pp. 146, 147–149	✔	✔

Preparación para el examen

On the exam you will be asked to . . .	Here are practice tasks similar to those you will find on the exam . . .	For review go to your print or digital textbook . . .
1 Escuchar Listen to and understand descriptions of bedrooms	You will be spending a month in a Spanish immersion camp. You go to the camp Web site and click on the audio descriptions of the student rooms. Which items are provided? Which items do you have to bring?	**pp. 94–99** *Vocabulario en contexto* **p. 100** Actividad 6 **p. 101** Actividad 8 **p. 102** Actividad 11

2 Hablar Ask and answer questions about your bedroom and that of a classmate	You are asked to survey several classmates about their bedrooms in order to describe the "typical" teenage room. Ask a partner at least three questions including: a) information about the color of his or her room; b) whether or not there is a TV or sound system in the room; c) whether he or she is able to study well in the room; d) what is on the walls.	**pp. 94–99** *Vocabulario en contexto* **p. 101** Actividad 8 **p. 102** Actividad 11
3 Leer Read and understand descriptions of bedroom colors that are associated with particular personality types	Decorators say that the colors of a room's walls should match the personality of the person living in it. Based on the descriptions of a "yellow personality" and a "blue personality," what kind of room best suits you? Why or why not? *A las personas más sociables les gustan los dormitorios amarillos. Es el color más popular para los jóvenes a quienes les gusta hablar y hablar por teléfono. ¡Ellos son los mejores amigos! Al contrario, a las personas más serias les gustan los dormitorios azules. Ellos son los mejores estudiantes y los peores cómicos.*	**p. 104** Actividad 14 **p. 105** Actividad 15 **pp. 116–117** *Lectura*

4 Escribir Write a short paragraph comparing your bedroom to a friend's bedroom	After surveying classmates, you are asked to write a comparison of your room to that of one of the people you surveyed. Use the information from Task 2 to practice. You might compare: a) the colors; b) the sizes; c) the types of furniture in the rooms; d) the number of different things on the walls.	**p. 101** Actividad 7 **p. 107** Actividad 19 **p. 119** *Presentación oral*
5 Pensar Demonstrate an understanding of cultural perspectives regarding a celebration	Explain the historical significance of *las luminarias*. What is the history of other decorations used in the celebrations of different cultures?	**p. 118** *La cultura en vivo*

Performance Tasks

Standards: 5.2

Student Resource: Realidades para hispanohablantes, p 229

Teacher Resources: Teacher's Resource Book: Audio Script, p. 93; Audio Program DVD: Cap. 6A, Track 16; Answer Keys: Student Edition, p. 122

1. Escuchar

Suggestions: Use the audio or read the script.

 **Script and Answers:**

¿Vas a pasar el verano con nosotros? Tenemos los mejores dormitorios. Después de un día de muchas actividades, puedes ver la tele o escuchar música. Hay un televisor y un equipo de sonido en todos los dormitorios.
TVs and stereos are provided. Other answers will vary.

2. Hablar

Suggestions: Have students write their questions and the answers to their partner's questions. Let them practice until they can perform without consulting their notes.

Answers will vary.

3. Leer

Suggestions: Point out that students will be asked about two personality types and their associated colors. If they have difficulty reading and understanding the text, refer them to the vocabulary list.

Answers will vary.

4. Escribir

Suggestions: Have students create a graphic organizer before they begin. Refer them to the chart on p.106 for comparisons.

Answers will vary.

5. Pensar

Suggestions: Have students refer to p.118 to review information on *luminarias.*

Answers will vary.

DIFFERENTIATED ASSESSMENT

CORE ASSESSMENT
- **Assessment Program:** Examen del capítulo 6A, pp. 154–161
- **Audio Program DVD:** Cap. 6A, Track 17
- **ExamView:** Chapter Test, Test Banks A and B

ADVANCED/PRE-AP*
- **ExamView:** Pre-AP* Test Bank
- **Pre-AP* Resource Book,** pp. 82–85

STUDENTS NEEDING EXTRA HELP
- **Alternate Assessment Program:** Examen del capítulo 6A
- **Audio Program DVD:** Cap. 6A, Track 17

HERITAGE LEARNERS
- **Assessment Program: Realidades para hispanohablantes:** Examen del capítulo 6A
- **ExamView: Heritage Learner Test Bank**

Objectives

- Talk, write, and listen to conversations about household chores
- Read housing ads
- Write a description of a house or apartment
- Exchange information while giving advice
- Understand cultural perspectives regarding homes and privacy
- Explain how houses in the Spanish-speaking world compare to those in the United States

Vocabulary

- Houses and apartments
- Rooms
- Household chores

Grammar

- Affirmative *tú* commands
- The present progressive tense

Culture

- *la arpillera,* p. 125
- *el patio,* p. 135
- Percentages of people living in houses and apartments in Caracas, Venezuela, p. 145
- The story of Cinderella, p. 147
- Cultural perspectives on architectural features, p. 148

Recycle ♺

- *estar*
- *ir + a* + infinitive
- *-ar, -er,* and *-ir* verbs
- Comparatives
- Affirmative commands in direction lines
- Adjective agreement
- The present tense

RESOURCES

	FOR THE STUDENT	ONLINE	DVD	PRINT	FOR THE TEACHER	ONLINE	PREEXP	DVD	PRINT
Plan					Interactive TE and Resources DVD	•		•	
					Teacher's Resource Book, pp. 122–157	•		•	•
					Pre-AP* Resource Book, pp. 82–85	•		•	•
					Mapa global interactivo	•			
					Lesson Plans	•			•
Introducción PP. **124–125**									
Present	Student Edition, pp. 124–125	•	•	•	Interactive TE and Resources DVD	•		•	
	DK Reference Atlas	•	•		Teacher's Resource Book, pp. 122–123	•		•	•
	Videocultura	•	•		Galería de fotos		•		
	Hispanohablantes WB, pp. 230–231			•	Map Transparencies, 12, 14–18, 20	•	•	•	
Vocabulario en contexto PP. **126–131**									
Present & Practice	Student Edition, pp. 126–131	•	•	•	Interactive TE and Resources DVD	•		•	
	Audio	•	•		Teacher's Resource Book, pp. 124–126, 129, 138–140	•		•	•
	Videohistoria	•	•		Vocabulary Clip Art	•	•	•	•
	Flashcards	•	•		Audio Program	•	•	•	•
	Instant Check	•			Video Program: Videohistoria	•		•	
	Guided WB, pp. 49–58	•	•	•	Video Program Teacher's Guide: Cap. 6B	•		•	•
	Core WB, pp. 28–31	•	•	•	Vocabulary and Grammar Transparencies, 120–123	•	•	•	•
	Comm. WB, pp. 33–36, 39	•	•	•	Answer Keys: Student Edition, pp. 123–125	•	•	•	
	Hispanohablantes WB, pp. 232–233			•	TPR Stories, pp. 77–91	•		•	
Assess and Remediate					Prueba 6B–1: Assessment Program, pp. 162–163	•		•	•
					Assessment Program para hispanohablantes, pp. 162–163	•		•	•

RESOURCES

FOR THE STUDENT	ONLINE	DVD	PRINT	FOR THE TEACHER	ONLINE	PREEXP	DVD	PRINT
Vocabulario en uso PP. **132–137**								
Present & Practice								
Student Edition, pp. 132–137	•	•	•	Interactive Whiteboard Vocabulary Activities	•		•	
Instant Check	•			Interactive TE and Resources DVD	•		•	
Comm. WB, p. 36	•	•	•	Teacher's Resource Book, pp. 125–126, 132–133, 137	•		•	•
Hispanohablantes WB, pp. 234–235			•	Communicative Pair Activities, pp. 132–133	•		•	
Communicative Pair Activities	•			Audio Program	•	•	•	
				Videomodelos	•		•	
				Vocabulary and Grammar Transparencies, 120–121, 126	•	•	•	
				Answer Keys: Student Edition, pp. 126–130	•	•	•	•
Assess and Remediate								
				Prueba 6B–2 with Study Plan	•			
				Prueba 6B–2: Assessment Program, pp. 164–165	•		•	•
				Assessment Program para hispanohablantes, pp. 164–165	•		•	•
Gramática PP. **138–145**								
Present & Practice								
Student Edition, pp. 138–145	•	•	•	Interactive Whiteboard Grammar Activities	•		•	
Instant Check	•			Interactive TE and Resources DVD	•		•	
Animated Verbs	•			Teacher's Resource Book, pp. 126–127, 129–130, 134–135	•		•	•
Tutorial Video: Grammar	•			Communicative Pair Activities, pp. 134–135	•		•	
Canción de hip hop	•			Audio Program	•	•	•	
Guided WB, pp. 59–62	•	•	•	Videomodelos	•		•	
Core WB, pp. 32–34	•	•	•	Video Program: GramActiva	•		•	
Comm. WB, pp. 37–38, 40–41, 150	•	•	•	Vocabulary and Grammar Transparencies, 124–125, 127	•	•	•	
Hispanohablantes WB, pp. 236–241			•	Answer Keys: Student Edition, pp. 130–134	•	•	•	
Communicative Pair Activities	•							
Assess and Remediate								
				Pruebas 6B–3 and 6B–4 with Study Plans	•			
				Pruebas 6B–3, 6B–4: Assessment Program, pp. 166, 167	•		•	•
				Assessment Program para hispanohablantes, pp. 166, 167	•		•	•
¡Adelante! PP. **146–151**								
Application								
Student Edition, pp. 146–151	•	•	•	Interactive TE and Resources DVD	•		•	
Online Cultural Reading	•			Teacher's Resource Book, pp. 130–131	•		•	•
Guided WB, pp. 63–64	•	•	•	Video Program: Videomisterio ¿Eres tú, María?	•		•	
Comm. WB, pp. 42, 151	•	•	•	Video Program Teacher's Guide: Cap. 6B	•		•	
Hispanohablantes WB, pp. 242, 247			•	Videomisterio Quiz			•	
¿Eres tú, María? Video WB, pp. 24–33	•	•	•	Answer Keys: Student Edition, pp. 134–135	•	•	•	
Repaso del capítulo PP. **152–153**								
Review								
Student Edition, pp. 152–153	•	•	•	Interactive TE and Resources DVD	•		•	
Online Puzzles and Games	•			Teacher's Resource Book, pp. 127, 136, 138–140	•		•	•
Core WB, pp. 35–36	•	•	•	Audio Program	•	•	•	
Comm. WB, pp. 152–155	•	•	•	Answer Keys: Student Edition, p. 135	•	•	•	
Hispanohablantes WB, pp. 248–249			•					
Instant Check	•							
Chapter Assessment								
Assess								
				Examen del capítulo 6B	•		•	•
				Assessment Program, pp. 168–174	•		•	•
				Alternate Assessment Program, pp. 73–78	•		•	•
				Assessment Program para hispanohablantes, pp. 168–174	•		•	•
				Audio Program, Cap. 6B, Examen	•		•	
				ExamView: Test Banks A and B questions only online	•			
				Heritage Learner Test Bank	•			
				Pre-AP* Test Bank	•			

6B Lesson Plans

REGULAR SCHEDULE (50 MINUTES)

DAY	Warm-up / Assess	Preview / Present / Practice / Communicate	Wrap-up / Homework Options
1	Return Examen del capítulo (10 min.)	**Vocabulario en contexto (35 min.)** • Objectives • Presentation • *Actividades* 1, 2 • Arte y cultura • Videocultura: *La casa*	**Wrap-up and Homework Options (5 min.)** • Core Practice • Vocabulary Clip Art
2	**Warm-up (5 min.)** • Homework check	**Vocabulario en contexto (40 min.)** • Review: *Vocabulario en contexto* • Presentation: *Videohistoria Los quehaceres de Elena* • View: Video *Los quehaceres de Elena* • Video Activities • *Actividades* 3, 4, 5	**Wrap-up and Homework Options (5 min.)** • *Prueba* 6B-1: Vocabulary recognition • Core Practice
3	**Warm-up (5 min.)** • Homework check ✔**Formative Assessment (10 min.)** • *Prueba* 6B-1: Vocabulary recognition	**Vocabulario en uso (30 min.)** • Objectives • Interactive Whiteboard Vocabulary Activities • *Actividades* 7, 8, 9	**Wrap-up and Homework Options (5 min.)** • *Actividad* 6
4	**Warm-up (5 min.)** • Homework check • Return *Prueba* 6B-1: Vocabulary recognition	**Vocabulario en uso (40 min.)** • *Actividades* 11, 12, 13 • *Fondo cultural* • Communicative Pair Activities	**Wrap-up and Homework Options (5 min.)** • *Actividad* 10
5	**Warm-up (5 min.)** • Homework check	**Vocabulario en uso (40 min.)** • *Actividades* 14, 15, 16 • *Exploración del lenguaje*	**Wrap-up and Homework Options (5 min.)** • *Exploración del lenguaje:* Try it out!
6	**Warm-up (5 min.)** • Homework check	**Gramática y vocabulario en uso (40 min.)** • Presentation: Affirmative *tú* commands • *GramActiva* Video • Interactive Whiteboard Grammar Activities • *Actividades* 17, 18, 20	**Wrap-up and Homework Options (5 min.)** • *Actividad* 19
7	**Warm-up (5 min.)** • Homework check	**Gramática y vocabulario en uso (40 min.)** • Review: Affirmative *tú* commands • *Actividades* 21, 22, 23 • *Pronunciación*	**Wrap-up and Homework Options (5 min.)** • Core Practice • *Prueba* 6B-3 with Study Plan: Affirmative *tú* commands
8	**Warm-up (5 min.)** • Homework check ✔**Formative Assessment (10 min.)** • *Prueba* 6B-3 with Study Plan: Affirmative *tú* commands	**Gramática y vocabulario en uso (30 min.)** • Presentation: The present progressive tense • *GramActiva* Video • Interactive Whiteboard Grammar Activities • *Actividades* 25, 26 • *Juego: Actividad* 27 • Communicative Pair Activities	**Wrap-up and Homework Options (5 min.)** • *Actividad* 24 • *Prueba* 6B-2 with Study Plan: Vocabulary production

REGULAR SCHEDULE (50 MINUTES)

DAY	Warm-up / Assess	Preview / Present / Practice / Communicate	Wrap-up / Homework Options
9	**Warm-up (5 min.)** • Homework check • Return *Prueba* 6B-3 with Study Plan: Affirmative *tú* commands ✔**Formative Assessment (10 min.)** • *Prueba* 6B-2 with Study Plan: Vocabulary production	**Gramática y vocabulario en uso (30 min.)** • Review: The present progressive tense • *Actividad 28* • *El español en el mundo del trabajo*	**Wrap-up and Homework Options (5 min.)** • Core Practice • *Prueba* 6B-4 with Study Plan: The present progressive tense
10	**Warm-up (5 min.)** • Homework check ✔**Formative Assessment (10 min.)** • *Prueba* 6B-4 with Study Plan: The present progressive tense	**Gramática y vocabulario en uso (30 min.)** • *Actividad 30* • *El español en el mundo del trabajo* • *Conexiones: Actividad 29*	**Wrap-up and Homework Options (5 min.)** • Core Practice
11	**Warm-up (5 min.)** • Homework check • Return *Prueba* 6B-4 with Study Plan: The present progressive tense	**¡Adelante! (40 min.)** • *Presentación escrita:* Prewrite • *Lectura* • *Fondo cultural*	**Wrap-up and Homework Options (5 min.)** • *¿Comprendes?*
12	**Warm-up (5 min.)** • Homework check	**¡Adelante! (40 min.)** • *Presentación escrita:* Draft, revise • *Perspectivas del mundo hispano*	**Wrap-up and Homework Options (5 min.)** • *Presentación escrita:* Publish
13	**Warm-up (5 min.)** • Homework check	**¡Adelante! (40 min.)** • *Presentación escrita:* Present	**Wrap-up and Homework Options (5 min.)** • Writing Activities • Core Practice Organizer
14	**Warm-up (5 min.)** • Homework check • Core Practice Organizer	**¡Adelante! (20 min.)** • *Videomisterio* **Repaso (20 min.)** • *Vocabulario y gramática* • *Preparación para el examen*	**Wrap-up and Homework Options (5 min.)** • Instant Check • *Examen del capítulo*
15	**Warm-up (5 min.)** • Answer questions ✔**Summative Assessment (45 min.)** • *Examen del capítulo*		

Standards for *Capítulo* 6B

- To achieve the goals of the Standards, students will:

Communication

1.1 Interpersonal
- Talk about the locations of rooms in a house
- Talk about furniture found in homes
- Talk about household chores
- Give advice to another person

1.2 Interpretive
- Read and listen to information about rooms in a house
- Read and listen to information about household chores
- Read a picture-based story
- Listen to and watch a video about household chores
- Read a letter asking for personal advice
- Read a real estate advertisement
- Listen to and watch a video about household chores

1.3 Presentational
- Present information about household chores
- Present information about rooms in a house
- Write a letter giving advice

Culture

2.1 Practices and Perspectives
- Learn how architecture design promotes privacy in Spanish-speaking countries

2.2 Products and Perspectives
- Learn about *la arpillera* patchwork appliqué in Chile
- Learn about *patios* in Spain and the Americas
- Understand the use of home features such as patios

Connections

3.1 Cross-curricular
- Reinforce graphing and math skills

Comparisons

4.1 Language
- Learn new vocabulary through the recognition of cognates
- Understand the use of *tú* commands
- Compare nouns formed from verbs as their roots
- Learn the progressive tense
- Understand the pronunciation of *n* and *ñ*

4.2 Culture
- Compare crafts from different regions
- Compare idioms for names of house sections
- Compare types of patios
- Compare versions of "Cinderella" tales

Communities

5.1 Beyond the School
- Identify local increase in Spanish-language advertising

5.2 Lifelong Learner
- View a video mystery series

Capítulo
6B ¿Cómo es tu casa?

▼ Chapter Objectives

Communication
By the end of this chapter you will be able to:
- Talk, write, and listen to conversations about household chores
- Read housing ads
- Write a description of a house or apartment
- Exchange information while giving advice

Culture
You will also be able to:
- Understand cultural perspectives regarding homes and privacy
- Explain how houses in the Spanish-speaking world compare to those in the United States

You will demonstrate what you know and can do:
- Presentación escrita, p. 149
- Preparación para el examen, p. 153

You will use:

Vocabulary	Grammar
• Houses and apartments	• Affirmative *tú* commands
• Rooms	• The present progressive tense
• Household chores	

Exploración del mundo hispano

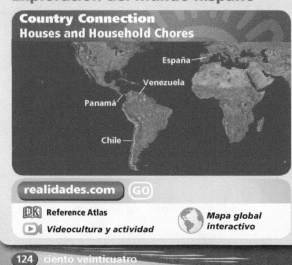

Country Connection
Houses and Household Chores

España
Venezuela
Panamá
Chile

realidades.com GO

📖 Reference Atlas
▶ Videocultura y actividad
🌐 Mapa global interactivo

Una casa en Tenerife, Islas Canarias, España

ENRICH YOUR TEACHING

Using Backward Design
Have students preview the sample performance tasks on *Preparación para el examen*, p. 153, and connect them to the Chapter Objectives. Explain to students that by completing the sample tasks they can self-assess their learning progress.

Mapa global interactivo
Download the *Mapa global interactivo* files for Chapter 6B and preview the activities. In Activity 1, you look at a small village in Chile. In Activity 2, you visit Seville, Spain, and in Activity 3 you compare neighborhoods in Caracas, Venezuela.

Tema 6 • La casa

Arte y cultura | Chile

La arpillera is a popular textile folk art of rough patchwork appliqués created by women in Chile. Done in brilliant colors, the themes show the story of daily life, traditions, and values in the country.

• What other types of crafts have you seen that portray life in a region or country?

Arpillera de Chile ▶

ciento veinticinco **125**
Capítulo 6B

Chapter Opener
Core Instruction

Resources: Map Transparencies 12, 14–18, 20

Suggestions: Introduce students to the chapter theme and review the objectives. Brainstorm a list of chores students do in their homes. Point out to students that they will learn about cultural differences in housing. The *A primera vista* video will present a comical episode about a sister who gets her little brother to do her chores. Since students will be learning about chores, they'll learn how to give orders and tell what they're doing.

▶ **Videocultura** View *La Casa* with the class to learn how people in various Spanish-speaking countries live.

Arte y cultura

Standards: 2.2, 4.1

Suggestions: Point out that crafts are often a reflection of a country and its history. **Arpilleras,** named for their burlap backing, were first made as folk art by Chilean women to show the difficult conditions in which they lived. Wives of political prisoners or mothers who were trying to feed their families made and sold **arpilleras.** In addition to providing a small income, these bright designs were banners of hope.

Answers will vary but may include murals, primitive paintings, quilts, collages, and so forth.

🌐 **Mapa global interactivo, Actividad 1** Look at a small village such as the ones on the *arpilleras* of Chile.

Teaching with Photos
Have students compare homes in their community with the home pictured. Ask: How is this home similar to homes you know? How is it different?

DIFFERENTIATED INSTRUCTION

Digital resources such as the *Interactive Whiteboard* activity banks, *Videomodelos*, additional *Online Activities*, *Study Plans*, automatically graded *Leveled Workbook*, animated *Grammar Tutorials*, *Flashcards*, and *Vocabulary and Grammar Videos* will help you reach students of different ability levels and learning styles.

STUDENTS NEEDING EXTRA HELP

Guided Practice Activities
• Flashcards, pp. 49–54
• Vocabulary Check, pp. 55–58
• Grammar Support, pp. 59–62

HERITAGE LEARNERS

Realidades para hispanohablantes
• Chapter Opener, pp. 230–231
• A primera vista, p. 232
• Videohistoria, p. 233
• Manos a la obra, pp. 234–241
• ¡Adelante!, pp. 242–247
• Repaso del capítulo, pp. 248–249

ADVANCED/PRE-AP*

Pre-AP* Resource Book,
• pp. 82–85

Communications Workbook
• Integrated Performance Assessment, p. 152

125

Vocabulario en contexto

Core Instruction

Standards: 1.2, 4.1

Resources: Teacher's Resource Book: Input Script, p. 124, Clip Art, pp. 138–140, Audio Script, p. 125; Voc. and Gram. Transparencies 120–121; TPR Stories Book, pp. 77–91; Audio Program DVD: Cap. 6B, Tracks 1–2

Focus: Presenting visualized vocabulary for rooms in a house and household chores; presenting verbs that tell someone to do something

Suggestions: Use the story in *TPR Stories Book* to present the new vocabulary and grammar or use the Input Script from the *Teacher's Resource Book*.

Present the vocabulary in three sets: the structure of a house, the rooms in a house, and household chores (including **dar, lavar, poner**). Say each word on the transparencies, but wait to point to each picture until students point to the correct picture in the book. Have volunteers come up and point to pictures on the transparencies after you describe the picture (say who is in the room, what chore you are going to do, etc.).

Ask questions that require limited verbal response, such as: *¿Generalmente, la sala está en la planta baja? ¿Comes el desayuno en la cocina?*

Read, listen to, and understand information about
▶ rooms in a house
▶ household chores
▶ how to tell someone to do something

Vocabulario en contexto

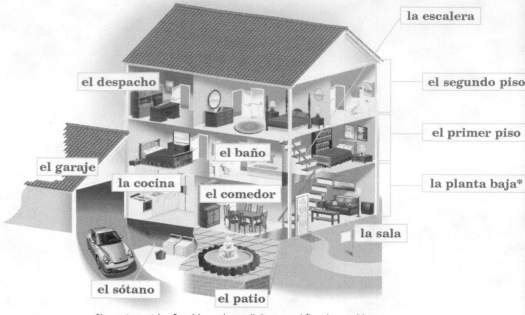

la escalera

el segundo piso

el primer piso

la planta baja*

el despacho

el garaje

el baño

la cocina

el comedor

la sala

el sótano

el patio

*In most countries, Spanish speakers call the ground floor in a multistory building *la planta baja*, the second floor *el primer piso*, the third floor *el segundo piso*, the fourth floor *el tercer piso*, and so on.

—Me gustaría ver esta casa. Es grande y bonita.
—Sí, tiene tres dormitorios y un despacho. Y también tiene una cocina moderna, si te gusta cocinar.

Se vende
Casa particular de tres pisos y sótano. Sala grande, cocina moderna, comedor, despacho, 2 baños, 3 dormitorios, garaje.
Llama al 555-37-89.

Más vocabulario
el apartamento   apartment
cerca (de)   close (to), near
lejos (de)   far (from)
bastante   enough, rather

126 ciento veintiséis
Tema 6 • La casa

DIFFERENTIATED INSTRUCTION

Heritage Language Learners

Have students pretend they are real estate agents. Have them create a flyer for a mansion they are selling. Encourage them to describe outrageous houses. After correcting the flyers, discuss any grammar and spelling concerns and have them make revisions as needed. Post the flyers and ask students to decide which house they would like to buy.

lavar los platos sucios

Hijos —
¡Tienen que hacer **los quehaceres** esta mañana!

Anita | Juanito

cortar el césped

poner la mesa

lavar el coche

pasar la aspiradora

dar de comer al perro

lavar la ropa

sacar la basura

cocinar

hacer la cama

—¡Ay! ¡Mira todos los quehaceres! Mamá sabe que tengo que ir de compras con Cristina. No puedo . . .

—Yo voy a jugar al fútbol a la una. Y tengo más quehaceres que tú.

quitar el polvo

arreglar el cuarto

limpiar el baño

▼1 🔊 Escuchar

La casa de Elena

Escucha a Elena describir su casa. Señala cada cuarto que describe.

▼2 🔊 Escuchar

¿Es lógico o no?

Escucha cada frase. Si es lógica, haz el gesto del pulgar hacia arriba (*"thumbs-up" sign*). Si no es lógica, haz el gesto del pulgar hacia abajo (*"thumbs-down" sign*).

Más práctica	GO

realidades.com | print

Instant Check	✔	
Guided WB pp. 49–54	✔	✔
Core WB pp. 28–29	✔	✔
Comm. WB p. 39	✔	✔
Hispanohablantes WB p. 232		✔

ciento veintisiete **127**
Capítulo 6B

ENRICH YOUR TEACHING

Teacher-to-Teacher
Have groups draw floor plans on butcher paper. Have them draw or glue magazine photos on index cards to represent the chores and write sentences on the cards such as: *Tengo que dar de comer al perro.* Students draw a card, read the sentence aloud, and place it in a room where the chore would be done.

21st Century Skills

Communication Have students use the announcement on page 126 as a model to create a For Sale ad for their own homes. Their ads should include information about the general layout of the house, number of rooms, and a contact number. After, have them choose one of the ads, and recreate the dialogue between a potential buyer and a real estate agent, who will try to sell the house to the buyer.

1 Standards: 1.2

Resources: Teacher's Resource Book: Audio Script, p. 125; Audio Program DVD: Cap. 6B, Track 3; Answer Keys: Student Edition, p. 123

Focus: Listening comprehension about chores and rooms in a house

Suggestions: Play the audio or read the script. Allow students to listen more than once. Pause to monitor students, making sure they are identifying the correct rooms.

🔊 **Script and Answers:**

1. Mi casa tiene una cocina muy moderna. *(cocina)*
2. El comedor está al lado de la cocina. *(comedor, cocina)*
3. El televisor está en la sala. *(sala)*
4. Hay un baño en la planta baja. *(baño)*
5. A veces mi mamá trabaja en casa en el despacho. *(despacho)*
6. Tengo que poner la mesa en el comedor. *(comedor)*
7. Mi dormitorio está en el primer piso. *(dormitorio)*
8. No me gusta limpiar el sótano. *(sótano)*

BELLRINGER REVIEW

To review names of activities, ask students to complete sentences about things they do in different rooms. Say or write a phrase like *En el comedor, me gusta ____.* Have students think of logical infinitives, such as **comer** or **cenar.**

2 Standards: 1.2

Resources: Teacher's Resource Book: Audio Script, p. 125; Audio Program DVD: Cap. 6B, Track 4; Answer Keys: Student Edition, p. 124

Focus: Listening comprehension

Suggestions: Before doing the activity, have students decide which chores on p. 127 go with which rooms on p. 126. Use the audio or read the script.

🔊 **Script and Answers:**

1. Me gusta dormir en el comedor. *(down)*
2. Hago la cama en mi dormitorio. *(up)*
3. Paso la aspiradora en la sala. *(up)*
4. Lavo los platos sucios en el baño. *(down)*
5. Doy de comer al perro en la cocina. *(up)*
6. Tengo que cortar el césped en el garaje. *(down)*
7. Comemos la cena en el baño. *(down)*
8. Saco la basura en el garaje. *(up)*

127

Videohistoria 🔊

Core Instruction

Standards: 1.2

Resources: Voc. and Gram. Transparencies 122–123; Audio Program DVD: Cap. 6B, Track 5; Answer Keys: Student Edition, p. 124

Focus: Reading comprehension of contextualized vocabulary about chores

Suggestions:

Pre-reading: Using the transparencies, go panel by panel and ask students to predict the outcome. Direct students' attention to the *Strategy* and have them determine which chores Elena has to complete. Ask them to guess why Jorgito is in trouble.

Answers:
1. Elena has chores to do and doesn't want to do them.
2. Jorgito wants money in return for doing Elena's chores.
3. Their parents are pleased and think Elena did the work. The chores were Elena's jobs.

Videohistoria | 🔊 | 📷

Los quehaceres de Elena

Elena no quiere hacer sus quehaceres. ¿Qué hace ella?

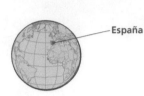
España

Mamá — Papá — Elena — Jorgito

Antes de leer

Strategy **Using language knowledge** Using what you already know about a language can help you understand better when you read.

- You have just learned the infinitives for various household chores. Can you list the four activities that Elena tells Jorgito to do in photo 5?

Before reading the *Videohistoria*, use the photos to consider the following:

1. What does Elena have to do? How does she feel about this?
2. What do you think Jorgito expects in return for doing Elena's chores?
3. How do their parents react to the condition of the house when they arrive home? Who do they think has done all the work? Why?

DIFFERENTIATED INSTRUCTION

Heritage Language Learners
Have students write a short paragraph about who among their siblings has household chores and who does the most work. They can include ways that family members try to get out of doing chores. When necessary, talk to students on an individual basis about spelling or grammatical errors they made in writing their paragraphs.

Students with Special Needs
Have students look at the photos and identify chores that need to be done. Highlight key words and phrases for them.

Language Input 6B

1

Elena: ¡Hola! Bienvenidos a mi casa. **Vivo** en el número 12 de la calle Apodaca. Vamos a entrar. Mi casa es su casa.

2

Elena: ¡Ay, no! Veo que tengo más quehaceres. Siempre lavo los platos sucios y **pongo** la mesa para la cena. ¡Y ahora necesito hacer más trabajo!

3

Elena: ¿Me **ayudas** con los quehaceres?
Jorgito: Quiero **dinero**.
Elena: No te **doy** dinero, pero puedes escuchar discos compactos en mi dormitorio.

4

Jorgito: A ver. Si hago unos de los quehaceres, me **das** los discos y escucho música por una hora.
Elena: Media hora.
Jorgito: Cuarenta y cinco minutos.
Elena: Está bien.

ciento veintinueve **129**
Capítulo 6B

Suggestions:

Reading: Read the captions with students or use the audio. Using the transparencies and non-verbal clues, help students understand the new words in blue type. Point out the different forms of the verb *dar* in panels 3 and 4. Ask students the comprehension questions found on the transparencies.

Post-reading: Complete the activities on p. 131 to check comprehension.

Pre-AP* Support

- **Learning Objective:** Interpretive Print and Audio
- **Activity:** Distribute Clip Art of the rooms of a house (including the patio and the garage) so that students can cut them into squares. Have volunteers tell what activities one can do in one of the rooms, and ask the class to respond by holding up the appropriate clip art. (Ex. *Podemos cocinar en la cocina.*)
- **Pre-AP* Resource Book:** Comprehensive guide to Pre-AP* vocabulary skill development, pp. 51–57

ENRICH YOUR TEACHING

Culture Note

In many Spanish-speaking countries, children are expected to help out in the home but are not paid for their help. As members of the family, it is their responsibility to do as their parents ask. They are given spending money when needed, but it is not usually seen as a *quid quo pro* exchange for labor.

Teacher-to-Teacher

Call on students and have them tell which chore they like more than others. Then have students tell which chore they dislike the most. They can begin their statements with *Me gusta* or *No me gusta*.

Video ▶

Core Instruction

Standards: 1.2

Resources: Teacher's Resource Book: Video Script, p. 129; Video Program: Cap. 6B; Video Program Teacher's Guide: Cap. 6B

Focus: Listening comprehension of contextualized vocabulary about chores

Suggestions:

Pre-viewing: Review the *Videohistoria* reading, and have students make a list of key ideas. Play an excerpt of the video with the sound down, and ask students to tell what panel of the *Videohistoria* it corresponds to.

Viewing: Show the video without pausing, then go back and show it again, pausing along the way to check for comprehension of new vocabulary. Ask students to discuss the bargaining between Elena and Jorgito. Is this something they do with their siblings?

Post-viewing: Complete the Video Activities in the *Communication Workbook*.

Pre-AP* Support

- **Learning Objective:** Presentational Writing and Speaking
- **Activity:** As a post-viewing activity, have pairs of students rewrite the third and fifth frames of the video. Ask them to imagine Elena offers a different compensation in exchange for doing the chores, and that the chores have changed. Have students act out their new version of the third, fourth, and fifth frames of the scene.
- **Pre-AP* Resource Book:** Comprehensive guide to Pre-AP* vocabulary skill development, pp. 51–57

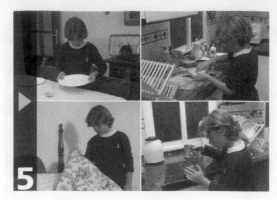

5

Jorgito: ¿**Cuáles** son los quehaceres que necesito hacer?
Elena: Pon la mesa, lava los platos sucios en la cocina, **haz** la cama en mi dormitorio y da de comer al perro.

6

Mamá: Elena, ¡qué **trabajadora** eres!
Papá: ¡Cómo ayudas en casa! Das de comer al perro, lavas los platos, **pones la mesa** . . .
Elena: Ah, . . . ¿**Recibo** mi dinero?
Mamá: Un momento. ¿Tu dormitorio está **limpio?**

7

Mamá: ¡Jorgito! ¡Qué **perezoso** eres! ¿Qué estás **haciendo?**
Jorgito: Pero, . . . pero, . . .
Papá: Ni pero ni nada. ¡Jorgito, a tu dormitorio! Vamos a ver . . .

8

Mamá: Elena, tu dinero.
Elena: Gracias, mamá.
Papá: Jorgito, ¿cómo puedes vivir así? Tienes que arreglar tu cuarto, hijo: haz la cama, quita el polvo, pasa la aspiradora . . .
Jorgito: Pero, Elena . . .
Elena: ¡Adiós! ¡Voy al cine!

 130 ciento treinta
Tema 6 • La casa

DIFFERENTIATED INSTRUCTION

Multiple Intelligences

Bodily/Kinesthetic: Ask students to come to the front of the class and role-play the parts of Jorgito, Elena, and the parents. Encourage them to be dramatic and to act out the various chores as they are being described. Give them a few minutes to practice beforehand.

▼3 Leer • Escribir

La lista de quehaceres

Lee esta lista de quehaceres y escoge los que necesitan hacer Elena y Jorgito. En una hoja de papel, escribe la lista de todos los quehaceres que tienen que hacer.

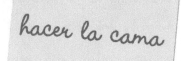

hacer la cama

cortar el césped	quitar el polvo
dar de comer al perro	pasar la aspiradora
lavar los platos	poner la mesa
limpiar el baño	sacar la basura

▼4 Leer • Pensar

¿Para quién trabaja?

Jorgito hace unos quehaceres para Elena y unos para arreglar su propio dormitorio. Lee estas frases y escribe *C* (cierto) o *F* (falso) según lo que hace en la *Videohistoria*.

1. Jorgito tiene que hacer la cama de Elena y también su propia cama.
2. Elena tiene que quitar el polvo.
3. Jorgito da de comer al perro para Elena.
4. Jorgito tiene que pasar la aspiradora en el dormitorio de Elena.
5. Jorgito lava los platos para Elena.
6. Jorgito pone la mesa en su dormitorio.

▼5 Leer • Escribir

¿Comprendes?

Todas estas frases son falsas. Para cada una, escribe una frase nueva con la información correcta según la *Videohistoria*.

1. Elena nunca pone la mesa en su casa.
2. A Jorgito no le gusta escuchar los discos compactos.
3. Si hace unos de los quehaceres, Jorgito puede escuchar una hora de música.
4. Según los padres, Elena es muy perezosa.
5. Según los padres, Jorgito es trabajador.
6. Ahora Jorgito va al cine.

Más práctica (GO)

realidades.com | print

Instant Check	✔	
Guided WB pp. 55–58	✔	✔
Core WB pp. 30–31	✔	✔
Comm. WB pp. 33–35, 36	✔	✔
Hispanohablantes **WB** p. 233	✔	

ciento treinta y uno **131**
Capítulo 6B

▼**3** Standards: 1.2, 1.3

Resources: Answer Keys: Student Edition, p. 125

Focus: Verifying understanding of the *Videohistoria*

Suggestions: Explain that not all of the chores will be on the list.

Answers: dar de comer al perro, lavar los platos, poner la mesa

▼**4** Standards: 1.2

Resources: Answer Keys: Student Edition, p. 125

Focus: Verifying understanding of the *Videohistoria*

Suggestions: Have volunteers read the statements out loud. Allow a moment for students to write each answer. Go over the answers in class.

Answers: 1. C   2. F   3. C   4. F   5. C   6. F

▼**5** Standards: 1.2, 1.3

Resources: Answer Keys: Student Edition, p. 125

Focus: Verifying understanding of the *Videohistoria*

Suggestions: Review the *Videohistoria* with students before they begin.

Answers:

1. **Elena siempre pone la mesa en su casa.**
2. **A Jorgito le gusta escuchar los discos compactos.**
3. **Si hace unos de los quehaceres, Jorgito puede escuchar cuarenta y cinco minutos de música.**
4. **Según los padres, Elena es muy trabajadora.**
5. **Según los padres, Jorgito es perezoso.**
6. **Ahora Elena va al cine.**

Additional Resources

• Communication Wbk.: Audio Act. 5, p. 36
• Teacher's Resource Book: Audio Script, p. 126
• Audio Program DVD: Cap. 6B, Track 7

ENRICH YOUR TEACHING

Teacher-to-Teacher

Use the vocabulary on chores to play charades. Write the expressions on index cards and place in a box. Ask volunteers to take a card from the box and act out the chore. Other students will guess which chore the student is doing. Ask questions such as: *Y en tu casa, ¿quién pone la mesa?*

21st Century Skills

Technology Literacy Encourage students to use the various tools available at **realidades.com** for learning this vocabulary (such as the eBook with embedded audio). Then have students create a weekly calendar of household chores. If possible, they should set up an electronic calendar on a computer, to remind themselves when it is time to do something.

✓ASSESSMENT

Quiz: Vocabulary Recognition
• Prueba 6B-1: pp. 162–163

INTERACTIVE WHITEBOARD
Vocabulary Activities 6B

BELLRINGER REVIEW

Show *Voc. and Gram. Transparency 120.* Ask students to name the rooms on *la planta baja, el primer piso,* and *el segundo piso.*

6 Standards: 1.2, 1.3

Resources: Answer Keys: Student Edition, p. 126

Focus: Practicing vocabulary and grammar about rooms in a house

Recycle: Classroom objects vocabulary

Suggestions: Have students write all the rooms in the word box at the top of their papers. As they read each description, they can cross their answer off the list of rooms.

Answers:
1. el dormitorio 4. la cocina 6. el despacho
2. el garaje   5. el baño   7. el comedor
3. la sala

7 Standards: 1.3

Resources: Answer Keys: Student Edition, p. 126

Focus: Writing visualized vocabulary

Recycle: *Ordinal numbers: primero, segundo, tercero, cuarto, quinto, sexto; vivir*

Suggestions: Suggest that students write the *Recycle* words at the top of their page as a word box. Discuss the *Nota* on p.133.

Answers:
1. Javier y Ana Ríos viven en el cuarto piso.
2. Luis Méndez vive en el quinto piso.
3. Jorge y Carmen Benítez viven en el sexto piso.
4. Marta Herrera vive en el tercer piso.
5. La Sra. Lopera vive en la planta baja.
6. Paco y Juana Ramos viven en el sótano.

Additional Resources

• Teacher's Resource Book: GramActiva BLM, p. 137

✓ASSESSMENT

Go over the answers together in class, having volunteers read their answers. Students can check their own papers.

Manos a la obra

▼ Objectives
▶ Listen to and write descriptions of a house
▶ Write about and discuss furniture and chores
▶ Read and respond to a survey
▶ Exchange information about homes

Vocabulario en uso

▼6 | ♻ | Leer • Escribir

¿Dónde estás?

Lee las frases para decidir en qué cuarto estás. Escribe los números del 1 al 7 en una hoja de papel y completa las frases con la palabra apropiada de la lista.

1. Hay una cama y dos mesitas en ___.
2. El coche siempre está en ___.
3. Hay un sofá y dos sillas en ___.
4. Los tenedores y los cuchillos están en ___.
5. Hay un espejo muy grande en ___.
6. La computadora y el escritorio están en ___.
7. Hay una mesa y cuatro sillas en ___.

el comedor	el garaje
el baño	el dormitorio
la sala	el despacho
la cocina	

▼7 Escribir

¿En qué piso viven?

You are in front of the apartment building from where the Ramírez family will be moving. Look at the buzzer panel to identify on what floor their neighbors live. Write your answers on a separate sheet of paper.

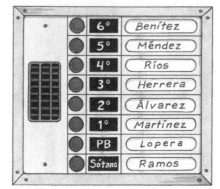

Modelo
El Sr. Álvarez
El Sr. Álvarez vive en el segundo piso.

1. Javier y Ana Ríos
2. Luis Méndez
3. Jorge y Carmen Benítez
4. Marta Herrera
5. La Sra. Lopera
6. Paco y Juana Ramos

132 ciento treinta y dos
Tema 6 • La casa

DIFFERENTIATED INSTRUCTION

Heritage Language Learners

Have students describe to the class one or two rooms in their homes following the descriptions in *Actividad* 6. If a student uses another word for a room, such as **salón** instead of **sala,** or **alcoba** instead of **dormitorio,** have them share these different words with the class.

Students with Learning Difficulties

You may need to simplify or explain in detail *Actividad* 8 for students with visual or spatial difficulties. Having them focus on just one floor may be helpful.

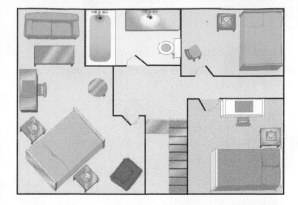
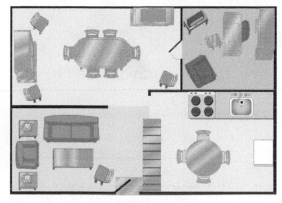
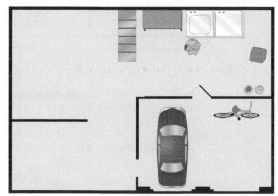

▼**8** | 🔊 ⟩⟩ | **Escuchar • Escribir**

La casa de los Ramírez

Los Ramírez van a comprar la casa que ves aquí. En una hoja de papel escribe los números del 1 al 8 y escribe el nombre de cada cuarto que describen.

> **Nota**
>
> *Primero(a)* and *tercero(a)* become *primer* and *tercer* before a masculine singular noun.
>
> • Mi dormitorio está en el **primer** piso.
> • Su apartamento está en el **tercer** piso.

▼**9** | 🗨 👥 | **Escribir • Escuchar • Hablar**

¿Cierto o falso?

Escribe cinco frases para indicar dónde están los cuartos en la casa de los Ramírez. Las frases pueden ser ciertas o falsas. Lee tus frases a otro(a) estudiante, quien va a indicar si las frases son ciertas o falsas. Si son falsas, tiene que dar la información correcta.

▶ **Modelo**

A —*La sala está en el primer piso.*
B —*Falso. La sala está en la planta baja.*

> **También se dice . . .**
>
> **la sala** = el salón *(muchos países);*
> el living *(España)*
>
> **el despacho** = la oficina *(muchos países)*
>
> **el piso** = la planta *(muchos países)*
>
> **el apartamento** = el piso *(España);*
> el departamento *(muchos países)*

ciento treinta y tres **133**
Capítulo 6B

▼**8** Standards: 1.2, 1.3

Resources: Teacher's Resource Book: Audio Script, p. 125; Audio Program DVD: Cap. 6B, Track 6; Answer Keys: Student Edition, p. 127

Focus: Locating the rooms in a house based on an oral description

Suggestions: Have students describe the floor plan and brainstorm a list of location words that they will need to listen for. Write the words on the board. Emphasize that students should look at each floor as if the side closest to the bottom of the page were the front of the house. Play the audio or read the script aloud.

🔊 ⟩⟩ **Script and Answers:**

1. Está en la planta baja, al lado del comedor. *(el despacho)*
2. Está en el primer piso, a la derecha del baño. *(el dormitorio)*
3. Está a la derecha del dormitorio grande en el primer piso. *(el baño)*
4. Está en la planta baja, detrás de la sala. *(el comedor)*
5. El coche está aquí. *(el garaje)*
6. Está delante del despacho en la planta baja. *(la cocina)*
7. La ropa sucia está aquí, debajo de la planta baja. *(el sótano)*
8. Está en la planta baja a la izquierda de la cocina. *(la sala)*

▼**9** Standards: 1.1, 1.2, 1.3

Focus: Using contextualized vocabulary in written and oral formats

Suggestions: Model a true and a false sentence. Have a volunteer correct the false statement. When students complete the activity, have pairs say their sentences to the class. Other students should say whether or not the statement is true or false before the volunteer provides the correct information.

Answers will vary.

ENRICH YOUR TEACHING

Teacher-to-Teacher

Have students design a floor plan for their dream house. It should include a Spanish-type patio. (Students may need to do some research in order to identify an appropriate design.) Have students draw the design on poster board. On the side, students should list what will be in the patio (plants, animals, etc.), the colors they will use, and which rooms in the house will have access to the patio. Have students vote on the best floor plans and display them in the classroom.

10 Standards: 1.3

Resources: Answer Keys: Student Edition, p. 128

Focus: Practicing new vocabulary for chores and rooms of the house

Suggestions: Point out that students will answer in the first person singular and need to know the correct form of **poner** and **hacer.** Call on a volunteer to read the *Nota* in *Actividad* 11.

Answers:
1. Pongo la mesa en el comedor (la cocina).
2. Hago la cama en el dormitorio.
3. Lavo los platos sucios en la cocina.
4. Lavo la ropa en el sótano (el garaje).
5. Quito el polvo en la sala (el dormitorio).
6. Paso la aspiradora en la sala (el dormitorio, el despacho, el comedor).

11 Standards: 1.1

Resources: Answer Keys: Student Edition, p. 128

Focus: Practicing familiar vocabulary in the context of rooms in a house

Recycle: Furnishings and electronics

Suggestions: Ask volunteers to read the model and point out the different verbal expressions used in each sentence. Encourage students to use as many different rooms as possible.

Answers:
Student A:
1. ¿Dónde pongo la cama?
2. ¿Dónde pongo el espejo?
3. ¿Dónde pongo el televisor?
4. ¿Dónde pongo la bicicleta?
5. ¿Dónde pongo la computadora?
6. ¿Dónde pongo la mesa?
7. ¿Dónde pongo la lámpara?
Student B:
Answers will vary.

Common Errors: Students may say *Vamos a pongo* or use the wrong articles before new vocabulary. Remind them to use the infinitive after **ir a.** Monitor the pairs, then correct errors with the whole class.

Extension: Ask students to provide additional details when describing where to put things, such as *Vamos a poner la silla en el comedor, cerca de la mesa.*

▼10 Escribir

¿En qué cuarto?

Siempre ayudas a tu familia con los quehaceres. Escribe una frase para decir dónde haces estos *(these)* quehaceres.

Modelo
Saco la basura en el garaje.

1.
2.
3.

4.
5.
6.

▼11 Hablar

¿Dónde pongo la silla?

Ayudas a tu amigo(a) a mudarse *(move)* a su nueva casa pero no sabes dónde poner sus posesiones. Con otro(a) estudiante, pregunta y contesta según el modelo.

▶ Modelo
A —*¿Dónde pongo la silla?*
B —*Vamos a poner la silla en el comedor.*

> **Nota**
> *Poner,* "to put," is also used in the expression *poner la mesa,* "to set the table." It has an irregular *yo* form: *pongo.*
> • En la mañana **pongo** la mesa.

Estudiante A

Estudiante B

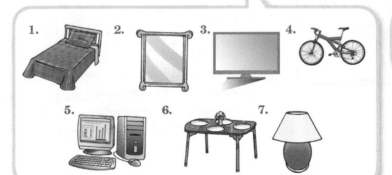

> ¡Respuesta personal!

134 ciento treinta y cuatro
Tema 6 • La casa

DIFFERENTIATED INSTRUCTION

Advanced Learners/Pre-AP*

Have students prepare and present a brief description of their homes or an ideal home: the rooms, the location of the rooms, and the furniture. Have them take turns reading their descriptions to a partner, who will draw a sketch based on the description. Students who are drawing the picture should be encouraged to ask questions that will provide details for the illustration.

▼**12** | | **Escribir**

En mi casa hay . . .

Haz una lista de los cuartos en tu casa o apartamento. Al lado de cada cuarto, escribe por lo menos *(at least)* dos cosas que hay en el cuarto.

Los cuartos	Las cosas
mi dormitorio	una cama

 12 Standards: 1.3

Focus: Writing home vocabulary in a personalized context

Recycle: Furniture

Suggestions: Have students make a chart and have them complete it with things that are in their own homes.

Answers will vary.

BELLRINGER REVIEW

Show Voc. and Grammar Transparency 121. Have students work in pairs to tell each other where they do three of the activities.

▼**13** |  | **Hablar**

¿Qué hay en nuestras casas?

Con otro(a) estudiante, usa tu lista de la Actividad 12 para hablar de los cuartos en su casa o apartamento, y de las cosas que hay en cada uno.

▶ **Modelo**

A —¿Hay <u>un comedor</u> en tu casa?
B —Sí, hay <u>un comedor</u>.
A —¿Qué hay en <u>tu comedor</u>?
B —Hay <u>una mesa y unas sillas</u>.

13 Standards: 1.1

Focus: Talking with a partner using home vocabulary

Suggestions: Read the *Modelo* with a student volunteer reading the part of Student B. Pair the class for the activity and tell them to alternate being Student A. You may want to help with pronunciation.

Answers will vary.

Fondo Cultural | España

El patio in an apartment building in a large Spanish city is usually just an open area in the center of the building. In southern Spain, however, houses are often built around *patios*, which may have gardens as well as a fountain. The Moors brought this architectural style to Spain, and the Spaniards then carried it over to the Americas.

• How does the Spanish patio differ from what a patio is in your community? How is it similar?

Un patio típico en Córdoba, España ▶

Fondo cultural

Standards: 2.2, 4.2

Suggestions: Explain that enclosed patios were often used by the Moors who occupied Spain for over 700 years. The Moors were Muslim and used patios as places for prayer and meditation. Have students discuss how they use patios and yards and contrast this with how they might use an enclosed patio like the one in the picture. Ask them to try to determine historical, cultural, or social variations that would lead to these different uses.

Answers will vary.

Mapa global interactivo, Actividad 2 Visit Seville, Spain and learn about the tradition of *patios* in houses.

ciento treinta y cinco **135**
Capítulo 6B

ENRICH YOUR TEACHING

Culture Note

Because the climate of southern Spain is so warm throughout the year, many homes have a patio within the house that is open to the sky. These patios often contain a fountain, small pool, or garden to help cool the home. Usually this is a place for private relaxation, but every May the city of Córdoba has a festival during which each homeowner proudly displays his or her patio. Thousands of flowers and plants are used for decoration. People open their homes for several weeks so friends, neighbors, and tourists can come and enjoy their patios. A prize is awarded to the most beautiful one.

Pre-AP* Support

• **Learning Objective:** Interpersonal Speaking
• **Activity:** Have students work with a partner to tell what they would and would not be able to do in the patio pictured on this page. (Ex. *No puedo jugar al fútbol.*) Allow each student to talk for 30 seconds.

14

Standards: 1.1

Resources: Answer Keys: Student Edition, p. 129

Focus: Describing household chores from a personal point of view

Suggestions: Point out that the question will use the familiar form of **tener que** + **infinitive,** but that Student B will have to conjugate the verb pictured. Ask volunteers to model a negative response from Student B: No, no lavo nunca el coche.

Answers:

Student A:
1. ¿Tienes que cocinar?
2. ¿Tienes que cortar el césped?
3. ¿Tienes que dar de comer al perro?
4. ¿Tienes que lavar los platos sucios?
5. ¿Tienes que hacer la cama?
6. ¿Tienes que quitar el polvo?

Student B answers will vary but verbs should be in the *yo* form.

Common Errors: Students may say: *Tengo que lavo, Tengo que cocino, etc.* Remind them that the second verb should be in the infinitive.

Extension: Have students work in pairs to make a four-column chart labeled: *Todos los días, El fin de semana, A veces,* and *Nunca.* They should then write the chores pictured in the Student A bubble along the left-hand side. Have them place a check in the column indicating how often they do the chore. Then have them work with a partner to talk about their activities. Ask students to be prepared to present the discussion to the class.

Exploración del lenguaje
Core Instruction

Standards: 4.1

Resources: Answer Keys: Student Edition, p. 129

Suggestions: Have students brainstorm a list of other English words whose noun form ends in **-er** or **-or** (teacher, actor, painter, operator, vendor, etc.). Ask students to match the answers for *Try it out!* at their seats before you review them as a class.

Answers:
1. d   2. a   3. b   4. c

▼14 | | | Hablar

¿Cómo ayudas en casa?

¿Ayudas mucho en casa? Habla de tus quehaceres con otro(a) estudiante.

▶ **Modelo**

A —¿Tienes que *lavar el coche*?
B —Sí, *lavo el coche* todos los sábados.

Nota

Dar means "to give" and is used in the expression *dar de comer,* "to feed." It has an irregular *yo* form: *doy.*

• En mi casa **doy** de comer al perro.

Estudiante A

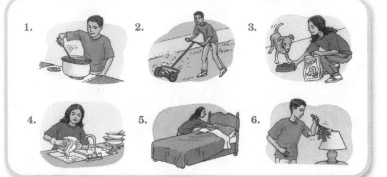

Estudiante B

a veces
mucho
todos los días
todos los (sábados)
en el (verano)
los fines de semana
nunca

▼ Exploración del lenguaje

Nouns that end in *-dor* and *-dora*

Every day you use appliances and gadgets to help with different tasks: a calculator, a computer, a stapler, a copier, a dryer, etc. Many of these words in English add the ending *-er* or *-or* to the verb that tells what the device is for. Spanish follows a similar pattern. Look at these words you already know and identify the pattern: *despertador, computadora, calculadora, aspiradora.* Can you guess what the corresponding verbs are and what they mean?

Try it out! Read each statement on the left and decide which appliance is needed.

1. Tengo calor.
2. ¿Dónde está el pan tostado?
3. Mi ropa está sucia.
4. Necesito leche para el cereal.

a. Está en la tostadora.
b. Ponla en la lavadora.
c. Está en el refrigerador.
d. Necesitas el ventilador.

DIFFERENTIATED INSTRUCTION

Advanced Learners
Have students make a map of their community or neighborhood, labeling the places they include. Ask them to write a short paragraph about where the places on the map are located in relation to their house.

Heritage Language Learners
Have students search U.S. magazines or the Internet to see if they can find information similar to that in *Actividad* 15. Have them compare the information and report the similarities or differences.

Practice and Communicate 6B

▼15 | ♻ | Leer • Escribir • Hablar

¿Quién hace los quehaceres?

Un artículo de la revista española *Muy interesante* explica quién hace la mayoría de *(most of)* los quehaceres de la casa. Estudia las gráficas a la derecha y haz comparaciones entre *(between)* las mujeres y los hombres españoles. Después, explica si las mujeres hacen los siguientes quehaceres mucho más, un poco más, o menos que los hombres.

Modelo
lavar los platos
Según el artículo, las mujeres lavan los platos mucho más que los hombres.

1. comprar cosas para la familia cada día
2. preparar la comida y la cena
3. cuidar *(to take care of)* el coche
4. cuidar a las personas enfermas de la familia
5. lavar y planchar *(iron)* la ropa
6. ir al banco
7. limpiar la casa

¿Quién hace los quehaceres?

Lavar y planchar la ropa — Mujeres 88%, Hombres 4%, Juntos* 8%
Comprar la comida — Mujeres 73%, Hombres 8%, Juntos 19%
Preparar comidas — Mujeres 68%, Hombres 13%, Juntos 19%
Cuidar el coche — Mujeres 14%, Hombres 78%, Juntos 8%
Limpiar la casa — Mujeres 60%, Hombres 13%, Juntos 19%
Ir al banco — Mujeres 37%, Hombres 26%, Juntos 36%
Lavar los platos — Mujeres 67%, Hombres 10%, Juntos 23%
Cuidar a los enfermos — Mujeres 31%, Hombres 10%, Juntos 30%

*Together

▼16 | 💬 | ♻ | Escribir • Hablar

¿Dónde vives?

Escribe una lista de cinco lugares *(places)* en tu comunidad, como la escuela, el centro comercial, la biblioteca, etc. Pregunta a otro(a) estudiante si vive cerca o lejos de estos lugares.

▶ Modelo
El cine Rex
A —¿Vives cerca del cine Rex?
B —Sí, vivo bastante cerca del cine.
o: —No, vivo muy lejos.

ciento treinta y siete **137**
Capítulo 6B

▼15 Standards: 1.1, 1.2, 1.3

Resources: Voc. and Gram. Transparency 126; Answer Keys: Student Edition, p. 130

Focus: Reading and writing about household chores

Recycle: Numbers 1–80

Suggestions: Ask students to look at the graphs before beginning and have them write down the percentages for each box before writing a sentence.

Answers:
1. Las mujeres compran cosas para la familia mucho más que los hombres.
2. … preparan la comida y la cena mucho más.
3. … cuidan el coche mucho menos.
4. … cuidan a las personas enfermas de la familia un poco más.
5. … lavan y planchan la ropa mucho más.
6. … van al banco un poco más.
7. … limpian la casa mucho más.

▼16 Standards: 1.1, 1.3

Focus: Writing and speaking about the location of one's home

Recycle: Names of places in the community

Suggestions: Brainstorm a list of place names on the board to use as a word bank. Have two volunteers read the model and then repeat it, substituting the name of a movie theater in your community.

Answers will vary.

Additional Resources
- Communication Wbk.: Audio Act. 6, p. 36
- Teacher's Resource Book: Audio Script, p. 126, Communicative Pair Activity BLM, pp. 132–133
- Audio Program DVD: Cap. 6B, Track 8

ENRICH YOUR TEACHING

Culture Note
In the cities of Spain, most people live in apartment buildings called **bloques.** These buildings are usually between five and eleven stories high. There is normally a large patio shared by several buildings where children play. The lower levels of the buildings are generally occupied by businesses such as bakeries, restaurants, or video stores. Have students go online and look at some of the apartments for rent in Spanish cities.

✔ ASSESSMENT

Prueba 6B-2 with Study Plan (online only)

Quiz: Vocabulary Production
- Prueba 6B-2: pp. 164–165

137

Gramática

Core Instruction

Standards: 4.1

Resources: Voc. and Gram. Transparency 124; Teacher's Resource Book: Video Script, p. 129; Video Program: Cap. 6B

INTERACTIVE WHITEBOARD

Grammar Activities 6B

Suggestions: Direct attention to the *¿Recuerdas?* Ask what form of the verb the words in bold type resemble. Build upon students' knowledge of English grammar to discuss the meanings of these words. Use the transparency to reinforce the affirmative *tú* commands. Remind students that this form should be used only with friends or family. Use the *GramActiva* Video as an introduction to the structure or as a follow-up.

▼ 17 Standards: 1.2

Focus: Listening to affirmative *tú* commands and following directions

Recycle: Activities

Suggestions: Prepare a set of commands before beginning the activity. As you give the first command, pantomime the activity.

Script:
Simón dice... escribe tu nombres. / ...baila. / ...toca tu cabeza. / ...toca la silla.

Answers will vary.

BELLRINGER REVIEW

Review the household chores on p. 127. Read them, making each infinitive verb an affirmative *tú* command.

▼ 18 Standards: 1.3

Resources: Answer Keys: Student Edition, p. 130

Focus: Writing informal commands about cleaning the house

Suggestions: Tell students that they will create *tú* commands for the list.

Answers:

1. Quita ...
2. Limpia ...
3. Arregla ...
4. Haz ...
5. Pasa ...
6. Pon ..

Gramática

Affirmative *tú* commands

When you tell friends, family members, or young people to do something, you use an affirmative *tú* command. To give these commands, use the same present-tense forms that you use for *Ud., él, ella.*

Infinitive	Ud./él/ella	Affirmative *tú* commands
hablar	habla	¡Habla!
leer	lee	¡Lee!
escribir	escribe	¡Escribe!

- Certain verbs, like *poner* and *hacer*, have irregular command forms.

  Jorgito, ¡pon la mesa!

  Jorgito, ¡haz tu cama!

¿Recuerdas?

In the direction lines of many activities, you have already seen many affirmative commands.

- **Habla** con otra persona.
- **Lee** las frases.
- **Escribe** la palabra apropiada.

Más ayuda   **realidades.com**

 GramActiva Video
Tutorial: Formation of regular *tú* commands

 Canción de hip hop: Cenicienta

 GramActiva Activity

▼ 17 | Escuchar • GramActiva

"Simón dice . . . "

Escucha y sigue *(follow)* las instrucciones de tu profesor(a) o de otro(a) estudiante. Si no dicen *"Simón dice,"* no debes hacer la acción.

▼ 18 Escribir

¿Me ayudas?

Vienen unos amigos a tu casa para almorzar y tu madre necesita ayuda con los quehaceres. Completa la nota con la forma correcta del verbo apropiado para saber qué tienes que hacer. Escribe las frases completas en una hoja de papel.

Modelo

Saca la basura.

> Viene la familia Sánchez a casa para almorzar. Voy al trabajo esta mañana.
> ¿Me ayudas con los quehaceres?
> Por favor:
> 1. ____ el polvo del despacho.
> 2. ____ el baño.
> 3. ____ tu dormitorio.
> 4. ____ la cama en mi dormitorio.
> 5. ____ la aspiradora en la sala.
> 6. ____ la mesa para el almuerzo.
>
> ¡Muchísimas gracias!
> Mamá

DIFFERENTIATED INSTRUCTION

Advanced Learners

Have students model affirmative *tú* commands by writing and acting out a dialogue between either teacher and student or brother and sister. In the dialogue, one person should be giving orders, and the other should be responding. Suggest that students write at least five lines. Encourage humor and creativity!

Heritage Language Learners

Discuss with students with whom they would typically use *tú* in their heritage culture. Be sure to note that familiarity may not necessarily require the use of *tú,* and using **usted** or **vos** may be acceptable. Ask students to compare how respect / familiarity is shown in Spanish with how it is shown in English.

▼**19** | ♻ | Pensar • Escribir

¿Responsable o irresponsable?

You need to make a decision: be responsible and do the household chores that need to be done, or be irresponsible and do things that are more fun. On a separate sheet of paper, make two lists: one titled *Responsable* and the other titled *Irresponsable*. For each list, write five sentences using the words in the box.

cocinar	limpiar
cortar	leer
escuchar	poner
hacer la tarea	ver
lavar	

¡Respuesta personal!

También se dice . . .

cocinar = guisar *(España)*

cortar el césped = cortar la hierba, cortar el pasto *(muchos países);* cortar el zacate *(México)*

lavar los platos = fregar los platos *(España)*

quitar el polvo = sacudir los muebles *(México);* desempolvar *(Bolivia)*

▼**20** | 🗨 | ♻ | Hablar

Un(a) niño(a) difícil

Estás cuidando a un(a) niño(a) difícil que quiere hacer muchas cosas. Tienes que indicar dónde él (ella) debe hacer estas actividades. Con otro(a) estudiante, explica dónde debe hacer varias actividades.

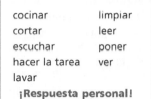 **Modelo**

A —*Yo quiero comer el almuerzo.*
B —*Está bien, pero por favor, come el almuerzo en la cocina.*

Estudiante A

1. hablar por teléfono
2. tocar la guitarra
3. limpiar los zapatos sucios
4. escuchar la radio
5. ver una película en el lector DVD
6. jugar videojuegos

Estudiante B

el baño
la cocina
el comedor
el cuarto
el despacho
el garaje
la sala
el sótano

¡Respuesta personal!

ciento treinta y nueve **139**
Capítulo 6B

---

19 Standards: 1.3

Resources: Answer Keys: Student Edition, p. 131

Focus: Thinking and writing about your actions in a personalized context

Recycle: *Escuchar, hacer la tarea, leer, ver*

Suggestions: Remind students that *hacer* and *poner* have irregular *tú* commands. This activity could be done in pairs, which allows students to brainstorm together and create one list.

Answers will vary but verbs will be:

cocina	haz	lee
corta	lava	pon
escucha	limpia	ve

Common Errors: Some students will want to use negative commands, saying that it is irresponsible *not* to cook dinner. Warn them that negative commands use a different verb form and that they must use affirmative *tú* commands for all of their sentences.

20 Standards: 1.1

Resources: Answer Keys: Student Edition, p. 131

Focus: Talking about where to do household activities using affirmative *tú* commands

Recycle: Activities vocabulary

Suggestions: Review the leisure activity verbs with students. Explain that Student A wants to do these activities and Student B is going to tell him or her where to do them using an affirmative *tú* command. Read the *Modelo* with a student volunteer. Tell students to alternate the roles. Circulate around the room to help with pronunciation and grammar.

Answers will vary but answers for Student B should include:

1. ...habla por teléfono...
2. ...toca la guitarra...
3. ...limpia los zapatos sucios...
4. ...escucha la radio...
5. ...ve una película en el lector DVD...
6. ...juega videojuegos...

ENRICH YOUR TEACHING

Teacher-to-Teacher

Have students write a letter to their parents. The letter should state why they won't be able to complete their household chores this weekend. Encourage students to be creative and outrageous with their reasons. Read the letters in class and vote on the best excuses for each chore or the best overall letter. As an extension, have students pretend to be the parents and answer the letter, stating that the chores have to get done.

Theme Project

Students can perform Step 4 at this point. Be sure they understand your corrections and suggestions. (For more information, see p. 92-b.)

BELLRINGER REVIEW

Have students list suggestions for how to be healthy, including advice on eating, sleeping, and exercising.

▼ **21** Standards: 1.2, 1.3

Resources: Answer Keys: Student Edition, p. 131

Focus: Reading comprehension and writing accuracy with *tú* commands and vocabulary

Recycle: Vocabulary for food and drink; vocabulary for exercise; adjectives describing feeling

Suggestions: Have a volunteer read the letter aloud, and ask follow-up questions such as *¿Cuál es el problema de Carmen?* In their responses, encourage students to use verbs and recommendations in addition to those in the box.

Answers will vary but the verbs should be:

corre	juega
duerme	levanta
estudia	ve
haz	

Extension: Have students peer-edit each other's letters.

▼ **22** Standards: 1.1, 1.3

Resources: Answer Keys: Student Edition, p. 132

Focus: Practicing conversation

Recycle: Items in a bedroom

Suggestions: Refer students to the *¿Recuerdas?* and point out that there are two parts to the activity. First, they must identify what is dirty. Then they must form an affirmative command to tell their sibling to clean the item.

Answers
1. La alfombra está sucia. Pasa la aspiradora, por favor.
2. El espejo está sucio. Limpia el espejo, por favor.
3. El cuarto (dormitorio) está sucio (desordenado). Arregla el cuarto (dormitorio), por favor.
4. Las ventanas están sucias. Limpia las ventanas, por favor.
5. La ropa está sucia. Lava la ropa, por favor.
6. La cocina está sucia. Saca la basura, por favor.

▼ **21** | ♻ | Leer · Escribir

Menos quehaceres, más tiempo libre

Tu amiga Carmen tiene un problema y te escribe una carta *(letter)*. Lee su carta y escribe tus recomendaciones en otra carta, usando los verbos de la lista.

Modelo
Mi querida Carmen, aquí están mis recomendaciones: Corre en el parque, . . .

correr	jugar
dormir	levantar pesas
estudiar	ver
hacer ejercicio	
¡Respuesta personal!	

> ¡Hola!
>
> Tengo un problema grande. Nunca paso tiempo con mis amigos y no estoy en buena forma. ¡No tengo tiempo libre! Durante la semana tengo clases y en los fines de semana arreglo mi cuarto, limpio el baño, quito el polvo de toda la casa . . . ¡Hago quehaceres todo el día! Quisiera hacer cosas más divertidas. Siempre tengo mucho sueño y poca energía. Nunca hago ejercicio. No estoy muy enferma pero quisiera estar mejor de salud. ¿Qué debo hacer?
>
> Tu amiga desesperada,
>
> Carmen

▼ **22** | ♻ | Hablar · Escribir

Muchos quehaceres

Tienes muchos quehaceres en casa, pero no los quieres hacer. ¡A ver si tu hermanito(a) puede hacer todo! Primero di *(say)* lo que está sucio (o lo que no está limpio). Luego di lo que tiene que hacer.

Modelo
Los platos están sucios.
o: *Los platos no están limpios.*
Lava los platos, por favor.

¿Recuerdas?
Adjectives agree in number and gender with the nouns they modify.
• La casa está sucia.
• Los platos están limpios.

1.
2.
3.
4.
5.
6.

DIFFERENTIATED INSTRUCTION

Students with Learning Difficulties

Have students make a three-column chart to use as a reference. They should put the infinitive in the first column, the present tense form used for *Ud., él, and ella* in the second column, and the affirmative *tú* command in the third column. They can add to the chart and use it as a reference throughout the chapter.

▼23 | 🗣️👥 | Hablar

Compartir el trabajo

Tú y tus amigos van a tener una fiesta en tu casa. Tus padres están de acuerdo, pero Uds. tienen que arreglar la casa antes de la fiesta. Lee la lista de todos los quehaceres que necesitas hacer. Trabaja con otro(a) estudiante para decidir cómo compartir el trabajo.

▶️ **Modelo**

A —*Limpia el baño.*
B —*No me gusta nada limpiar el baño. ¿Por qué no limpias tú el baño? Yo paso la aspiradora.*
A —*Está bien. Pasa la aspiradora y yo puedo limpiar el baño.*
o: —*Bueno, pasa la aspiradora pero yo quiero hacer las camas.*

Antes de la fiesta necesitan:

cortar el césped

hacer todas las camas

arreglar los dos dormitorios

limpiar el baño

pasar la aspiradora en el despacho

sacar la basura de la cocina

quitar el polvo de la sala

poner las bicicletas en el garaje

Más práctica GO realidades.com | print

Instant Check	✔	
Guided WB pp. 59–60	✔	✔
Core WB p. 32	✔	✔
Comm. WB pp. 37, 40	✔	✔
Hispanohablantes WB pp. 234–237, p. 240		✔

▼ Pronunciación | 🔊 | 🗣️

The letters *n* and *ñ*

In Spanish, the letter *n* sounds like the *n* in *no*. Listen to and say these words:

anaranjado	nieva	nadar	joven	desayuno
necesito	encantado	número	nombre	donde

However, the sound changes when there is a tilde (~) over the *n*. The *ñ* then sounds like the *-ny-* of the word *canyon*. Listen to and say these words:

señor	otoño	español	enseñar	año
montañas	niña	mañana	piñata	cumpleaños

Try it out! Listen to this *trabalenguas* and then try to say it.

El Sr. Yáñez come ñames[1] en las mañanas con el niño.

[1] yams

▼23 Standards: 1.1

Focus: Reading and talking about household chores using the affirmative *tú* commands, questions, and answers

Suggestions: Review the words *(no) me gusta.* Read the list of chores with the students. Explain that they will work in pairs to decide who will do each of the eight chores. Read the *Modelo* with a student volunteer. Pair the students to complete the activity. Circulate around the room to help with pronunciation, grammar, and vocabulary problems.

Answers will vary but may include affirmative *tú* commands.

Extension: Have each pair role-play one of their conversations about the chores for the rest of the class.

Pronunciación
Core Instruction

Standards: 4.1

Resources: Teacher's Resource Book: Audio Script, p. 126; Audio Program DVD: Cap. 6B, Track 9

Suggestions: Read the *Pronunciación* with the students or use the audio. Model the two distinct sounds, exaggerating them somewhat for clarity. Have students repeat the words after you. Say the tongue twister and then ask volunteers to say it for the class.

Additional Resources
- Communication Wbk.: Audio Act. 7, p. 37
- Teacher's Resource Book: Audio Script, pp. 126–127
- Audio Program DVD: Cap. 6B, Track 10

✓ASSESSMENT

Prueba 6B-3 with Study Plan (online only)

Quiz: Affirmative *tú* commands
- Prueba 6B-3: p. 166

ENRICH YOUR TEACHING

Teacher-to-Teacher
Have students prepare a skit in which two of them are the parents and two are the children. The parents ask the children to do their chores and the children refuse or agree reluctantly. Encourage students to be creative and funny. Have students act it out in class.

21st Century Skills

Communication After students review affirmative commands, have them take turns giving each other orders about cleaning the classroom, using the applicable chores and the *tú* command forms.

Gramática

Core Instruction

Standards: 4.1

Resources: Voc. and Gram. Transparency 125; Teacher's Resource Book: Video Script, p. 130; Video Program: Cap. 6B

INTERACTIVE WHITEBOARD
Grammar Activities 6B

Suggestions: Direct attention to the *¿Recuerdas?* Be sure students understand that the present tense in Spanish already includes the meaning of doing something now. However, the present progressive tense puts stronger emphasis on the fact that the action is taking place as one speaks. Use the transparency to reinforce the forms of the present progressive tense. Use the *GramActiva* Video either as an initial introduction to the structure or as a follow-up after your own grammar explanation.

24 Standards: 1.3

Resources: Answer Keys: Student Edition, p. 132

Focus: Writing practice using the present progressive tense

Recycle: Activities and household items vocabulary

Suggestions: Read the *Modelo* with the class. Tell them that they will write six complete sentences using the present progressive tense. Remind students to note the different endings for the **-ar** verbs and for the **-er** and **-ir** verbs.

Answers:

Mercedes está pasando la aspiradora.
Papá está limpiando el baño.
Rita está haciendo la cama.
Gilberto está cocinando.
Ángel está sacando la basura.
Mamá está poniendo la mesa.

Portfolio

Assign *Actividad* 24 as homework and go over it at the beginning of the next class or grade it and include it in the portfolio as a writing sample.

▼ Objectives
► Listen to a conversation about chores
► Talk and write about what people are doing
► Read and respond to a housing ad and a survey

Gramática

The present progressive tense

When you want to emphasize that an action is happening *right now*, you use the present progressive tense.

Paco está lavando los platos.	Paco **is washing** dishes **(now)**.
Estoy haciendo la cama.	**I'm making** the bed **(now)**.

To form the present progressive tense, use the present-tense forms of *estar* + the present participle. The present participle is formed by dropping the ending of the infinitive and adding *-ando* for *-ar* verbs or *-iendo* for *-er* and *-ir* verbs.

¿Recuerdas?

You use the present tense to talk about an action that regularly takes place, or that is happening now.

• Paco lava los platos.
  *Paco **washes** the dishes.*
  OR
  *Paco **is washing** the dishes.*

(yo)	estoy	lav**ando** com**iendo** escrib**iendo**	(nosotros) (nosotras)	estamos	lav**ando** com**iendo** escrib**iendo**
(tú)	estás	lav**ando** com**iendo** escrib**iendo**	(vosotros) (vosotras)	estáis	lav**ando** com**iendo** escrib**iendo**
Ud. (él) (ella)	está	lav**ando** com**iendo** escrib**iendo**	Uds. (ellos) (ellas)	están	lav**ando** com**iendo** escrib**iendo**

• *Leer* has an irregular spelling in the present participle: *leyendo*.

Más ayuda   **realidades.com**

▶ **GramActiva Video**
Tutorial Formation of the present progressive

📝 **GramActiva Activity**

▼24 | ♻ | Escribir

¿Qué están haciendo ahora?

Mira este dibujo y en una hoja de papel, escribe seis frases para decir cuáles quehaceres están haciendo estas personas.

Modelo
Roberto está quitando el polvo.

Papá · Roberto · Rita · Mercedes · Mamá · Ángel · Gilberto

(142) ciento cuarenta y dos
Tema 6 • La casa

DIFFERENTIATED INSTRUCTION

Multiple Intelligences

Visual/Spatial: Have students take pictures, or cut out pictures from magazines, of people doing chores or other activities. Have students give a name to each person and, underneath each photo, use the present progressive to write what he or she is doing. Display their work for the class to enjoy.

Students with Learning Difficulties

Use index cards as manipulatives to help students practice the present progressive. Make cards with the forms of ***estar,*** and the endings **-ando** and **-iendo** written on them. Make additional cards showing verbs with their infinitive endings removed. Students can use these cards to practice this new tense.

▼25 | ♻ | 🔊 | Escuchar • Escribir

Escucha y escribe

Estos hermanos tienen muchos quehaceres. Escucha y escribe la pregunta de la madre y las excusas de los hijos.

▼26 | 💬🧑🧑 | ♻ | Escribir

Un momento, por favor

A veces no podemos hacer los quehaceres porque estamos haciendo otras cosas. Trabaja con otro(a) estudiante para dar un mandato y una excusa.

▶ Modelo

A —*Por favor, da de comer al perro.*
B —*No puedo. Estoy estudiando para un examen.*

Estudiante A

1.
2.
3.
4.
5.
6.

Estudiante B

Un momento . . .	estudiar
No puedo . . .	hacer
Lo siento . . .	jugar
Me gustaría	escuchar
pero . . .	tocar
	escribir
	comer
	beber
	hablar

¡Respuesta personal!

▼27 | 🧑🧑 | ♻ | Escribir • Hablar • GramActiva

Juego

❶ En una hoja de papel, escribe una frase para explicar lo que está haciendo una persona (usa la forma tú). En otra hojita, escribe una frase para explicar lo que están haciendo dos personas (usa la forma Uds.).

Modelo
Estás levantando pesas.
Uds. están esquiando.

❷ Todas las frases van boca abajo *(facedown)* encima de una mesa. Toma una frase. Si la frase usa la forma tú, haz la acción solo(a). Si la frase usa la forma Uds., haz la acción con otro(a) estudiante. Los compañeros tienen que adivinar *(guess)* lo que estás (están) haciendo.

ciento cuarenta y tres **143**
Capítulo 6B

---

25 Standards: 1.2, 1.3

Resources: Teacher's Resource Book: Audio Script, p. 127; Audio Program DVD: Cap. 6B, Track 11; Answer Keys: Student Edition, p. 133

Focus: Listening comprehension and writing accuracy

Suggestions: Use the audio or read the script aloud. Have students listen to the script once without writing. Encourage students to use the art to help them.

🔊 **Script and Answers:**

1. Hijos, ¿están haciendo sus quehaceres? *(female adult)*
2. Un momento. Estamos jugando videojuegos. *(male teen)*
3. No puedo. Estoy escribiendo un cuento. *(male teen)*
4. Lo siento. Estoy comiendo un sándwich. *(female teen)*

26 Standards: 1.1, 1.3

Resources: Answer Keys: Student Edition, p. 133

Focus: Using *tú* commands and present progressive tense in writing and speaking

Recycle: Leisure activities

Suggestions: Remind students to use affirmative *tú* commands when they are Student A and the present progressive tense when Student B.

Answers:
Student A:
1. Por favor, pon la mesa.
2. Por favor, lava el coche.
3. Por favor, pasa la aspiradora.
4. Por favor, haz la cama.
5. Por favor, saca la basura.
6. Por favor, corta el césped.
Student B: Answers will vary.

27 Standards: 1.1, 1.3

Focus: Using the present progressive tense in writing and speaking

Recycle: Leisure activities

Suggestions: Brainstorm a list of activities that students can write on their papers.

Answers will vary.

ENRICH YOUR TEACHING

Teacher-to-Teacher

Have students prepare a dialogue of a phone call in which a telemarketer is on the line, wishing to speak to anyone available. The person who answers should use the present progressive tense to make excuses for everyone else in the house, saying what they're doing at the moment. Ask students to add details, such as where they are in the house, or who they're with. If possible, have students record their conversations to play for the class.

28

Standards: 2.1

Resources: Voc. and Gram. Transparency 127

Focus: Reading comprehension

Recycle: Items found in the home; family members

Suggestions: Have students read silently, then ask volunteers to read the passages aloud. Assign small groups to focus on one of the people looking for a house. Each group should discuss the ad and decide if the house suits the needs of that person. Have students justify their answers, and have groups present their findings to the class.

Answers: Dora Peña

Extension: Have students write a short paragraph telling what their requirements for a house are. Suggest that they use the passages in the activities as models.

El español en el mundo del trabajo

Core Instruction

Standards: 5.1

Suggestions: Write the expressions *se vende* and *se alquila* on the board and explain them or ask students to guess what these words mean.

Theme Project

Students can perform Step 5 at this point. Record their presentations for inclusion in their portfolios. (For more information, see p. 92-b.)

Additional Resources

- Communication Wbk.: Audio Act. 8–9, pp. 37–38
- Teacher's Resource Book: Audio Script, p. 127, Communicative Pair Activity BLM, pp. 134–135
- Audio Program DVD: Cap. 6B, Tracks 12–13

▼ 28 | ♻ | Leer • Pensar

¿Qué casa están buscando?

En Santiago, Chile, tres personas están buscando *(looking for)* una nueva casa y leen el anuncio a la derecha. ¿Quién crees que va a comprar *(buy)* la casa?

José Guzmán: "Quiero vivir bastante cerca de mi trabajo. Para mi esposa es importante tener una cocina equipada. Prefiero una casa con sólo un piso porque mis padres van a vivir con nosotros y las escaleras son muy difíciles para ellos".

Alejandro Lara: "Mis padres y yo vivimos en un apartamento ahora. Quiero una casa con tres dormitorios porque mis primos vienen a nuestra casa a veces. No quiero una casa muy grande porque no me gusta ni pasar la aspiradora ni limpiar los baños".

Dora Peña: "Mi familia y yo estamos buscando una casa nueva. Tenemos dos hijas y mi mamá vive con nosotros. Quiero una casa con un dormitorio un poco separado para mi mamá. Prefiero tener alfombra en los dormitorios porque nuestras hijas juegan mucho allí".

Chile

LAS MEJORES CASAS
EN LA AVENIDA LA FLORIDA

CASA VENEZIA: 310 m² 3 PISOS
DESDE CHP¹ 40.000.000

Planta baja: Amplia sala • Comedor separado • Cocina y baño de visitas

Primer piso: Dormitorio principal, más 2 dormitorios y otro baño

Segundo piso: Amplio dormitorio con baño completo y una gran sala de estar

«VISITE NUESTRA OFICINA Y COMPRE HOY MISMO»

- Cerámica en el primer piso
- Alfombra en dormitorios
- Cocina equipada
- Papel vinílico en paredes
- Armarios terminados
- Ventanas de aluminio
- Amplio jardín

CASAS ROJAS

MAGALLANES 3400

¡Llame hoy! 232 9980

¹ Pesos chilenos

El español en el mundo del trabajo

In lawns and in front of apartment buildings across the country, you can find "For Sale" signs in English and Spanish. With the increase of Hispanic homebuyers in the United States, the demand for Spanish speakers in jobs related to housing has grown.

- Look for ads in Spanish in the real-estate section of your local newspaper, or at a local house and garden store. How would knowledge of Spanish help real-estate agents, architects, builders, and retailers?

se vende

144 ciento cuarenta y cuatro
Tema 6 • La casa

DIFFERENTIATED INSTRUCTION

Advanced Learners

Ask students to use the Internet or other resources to find information on how living arrangements in Spanish-speaking countries differ between rural areas and urban ones. Suggest that students compare their findings to trends in the United States. Have students present their information to the class.

Heritage Language Learners

Have students use the Internet to find for-sale ads in three different Spanish-speaking countries. Have them investigate size, location, and prices, and prepare a chart indicating the advantages and disadvantages of the houses. Have them present the results to the class.

29 | | Leer · Pensar |

¿Dónde viven?

En Caracas, la capital de Venezuela, analizaron *(they analyzed)* dónde viven algunos habitantes. Según los estudios, ¿viven más personas en casas o en apartamentos? ¿Viven en casas y apartamentos grandes o pequeños? Estudia las gráficas y contesta las preguntas.

Nota

Do you see the pattern in the following numbers?

100,000 = cien mil
200,000 = doscientos mil
300,000 = trescientos mil

But watch out for 500,000:

542,656 = quinientos cuarenta y dos mil, seiscientos cincuenta y seis

1,000,000 = un millón

Conexiones | Las matemáticas

Venezuela

1. ¿Cuántas personas viven en una casa con dos cuartos? ¿Cuántas viven en un apartamento con dos cuartos?

2. ¿Cuántas personas viven en una casa con ocho o más cuartos? ¿Cuántas viven en un apartamento con ocho o más cuartos?

3. Calcula el porcentaje de personas que viven en una casa con cuatro cuartos. Calcula el porcentaje de personas que viven en un apartamento con cuatro cuartos.

▼30 | Dibujar · Escribir · Hablar

¿Qué están haciendo todos?

Haz un dibujo de tres personas que están haciendo diferentes actividades. En otra hoja de papel, escribe dos preguntas sobre lo que está haciendo cada persona. Trabaja en un grupo de tres. Da tu dibujo a los otros estudiantes y lee tus preguntas. Tus compañeros tienen que contestar.

▶ **Modelo**

A —¿Qué *está haciendo la chica?*
B/C —Está *lavando los platos sucios*.

Más práctica GO

realidades.com | print

Instant Check	✔	
Guided WB pp. 61–62	✔	✔
Core WB pp. 33–34	✔	✔
Comm. WB pp. 41–150	✔	✔
Hispanohablantes WB p. 238–241		✔

ENRICH YOUR TEACHING

Teacher-to-Teacher
Have students create their own ads for a newspaper listing. They can write an ad for a house or an apartment. Have them refer to sample ads in the textbook or, if possible, bring in some from a Spanish-language newspaper or Web site.

21st Century Skills
Critical Thinking and Problem Solving To expand the suggestion for Activity 29, guide students on a brief investigation about urban living arrangements in their own city or community. Have them discuss the results with a partner and compare living habits (apartment vs. family home) between their own community, and the city of Caracas.

Practice and Communicate 6B

29 Standards: 1.2, 1.3, 3.1
Resources: Answer Keys: Student Edition, p. 134
Mapa global interactivo, Actividad 3 Compare neighborhoods in Caracas, Venezuela.
Focus: Reading comprehension; cultural understanding
Recycle: Numbers
Suggestions: Point out the *Nota* and work with students to practice forming these large numbers. Have students scan the graphs to predict what the activity is about. Then read the activity aloud and review the statistics. Discuss the answers to the questions. Ask students to compare these statistics with what they know about urban living arrangements in the United States, then ask them to compare these statistics with what they can find out about their own community.
Answers: 1. 400,000; 50,000
2. 100,000; 10,000 **3.** 51%, 73.7% (74%)

30 Standards: 1.1, 1.3
Focus: Reading comprehension
Recycle: Activities vocabulary
Suggestions: Point out that student drawings can be stick drawings and set a time limit for preparing them.
Answers will vary but should use the present progressive tense.

Pre-AP* Support
- **Learning Objective:** Presentational Writing
- **Activity:** Have students prepare a brief paragraph describing their dream home. Encourage them to be creative in their description of their fantasy house, and to give details such as location (town *vs.* city), amenities, etc. Have them exchange paragraphs with a partner, and comment on their respective ideas.
- *Pre-AP* Resource Book:* Comprehensive guide to Pre-AP* communication skill development, pp. 27–38

✔ASSESSMENT
Prueba 6B-4 with Study Plan (online only)
Quiz: Present Progressive
- Prueba 6B-4: p. 167

145

Lectura

Core Instruction

Standards: 1.2

Focus: Reading comprehension of a Cinderella-like story, using vocabulary for household chores

Suggestions:

Pre-reading: Read the *Strategy* aloud. Students may want to briefly discuss the plot of "Cinderella" before they begin skimming. Have students skim the story to look for a Cinderella story line and dialogue.

Reading: Have students read the selection. Point out that familiarity with the story line will help them understand the story, although there are differences. As they read, have them take brief notes about Cantaclara to compare her with Cinderella.

Post-reading: Have the class list comparisons between the two stories as you write them on the board. Then have students reread the last paragraph on p. 146. How does this story deviate from that of Cinderella? Ask students if they can explain the pun in Cantaclara's name. (Cantaclara = "sings clearly")

Extension: Have students write a different ending to the story: After Cantaclara's stepmother and stepsisters see her on television, what happens next?

BELLRINGER REVIEW

Have students pantomime several of the household chores as you say them using the **tú** command form.

Pre-AP* Support

- **Learning Objective:** Interpretive: Print
- **Activity:** As a pre-reading activity, have students work in pairs to write as many true/false statements as possible about the illustrations on these pages. Students can then choose two or three of their statements and ask the class to respond with *Cierta* or *Falsa*.
- **Pre-AP* Resource Book:** Comprehensive guide to Pre-AP* reading skill development, pp. 19–26

▼ Objectives

▶ Read a version of "Cinderella"
▶ Skim to find characters and dialogue to aid comprehension
▶ Analyze the "Cinderella" story across cultures

Lectura

Lee esta historia sobre una joven que se llama Cantaclara.

Cantaclara

Strategy

Skimming
This reading is based on the story of Cinderella. Quickly skim the story and find characters and dialogue that remind you of *Cinderella*.

Hay una muchacha que se llama Cantaclara. Ella vive con su madrastra y sus dos hermanastras, Griselda y Hortencia. Las cuatro viven en una casa grande y Cantaclara hace todos los quehaceres. Sus dos hermanastras y su madrastra no hacen nada.

—Cantaclara, saca la basura. Y después, pon la mesa —dice la madrastra.

—Cantaclara, haz mi cama y limpia el baño —dice Griselda.

—Haz mi cama también —dice Hortencia.

—Un momento. Estoy lavando los platos ahora mismo —dice Cantaclara.

¡Pobre[1] Cantaclara! Hace todos los quehaceres y cuando trabaja, ella canta. Tiene una voz[2] muy clara y le encanta cantar.

Un día, Cantaclara entra en el dormitorio de Griselda para hacer la cama. Ve en la televisión un anuncio[3] para un programa muy popular que se llama *La estrella[4] del futuro*. En la televisión hay un señor que dice: "¡Hola, amigos! ¿Tienen talento? ¿Cantan bien? ¿Por qué no cantan para nosotros? ¡Pueden tener un futuro fantástico y recibir muchísimo dinero!"

Cantaclara está muy contenta. Ella puede cantar. Ella quiere un futuro fantástico. En este momento, ella decide cantar para el programa *La estrella del futuro*.

[1]Poor   [2]voice   [3]ad   [4]star

DIFFERENTIATED INSTRUCTION

Heritage Language Learners

Have students write a brief summary of one of their favorite fairy tales or tall tales using the present tense and the present progressive. Encourage students to include pictures or drawings. Distribute the story to the class to read aloud and discuss.

Students with Learning Difficulties

Point out that in Spanish, dialogue is set off by dashes, whereas in English, dialogue is set off by quotation marks. Speaker tags are used similarly: sometimes they are provided, sometimes they are not. Work through the story with students and help them see where speakers change.

Es la noche del programa. Después de hacer todos los quehaceres, Cantaclara está saliendo[5] de casa cuando su madrastra le habla.

—Cantaclara, ¿adónde vas?

—Quiero salir por unas horas, madrastra. ¿Está bien?

—Ahora no. Tienes que limpiar la cocina —contesta la madrastra. —Está muy sucia.

— Pero, madrastra, tengo que . . .

—¡No importa, Cantaclara! ¡Limpia la cocina!

Cantaclara mira su reloj. Sólo tiene una hora. Va a la cocina y limpia todo. Trabaja muy rápidamente. Después de cuarenta y cinco minutos, termina el trabajo.

Cantaclara llega[6] al programa y canta su canción favorita. ¡Por supuesto ella canta mejor que todos![7] Ella va a tener un futuro fantástico y va a recibir muchísimo dinero.

Son las ocho de la noche. La madrastra y las dos hermanastras están en la sala y ven su programa favorito. Pero, ¿qué es esto? ¡Ven a Cantaclara en la pantalla!

—Mira, mamá. ¡Es Cantaclara! —dice Hortencia.

—¡Oh, no! Si Cantaclara es la nueva estrella del futuro, ¿quién va a hacer los quehaceres? —pregunta Griselda.

[5]is leaving   [6]arrives   [7]anyone else

¿Comprendes?

Pon las frases en orden según la historia.

1. Ella decide cantar en el programa *La estrella del futuro*.
2. Cantaclara es la persona que canta mejor en el programa.
3. Ella está lavando los platos.
4. Ella tiene que limpiar la cocina.
5. Ella ve el anuncio para *La estrella del futuro*.
6. Griselda no sabe quién va a hacer los quehaceres.
7. Cantaclara vive en una casa grande con su madrastra y dos hermanastras.
8. Son las ocho de la noche y la madrastra y las hermanastras están viendo la tele.

▼ **Fondo Cultural** | El mundo hispano

La Cenicienta The story of Cinderella (*La Cenicienta*) is perhaps the best-known fairy tale in the world. Almost every culture seems to have its own version and there may be over 1,500 variations. The tale appears to date back to a Chinese story from the ninth century, "Yeh-Shen."

• What aspects of the story might change from culture to culture?

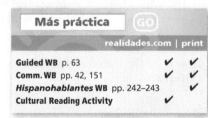

Más práctica	GO

realidades.com | print

Guided WB p. 63	✔	✔
Comm. WB pp. 42, 151	✔	✔
Hispanohablantes **WB** pp. 242–243		✔
Cultural Reading Activity	✔	

ciento cuarenta y siete **147**
Capítulo 6B

Reading 6B

▼**¿Comprendes?** Standards: 1.2, 1.3

Resources: Answer Keys: Student Edition, p. 134

Focus: Reading comprehension

Suggestions: Have students read all the statements. Ask them to say whether each sentence they read takes place in the beginning, the middle, or the end of the story. Then, have them put each section of the story in order to get their finished product, which will be a summary of the story.

Answers:

(7) Cantaclara vive en una casa grande con su madrastra y dos hermanastras. (3) Ella está lavando los platos. (5) Ella ve el anuncio para *La estrella del futuro*. (1) Ella decide cantar en el programa *La estrella del futuro*. (4) Ella tiene que limpiar la cocina. (2) Cantaclara es la persona que canta mejor en el programa. (8) Son las ocho de la noche y la madrastra y las hermanastras están viendo la tele. (6) Griselda no sabe quién va a hacer los quehaceres.

Fondo cultural

·Standards: 4.2

Suggestions: Point out to students that the name for Cinderella in Spanish is *Cenicienta.* (It is interesting to note that in most European versions, the girl's name includes something about ashes or cinders.) Use the question to have students predict how the variation of the fairy tale may be different. Have them research variants of the tale on the Internet or in the library.

Answers will vary but may include the culture in which the story is set, the tasks the young girl does, or the reward she earns.

For Further Reading

Student Resource: Realidades para hispanohablantes: Lectura 2, pp. 244–245

ENRICH YOUR TEACHING

Teacher-to-Teacher

Write a brief summary of "*Caperucita Roja*" ("Little Red Riding Hood"), or another familiar fairy tale, leaving out the title. Make it as simple and comprehensible as possible, though some unfamiliar words are fine.

Distribute copies to students, and read the passage as a class. Have students guess which fairy tale they are reading. For a variation of this activity, have students act out the fairy tale or use a cloze passage to fill in the reading.

Perspectivas del mundo hispano

Core Instruction

Standards: 2.1, 2.2, 4.2

Focus: Reading about homes in Spanish-speaking countries

Suggestions: Tell students that there are many types and styles of architecture but that buildings usually have a form that is functional. One thing that influences the form is the local climate. An example is slanted roofs in places where it snows a lot. This lets the snow fall off, instead of building up and threatening a collapse from the weight.

Have students read the text. Discuss how the climate in many Spanish-speaking countries is warm enough to allow an outdoor patio where meals are often served. Discuss how the patio fits into the social aspects of the culture. It is private, yet open and relaxed. Note that acquaintances are not usually entertained in the home. Discuss other privacy-oriented characteristics of homes in Spanish-speaking countries, such as tall walls and bars on windows. Have students complete the *Check it out!* section and discuss the question with the class.

Students may have difficulty envisioning the patios in Spanish-speaking countries. Although uncovered, they are nonetheless inside the house. The rest of the house is built around the patio, and many rooms will have a door leading to it. Remind students that in many countries the climate is warm, and going outdoors to eat and socialize is pleasant.

Direct attention to the *Think about it!* section and have students discuss the questions.

Answers will vary.

Additional Resources

Student Resource: Realidades para hispanohablantes, p. 246

Perspectivas del mundo hispano

¿Cómo son las casas en el mundo hispano?

In many Spanish-speaking countries the architectural features of houses are very different from those in the United States. Houses tend to be separated from the outside by a barrier such as a tall wall or fence. The owner would open a gate to enter the property where there may be a carport or small outside area. In many communities, the outside wall of the house is located directly on the sidewalk and the front windows may contain bars or *rejas*. The doors may be large wooden or metal doors. A plain walled exterior gives no hints about what may be a beautiful, comfortable interior.

Inside, a home will often have an open space in the middle called the *patio*. Many rooms of the house open onto the *patio*, and it is a place for the family to meet, eat meals, talk, and spend time together. Privacy is valued, and the home and family activities are shielded from view from the outside.

El patio de una casa en Córdoba, España

Homes in Spanish-speaking countries are used for the family and to entertain very close relatives and friends. It is unusual to invite non-family members such as coworkers or casual friends into the home. Parties often take place in restaurants or small reception halls.

Check it out! Look around your neighborhood. How does the architecture of houses compare with the design of houses in the Spanish-speaking world?

Think about it! If architectural features of houses in Spanish-speaking countries imply a desire for privacy, what do the architectural features of houses in the United States imply? How does the concept of a *patio* compare in these cultures?

Una casa en Santo Domingo de Silos, España

DIFFERENTIATED INSTRUCTION

Advanced Learners

Have students choose a Spanish-speaking country and research the style of the houses. They should find out if the houses usually have a patio and the origins of the style of architecture. Have them share their findings with the class, showing pictures if possible.

Students with Learning Difficulties

Students may have difficulty understanding the basic layout of the homes described here. Show pictures or diagrams, but if using diagrams, make sure students understand the perspective.

Presentación escrita

Se vende casa o apartamento

Task
Design a flyer in Spanish to promote the sale of your family's house or apartment. Create an attractive flyer that will make your home (or dream house) appealing to a potential buyer.

1 Prewrite Think about the information you want to include, then jot down your answers to these questions.

- En general, ¿cómo es la casa o el apartamento?
- ¿Qué cuartos hay? ¿Cómo son? ¿De qué colores son?
- ¿Hay algo especial en la casa (piscina, cuarto especial)?
- Incluye (*Include*) otra información importante como la dirección (*address*) y el precio (*price*).

2 Draft Use the ad on p. 310 and your Prewrite answers to design the flyer. Include illustrations and other features to make it attractive. Begin with *Se vende casa / apartamento*.

3 Revise Read your ad to see that you have included all the information a potential buyer might want. Check for correct spelling. Share your flyer with a partner, who will check the following:

- Is the flyer neat and attractive? Does it include a visual?
- Is the key information provided?
- Does it make you want to look at the property?

4 Publish Write a final copy, making any necessary changes. You may want to include it in a class collection called *Se vende* or in your portfolio.

5 Evaluation The following rubric will be used to grade your flyer.

Strategy
Using key questions

Answering key questions can help you think of ideas for writing.

Una casa típica, Coclé, Panamá

Rubric	Score 1	Score 3	Score 5
Neatness and attractiveness	You use no visual and your ad contains visible error corrections and smudges.	You use a visual, but your ad contains visual error corrections and smudges.	You use a visual, have no error corrections or smudges, and your ad is attractive.
Use of vocabulary expressions	You use very little variation of vocabulary and have frequent usage errors.	You use limited vocabulary, with some usage errors.	You use an extended variety of vocabulary with very few usage errors.
Amount of information provided	You only describe rooms.	You describe rooms plus special features.	You describe rooms, special features, and provide price and address.

Presentación escrita

Core Instruction

Standards: 1.3

Focus: Writing using vocabulary related to homes

Suggestions: Review the task and the five-step approach with students. Point out that there are key ideas that the flyer must include, such as number of bedrooms and baths, size, location, etc. Encourage students to make their flyers eye-catching as well as persuasive. Review the rubric with the class to explain how you will grade the flyers. Bring in flyers from a local realtor. Internet sites for realtors can be a good source for samples.

Suggestions: Have students present their flyers to the class. Students can decide which house would be the most expensive, the most modern, etc.

Pre-AP* Support

- **Learning Objective:** Interpersonal Writing
- **Activity:** Draft an e-mail to a friend summarizing the flyer from *Presentación oral*. Say why you think the house is right for you (or not), and ask your friend's opinion.
- **Pre-AP* Resource Book:** Comprehensive guide to Pre-AP* writing skill development, pp. 27–38

Portfolio

Invite students to review the activities they completed in this chapter, including written reports, posters, or other visuals, and recordings of oral presentations or other projects. Have them select one or two items to include in their portfolios.

Additional Resources

Student Resources: Realidades para hispanohablantes, p. 247; Guided Practice: Presentación escrita, p. 64

✓ ASSESSMENT

Presentación escrita
- Assessment Program: Rubrics, p. T32
  Go over the descriptions of the different levels of performance. After assessing students, help individuals understand how their performance could be improved.

ENRICH YOUR TEACHING

21st Century Skills

Technology Literacy Encourage students to make their flyers electronic, combining online images, audio, and video. As part of their pre-writing task, have them ask and answer the questions with a partner, to make sure they include as much pertinent information as possible with accuracy.

6B Video

Videomisterio ▶

Core Instruction

Standards: 1.2, 4.1, 5.2

Resources: Teacher's Resource Book: Video Script, pp. 130–131; Video Program: Cap. 6B; Video Program Teacher's Guide: Cap. 6B

Focus: Introducing events and vocabulary; scanning and reading the episode summary

Personajes importantes:

Lola Lago, detective
Paco, colega de Lola
Margarita, la secretaria de la oficina de Lola
Doña Lupe Aguirre, portera
Carmela, una buena amiga de Lola
Pedro Requena, nieto de doña Gracia Requena

Synopsis: Lola visits doña Lupe to find out more news about doña Gracia, who is getting better at the hospital. Doña Gracia does not remember anything about the incident. Then Lola meets her best friend, Carmela, at a café. Lola explains the events that led doña Gracia to the San Carlos hospital. Carmela has a friend, Rosalinda, who works at the hospital. Lola and Carmela agree to meet the next morning in the hospital to ask Rosalinda for information. Later, Lola meets Pedro as he inquires about his grandmother in the hospital. Lola offers her services as a detective and gives him her card.

Suggestions:

Pre-viewing: Review with students the events of the previous episode. Lola questioned doña Lupe, who found doña Gracia on the floor. There are three mysteries at hand: (1) What caused doña Gracia's incident? (2) Where is her niece, María? (3) Where are doña Gracia's jewels? María, a professional model, spent three months in the hospital after a car accident. Doña Gracia's only other relative is her grandson, Pedro Requena, who lives in Italy. His father did not get along with his father, doña Gracia's husband.

Review the *Nota cultural* with the class. You may want to show a picture of a **tapa,** such as a piece of **tortilla española.** Point out the *Palabras para comprender,* giving examples in context and writing the sentences on the board. Remind students that these words are only used to help them understand the episode and that they are not responsible for that vocabulary.

¿Eres tú, María?
Episodio 4

Antes de ver el video
Personajes importantes

Carmela, una buena amiga de Lola

Pedro Requena, el nieto de doña Gracia. Está en Madrid para visitar a su abuela en el hospital.

Resumen del episodio

Doña Gracia está mucho mejor y puede ir a casa en unos días. Pero no recuerda mucho del incidente. Lola llama por teléfono a su buena amiga, Carmela. Las dos van a un café para hablar y Carmela le dice a Lola que una de sus amigas, Rosalinda, trabaja en el hospital San Carlos. Es el hospital donde está doña Gracia. Deciden ir al hospital para hablar con Rosalinda y ver a doña Gracia. A la mañana siguiente,[1] Lola habla con Pedro Requena.

[1] next

150 **ciento cincuenta**
Tema 6 • La casa

Nota cultural *Tapas* are popular appetizers in Spain. *Tapas* come in small servings called *raciones*, and can be almost anything: olives, seafood, meat, cheese, vegetables, shellfish, or any dish the chef cares to prepare. Eating *tapas* is a social event. Friends eat, drink, and relax as they talk. When you are done, you are charged according to how many platefuls of *tapas* you ate.

Palabras para comprender

fui a visitarla	I went to visit her
¿Habló del incidente?	Did she talk about the incident?
¿Sabe . . .	Does she know . . . ?
Lo único que recuerda . . .	The only thing she remembers . . .
un golpe	hit, blow
ahora mismo	right away
preguntar por	to ask about
los churros	fried dough pastries
No estoy pensando en . . .	I'm not planning to . . .
Voy a pensarlo.	I'll think about it.

DIFFERENTIATED INSTRUCTION

Heritage Language Learners

Ask students to use the vocabulary from *Palabras para comprender* to tell what happened in this episode. Encourage them to go back and use vocabulary from previous chapters.

"Lo único que recuerda es un golpe aquí, en la cabeza. ¿La verdad? No sabe nada".

"Soy Pedro Requena. Exacto, el nieto de la Sra. Gracia Requena. Voy ahora mismo para el hospital".

—Si necesita más información, aquí tiene mi número de teléfono.

—Gracias, señorita. Voy a pensarlo.

Después de ver el video

¿Comprendes?

A. Lee las frases y ponlas *(put them)* en el orden cronológico.

1. Pedro no sabe si quiere contratar a una detective.
2. Lola y Carmela van al café a comer unas tapas.
3. Lola habla con Pedro y le da su número de teléfono.
4. Paco y Lola hablan en la oficina.
5. Pedro Requena habla por teléfono con el Dr. Sánchez Mata.
6. Doña Lupe dice que fue al hospital y habló con doña Gracia.
7. Carmela dice que su amiga, Rosalinda, trabaja en el hospital San Carlos.

B. Lee las frases y escribe el nombre de la persona que dice cada frase: Pedro, Carmela, Lola, doña Lupe o Paco.

1. No podemos trabajar si no hay cliente y no hay dinero.
2. Buenas noticias. Doña Gracia está mejor.
3. ¿Quieres tomar un café conmigo?
4. Mi amiga trabaja allí. Puedes hablar con doña Gracia.
5. No estoy pensando en contratar a un detective.

Más práctica (GO)

realidades.com | print

Actividades ✔

ciento cincuenta y uno (151)
Capítulo 6B

ENRICH YOUR TEACHING

Culture Note
Spaniards usually have a light breakfast, sometimes just coffee. Then they may have a mid-morning snack, which is called *almuerzo.* The early-afternoon meal—the largest of the day—is *la comida.* Spaniards sometimes go out to eat *tapas* as dinner. Otherwise, *la cena* is a light meal.

Teacher-to-Teacher
Have students look for information about *tapas,* their origin, and the different types served in cafés and restaurants. Inquire about a local restaurant that may have them on their menu. Some examples of *tapas* include *tortilla española,* sausage *(chorizo),* octopus *(pulpo),* and cheese *(queso).*

Visual scanning: Direct students' attention to the two photos on p. 150 and ask who they are (Carmela and Pedro) and what relationship they have to Lola (Lola's best friend and a potential client). Before students read the *Resumen del episodio,* have them scan the text and find three cognates. *(teléfono, café, hospital, deciden)* Then ask them to read the *Resumen del episodio* carefully and ask questions about what will happen in this episode.

Viewing: If there is time after viewing the full episode, select some key moments you wish to highlight, such as the scene in which Lola introduces herself to Pedro.

Post-viewing: Have students look at the pictures at the top of the page and use them to summarize the scenes in this episode. Write the vocabulary presented in this episode on the board to help students create sentences for each important scene that adds new information to the plot. Direct students' attention to the *¿Comprendes?* section.

▼ **¿Comprendes?** Standards: 1.1, 1.2
Resources: Answer Keys: Student Edition, p. 135
Focus: Verifying comprehension by answering questions; reviewing the plot
Suggestions: For part A, have students read all the sentences, then show the video again, pausing to allow them to make sentences as events occur. For part B, tape large photocopies of the characters' faces on the board and have volunteers point to the correct image.
Answers:
Part A: The sequence of events is 4, 6, 2, 7, 5, 1, 3.
Part B: 1. Paco; 2. doña Lupe; 3. Lola; 4. Carmela; 5. Pedro

Additional Resources
• *¿Eres tú, María?* Video Workbook, Episode 4
• *¿Eres tú, María?* Teacher's Video Guide: Answer Key

Repaso del capítulo

Vocabulario y gramática

Review Activities

To talk about houses or apartments:
Student A can draw a house plan and write the vocabulary words in English. Student A points to the room, and Student B says the word in Spanish. Have students exchange roles.

To name household chores: Students work in pairs to make sketches of household chores on note cards. Have them shuffle the cards and take turns saying the chore in Spanish, including a sentence about who does that chore in their house. Students may have "time trials" to see who can answer the fastest.

Affirmative tú commands and present progressive tense: After practicing household chores, Student A will be the "parent" and use commands to tell Student B to clean. Student B will have an excuse and must use present progressive tense in the reply. Students will reverse roles.

Portfolio

Invite students to review the activities they completed in this chapter, including written reports, posters, or other visuals, and recordings of oral presentations or other projects. Have them select one or two items that they feel best demonstrate their achievements in Spanish to include in their portfolios.

Teacher-to-Teacher

Careers: *Tema* 6 has focused on houses. Have students work in groups to talk about a career in the construction business. Have them write a list of words and expressions that would be useful for discussing the construction of a new home or apartment. Ask groups to share their lists.

Additional Resources

Student Resources: Realidades para hispanohablantes, p. 248

Teacher Resources:
- Teacher's Resource Book: Situation Cards, p. 136, Clip Art, pp. 138–140
- Assessment Program: Chapter Checklist and Self-Assessment Worksheet, pp. T56–T57

to talk about where someone lives

cerca (de)	close (to), near
lejos (de)	far (from)
vivir	to live

to talk about houses or apartments

el apartamento	apartment
el baño	bathroom
la cocina	kitchen
el comedor	dining room
el cuarto	room
el despacho	home office
la escalera	stairs, stairway
el garaje	garage
el piso	story, floor
la planta baja	ground floor
el primer piso	second floor
la sala	living room
el segundo piso	third floor
el sótano	basement

to name household chores

arreglar el cuarto	to straighten up the room
ayudar	to help
cocinar	to cook
cortar el césped	to cut the lawn
dar (yo doy, tú das)	to give
dar de comer al perro	to feed the dog
hacer la cama	to make the bed
lavar (el coche, los platos, la ropa)	to wash (the car, the dishes, the clothes)
limpiar el baño	to clean the bathroom
pasar la aspiradora	to vacuum
poner (yo pongo, tú pones)	to put, place
poner la mesa	to set the table
los quehaceres	chores
quitar el polvo	to dust
sacar la basura	to take out the trash

to describe household items

limpio, -a	clean
sucio, -a	dirty

other useful words and expressions

bastante	enough; rather
¿Cuáles?	Which (ones)?
el dinero	money
un momento	a moment
¿Qué estás haciendo?	What are you doing?
recibir	to receive
si	if, whether

affirmative tú commands

For regular verbs, use the *Ud./él/ella* form:

-ar:	habla
-er:	lee
-ir:	escribe

For *hacer* and *poner*:

hacer	haz
poner	pon

present progressive tense

Use the present-tense forms of *estar* + the present participle to say that you are doing something right now.

present participles:

-ar:	stem + -ando → lavando
-er:	stem + -iendo → comiendo
-ir:	stem + -iendo → escribiendo

For *Vocabulario adicional,* see pp. 336–337.

DIFFERENTIATED INSTRUCTION

Students with Learning Difficulties

Have students review the *Repaso del capítulo* and create flashcards for any words that they do not know. Pair them with a student who is more confident with the vocabulary to practice. Before the test, provide students with a practice test, so they can become comfortable with the format.

Heritage Language Learners

Have students write a few paragraphs telling about their perfect birthday celebration: Where are they going to have it? Whom are they going to invite? What food are they going to eat? What kind of music are they going to play? Encourage them to use as many vocabulary words from this chapter as they can.

Más repaso (GO) realidades.com | print

Instant Check	✔
Puzzles	✔
Core WB pp. 35–36	✔ ✔
Comm. WB pp. 152, 153–155	✔ ✔

Preparación para el examen

On the exam you will be asked to . . .	Here are practice tasks similar to those you will find on the exam . . .	For review go to your print or digital textbook . . .
1 **Escuchar** Listen to and understand teenagers' excuses for not doing a particular chore at the moment they are asked to do it	As you listen to a teenager explain to his mother why he can't do a particular chore at the moment, identify: a) what the mother wants the teenager to do; b) what the teenager says he is busy doing.	**pp. 126–131** *Vocabulario en contexto* **p. 134** Actividad 10 **p. 136** Actividad 14 **p. 143** Actividades 25–26
2 **Hablar** Give advice to others about how to be successful in school	Your school counselors have asked you to participate in an orientation for new Spanish-speaking students. Offer each student in the group a piece of advice. For example, you might say *Escucha bien en clase* or *Haz la tarea.*	**p. 140** Actividad 21
3 **Leer** Read and understand ads for apartments that you might find in the classified section of a Spanish-language newspaper	A friend is moving to Spain and asks you to help find an apartment. He wants a two-bedroom, two-bath apartment with a small kitchen. He wants to live near a gym and a library. Read this ad and answer the following: a) Is this a good apartment for him?; b) How many of his requested features does it have?; c) What other features that are mentioned might he like?	**pp. 126–131** *Vocabulario en contexto* **p. 133** Actividades 8–9 **p. 144** Actividad 28 **p. 149** *Presentación escrita*

> Este maravilloso apartamento tiene todo. Está cerca de un parque y un gimnasio moderno. Tiene una cocina pequeña, pero totalmente equipada. Tiene dos dormitorios con estantes y un baño muy grande. También tiene televisión por satélite y un garaje privado. No se permiten animales.

4 **Escribir** Write a list of household chores that you are willing to do	You and your classmates are offering to do chores to earn money for your Spanish club. Make a list of at least eight chores that you would be willing to do.	**pp. 126–131** *Vocabulario en contexto* **p. 134** Actividades 10–11 **p. 136** Actividad 14 **p. 137** Actividad 15 **p. 140** Actividad 22
5 **Pensar** Demonstrate an understanding of cultural perspectives regarding houses	Explain how the architechtural features of many houses in the Spanish speaking world reflect the importance the owners place on privacy. How do these features compare to those in homes in the United States?	**p. 135** *Fondo cultural* **p. 148** *Perspectivas del mundo hispano*

DIFFERENTIATED ASSESSMENT

CORE ASSESSMENT
- **Assessment Program:** Examen del capítulo 6B, pp. 168–174
- **Audio Program DVD:** Cap. 6B, Track 16
- **ExamView:** Chapter Test, Test Banks A and B

ADVANCED/PRE-AP*
- **ExamView: Pre-AP* Test Bank**
- **Pre-AP* Resource Book,** pp. 82–85

STUDENTS NEEDING EXTRA HELP
- **Alternate Assessment Program:** Examen del capítulo 6B
- **Audio Program DVD:** Chap. 6B, Track 16

HERITAGE LEARNERS
- **Assessment Program: Realidades para hispanohablantes:** Examen del capítulo 6B
- **ExamView: Heritage Learner Test Bank**

Review 6B

Performance Tasks

Standards: 1.1, 1.2, 1.3, 2.2, 4.2

Student Resource: Realidades para hispanohablantes, p. 249

Teacher Resources: Teacher's Resource Book: Audio Script, p. 127; Audio Program DVD: Cap. 6B, Track 15; Answer Keys: Student Edition, p. 135

1. Escuchar

Suggestions: Use the audio or read the script.

Script:

Madre: Miguel, da de comer al perro. Son las siete de la tarde y pobre Rufus no tiene comida.

Miguel: Mamá, el perro está jugando con el gato. No quiere comer ahora. Y yo estoy estudiando para mi examen de matemáticas. No puedo dar de comer a Rufus ahora.

Answers: a) She tells Miguel to feed the dog; b) He says he is studying for a math exam.

2. Hablar

Suggestions: Remind students that their advice should use affirmative *tú* commands. Students may want to first write their tips.

Answers will vary.

3. Leer

Suggestions: Students should make two columns on a sheet of paper. One side will have the friend's criteria for an apartment; the other will be a list of what the aparment actually has.

Answers:

a. yes; b. three; c. satellite television, private garage

4. Escribir

Suggestions: Have students number their chores. They can include how much each chore will cost and make a small poster.

Answers will vary.

5. Pensar

Suggestions: Have students reread the appropriate *Fondos culturales* and the *Perspectivas del mundo hispano*.

Answers will vary.

De compras

7A ¿Cuánto cuesta?

• **Shopping and clothing**

Vocabulary: clothing; shopping; numbers 200–1,000

Grammar: stem-changing verbs: *pensar, querer,* and *preferir;* demonstrative adjectives

Cultural Perspectives: shopping

7B ¡Qué regalo!

• **Buying gifts and places to shop**

Vocabulary: places to shop; gifts; accessories; buying and selling

Grammar: preterite of *-ar, -car,* and *-gar* verbs; direct object pronouns *lo, la, los, las*

Cultural Perspectives: gift-giving

THEME SUPPORT

Bulletin Boards

Theme: *De compras*

Ask students to cut out, copy, or download photos of clothing, accessories, currencies, and different types of storefronts and markets in Spanish-speaking countries. Cluster photos in three groups: clothing and accessories, currencies, and places to shop.

Hands-on Culture

Craft: *Pulseras de amistad*

Materials for one bracelet:
4 30" strands of yarn of different colors

Directions:

1. Join the four strands of yarn together, and make an overhand knot 8" from one end. Tie the end to the strap of a backpack or the back of a chair.

2. Hold the first strand of yarn in one hand (Color 1) and the second strand (Color 2) in the other. Wrap Color 1 over and under Color 2, then pull the end of Color 1 through the loop.

3. Hold Color 2 so that it doesn't move. Pull up on Color 1 to form a knot.

4. Repeat Steps 2 and 3 to do a second knot.

5. Let go of Color 2 and pick up the third strand of yarn (Color 3). Repeat Steps 2–4 with Colors 1 and 3. Let go of Color 3 and pick up the fourth strand of yarn (Color 4). Repeat Steps 2–4 with Colors 1 and 4.

6. To make the next row in the bracelet, repeat Steps 2–5, making the knots with Color 2. (Knot Color 2 over Color 3, Color 4, then Color 1.) Continue until the bracelet has reached the desired length, then tie an overhand knot. Trim the ends and tie the bracelet around your wrist.

Game

¿Qué vas a comprar?

Play this game in *Capítulo* 7B, after students have learned definite object pronouns.

Players: the whole class

Materials: index cards, two for each student

Rules:

1. Count out two index cards for each student. Divide the cards into two sets. Write an article of clothing, accessory, or gift on each index card in the first set. Write the corresponding places where each item can be purchased on the second set of cards. Shuffle each set of cards separately.

2. Give each student one card from each set. Divide students into two teams.

3. To find a match to their cards, students circulate, asking their classmates what they are going to buy and where they are going to buy it.
   Student 1: ¿Qué vas a comprar?
   Student 2: Voy a comprar unos zapatos.
   Student 1: ¿Dónde vas a comprarlos?
   Student 2: Voy a comprarlos en la zapatería. ¿Sabes dónde está?
   If Student 1 does not have the card: No, no sé dónde está.
   If Student 1 has the card: Está aquí. (The student hands over the card.)

4. After students get rid of their shopping location card, they must wait to be approached to match their item card. When a match is made, they sit down. Call time after four to five minutes. The winner is the team with the most members sitting down.

Variation: Make one set of cards, with two cards depicting the same items. Give each student a card. Students circulate, asking their classmates if they have the item on their card.
   Student 1: ¿Tienes los zapatos?
   Student 2: Sí, los tengo, *or* No, no los tengo.

THEME PROJECT

Catálogo de ventas por correo

Overview: Students create two pages from a catalog featuring photos of three clothing items and three gift items, each accompanied by a brief description. Students can create their catalog pages digitally or by hand, or using a combination of resources. They present their catalog to the class, describing each item in complete sentences.

Resources: online or print clothing and accessory catalogs and fashion magazines; image editing and page layout software, and/or scissors, glue, markers, construction paper

Sequence: (suggestions for when to do each step appear throughout the chapters)

 7A

STEP 1. Review instructions so students know what is expected of them. Hand out the "Theme 7 Project Instructions and Rubric" from the *Teacher's Resource Book*.

STEP 2. Students look through catalogs for layout ideas, price ranges, and sizes. They then submit a rough sketch of their two-page layout. Return the drafts with your suggestions.

STEP 3. Students create their two-page layout, leaving room for their descriptions. Teach students the following vocabulary for sizes: *talla* ("size"), *pequeño* ("small"), *mediano* ("medium"), *grande* ("large").

7B

STEP 4. Students submit a draft of their clothing and gift descriptions. Note your corrections and suggestions, then return drafts to students. Students partner to practice their catalog presentations.

STEP 5. Students present their catalog pages to the class, describing each item on the pages in complete sentences.

Options:

1. Students use a different currency and metric sizes in their catalogs, looking up conversions on the Internet.
2. Students feature only clothing or only gift items in their catalogs.

Assessment:

Here is a detailed rubric for assessing the Theme 7 project

RUBRIC	Score 1	Score 3	Score 5
Evidence of planning	You didn't submit a sketch and draft.	You submitted the sketch and draft, but didn't correct them.	You submitted and corrected your draft and layout.
Use of illustrations	You didn't include any photos.	You included photos for most items. Your layout was somewhat effective.	You included photos for all items. Your layout was effective.
Presentation	You listed items, but didn't describe them. You rarely use complete sentences.	You described some but not all items completely. You included some incomplete sentences.	You described each item completely, using complete sentences.

21st Century Skills

Look for tips throughout *Tema 7* to enrich your teaching by integrating 21st Century Skills. Suggestions for the Theme Project and Theme Culture follow below.

Theme Project

Modify the Theme Project with one or more of these suggestions:

Increase Collaboration

Have students work together in groups of three to increase their collaboration skills. Provide them with the handout "Work in teams" to help them organize their group and divide the tasks.

Develop Media Literacy

The instructions for the Theme Project give students the option to do their research online. Provide students with the handout "Analyze Media Content" to help them analyze Web sites. Tell students to think about what makes a Web site attractive and how the design of a site affects its message.

Support Critical Thinking and Problem Solving

As students plan their project, tell them to consider the following questions: Who are the potential buyers of your clothing? What kinds of items will you offer? What will be the price range and why?

Theme Culture

Foster Social and Cross-Cultural Skills

Help students bridge cultural differences by offering opportunities for them to discuss the culture highlighted throughout the chapter. Use the teaching suggestions for the *Fondo cultural* on page 155 to support discussion of cultural perspectives about fashion and clothing.

▶ **Videocultura** View *Los mercados* online with the class to learn more about shopping in Spanish-speaking countries.

AT A GLANCE

Objectives
- Listen to conversations and read about clothes and shopping
- Talk and write about shopping plans and gifts
- Exchange information while purchasing an item of clothing
- Understand the role of *molas* in the Kuna culture
- Compare the significance of crafts and clothing in Panama and the United States

Vocabulary
- Shopping
- Clothing
- Prices and numbers

Grammar
- Stem-changing verbs: *pensar, querer,* and *preferir*
- Demonstrative adjectives

Culture
- Joan Miró, p. 155
- Fernando Botero, p. 162
- Currencies of the Spanish-speaking world, p. 165
- Nonverbal language, p. 166
- Carolina Herrera, p. 175
- Traditional clothing of Panama, pp. 177–178
- *Carnaval,* p. 177
- Make a *mola,* p. 178

Recycle ♻
- *quiero, quieres* and *prefiero, prefieres*
- *me gusta(n), me encanta(n)*
- Places
- Colors
- Activities
- Infinitives
- Numbers

RESOURCES

FOR THE STUDENT	ONLINE	DVD	PRINT	FOR THE TEACHER	ONLINE	PREEXP	DVD	PRINT
Plan				Interactive TE and Resources DVD	•		•	
				Teacher's Resource Book, pp. 160–197	•		•	•
				Pre-AP* Resource Book, pp. 86–89	•		•	•
				Mapa global interactivo	•			
				Lesson Plans	•			•

Introducción PP. 154–155

Present								
Student Edition, pp. 154–155	•	•	•	Interactive TE and Resources DVD	•		•	
DK Reference Atlas	•	•		Teacher's Resource Book, pp. 160–163	•		•	•
Videocultura	•	•		Galería de fotos		•		
Hispanohablantes WB, pp. 250–251			•	Fine Art Transparencies, 39	•	•	•	
				Map Transparencies, 12–18, 20	•	•	•	

Vocabulario en contexto PP. 156–161

Present & Practice								
Student Edition, pp. 156–161	•	•	•	Interactive TE and Resources DVD	•		•	
Audio	•	•		Teacher's Resource Book, pp. 164–166, 177–179, 199	•		•	•
Videohistoria	•	•		Vocabulary Clip Art	•	•	•	•
Flashcards	•	•		Audio Program	•	•	•	
Instant Check	•			Video Program: Videohistoria	•		•	
Guided WB, pp. 65–74	•	•	•	Video Program Teacher's Guide: Cap. 7A	•		•	
Core WB, pp. 37–40	•	•	•	Vocabulary and Grammar Transparencies, 128–131	•	•	•	
Comm. WB, pp. 43–46, 49	•	•	•	Answer Keys: Student Edition, pp. 136–137	•			•
Hispanohablantes WB, pp. 252–253			•	TPR Stories, pp. 92–106	•		•	•
Assess and Remediate				Prueba 7A–1: Assessment Program, pp. 175–176	•		•	•
				Assessment Program para hispanohablantes, pp. 175–176	•		•	•

RESOURCES

FOR THE STUDENT	ONLINE	DVD	PRINT	FOR THE TEACHER	ONLINE	PREEXP	DVD	PRINT
Vocabulario en uso PP. **162–167**								
Present & Practice								
Student Edition, pp. 162–167	•	•	•	Interactive Whiteboard Vocabulary Activities	•		•	
Instant Check	•			Interactive TE and Resources DVD	•		•	
Comm. WB, p. 46	•	•	•	Teacher's Resource Book, pp. 166, 171–172	•		•	•
Hispanohablantes WB, pp. 254–255			•	Communicative Pair Activities, pp. 171–172	•		•	•
Communicative Pair Activities	•			Audio Program	•	•	•	
				Videomodelos	•		•	
				Fine Art Transparencies, 8	•	•	•	
				Answer Keys: Student Edition, pp. 138–140	•	•	•	
Assess and Remediate				Prueba 7A–2 with Study Plan	•			
				Prueba 7A–2: Assessment Program, pp. 177–178	•		•	•
				Assessment Program para hispanohablantes, pp. 177–178	•		•	•
Gramática PP. **168–175**								
Present & Practice								
Student Edition, pp. 168–175	•	•	•	Interactive Whiteboard Grammar Activities	•		•	
Instant Check	•			Interactive TE and Resources DVD	•		•	
Animated Verbs	•			Teacher's Resource Book, pp. 166–170	•		•	•
Tutorial Video: Grammar	•			Communicative Pair Activities, pp. 173–174	•		•	•
Canción de hip hop	•			Audio Program	•	•	•	
Guided WB, pp. 75–78	•	•	•	Videomodelos	•		•	
Core WB, pp. 41–43	•	•	•	Video Program: GramActiva	•		•	
Comm. WB, pp. 47–48, 50–51, 156	•	•	•	Vocabulary and Grammar Transparencies, 132–135	•	•	•	
Hispanohablantes WB, pp. 256–261			•	Answer Keys: Student Edition, pp. 141–143	•	•	•	
Communicative Pair Activities	•							
Assess and Remediate				Pruebas 7A–3 and 7A–4 with Study Plans	•			
				Pruebas 7A–3, 7A–4: Assessment Program, pp. 179, 180	•		•	•
				Assessment Program para hispanohablantes, pp. 179, 180	•		•	•
¡Adelante! PP. **176–181**								
Application								
Student Edition, pp. 176–181	•	•	•	Interactive TE and Resources DVD	•		•	
Online Cultural Reading	•			Teacher's Resource Book, pp. 170, 176	•		•	
Guided WB, pp. 79–80	•	•	•	Video Program: Videomisterio ¿Eres tú, María?	•		•	
Comm. WB, pp. 52, 157	•	•	•	Video Program Teacher's Guide, Cap. 7A	•		•	
Hispanohablantes WB, pp. 262–267			•	Videomisterio Quiz		•		
¿Eres tú, María? Video WB, pp. 34–40	•	•	•	Answer Keys: Student Edition, pp. 143–144	•	•	•	
Repaso del capítulo PP. **182–183**								
Review								
Student Edition, pp. 182–183	•	•	•	Interactive TE and Resources DVD	•		•	
Online Puzzles and Games	•			Teacher's Resource Book, pp. 168, 175, 177–179	•		•	•
Core WB, pp. 44–45	•	•	•	Audio Program	•	•	•	
Comm. WB, pp. 158–161	•	•	•	Answer Keys: Student Edition, p. 144	•	•	•	
Hispanohablantes WB, pp. 268–269			•					
Instant Check	•							
Chapter Assessment								
Assess				Examen del capítulo 7A	•		•	•
				Assessment Program, pp. 181–187	•		•	•
				Alternate Assessment Program, pp. 79–83	•		•	•
				Assessment Program para hispanohablantes, pp. 181–187	•		•	•
				Audio Program, Cap. 7A, Examen	•		•	•
				ExamView: Test Banks A and B questions only online	•			
				Heritage Learner Test Bank	•			
				Pre-AP* Test Bank	•			

REGULAR SCHEDULE (50 MINUTES)

DAY	Warm-up / Assess	Preview / Present / Practice / Communicate	Wrap-up / Homework Options
1	Return Examen del capítulo (10 min.)	Vocabulario en contexto (35 min.) • Objectives • Presentation • *Actividades* 1, 2 • Arte y cultura • Videocultura: *Los mercados*	Wrap-up and Homework Options (5 min.) • Core Practice • Vocabulary Clip Art
2	Warm-up (5 min.) • Homework check	Vocabulario en contexto (40 min.) • Review: *Vocabulario en contexto* • Presentation: *Videohistoria Una noche especial* • View: Video *Una noche especial* • Video Activities • *Actividades* 3, 4, 5	Wrap-up and Homework Options (5 min.) • *Prueba* 7A-1: Vocabulary recognition • Core Practice
3	Warm-up (5 min.) • Homework check ✔Formative Assessment (10 min.) • *Prueba* 7A-1: Vocabulary recognition	Vocabulario en uso (30 min.) • Objectives • Interactive Whiteboard Vocabulary Activities • *Actividades* 7, 8, 9 • *Fondo cultural* • Communicative Pair Activities	Wrap-up and Homework Options (5 min.) • *Actividad* 6
4	Warm-up (5 min.) • Homework check • Return *Prueba* 7A-1: Vocabulary recognition	Vocabulario en uso (40 min.) • Review: *Vocabulario* • *Actividades* 10, 12, 13 • *Juego: Actividad* 11	Wrap-up and Homework Options (5 min.) • *Fondo cultural*
5	Warm-up (5 min.) • Homework check	Vocabulario en uso (40 min.) • Review: *Vocabulario* • *Exploración del lenguaje* • *Actividades* 14, 15 • Communicative Pair Activities	Wrap-up and Homework Options (5 min.) • *Actividad* 16
6	Warm-up (5 min.) • Homework check	Gramática y vocabulario en uso (40 min.) • Presentation: Stem-changing verbs: *pensar, querer, preferir* • *GramActiva* Video • Interactive Whiteboard Grammar Activities • *Actividades* 17, 18	Wrap-up and Homework Options (5 min.) • *Actividad* 19
7	Warm-up (5 min.) • Homework check	Gramática y vocabulario en uso (40 min.) • Review: Stem-changing verbs: *pensar, querer, preferir* • *Actividades* 20, 21, 22, 23 • *Pronunciación*	Wrap-up and Homework Options (5 min.) • Core Practice • *Prueba* 7A-3 with Study Plan: Stem-changing verbs: *pensar, querer, preferir*
8	Warm-up (5 min.) • Homework check ✔Formative Assessment (10 min.) • *Prueba* 7A-3 with Study Plan: Stem-changing verbs: *pensar, querer, preferir*	Gramática y vocabulario en uso (30 min.) • Presentation: Demonstrative adjectives • *GramActiva* Video • Interactive Whiteboard Grammar Activities • *Actividades* 24, 25 • *Juego: Actividad* 26	Wrap-up and Homework Options (5 min.) • *Prueba* 7A-2 with Study Plan: Vocabulary production

REGULAR SCHEDULE (50 MINUTES)

DAY	Warm-up / Assess	Preview / Present / Practice / Communicate	Wrap-up / Homework Options
9	**Warm-up (5 min.)** • Homework check • Return *Prueba* 7A-3 with Study Plan: Stem-changing verbs *pensar, querer, preferir* ✔**Formative Assessment (10 min.)** • *Prueba* 7A-2 with Study Plan: Vocabulary production	**Gramática y vocabulario en uso (30 min.)** • *Actividades 27, 29* • *Conexiones: Actividad 28* • *El español en la comunidad* • *Fondo cultural*	**Wrap-up and Homework Options (5 min.)** • Core Practice • *Prueba* 7A-4 with Study Plan: Demonstrative adjectives
10	**Warm-up (5 min.)** • Homework check • Return *Prueba* 7A-2 with Study Plan: Vocabulary production ✔**Formative Assessment (10 min.)** • *Prueba* 7A-4 with Study Plan: Demonstrative adjectives	**¡Adelante! (30 min.)** • *Lectura* • *Fondo cultural*	**Wrap-up and Homework Options (5 min.)** • *¿Comprendes?*
11	**Warm-up (5 min.)** • Homework check • Return *Prueba* 7A-4 with Study Plan: Demonstrative adjectives	**¡Adelante! (40 min.)** • *Presentación oral:* Prepare • *La cultura en vivo*	**Wrap-up and Homework Options (5 min.)** • *Presentación oral:* Prepare
12	**Warm-up (5 min.)** • Homework check	**¡Adelante! (40 min.)** • *Presentación oral:* Practice	**Wrap-up and Homework Options (5 min.)**
13	**Warm-up (5 min.)** • Homework check	**¡Adelante! (40 min.)** • *Presentación oral:* Present	**Wrap-up and Homework Options (5 min.)** • Writing Activities • Core Practice Organizer
14	**Warm-up (5 min.)** • Homework check • Core Practice Organizer	**¡Adelante! (20 min.)** • *Videomisterio* **Repaso (20 min.)** • *Vocabulario y gramática* • *Preparación para el examen*	**Wrap-up and Homework Options (5 min.)** • *Examen del capítulo* • Instant Check
15	**Warm-up (5 min.)** • Answer questions ✔**Summative Assessment (45 min.)** • *Examen del capítulo*		

Standards for *Capítulo* 7A

• To achieve the goals of the Standards, students will:

Communication
1.1 Interpersonal
• Talk about: shopping and clothes; preferences and plans; traditional clothing of Panama
• Extend and accept invitations
• Discuss the plot of a video mystery series

1.2 Interpretive
• Read and listen to information about shopping and clothes
• Read a picture-based story
• Listen to and watch a video about shopping and clothes
• Read about: preferences and plans; an advertisement for a variety store; traditional clothing of Panama
• View a video mystery series

1.3 Presentational
• Present information about: shopping and clothes; money and currency; preferences and plans
• Write about Botero's painting, *"En Familia"*

Culture
2.1 Practices and Perspectives
• Understand etiquette of dress at social functions
• Learn about the growing influence of Latin American fashion designers
• Learn about traditional Panamanian festivals
• Learn about Carnaval in Latin American countries

2.2 Products and Perspectives
• Learn about: Joan Miró and his painting; Fernando Botero, his painting and sculpture
• Learn about the *garibaldina*
• Learn about currency in Spanish-speaking countries
• Learn about Panamanian festival costumes; the fabric artwork style, *mola*

Connections
3.1 Cross-curricular
• Learn about important artists and their work: Miró, Botero, Herrera
• Reinforce mathematics skills; knowledge of geography

3.2 Target Culture
• Read a poem of Puerto Rico, *"En la puerta del cielo"*

Comparisons
4.1 Language
• Understand the pronunciation of the letter *z*
• Learn the verbs *pensar, querer,* and *preferir*
• Learn to use demonstrative adjectives
• Learn a non-verbal expression for "That's expensive!"

4.2 Culture
• Compare changing fashions
• Compare artwork and symbolism of currency
• Compare celebrations in the United States to *Carnaval*
• Compare personalized decorative clothing

Communities
5.1 Beyond the School
• Identify local stores that sell products from Spanish-speaking countries

5.2 Lifelong Learner
• View a video mystery series

Capítulo
7A ¿Cuánto cuesta?

▼ Chapter Objectives

Communication
By the end of this chapter you will be able to:
• Listen to conversations and read about clothes and shopping
• Talk and write about shopping plans and gifts
• Exchange information while purchasing an item of clothing

Culture
You will also be able to:
• Understand the role of *molas* in the Kuna culture
• Compare the significance of crafts and clothing in Panama and the United States

You will demonstrate what you know and can do:
• Presentación oral, p. 179
• Preparación para el examen, p. 183

You will use:

Vocabulary	**Grammar**
• Shopping	• Stem-changing verbs: *pensar, querer,* and *preferir*
• Clothing	
• Prices and numbers	• Demonstrative adjectives

Exploración del mundo hispano

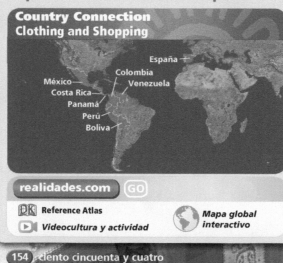

Country Connection
Clothing and Shopping

España
Colombia
México
Costa Rica
Venezuela
Panamá
Perú
Bolivia

realidades.com [GO]

🅳🅺 **Reference Atlas**

▶ **Videocultura y actividad**

🌐 **Mapa global interactivo**

(154) **ciento cincuenta y cuatro**
Tema 7 • De compras

Mercado de artesanías, Playa del Carmen, México

ENRICH YOUR TEACHING

Using Backward Design
Have students preview the sample performance tasks on *Preparación para el examen*, p. 183, and connect them to the Chapter Objectives. Explain to students that by completing the sample tasks they can self-assess their learning progress.

Mapa global interactivo
Download the *Mapa global interactivo* files for Chapter 7A and preview the activities. Activity 1 takes you to Barcelona, Spain. In Activity 2, visit the Islas de San Blas and the Panama Canal.

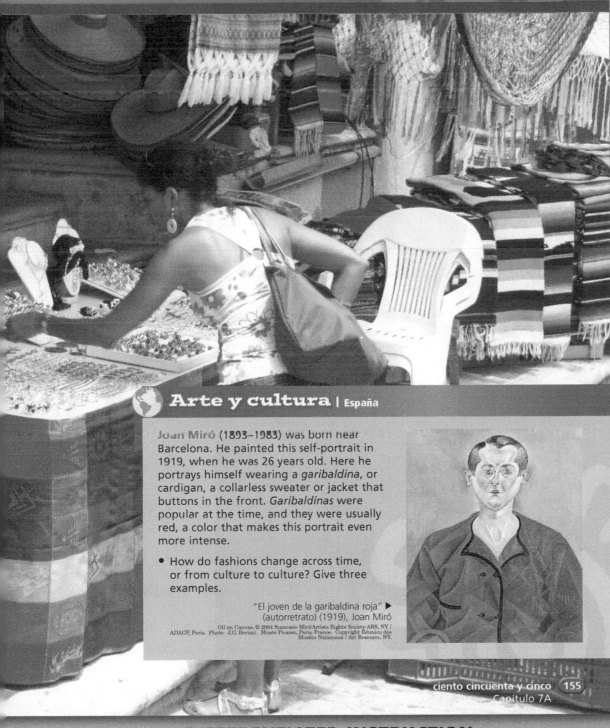

Arte y cultura | España

Joan Miró (1893–1983) was born near Barcelona. He painted this self-portrait in 1919, when he was 26 years old. Here he portrays himself wearing a *garibaldina*, or cardigan, a collarless sweater or jacket that buttons in the front. *Garibaldinas* were popular at the time, and they were usually red, a color that makes this portrait even more intense.

• How do fashions change across time, or from culture to culture? Give three examples.

"El joven de la garibaldina roja" ▶
(autorretrato) (1919), Joan Miró

Oil on Canvas. © 2004 Successio Miró/Artists Rights Society ARS, NY / ADAGP, Paris. Photo: J.G. Berizzi. Musée Picasso, Paris, France. Copyright Réunion des Musées Nationaux / Art Resource, NY.

Chapter Opener

Core Instruction

Resources: Map Transparencies 12–18, 20

Suggestions: Explain that students will learn how to talk about clothing, shopping, and prices. Brainstorm a list of words and expressions used to talk about shopping. Have them keep the list and check off the items covered in *Capítulo* 7A. The video story is about teenagers helping their friend dress appropriately for a party. The *GramActiva* Videos will help students learn to use *e → ie* stem-changing verbs and demonstrative adjectives.

▶ **Videocultura** View *Los mercados* online with the class to learn more about shopping in Spanish-speaking countries.

Arte y cultura

Standards: 2.2, 3.1, 4.2

Resources: Fine Art Transparencies, p. 39

Mapa global interactivo, Actividad 1 Explore Barcelona, Spain, home of the Miró Museum.

Suggestions: Talk about the fact that clothes are often worn as a statement. Have students provide examples. Why are some articles of clothing more popular than others? Who sets clothing trends? Ask if students could imagine someone wearing a *garibaldina* today. Are there differences in dress from region to region within the students' own country?

Answers might include the following: Clothing styles have become less formal and more comfortable over time. Possible examples include the almost universal wearing of jeans and men wearing suits and ties less frequently.

▶ **TEACHING WITH ART**

Resources: Fine Art Transparencies, p. 39

DIFFERENTIATED INSTRUCTION

Digital resources such as the *Interactive Whiteboard* activity banks, *Videomodelos*, additional *Online Activities*, *Study Plans*, automatically graded *Leveled Workbook*, animated *Grammar Tutorials*, *Flashcards*, and *Vocabulary and Grammar Videos* will help you reach students of different ability levels and learning styles.

STUDENTS NEEDING EXTRA HELP

Guided Practice Activities
• Flashcards, pp. 65–70
• Vocabulary Check, pp. 71–74
• Grammar Support, pp. 75–78

HERITAGE LEARNERS

Realidades para hispanohablantes
• Chapter Opener, pp. 250–251
• A primera vista, p. 252
• Videohistoria, p. 253
• Manos a la obra, pp. 254–261
• ¡Adelante!, pp. 262–267
• Repaso del capítulo, pp. 268–269

ADVANCED/PRE-AP*

Pre-AP* Resource Book,
• pp. 86–89
Communications Workbook
• Integrated Performance Assessment, p. 158

Read, listen to, and understand information about
▶ shopping for clothes
▶ plans, desires, and preferences

Vocabulario en contexto

Core Instruction

Standards: 1.2a

Resources: Teachers Resource Book: Input Script, p. 164, Clip Art, pp. 177–179, Audio Script, p. 165; Voc. and Gram. Transparencies 128–129; TPR Stories Book, pp. 92–106; Audio Program DVD: Cap. 7A, Tracks 1–2

Focus: Presenting new vocabulary about clothes and shopping

Suggestions: Use the story in the *TPR Stories Book* to present the new vocabulary and grammar or use the Input Script from the *Teacher's Resource Book*. Present the vocabulary in four sets: *ropa deportiva, ropa elegante, ¿Cómo me queda?,* and *precios.* Substitute the various clothing articles in the dialogues, using the transparencies as cues. Say each word on the transparencies, but wait to point to each picture until students point to the correct picture in the book. Have students write the words *ropa elegante* in large red letters on one sheet of paper and *ropa deportiva* in blue letters on another. As you mention items, have students hold up the appropriate paper. Have volunteers point to clothing articles that they or classmates are wearing as you mention items. If you prefer, bring in examples of each article of clothing and set up your own "store" in which you are the clerk selling items to student customers.

BELLRINGER REVIEW

Have students review numbers by counting aloud in unison from 10 to 100 by tens.

Vocabulario en contexto

—Buenos días. ¿En qué puedo servirle?

—Necesito **comprar** una blusa. Y también **busco** unos jeans **nuevos.**

—¿Prefiere Ud. **llevar** una blusa deportiva o elegante?

—¡Me encantan las blusas deportivas!

156 ciento cincuenta y seis
Tema 7 • De compras

DIFFERENTIATED INSTRUCTION

Heritage Language Learners
Give each student a photograph cut from a magazine of people dressed either casually or formally. Have students write complete descriptions of the outfits. Encourage the use of descriptive adjectives. Check agreements carefully.

Students with Learning Difficulties
Numbers are a challenge for most students. Spend extra time practicing them. Bring in mail order catalogs and have students practice saying the prices in Spanish.

el abrigo

el suéter   la chaqueta

—¿Qué **piensas** comprar hoy?

—Necesito comprar un abrigo. Me gusta ese abrigo. **¿Entramos en la tienda?**

—¡Uf! **Me queda mal.**

—Tienes razón. Es demasiado grande.

—¿Cómo me queda este abrigo?

—**Te queda bien.** Me gusta. ¿Qué piensas?

—Me gusta también. **¿Cuánto cuesta?**

—A ver . . . Cuesta ochocientos pesos. Es un buen **precio**, ¿no?

$200 La Preferida	$300 La Preferida	$400 La Preferida	$500 La Preferida	$600 La Preferida
doscientos **pesos**	trescientos **pesos**	cuatrocientos **pesos**	quinientos **pesos**	seiscientos **pesos**
$700 La Preferida	$800 La Preferida	$900 La Preferida	$1000 La Preferida	
setecientos **pesos**	ochocientos **pesos**	novecientos **pesos**	mil **pesos**	

1 | Escuchar

¿Qué ropa llevan?

Listen to what different people are wearing today. Point to the picture of each clothing item as you hear it.

2 | Escuchar

¿Verano o invierno?

On a sheet of paper, draw a snowman on one side and the sun on the other. If a statement you hear is most logical for winter, hold up the snowman. If it is most logical for summer, hold up the sun.

Más práctica	GO
	realidades.com | print
Instant Check	✔
Guided WB pp. 65–70	✔ ✔
Core WB pp. 37–38	✔ ✔
Comm. WB p. 49	✔ ✔
Hispanohablantes WB p. 252	✔

ciento cincuenta y siete **157**
Capítulo 7A

1 Standards: 1.2

Resources: Teacher's Resource Book: Audio Script, 165; Audio Program DVD: Cap. 7A, Track 3; Answer Keys: Student Edition, p. 136

Focus: Listening comprehension

Suggestions: Play the audio or read the script. Pause to monitor that students are pointing to the correct pictures.

Suggestions: Bring in articles of clothing. Put price tags on them, explaining that different countries use different currencies. Mention that depending on what monetary unit a country uses, the number may be quite large. Give students a supply of paper money. Play the role of the clerk quoting prices. Students demonstrate comprehension by handing you the appropriate number of bills.

Script and Answers:

1. El profesor Ramírez lleva un traje. *(suit)*
2. Leonardo lleva una gorra. *(cap)*
3. Gerardo lleva pantalones cortos. *(shorts)*
4. La dependienta lleva una falda azul. *(skirt)*
5. Los zapatos que lleva José son negros. *(shoes)*
6. Hace calor y Carlos lleva una camiseta. *(T-shirt)*
7. Carmen lleva unas botas muy bonitas. *(boots)*
8. Mi hermana lleva unos jeans nuevos. *(jeans)*

2 Standards: 1.2

Resources: Teacher's Resource Book: Audio Script, p. 165; Audio Program DVD: Cap. 7A, Track 4; Answer Keys: Student Edition, p. 136

Focus: Listening comprehension

Suggestions: Ask students to draw their pictures large enough so you will be able to see them. If students use blue for the snowman and orange for the sun you can spot errors easily.

Script and Answers:

1. ¿Dónde está tu suéter? *(winter)*
2. Necesito comprar un traje de baño nuevo. *(summer)*
3. ¿Por qué llevas pantalones cortos? *(summer)*
4. Voy a llevar una sudadera hoy. *(winter)*
5. ¿Cuánto cuesta el abrigo? *(winter)*
6. Mamá, ¿dónde está mi camiseta amarilla? *(summer)*
7. Las botas son muy pequeñas. *(winter)*

ENRICH YOUR TEACHING

Teacher-to-Teacher

Have groups of students draw an outfit and ask them to label each piece of clothing with an estimated price in dollars. Then have them do an Internet search for the term "currency converter." Have students go to one of the sites and find out how much the outfit they created would cost in the currency of the Spanish-speaking country of their choice.

21st Century Skills

Creativity and Innovation Have students plan the clothing they will need to visit a Spanish-speaking country in each of the country's seasons. (First, they should research the seasons of the country they have chosen!) Have them make a list of items they are bringing for each season and then write an e-mail to friends in that country, explaining what they plan to bring and asking if their choices are correct.

Videohistoria 🔊

Videohistoria | 🔊 | ▶️

Core Instruction

Standards: 1.2, 2.1

Resources: Voc. and Gram. Transparencies 130–131; Audio Program DVD: Cap. 7A, Track 5

Focus: Presenting additional contextualized vocabulary and grammar; previewing the video

Suggestions:

Pre-reading: Discuss the pre-reading questions. Direct students' attention to the *Strategy*. Have them read the *¿Comprendes?* questions. Point out that this *Strategy* allows students to read with a purpose. Using the transparencies, go panel by panel and ask students to summarize the events. Ask students to identify problems the characters encounter.

Una noche especial

¿Por qué necesita ir de compras Teresa? Lee la historia.

México

Berta

Manolo

Teresa

Ramón

Claudia

Antes de leer

Strategy — **Using questions as a guide for reading**
Before you read the *Videohistoria*, read the questions in *Actividad 5* to help you focus on the information that is most important.

- What are three specific things that you should be thinking about as you read the *Videohistoria*?

1. Think about the last time you went clothes shopping. What were you looking for? Did you buy something? If so, was it expensive? If not, why didn't you buy anything? What do you expect Teresa and Claudia to talk about when Teresa tries to buy something to wear to the party?

2. Compare how Ramón is dressed in photo 6 and how he is dressed in photo 8. What are the differences? What are the similarities?

 158 ciento cincuenta y ocho
Tema 7 • De compras

DIFFERENTIATED INSTRUCTION

Students with Learning Difficulties
To help students with the *Strategy*, make a transparency with the questions from *Actividad* 5. Highlight key words in color, and display the transparency for reference while students search the text.

Multiple Intelligences
Intrapersonal/Introspective: Use the photos to review physical characteristics and personality traits. Have groups of students look at one photo and work together to write a description of each person in it. Tell students to use their imaginations to describe each person's personality.

Language Input 7A

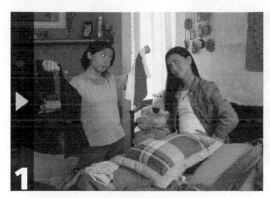

Teresa: **Esta** falda no me queda bien y este vestido no me gusta. No sé qué llevar para la fiesta.

Claudia: Pues, puedes comprar ropa nueva. Hay una tienda de **ropa** aquí cerca y tienen ropa muy bonita.

Teresa: Sí, **quizás** una falda nueva . . . ¡**Vamos!**

Claudia: ¡Mira esta tienda!

Teresa: Mmmm . . . No sé. No tengo mucho dinero y **esa** ropa es muy cara.

Claudia: ¡Vamos! ¡**Queremos** ver qué tienen!

Teresa: **Perdón,** ¿señora?

Dependienta: ¿Sí? ¿En qué puedo servirle, señorita?

Teresa: **Busco** ropa para llevar a una fiestá. Me gustaría comprar esta falda y esta blusa.

Claudia: A ver . . . ¿Cuánto **cuestan?**

Teresa: ¡Seiscientos pesos! Pero, ¡es mucho dinero!

Dependienta: Bueno, aquí hay ropa que no cuesta **tanto.**

Claudia: Mira, Teresa. Esta falda cuesta trescientos pesos. ¿Qué piensas?

Teresa: ¡Genial! Y este suéter cuesta doscientos pesos. **Los dos** no cuestan tanto.

ciento cincuenta y nueve **159**
Capítulo 7A

Suggestions:

Reading: Read the captions with students or play the audio. Using the transparencies and nonverbal clues, help students understand the new words in blue type. Use the pictures to help establish the difference between *esa* and *esta,* which is explained later in the chapter.

Post-reading: Complete *Actividades* 3–5 to check comprehension.

Pre-AP* Support

- **Learning Objective:** Presentational Writing and Speaking
- **Activity:** As a post-viewing activity, have groups of students rewrite the sixth frame of the scene, imagining that Ramón is dressed too formally instead of too casually. Then have them act out their new version of the sixth, seventh, and eighth frames of the scene. You may want to make a video of the new scene to share with other classes.
- *Pre-AP* Resource Book:* Comprehensive guide to Pre-AP* vocabulary skill development, pp. 51–57

ENRICH YOUR TEACHING

Culture Note

It is common in many Spanish-speaking countries for young adults to dress more formally than do young people in the United States. This may apply even to concerts, walks in the park, or just visiting family in the next town.

Teacher-to-Teacher

If students notice the structure *¿En qué puedo servirle?*, you might want to explain it to them. Do they see the infinitive **servir?** Do they recognize **le** from **le gusta?**

Video ▶️

Core Instruction

Standards: 1.2, 2.1

Resources: Teacher's Resource Book: Video Script, p. 169; Video Program: Cap. 7A; Video Program Teacher's Guide: Cap. 7A

Focus: Comprehending a story about culturally appropriate clothing

Suggestions:

Pre-viewing: Ask students if they worry about what they wear to parties. Explain that the video deals with teens facing this dilemma.

Viewing: Show the video without the sound, stopping to ask what information students have learned from the images. Before playing the video with sound, remind students that they will not understand every word, but that they should listen and watch for overall understanding. Show the video once without pausing. Show it again, stopping to check comprehension.

Post-viewing: Complete the Video Activities in the *Communication Workbook*.

3 Standards: 1.2, 1.3

Resources: Answer Keys: Student Edition, p. 137

Focus: Reading comprehension

Suggestions: Have students read and list the items that Berta and Manolo say are appropriate. This will serve as a list to check against.

Answers:

1. no puedes   4. sí puedes
2. sí puedes   5. no puedes
3. no puedes

5

Manolo: Ramón, son las ocho. La fiesta es a las nueve, ¿recuerdas?

Ramón: Sí, sí, tienes razón. Vamos.

6

Berta: Ramón, ¿tú piensas llevar esa ropa a la fiesta de Teresa? ¡Esos jeans y esa camiseta y . . . esa gorra! No, no puedes.

Ramón: ¿Y por qué no?

Berta: Uhm . . . Pues, aquí en México no llevamos esa ropa a las fiestas.

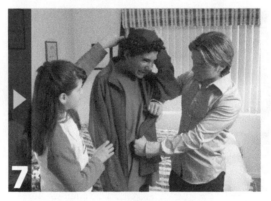

7

Ramón: ¡Yo quiero llevar mi gorra favorita, y me gustan **estos** jeans!

Manolo y Berta: Te ayudamos.

8

Teresa: ¡Hola! Buenas noches. Pero, ¿dónde está la gorra?

DIFFERENTIATED INSTRUCTION

Heritage Language Learners

Have students imagine the conversation Ramón and Claudia would have if Ramón had not changed into nice clothing. Students can brainstorm the conversation and write the dialogue together. They could record their scenes on video to include in their portfolios.

▼3 Leer • Escribir

¿Sí puedes o no puedes?

Lee estas frases de Ramón. En una hoja de papel, escribe *sí puedes* si según Berta y Manolo es algo que Ramón puede llevar a la fiesta o *no puedes* si según ellos es algo que no puede llevar a la fiesta.

1. Quiero llevar mis jeans a la fiesta.
2. Pienso llevar unos pantalones negros a la fiesta.
3. Pienso llevar mi gorra favorita a la fiesta.
4. Voy a llevar una camisa blanca a la fiesta.
5. Quiero llevar una camiseta a la fiesta.

▼4 Leer • Pensar

¿Cierto o falso?

Lee las frases y escribe *C* (cierto) o *F* (falso), según la *Videohistoria*.

1. Claudia y Teresa buscan ropa para una fiesta.
2. Teresa tiene un vestido que le gusta mucho y no quiere ropa nueva.
3. A Ramón le encanta llevar su gorra.
4. La tienda no tiene ropa que cuesta menos que seiscientos pesos.
5. Teresa puede comprar un suéter con doscientos pesos.
6. Para Berta y Manolo, no es importante la ropa que lleva Ramón a la fiesta.

▼5 Hablar • Escribir

¿Comprendes?

1. ¿Por qué no está contenta Teresa? ¿Adónde va ella?
2. Según Claudia, ¿qué puede hacer Teresa?
3. ¿Adónde van las dos?
4. ¿Tiene Teresa mucho o poco dinero?
5. ¿Por qué no compra Teresa la primera falda y blusa?
6. ¿Cuánto cuestan la segunda falda y blusa?
7. ¿Qué quiere llevar Ramón a la fiesta?
8. Cuando Ramón entra en la casa de Teresa, ¿qué lleva?

Más práctica	GO
realidades.com | print	
Instant Check	✔
Guided WB pp. 71–74	✔ ✔
Core WB pp. 39–40	✔ ✔
Comm. WB pp. 43–45, 46	✔ ✔
Hispanohablantes WB p. 253	✔

ciento sesenta y uno **161**
Capítulo 7A

▼4 Standards: 1.2
Resources: Answer Keys: Student Edition, p. 137
Focus: Reading comprehension
Suggestions: Have students tell you which panels of the story support each answer.

Answers:

1. C   4. F
2. F   5. C
3. C   6. F

▼5 Standards: 1.1, 1.3
Resources: Answer Keys: Student Edition, p. 137
Focus: Reading comprehension
Suggestions: Remind students to search for key words in the questions. For example, if they see **adónde,** they need to look for a location. Have them work in groups of three or four to check their answers.

Answers:

1. No está contenta porque no sabe qué llevar. Va a una fiesta.
2. Puede comprar ropa (una falda) nueva.
3. Van a una tienda de ropa.
4. Teresa no tiene mucho (tiene poco) dinero.
5. Porque cuestan mucho.
6. Cuestan quinientos pesos.
7. Quiere llevar su ropa favorita, unos jeans y una gorra.
8. Lleva una camisa y pantalones, y tiene su gorra.

Additional Resources

• Communication Wbk.: Audio Act. 5, p. 46
• Teacher's Resource Book: Audio Script, p. 166
• Audio Program DVD: Cap. 7A, Track 8

ENRICH YOUR TEACHING

Culture Note

Tell students that the clothing associated with American cowboys evolved from the clothing worn by the Mexican **vaqueros** or **charros** who worked on the ranches created by Spanish colonists. American frontier dwellers eventually adopted the **vaquero** "look," which included cowboy boots, cowboy hats, leather vests, and chaps.

Teacher-to-Teacher

Write different events on index cards (a wedding, a rock concert, the first day of school, a day at an amusement park). Divide the class into groups and give each group a card. Each group will prepare a chart listing the *dos* and *don't*s of what to wear for the event on their card.

✔ASSESSMENT

Quiz: Vocabulary Recognition
• Prueba 7A-1: pp. 175–176

BELLRINGER REVIEW

Go around the room and point to different items students are wearing. Ask others to name them.

6 Standards: 1.3

Focus: Writing about clothing in a personalized context

Recycle: Leisure activities

Suggestions: Discuss why *jeans y una camiseta* would be appropriate at a friend's house. Have students consider the activities for each location to help them decide what to wear.

Answers will vary.

Common Errors: Not correctly matching the indefinite articles to nouns in gender and number. Before beginning the activity, have students give the appropriate article for each item of clothing.

Extension: Have students list five of their favorite places or activities and describe the appropriate clothing for each situation.

7 Standards: 1.3

Resources: Answer Keys: Student Edition, p. 138

Focus: Writing a description using clothing vocabulary

Recycle: Colors

Suggestions: Encourage students to brainstorm before they write. Have students write their responses for homework.

Answers:
la madre: un vestido negro, zapatos negros; *el padre:* un traje marrón, una camisa blanca, zapatos negros; *el hijo:* pantalones cortos marrones, zapatos blancos, calcetines azules, un suéter rosado; *la hija:* una falda verde, un suéter amarillo, una blusa blanca, calcetines azules, zapatos marrones

---

Manos a la obra

▼ Objectives
▶ Listen to shoppers and clerks comment on clothes and prices
▶ Write and talk about the clothes you wear and buy
▶ Describe the clothes in a painting
▶ Discuss how clothes fit and how much they cost

Vocabulario en uso

▼6 | ♻ | Escribir

¿Qué piensas llevar?

¡Es importante llevar ropa diferente en diferentes ocasiones! ¿Qué ropa piensas llevar a estos lugares (*places*) o actividades? Escribe las frases.

Modelo
la casa de un amigo
Pienso llevar unos jeans y una camiseta.

1. la playa
2. un baile formal
3. un concierto
4. las montañas
5. un partido de béisbol

▼7 | ♻ | Escribir

¿Qué ropa llevan en el cuadro?

Escribe cuatro o más frases que describen la ropa que lleva la familia en este cuadro de Fernando Botero.

Modelo
La madre lleva . . .

▼ Fondo Cultural | Colombia

Fernando Botero (1932–) is a very famous artist from Medellín, Colombia. His paintings and sculptures feature people and objects that are puffed up to an exaggerated size. The figures celebrate life while making fun of what they represent.

● What statement might an artist like Botero be making when his artwork presents humorous portrayals of politicians and prominent people?

"En familia" (1983), Fernando Botero ▶
Courtesy of the Marlborough Gallery, New York.

DIFFERENTIATED INSTRUCTION

Students with Learning Difficulties
Some students will have more success with *Actividad* 6 if you use the Clip Art from the *Teacher's Resource Book*. Give them pictures of the items that they can physically sort into piles according to the events listed.

Advanced Learners
Have students find an image on the Internet of another Botero painting or sculpture. Ask them to save the image as a file and write down the Web address. Have them insert the image and the URL into a text document and type a description of the painting and the people in it. What do they think Botero was trying to communicate?

▼8 | ♻ | ◀)) | **Escuchar • Escribir**

Escucha y escribe

Trabajas en una tienda de ropa y escuchas los comentarios de diferentes personas que buscan ropa. Escribe los números del 1 al 6 en una hoja de papel y escribe las frases que escuchas. Después indica con (+) o (–) si piensas que las personas van a comprar la ropa.

También se dice...

la camiseta = la playera (México); la polera (Chile); la remera (Argentina)

la chaqueta = la chamarra (México, Bolivia); la campera (Argentina, Chile, Paraguay, Uruguay)

los jeans = los mahones (el Caribe); las mezclillas (México); los vaqueros (Argentina, España); el pantalón vaquero (España)

el suéter = el jersey (España); la chompa (Bolivia, Ecuador, Paraguay, Perú, Uruguay)

▼9 | 👥 | ♻ | **Escribir • Hablar**

En el almacén Buenprecio

Haz una lista de seis artículos de ropa que te gustaría comprar. Después, con otro(a) estudiante, mira el directorio del almacén Buenprecio y decide dónde puedes encontrar *(find)* la ropa en tu lista.

▶ **Modelo**

A —*¿Dónde están las botas?*
B —*Están en la planta baja.*

BIENVENIDOS AL ALMACÉN
BUENPRECIO

3 ROPA PARA MUJER. VESTIDOS. FALDAS Y BLUSAS. ABRIGOS. FUTURA MAMÁ.

2 ROPA PARA HOMBRE. PANTALONES. CAMISAS. TRAJES. CHAQUETAS.

1 ROPA DEPORTIVA. CAMISETAS. GORRAS. SUDADERAS. ZAPATOS DE TENIS.

PB ZAPATOS. BOTAS. CALCETINES.

S CAFÉ. DISCOS. LIBROS. VIDEOS.

ciento sesenta y tres **163**
Capítulo 7A

Fondo cultural

Standards: 2.2, 3.1
Resources: Fine Art Transparencies, p. 8
Suggestions: Bring in political cartoons and discuss what the artist is saying about the personal qualities of the politician through caricature.

Answers will vary but might include the idea that prominent people tend to take themselves very seriously and make themselves appear larger than life. The artist shows that these "important" people are human, too.

▼**8** Standards: 1.2

Resources: Teacher's Resource Book: Audio Script, p. 166; Audio Program DVD: Cap. 7A, Track 6; Answer Keys: Student Edition, p. 138
Focus: Listening comprehension and writing accurately using shopping vocabulary
Recycle: Adjectives; *me gusta*
Suggestions: Clarify the use of the (+) and (–) signs. Play the audio or read the script aloud.

◀)) **Script and Answers:**

1. Esta blusa me queda muy bien. *(+)*
2. Esta camisa cuesta demasiado. *(–)*
3. Tienes razón. Estas botas son muy bonitas. *(+)*
4. Estos zapatos me quedan mal. *(–)*
5. No sé. Vamos a otra tienda. *(–)*
6. Quizás, pero no me gusta mucho. *(–)*

▼**9** Standards: 1.1, 1.2

Focus: Reading in authentic context; telling where to find specific clothing items in a department store
Recycle: *Estar;* ordinal numbers
Suggestions: Have students read the directory and brainstorm a list of items associated with each department.

Answers will vary.

ENRICH YOUR TEACHING

Culture Note
Students may not remember that "PB" means Planta Baja, or what is considered in the United States as the "ground floor." Remind them that "3" really is the fourth floor!

Teacher-to-Teacher
Name an article of clothing and ask students wearing that item to stand. Specify a color. Students wearing an article of that color should then sit down. Continue naming colors until all students are sitting down. Repeat with another article of clothing.

10 Standards: 1.1

Focus: Using vocabulary in a conversation; practicing making clothing purchases

Recycle: *Me gustaría;* colors; present progressive

Suggestions: Practice the model with a student volunteer. Students can take turns being the salesperson and the customer. Walk around the room and help students with adjective use.

Answers will vary.

Extension: Have students add to the conversation. The clothing might be too expensive or the salesperson might say the item does not fit well.

11 Standards: 1.1, 1.3

Focus: Writing a description of what classmates are wearing

Recycle: Colors; adjective agreement

Suggestions: Suggest that students choose a person to describe, and then list that person's clothing items and their colors before writing sentences. Write an example on the board. Encourage students not to guess randomly who the person is without listening to your description. Stress that students should ask three questions before guessing a name.

Answers will vary.

Fondo cultural

Standards: 2.2, 3.1

Resources: Answer Keys: Student Edition, p. 139

Suggestions: Help students with the discussion question by asking them who appears on the one-, five-, ten-, twenty-, fifty-, and one hundred-dollar bills.

Answers: Bolivia, Peru, Costa Rica, and the United States all honor people important to their history and culture. In the United States, we usually honor presidents on our money. We also honor our history, as on the state quarters.

▼10 | (Talk!) 👥 | ♻ | Hablar

¿En qué puedo servirle?

Tú vas de compras y hablas con un(a) dependiente(a). Con otro(a) estudiante, pregunta y contesta según el modelo. Escoge *(choose)* cinco artículos de ropa.

▶ Modelo

A —¿*En qué puedo servirle, señor (señorita)?*
B —*Me gustaría comprar una camisa nueva.*
A —¿*De qué color?*
B —*Estoy buscando una camisa blanca.*

▼11 | (Talk!) 👥 | ♻ | Escribir • Hablar

Juego

1 Escribe una descripción de la ropa de una persona en tu clase. Incluye dos o más cosas que lleva y los colores de la ropa.

2 Juega con otro(a) estudiante. Lee tu descripción. Tu compañero(a) tiene que identificar a la persona que describes. Antes de decir *(Before saying)* su nombre, él o ella tiene que hacer tres preguntas para saber más cosas. Por ejemplo: ¿*Lleva una sudadera azul? ¿Tiene zapatos negros? ¿Sus calcetines son blancos? ¿Es Mateo?*

164 **ciento sesenta y cuatro**
Tema 7 • De compras

DIFFERENTIATED INSTRUCTION

Advanced Learners

Have students choose a Spanish-speaking country and locate an example or picture of its currency. Have them copy or draw an example of one of the bills and tape it to a map, with a string stretching from the bill to the appropriate country.

Heritage Language Learners

Have students research the currency of their heritage country. What is it called? Where does the name come from? What is its exchange rate against the U.S. dollar?

▼ Fondo Cultural | Bolivia | Costa Rica | Perú

El dinero The currencies of Bolivia, Peru, and Costa Rica are all different. Just as the United States has the dollar, Spanish-speaking countries have their own national currencies.* In Bolivia, the official currency is the *boliviano*; in Peru it's the *nuevo sol*, and in Costa Rica, people use the *colón*. The images on the printed money honor each country's history and culture.

* How do the images that appear on bills and coins in Spanish-speaking countries compare to those in the United States?

*Puerto Rico and Ecuador use the United States dollar.

BELLRINGER REVIEW

Use Transparency 134 to quickly review clothing items in a personalized context.

▼12 | 🔊 | Escuchar • Escribir

¿Cuánto cuesta en Montevideo?

Estás comprando ropa en Montevideo, Uruguay. Escucha los precios en pesos uruguayos. Escribe en tu hoja de papel el precio que escuchas.

1. la camiseta
2. la blusa
3. el traje de baño
4. el suéter
5. el vestido
6. la chaqueta

Modelo

los zapatos
Escuchas: *Los zapatos cuestan mil ochocientos veinte pesos.*
Escribes: *1.820 pesos*

Uruguay

12 Standards: 1.2, 1.3

Resources: Teacher's Resource Book: Audio Script, p. 166; Audio Program DVD: Cap. 7A, Track 7; Answer Keys: Student Edition, p. 139

Focus: Listening for comprehension

Suggestions: Ask students to name the average price of each item. Convert the price into **pesos uruguayos** so that students know what prices to expect.

🔊 **Script and Answers:**

1. La camiseta cuesta 336 pesos.
2. ¿Cuánto cuesta la blusa? 1.260 pesos.
3. El traje de baño sólo cuesta 980 pesos.
4. El suéter cuesta 1.568 pesos.
5. ¿Cuánto cuesta el vestido? 1.680 pesos.
6. La chaqueta cuesta 1.764 pesos.

▼13 | 💬 | Hablar

¿Cuánto cuesta esa ropa?

Tú y tu amigo(a) van de compras. Con otro(a) estudiante, pregunta y contesta cuánto cuesta esta ropa. Los precios están en nuevos pesos uruguayos (UYU).

195 pesos

▶ **Modelo**

A —¿Cuánto cuestan <u>los calcetines</u>?
B —Cuestan <u>cuatrocientos pesos</u>.

1. 800 pesos

2. 775 pesos

3. 950 pesos

4. 2100 pesos

5. 700 pesos

6. 625 pesos

13 Standards: 1.1

Resources: Answer Keys: Student Edition, p. 140
Focus: Asking and telling prices of clothing items

Suggestions: Put price tags on three articles of clothing you have brought in and model the exchange.

🔊 **Script and Answers:**

1. A: ¿Cuánto cuesta la camisa verde?
   B: Cuesta ochocientos pesos.
2. A: ¿Cuánto cuesta la sudadera amarilla?
   B: Cuesta dos mil pesos.
3. A: ¿Cuánto cuesta el traje de baño rojo?
   B: Cuesta novecientos cincuenta pesos.
4. A: ¿Cuánto cuesta el traje gris?
   B: Cuesta seiscientos veinticinco pesos.
5. A: ¿Cuánto cuestan los jeans azules?
   B: Cuestan quinientos setenta y cinco pesos.
6. A: ¿Cuánto cuesta la falda gris?
   B: Cuesta mil cien pesos.

ciento sesenta y cinco **165**
Capítulo 7A

ENRICH YOUR TEACHING

Culture Note

A few Spanish-speaking countries accept the U.S. dollar in addition to their own currency. This is generally done to attract investment and tourism, and may be limited to major cities and tourist areas. The countries that accept the dollar include Mexico, Ecuador, El Salvador, Costa Rica, Panama, Bolivia, and Argentina.

21st Century Skills

Social and Cross-Cultural Skills Have students talk with a native Spanish speaker about how much various articles of clothing cost in the Spanish-speaker's native city. Then, they should decide what factors might be responsible for any price differences. (They can ask the Spanish-speakers for input!)

▼14 Standards: 1.1, 1.2

Resources: Answer Keys: Student Edition, p. 140

Focus: Reading for comprehension

Suggestions: Have students read all the choices the *joven* has. Once students have made their matches, have them practice the conversation, then reverse roles.

Answers:

1. c **2.** e **3.** f **4.** a **5.** d **6.** b

Extension: For homework, have students write a similar conversation, with each sentence on a separate slip of paper. They then exchange their conversations with another student and put each other's sentences in the correct order.

Exploración del lenguaje
Core Instruction

Standards: 4.1

Focus: Understanding common gestures and nonverbal language

Suggestions: Demonstrate the gesture and have students imitate it. Hold up various articles and say: *¡Ay! ¡¿(300) dólares?! ¡Es mucho!* Then make the gesture. To apply it to people, say: *(El Sr. Bill Gates) tiene mucho, mucho dinero,* and make the gesture. Have students create their own examples.

▼14 | Pensar • Leer • Hablar

En la tienda

Con otro(a) estudiante lee la conversación entre un(a) dependiente(a) y un(a) joven. Empareja *(Match)* lo que dice el(la) dependiente(a) con lo que contesta el(la) joven.

el(la) dependiente(a)

1. Buenas tardes. ¿En qué puedo servirle?
2. ¿Qué color prefiere Ud.?
3. Pues, estos pantalones son muy populares.
4. Sólo 50 dólares.
5. Pues, hay otros pantalones que no cuestan tanto.
6. Creo que te quedan muy bien.

el(la) joven

a. Perdón . . . ese precio es demasiado para mí.
b. Entonces voy a comprar estos pantalones.
c. Quiero comprar unos pantalones nuevos.
d. Son bonitos. A ver si me quedan bien.
e. No sé—quizás negro.
f. Me gustan. ¿Cuánto cuestan?

▼ Exploración del lenguaje

Nonverbal language

You've already learned about the gesture *¡Ojo!*, which means "be careful." Another common gesture used by Spanish speakers conveys the meaning "a lot of money." This gesture is made by holding the hand palm-up and rubbing the fingertips together. It is often accompanied by expressions such as *¡Cuesta muchísimo!* or *Es mucho dinero*. It can even be used when you're describing someone who is rich.

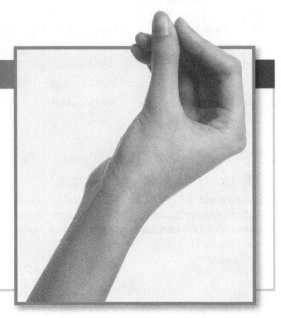

DIFFERENTIATED INSTRUCTION

Students with Special Needs

To make *Actividad* 15 more accessible, enlarge the pictures so details will be more evident. Some students will need to be told what features to focus on.

Advanced Learners

Tell students they have $100 to spend on clothing. Ask them to write sentences telling what items they would like to buy and their cost.

▼15 | 👥 | Hablar

¿Cómo me queda?

Estás en una tienda de ropa. Te pruebas *(You're trying on)* la ropa y necesitas la opinión honesta de tu amigo(a). Tu amigo(a) siempre te hace *(gives you)* comentarios. Escoge dos artículos de ropa.

> **Nota**
>
> *Me/te queda(n)* follows the same pattern as *me/te gusta(n)*.
>
> • La camisa **me** queda bien pero los jeans **me quedan** mal.

▶ Modelo

A —¿*Me queda bien el traje*? *¿Qué piensas?*

B —*Te queda bien. ¡Qué guapo estás!*

Estudiante A

Estudiante B

> Te queda(n) bien/mal.
>
> Es/son muy/bastante/ demasiado . . .
>
> ¡Qué guapo/bonita estás!
>
> (No) me gusta(n) mucho.

▼16 | ♻ | 💬 | Escribir • Hablar

Y tú, ¿qué dices?

1. ¿Qué ropa llevas en el verano? ¿Y en el invierno? Incluye tres artículos de ropa para cada estación.

2. Describe qué llevas hoy. ¿Cuál de los artículos que llevas es tu favorito?

3. Describe qué llevas cuando estás en casa. ¿Cómo es diferente de la ropa que llevas a clases?

4. ¿Quién compra ropa, tú o tus padres? ¿Dónde te gusta ir de compras?

5. ¿Cuáles son tres artículos de ropa que te gustaría comprar? ¿Cuánto cuesta cada uno? ¿Cuál es el total?

6. Describe alguna ropa nueva que tienes.

ENRICH YOUR TEACHING

Teacher-to-Teacher

Ask students to bring unwanted clothing items to class. Make fake bills and give each student 20 **pesos** (or other currency). Auction off a few items, then ask a student to be the auctioneer. Start by describing the item.

Es una corbata roja. Cuesta tres pesos. ¿Quién da más? Explain that in this context *¿Quién da más?* means "Who will bid more?" Have the class choose a charity and donate the clothes to it.

▼15 Standards: 1.1

Focus: Using *quedar* to express opinions about how clothing looks and fits

Suggestions: Point out the *Nota.* Students will need this structure when they give their opinion about friends' clothing.

Answers will vary.

Common Errors: While attempting to comprehend a word, students may forget to be attentive to forms. Remind students that if they hear a question using **gustan** or **quedan,** they can often use that form of the verb in their response.

▼16 Standards: 1.1, 1.3

Focus: Using clothing vocabulary in a personalized context

Recycle: Seasons

Suggestions: Pair students and let them edit one another's work.

Answers will vary.

Pre-AP* Support

• **Learning Objective:** Interpersonal Writing

• **Activity 16:** Have students send an e-mail to a friend in a Spanish-speaking country, asking how people dress in that country at home, at school, and on special occasions.

• *Pre-AP* Resource Book:* Comprehensive guide to Pre-AP* writing skill development, pp. 27–36

Additional Resources

• Communication Wbk.: Audio Act. 6, p. 46

• Teacher's Resource Book: Audio Script, p. 166, Communicative Pair Activity BLM, pp. 171–172

• Audio Program DVD: Cap. 7A, Track 9

✓ASSESSMENT

Prueba 7A-2 with Study Plan (online only)

Quiz: Vocabulary Production

• Prueba 7A-2: pp. 177–178

Gramática

Core Instruction

Standards: 4.1

Resources: Voc. and Gram. Transparency 132; Teacher's Resource Book: Video Script, p. 169; Video Program: Cap. 7A

INTERACTIVE WHITEBOARD
Grammar Activities 7A

Suggestions: Direct attention to the *¿Recuerdas?* Use the transparency to introduce the structure and a highlighter to demonstrate stem changes. The *GramActiva* Video can serve as reinforcement of your explanation.

▼17 Standards: 1.3

Resources: Answer Keys: Student Edition, p. 141

Focus: Writing sentences using forms of *querer* and *pensar*

Suggestions: Have students first tell you which verb forms to use for each subject. Be sure they understand that there is more than one option for each answer. Tell them that they may not use the same choices twice.

Answers will vary but will include:
1. quiero / pienso
2. quiere / piensa
3. quiere / piensa
4. quieren / piensan
5. queremos / pensamos

Manos a la obra | ▼ **Objectives**
► Listen to clothing choices and write about shopping plans
► Exchange information while discussing what you and others plan and want to do

Gramática

Stem-changing verbs: *pensar, querer, preferir*

Verbs like *pensar* ("to think," "to plan"), *querer* ("to want"), and *preferir* ("to prefer") are *e→ie* stem-changing verbs. The *-e-* of the stem changes to *-ie-* in all forms except *nosotros* and *vosotros*. Here are the forms:

(yo)	pienso quiero prefiero	(nosotros) (nosotras)	pensamos queremos preferimos
(tú)	piensas quieres prefieres	(vosotros) (vosotras)	pensáis queréis preferís
Ud. (él) (ella)	piensa quiere prefiere	Uds. (ellos) (ellas)	piensan quieren prefieren

¿Recuerdas?
You have used *quiero/quieres* and *prefiero/prefieres* to say what you want or prefer.

- Use the infinitive for any verb that follows pensar, querer, or preferir.

  ¿Piensas comprar esa blusa?
  Do you plan to buy that blouse?

Más ayuda  **realidades.com**

▶ *GramActiva* Video
Tutorial: *Querer*
Animated Verbs

◀)) *Canción de hip hop:* ¿Quieres ir de compras?

🖊 *GramActiva* Activity

▼17 Escribir

Ropa para el fin de semana

Tú y tus amigos piensan comprar ropa para las cosas que quieren hacer este fin de semana. En una hoja de papel, escribe frases para decir qué quieren hacer y qué ropa piensan comprar.

Modelo
Mi amigo Manuel quiere ir a una fiesta y piensa comprar una camisa y unos pantalones.

1. Yo		un partido de béisbol	un traje
2. Mi amigo	querer	la playa	unos pantalones
3. Mi amiga	ir a	las montañas	una camisa
4. Mis amigos		un restaurante elegante	una falda
5. Mis amigos y yo		un baile en la escuela	una camiseta
		la biblioteca	un traje de baño
		¡Respuesta personal!	unas botas
	pensar + comprar		una sudadera
			un vestido
			un suéter
			¡Respuesta personal!

 ciento sesenta y ocho
Tema 7 • De compras

DIFFERENTIATED INSTRUCTION

Heritage Language Learners

Ask students to write six sentences telling what young people usually want, plan, or prefer to do on weekends and after school in their heritage countries. Have them use the *Gramática* chart to guide them in grammar and writing accuracy. Have students read their work aloud.

Advanced Learners/Pre-AP*

Have students invent a dialogue in which they go shopping. They can describe what they plan to buy, what clothes their parents prefer, and what kinds of clothes they prefer to wear. Their shopping partner can provide opinions about fit and cost.

▼**18** | ♻ | ◀)) | **Escuchar • Escribir**

¿Qué piensan llevar?

❶ En una hoja de papel, escribe los números del 1 al 6. Escucha lo que quieren o piensan hacer diferentes personas y escribe las frases.

❷ Escribe otra frase para decir qué piensan llevar las personas para sus actividades.

Modelo
Mis primas quieren ir a un baile el viernes. Piensan llevar una falda y una blusa.

▼**19** **Escribir**

¿Qué prefieren comprar?

Después de dos semanas de trabajo, todos los jóvenes tienen dinero y quieren ir de compras. Escribe frases para decir qué prefieren comprar y cuándo piensan ir de compras.

Modelo
Catalina quiere ir de compras. Prefiere comprar unos pantalones cortos. Piensa ir a la tienda de ropa el sábado.

Catalina/el sábado

1. Isidoro y Lorenzo/esta tarde

2. Julia y yo/mañana

3. Javier/este fin de semana

4. yo/¿?

ciento sesenta y nueve **169**
Capítulo 7A

---

18 Standards: 1.2, 1.3

Resources: Teacher's Resource Book: Audio Script, pp. 166–167; Audio Program DVD: Cap. 7A, Track 10; Answer Keys: Student Edition, p. 141

Focus: Listening comprehension

Recycle: Leisure activities; places

Suggestions: Have students skip a line between each sentence to leave space for Step 2. Remind students that they must conjugate the verb *pensar* for Step 2.

◀)) **Script and Answers:**

1. El sábado mis amigos y yo pensamos ir a la playa.
2. Esta tarde Elena piensa jugar al tenis con su hermano.
3. Juan y Felipe quieren ir a las montañas para esquiar.
4. Carlos y su familia piensan ir a un partido de béisbol.
5. Rosa quiere buscar un trabajo en el centro comercial.
6. Fernando y yo queremos jugar al fútbol esta tarde.

Answers for Step 2 will vary.

Extension: Have students write what they are thinking of wearing to the following locations: *el gimnasio, el parque de diversiones, la escuela, el campo, la playa, una fiesta.*

19 Standards: 1.3

Resources: Answer Keys: Student Edition, p. 142

Focus: Using *pensar, querer,* and *preferir* to express what people would like to buy

Suggestions: Write the model on the board and underline the parts students will need to fill in.

Answers:

1. Isidoro y Lorenzo quieren ir de compras. Prefieren comprar unas gorras. Piensan ir a la tienda de ropa esta tarde.
2. queremos / preferimos ... zapatos / pensamos
3. quiere / prefiere ... un suéter / piensa
4. quiero / prefiero ... / pienso

Extension: Have students use the model to plan a shopping trip for vacation clothes. They should state where they want to go on vacation, what clothing they would like to buy for the trip, and when they think they'll go shopping.

ENRICH YOUR TEACHING

Teacher-to-Teacher
Have students imagine that they are taking a trip to the coast of Mexico for three days. They can take only a very small suitcase (*una maleta*) that is about the size of their backpacks. What do they pack and why?

Teacher-to-Teacher
Have students develop a survey about where classmates like to shop for clothing. They could break their survey down into categories such as: *Prefiero comprar los jeans (las camisetas, los zapátos) en ___.* Have them share the results with the class.

20 Standards: 1.1

Focus: Using *pensar* + **infinitive** in a personalized context

Recycle: Time expressions; leisure activities

Suggestions: Brainstorm with students a list of activities that Student B might mention. Write them on the board for quick reference.

Answers will vary.

21 Standards: 1.1, 1.3

Focus: Exchanging information using *con quién, adónde,* and *qué*

Recycle: Names for places and leisure activities

Suggestions: Draw the chart on the board and fill in the information for three students. Allow students to ask two questions to guess the correct activity in Step 2.

Answers will vary.

Theme Project

Give students copies of the Theme Project outline and rubric from the *Teacher's Resource Book.* Explain the task to them, and have them perform Step 1. (For more information, see p. 154-b.)

Additional Resources

- Communication Wbk.: Audio Act. 7, p. 47
- Teacher's Resource Book: Audio Script, p. 167
- Audio Program DVD: Cap. 7A, Track 12

▼**20** | Talk! 👥 | **Hablar**

¿Qué piensas hacer?

Habla con otro(a) estudiante sobre qué piensas hacer tú y qué piensan hacer otras personas.

▶ **Modelo**

tu amigo(a)/después de las clases

A —*¿Qué piensa hacer tu amigo después de las clases?*

B —*Mi amigo David piensa montar en monopatín.*

Estudiante A

1. tus amigos(as)/mañana
2. tu familia/este fin de semana
3. tus amigos y tú/esta tarde
4. tú / el domingo
5. tu amigo(a)/esta noche

Estudiante B

¡Respuesta personal!

▼**21** | Talk! 👥 | ♻ | **Escribir • Hablar**

¿Adónde quieren ir?

1 Copia la gráfica en una hoja de papel y escribe los nombres de tres personas con quienes vas a salir. ¿Adónde quieren ir Uds. y qué piensan hacer?

¿Con quién?	¿Adónde?	¿Qué?
Pepe	al gimnasio	levantar pesas

Pensamos comprar algo en el mercado.

2 Dile *(Tell)* a otro(a) estudiante adónde quieren ir tú y la otra persona. Tu compañero(a) va a adivinar *(guess)* qué piensan hacer Uds. Puede continuar adivinando hasta *(until)* decir la actividad correcta.

▶ **Modelo**

A —*Pepe y yo queremos ir al gimnasio.*

B —*¿Uds. piensan jugar al básquetbol?*

A —*No, no pensamos jugar al básquetbol.*

B —*¿Uds. piensan levantar pesas?*

A —*Sí, tienes razón. Pensamos levantar pesas.*

DIFFERENTIATED INSTRUCTION

Students with Learning Difficulties

Some students will benefit from further explanation of *Actividad* 21. Demonstrate how the first statement is based on columns 1 and 2. Student B's questions are guesses. Student A's answers are based on column 3.

▼22 | 🗣👥 | Hablar

¿Qué prefieres llevar cuando . . . ?

Invita a un(a) compañero(a) a hacer estas actividades, y habla de la ropa que prefieren llevar.

1. la piscina
2. el parque
3. el gimnasio
4. un partido de fútbol
5. una fiesta
6. un concierto de rock

▶ Modelo

A —¿Quieres ir <u>al cine</u> conmigo?
B —Sí, quiero ir. ¿Qué piensas llevar?
A —Generalmente cuando voy <u>al cine</u> prefiero llevar <u>unos jeans y una camiseta</u>.
B —Bueno, yo pienso llevar <u>una camiseta</u> también, pero pienso llevar <u>pantalones negros</u>.

▼ Pronunciación | 🔊 | 💬

The letter z

In most Spanish-speaking countries, the letter z sounds like the s in see. Listen to and say these words:

zapato	arroz	almuerzo	cabeza
izquierda	haz	razón	nariz
zanahoria	azul	quizás	perezoso

In many parts of Spain, however, the letter z is pronounced something like the th in think. Listen again to the words as a Spaniard says them. Then practice saying the words as if you were in Spain.

Try it out! Listen to "En la puerta del cielo" ("At Heaven's Gate"), a traditional poem from Puerto Rico. Then say the poem aloud.

> En la puerta del cielo,
> venden zapatos
> para los angelitos
> que andan descalzos.

▼23 | 🗣 | Escribir • Hablar

Y tú, ¿qué dices?

1. ¿Qué piensas hacer después de clases hoy? ¿Qué ropa piensas llevar?
2. ¿Qué ropa piensas llevar a clase mañana?
3. ¿Dónde prefieres comprar ropa elegante? ¿Ropa deportiva?
4. ¿Con quién prefieres ir de compras? ¿Por qué?
5. ¿Quieres comprar ropa nueva? ¿Por qué sí o por qué no? ¿Cuándo piensas ir de compras?

Más práctica GO

realidades.com | print

Instant Check	✔	
Guided WB pp. 75–76	✔	✔
Core WB p. 41	✔	✔
Comm. WB p. 50	✔	✔
Hispanohablantes WB pp. 254–257		✔

ciento setenta y uno **171**
Capítulo 7A

▼22 Standards: 1.1

Focus: Inviting someone to go somewhere; discussing appropriate clothing

Suggestions: Before students begin, have them make notes of what clothes they wear for each place or event. Explain that Student B must listen carefully to what Student A plans to wear.

Answers will vary.

Pronunciación
Core Instruction

Standards: 4.1

Resources: Teacher's Resource Book: Audio Script, p.167; Audio Program DVD: Cap. 7A, Track 11

Suggestions: Have students read the words aloud twice to practice pronouncing the **z** both ways. Then say a word and ask students to tell you whether the word is pronounced as it would be in Spain or not. You may have to exaggerate the sound at first.

▼23 Standards: 1.1, 1.3

Focus: Describing plans and preferences
Suggestions: Have students interview one another. Then have them write a short report about what they learned from their partners.

Answers will vary.

ENRICH YOUR TEACHING

Culture Note

Tell students that Spain's most famous department store is **El Corte Inglés.** Have students go online and locate the store's Web site. Ask students to compare and contrast the ads on the Web site with those of department stores in the United States.

21st Century Skills

Initiative and Self-Direction Have students use the many tools available in **realidades.com** to support grammar learning, such as the online text with audio, the *Canción de hip-hop*, and the *GramActiva video*, as well as the online games. Have students track the different tools they use and how effective each is, so they can establish over time what type of learners they are. This will help them in all areas of learning.

✔ASSESSMENT

Prueba 7A-3 with Study Plan (online only)

Quiz: Stem-changing verbs: *pensar, querer,* and *preferir*
• Prueba 7A-3: p. 179

Gramática

Core Instruction

Standards: 4.1

Resources: Voc. and Gram. Transparency 133; Teacher's Resource Book: Video Script, pp. 169–170; Video Program: Cap. 7A

INTERACTIVE WHITEBOARD
Grammar Activities 7A

Suggestions: Discuss usage of *this, that, these,* and *those* in English. Remind students that demonstrative adjectives come before the noun and must have the same gender and number as the nouns that follow them. Use the *GramActiva* Video to reinforce your presentation. Practice the concept by placing similar objects in different parts of the room, pointing to an object, and asking students to bring it to you. (*Quiero esta gorra* or *Quiero esa gorra.*)

▼24 Standards: 1.2, 1.3

Resources: Answer Keys: Student Edition, p. 142

Focus: Reading for comprehension and using demonstrative adjectives in a guided context

Suggestions: Remind students that they will only be using **este(a)** and **estos(as).** They should identify the clothing items in each sentence, then determine if they are masculine or feminine, singular or plural.

Answers:

1. Estas	3. esta	5. esta
2. estos	4. Estos	6. Este

Pre-AP* Support

- **Learning Objective:** Presentational Speaking
- **Activity:** Have students bring in a family photo or an illustration from a magazine or the Internet that shows several people in the foreground and background. Have them describe the scene in front of the class, using demonstrative adjectives.
- *Pre-AP* Resource Book:* Comprehensive guide to Pre-AP* speaking skill development, pp. 39–50

| ▼ Objectives
▶ Point out items of clothing
▶ Read and discuss a clothing ad
▶ Exchange information while discussing prices and planning a fashion show

Gramática

Demonstrative adjectives

You use demonstrative adjectives to point out nouns: ***this*** *cap,* ***these*** *socks,* ***that*** *shirt,* ***those*** *shoes.* Notice that "this" and "these" refer to things that are close to you, while "that" and "those" refer to things that are at some distance from you.

Here are the corresponding demonstrative adjectives in Spanish. Like other adjectives, demonstrative adjectives agree in gender and number with the nouns that follow them.

	"this," "these"	"that," "those"
SINGULAR	este suéter esta falda	ese vestido esa chaqueta
PLURAL	estos suéteres estas faldas	esos vestidos esas chaquetas

> **Strategy**
>
> **Using rhymes to remember meaning**
> To remember the difference between these demonstrative adjectives that are spelled very similarly, memorize this rhyme:
>
> "This" and "these" both have *t's,*
> "That" and "those" don't.

Más ayuda — **realidades.com**

 GramActiva Video
Tutorial: Demonstrative adjectives

 GramActiva Activity

▼24 Leer · Escribir

En la tienda de ropa

Carmen y su amiga están en una tienda y hablan de la ropa que se están probando *(trying on).* Escribe la forma correcta de *este(a)* o *estos(as)* para cada número.

Carmen: __1.__ botas son bonitas, ¿no?

Mariel: Sí, pero creo que __2.__ zapatos son bastante feos.

Carmen: ¿Qué piensas de __3.__ blusa? A mí me gusta mucho.

Mariel: A mí también. __4.__ jeans son demasiado cortos, ¿no?

Carmen: Tienes razón. Y pienso que __5.__ falda es muy corta también.

Mariel: Quizás. __6.__ suéter no cuesta mucho. ¡Qué bueno!

172 **ciento setenta y dos**
Tema 7 • De compras

DIFFERENTIATED INSTRUCTION

Students with Learning Difficulties

Many students will benefit from physical demonstrations of the spatial distinctions between the demonstrative adjectives. Use actual items such as clothing or classroom objects. Stand directly beside students and point with them to nearby and far-away items that are the same, while using the demonstratives. Exaggerated pointing for *ese* will help reinforce the idea. Have pairs of students do the same thing until they begin to grasp the distinction.

▼25 | Hablar

¡Un día con tu hermanito!

Tienes que cuidar *(to take care of)* a tu hermanito. Tus padres tienen toda la ropa para él encima de la cama, pero ¡tu hermanito tiene sus propias ideas!

▶ **Modelo**

A (tú) —*Tienes que llevar esta ropa.*
B (tu hermanito) —*¡No! No quiero llevar esa ropa. Prefiero esta ropa que está en el armario.*

▼26 | Escribir • Hablar

Juego

¿Quién en tu clase sabe mejor cuánto cuestan diferentes cosas?

1 Trabaja con otro(a) estudiante. Escojan un objeto o una foto de un objeto. Puede ser ropa, algo de la casa, algo de la escuela, o de otro lugar. Escriban una descripción de ese objeto y determinen cuánto cuesta.

Modelo

Este suéter azul y amarillo es.... Puedes llevar este suéter a.... Puedes comprar este suéter en.... ¿Cuánto cuesta este suéter? (Cuesta 55 dólares.)

2 Ahora, trabajen con un grupo de cuatro parejas (ocho estudiantes). Lean la descripción de su objeto sin decir cuánto cuesta. La pareja que da el precio más aproximado *(closest)* sin exceder *(without exceeding)* el precio, gana.

Modelo

—*Pensamos que el suéter cuesta 50 dólares.*
—*Daniel y Eva, Uds. ganan. El suéter cuesta 55 dólares.*

ciento setenta y tres **173**
Capítulo 7A

▼**25** Standards: 1.1

Resources: Answer Keys: Student Edition, p. 142
Focus: Using demonstrative adjectives
Suggestions: Dramatize the model. Remind the students what adjectives to use for nearby objects and for those far away.

Answers:

1. **estos pantalones / esos / estos**
2. **esta camiseta / esa / esta**
3. **estos calcetines / esos / estos**
4. **este suéter / ese / este**
5. **estos zapatos / esos / estos**

▼**26** Standards: 1.1, 1.3

Focus: Using demonstrative adjectives and numbers in creative context
Recycle: Numbers; school supplies; furniture
Suggestions: Model the activity for students and have them guess the price of an object. After partners complete their descriptions, break the class into groups for Step 2.

Answers will vary.

ENRICH YOUR TEACHING

Culture Note

For over 130 years, Spain used the *peseta* as its currency. In 2002, the euro replaced the *peseta* as Spain joined eleven other members of the European Union to create a common currency. Euros are similar to dollars in that 100 cents make one euro or one dollar, respectively.

A euro coin or bill has an image from its country of origin on one side but can be spent in any country in the E.U.

Portfolio

Students might include their comparison-shopping report in their portfolios.

173

27 Standards: 1.1

Focus: Practicing buying gifts; using vocabulary in conversation

Suggestions: Be sure that Student A understands that he or she must choose an item that is shown in the clothing ad. Remind Student B to specify the clothing item and its color. Then have students reverse roles.

Answers will vary.

BELLRINGER REVIEW

Have individual students tell classmates the colors of duplicate clothing items in the room. As they point to themselves they say, *"Este suéter es azul."* As they point to a classmate, they say, *"(María), ese suéter es blanco."*

28 Standards: 1.1, 3.1

Resources: Answer Keys: Student Edition, p. 143
Focus: Cross-curricular math activity

Suggestions: Ask volunteers to explain about percentages and calculate one based on the information in the clothing ad for *Actividad* 27. Suggest that students calculate the discount to all items before they begin their conversations.

Answers will vary, but percentages are:
1. falda marrón: 30%
2. blusa morada: 34%
3. sudadera gris: 40%
4. camisa blanca: 32%
5. camiseta azul: 39%
6. suéter rosado: 29%
7. pantalones cortos verdes: 33%
8. gorra roja: 43%

Theme Project

Students can perform Step 2 at this point. Be sure students understand your corrections. (For more information, see p. 154-b.)

Teacher-to-Teacher

Have students create labels and price tags in Spanish for items in the school store. You might have them create a conversion chart for the different currencies used in Spanish-speaking countries.

▼27 | 🗣👥 | Leer • Hablar

¡Muchos regalos!

Muchas personas en tu familia y unos amigos tienen cumpleaños este mes y tienes que comprar regalos. Tú y un(a) compañero(a) miran este anuncio para una tienda de ropa. Habla con tu compañero(a) sobre qué necesitas comprar.

▶ **Modelo**

tu tía o tío
A —*Necesito un regalo para mi tía. Voy a buscar un suéter para ella.*
B —*Buena idea. ¿Te gusta este suéter rosado? Sólo cuesta 32 dólares.*
A —*Sí. Vamos a la tienda a buscar este suéter.*

1. tu hermano o amigo
2. tu hermana o amiga
3. tu abuelo o abuela
4. tu mamá o papá

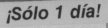

La tienda de ropa Perfección
¡Sólo 1 día!

$35 orig. $50 $25 orig. $38 $18 orig. $30

$19 orig. $28 $11 orig. $18 $32 orig. $45

$16 orig. $24 $8 orig. $14

▼28 | 🗣👥 | Pensar • Hablar

Los descuentos

Conexiones | Las matemáticas

Estás ahora en la tienda de ropa Perfección de la Actividad 27.

① Calcula el porcentaje de descuento de la ropa en el anuncio. La fórmula para calcular el porcentaje de descuento es:

el precio original – el precio nuevo = la diferencia
la diferencia ÷ el precio original = la respuesta
la respuesta x 100 = el porcentaje de descuento

② Habla con otro(a) estudiante de los descuentos que hay en la tienda. Una persona hace el papel *(plays the role)* de cliente, y la otra, un(a) dependiente(a). Pregunta y contesta según el modelo.

▶ **Modelo**
A —*Perdón, señor (señorita). ¿Cuánto cuesta ese suéter rosado?*
B —*Hoy este suéter cuesta sólo 32 dólares. Es un descuento del 29 por ciento.*
A —*¡Genial! Quiero comprar el suéter. ¡Qué buen precio!*

174 ciento setenta y cuatro
Tema 7 • De compras

DIFFERENTIATED INSTRUCTION

Students with Special Needs
Some students will have difficulty calculating percentages. You might have them work with other students who can do this or have them play Student A.

Multiple Intelligences
Logical/Mathematical: Give students a list of four discount percentages. Have them break into pairs. Each student writes an item and its price beside the discount amount. Students then exchange papers and calculate the amount of the discount for each of the four items. Encourage them to calculate with paper and pencil and not with a calculator.

▼29 | 👥 | ♻ | **Escribir · Hablar** _____

Un desfile de modas

Trabaja con un grupo de tres. Una persona de los tres va a ser el/la modelo en un desfile de modas *(fashion show)*. Decidan qué va a llevar el/la modelo. En una hoja de papel, describan tres o más cosas que lleva el/la modelo. Pueden incluir los colores, cuánto cuesta, dónde pueden comprar la ropa y en qué ocasión o estación pueden llevar la ropa.

Su modelo va a participar con los/las otros(as) modelos de la clase en el desfile de modas. Los otros dos leen su descripción de la ropa.

Modelo

El (La) modelo que entra en este momento lleva . . .

> **Para decir más . . .**
> **cómodo(a)** comfortable
> **elegante** elegant
> **de algodón** cotton
> **de lana** wool
> **de seda** silk

▼ Fondo Cultural | Venezuela

Carolina Herrera is one of the world's leading fashion designers. This Venezuelan designer makes clothes, perfume, accessories for women, and cologne for men as well. She is one of many creative Spanish-speaking designers who are making their mark in the fashion world.

• Think of the names of some fashion designers from the United States. In what ways do you think they influence everyday culture?

BOUTIQUE GUADALAJARA

Vestidos y accesorios para toda ocasión

Ropa sport y vaquera; sombreros, botas

Invitaciones y regalos
Libros y revistas
Envío de dinero y tarjetas telefónicas

1819 First Street Sonora, Arizona

El español en la comunidad

Locate a store in your community or on the Internet that sells products from Spanish-speaking countries. Visit the store or Web site and list the types of items you find there. Are they similar to the items listed in the ad? Bring your list to class and compare it with other students' lists. What are the most common types of items found in these stores?

Más práctica	GO

	realidades.com	print
Instant Check	✔	
Guided WB pp. 77–78	✔	✔
Core WB pp. 42–43	✔	✔
Comm. WB pp. 47–48, 51, 156	✔	✔
Hispanohablantes **WB** pp. 258–261		✔

ciento setenta y cinco **175**
Capítulo 7A

ENRICH YOUR TEACHING

Culture Note
One of the best-known names in fashion design is Oscar de la Renta. He was born in 1932 in Santo Domingo, the capital city of the Dominican Republic. He moved to United States and formed his own business in 1965. He is one of the top Spanish-speaking fashion designers, in the world.

21st Century Skills

Communication Have students who are having difficulty with the concept of demonstrative adjectives work with the *GramActiva* video, the tutorials, and the auto-scored online practice. Then have each student bring five small objects or pictures to class and work with a group to place the objects in different places, ask questions about them, and identify them, using the demonstrative adjectives.

---

29 Standards: 1.1, 1.3

Focus: Writing and speaking in a contextualized situation

Recycle: Events and places

Suggestions: Bring in outrageous clothes. Direct students to the *Para decir más....* If possible, record the fashion shows.

Fondo cultural

Standards: 3.1, 2.1

Suggestions: Ask how many students have heard of Carolina Herrera and Oscar de la Renta (see *Culture Note* below). If students are not familiar with the names, show magazine photos of celebrities wearing outfits by these designers.

Answers will vary but may include that fashion designers influence everyday culture by suggesting through TV and magazine ads what people should be wearing. Because they continually change what is "in" and "out," they affect how people spend their money on clothing.

▼ El español en la comunidad

Core Instruction
Standards: 1.2, 5.1

Resources: Voc. and Gram. Transparency 135
Suggestions: Help students come up with ideas for finding stores in your area or online. Allow time for students to present their findings.

Additional Resources
• Communication Wbk.: Audio Act. 8–9, pp. 47–48
• Teacher's Resource Book: Audio Script, pp. 167–168, Communicative Pair Activity BLM, pp. 173–174
• Audio Program DVD: Cap. 7A, Tracks 13–14

✔ASSESSMENT

Prueba 7A-4 with Study Plan (online only)

Quiz: Demonstrative Adjectives
• Prueba 7A-4: p. 180

Lectura

Core Instruction

Standards: 1.1, 1.2, 2.1, 2.2, 3.1

Resources: Map Transparency 13

🌐 **Mapa global interactivo, Actividad 2**
Visit Panama's Islas de San Blas and the Canal.

Focus: Reading for comprehension and cultural perspectives

Suggestions:

Pre-reading: Read the information in the *Strategy* with students. Have them read the title and connect it with the photos and their prediction of what the reading is about. Ask them to focus their reading on discovering if their prediction was correct or not. Remind them that they need not understand all the details to do this.

Reading: Have student volunteers read sections of the article aloud. Stop after major sections and have students discuss what they have read. Students should try to get the main idea from the context and cognates. When they come across words they do not know, encourage them to look at surrounding words.

Post-reading: Have students review their predictions and see how accurate they were. Have them identify five words they think they have learned by using context clues.

BELLRINGER REVIEW

Have students refer to pp. xvi–xvii and have them mention each country, its capital and the color of its flag.

Pre-AP* Support

- **Learning Objective:** Interpretive: Print
- **Activity:** Have students follow along as you read the selection aloud. Then assign pairs of students one of the three specific sections. For their section, ask that each pair first write, in their own words, a brief summary of the main points. Then they should be ready to share decoding strategies for any unfamiliar vocabulary. Finally, they should create two multiple-choice questions. Have each pair share their summary. Collect and compile the questions into a longer activity for later use.
- **Pre-AP* Resource Book:** Comprehensive guide to Pre-AP* reading skill development, pp. 19–26

¡Adelante!

▼ Objectives
- ▶ Read about traditional clothing in Panama
- ▶ Use maps and photos to predict content
- ▶ Compare and contrast *carnaval* celebrations to those in your community

Lectura 🌐

Tradiciones de la ropa panameña

Una tradición panameña de mucho orgullo[1] es llevar el vestido típico de las mujeres, "la pollera". Hay dos tipos de pollera, la pollera montuna[2] y la pollera de gala, que se lleva en los festivales. La pollera de gala se hace a mano y cuesta muchísimo por la cantidad de joyas[3] que adornan el vestido. ¿Cuánto cuesta una pollera de gala? Puede costar unos 1.850 dólares americanos, y requiere aproximadamente siete meses de trabajo. La pollera es tan importante que en la ciudad de Las Tablas celebran el Día Nacional de La Pollera el 22 de julio.

Si quieres celebrar con los panameños, puedes visitar la ciudad de Las Tablas en la provincia de Los Santos. Las Tablas es famosa por ser el mejor lugar para celebrar los carnavales. Durante el carnaval y en otros festivales, puedes admirar los vestidos y los bailes tradicionales.

El canal de Panamá conecta el océano Pacífico con el mar Caribe y el océano Atlántico.

El istmo de Panamá es la conexión entre dos continentes, y tiene costas sobre el océano Pacífico y el mar Caribe. Es famoso por el canal en el que navegan barcos[4] de todo el mundo. El folklore panameño es muy variado. La música, los bailes y los vestidos son importantes en la vida[5] social, especialmente en las provincias del centro del país.

176   [1]pride   [2]from the mountains   [3]jewels   [4]ships   [5]life

---

DIFFERENTIATED INSTRUCTION

Heritage Language Learners
Have students write a paragraph about a tradition from their heritage country and whether they continue celebrating it here. Have them read their paragraphs in small groups and talk about why they think they will or will not continue the tradition.

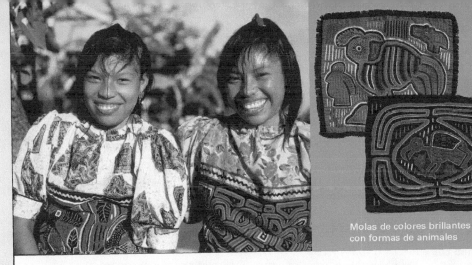

Molas de colores brillantes con formas de animales

Otro tipo de ropa auténtica de Panamá viene de los indios Kuna, un grupo de indígenas que viven en las islas de San Blas. Las mujeres llevan una blusa hecha[6] de molas. Las molas son paneles decorativos que forman la parte de adelante y de atrás de las blusas. Las mujeres demuestran[7] su talento y expresión personal con los diseños[8] originales de las molas. Los diseños representan formas humanas y animales. Hoy día, puedes ver y admirar molas como objetos de arte en muchos museos y colecciones.

[6]made [7]demonstrate [8]designs

▼ Fondo Cultural | El mundo hispano

Carnaval is a traditional celebration in many Latin American countries. It takes place in the weeks before the season of Lent. *Carnaval* normally includes the coronation of a beauty queen, parades, elaborate costumes, street music, and dancing. The *Carnaval* in Las Tablas, a town near the Pacific coast in Panama, is very popular and attracts thousands of visitors every year.

• What traditional parades or celebrations take place in your community? How do they compare to the celebration of *Carnaval*?

Unos niños panameños tocan música durante el Carnaval.

¿Comprendes?

1. ¿Por qué es importante el canal de Panamá en el comercio global?

2. ¿Cuáles son las dos formas de ropa auténtica de Panamá en el artículo?

3. ¿Qué puedes celebrar si visitas Las Tablas?

4. ¿Cuánto puede costar una pollera de gala? En tu opinión, ¿es mucho o poco dinero?

5. ¿Cómo se llama el grupo de indígenas que viven en las islas de San Blas?

6. ¿Quiénes llevan las molas, los hombres o las mujeres?

7. ¿Por qué es diferente cada mola?

Más práctica	GO
	realidades.com | print
Guided WB p. 79	✔ ✔
Comm. WB pp. 52, 157	✔ ✔
Hispanohablantes WB pp. 262–263	✔
Cultural Reading Activity	✔

ciento setenta y siete **177**
Capítulo 7A

¿Comprendes? Standards: 1.2, 1.3

Resources: Answer Keys: Student Edition, p. 143

Focus: Demonstrating reading comprehension

Suggestions: Ask students to review the questions before reading.

Answers:
1. Porque conecta el océano Pacífico con el mar Caribe y el océano Atlántico.
2. La pollera y la mola.
3. Los carnavales y el Día Nacional de la Pollera.
4. Puede costar unos 1.850 dólares. Answers will vary.
5. Se llaman los indios Kuna.
6. Las mujeres.
7. Porque son originales.

Fondo cultural

Standards: 2.1, 4.2

Suggestions: Ask students if they have ever heard of or participated in the Mardi Gras ("Fat Tuesday" in French) celebration in New Orleans. Explain that *Carnaval* is a celebration that ends on the Tuesday before the Christian observance of Lent, which begins on Ash Wednesday and continues throughout 40 days of solemn preparation for Easter.

Answers will vary.

Teaching with Photos

Have students carefully examine the photos on pp. 176–177. Ask if certain colors are used more than others and if these are light or dark colors. Ask about the subjects of the *molas,* e.g., designs, animals, etc. Then ask how these traditional clothes are different from everyday dress in both students' heritage countries and the United States.

Theme Project

Students can perform Step 3 at this point. (For more information, see p. 154-b.)

For Further Reading

Student Resource: Realidades para hispanohablantes: Lectura 2, pp. 264–265

ENRICH YOUR TEACHING

Culture Note

Few human endeavors have changed the face of the planet as did the completion of the Panama Canal in 1914. The Canal became a vital link for the entire world. Where others had failed, the United States overcame numerous difficulties to build one of the great engineering marvels of the world.

21st Century Skills

Initiative and Self-Direction Remind students of the tools available for extra reading support in **realidades.com.** Computer-corrected activities use different strategies to help students comprehend the new vocabulary, monitor their learning needs, and progress at their own pace through the reading.

177

La cultura en vivo

Core Instruction

Standards: 2.2, 4.2

Resources: Teacher's Resource Book: GramActiva BLM, p. 176

Focus: Reading about *molas* and learning the process of creating one

Suggestions: Before class, gather the supplies, making sure you have two pencils for each project and a lot of brightly colored construction paper. Direct students' attention to the photo. Ask the class to describe the clothing. Have them notice and comment on the colors and designs. Ask them if they have any idea of the process used and how long they think it takes. Then explain that making a *mola* can take up to 100 hours.

Have students work in pairs or as individuals. Walk around and monitor the steps you think might be troublesome, such as cutting out all spaces not between the double lines and creating borders of different colors. Show an example of a contrasting background.

Ask students to show their work to the class. Direct attention to the *Think about it!* section and have students discuss the questions.

Answers will vary.

Pre-AP* Support

- **Learning Objective:** Presentational Speaking (Cultural Comparisons)
- **Background:** This task prepares students for the Spoken Presentational Communication tasks that focus on cultural comparisons in the exam.
- **Activity:** Have students prepare a two-minute (maximum) presentation in English (or Spanish, if possible) on how clothing can showcase the beliefs and values of a culture. Think of how *molas* reflect the Kuna Indians' culture. Compare this with an example of how clothing represents the values of your own culture.
- *Pre-AP* Resource Book:* Comprehensive guide to Pre-AP* speaking skill development, pp. 39–50

Additional Resources

Student Resource: Realidades para hispanohablantes, p. 266

¡Adelante!

La cultura en vivo

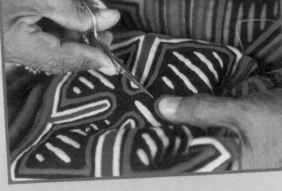

Las molas

Molas are the bright fabric artwork created by the Kuna Indians of the San Blas Islands, a group of islands off the Panama coast in the Caribbean Sea. *Mola* is a Kuna word meaning "blouse." This art form was originally used to make clothing, but today the term *mola* refers to any piece of fabric made using this method.

Kuna women cut out a cloth pattern and sew it onto layers of cloth that have been sewn together. Pieces of the upper layers are cut away to expose the underlying colors and create a design. Later, the women embroider details. Many designs on *molas* represent nature or animals. Each *mola* may take many weeks to complete.

Try it out! Here's how you can make *molas* out of paper.

Figure 1

Materials:

- 2 pencils
- rubber bands
- construction paper
- paste or glue
- scissors

Figure 2

Directions:

1 Your teacher will provide a pattern to trace on a piece of construction paper. You may prefer to trace around a cookie cutter or draw a simple design found in nature (for example, a leaf, flower, or fir tree). *(Fig. 1)*

2 Double all the lines by drawing with two pencils fastened together with rubber bands. *(Fig. 2)*

Figure 3

3 Cut out all spaces that do NOT fall between the double lines. *(Fig. 3)*

4 Paste the cutout figure onto construction paper of a contrasting color.

5 Cut around the pasted figure, leaving a border of the second color. *(Fig. 4)*

6 Paste this cutout figure onto another piece of construction paper and cut around it, leaving a border of the new color. Paste the entire piece on a contrasting background.

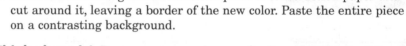

Figure 4

Think about it! Do you or anyone in your family practice a traditional handicraft? Do you have any clothes or outfits that you have made or customized to express your interests or personality?

DIFFERENTIATED INSTRUCTION

Students with Special Needs

You may need to provide construction paper already traced or cut out to accommodate some students.

Students with Learning Difficulties

If students have difficulty following these directions, provide models of each stage of production so that students can see what their own version should look like. Create your own **mola** along with students, circulating it so they can see how you are doing it.

Presentación oral 📢👥

¿En qué puedo servirle?

Objectives
▸ Demonstrate how to buy and sell clothing in a store
▸ Use feedback from your partner to improve your performance

Task
You and a partner will play the roles of a customer and a sales clerk in a clothing store. You will ask and answer questions about the articles of clothing sold in the store. The customer will then decide whether or not to buy the articles.

1 Prepare Work with a partner to prepare the skit. One of you will play the role of the salesperson, and the other will be the shopper. Be prepared to play both roles. Decide the type of clothing the store will sell and bring to class real articles of clothing or pictures from a magazine. Give the store a name.

Cliente: Make a list of expressions and questions you can use to ask about, describe, and say whether you will buy an article of clothing.

Dependiente(a): Make a list of expressions and questions you can use to help your client, answer his or her questions, and show him or her the clothing.

2 Practice Work with your partner and practice both roles. You might want to review *A primera vista,* the *Videohistoria,* and Actividad 14 for ideas. You can use your written notes when you practice, but not during the actual role-play.

3 Present Your teacher will assign the roles. The clerk will begin the conversation. Keep talking until the customer has made a decision to buy or not to buy the article of clothing.

4 Evaluation The following rubric will be used to grade your presentation.

Strategy

Seeking feedback
As you practice with a partner, seek his or her feedback to correct errors you have made and to improve your overall performance.

Rubric	Score 1	Score 3	Score 5
How well you sustain a conversation	You provide no conversational response or follow-up to what your partner says.	You provide frequent responses or follow-up to what your partner says.	You always respond to your partner, listen and ask follow-up questions, or volunteer additional information.
Completeness of presentation	You only describe the clothing.	You describe the clothing and price.	You describe the clothing, price, and the decision to purchase.
Use of new and previously learned vocabulary	You use very limited and repetitive vocabulary.	You use only recently acquired vocabulary.	You use recently acquired and previously learned vocabulary.

Presentación oral

Core Instruction

Standards: 1.3

Focus: Practicing buying or selling clothing in a personalized context

Suggestions: Review the task and steps with students. After reading the *Strategy,* model how to give specific advice instead of only positive or negative comments. Review the rubric with the class to explain how you will grade the performance task.

Pre-AP* Support

- **Learning Objective:** Presentational Speaking
- **Activity:** Remind students to focus on the presentational speaking skills used in this task such as fluency, pronunciation, and comprehensibility.
- **Pre-AP* Resource Book:** Comprehensive guide to Pre-AP* speaking skill development, pp. 39–50

Portfolio

Make video or audio recordings of student presentations in class, or assign the RealTalk activity so they can record their presentations online. Include the recording in their portfolios.

Additional Resources

Student Resource: Realidades para hispanohablantes, p. 267; Guided Practice: Presentación oral, p. 80

ENRICH YOUR TEACHING

Teacher-to-Teacher

As each pair presents, take notes of the positive aspects of their presentation. Note aspects such as vocabulary use, grammar, pronunciation, and intonation. Set up a brief meeting time to discuss your feedback. Aside from helping students to become more confident about speaking, this can help them to know their strengths and to concentrate on aspects that need work.

21st Century Skills

Creativity and Innovation Have students brainstorm ideas for expanding their basic skits to make them more varied or creative. Have students consider changing the location to a shoe store, using pretend money, and adding traits to their characters in the skit, such as an indecisive customer, or an impatient salesperson.

✓ASSESSMENT

Presentación oral
- Assessment Program: Rubrics, p. T32
  Go over the descriptions of the different levels of performance. After assessing students, help individuals understand how their performance could be improved.

7A Video

Videomisterio ▶

Core Instruction

Standards: 1.2, 1.3, 5.1

Resources: Teacher's Resource Book: Video Script, p. 170; Video Program: Cap. 7A; Video Program Teacher's Guide: Cap. 7A

Focus: Introducing the events and vocabulary of this episode; scanning and reading the episode summary

Personajes importantes:

Lola Lago, detective
Carmela, Lola's best friend
Rosalinda, Carmela's friend who works at San Carlos Hospital

Synopsis: Lola and Carmela meet at the San Carlos hospital, where they ask Rosalinda for help in getting information about María Requena, who spent three months in the hospital as a result of a car accident. Mysteriously, the medical record cannot be found. They inquire about María's friend, Julia, who was also in the accident. Julia died in the hospital, but her file cannot be found, either.

Suggestions:

Pre-viewing: Review with students the events of the previous episode. Doña Gracia was getting better at the hospital, although she did not remember anything about the incident that put her there. Then Lola met her best friend, Carmela, at a café. Lola explained the events that led to doña Gracia being in the San Carlos hospital. Carmela's friend, Rosalinda, works at the hospital so Carmela and Lola met the next morning in the hospital to ask Rosalinda for information. Later, Lola met Pedro as he inquired about his grandmother in the hospital. Lola offered her services as a detective and gave him her card.

Point out the *Palabras para comprender* to the class, saying examples in context and writing the sentences on the board. Remind students that these words are only used to help them understand the episode, and are not vocabulary words.

Visual scanning: Direct students' attention to the picture on p. 180 and ask who this character is (Rosalinda), what relationship she has to Lola (a friend of Carmela, Lola's

¿Eres tú, María?
Episodio 5

Antes de ver el video

Personajes importantes

Resumen del episodio

Lola y Carmela van al hospital para hablar con Rosalinda sobre doña Gracia y María. Aprenden más sobre el accidente de coche de María. Ocurrió entre María y otra joven, Julia. Las dos fueron llevadas[1] al Hospital San Carlos. Desafortunadamente,[2] Julia murió. Rosalinda va a los archivos para buscar los historiales clínicos de Julia y María. Pero hay un problema.

[1] were brought   [2] unfortunately

Rosalinda, una amiga de Carmela, trabaja en el hospital San Carlos

Palabras para comprender

Estuvo aquí . . .	She was here . . .
¿Te acuerdas de ella?	Do you remember her?
Sí, me acuerdo de María.	Yes, I remember María.
Dos coches chocaron . . .	Two cars crashed . . .
la carretera	highway
murió	died
Las ayudó a las dos.	He helped the two of them.
No viene a trabajar.	He hasn't been coming to work.
el archivo	records
los historiales clínicos	medical records
los visitantes	visitors

180 ciento ochenta
Tema 7 • De compras

DIFFERENTIATED INSTRUCTION

Advanced Learners

As a special project, have advanced learners collect all of the expressions from the past episodes, or from the book, that are used in Spain. Do this in conjunction with the Heritage Language Learners suggestion.

Heritage Language Learners

Have students who are not from Spain use the list compiled by Advanced Learners and suggest equivalent colloquialisms in their heritage countries. Using a world map, create a bulletin board of idiomatic expressions listed next to the countries that use them.

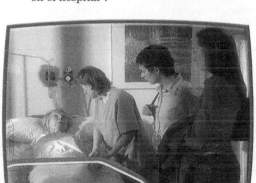

"Primero, quiero hablar de una paciente que se llama María Requena. Estuvo aquí, en el hospital".

"Pues, no está su historial clínico. Ni un papel. Nada, absolutamente nada sobre María Requena".

"¿Eres tú, María?"

Después de ver el video

¿Comprendes?

Lee las frases. Decide a quién(es) describe cada frase: Lola, Rosalinda, Carmela, doña Gracia, Julia, María o Luis Antonio.

1. Dos coches y dos chicas. Fue muy triste.
2. Ella murió en el accidente.
3. Hay un enfermero que ayudó a las dos.
4. Es muy simpática tu amiga.
5. No hay nada sobre ellas en los archivos.
6. Está bastante mal.
7. Las amigas de Carmela son amigas mías.

> **Nota gramatical** Rosalinda uses two *vosotros* commands when she is talking with Carmela and Lola: *esperad* ("wait") and *venid* ("come"). You will hear this verb form often when you go to Spain.

Más práctica GO

realidades.com | print

Actividades ✔

ciento ochenta y uno 181
Capítulo 7A

ENRICH YOUR TEACHING

Culture Note

Most hospitals in Spain are state-run. Doctors take a national examination at the end of their studies to be selected as certified professionals to work in the national health system. Students may comment on the breach of privacy that the hospital worker, Rosalinda, is committing by looking for a patient's private records (Julia / María). You may want to discuss this in class, and to debate whether a detective's search for the records justifies this sort of breach. Do students know what is required in the United States to open private medical records?

Review Activities

To talk about shopping: Have students ask each other questions that incorporate these terms and useful expressions. For example, Student A might ask: *¿Qué dice el dependiente de la tienda?* Student B responds, *¿En qué puedo servirle?*

To talk about clothing: Have Student A draw a stick figure. Student B will name a piece of clothing. Student A draws the item on the stick figure. When the figure is dressed, have students reverse roles.

To talk about prices: Have Student A point to items and ask *¿Cuánto cuesta(n)?* Student B answers with a price, which Student A writes down. Student B then checks the spelling and says *Sí, tienes razón* or *No, no tienes razón.*

To indicate specific items: Bring to class objects such as different colored pens and pencils. Go to students' desks and put the objects in different proximity to them. Ask questions using demonstrative adjectives. For example, *¿Te gusta este lápiz o ese lápiz?*

Portfolio

Invite students to review the activities they completed in this chapter, including written reports, posters or other visuals, recordings of oral presentations, or other projects. Have them select one or two items that they feel best demonstrate their achievements in Spanish to include in their portfolios. Have them include this with the Chapter Checklist and Self-Assessment Worksheet.

Additional Resources

Student Resources: Realidades para hispanohablantes, p. 268

Teacher Resources:
- Teacher's Resource Book: Situation Cards, p. 175, Clip Art, pp. 177–179
- Assessment Program: Chapter Checklist and Self-Assessment Worksheet, pp. T56–T57

Repaso del capítulo

Vocabulario y gramática

▼ **Objectives**
▶ Review the vocabulary and grammar
▶ Demonstrate you can perform the tasks on p. 183

to talk about shopping

buscar	to look for
comprar	to buy
el dependiente, la dependienta	salesperson
¿En qué puedo servirle?	How can I help you?
entrar	to enter
la tienda	store
la tienda de ropa	clothing store

to talk about clothing

el abrigo	coat
la blusa	blouse
las botas	boots
los calcetines	socks
la camisa	shirt
la camiseta	T-shirt
la chaqueta	jacket
la falda	skirt
la gorra	cap
los jeans	jeans
los pantalones	pants
los pantalones cortos	shorts
la sudadera	sweatshirt
el suéter	sweater
el traje	suit
el traje de baño	swimsuit
el vestido	dress
los zapatos	shoes
¿Cómo me/te queda(n)?	How does it (do they) fit (me/you)?
Me/Te queda(n) bien/mal.	It fits (They fit) me/you well/poorly.
llevar	to wear
nuevo, -a	new

other useful words

quizás	maybe
Perdón.	Excuse me.
¡Vamos!	Let's go!

to talk about prices

¿Cuánto cuesta(n)...?	How much does (do)...cost?
costar (o → ue)	to cost
el precio	price
tanto	so much
doscientos, -as	two hundred
trescientos, -as	three hundred
cuatrocientos, -as	four hundred
quinientos, -as	five hundred
seiscientos, -as	six hundred
setecientos, -as	seven hundred
ochocientos, -as	eight hundred
novecientos, -as	nine hundred
mil	a thousand

to indicate if someone is correct

tener razón	to be correct

to indicate specific items

los/las dos	both
este, esta	this
estos, estas	these
ese, esa	that
esos, esas	those

pensar *to think, to plan*

pienso	pensamos
piensas	pensáis
piensa	piensan

preferir *to prefer*

prefiero	preferimos
prefieres	preferís
prefiere	prefieren

querer *to want*

quiero	queremos
quieres	queréis
quiere	quieren

For *Vocabulario adicional,* see pp. 336–337.

 182 ciento ochenta y dos
Tema 7 • De compras

DIFFERENTIATED INSTRUCTION

Students with Learning Difficulties

Have students review the *Repaso del capítulo* and create flashcards for any words that they do not know. Pair them with a student who is more confident with the vocabulary to practice. Before the test, provide students with a practice test, so they can become comfortable with the format.

Heritage Language Learners

Have students write a few paragraphs telling about their perfect birthday celebration: Where are they going to have it? Whom are they going to invite? What food are they going to eat? What kind of music are they going to play? Encourage them to use as many vocabulary words from this chapter as they can.

Más repaso (GO) realidades.com | print

Instant Check	✔	
Puzzles	✔	
Core WB pp. 44–45	✔	✔
Comm. WB pp. 158, 159–161	✔	✔

Preparación para el examen

On the exam you will be asked to . . .	Here are practice tasks similar to those you will find on the exam . . .	For review go to your print or digital textbook . . .
1 Escuchar Listen and understand why people are returning clothing items	Listen as people explain to the clerk in a department store why they are returning or exchanging clothing they received as gifts. Try to decide if the reason is: a) it doesn't fit well; b) it's the wrong color or style; c) it's too expensive; d) they just didn't like it.	pp. 156–161 *Vocabulario en contexto* **p. 163** Actividad 8 **p. 165** Actividad 12 **p. 167** Actividad 15 **p. 172** Actividad 24
2 Hablar Describe what you are planning to buy with gift certificates from your favorite clothing store	You got gift certificates from your favorite clothing store for your birthday. Describe at least four items you would like to buy. You could say something like: *Me gustaría comprar un suéter rojo. Prefiero esos suéteres que me quedan grandes.*	pp. 156–161 *Vocabulario en contexto* **p. 164** Actividad 10 **p. 166** Actividad 14 **p. 169** Actividades 18–19 **p. 174** Actividad 27 **p. 179** *Presentación oral*
3 Leer Read and understand an online order form for a popular department store	You want to apply for a job at a department store. They need someone who understands Spanish to interpret the online orders that come in. Read the entries to see if you can tell them: a) the description of the item ordered; b) the color; c) the price.	pp. 156–161 *Vocabulario en contexto* **p. 165** Actividad 12 **p. 174** Actividad 27

Artículo	Color	Precio
sudadera	rojo/azul	355 pesos
abrigo	negro	801 pesos
falda	blanco/marrón/verde	506 pesos

4 Escribir Fill in an order form for specific clothing items you might purchase as gifts	Order the following items using the online order form: a) black boots for your sister, who is very little; b) a blue-and-white baseball cap for your brother, who would need a small size; c) three pairs of gray socks for your dad, who has VERY big feet!	pp. 156–161 *Vocabulario en contexto* **p. 162** Actividades 6–7 **p. 164** Actividad 11 **p. 167** Actividad 16 **p. 169** Actividad 19

Descripción del artículo	Color	Tamaño

5 Pensar Demonstrate an understanding of cultural perspectives and clothing	Give an example of American folk art that is handed down from generation to generation. How is it similar to or different from the *molas* made by the Kuna Indians?	pp. 176–177 *Lectura* **p. 178** *La cultura en vivo*

ciento ochenta y tres **183**
Capítulo 7A

Performance Tasks

Standards: 1.1, 1.2, 1.3, 2.2, 4.2

Student Resource: Realidades para hispanohablantes, p. 269

Teacher Resources: Teacher's Resource Book: Audio Script, p. 168; Audio Program DVD: Cap. 7A, Track 16; Answer Keys: Student Edition, p. 144

1. Escuchar
Suggestions: Use the audio or read the script.

Script:
Salesclerk: Buenas tardes, señora.
Señora: Buenas tardes, señor. Esta falda no me queda bien. Yo soy baja, y la falda es demasiado larga.
Salesclerk: No hay problema, señora. Un momento. *[pause]* Aquí hay otra más corta.
Answer: a) It doesn't fit well.

2. Hablar
Suggestions: Remind students to use adjectives to describe items and to make adjectives and nouns agree.
Answers will vary.

3. Leer
Suggestions: Students may need to review colors.
Answers: A. sweatshirt; red and blue; 355 pesos
B. overcoat; black; 801 pesos
C. skirt; white, brown, and green; 506 pesos

4. Escribir
Suggestions: Have students try this activity without consulting the vocabulary list.
Answers:

a. unas botas	negro	pequeño
b. una gorra	azul y blanco	pequeño
c. tres calcetines	gris	grande

5. Pensar
Suggestions: Have students refer to the appropriate parts of the chapter. Reflect with them on the question.

DIFFERENTIATED ASSESSMENT

CORE ASSESSMENT
- **Assessment Program:** Examen del capítulo 7A, pp. 181–187
- **Audio Program DVD:** Cap. 7A, Track 17
- **ExamView:** Chapter Test, Test Banks A and B

ADVANCED/PRE-AP*
- **ExamView: Pre-AP* Test Bank**
- **Pre-AP* Resource Book,** pp. 86–89

STUDENTS NEEDING EXTRA HELP
- **Alternate Assessment Program:** Examen del capítulo 7A
- **Audio Program DVD:** Cap. 7A, Track 17

HERITAGE LEARNERS
- **Assessment Program: Realidades para hispanohablantes:** Examen del capítulo 7A
- **ExamView: Heritage Learner Test Bank**

AT A GLANCE

Objectives

- Listen to and read descriptions of gifts and gift stores
- Talk and write about items you've bought and their prices
- Exchange information while comparing gifts and prices
- Compare cultural perspectives about shopping malls in Chile and the United States
- Explain the role of markets and specialty stores in Spanish-speaking countries
- Compare the significance of gifts in Mexican festivals and in holidays in the United States

Vocabulary

- Stores and online shopping
- Gifts and clothing accessories
- Expressions to describe past events

Grammar

- The preterite of *-ar* verbs
- The preterite of verbs ending in *-car* and *-gar*
- Direct object pronouns

Culture

- *ñandutí,* p. 185
- Shopping habits in Spanish-speaking countries, p. 192
- *Museo del Oro* in Bogotá, p. 198
- Song, *"El coquí",* p. 199
- Zapotecs, p. 205
- Guelaguetza festival, p. 205
- *El Rastro,* p. 206
- *artesanías,* p. 209
- Chilean and United States consumer practices, p. 210

Recycle ♻

- Prepositions of location
- Information given in verb endings
- *-ar* verbs
- Verbs that end in *-car* and *-gar*
- *tener*
- Family members

RESOURCES

	FOR THE STUDENT	ONLINE	DVD	PRINT	FOR THE TEACHER	ONLINE	PREEXP	DVD	PRINT
Plan					Interactive TE and Resources DVD	•		•	
					Teacher's Resource Book, pp. 198–230	•		•	•
					Pre-AP* Resource Book, pp. 86–89	•		•	•
					Mapa global interactivo	•			
					Lesson Plans	•			
Introducción PP. **184–185**									
Present	Student Edition, pp. 184–185	•	•	•	Interactive TE and Resources DVD	•		•	
	DK Reference Atlas	•	•		Teacher's Resource Book, pp. 198–201	•		•	•
	Videocultura	•	•		Galería de fotos			•	
	Hispanohablantes WB, pp. 270–271			•	Map Transparencies, 12–18, 20	•	•	•	
Vocabulario en contexto PP. **186–191**									
Present & Practice	Student Edition, pp. 186–191	•	•	•	Interactive TE and Resources DVD	•		•	
	Audio	•	•		Teacher's Resource Book, pp. 200–202, 205, 214–215	•		•	•
	Videohistoria	•	•		Vocabulary Clip Art	•	•	•	•
	Flashcards	•	•		Audio Program	•	•	•	
	Instant Check	•			Video Program: Videohistoria	•		•	
	Guided WB, pp. 81–88	•	•	•	Video Program Teacher's Guide: Cap. 7B	•		•	
	Core WB, pp. 46–49	•	•	•	Vocabulary and Grammar Transparencies, 136–139	•	•	•	
	Comm. WB, pp. 53–56, 59	•	•	•	Answer Keys: Student Edition, pp. 145–147	•	•		
	Hispanohablantes WB, pp. 272–273			•	TPR Stories, pp. 92–106	•		•	
Assess and Remediate					Prueba 7B–1: Assessment Program, pp. 188–189	•		•	•
					Assessment Program para hispanohablantes, pp. 188–189	•		•	

RESOURCES

	FOR THE STUDENT	ONLINE	DVD	PRINT	FOR THE TEACHER	ONLINE	PREEXP	DVD	PRINT
Vocabulario en uso PP. **192–195**									
Present & Practice	Student Edition, pp. 192–195	•	•	•	Interactive Whiteboard Vocabulary Activities	•		•	
	Instant Check	•			Interactive TE and Resources DVD	•		•	
	Comm. WB, p. 56	•	•	•	Teacher's Resource Book, pp. 201–202, 208–209	•		•	•
	Hispanohablantes WB, pp. 274–275, 277			•	Communicative Pair Activities, pp. 208–209	•		•	•
	Communicative Pair Activities	•			Audio Program	•	•	•	
					Videomodelos	•		•	
					Vocabulary and Grammar Transparencies, 137, 142	•	•	•	
					Answer Keys: Student Edition, pp. 148–149	•	•	•	•
Assess and Remediate					Prueba 7B–2 with Study Plan	•			
					Prueba 7B–2: Assessment Program, pp. 190–191	•		•	•
					Assessment Program para hispanohablantes, pp. 190–191	•		•	•
Gramática PP. **196–207**									
Present & Practice	Student Edition, pp. 196–207	•	•	•	Interactive Whiteboard Grammar Activities	•		•	
	Instant Check	•			Interactive TE and Resources DVD	•		•	
	Animated Verbs	•			Teacher's Resource Book, pp. 202–206, 210–211, 213	•		•	•
	Tutorial Video: Grammar	•			Communicative Pair Activities, pp. 210–211	•		•	•
	Canción de hip hop	•			Audio Program	•	•	•	
	Guided WB, pp. 89–92	•	•	•	Videomodelos	•		•	
	Core WB, pp. 50–52	•	•	•	Video Program: GramActiva	•		•	
	Comm. WB, pp. 57–58, 60–61, 162	•	•	•	Vocabulary and Grammar Transparencies, 140–141	•	•	•	
	Hispanohablantes WB, pp. 276–281			•	Map Transparencies, 12–14, 20	•	•	•	
	Communicative Pair Activities	•			Answer Keys: Student Edition, pp. 149–153	•	•	•	
Assess and Remediate					Pruebas 7B–3 to 7B–5 with Study Plans	•			
					Pruebas 7B–3 to 7B–5: Assessment Program, pp. 192–194	•		•	•
					Assessment Program para hispanohablantes, pp. 192–194	•		•	•
¡Adelante! PP. **208–213**									
Application	Student Edition, pp. 208–213	•	•	•	Interactive TE and Resources DVD	•		•	
	Online Cultural Reading	•			Teacher's Resource Book, pp. 162–163	•		•	•
	Guided WB, pp. 93–94	•	•	•	Video Program: Videomisterio ¿Eres tú, María?	•		•	
	Comm. WB, pp. 62, 163	•	•	•	Video Program Teacher's Guide: Cap. 7B	•		•	
	Hispanohablantes WB, pp. 282–287			•	Videomisterio Quiz		•		
	¿Eres tú, María? Video WB, pp. 41–49	•	•	•	Answer Keys: Student Edition, p. 154	•	•	•	
Repaso del capítulo PP. **214–215**									
Review	Student Edition, pp. 214–215	•	•	•	Interactive TE and Resources DVD	•		•	
	Online Puzzles and Games	•			Teacher's Resource Book, pp. 204, 212, 214–215	•		•	•
	Core WB, pp. 53–54	•	•	•	Audio Program	•	•	•	
	Comm. WB, pp. 164–167	•	•	•	Answer Keys: Student Edition, p. 155	•	•	•	
	Hispanohablantes WB, pp. 288–289	•							
	Instant Check	•							
Chapter Assessment									
Assess					Examen del capítulo 7B	•		•	•
					Assessment Program, pp. 195–200	•		•	•
					Alternate Assessment Program, pp. 84–88	•		•	•
					Assessment Program para hispanohablantes, pp. 195–200	•		•	•
					Audio Program, Cap. 7B, Examen	•		•	
					ExamView: Test Banks A and B questions only online	•		•	
					Heritage Learner Test Bank	•		•	
					Pre-AP* Test Bank	•			

REGULAR SCHEDULE (50 MINUTES)

DAY	Warm-up / Assess	Preview / Present / Practice / Communicate	Wrap-up / Homework Options
1	Return Examen del capítulo (10 min.)	Vocabulario en contexto (35 min.) • Objectives • Presentation • *Actividades* 1, 2 • Arte y cultura • Videocultura: *Los mercados*	Wrap-up and Homework Options (5 min.) • Core Practice • Vocabulary Clip Art
2	Warm-up (5 min.) • Homework check	Vocabulario en contexto (40 min.) • Review: *Vocabulario en contexto* • Presentation: *Videohistoria Un regalo especial* • View: Video *Un regalo especial* • Video Activities • *Actividades* 3, 4, 5	Wrap-up and Homework Options (5 min.) • *Prueba* 7B-1: Vocabulary recognition • Core Practice
3	Warm-up (5 min.) • Homework check ✔Formative Assessment (10 min.) • *Prueba* 7B-1: Vocabulary recognition	Vocabulario en uso (30 min.) • Objectives • Interactive Whiteboard Vocabulary Activities • *Actividades* 6, 9	Wrap-up and Homework Options (5 min.) • *Actividad* 7
4	Warm-up (5 min.) • Homework check • Return *Prueba* 7B-1: Vocabulary recognition	Vocabulario en uso (40 min.) • *Actividades* 8, 10, 11 • *Exploración del lenguaje* • Communicative Pair Activities	Wrap-up and Homework Options (5 min.) • *Actividad* 12
5	Warm-up (5 min.) • Homework check	Gramática y vocabulario en uso (40 min.) • Presentation: The preterite of *-ar* verbs • *GramActiva* Video • Interactive Whiteboard Grammar Activities • *Actividades* 13, 14, 16 • *Juego: Actividad* 15	Wrap-up and Homework Options (5 min.) • Core Practice
6	Warm-up (5 min.) • Homework check	Gramática y vocabulario en uso (40 min.) • Presentation: The preterite of verbs ending in *-car* and *-gar* • *GramActiva* Video • Interactive Whiteboard Grammar Activities • *Juego: Actividad* 18 • *Fondo cultural* • Communicative Pair Activities	Wrap-up and Homework Options (5 min.) • *Actividad* 17
7	Warm-up (5 min.) • Homework check	Gramática y vocabulario en uso (40 min.) • Review: The preterite of *-ar*, *-car*, and *-gar* verbs • *Conexiones: Actividad* 19 • *Actividad* 20 • *Pronunciación*	Wrap-up and Homework Options (5 min.) • Core Practice • *Pruebas* 7B-3, 7B-4 with Study Plans: The preterite of *-ar*, *-car*, and *-gar* verbs
8	Warm-up (5 min.) • Homework check ✔Formative Assessment (10 min.) • *Pruebas* 7B-3, 7B-4 with Study Plans: The preterite of *-ar*, *-car*, and *-gar* verbs	Gramática y vocabulario en uso (30 min.) • Presentation: Direct object pronouns • *GramActiva* Video • Interactive Whiteboard Grammar Activities • *Actividades* 21, 23	Wrap-up and Homework Options (5 min.) • *Actividad* 22 • *Prueba* 7B-2 with Study Plan: Vocabulary production

REGULAR SCHEDULE (50 MINUTES)

DAY	Warm-up / Assess	Preview / Present / Practice / Communicate	Wrap-up / Homework Options
9	**Warm-up (5 min.)** • Homework check • Return *Pruebas* 7B-3, 7B-4 with Study Plans: The preterite of *-ar, -car,* and *-gar* verbs ✔**Formative Assessment (10 min.)** • *Prueba* 7B-2 with Study Plan: Vocabulary production	**Gramática y vocabulario en uso (30 min.)** • Review: Direct object pronouns • *Actividades* 24, 25, 26, 27 • *Fondo cultural*	**Wrap-up and Homework Options (5 min.)** • *Actividad* 29 • *Prueba* 7B-5, with Study Plan: Direct object pronouns
10	**Warm-up (5 min.)** • Homework check • Return *Prueba* 7B-2 with Study Plan: Vocabulary production ✔**Formative Assessment (10 min.)** • *Prueba* 7B-5 with Study Plan: Direct object pronouns	**Gramática y vocabulario en uso (30 min.)** • *Juego: Actividad* 28 • *El español en el mundo del trabajo* • *Actividades* 30, 31 • *Fondo cultural*	**Wrap-up and Homework Options (5 min.)** • Core Practice
11	**Warm-up (5 min.)** • Homework check • Return *Prueba* 7B-5, with Study Plan: Direct object pronouns	**¡Adelante! (40 min.)** • *Presentación escrita:* Prewrite • *Lectura* • *Fondo cultural*	**Wrap-up and Homework Options (5 min.)**
12	**Warm-up (5 min.)** • Homework check	**¡Adelante! (40 min.)** • *Presentación escrita:* Draft, revise • *Perspectivas del mundo hispano*	**Wrap-up and Homework Options (5 min.)** • *Presentación escrita:* Publish
13	**Warm-up (5 min.)** • Homework check	**¡Adelante! (40 min.)** • *Presentación escrita:* Present	**Wrap-up and Homework Options (5 min.)** • Writing Activities • Core Practice Organizer
14	**Warm-up (5 min.)** • Homework check • Core Practice Organizer	**¡Adelante! (20 min.)** • *Videomisterio* **Repaso (20 min.)** • *Vocabulario y gramática* • *Preparación para el examen*	**Wrap-up and Homework Options (5 min.)** • Instant Check • *Examen del capítulo*
15	**Warm-up (5 min.)** • Answer questions ✔**Summative Assessment (45 min.)** • *Examen del capítulo*		

Standards for *Capítulo* 7B

• To achieve the goals of the Standards, students will:

Communication
1.1 *Interpersonal*
• Talk about shopping and gifts
• Talk about stores and malls
• Talk about leisure activities, work, and chores
• Talk about historical events and dates
• Talk about things using direct object pronouns
• Talk about U.S. Hispanic commercial centers

1.2 *Interpretive*
• Read and listen to information about stores and malls
• Read and listen to information about shopping and gifts
• Read a picture-based story
• Listen to and watch a video about shopping and gifts
• Read a jewelry store advertisement
• Listen to information about work and chores
• Read about historical events and dates
• Read about Hispanic commercial centers in the U.S.
• View a video mystery series

1.3 *Presentational*
• Present information about shopping and gifts
• Present information about historical events and dates
• Present information about stores and malls
• Present information about activities, work, and chores

Culture
2.1 *Practices and Perspectives*
• Understand contrast of specialty shops and malls
• Learn about the Zapotec Guelaguetza festival
• Understand using tutear to invite informal address

2.2 *Products and Perspectives*
• Learn about *ñandutí* weavings of Paraguay
• Learn about **El Museo del Oro**
• Learn about Madrid's flea market, **El Rastro**
• Learn about **las artesanías** of Spanish-speaking countries
• Learn that the euro is the currency of Spain

Connections
3.1 *Cross-curricular*
• Read about Hispanic communities and commercial centers in United States cities
• Learn about historical events and dates

Comparisons
4.1 *Language*
• Learn vocabulary through the recognition of cognates
• Learn about nouns that end in *-ería*
• Understand forming the preterite tense of *-ar* verbs
• Learn the preterite of verbs ending in *-car* and *-gar*
• Learn the pronunciation of **gue, gui, que,** and **qui**
• Learn about direct object pronouns

4.2 *Culture*
• Compare selections of shopping destinations
• Compare museums and artifacts
• Compare local flea markets to **El Rastro**
• Compare gift-giving festivals
• Compare attitudes about shopping mall experiences

Communities
5.1 *Beyond the School*
• Learn of opportunities for Spanish-speaking international buyers

5.2 *Lifelong Learner*
• View a video mystery series

184

Capítulo
7B ¡Qué regalo!

▼ Chapter Objectives

Communication
By the end of this chapter you will be able to:
• Listen to and read descriptions of gifts and gift stores
• Talk and write about items you've bought and their prices
• Exchange information while comparing gifts and prices

Culture
You will also be able to:
• Compare cultural perspectives about shopping malls in Chile and the United States
• Explain the role of markets and specialty stores in Spanish-speaking countries
• Compare the significance of gifts in Mexican festivals and in holidays in the United States

You will demonstrate what you know and can do:
• Presentación escrita, p. 211
• Preparación para el examen, p. 215

You will use:

Vocabulary
• Stores and online shopping
• Gifts and clothing accessories
• Expressions to describe past events

Grammar
• The preterite of *-ar* verbs
• The preterite of verbs ending in *-car* and *-gar*
• Direct object pronouns

Exploración del mundo hispano

Country Connection
Shopping for Gifts

California — Texas — Nueva York — España
Florida
Cuba
México
El Salvador — República Dominicana
Panamá — Puerto Rico
Colombia
Paraguay
Chile — Argentina

realidades.com (GO)

📖 **Reference Atlas**
▶ **Videocultura y actividad**
🌎 **Mapa global interactivo**

El centro comercial Galerías Pacífico, Buenos Aires, Argentina

---

ENRICH YOUR TEACHING

Using Backward Design
Have students preview the sample performance tasks on Preparación para el examen, p. 215, and connect them to the Chapter Objectives. Explain to students that by completing the sample tasks they can self-assess their learning progress.

Mapa global interactivo
Download the *Mapa global interactivo* files for Chapter 7B and preview the activities. Activity 1 takes you to San Luis Potosí, Mexico. In Activity 2, you look at several of the states in Mexico. In Activity 3, explore El Rastro in Madrid, Spain. In Activity 4, visit shopping areas in New York, Miami, Los Angeles, and San Antonio.

Tema 7 • De compras

Arte y cultura | Paraguay

Ñandutí, which means "spider web" in the Guaraní language, refers to the fine lace weavings from the South American country of Paraguay. Wall hangings and table linens are just a few of the intricately woven and multicolored items made from this fabric. *Ñandutí* looms are routinely found outside the doorways of houses in Itauguá, a small town where much of the country's *ñandutí* is made.

• Handmade items are usually more expensive than mass-produced ones. Why do you think some people are willing to pay more for these items?

Mantel (*Tablecloth*) de ñandutí, Itauguá, Paraguay ▶

ciento ochenta y cinco 185
Capítulo 7B

Chapter Opener
Core Instruction

Resources: Map Transparencies 12–18, 20

Suggestions: Brainstorm a list of things that teenagers buy when they go shopping. Prompt students to include accessories and gift items. The video in this chapter is about a teenage boy who needs help shopping for a birthday present. The *GramActiva* Videos will help students learn the preterite of *-ar* verbs, verbs ending in *-car* and *-gar*, and direct object pronouns.

▶ **Videocultura** View *Los mercados* online with the class to learn more about shopping in Spanish-speaking countries.

Arte y cultura

Standards: 2.1

Suggestions: Discuss the tradition of making crafts and clothing by hand. Point out that many such crafts are taught within a community and passed on from one generation to the next. Ask if there are any types of crafts or artwork that are typical of their community or region or of particular ethnic groups who live there.

Answers will vary but may include the following: People are more willing to buy handmade items at a higher price because they are one-of-a-kind. They may also be of higher quality and reflect traditional craftsmanship.

Teaching with Photos

How does *Galerías Pacífico* compare to shopping centers you have visited? Take a few minutes to make a list of similarities and differences. What attracts you in the photo? What don't you like about this shopping center?

DIFFERENTIATED INSTRUCTION

Digital resources such as the *Interactive Whiteboard* activity banks, *Videomodelos*, additional *Online Activities*, *Study Plans*, automatically graded *Leveled Workbook*, animated *Grammar Tutorials*, *Flashcards*, and *Vocabulary and Grammar Videos* will help you reach students of different ability levels and learning styles.

STUDENTS NEEDING EXTRA HELP

Guided Practice Activities
• Flashcards, pp. 81–84
• Vocabulary Check, pp. 85–88
• Grammar Support, pp. 89–92

HERITAGE LEARNERS

Realidades para hispanohablantes
• Chapter Opener, pp. 270–271
• A primera vista, p. 272
• Videohistoria, p. 273
• Manos a la obra, pp. 274–281
• ¡Adelante!, pp. 282–287
• Repaso del capítulo, pp. 288–289

ADVANCED/PRE-AP*

Pre-AP* Resource Book,
• pp. 86–89

Communications Workbook
• Integrated Performance Assessment, p. 164

Vocabulario en contexto

Core Instruction

Standards: 1.2

Resources: Teacher's Resource Book: Input Script, p. 200, Clip Art, pp. 214–215, Audio Script, p. 201; Voc. and Gram. Transparencies 136–137; TPR Stories Book, pp. 92–106; Audio Program DVD: Cap. 7B, Tracks 1–2

Focus: Learning new vocabulary about stores and shopping for gifts and accessories

Suggestions: Use the *TPR Stories Book* to present the new vocabulary and grammar, or use the Input Script from the *Teacher's Resource Book*. Present the vocabulary in three parts: specialty stores, gifts and accessories, and talking about buying things. You might bring in some of the gift items and dramatize the two dialogues using the props. Use gestures and a calendar to help convey *hace una semana* and *pagué*.

Extension: Make logical and illogical statements about items you are going to buy and the stores where you will buy them. Have students give a "thumbs-up" sign for logical statements (*Voy a comprar un collar en la joyería.*) and a "thumbs-down" sign for illogical ones (*Voy a compar unos zapatos en la tienda de electrodomésticos.*). Use the transparencies to confirm the responses.

BELLRINGER REVIEW

Have students complete this sentence (from the board) to suggest a good gift choice for one member of their family or a friend.

Un regalo bueno para _____ es un/una _____.

Share with the class.

A primera vista | 🔊 | 📖

Vocabulario en contexto

▼ Objectives
Read, listen to, and understand information about
▶ stores
▶ shopping for gifts and accessories
▶ things done in the past

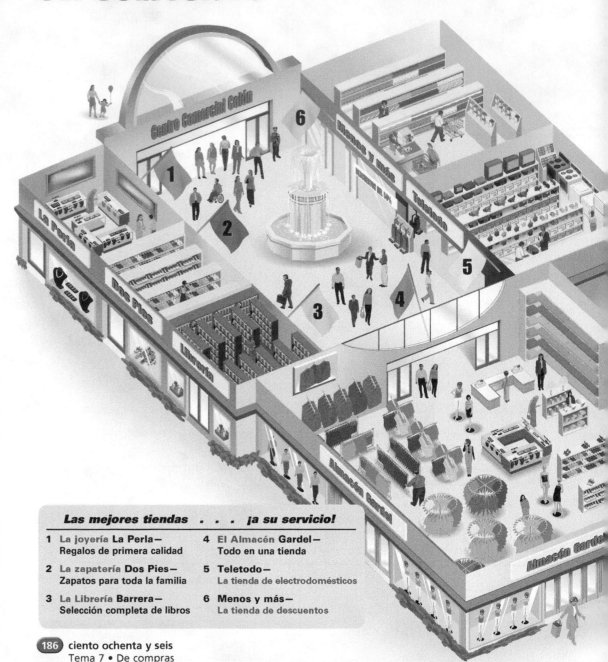

Las mejores tiendas . . . ¡a su servicio!

1 La joyería **La Perla**— Regalos de primera calidad

2 La zapatería **Dos Pies**— Zapatos para toda la familia

3 La Librería **Barrera**— Selección completa de libros

4 El Almacén **Gardel**— Todo en una tienda

5 **Teletodo**— La tienda de electrodomésticos

6 **Menos y más**— La tienda de descuentos

186 ciento ochenta y seis
Tema 7 • De compras

DIFFERENTIATED INSTRUCTION

Heritage Language Learners

Have students write a paragraph in which they describe their ideal birthday gift. They should include details such as who bought it, what it looks like, and what they plan to do with it. Allow students to turn in a rough draft first, and determine if they want to include the paragraph in their portfolio.

Students with Learning Difficulties

Provide students with a copy of the *centro comercial* illustration on this page and have them write store labels directly on it. Ask them to keep it in their notebooks for future reference.

Language Input 7B

—¡Mira! Todo cuesta menos aquí. ¡Qué **barato**!

—¡No puede ser! Yo **compré** esta cartera en el Almacén Gardel **hace una semana** y **pagué** mucho más. ¡Uf!

la cartera

el bolso

MENOS Y MÁS

los anteojos de sol

el llavero

los guantes

el perfume

la corbata

la cadena

el reloj pulsera

Joyería La Perla

el collar

la pulsera

los aretes

el anillo

—Mi **novio** necesita un reloj pulsera.

—¿Por qué no **lo** compras? Cuesta 30 dólares. No es muy **caro.**

—¡Buena idea! Vamos a entrar.

▾1 | 🔊 | Escuchar

¿Qué vas a hacer?

Estás de compras con tu hermana en un centro comercial. Tu hermana te está diciendo todo lo que quiere hacer, o lo que necesita, en el centro comercial. Para cada cosa que dice, señala dónde en el centro comercial tiene que ir.

▾2 | 🔊 | Escuchar

¿Dónde lo llevas?

Escucha cada una de estas frases. Señala la parte del cuerpo en la que una persona lleva cada artículo que se menciona.

Más práctica	GO
realidades.com | print	

Instant Check	✓	
Guided WB pp. 81–84	✓	✓
Core WB pp. 46–47	✓	✓
Comm. WB p. 59	✓	✓
Hispanohablantes WB p. 272		✓

ciento ochenta y siete **187**
Capítulo 7B

---

1 Standards: 1.2

Resources: Teacher's Resource Book: Audio Script, p. 201; Audio Program DVD: Cap. 7B, Track 3; Answer Keys: Student Edition, p. 145

Focus: Listening comprehension of specialty shop vocabulary

Suggestions: Play the audio or read the script aloud. Brainstorm items sold in each store pictured.

🔊 Script and Answers:

1. Primero, necesito comprar unos aretes. *(Joyería La Perla)*
2. Quiero comprar un televisor nuevo. *(Teletodo)*
3. Necesito comprar ropa, unos zapatos y cosas para la casa y quiero ir a sólo una tienda. *(Almacén Gardel)*
4. Busco un libro para mamá. *(Librería Barrera)*
5. Necesito unas botas para el invierno. *(Zapatería Dos Pies)*
6. Quiero comprar algo muy barato para Miguelito. *(Menos y más)*
7. Tengo que comprar un vestido nuevo. *(Almacén Gardel)*
8. ¿Dónde puedo comprar unos anteojos de sol muy baratos? *(Menos y más)*

---

2 Standards: 1.2

Resources: Teacher's Resource Book: Audio Script, p. 201; Audio Program DVD: Cap. 7B, Track 4; Answer Keys: Student Edition, p. 146

Focus: Listening to identify on what part of the body one wears accessories

Suggestions: Make sure students understand the task. Say one of the gifts; have students repeat it and point to the part of the body where it is worn. Play the audio or read the script aloud.

🔊 Script and Answers:

1. ¡Qué bonito es este anillo! *(finger)*
2. Mira estos aretes que compré anoche. *(ears)*
3. ¿Qué piensas de la corbata azul? *(neck)*
4. Ese reloj pulsera es demasiado caro. *(wrist)*
5. Vamos a mirar los anteojos de sol en esa tienda. *(eyes)*
6. ¡Sólo pagué 15 dólares por estos guantes! *(hands)*
7. Un collar es un regalo perfecto. *(neck)*
8. Mira la pulsera que compré hace una semana. *(wrist)*

ENRICH YOUR TEACHING

Culture Note

One of the largest shopping centers in Spain is *Diagonal Mar* in Barcelona. Built within sight of the Mediterranean for the 1992 Olympic Games, it contains 220 shops and houses a 20-screen movie theater. Because the parking lot is so large, complimentary golf carts are available for shoppers to drive to their cars.

21st Century Skills

Information Literacy Have students locate Web sites for department stores in both the United States and in some Spanish-speaking countries. After they review the sites, have them comment on similarities and differences between the samples in terms of presentation, format, or content. Are similar strategies used to present the information? What may account for this?

187

7B Language Input

Videohistoria 🔊

Core Instruction

Standards: 1.2

Resources: Voc. and Gram. Transparencies 138–139; Audio Program DVD: Cap. 7B, Track 5; Answer Keys: Student Edition, p. 146

Focus: Learning contextualized vocabulary and grammar; previewing the video

Suggestions:

Pre-reading: Direct attention to the *Antes de leer.* Using the transparencies, go panel by panel, asking students to predict what happens at each point in Manolo's and Claudia's shopping trip. Direct attention to panel 6 on p. 190. Do students see that there are two identical bags, and that Claudia is not picking up the one closest to her? Point out the preterite of the verbs in the story and use these to preteach the structure.

Answers:

Strategy: disbelief
1. Answers will vary.
2. Books; gloves; ties; videogames; software; jewelry; Manolo's aunt would probably like books, gloves, or jewelry.

Un regalo especial

¿Qué pasó cuando Manolo compró un regalo para su tía? Lee la historia.

México
la tía de Manolo
Claudia
Manolo

Antes de leer

Strategy **Using visuals** Look at each picture before you read the text below it to help you understand the story.

- Look at photo 3. Can you guess what Claudia's reaction is to Manolo's suggestion to give his aunt computer software for her birthday?

1. Think about gifts that you've bought. Were they for friends or family? Of the people you know, for whom is it most difficult to buy gifts?

2. Skim the *Videohistoria* and make a list of the items that could be given as gifts. To whom would you give them? Which of those items would make a good gift for Manolo's aunt?

188 **ciento ochenta y ocho**
Tema 7 • De compras

DIFFERENTIATED INSTRUCTION

Heritage Language Learners

Have students write a sequel to the *Videohistoria*, featuring the dog. Have them think about how receiving the beautiful "collar" affects the dog's life. Encourage humor and creativity. For example, students might suggest that the collar has magic powers or belonged to someone famous who is looking for it.

Language Input 7B

Manolo: Necesito comprar un regalo para mi tía. Mañana es su cumpleaños.

Claudia: ¿Qué compraste el año pasado?

Manolo: Compré un libro. Quizás otro libro.

Claudia: ¡Qué aburrido! Vamos al centro comercial . . .

Manolo: Aquí venden guantes, corbatas . . .

Claudia: ¿Corbatas para tu tía? ¿No tienes otra idea? Mira, aquí hay otras cosas . . .

Manolo: ¡Ah! Tengo una idea. **Anoche** compré un videojuego **en la Red** con mi computadora. ¿Quizás podemos comprar **software?**

Claudia: Para un amigo, sí, pero para tu tía, ¡no!

Claudia: Yo prefiero la joyería: una pulsera, un collar, un anillo. A ver. Señorita, ¿cuánto cuesta ese collar?

Dependienta: Cuesta 200 pesos con el descuento.

Claudia: ¡Qué barato! **La semana pasada** yo **pagué** 300 pesos **por** un collar.

ciento ochenta y nueve 189
Capítulo 7B

Reading: Read the captions or play the audio. Using the transparencies and nonverbal clues, help students understand the new words.

Post-reading: Complete *Actividades* 3–5 to check comprehension.

Pre-AP* Support

- **Learning Objective:** Interpersonal Speaking
- **Activity:** Have students create a short conversation based on Scene 4 in this video. One student will assume the role of the client. The other student will be the vendor. In the new scene, the client needs to buy something other than *el collar*.
- **Pre-AP* Resource Book:** Comprehensive guide to Pre-AP* vocabulary skill development, pp. 51–57

ENRICH YOUR TEACHING

Culture Note

In Latin America, certain gifts are considered inappropriate. Knives and scissors are rarely given, because they indicate severing of a relationship. Avoid yellow flowers in Mexico (used for **el Día de los Muertos**). Handkerchiefs are associated with weeping and sorrow. Black and purple wrapping paper are usually not used because the colors are associated with Holy Week.

189

Video ▶️

Core Instruction

Standards: 1.2

Resources: Teacher's Resource Book: Video Script, p. 205; Video Program: Cap. 7B; Video Program Teacher's Guide: Cap. 7B

Focus: Comprehending a story about buying a gift

Suggestions:

Pre-viewing: Ask students if they have ever received someone else's gift by mistake. If so, what happened? Explain that as they watch the video there will be references to the past, so they will need to pay close attention to the sequence of events.

Viewing: Remind students that they will not understand every word, but they should listen and watch for overall meaning. Play the video once without pausing, then again, stopping to check comprehension. Show it a third time without pausing. See the *Teacher's Resource Book* for additional ideas.

Post-viewing: Complete the Video Activities in the *Communication Workbook*.

3 Standards: 1.2

Resources: Answer Keys: Student Edition, p. 147

Focus: Reading comprehension

Suggestions: Have students identify the objects before they begin the activity.

Answers:

1. mala idea
2. buena idea
3. mala idea
4. buena idea
5. mala idea
6. mala idea

5

Claudia y Manolo están esperando el autobús. Tienen el regalo para la tía. A su derecha hay otra chica con un perro y otro regalo también.

6

Manolo: ¡Vamos, Claudia! Aquí viene el autobús.

Claudia: Bueno . . . bueno.

7

Manolo: ¡Feliz cumpleaños, tía! Te compré este regalo **ayer.**

Tía: ¿Para mí? Ah, es muy bonito, pero . . . sabes que no tenemos un perro.

Manolo: ¡No entiendo . . . !

8

Perro: ¡Me gusta mucho este collar nuevo! Me queda bien, ¿no crees?

DIFFERENTIATED INSTRUCTION

Multiple Intelligences

Visual/Spatial: Have students work independently or in small groups to draw their ideal mall. It should include their favorite stores, as well as any desirable extras (indoor ice-skating rinks, movie theaters, etc.). Have them label the specialty shops and window displays in Spanish.

Advanced Learners

Have students change the story by replacing the dog collar with another item and describing Manolo's aunt's reaction.

▼3 Leer · Pensar

¿Buena o mala idea?

Mira estos dibujos. Escribe los números del 1 al 6 en una hoja de papel. Para cada dibujo, escribe *buena idea* si según Claudia es un buen regalo para la tía de Manolo, o *mala idea* si no es un buen regalo.

1.

2.

3.

4.

5.

6.

▼4 Escribir

¿Qué compraron?

¿Qué compraron estas personas de la *Videohistoria?* Usa las palabras de la lista para completar sus frases. Escribe las frases completas en una hoja de papel.

Manolo: Yo compré ___, ___ y ___.

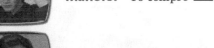

Claudia: Yo compré ___.

La chica: Yo compré ___.

> un libro
> un collar por 300 pesos
> un collar por 200 pesos
> un collar para un perro
> un videojuego

▼5 Escribir · Hablar

¿Comprendes?

1. ¿Por qué van de compras Manolo y Claudia?
2. ¿Qué compró Manolo para su tía el año pasado?
3. ¿Qué piensa Claudia de comprar otro libro?
4. ¿Qué regalo compran y cuánto pagan?
5. ¿A la tía le gusta el collar? ¿Por qué?
6. Al final *(At the end),* ¿quién tiene el mejor collar?

Más práctica	GO	
**realidades.com	print**		
Instant Check	✔	
Guided WB pp. 85–88	✔	✔
Core WB pp. 48–49	✔	✔
Comm. WB pp. 53–55, 56	✔	✔
Hispanohablantes WB p. 273	✔	

4 Standards: 1.2, 1.3

Resources: Answer Keys: Student Edition, p. 147

Focus: Reading comprehension

Suggestions: Point out that students will need to distinguish between two of the *collares* based on their prices.

Answers:

Manolo: un libro; un collar por 200 pesos; un videojuego
Claudia: un collar por 300 pesos
La chica: un collar para un perro

Extension: Have students use the sentences as models to tell what they bought recently.

5 Standards: 1.2, 1.3

Resources: Answer Keys: Student Edition, p. 147

Focus: Reading for understanding

Suggestions: Have students identify the panel in which they found the answer.

Answers:

1. **Porque Manolo necesita comprar un regalo para su tía.**
2. **un libro**
3. **Es muy aburrido.**
4. **un collar; 200 pesos**
5. **Sí, le gusta, pero dice que no tienen un perro.**
6. **el perro**

Additional Resources

- Communication Wbk.: Audio Act. 5, p. 56
- Teacher's Resource Book: Audio Script, p. 202
- Audio Program DVD: Cap. 7B, Track 7

ENRICH YOUR TEACHING

Culture Note

Although bargaining once was common in the United States, it is used less today. But it is still common in Latin America. In a marketplace, you can ask for **una rebaja** if you want the vendor to lower the price. However, in a mall, you are expected to pay the set price, just as in the United States.

21st Century Skills

Technology Literacy Encourage students to use the various digital tools available at **realidades.com,** like the eBook with embedded audio and the flashcards, to learn this vocabulary. Then have them conduct Internet searches on shopping sites from Spanish-speaking countries, using the new vocabulary.

✔**ASSESSMENT**

Quiz: Vocabulary Recognition
- Prueba 7B-1: pp. 188–189

191

6 Standards: 1.1, 1.3

Resources: Teacher's Resource Book: Audio Script, p. 201; Audio Program DVD: Cap. 7B, Track 6; Answer Keys: Student Edition, p. 148

Focus: Listening comprehension

Suggestions: For Step 2, have students draw on personal experience and think about the things they have seen when shopping in these types of stores.

Script and Answers:

Step 1:
1. La ropa es más barata en una tienda de descuentos.
2. Prefiero un almacén porque venden muchas cosas diferentes.
3. Después de las clases voy a la librería con una amiga.
4. Me encanta mirar las cosas bonitas en una joyería.
5. Prefiero ir a una tienda de electrodomésticos.
6. Siempre puedo buscar algo en una zapatería.
Step 2 answers will vary.

7 Standards: 1.1, 1.3

Focus: Writing about specialty shops

Recycle: Clothing; electronics

Suggestions: Tell students to keep their sentences to use in *Actividad* 8.

Answers will vary but may include:
1. libros, revistas
2. ropa, joyas, discos compactos, etc.
3. aspiradoras, equipos de sonido, lectores DVD, televisores
4. cadenas, collares, relojes pulseras, pulseras, anillos, aretes
5. ropa, joyas, perfumes, corbatas, guantes, etc.
6. zapatos, botas, calcetines, bolsos

Fondo cultural

Standards: 2.1, 4.2

Suggestions: Ask what kinds of stores students like. Discuss the differences between shopping in a specialty store and a mall. Do students know of any family-owned stores in their community?

Answers will vary.

Mapa global interactivo, Actividad 1
Visit a specialty store in San Luis Potosí, Mexico.

192

▼ Objectives
▶ Listen to comments about stores and talk about where you shop
▶ Write about and discuss stores, gifts, and shopping trips
▶ Read and analyze an ad for a jewelry store
▶ Exchange information about shopping malls and gifts

Vocabulario en uso

▼6 | 🔊 | Escuchar · Escribir

Escucha y escribe

1 Vas a escuchar lo que unos jóvenes dicen de algunas tiendas. En una hoja de papel, escribe los números del 1 al 6. Escribe lo que escuchas.

2 Escribe frases para describir lo que crees que van a comprar los jóvenes en cada tienda.

Modelo
Creo que él (ella) va a comprar . . .

▼7 | ♻ | Escribir

En tu comunidad

Para cada tienda de la lista, piensa en una que está en tu comunidad. Escribe una frase para describir dos o más cosas que venden allí y explica dónde está la tienda.

Modelo
una tienda de ropa
En la tienda de ropa Ávila venden pantalones, camisas y corbatas. Está en el centro comercial Mill Valley.

1. una librería
2. una tienda de descuentos
3. una tienda de electrodomésticos
4. una joyería
5. un almacén
6. una zapatería

192 ciento noventa y dos
Tema 7 • De compras

Fondo Cultural | El mundo hispano

Centros comerciales and *grandes almacenes* are popular in Spanish-speaking countries, but many people still shop in traditional specialty stores. These stores are often owned and operated by families, and customer loyalty is built over generations.

● Why do you think small specialty stores continue to survive when large, one-stop superstores and malls are very popular? Where do you prefer to shop? Why?

¿Qué venden en esta sombrería de Barcelona, España?

DIFFERENTIATED INSTRUCTION

Heritage Language Learners
Ask students to write a commercial for a specialty shop owned by a family member or friend. They should name the store and the products they sell and tell why people should shop there. If possible, have students record their commercials.

Students with Learning Difficulties
For *Actividad* 7, give students a list of local retailers and have them think of two items sold in each shop. Have them match these shops to the categories listed.

8 | 👥 | ♻ | Hablar

¿Sabes dónde ir para comprar . . . ?

Trabaja con otro(a) estudiante. Lee lo que escribiste en la Actividad 7, sin decir qué tipo de tienda es. Tu compañero(a) tiene que identificar qué tienda es.

▶ **Modelo**

A —*Es una tienda que vende pantalones, camisas y corbatas. Está en el centro comercial Mill Valley.*

B —*Es una tienda de ropa. ¿Es la tienda Ávila?*

A —*Sí. Es la tienda de ropa Ávila.*

8 Standards: 1.1
Focus: Talking about where to shop for different merchandise
Recycle: Clothing; electronics
Suggestions: Remind students to refer to their sentences for *Actividad* 7.
Answers will vary.

9 | 👥 | ♻ | Dibujar · Escribir · Hablar

¿Dónde está el almacén La Galería?

Habla con otro(a) estudiante sobre dónde están las tiendas en un centro comercial.

1 Haz un dibujo de un centro comercial. Incluye *(include)* estos lugares en tu dibujo y, para cada uno, inventa un nombre.

> una zapatería
> un almacén
> un restaurante
> una librería
> una tienda de descuentos
> una tienda de regalos
> una tienda de electrodomésticos
> una tienda de ropa
>
> **¡Respuesta personal!**

2 Muestra *(Show)* el dibujo a otro(a) estudiante. Usa las palabras en esta lista para hacer seis preguntas sobre su centro comercial. Tu compañero(a) debe contestar.

> uvas/voy a . . .
> quieres/quiero . . .
> necesitas/necesito . . .
> te/me gustaría . . .
> piensas/pienso . . .
> comer . . .
> buscar . . .
> comprar . . .
> mirar . . .

¿Recuerdas?
To tell the location of something, use *está . . . :*

a la derecha de   delante de
a la izquierda de   detrás de
al lado de   lejos de
cerca de

Para decir más . . .
entre   between
enfrente de   across from

▶ **Modelo**

A —*¿Dónde está el restaurante La Mariposa?*

B —*Está detrás de la zapatería y la librería.*

A —*¿Por qué quieres ir allí?*

B —*Quiero comer con mi amigo.*

ciento noventa y tres **193**
Capítulo 7B

9 Standards: 1.1, 1.2, 1.3
Focus: Writing and speaking about malls
Recycle: Locations; *estar*
Suggestions: Supply colored pencils or markers for the students' drawings. Encourage them to think of creative names for their shops that indicate what items are sold there. Use one of the student drawings to introduce the new location expressions in *Para decir más....* Practice the model for Step 2 with a volunteer, using his or her drawing.
Answers will vary.

BELLRINGER REVIEW

Show Voc. and Gram. Transparency 137 and have the students unscramble these three words for items found in either of the display windows.

veallor   meferpu   daacen

(Answers: *llavero, perfume, cadena*)

ENRICH YOUR TEACHING

Teacher-to-Teacher
Have students prepare an advertisement for a store. They should include the store's name, what is on sale, store hours, and location. Display their advertisements in the classroom.

21st Century Skills
Critical Thinking and Problem Solving Have students find Web sites for department stores in both the United States and in Spanish-speaking countries. In groups, they should create an ad for one of the department stores, combining print, audio, and video. Some groups create ads for a United States department store and others for a department store in a Spanish-speaking country.

▼10 Standards: 1.1

Focus: Exchanging information about gift ideas

Recycle: Clothing vocabulary

Suggestions: Ask what things students consider when buying a gift. Do they tend to think more about what they like or what the person they are buying the gift for likes? Have them use this information to answer the questions. When asking questions in items 3–6, Student A might use the possessive *tu* instead of *mi* in the first speaking line. Clarify that students should be asking about their own friends or family members.

Answers will vary.

▼11 Standards: 1.1, 1.2, 1.3, 4.1

Resources: Voc. and Gram. Transparency 142; Answer Keys: Student Edition, p. 148

Focus: Reading authentic material for comprehension

Recycle: Expressing preferences; using cognates

Suggestions: Have students note unknown words, look for cognates, and use context clues to guess their meaning. Suggest that students think about jewelry stores they may have visited to help them answer item 3.

Answers:
1. relojes variados y todo tipo de joyas
2. Cuestan poco.
3. instalación de baterías de reloj; reparaciones de joyas y cadenas; arreglos de pulseras
4. Answers will vary.

Teacher-to-Teacher

Bring in copies of ads for specialty shops from Spanish-language newspapers or magazines. Distribute the ads and have each student write five questions based on the ad they received. Have the students exchange ads and questions, and take turns asking and answering each other's questions.

194

▼10 | 👥 | ♻ | Hablar

Un buen regalo

Habla con otro(a) estudiante sobre los buenos regalos para diferentes personas.

▶ Modelo

un señor que trabaja en una oficina

A —¿Cuál es un buen* regalo para un señor que trabaja en una oficina?

B —Creo que una corbata es el mejor regalo para él.

A —¿Sabes dónde venden corbatas?

B —Por supuesto. En la tienda de ropa.

Estudiante A

Estudiante B

1. un(a) joven que no es puntual
2. un(a) joven que trabaja en un almacén
3. tu hermano(a) mayor (menor)
4. tu mejor amigo(a)
5. tu novio(a)
6. tu abuelo(a)

¡Respuesta personal!

*Buen is used in front of a masculine singular noun.

▼11 | 👥 | ♻ | Leer · Escribir · Hablar

Vamos a la joyería

Lee el anuncio de una joyería en Tegucigalpa, Honduras y luego contesta las preguntas.

1. ¿Qué venden en la tienda?
2. Según el anuncio, ¿las cosas que venden en la tienda cuestan mucho o poco?
3. Además de *(In addition to)* vender, ¿qué otros servicios hay en la joyería?
4. Pregunta a dos personas diferentes: ¿Qué te gustaría comprar en una joyería? ¿Qué joyas tienes?

Strategy

Using cognates and context clues
Try to figure out the meanings of unknown words by looking for cognates or by seeing how other words are used in the sentence.

- Can you guess the meanings of *bajos, diamantes, piedras preciosas, baterías,* and *arreglos* in this ad?

JOYERÍA HERMANOS SILVA

Vendemos relojes variados y todo tipo de joyas para toda ocasión

- Anillos y collares de diamantes y otras piedras preciosas
- Baterías de reloj, incluyendo instalación
- Hacemos reparaciones y joyas nuevas de su oro* viejo
- Reparación de cadenas y arreglos de pulseras

¡Precios bajos todos los días!

MENCIONE ESTE ANUNCIO Y RECIBA UN DESCUENTO DEL 10%

Abierto lunes a sábado de 10:00 hs. a 18:00 hs.

*gold

194 ciento noventa y cuatro
Tema 7 • De compras

DIFFERENTIATED INSTRUCTION

Heritage Language Learners

Explain such advertising tactics as bandwagon ("Everybody drinks Super Soda!"), snob appeal ("Super Soda, for the sophisticated!"), and expert opinion ("Take it from me, Joe Football-Player, Super Soda is the best!"). Have students find such ads in Spanish-language magazines, and share examples with the class.

Multiple Intelligences

Musical/Rhythmic: Have students create a short radio or TV ad for a jewelry store. The ad may contain a jingle to be sung or chanted.

▼ Exploración del lenguaje

Nouns that end in *-ería*

The Spanish word ending, or suffix, *-ería* usually indicates a place where something is sold, made, or repaired. This suffix is added to a form of the word that names the specialty item. For example, if you know that *una joya* is a piece of jewelry, you understand that you can buy jewelry at *la joyería*.

Try it out! You will often see these signs over stores. Tell what each one sells.

heladería	librería	pastelería
papelería	panadería	zapatería

Modelo
joyería
En la joyería venden joyas como anillos, pulseras y collares.

Esta joyería vende pulseras, anillos y collares.

Muchos españoles compran pan en una panadería.

Venden flores para todas las ocasiones en esta florería en España.

Muchos mexicanos compran tortillas frescas en una tortillería cerca de su casa.

▼12 | 💬 | Escribir • Hablar

Y tú, ¿qué dices?

1. ¿En qué tiendas vas de compras? ¿Qué te gusta comprar?
2. ¿Para quiénes compras regalos? ¿Qué tipo de regalos compras?
3. ¿Qué regalo compraste recientemente *(recently)*? ¿Cuándo y dónde compraste el regalo? ¿Pagaste mucho o poco dinero?

ciento noventa y cinco **195**
Capítulo 7B

Practice and Communicate | 7B

ENRICH YOUR TEACHING

Gramática

Core Instruction

Standards: 4.1

Resources: Voc. and Gram. Transparency 140; Teacher's Resource Book: Video Script, p. 205; Video Program: Cap. 7B

INTERACTIVE WHITEBOARD

Grammar Activities 7B

Suggestions: Call students' attention to the ¿Recuerdas? Use the transparency to introduce the structure. The *GramActiva* Video can serve as reinforcement. Point out that students must look for context clues to tell whether **nosotros** forms are in the present or in the preterite.

▶13 Standards: 1.2

Resources: Teacher's Resource Book: Audio Script, p. 202; Audio Program DVD: Cap. 7B, Track 9; Answer Keys: Student Edition, p. 149

Focus: Listening to and identifying present and past tenses

Recycle: Household chores

Suggestions: Play the audio or read the script. Remind students to listen for verb endings and context clues such as **la semana pasada** and **ayer.**

Script and Answers:

1. Ella cocina para la familia cada día. *(presente)*
2. Mis padres trabajan todos los días excepto los fines de semana. *(presente)*
3. Corté el césped después de las clases. *(pasado)*
4. ¿Ayudaste mucho a tus padres la semana pasada? *(pasado)*
5. Mis hermanos limpiaron el baño y yo lavé los platos. *(pasado)*
6. Mi hermano y yo lavamos el coche ayer. *(pasado)*
7. Siempre arreglo mi cuarto en la mañana. *(presente)*
8. Mi abuela arregló el sótano hace un mes. *(pasado)*

▶14 Standards: 1.1, 1.2

Resources: Answer Keys: Student Edition, p. 150

Focus: Using the preterite to write and talk about buying.

Suggestions: Point out that students are using only *comprar.*

Answers:

1. compró unos aretes
2. compraron un videojuego
3. compró una cartera
4. compraste un collar
5. compraron una pulsera
6. compramos perfume

Gramática

▼ Objectives
▶ Listen to a description of family activities
▶ Write and talk about what you and others did
▶ Interview a classmate about activities last week

The preterite of -ar verbs

To talk about actions that were completed in the past, use the preterite tense. To form the preterite tense of a regular -ar verb, add the preterite endings to the stem of the verb. Here are the preterite forms of *comprar*:

(yo)	compré	(nosotros) (nosotras)	compramos
(tú)	compraste	(vosotros) (vosotras)	comprasteis
Ud. (él) (ella)	compró	Uds. (ellos) (ellas)	compraron

¿Recuerdas?

In Spanish, the endings of verbs identify both who is performing the action (the subject) and when it is being performed (the tense).

Notice the accent marks on the endings -é and -ó.

The *nosotros* form is the same in the present and preterite tenses. You will need to look for other context clues to tell which tense is intended.

Más ayuda realidades.com

▶ **GramActiva Video**
Tutorials: Past tense, Tense, *Hacer* in time expressions, Preterite

🔊 **Canción de hip hop:** ¿Qué compraste ayer?

📖 **GramActiva Activity**

▶13 | ♻ | 🔊 | Escuchar

¿El presente o el pasado?

En una hoja de papel, escribe los números del 1 al 8. Vas a escuchar ocho frases que describen los quehaceres de una familia. ¿Ocurren los quehaceres en el presente o el pasado *(past)?* Escribe *presente* o *pasado.*

▶14 Escribir · Hablar

El dinero es un buen regalo

Tus abuelos les regalaron *(gave)* a todos dinero y cada uno compró algo. Explica lo que compraron todos y cuándo compraron las cosas.

Modelo

Mi hermano ___ hace una semana.
Mi hermano compró un reloj pulsera hace una semana.

1. Mi madre ___ ayer.

2. Mis primos ___ anoche.

3. Mi papá ___ el año pasado.

4. Tú ___ hace tres días.

5. Mis tíos ___ hace un mes.

6. Mi hermana y yo ___ ayer.

DIFFERENTIATED INSTRUCTION

Heritage Language Learners

Have students write a short paragraph describing a special gift they bought for someone sometime in the past. Meet with individuals to review the spelling and grammar in their paragraphs.

Advanced Learners/Pre-AP*

Working in pairs, have students use one of the four pictures on p. 195 to create and tell a brief story. Encourage them to use the preterite of *comprar* and other appropriate -ar verbs. Allow each student to prepare for 30 seconds and talk for 30 seconds.

▼15 | 👥 | ♻ | Hablar · GramActiva

Juego

❶ Tu profesor(a) va a enseñar a todos cómo deben señalar *(point to)* a diferentes personas: *ella, nosotros, tú, ellos,* etc. Practica con tu profesor(a).

❷ Trabaja en un grupo de cuatro. Una persona es líder y dice un infinitivo de la lista y un sujeto *(subject)*. Por ejemplo: *cantar / ella.* Los otros tienen que señalar a la persona, o a las personas, y decir el verbo en el pretérito: *ella cantó.* Continúa así con tres sujetos más y el mismo verbo. Después, cambia de *(change)* líderes.

¿Recuerdas?

arreglar	cortar	hablar	nadar
bailar	dibujar	lavar	pasar
caminar	escuchar	levantar	patinar
cantar	esquiar	limpiar	trabajar
cocinar	estudiar	montar	usar

▼16 | 💬👥 | ♻ | Escribir · Hablar

Hace una semana

Usa el pretérito para escribir y hablar de tus actividades.

❶ Copia la tabla *(chart)* en una hoja de papel. Usa los verbos de la lista de la Actividad 15 para escribir seis actividades que hiciste *(you did)* en el pasado. Indica cuándo hiciste cada actividad.

¿Qué?	¿Cuándo?
patiné	la semana pasada

❷ Usa la información de la tabla para escribir frases sobre tus actividades. Incluye información para contestar *¿dónde?* y *¿con quién?* Después, lee tus frases a otro(a) estudiante y pregunta: *¿Y tú?* Tu compañero(a) debe contestar. Escribe la respuesta de tu compañero(a).

▶ Modelo
A —*Patiné en el parque con mis amigos la semana pasada.¿Y tú?*
B —*Monté en monopatín con mi hermana la semana pasada.*

❸ Escribe tres frases con la información del paso 2.

Modelo
Patiné en el parque con mis amigos la semana pasada, pero Luisa montó en monopatín con su hermana.

Nota

To say when something happened, use *hace* + a time expression. It's like saying "ago."

• Compré la pulsera **hace un año.**
  I bought the bracelet a year ago.

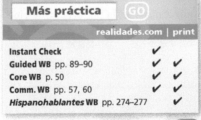

Más práctica GO

realidades.com | print

Instant Check	✔	
Guided WB pp. 89–90	✔	✔
Core WB p. 50	✔	✔
Comm. WB pp. 57, 60	✔	✔
***Hispanohablantes* WB** pp. 274–277		✔

ciento noventa y siete **197**
Capítulo 7B

▼15 Standards: 1.1

Focus: Talking about what people did

Recycle: Sports and activities; chores

Suggestions: Review subject pronouns and write them on the board. Use three volunteers to demonstrate part 2.

Answers will vary.

▼16 Standards: 1.1, 1.3

Focus: Writing and speaking about activities in the past

Recycle: Sports, leisure activities, and household chores

Suggestions: Write a sample chart on the board. Remind them to use ***hace*** + *period of time* when appropriate. Model writing sentences that answer ***¿Dónde?*** and ***¿Con quién?***

Answers will vary.

Pre-AP* Support

• **Learning Objective:** Presentational Writing
• **Activity:** Have students write a short paragraph about something they bought or a place they visited in the past and explain why they enjoyed the purchase or the trip.
• ***Pre-AP* Resource Book:** Comprehensive guide to Pre-AP* communication skill development, pp. 10–57

Additional Resources

• Communication Wbk.: Audio Act. 7, p. 57
• Teacher's Resource Book: Audio Script, pp. 202–203
• Audio Program DVD: Cap. 7B, Track 10

ENRICH YOUR TEACHING

Culture Note
There are many different customs involving gifts in South America. For example, Colombians generally do not unwrap a gift right away so as not to appear greedy, but in Chile, gifts usually are opened immediately.

Culture Note
In Latin America and Spain, if you are invited to someone's home for dinner, it is customary to bring a simple gift, such as flowers or chocolates. If you are visiting from another country, it is thoughtful to give a gift that is a product of your homeland.

✓ASSESSMENT

Prueba 7B-3 with Study Plan (online only)

Quiz: The preterite of *-ar* verbs
• Prueba 7B-3: p. 192

197

Gramática

Core Instruction

Standards: 4.1

Resources: Teacher's Resource Book: Video Script, pp. 205–206; Video Program: Cap. 7B

INTERACTIVE WHITEBOARD
Grammar Activities 7B

Focus: Presenting preterite of *-car* and *-gar* verbs

Suggestions: Direct attention to the *¿Recuerdas?* Point out that the *u* is added to keep the hard *c* and *g* sounds and that the *u* is not pronounced. Point out that verbs such as *jugar* that have a stem change in the present do *not* have a stem change in the preterite. Use the *GramActiva* Video to reinforce your presentation.

▼17 Standards: 1.3

Resources: Answer Keys: Student Edition, p. 150
Focus: Writing verbs in the preterite
Suggestions: Remind students to read the entire passage before writing their answers and to read each sentence carefully to determine the subject.

Answers:

1. jugaron   4. tocó   7. pagaron
2. jugué   5. jugamos 8. saqué
3. toqué   6. sacó

Common Errors: Using the verb *jugar*—not *tocar*—to talk about playing an instrument. Remind students that *jugar* is used for games and *tocar* for musical instruments.

Fondo cultural

Standards: 2.2, 4.2

Suggestions: Brainstorm items commonly found in museums and have students discuss the importance of these items in history.

Answers will vary.

▼ Objectives
▶ Write and talk about what you and others did
▶ Discuss gifts you bought
▶ Read a timeline to write and talk about historical events

Gramática

The preterite of verbs ending in -car and -gar

Verbs that end in *-car* and *-gar* have a spelling change in the *yo* form of the preterite.

buscar: c → qu   yo bus**qué**

Silvia y Rosa bus**car**on aretes pero yo busqué un collar.

pagar: g → gu   yo pa**gué**

¿Cuánto pa**gaste** por tu cadena? Pa**gué** 13 dólares.

Verbs such as *jugar* that have a stem change in the present tense do not have a stem change in the preterite.

El sábado pasado ju**gué** al tenis.
Mis hermanos ju**garon** al básquetbol.

> **¿Recuerdas?**
> You know these verbs that end in *-car* and *-gar*:
>
> buscar   practicar
> jugar   sacar
> pagar   tocar

> **Más ayuda**   **realidades.com**
>
> *GramActiva* Video Tutorial: Preterite
>
> *GramActiva* Activity

▼17 ♻ Escribir

El viernes pasado

El viernes pasado Juan invitó a unos amigos a su casa. Completa la descripción de sus actividades con la forma apropiada del pretérito de los verbos *jugar, pagar, sacar* y *tocar*.

El viernes pasado mis amigos pasaron tiempo conmigo en mi casa. Tomás y Fernando __1.__ videojuegos en mi dormitorio pero yo no __2.__ con ellos. Yo __3.__ la guitarra en la sala y todos cantamos. Jorge __4.__ el piano un poco también. Después de cantar, nosotros __5.__ al vóleibol. Mi amiga Ana __6.__ fotos de nosotros. ¡Qué graciosas son las fotos! A las nueve fuimos por pizza y ¡mis padres __7.__ la cuenta! ¡Qué bueno porque nunca tengo mucho dinero! Yo __8.__ fotos de todos mis amigos en la pizzería. ¡Qué bien lo pasamos nosotros!

▼ Fondo Cultural | Colombia

El Museo del Oro in Bogotá, Colombia, houses over 33,000 objects of gold, emeralds, and other precious stones made by pre-Columbian cultures—cultures that existed long before the arrival of Columbus in the Americas. These ancient civilizations viewed gold as life-giving energy from the sun.

• What kinds of specialized museums have you visited in your community or in other locations? What did you learn from the types of objects that were included there?

El Museo del Oro en Bogotá, Colombia

DIFFERENTIATED INSTRUCTION

Heritage Language Learners

Have students write a paragraph about a sports competition or a musical performance in which they participated or a fictional event. Have them include as many of the past tense forms of the *-car* and *-gar* verbs as they can.

Students with Learning Difficulties

For *Actividad 17*, remind students of the meanings of the four verbs used. Provide a copy of the paragraph so students can write directly on it. You may want to supply the infinitive forms of the verbs that belong in the spaces.

▼ Pronunciación | 🔊 | 🗣

The letter combinations *gue*, *gui*, *que*, and *qui*

You know that when the letter *g* appears before the letters *a*, *o*, or *u*, it is pronounced like the *g* in *go*, and that *g* before *e* and *i* is pronounced like the *h* in *he*.

To keep the sound of the *g* in *go* before *e* and *i*, add the letter *u: gue, gui*. Don't pronounce the *u*. Listen to and say these words:

Guillermo	guitarra	espaguetis
guisantes	hamburguesa	Miguel

You also know that the letter *c* before *a*, *o*, or *u* is pronounced like the *c* in *cat*, while the *c* before *e* and *i* is usually pronounced like the *s* in *Sally*.

To keep the sound of the *c* in "cat" before *e* and *i*, words are spelled with *qu: que, qui*. The *u* is not pronounced. Listen to and say these words:

queso	quince	quieres	riquísimo
quehacer	quinientos	quisiera	querer

Try it out! Listen to the first verse of this traditional song from Puerto Rico entitled *"El coquí." El coquí* is a little tree frog found in Puerto Rico, named for the *coquí, coquí* sound that it makes at night. Say the verse.

> El coquí, el coquí siempre canta.
> Es muy suave el cantar del coquí.
> Por las noches a veces me duermo
> con el dulce cantar del coquí.
> Coquí, coquí, coquí, quí, quí, quí,
> coquí, coquí, coquí, quí, quí, quí.

▼18 | 🗣 | ♻ | Escribir • Escuchar • Hablar • GramActiva

Juego

① Escribe en una hoja de papel una o dos frases para indicar qué regalo compraste, para quién es, dónde lo compraste y cuánto pagaste.

Modelo
Compré un collar para mi novia en la Red. Pagué 45 dólares.

② Trabaja con un grupo de cuatro. Pon tu hoja de papel en una bolsa *(bag)* con las otras hojas del grupo. Cada uno toma una hoja, que debe ser de otro(a) estudiante del grupo. Cambia una parte de la frase y lee la nueva frase al grupo. ¿Quién puede identificar el cambio?

▶ Modelo
A —*Esta persona compró un collar <u>para su madre</u> en la Red. Pagó 45 dólares.*
B —*No es cierto. Compré un collar <u>para mi novia</u>.*

ciento noventa y nueve **199**
Capítulo 7B

Practice and Communicate — 7B

Pronunciación
Core Instruction

Standards: 4.1

Resources: Teacher's Resource Book: Audio Script, p. 203; Audio Program DVD: Cap. 7B, Tracks 11–12

Suggestions: Point out that there are subtle pronunciation differences of these sounds and they may vary from region to region. Have students repeat the words after you or play the audio. Pair students to say the verse aloud. Have them record their presentations.

BELLRINGER REVIEW

Use the transparencies to ask and answer questions about gifts.

▼18 Standards: 1.1, 1.2, 1.3

Focus: Writing and talking about gifts purchased in the past.

Suggestions: Encourage students to include unique details in their sentences for Step 1. Remind students that they can make up sentences if they want, but that they must remember the details for Step 2.

Answers will vary.

Teacher-to-Teacher

Have students conduct an Internet search to find out what kinds of Latin American products can be bought online. They might look for handicrafts unique to a country or more expensive items, such as jewelry. The students should report the names of different businesses, the products they sell, and how much the products cost.

ENRICH YOUR TEACHING

Culture Note

The Spaniards' search for **El Dorado** in the Americas in the sixteenth century was the first major gold rush. It was set off by tales of indigenous people wearing gold ornaments and using gold tools. **El Dorado,** the "Golden Man" who covered himself with gold dust, was said to own the gold.

21st Century Skills

Technology Literacy Have students use the digital technology within **realidades.com** to access and manage the audio files, videos, and activities that support learning the new vocabulary.

19 Standards: 1.1, 1.2, 1.3, 3.1

Resources: Map Transparencies 12–14, 20; Answer Keys: Student Edition, p. 151

Focus: Interpreting maps and timelines; using the preterite to describe historical events

Suggestions: Tell students to look first at the timeline, find the corresponding number on the map, and identify that location. Remind students that they may need to use a history book to make sure their information is accurate. If available, copy pages from a Spanish history text for them to use.

Answers:

1. En 1492 Cristobal Colón llegó a la República Dominicana.
2. En 1513 Juan Ponce de León exploró la Florida.
3. En 1540 Francisco Vázquez de Coronado buscó las siete ciudades de Cibola en el suroeste de los Estados Unidos.
4. En 1769 Fray Junípero Serra fundó la misión de San Diego de Alcalá.
5. En 1848 el presidente James K. Polk y los Estados Unidos pagaron 15 millones de dólares a México según el Tratado de Guadalupe Hidalgo.
6. En 1898 el presidente William McKinley y los Estados Unidos ayudaron a Cuba y Puerto Rico a declarar su independencia de España.
7. En 1904 el presidente Theodore Roosevelt y los Estados Unidos empezaron la construcción del canal de Panamá.

▼**19** Leer • Pensar • Escribir • Hablar

Una lección de historia

Estudia la línea cronológica (*timeline*), los eventos y el mapa. Luego usa el pretérito para emparejar estos eventos históricos con las personas en la línea cronológica.

Modelo

En 1492 Cristóbal Colón llegó (arrived) *a la República Dominicana.*

> **Nota**
>
> Here is how you say dates:
> - **1500** mil quinientos
> - **1898** mil ochocientos noventa y ocho
> - **2005** dos mil cinco

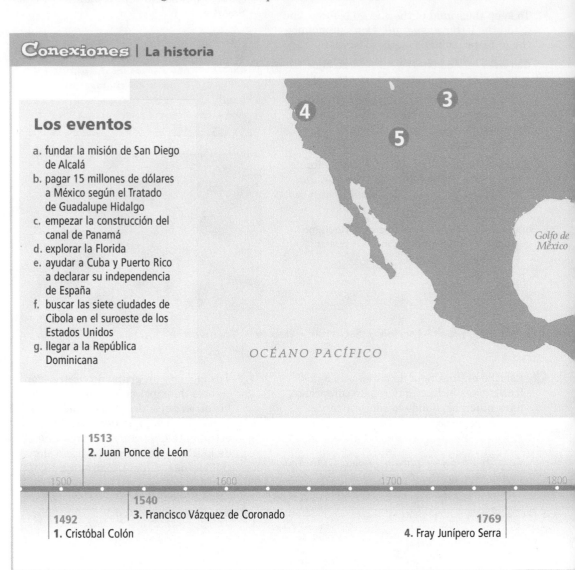

Conexiones | La historia

Los eventos

a. fundar la misión de San Diego de Alcalá
b. pagar 15 millones de dólares a México según el Tratado de Guadalupe Hidalgo
c. empezar la construcción del canal de Panamá
d. explorar la Florida
e. ayudar a Cuba y Puerto Rico a declarar su independencia de España
f. buscar las siete ciudades de Cibola en el suroeste de los Estados Unidos
g. llegar a la República Dominicana

OCÉANO PACÍFICO

Golfo de México

1513
2. Juan Ponce de León

1500 1600 1700 1800

1492
1. Cristóbal Colón

1540
3. Francisco Vázquez de Coronado

1769
4. Fray Junípero Serra

200 doscientos
Tema 7 • De compras

DIFFERENTIATED INSTRUCTION

Students with Learning Difficulties

You may want to provide students with a timeline that contains all of the events in *Actividad* 19 in English. Providing them with this background knowledge will make the task less intimidating.

Advanced Learners/Pre-AP*

Have students write five sentences about local or state historical events. They may need to make a trip to the library. Gather all the information and have the class make a mural timeline.

La misión de San Diego de Alcalá, California, fundada en 1769

El edificio más antiguo de los Estados Unidos está en San Agustín, en la Florida.

Fray Junípero Serra

OCÉANO ATLÁNTICO

Mar Caribe

1848
5. El presidente James K. Polk y los Estados Unidos

1900

1898
6. El presidente William McKinley y los Estados Unidos

1904
7. El presidente Theodore Roosevelt y los Estados Unidos

▼20 | (Talk!) | ♻ | Escribir • Hablar

Y tú, ¿qué dices?

1. ¿Qué deportes practicaste el fin de semana pasado?

2. ¿Con quién practicaste el español la semana pasada?

3. ¿Qué cumpleaños celebraste el mes pasado? ¿Quién sacó fotos en la fiesta?

4. Para el cumpleaños de tu amigo(a) el año pasado, ¿qué compraste? ¿Cuánto pagaste?

5. Cuando celebraste tu quinto cumpleaños, ¿qué jugaste con tus amigos?

Más práctica	(GO)
realidades.com	print	
Instant Check	✔
Guided WB p. 91	✔ ✔
Core WB p. 51	✔ ✔
Comm. WB pp. 61, 162	✔ ✔
Hispanohablantes WB pp. 280–281	✔

doscientos uno **201**
Capítulo 7B

Practice and Communicate 7B

▼**20** Standards: 1.1, 1.3

Resources: Answer Keys: Student Edition, p. 152

Focus: Using the preterite to talk about past activities

Recycle: Sports; musical instruments

Suggestions: Remind students that they can invent answers if the question does not apply to them or if they do not remember.

Answers will vary but should include:
1. practiqué
2. practiqué
3. celebré, saqué (sacó)
4. compré, pagué
5. jugué

Teaching with Photos
Have students compare and contrast the two buildings in the photos. Point out the rounded archways and the freestanding exterior walls that form a courtyard. Point out that these are features of Spanish colonial architecture and can be found in homes and buildings in Florida, California, and throughout the Southwest.

Theme Project
Students can perform Step 4 at this point. Be sure they understand your corrections and suggestions. (For more information, see p. 154-b.)

Additional Resources
• Communication Wbk.: Audio Act. 8, p. 57
• Teacher's Resource Book: Audio Script, p. 203
• Audio Program DVD: Cap. 7B, Track 13

ENRICH YOUR TEACHING

Culture Note
Ask the students to name as many cities as they can that begin with **San.** Tell them that **san** is the shortened form of the masculine **santo,** meaning "saint." **Santa** is the feminine form. Tell students that many cities were built around missions named for various saints.

21st Century Skills

Critical Thinking and Problem Solving Have students research a time period in the history of their city or state, decide which events are the most important ones, and create a timeline for those events. Have them compare their timeline with others and establish if similar events were selected to include in the timeline.

✓ASSESSMENT

Prueba 7B-4 with Study Plan (online only)

Quiz: The preterite of verbs ending in -car and -gar
• Prueba 7B-4: p. 193

201

Gramática

Core Instruction

Standards: 4.1

Resources: Voc. and Gram. Transparency 141; Teacher's Resource Book: Video Script, p. 206; Video Program: Cap. 7B

INTERACTIVE WHITEBOARD

Grammar Activities 7B

Focus: Presenting direct object pronouns

Suggestions: Bring in items to use as a demonstration. On the chalkboard, write the words for these items with the definite article underlined. Say: *Yo compré el libro. Lo compré anoche.* Hold up the item when saying the second sentence. Point out that the direct object pronoun is different from the definite article only in the masculine singular form. Use the *GramActiva* Video either as an initial introduction to the structure or as a follow-up after your own grammar explanation.

21 Standards: 1.2, 1.3

Resources: Answer Keys: Student Edition, p. 152
Focus: Reading and writing about buying gifts using direct object pronouns
Suggestions: Have students first identify the objects in the numbered sentences, then the direct object pronouns in the lettered sentences.

Answers:
1. b   2. c   3. d   4. e   5. f   6. a

Extension: Have students write one or two sentences about something they looked for to give to someone. They should use the sentences in *Actividad* 21 as models. Have them read their sentences to the class. A volunteer should respond with a question. For example, Student A: *Busqué unos discos compactos para mi papá.* Student B: *¿Los compraste en la tienda de música?* Student A will finish the exchange by responding: *Sí, los compré en la tienda de música.*

Gramática

Direct object pronouns

A direct object tells who or what receives the action of the verb.

> Busco una cadena.
> Compré unos guantes.

To avoid repeating a direct object noun, you can replace it with a direct object pronoun.

> ¿Dónde compraste **tus aretes**?
> *Where did you buy **your earrings**?*

> **Los** compré en la joyería Sánchez.
> *I bought **them** at Sánchez Jewelry.*

	SINGULAR		PLURAL	
M.	lo	it	los	them
F.	la	it	las	them

Direct object pronouns agree in gender and number with the nouns they replace.

> ¿Tienes mi pulsera? No, no **la** tengo.
> ¿Tienes mis anillos? No, no **los** tengo.

A direct object noun *follows* the conjugated verb. A direct object pronoun comes *before* the conjugated verb.

When an infinitive follows a conjugated verb, the direct object pronoun can either be placed before the conjugated verb or be attached to the infinitive.

> ¿Quieres comprar el llavero?
> Sí, **lo** quiero comprar.
> o: Sí, quiero comprar**lo**.

Más ayuda   **realidades.com**

▶ *GramActiva* Video
Tutorial: Direct object pronouns

GramActiva Activity

▼**21** Leer • Escribir

Los regalos de José

Tu amigo, José, buscó regalos para su familia y sus amigos. Él está hablando de lo que compró. Escribe los números del 1 al 6 en una hoja de papel. Para cada cosa que buscó José, escribe la frase que explica dónde la compró.

1. Busqué unos discos compactos para mi papá.
2. Busqué un libro nuevo para mi hermana.
3. Busqué unos aretes para mi mamá.
4. Busqué unas revistas para mi amigo Juan.
5. Busqué un equipo de sonido para mi hermano.
6. Busqué una pulsera para mi novia.

a. La compré en la joyería.
b. Los compré en la tienda de música.
c. Lo compré en la librería.
d. Los compré en la joyería.
e. Las compré en la librería.
f. Lo compré en la tienda de música.

DIFFERENTIATED INSTRUCTION

Heritage Language Learners

Have students write a paragraph about a shopping trip they made. They should write about what they bought and why they bought it, using direct object pronouns and the preterite. For example: *Compré un vestido y unos zapatos. Los compré porque voy a una fiesta.* Review grammar and spelling.

Students with Learning Difficulties

Write sentences on the board, circling object nouns and underlining object pronouns. Use colored chalk to establish relationships between the words. For *Actividad* 23, you may want to limit the task by having students focus only on items 1, 3, 6, and 7.

▼22 Escribir

¡No compraron nada!

Ayer muchas personas fueron *(went)* al centro comercial y miraron muchas cosas pero ¡no compraron nada! Escribe lo que no compraron.

Modelo
Carlos
Ayer Carlos miró unas carteras pero no las compró.

1. Juanita   4. nosotros

2. los novios   5. el señor Miró

3. tú    6. yo

También se dice . . .

el anillo	= la sortija *(muchos países)*
los aretes	= los pendientes *(España)*; los aros *(Argentina, Uruguay)*
la pulsera	= el brazalete *(muchos países)*
el bolso	= la cartera *(Argentina)*; la bolsa *(Chile, México)*
los anteojos de sol	= las gafas de sol *(Argentina, España)*
la cartera	= la billetera *(Argentina, Uruguay, Bolivia)*

▼23 Leer · Pensar · Escribir

¿Quién compró qué?

¿Te gusta ser detective? ¡Vamos a ver si puedes descubrir lo que compraron las personas, dónde compraron las cosas y cuánto costó cada cosa!

❶ Lee las pistas *(clues)*. Luego copia la tabla en una hoja de papel y completa la tabla.

Las pistas

1. José gastó *(spent)* $35 en la joyería.
2. El software costó $45.
3. Paco no compró una novela.
4. Isabel fue *(went)* de compras a la tienda de electrodomésticos.
5. Luisa gastó $20 en la librería.
6. Los guantes costaron $25.
7. Paco fue de compras al almacén, pero no compró el collar.

❷ Usa la información de la tabla y lee las frases completas.

Modelo
José compró . . . Los (Las/Lo/La) compró en . . . Costaron (Costó) . . .

Nombre	¿Qué compró?	¿Dónde lo compró?	¿Cuánto costó?

doscientos tres **203**
Capítulo 7B

ENRICH YOUR TEACHING

Teacher-to-Teacher

Have students work in groups to create logic puzzles like the one in *Actividad* 23. They could use store names and gift items, or they could use school schedules and subjects, chores and rooms of the house, or any other set of previously learned vocabulary. Collect, copy, and redistribute the puzzles.

21st Century Skills

Creativity and Innovation As an extension of the Teacher-to-Teacher suggestion, have students turn any logic puzzles they create into dialogues. Have students add additional details about each category (such as how cheap or expensive something was), and present their dialogues in front of the class.

▼22 Standards: 1.3

Resources: Answer Keys: Student Edition, p. 152

Focus: Writing sentences using direct object pronouns

Suggestions: Emphasize that direct object pronouns have the same gender and number as the nouns they replace.

Answers:

1. Ayer Juanita miró un bolso pero no lo compró.
2. Ayer los novios miraron un anillo pero no lo compraron.
3. Ayer tú miraste unos llaveros pero no los compraste.
4. Ayer nosotros miramos unos aretes pero no los compramos.
5. Ayer el señor Miró miró unos anteojos de sol pero no los compró.
6. Ayer yo miré unas pulseras pero no las compré.

Extension: Have students write a sentence on a note card about something they looked at while shopping. *(Ayer miré una corbata.)* Students will exchange cards and ask one another if they bought the item or items they specified. *(¿La compraste?)* Student B will answer *sí* or *no (No, no la compré).*

Common Errors: Students use *a* after *mirar*. Remind students that *mirar* means "to look at" and there is no need for a preposition in Spanish.

▼23 Standards: 1.2, 1.3

Resources: Teacher's Resource Book: GramActiva BLM, p. 213; Answer Keys: Student Edition, p. 153

Focus: Reading and writing using past tense and direct object pronouns

Suggestions: Students may not know where to begin to solve the puzzle. Have them copy the chart and suggest that they begin by writing each person's name and the store where each one shopped. Then they can fill in the logical item that could be bought in each store. Point out that the information for every category is present in the sentences for Step 1.

Answers:

José compró un collar. Lo compró en la joyería. Costó $35. Isabel compró el software. Lo compró en la tienda de electrodomésticos. Costó $45. Paco compró unos guantes. Los compró en el almacén. Costaron $25. Luisa compró una novela. La compró en la librería. Costó $20.

24 Standards: 1.1

Resources: Answer Keys: Student Edition, p. 153

Focus: Using direct object pronouns

Suggestions: Write the *Modelo* on the chalkboard and have students identify the direct object noun. (*botas*) Ask which direct object pronoun should replace it. (*las*) Remind students to attach the direct object pronoun to the infinitive in a structure with two verbs.

Answers may vary but will include:

1. ... voy a comprarlos.
2. ... quiero leerlo.
3. ... tengo que hacerla.
4. ... quiero jugarlos contigo.
5. ... puedes comerlo.
6. ... voy a hacerla.

BELLRINGER REVIEW

Have students copy from the board the Spanish words for these types of stores and then write next to them the word for an item they might buy there:

1. *florería*   2. *pescadería*

3. *taquería*   4. *panadería*

(**Answers** may vary but might include:
1. flores; 2. pescado, mariscos; 3. tacos, comida mexicana; 4. pan, galletas, pasteles)

25 Standards: 1.1

Focus: Talking about purchases

Suggestions: Tell students that they should make up prices if they haven't purchased similar items recently. If students are uncomfortable talking about money, encourage the class to pretend they went shopping in an expensive store, and make up extravagant prices.

Answers will vary but may include:

1. ¿... tu reloj pulsera nuevo? Lo compré...
2. ¿... tu anillo nuevo? Lo compré...
3. ¿... tu software nuevo? Lo compré...
4. ¿... tu llavero nuevo? Lo compré...
5. ¿... tu perfume nuevo? Lo compré...
6. ¿... tu videojuego nuevo? Lo compré...

▼24 |  | Hablar

¡Demasiadas preguntas!

Tu hermanito te hace muchas preguntas. Trabaja con otro(a) estudiante y contesta todas sus preguntas con mucha paciencia.

 Modelo

A —¿Necesito llevar botas en el invierno?
B —Sí, necesitas llevarlas.
o: —No, no necesitas llevarlas.

1. ¿Vas a comprar perritos calientes?
2. ¿Quieres leer este libro?
3. ¿Tienes que hacer la tarea?
4. ¿Quieres jugar videojuegos conmigo?
5. ¿Puedo comer este pastel?
6. ¿Vas a hacer mi cama?

▼25 | | Hablar

¡Qué barato! ¡Qué caro!

Compraste muchas cosas. Ahora un(a) amigo(a) quiere saber cuándo compraste todas estas cosas y cuánto pagaste.

Modelo

A —¿Cuándo compraste tu *suéter* nuevo?
B —Lo compré *la semana pasada*.
A —¿Cuánto pagaste?
B —Pagué *25* dólares.
A —¡Qué barato!
o: —¡Uf! ¡Qué caro!

Estudiante A

1. 2. 3. 4. 5. 6.

Estudiante B

¡Respuesta personal!

$25
$55

DIFFERENTIATED INSTRUCTION

Heritage Language Learners

Ask students to give a presentation on a traditional dance, type of music, or costume from their heritage culture. They may choose to bring in examples or to teach a song or dance to the rest of the class.

Multiple Intelligences

Visual/Spatial: Have students do research and create posters on the history and traditions of the Guelaguetza and Oaxaca. Display their posters in the room.

▼26 | (Talk!) 👥 | Escribir • Hablar

¿Dónde lo compraste?

Haz una lista de cinco regalos que compraste recientemente *(recently)* y los nombres de las personas para quienes los compraste. Con un(a) compañero(a), habla de las cosas en tu lista y dónde las compraste. Si no compraste nada, habla de un amigo(a) o un miembro de tu familia que compró regalos.

▶ Modelo

A —¿Qué regalos compraste recientemente?
B —Compré unas botas nuevas para Emily.
A —¿Dónde las compraste?
B —Las compré en la zapatería Azuelo.

Regalo	¿Para quién?
botas nuevas	Emily

▼27 | (Talk!) 👥 | Escribir • Hablar

¿Cuándo los compró?

❶ Escribe cuatro frases para indicar lo que compró una persona y cuándo lo compró.

❷ Lee tus frases a otro(a) estudiante sin decir cuándo la persona compró el artículo. Tu compañero(a) va a preguntar cuándo lo compró.

Modelo

Mi padre compró unos guantes la semana pasada.

▶ Modelo

A —Mi padre compró unos guantes.
B —¿Cuándo los compró?
A —Los compró la semana pasada.

 Fondo Cultural | México

The Zapotecs and other Indigenous groups in the Mexican state of Oaxaca have their own languages and cultures. However, every July they all gather to celebrate the *Guelaguetza*, a Zapotec word that means "offering" or "gift." The *Guelaguetza* was first celebrated more than 3,000 years ago with music, dance, and food products. Today the festivities last two weeks and celebrate regional dances, music, costumes, and foods.

• What celebration in your culture is similar?

La fiesta de la Guelaguetza en Oaxaca, México

doscientos cinco 205
Capítulo 7B

---

26 Standards: 1.1, 1.3
Focus: Writing and talking about gifts and where you bought them
Suggestions: Tell students they should make up their own list.
Answers will vary.
Extension: Have students make up a list of things they bought for you, for the school principal, or for a popular personality.

27 Standards: 1.1, 1.3
Focus: Writing and conversing using direct object pronouns
Suggestions: Tell students that they may write about family members and friends, or they can invent information for part 1. Practice the *Modelo* with a volunteer before students begin part 2.
Answers will vary.
Common Errors: In part 2, make sure that Student A understands that he or she should not read the complete sentence, but should omit when the item was bought.

Fondo cultural

Standards: 2.1, 4.2
Suggestions: Guide response to the question by directing attention to the meaning of the word Guelaguetza. Tell students that the offering or gift was originally to the gods whom the indigenous people worshipped. They wanted to show these gods their gratitude for sufficient rain and bountiful crops.
Answers will vary but may include Thanksgiving.
 Mapa global interactivo, Actividad 2 Look at several of the states in Mexico.

ENRICH YOUR TEACHING

Teacher-to-Teacher
Promote Spanish in the school by asking administrators, librarians, teachers, and other staff members to display students' projects in their offices.

Teacher-to-Teacher
Have students research the states of Mexico. They can list characteristics of the states, the capitals and other important cities, and the indigenous groups. They should point out where languages other than Spanish are spoken.

Fondo cultural

Standards: 2.2, 4.2

Suggestions: Preview the reading by asking students to list advantages and disadvantages of shopping at flea markets.

Answers will vary.

🌐 **Mapa global interactivo, Actividad 3**
Explore El Rastro in Madrid, Spain.

▼28 Standards: 1.1

Focus: Practicing direct object pronouns in a guessing game

Suggestions: Make sure that each group has five objects to put in the center. You may want to use Clip Art to make index cards for various items. Tell students that they must remember what the five objects are so that they will know which one is missing. You may want to give small prizes to the winners.

Answers will vary.

▼29 Standards: 1.3

Focus: Writing about things you want to buy

Suggestions: Brainstorm categories of vocabulary words before students begin.

Answers will vary.

▼ El español en el mundo del trabajo

Core Instruction

Standards: 5.1

Suggestions: To help students answer the question, list types of specialty shops on the chalkboard and have volunteers give the names of some of those types of shops in your community.

Fondo Cultural | España

Madrid's *El Rastro* is said to be the world's largest flea market. Located in one of the oldest sections of the city, *El Rastro* attracts thousands of visitors every Sunday of the year. Vendors line the streets with their stalls and offer everything from blue jeans to fine art. Everyone from teens to serious antiques collectors bargain with the vendors to get the best prices on the things they want to buy.

• Have you ever gone to a flea market in your community or state? What kind of things did you find there? How do you think that flea market would compare to Madrid's *el Rastro*?

El Rastro, en Madrid, España

▼28 | 👥 | Hablar

Juego

❶ Each student in a group of five puts an object in the center of the group. They must be items for which you have learned the Spanish word. One student turns around and another hides one of the objects.

❷ The student who turned around now guesses who has the object. Correct first guesses are worth five points; correct second guesses are worth three. If the second guess is wrong, the student who has the object must say that he or she has it. All take turns being the "guesser."

📹 **Modelo**

A —*Marta, ¿tienes el llavero?*
B —*No, no lo tengo.*
A —*Carlos, ¿tienes el llavero?*
C —*No, no lo tengo.*
A —*¿Quién tiene el llavero?*
D —*¡Yo lo tengo!*

▼29 Escribir

Lo quiero porque . . .

Escribe una lista de cinco cosas que quieres comprar. Para cada cosa, escribe una frase para explicar por qué la quieres y una frase para explicar por qué la necesitas.

Modelo

Quiero comprar un disco compacto nuevo.
Lo quiero porque me gusta la música jazz.
Lo necesito para mi clase de música.

El español en el mundo del trabajo

Large stores and mail-order companies employ buyers who search the world over for goods to offer their customers. Buyers often need to rely on their language skills when looking for products in places where English may not be spoken, and when negotiating prices.

• What stores in your community might employ buyers who travel the world (or the Internet) in search of products from Spanish-speaking countries?

DIFFERENTIATED INSTRUCTION

Heritage Language Learners

Ask students to describe a market similar to *el Rastro* in their heritage country. Have they visited the market? What is sold there? Do people bargain? Have students describe the general atmosphere of the market.

Advanced Learners

Have students write a letter to a relative or friend to tell them about a great purchase they made. In the letter, they should talk about what they bought, where they found it *(lo encontré)*, how much they paid for it, and why they bought it.

Practice and Communicate 7B

▼30 | 👥 | Hablar

Pero mamá, necesito . . .

Quieres ir de compras, pero primero debes hablar con tu madre o padre. Trabaja con un(a) compañero(a) y usa tu lista de la Actividad 29 para explicar lo que necesitas y ¡pide *(ask for)* dinero! Tu madre o padre va a explicar por qué no necesitas comprar nada. Tu profesor(a) te dará el papel *(will assign the role)* que vas a hacer.

❶ **Hijo(a):** Piensa en lo que quieres comprar y cómo vas a convencer *(convince)* a tu padre o madre.

Padre (Madre): Tienes que decir a tu hijo(a) que no necesita lo que pide. Piensa en razones *(reasons)* para convencerle de esto.

❷ Practica el drama con otro(a) estudiante.

❸ Presenta el drama a tus compañeros. Ellos van a decidir quién tiene las mejores razones: los padres o los hijos.

▼31 | ♻ | 💬 | Escribir • Hablar

Y tú ¿qué dices?

1. ¿Qué ropa compraste recientemente? ¿Por qué la compraste?

2. ¿De qué color son tus zapatos favoritos? ¿Dónde los compraste?

3. ¿Qué ropa llevaste ayer? ¿Cuándo la compraste?

4. ¿Qué cosas buscaste recientemente en el centro comercial? ¿En qué tiendas las buscaste?

▶ Modelo

A —*Mamá, necesito dinero para comprar un disco compacto nuevo.*
B —*¿Y por qué lo quieres?*
A —*Lo quiero porque me gusta la música jazz.*
B —*No, no lo necesitas. Tienes muchos discos compactos.*
A —*Pero mamá, también lo necesito para mi clase de música.*
B —*Sí, pero lo tienen en la biblioteca, ¿verdad?*

Más práctica GO

realidades.com | print

Instant Check	✔	
Guided WB p. 92	✔	✔
Core WB p. 52	✔	✔
Comm. WB p. 58	✔	✔
***Hispanohablantes* WB** pp. 279, 281		✔

---

30 Standards: 1.1

Focus: Using direct object pronouns in authentic speaking situations

Suggestions: Tell students to make a list of the things they want to buy. Have them think about reasons their parents might give for not being able to buy something. Remind them to use direct object pronouns in their skits.

Answers will vary.

31 Standards: 1.1, 1.3

Focus: Writing and talking about purchases and clothing

Recycle: Clothing

Suggestions: Have students include illustrations of the clothing they mention.

Answers will vary.

Theme Project

Students can perform Step 5 at this point. (For more information, see p. 154-b.)

Additional Resources

• Communication Wbk.: Audio Act. 9, p. 58
• Teacher's Resource Book: Audio Script, pp. 203–204, Communicative Pair Activity BLM, pp. 210–211
• Audio Program DVD: Cap. 7B, Track 14

ENRICH YOUR TEACHING

Culture Note

The name of the famous *el Rastro* comes from the time when that area of Madrid was used to butcher meat for the open-air market. The word *rastro* means "remains" or "traces" in English, and refers to the traces of blood left after the butchers finished their work.

Teacher-to-Teacher

If there is a large Spanish-speaking population in your community, find out if there are any outdoor markets where Spanish-speaking vendors sell products. If so, suggest that students visit the market and report back on the types of things available there.

✔ ASSESSMENT

Prueba 7B-5 with Study Plan (online only)

Quiz: Direct object pronouns
• Prueba 7B-5: p. 194

207

Lectura

Core Instruction

Standards: 1.1, 1.2, 3.1

Focus: Reading for comprehension and cultural perspectives

🌐 **Mapa global interactivo, Actividad 4**
Visit shopping areas in New York, Miami, Los Angeles, and San Antonio.

Suggestions: Direct students' attention to the Objectives to preview the goals of this section.

Pre-reading: Read the *Strategy* aloud and have students provide examples of how their prior experience has helped them with reading an unfamiliar text, listening to a news broadcast, or talking with a friend. For this assignment, they will need to think about a trip, shopping, and unique shopping items.

Reading: Have volunteers read the article aloud. After each paragraph, have students summarize what they have read. Then have them think of an experience they have had that was similar.

Post-reading: Ask students to say at which place they would like to shop. Complete the *¿Comprendes?* in class.

Extension: Have students write a paragraph telling which shopping site they would like to visit and why.

BELLRINGER REVIEW

Show the transparency for the map for the United States. As a class locate these cities: Nueva York, Miami, Los Ángeles, San Antonio. Ask several students, *¿Visitaste una de estas ciudades el verano pasado?*

Pre-AP* Support

- **Learning Objective:** Interpretive: Print and Audio
- **Activity:** Write the names for the four cities highlighted in this article on the board. After reading the article, read teacher-made statements about each one of the cities and have students indicate which city is being described.
- **Pre-AP* Resource Book:** Comprehensive guide to Pre-AP* reading skill development, pp. 19–26

¡Adelante!

> ▶ Read about shopping in four Hispanic communities in the United States
> ▶ Use prior experience to understand what you read
> ▶ Consider the relationship between handicrafts and artwork

Lectura

¡De compras!

Lee este artículo de una revista. A Luisa le encanta ir de compras. ¿Qué puede comprar en cada ciudad?

> **Strategy**
>
> **Using prior experience**
> Think about a trip that you took to another city. Did you go shopping? What items did you find that were unique to that city?

De COMPRAS
con Luisa, la compradora

¡Me encanta ir de compras! Hay muchos lugares donde me gusta ir de compras en los vecindarios[1] hispanos. Siempre es una experiencia divertida. Hay cosas que uno puede comprar que son muy baratas y que no hay en otros lugares. Voy a hablar de mis aventuras por las comunidades hispanas de Nueva York, Miami, Los Ángeles y San Antonio.

En el Barrio de Nueva York, en la calle[2] 116, venden ropa, comida típica del Caribe, discos compactos, libros y mucho más. Allí compré una camiseta con la bandera de Puerto Rico. En junio siempre hay una celebración grande que se llama el Festival de la calle 116. ¡Me encanta Nueva York!

La Pequeña Habana y la calle Ocho son el corazón[3] de la comunidad cubana en Miami. Hay bodegas[4] que venden productos típicos cubanos: frijoles[5] negros y frutas tropicales como el maguey y la papaya. Allí compré pasta de guayaba, un dulce delicioso que los cubanos comen con queso blanco. ¡Qué rico!

[1]neighborhoods [2]street [3]heart
[4]grocery stores [5]beans

La calle 116, en Nueva York

Tienda en la Pequeña Habana, Miami

Pasta de guayaba

DIFFERENTIATED INSTRUCTION

Students with Learning Difficulties

To help students understand the reading, display a map and highlight the four cities with large adhesive notes. Write key words from the descriptions on the notes. As students read, call their attention to the map to help provide context.

Advanced Learners

Have students write five sentences about a souvenir they or someone they know bought while on a trip. They can share their stories with a small group or set up displays for their stories. Have them bring the souvenir to class, if possible.

De compras en la calle Olvera, Los Ángeles

La calle Olvera es la calle más antigua[6] de la ciudad de Los Ángeles y allí uno puede ver la cultura mexicana. Hay muchos restaurantes y muchos lugares para comprar artesanías.[7] Me encanta ir de compras en las joyerías porque las joyas me fascinan. En las joyerías de la calle Olvera, venden joyas de plata:[8] aretes, collares, anillos y mucho más. En una joyería de allí compré una pulsera muy bonita a un precio muy bajo.

El Mercado en San Antonio, Texas

¡Ahora vamos a hablar de San Antonio! ¡Qué compras! En esta ciudad bonita de Texas, hay tiendas de artesanías mexicanas que son fabulosas. Mis favoritas están en el Mercado o como dicen en inglés, Market Square. Allí compré una piñata para mi hermano, una blusa bordada[9] para mi madre, una cartera para mi padre y un sarape[10] para decorar mi dormitorio… ¡y no pagué mucho!

[6]oldest [7]handicrafts [8]silver [9]embroidered [10]shawl; blanket

¿Comprendes?

1. De los cuatro lugares en *¡De compras!*, ¿adónde debe ir cada persona?

   Ana: Me gustaría comprar algo de Puerto Rico.
   Lorenzo: A mí me fascinan las artesanías mexicanas.
   Miguel: ¿Mi almuerzo favorito? El sándwich cubano.

2. ¿Qué compró Luisa en cada lugar?

Más práctica	GO
realidades.com	print

Guided WB p. 93	✔	✔
Comm. WB pp. 62, 163	✔	✔
Hispanohablantes WB pp. 282–283		✔
Cultural Reading Activity		✔

▼ Fondo Cultural

Las artesanías Handicrafts from Puerto Rico, Mexico, and other Spanish-speaking countries have been popular for years among tourists looking for gift ideas. Now these handicrafts are receiving recognition as museum-quality artwork. At the Mexican Fine Arts Center Museum in the Pilsen neighborhood of Chicago, visitors can see permanent collections of paintings, weavings, sculpture, pottery, and silver jewelry from all over Mexico. Other types of handmade items are for sale in the museum's gift shop.

• Do you think that handicrafts should be displayed in museums along with fine art? Why or why not?

Una caja pintada de El Salvador

doscientos nueve **209**
Capítulo 7B

ENRICH YOUR TEACHING

Culture Note

The first two weekends in December, Puerto Rico highlights its crafts with a huge cultural fair at which artisans set up booths to exhibit their work. Paintings, woodcarvings, embroidery, and ceramics are some of the crafts that are displayed.

Teacher-to-Teacher

Have a show-and-tell day. Ask students to bring to class any craft items they may have from a Spanish-speaking country. If they do not have any, perhaps you could loan items from your own travels to students who could then research and give a report on them.

Perspectivas del mundo hispano

Core Instruction

Standards: 4.2

Focus: Reading about shopping malls and how people use them

Suggestions: Discuss with students their reasons for going to the mall. Point to the photo and have them compare it to malls they have been to. Have them read the text. Compare the reasons people from Chile and from the United States go to malls.

Direct attention to the *Think about it!* section and have students discuss the questions.

Mention that some adults in the United States complain about young people hanging around in the mall. Ask students if this is a valid complaint, and based on what they have read, if they think it would be an issue in Chile.

Have students complete the *Check it out!* section for homework. Discuss the answers at a later date.

Answers will vary.

Teacher-to-Teacher

e-amigos: Have students e-mail their *e-amigos* to ask about recent gifts they have purchased. Have them print out or e-mail you the questions and responses.

Additional Resources

Student Resource: Realidades para hispanohablantes, p. 286

Perspectivas del mundo hispano

¿Por qué vas al centro comercial?

Why do people go to the mall? Note the differences between consumers in Chile and the United States.

In the United States many people go to the mall to see what merchandise is available and to spend time. In Chile, many people go to the mall because they want to make a specific purchase. They decide where to go according to the merchandise they need to buy.

For many in the United States, going to the mall is more than going shopping. The mall offers an opportunity to eat and to spend time with friends. For 50% of U.S. consumers, the atmosphere of a mall is very important. Only 13% of Chilean consumers think that atmosphere is important.

Although their motivation for going to the mall is different, 80% of both Chilean and U.S. consumers make a purchase once they are in the stores.

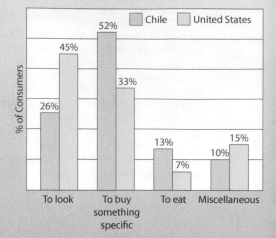

Check it out! Interview at least three people your age and at least three adults that you know and find out what their main reasons for going to a mall are, how they decide which mall to go to, and if they usually make a purchase while at the mall. Compare what you find out with the results above for shoppers in the United States and Chile.

Think about it! Why might shoppers in the United States consider the mall atmosphere an important factor in their decision about where to shop? Given what you have read about the reasons Chileans go shopping, what do you think a store clerk in a mall in Chile might expect you to do if you entered his or her store? How might a Chilean exchange student feel if he or she went to the mall with you and your friends?

En el centro comercial Galerías Pacífico, en Buenos Aires, Argentina

DIFFERENTIATED INSTRUCTION

Advanced Learners

Have students research malls in Spanish-speaking countries and in the United States. Ask them to prepare a visual comparison, using photos.

Heritage Language Learners

Have students conduct informal interviews of family or friends from their heritage country to find out when and why people go to malls. Do they go to spend time or only for a specific purchase?

Presentación escrita

Un regalo para mi . . .

▶ Write a letter about a gift for a relative
▶ Decide on a format and organize information before writing

Task
You recently bought a gift for a family member. Write a letter to a relative about the gift so that he or she will not buy the same item.

1 **Prewrite** A family member is celebrating a birthday. Think about the gift you bought. Answer the questions to organize your thoughts.

- ¿Para quién es el regalo?
- ¿Qué compraste y por qué?
- ¿Dónde lo compraste? ¿Cuánto pagaste?
- ¿Cuándo es la fiesta de cumpleaños?

2 **Draft** Use your Prewrite answers to write a first draft. Begin your letter with *Querido(a)...* or *Hola...*, and close it with *Tu primo(a)..., Saludos,* or *Hasta pronto.*

3 **Revise** Read the letter and check spelling, vocabulary choice, verb forms, and agreement. Share the letter with a partner, who will check the following:

- Is the letter easy to read and understand?
- Does it provide all the necessary information?
- Did you use appropriate letter form?
- Are there any errors?

4 **Publish** Rewrite the letter, making any necessary changes or additions. Share your letter with your teacher. You may also want to add it to your portfolio.

5 **Evaluation** The following rubric will be used to grade your letter.

Strategy

Organizing information
Thinking about the correct format and necessary information beforehand will help you write a better letter.

Querido Mauricio:

Compré un reloj pulsera para el abuelito. Lo compré en el almacén Génova que está en el centro comercial Plaza del Río. No pagué mucho por él. Creo que al abuelito le va a gustar. Voy a ver a toda la familia el 2 de octubre para la fiesta de cumpleaños del abuelito.

Tu primo,
Luis

Rubric	Score 1	Score 3	Score 5
How easily the letter is understood	Only a little of what you have written is comprehensible to others.	Most of what you have written is comprehensible.	All of what you have written is comprehensible to others.
Amount of information provided	You only give information about the gift and where it was purchased.	You give information about the gift, where you bought it, and why.	You provide all gift information and information about the party.
Appropriate greeting and closing are used	You use only a greeting or closing.	You use both a greeting and closing, but there are errors.	You use both a greeting and closing accurately.
Accurate use of the preterite	You use many incorrect verb forms.	You use incorrect verb forms.	You use very few incorrect verb forms.

doscientos once **211**
Capítulo 7B

Presentación escrita

Expository
Standards: 1.3

Focus: Writing a letter to describe a gift

Suggestions: Review the task and the steps with students. After reading the *Strategy*, suggest how they might organize information for a letter. Review the rubric to explain how you will grade their letters. Explain what is necessary for a top-scoring presentation, and have them use the model as a guide. Encourage students to write about a gift that was special, not necessarily expensive. Help them to work through each step of the writing process.

Pre-AP* Support

- **Learning Objective:** Interpersonal Writing
- **Activity:** Have students use the information in the letter they wrote to draft a reply e-mail from the recipient of the gift. Have them imagine the family member has received the gift, and writes to thank the gift-giver, and saying how much they enjoy the present.
- *Pre-AP* Resource Book:* Comprehensive guide to Pre-AP* writing skill development, pp. 27–38

Portfolio

Have students add this activity to their portfolios.

Additional Resources

Student Resources: Realidades para hispano-hablantes, p. 287; Guided Practice: Presentación escrita, p. 94

ENRICH YOUR TEACHING

Teacher-to-Teacher

Careers: *Tema 7* has focused on shopping. Have students work in small groups to talk about a career in retail. Ask students to generate a list of words, expressions, and sentences they have learned that would be useful for working in or managing a clothing store. Ask groups to share their lists.

21st Century Skills

Flexibility and Adaptability Using the letter on this page as a model, have students first discuss (in English) how the letter would be different if they wrote about a different gift or wrote to a different person--a younger brother, or a teacher. How would these changes affect the tone, the content, and the language of the letter?

✓ ASSESSMENT

Presentación escrita
- Assessment Program: Rubrics, p. T32
Go over the descriptions of the different levels of performance. After assessing students, help individuals understand how their performance could be improved.

7B Video

Videomisterio ▶

Core Instruction

Standards: 1.2, 2.1, 2.2, 5.2

Resources: Teacher's Resource Book: Video Script, pp. 162–163; Video Program: Cap. 7B; Video Program Teacher's Guide: Cap. 7B

Focus: Introducing the events and vocabulary of this episode; scanning and reading the episode summary

Personajes importantes:
Lola Lago, detective
Margarita, secretaria de Lola
Paco, colega de Lola
Pedro, nieto de doña Gracia

Synopsis: Pedro Requena decides to hire Lola to investigate what caused the incident at his grandmother's house that sent her to the hospital and who stole doña Gracia's jewels from her apartment. Inspector Gil suspects María, since she has disappeared. Lola accepts the job and they come to an agreement on the cost of her services.

Suggestions:

Pre-viewing: Review the events of the previous episode. Lola and Carmela met at the San Carlos hospital where they asked Rosalinda for help in getting information about María Requena, who spent three months there as a result of a car accident. But her medical record cannot be found. They inquired about María's friend, Julia, who also was in the accident. Julia died in the hospital, but her file cannot be found either.

Review the *Nota cultural* with the class. You may want to ask students if they know when it is appropriate to use or switch from *usted* to the informal *tú.* Point out the *Palabras para comprender,* saying examples in context and writing the sentences on the chalkboard. Remind students that these words are to help them understand the episode and that they are not responsible for learning them.

Visual scanning: Direct students' attention to the picture and ask who these characters are (Lola and Pedro), what their relationship is (he is Lola's client), and where they meet (at Lola's detective agency). Before students read the *Resumen del episodio,* have them scan the text and find three cognate words. *(oficina, detective, privado, preciosas, problema, robó)* Then ask them to read the *Resumen del episodio* carefully and ask questions about what they think will happen in this episode.

¿Eres tú, María?
Episodio 6

Antes de ver el video

Resumen del episodio

Lola llega a su oficina y hay un recado de Pedro Requena. Él viene a hablar con ella sobre su abuela, doña Gracia. Necesita un detective privado y quiere la ayuda de Lola y Paco. Pedro explica que su abuela es una mujer muy rica y que tiene joyas preciosas. Pero hay un problema. Las joyas de doña Gracia no están en el piso. Pedro cree que un ladrón robó las joyas. Pero, ¿cómo sabe el ladrón que hay joyas en el piso de doña Gracia?

"Por favor, ¿por qué no me tuteas?"

Nota cultural Lola quotes Pedro a price for her agency's services in euros. The euro is the currency in Spain and many other countries in Europe that are part of the European Union.

Nota cultural In Spain, it is customary for adults to speak to new acquaintances using the formal *Ud.* In most cases, the other person will then invite you to address them informally using the *tú* form. This is called *tutear.* In this scene, Pedro invites Lola to speak to him informally. When you visit Spain, you should address new adult acquaintances in the *Ud.* form and wait to be invited to *tutear.*

Palabras para comprender

un recado	a message
una cita	an appointment
Acabo de venir del hospital.	I just came from the hospital.
Vi a su abuela.	I saw your grandmother.
necesito saber	I need to know . . .
el ladrón robó	the burglar stole
nosotros cobramos	we charge

DIFFERENTIATED INSTRUCTION

Advanced Learners

Have students write three sentences summarizing the episode. They should include at least four new vocabulary words from this chapter and write the sentences using preterite *-ar* verbs.

"Mi abuela es una mujer rica. Tiene dinero y joyas de valor. Son de la familia".

"María va a recibir todo el dinero, todas las joyas, todo de mi abuela".

"Pedro, vamos a buscar las joyas".

Después de ver el video

¿Comprendes?

Termina las frases con la palabra más apropiada del recuadro.

fotos	sobrina
recado	abuela
joyas	teléfono
dinero	nieto

1. Lola, hay un ___ para ti de un tal Pedro Reteña, Resqueña o Retena. Algo así.

2. El ___ de doña Gracia viene a la una y media.

3. ¡Qué bueno! Un cliente con ___.

4. Acabo de venir del hospital. Vi a su ___.

5. Aquí tengo unas ___ de ella.

6. Mira, las ___ no están en el piso.

7. Aquí está el número de ___: 318-18-02.

Más práctica (GO)

realidades.com | print

Actividades ✔

Viewing: Play *Episodio* 6 for the class. If there is time after viewing the full episode, select some key moments that you wish to highlight, such as the scene in which Pedro explains to Lola that it is important to find the jewels because María is going to inherit everything from her aunt.

Post-viewing: Point out the list of words that appear in the box. Then have the students look at the pictures and the captions at the top of the page and use them to summarize the scenes in this episode. Write the vocabulary presented in this episode on the chalkboard to help students create sentences for each important scene that adds new information to the plot. Then direct students' attention to the *¿Comprendes?* section.

▼ ¿Comprendes? Standards: 1.2, 1.3

Resources: Answer Keys: Student Edition, p. 154

Focus: Verifying comprehension by answering questions; reviewing the plot

Suggestions: Remind students to read all of the sentences before choosing the best word from the box to fill in the blank.

Answers:

1. recado	5. fotos
2. nieto	6. joyas
3. dinero	7. teléfono
4. abuela	

Extension: Ask students to prepare questions to test the class's comprehension of the reading. Have them work in pairs or small groups. Have them ask who, what, when, where, and why questions. Give them an example to guide them.

Additional Resources

- *¿Eres tú, María?* Video Workbook, Episode 6
- *¿Eres tú, María?* Teacher's Video Guide: Answer Key

ENRICH YOUR TEACHING

Teacher-to-Teacher

Since English does not have the *tú* versus **usted** subject pronouns, what do English speakers use to establish formal and informal forms of address? You may want to discuss the notion of "register" with your students in order to develop their awareness of appropriate and inappropriate language in different situations in Spanish. Just as in English, the choice of formal versus informal words is another way Spanish speakers signal the form of address they expect from their counterparts in conversation.

Review Activities

To talk about places to shop: Let students work in pairs to quiz each other on the vocabulary. They can create flashcards, writing the Spanish word on one side and the English word on the other. They can also include drawings to help them remember the words.

To talk about gifts you might buy: Let students work in pairs and ask what gifts they have purchased, where they bought them, and how much they cost. This will also allow for practice of the preterite of ***comprar.*** Have students reverse roles.

To talk about buying and selling: Have students interview different pairs who have been practicing together to find out if their purchases were cheap or expensive and for whom they bought the gift. Students should use the preterite of ***buscar, comprar,*** and ***pagar.***

Direct object pronouns: Have students write five sentences about an item they bought. For each item, they must write where they purchased it and use a direct object pronoun. Example: *Compré un anillo para mi novia. Lo compré en la joyería.*

Portfolio

Invite students to review the activities they completed in this chapter, including written reports, posters or other visuals, and recordings of oral presentations or projects. Have them select one or two items that they feel best demonstrate their achievements in Spanish. Include these in students' portfolios. Have them include this with the Chapter Checklist and Self-Assessment Worksheet.

Additional Resources

Student Resources: Realidades para hispanohablantes, p. 288

Teacher Resources:
- Teacher's Resource Book: Situation Cards, p. 212, Clip Art, pp. 214–215
- Assessment Program: Chapter Checklist and Self-Assessment Worksheet, pp. T56–T57

Repaso del capítulo

Vocabulario y gramática

to talk about places where you shop

el almacén, *pl.* los almacenes	department store
en la Red	online
la joyería	jewelry store
la librería	bookstore
la tienda de descuentos	discount store
la tienda de electrodomésticos	household appliance store
la zapatería	shoe store

to talk about gifts you might buy

el anillo	ring
los anteojos de sol	sunglasses
los aretes	earrings
el bolso	purse
la cadena	chain
la cartera	wallet
el collar	necklace
la corbata	tie
los guantes	gloves
el llavero	key chain
el perfume	perfume
la pulsera	bracelet
el reloj pulsera	watch
el software	software

to talk about who might receive a gift

el novio	boyfriend
la novia	girlfriend

For *Vocabulario adicional,* see pp. 336–337.

to talk about buying or selling

barato, -a	inexpensive, cheap
caro, -a	expensive
mirar	to look (at)
pagar (por)	to pay (for)
vender	to sell

to talk about time in the past

anoche	last night
el año pasado	last year
ayer	yesterday
hace + *time expression*	ago
la semana pasada	last week

other useful expressions

¡Uf!	Ugh! Yuck!

preterite of regular *-ar* verbs

compré	compramos
compraste	comprasteis
compró	compraron

preterite of *-car* and *-gar* verbs

These verbs have a spelling change in the *yo* form of the preterite.

buscar	$c \rightarrow qu$	yo busqué
pagar	$g \rightarrow gu$	yo pagué
jugar	$g \rightarrow gu$	yo jugué

direct object pronouns

	SINGULAR	PLURAL
M.	lo it	los them
F.	la it	las them

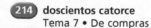

DIFFERENTIATED INSTRUCTION

Students with Learning Difficulties

Have students review the *Repaso del capítulo* and create flashcards for any words that they do not know. Pair them with a student who is more confident with the vocabulary to practice. Before the test, provide students with a practice test, so they can become comfortable with the format.

Heritage Language Learners

Have students write a few paragraphs telling about their perfect birthday celebration: Where are they going to have it? Whom are they going to invite? What food are they going to eat? What kind of music are they going to play? Encourage them to use as many vocabulary words from this chapter as they can.

Más repaso GO   realidades.com | print

Instant Check		✔
Puzzles		✔
Core WB pp. 53–54		✔ ✔
Comm. WB pp. 164, 165–167		✔ ✔

Preparación para el examen

On the exam you will be asked to . . .	Here are practice tasks similar to those you will find on the exam . . .	For review go to your print or digital textbook . . .
1 Escuchar Listen as someone describes what she bought as a gift and where she bought it	As a teenager tells what she bought for her friend's *quinceañera* (girl's fifteenth birthday party), see if you can tell: a) what she bought; b) where she bought it; c) how much she paid for it.	**pp. 186–191** *Vocabulario en contexto* **p. 187** Actividad 1 **p. 192** Actividad 6
2 Hablar Exchange opinions about whether certain items are expensive or inexpensive	Think about a gift you've bought. Tell your partner what you bought, for whom you bought it, and how much you paid. Then ask whether he or she thinks that it is expensive or inexpensive. Your partner will then share the same information and ask the same question about a gift he or she bought.	**p. 192** Actividad 7 **p. 193** Actividad 9 **p. 194** Actividad 10 **p. 203** Actividad 23 **p. 204** Actividad 25 **p. 205** Actividades 26–27
3 Leer Read and understand an online advertisement for a store you might find on the Internet	While surfing on the Internet, you find a Web site for a discount store in Mexico City. Can you list at least two advantages for customers who shop here?	**pp. 186–191** *Vocabulario en contexto* **p. 194** Actividad 11

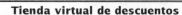

> **Tienda virtual de descuentos**
> Todos nuestros clientes reciben un descuento del 10%. Tenemos de todo —perfume para su novia, bolsos para su mamá, videojuegos para su hermano y software para Ud. Tenemos los mejores precios y descuentos de la Red. Si paga por algo en la Tienda virtual, va a recibir "ePesos". Puede usarlos en su próxima visita.

4 Escribir Write a short explanation about some items that you have bought this school year with your own money	As an entry for your class journal, explain how you spent your money last month. Describe: a) at least two new clothing items or accessories you bought; b) where you bought the items; c) how much you paid for them.	**p. 199** Actividad 18 **p. 203** Actividades 22–23 **p. 205** Actividad 27 **p. 211** *Presentación escrita*
5 Pensar Demonstrate an understanding of cultural perspectives regarding shopping	Think about what you do when you go to a shopping mall. Based on what you've learned in this chapter, would these be the same things that Chileans do? What similarities and differences would you expect to see in shopping malls and in attitudes of shoppers in both countries?	**p. 210** *Perspectivas del mundo hispano*

Performance Tasks

Standards: 1.1, 1.2, 1.3, 4.2

Student Resource: Realidades para hispanohablantes, p. 289

Teacher Resources: Teacher's Resource Book: Audio Script, p. 204; Audio Program DVD: Cap. 7B, Track 16; Answer Keys: Student Edition, p. 155

1. Escuchar

Suggestions: Use the audio or read the script. Students can create three columns on their papers: ¿Qué compró? ¿Dónde lo compró? ¿Cuánto costó?

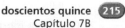 **Script:**

Yo compré este llavero para ella. Lo busqué en un almacén la semana pasada y pagué doscientos pesos. Es muy bonito, ¿no?

Answers:

a) The person bought a key ring.
b) The person bought it in a department store.
c) The person paid 200 pesos.

2. Hablar

Suggestions: Give students time to brainstorm before starting their conversation. They can make up prices for different items to use both **barato** and **caro.**

Answers will vary.

3. Leer

Suggestions: Have students read the ad silently, then have a volunteer read it aloud. Remind students that cognates will help them understand it.

Answers:

1. You can get a 10% discount.
2. You can accumulate "ePesos."

4. Escribir

Suggestions: Have students pre-write and write answers to a–c. Then they should expand their notes into a paragraph.

Answers will vary.

5. Pensar

Suggestions: Have students refer to the *Perspectivas del mundo hispano* on p. 210.

Answers will vary.

DIFFERENTIATED ASSESSMENT

CORE ASSESSMENT

- **Assessment Program:** Examen del capítulo 7B, pp. 195–200
- **Audio Program DVD:** Cap. 7B, Track 17
- **ExamView:** Chapter Test, Test Banks A and B

ADVANCED/PRE-AP*

- **ExamView:** Pre-AP* Test Bank
- **Pre-AP* Resource Book,** pp. 86–89

STUDENTS NEEDING EXTRA HELP

- **Alternate Assessment Program:** Examen del capítulo 7B
- **Audio Program DVD:** Cap. 7B, Track 17

HERITAGE LEARNERS

- **Assessment Program: Realidades para hispanohablantes:** Examen del capítulo 7B
- **ExamView: Heritage Learner Test Bank**

8A De vacaciones

- **Travel, vacations, and past events**

Vocabulary: vacation places and activities; modes of transportation

Grammar: preterite of *-er* and *-ir* verbs; preterite of *ir;* the personal *a*

Cultural Perspectives: travel and vacations

8B Ayudando en la comunidad

- **Volunteer work, community service tasks, what people do to help others**

Vocabulary: recycling and volunteer work; places in a community

Grammar: the verb *decir;* indirect object pronouns; preterite of *hacer* and *dar*

Cultural Perspectives: volunteer work

THEME SUPPORT

Bulletin Boards

Theme: *Experiencias*

Ask students to cut out, copy, or download photos of famous tourist destinations and attractions from around the world, and of people engaged in recreational and volunteer activities. Cluster photos according to the three above-mentioned themes.

Hands-on Culture

Chant: *Invito a...*

Jumping rope is a popular pastime, while on vacation or at home, of children throughout the Spanish-speaking world. The following is a chant sung by the person jumping rope to invite someone else to jump with him or her.

> *Invito a...* (the name of the person).
> —¿A qué?   —A un pastel.
> —¿A qué hora?   —A las tres.
> *Que una, que dos, que tres.*

The person who has been invited jumps in.

Suggestions for using the chant:
1. Teach students the jumping chant, and explain how the game is played.
2. Bring in a long jump-rope. Ask two volunteers to swing the jump-rope and a third volunteer to jump.
3. Have the volunteer jumping begin the chant, then ask the class to join in on the second line.
4. Have the class clap out a rhythm for the jumpers after they say the last line of the chant until one of the jumpers steps on the rope, and is out.
5. Play again, until everyone who wants to take a turn has had one.

Game

¡Cuéntame!

Play this game to review the material from *Capítulo* 8A.

Players: the whole class

Materials: index cards

Rules:
1. On index cards, write vocabulary words and expressions from *Capítulo* 8A as well as other *-er* and *-ir* verbs students have learned. Place the cards in a box.
2. Have every student draw an index card from the box.
3. Ask for a volunteer to begin a story, using the word on his or her card in a sentence. Write the student's sentence on the board or a transparency. Ask the class to make any necessary corrections.
4. Call on another volunteer to continue the story, using his or her word. Write the second volunteer's sentence on the board, and have the class make any necessary corrections. Continue in this manner until the class feels the story has reached a logical conclusion. If every student has not had the chance to contribute to the story, begin a second story.

   Student 1: (drew **zoológico**) Ayer visité el zoológico.
   Student 2: (drew **autobús**) Fui al zoológico en autobús.
   Student 3: (drew **animal**) Hay muchos animales en el zoológico.

Variation: Play the game at the end of *Capítulo* 8B, writing only verbs on the index cards. Have students tell the story in the preterite tense.

THEME PROJECT

Diario ilustrado

Overview: On construction paper or using electronic tools, students create illustrated journal entries for an imaginary one-week volunteer vacation they took. They then present their journals to the class, describing how they traveled, where they went, and what they did.

Resources: magazines, scissors, glue, markers, colored pencils or crayons, construction paper; or page layout tools, electronic photos and Internet access

Sequence: (suggestions for when to do each step appear throughout the chapters)

8A

STEP 1. Review instructions so students know what is expected of them. Hand out the "Theme 8 Project Instructions and Rubric" from the *Teacher's Resource Book.*

STEP 2. Students submit an outline and sketch of their journal entries. Return the drafts with your suggestions.

STEP 3. Students cut out or draw the illustrations they need, then create the layout for their journals on construction paper. Encourage students to think through the details of their designs before implementing them.

8B

STEP 4. Students submit drafts of their journal entries. Note your corrections and suggestions, then return drafts to students. Students correct their drafts, then partner to describe their trips.

STEP 5. Students present their journals to the class, describing where they went, what they did, and how they traveled.

Options:

1. Students present a slide show of a volunteer vacation, using transparencies or a computer.
2. Students create an illustrated itinerary of a real or imaginary vacation.

Assessment:

Here is a detailed rubric for assessing this project:

Theme 8 Project: *Diario ilustrado*

RUBRIC	Score 1	Score 3	Score 5
Evidence of planning	You didn't submit a sketch and draft.	You submitted the sketch and draft, but didn't correct them.	You submitted and corrected your sketch and draft.
Use of illustrations	You didn't include photos / illustrations.	You included photos / illustrations for most entries.	You included photos / illustrations for all entries.
Presentation	You listed places, activities, and transport; you had no description or complete sentences.	You listed places, activities, and transport; some description; some complete sentences.	You listed and described places, activities, and transport; you had complete sentences.

21st Century Skills

Look for tips throughout *Tema* 8 to enrich your teaching by integrating 21st Century Skills. Suggestions for the Theme Project and Theme Culture follow below.

Theme Project

Modify the Theme Project with one or more of these suggestions:

Develop Technology Literacy

To meet the goal of creating a journal that is not only informative but also appealing and attractive, have students enhance their journals by combining print, audio, and video images.

Encourage Collaboration

Have students work in small groups to compare their volunteer vacations, choosing the best proposal to present to the class. The class then chooses a plan to take on as a class project. The handout "Make Decisions" will guide the team to choose the best proposal.

Support Critical Thinking and Problem Solving

As students evaluate their classmates' proposals, ask them to consider the following questions: What elements make for the strongest or most interesting projects? Impact of the volunteer work on the community? Location? Community need?

Theme Culture

Foster Social and Cross-Cultural Skills

Have students act as travel agents whose job it is to find a suitable vacation spot for a family that cannot decide between going to Mexico or to Peru. After reviewing the cultural information about both countries in the chapter, have students prepare a helpful report for their clients.

▶ **Videocultura** View *Las vacaciones* with the class to learn about places to visit in Spanish-speaking countries.

AT A GLANCE

Objectives

- Listen to and read descriptions of trips and vacations
- Talk and write about favorite and imaginary trips
- Talk about and describe your best vacation
- Explain the tradition of the *ojo de Dios* and compare it to crafts in the United States
- Identify places of geographical and historical importance in Spanish-speaking countries, and compare them to places in the United States

Vocabulary

- Vacation destinations and activities
- Modes of transportation
- Attractions, parks, and animals
- Expressions to talk about a trip or vacation

Grammar

- The preterite of *-er* and *-ir* verbs
- The preterite of *ir*
- The personal *a*

Culture

- Joaquín Sorolla, p. 217
- El Yunque National Park, p. 224
- Places in Mexico City, p. 228
- Public transportation in Mexico City, p. 228
- Song *"Cielito Lindo"*, p. 229
- Patagonia, p. 235
- Geographic facts about the Americas, p. 238
- Cuzco, Machu Picchu, Lake Titicaca, Nazca lines, pp. 240–241
- *El ojo de Dios,* p. 242

Recycle ♻

- The preterite of *-ar* verbs
- Direct object pronouns lo, *la, los, las*
- Question words
- *-er* and *-ir* verbs
- *estar*
- *ir; ir a* + infinitive
- *me gusta(n)*

RESOURCES

FOR THE STUDENT	ONLINE	DVD	PRINT	FOR THE TEACHER	ONLINE	PREEXP	DVD	PRINT
Plan				Interactive TE and Resources DVD	•		•	
				Teacher's Resource Book, pp. 232–267	•		•	•
				Pre-AP* Resource Book, pp. 90–93	•		•	•
				Mapa global interactivo	•			
				Lesson Plans	•			•
Introducción PP. **216–217**								
Present Student Edition, pp. 216–217	•	•	•	Interactive TE and Resources DVD	•		•	
DK Reference Atlas	•	•		Teacher's Resource Book, pp. 232–235	•		•	•
Videocultura	•	•		Galería de fotos		•		
Hispanohablantes WB, pp. 290–291			•	Fine Art Transparencies, 18	•	•	•	
				Map Transparencies, 12–16, 18	•	•	•	
Vocabulario en contexto PP. **218–223**								
Present & Practice Student Edition, pp. 218–223	•	•	•	Interactive TE and Resources DVD	•		•	
Audio	•	•		Teacher's Resource Book, pp. 236–238, 241, 250–251	•		•	•
Videohistoria	•	•		Vocabulary Clip Art	•	•	•	
Flashcards	•	•		Audio Program	•	•	•	
Instant Check	•			Video Program: Videohistoria	•		•	
Guided WB, pp. 95–104	•	•	•	Video Program Teacher's Guide: Cap. 8A	•		•	
Core WB, pp. 55–58	•	•	•	Vocabulary and Grammar Transparencies, 143–146	•	•	•	
Comm. WB, pp. 63–66	•	•	•	Answer Keys: Student Edition, pp. 156–158	•	•	•	
Hispanohablantes WB, pp. 292–293			•	TPR Stories, pp. 107–121	•		•	•
Assess and Remediate				Prueba 8A–1: Assessment Program, pp. 201–202	•		•	•
				Assessment Program para hispanohablantes, pp. 201–202	•		•	•

RESOURCES

Vocabulario en uso PP. 224–229

FOR THE STUDENT	ONLINE	DVD	PRINT	FOR THE TEACHER	ONLINE	PREEXP	DVD	PRINT
Present & Practice								
Student Edition, pp. 224–229	•	•	•	Interactive Whiteboard Vocabulary Activities	•		•	
Instant Check	•			Interactive TE and Resources DVD			•	
Comm. WB, p. 66	•	•	•	Teacher's Resource Book, pp. 237–238, 244–245	•		•	•
Hispanohablantes WB, pp. 294–295			•	Communicative Pair Activities, pp. 244–245	•		•	•
Communicative Pair Activities	•			Audio Program	•	•	•	
				Videomodelos	•		•	
				Vocabulary and Grammar Transparencies, 149	•	•	•	
				Answer Keys: Student Edition, pp. 159–161	•	•	•	
Assess and Remediate								
				Prueba 8A–2 with Study Plan	•			
				Prueba 8A–2: Assessment Program, pp. 203–204	•		•	•
				Assessment Program para hispanohablantes, pp. 203–204	•		•	•

Gramática PP. 230–239

FOR THE STUDENT	ONLINE	DVD	PRINT	FOR THE TEACHER	ONLINE	PREEXP	DVD	PRINT
Present & Practice								
Student Edition, pp. 230–239	•	•	•	Interactive Whiteboard Grammar Activities	•		•	
Instant Check	•			Interactive TE and Resources DVD			•	
Animated Verbs	•			Teacher's Resource Book, pp. 238–239, 242, 246–247	•		•	•
Tutorial Video: Grammar	•			Communicative Pair Activities, pp. 246–247	•		•	•
Canción de hip hop	•			Audio Program	•	•	•	
Guided WB, pp. 105–108	•	•	•	Videomodelos	•		•	
Core WB, pp. 59–61	•	•	•	Video Program: GramActiva	•		•	
Comm. WB, pp. 67–68, 70–71, 168	•	•	•	Vocabulary and Grammar Transparencies, 147–148	•	•	•	
Hispanohablantes WB, pp. 296–301			•	Answer Keys: Student Edition, pp. 159–165	•	•	•	
Communicative Pair Activities	•							
Assess and Remediate								
				Pruebas 8A–3, 8A–4, and 8A–5 with Study Plans	•			
				Pruebas 8A–3, 8A–4, 8A–5: Assessment Program, pp. 205–208	•		•	•
				Assessment Program para hispanohablantes, pp. 205–208	•		•	•

¡Adelante! PP. 240–245

FOR THE STUDENT	ONLINE	DVD	PRINT	FOR THE TEACHER	ONLINE	PREEXP	DVD	PRINT
Application								
Student Edition, pp. 240–245	•	•	•	Interactive TE and Resources DVD	•		•	
Online Cultural Reading	•			Teacher's Resource Book, pp. 242–243, 249	•		•	•
Guided WB, pp. 109–110	•	•	•	Video Program: Videomisterio ¿Eres tú, María?	•		•	
Comm. WB, pp. 72, 169	•	•	•	Video Program Teacher's Guide: Cap. 8A	•		•	
Hispanohablantes WB, pp. 302–307			•	Videomisterio Quiz			•	
¿Eres tú, María? Video WB, pp. 50–57	•	•	•	Map Transparencies, 15	•		•	
				Answer Keys: Student Edition, p. 166	•		•	

Repaso del capítulo PP. 246–247

FOR THE STUDENT	ONLINE	DVD	PRINT	FOR THE TEACHER	ONLINE	PREEXP	DVD	PRINT
Review								
Student Edition, pp. 246–247	•	•	•	Interactive TE and Resources DVD	•		•	
Online Puzzles and Games	•			Teacher's Resource Book, pp. 240, 248, 250–251	•		•	•
Core WB, pp. 62–63	•	•	•	Audio Program	•	•	•	
Comm. WB, pp. 170–174	•	•	•	Answer Keys: Student Edition, p. 166	•	•	•	
Hispanohablantes WB, pp. 308–309			•					
Instant Check	•							

Chapter Assessment

FOR THE STUDENT	ONLINE	DVD	PRINT	FOR THE TEACHER	ONLINE	PREEXP	DVD	PRINT
Assess								
				Examen del capítulo 8A	•		•	•
				Assessment Program, pp. 208–214	•		•	•
				Alternate Assessment Program, pp. 88–94	•		•	•
				Assessment Program para hispanohablantes, pp. 208–214	•		•	•
				Audio Program, Cap. 8A, Examen	•		•	
				ExamView: Test Banks A and B questions only online	•		•	
				Heritage Learner Test Bank	•		•	
				Pre-AP* Test Bank	•		•	

REGULAR SCHEDULE (50 MINUTES)

DAY	Warm-up / Assess	Preview / Present / Practice / Communicate	Wrap-up / Homework Options
1	Return Examen del capítulo (10 min.)	**Vocabulario en contexto (35 min.)** • Objectives • Presentation • *Actividades* 1, 2 • Arte y cultura • Videocultura: *Las vacaciones*	**Wrap-up and Homework Options (5 min.)** • Core Practice • Vocabulary Clip Art
2	**Warm-up (5 min.)** • Homework check	**Vocabulario en contexto (40 min.)** • Review: *Vocabulario en contexto* • Presentation: *Videohistoria ¿Qué te pasó?* • View: Video *¿Qué te pasó?* • Video Activities • *Actividades* 3, 4, 5	**Wrap-up and Homework Options (5 min.)** • *Prueba* 8A-1: Vocabulary recognition • Core Practice
3	**Warm-up (5 min.)** • Homework check ✔**Formative Assessment (10 min.)** • *Prueba* 8A-1: Vocabulary recognition	**Vocabulario en uso (30 min.)** • Objectives • Interactive Whiteboard Vocabulary Activities • *Actividades* 7, 8, 9	**Wrap-up and Homework Options (5 min.)** • *Actividad* 6
4	**Warm-up (5 min.)** • Homework check • Return *Prueba* 8A-1: Vocabulary recognition	**Vocabulario en uso (40 min.)** • Review: *Vocabulario* • *Actividades* 11, 12, 13 • Communicative Pair Activities	**Wrap-up and Homework Options (5 min.)** • *Actividad* 10
5	**Warm-up (5 min.)** • Homework check	**Vocabulario en uso (40 min.)** • Review: *Vocabulario* • *Actividad* 14 • *Pronunciación* • *Fondo cultural*	**Wrap-up and Homework Options (5 min.)** • *Actividad* 15
6	**Warm-up (5 min.)** • Homework check	**Gramática y vocabulario en uso (40 min.)** • Presentation: The preterite of *-er* and *-ir* verbs • *GramActiva* Video • Interactive Whiteboard Grammar Activities • *Actividades* 16, 17, 18	**Wrap-up and Homework Options (5 min.)** • Core Practice • *Prueba* 8A-3 with Study Plan: The preterite of *-er* and *-ir* verbs
7	**Warm-up (5 min.)** • Homework check ✔**Formative Assessment (10 min.)** • *Prueba* 8A-3 with Study Plan: The preterite of *-er* and *-ir* verbs	**Gramática y vocabulario en uso (30 min.)** • Presentation: The preterite of *ir* • *GramActiva* Video • Interactive Whiteboard Grammar Activities • *Actividades* 19, 20, 21	**Wrap-up and Homework Options (5 min.)**
8	**Warm-up (5 min.)** • Homework check • Return *Prueba* 8A-3 with Study Plan: The preterite of *-er* and *-ir* verbs	**Gramática y vocabulario en uso (40 min.)** • Review: The preterite of *ir* • *Actividades* 23, 24, 25 • *Juego: Actividad* 22 • *Fondo cultural*	**Wrap-up and Homework Options (5 min.)** • *Prueba* 8A-2 with Study Plan: Vocabulary production • Core Practice

REGULAR SCHEDULE (50 MINUTES)

DAY	Warm-up / Assess	Preview / Present / Practice / Communicate	Wrap-up / Homework Options
9	**Warm-up (5 min.)** • Homework check ✔**Formative Assessment (10 min.)** • *Prueba* 8A-2 with Study Plan: Vocabulary production	**Gramática y vocabulario en uso (30 min.)** • Presentation: The personal *a* • Interactive Whiteboard Grammar Activities • *Actividades 26, 27* • *El español en la comunidad*	**Wrap-up and Homework Options (5 min.)** • *Pruebas* 8A-4, 8A-5 with Study Plans: The preterite of *ir;* the personal *a*
10	**Warm-up (5 min.)** • Homework check • Return *Prueba* 8A-2 with Study Plan: Vocabulary production ✔**Formative Assessment (10 min.)** • *Pruebas* 8A-4, 8A-5 with Study Plans: The preterite of *ir;* the personal *a*	**Gramática y vocabulario en uso (30 min.)** • *Conexiones: Juego: Actividad 28* • *Exploración del lenguaje* • *Actividad 29* • Communicative Pair Activities	**Wrap-up and Homework Options (5 min.)** • Core Practice
11	**Warm-up (5 min.)** • Homework check • Return *Pruebas* 8A-4, 8A-5 with Study Plans: The preterite of *ir;* the personal *a*	**¡Adelante! (40 min.)** • *Lectura* • *Fondo cultural* • *Presentación oral:* Prepare	**Wrap-up and Homework Options (5 min.)** • *Presentación oral:* Prepare
12	**Warm-up (5 min.)** • Homework check	**¡Adelante! (40 min.)** • *La cultura en vivo* • *Presentación oral:* Practice	**Wrap-up and Homework Options (5 min.)**
13	**Warm-up (5 min.)** • Homework check	**¡Adelante! (40 min.)** • *Presentación oral:* Present	**Wrap-up and Homework Options (5 min.)** • Writing Activities • Core Practice Organizer
14	**Warm-up (5 min.)** • Homework check • Core Practice Organizer	**¡Adelante! (20 min.)** • *Videomisterio* **Repaso (20 min.)** • *Vocabulario y gramática* • *Preparación para el examen*	**Wrap-up and Homework Options (5 min.)** • Instant Check • *Examen del capítulo*
15	**Warm-up (5 min.)** • Answer questions ✔**Summative Assessment (45 min.)** • *Examen del capítulo*		

Standards for *Capítulo 8A*

• To achieve the goals of the Standards, students will:

Communication

1.1 Interpersonal
• Talk about: travel and vacation activities; a scuba diving school; leisure activities, work, and chores; historical events and dates; leisure activities; local attractions of their community

1.2 Interpretive
• Read and listen to information about: travel and vacations; past events; El Yunque, Puerto Rico
• Read: a picture-based story; an advertisement for a scuba diving school; a version of "Goldilocks and the Three Bears"; a traditional rhyme; journal entries about a trip to Perú
• Listen to and watch a video about Sarapiquí, Costa Rica
• Read about the río Paraná
• View a video mystery series

1.3 Presentational
• Present information about: a trip to Sarapiquí; El Yunque, Puerto Rico; local attractions; history and geography of Perú
• Write about a scuba diving school
• Recite a traditional rhyme

Culture

2.1 Practices and Perspectives
• Learn about Perú's Independence Day celebrations
• Understand Spain's method of writing addresses

2.2 Products and Perspectives
• Learn about: Joaquín Sorolla; and his painting; Mexico's transportation system; Machu Picchu, Nazca Lines and Titicaca; history and geography of Perú; the *ojos de Dios* weaving of Mexico

Connections

3.1 Cross-curricular
• Learn about: Joaquín Sorolla; the Patagonia region of Argentina; the history and geography of Perú
• Reinforce geography skills

Comparisons

4.1 Language
• Learn: vocabulary through the recognition of cognates; the preterite of *–er* and *–ir* verbs
• Learn about: diphthongs; the personal *a;* nouns that end in *–io* and *–eo*
• Understand: the irregular preterite form of the verb *ir; -ar* verbs

4.2 Culture
• Compare *ojos de Dios* to traditional handicrafts of the United States

Communities

5.1 Beyond the School
• Learn of services available to Spanish-speakers at local tourist attractions

5.2 Lifelong Learner
• View a video mystery series

▼ Chapter Objectives

Communication

By the end of this chapter you will be able to:
• Listen to and read descriptions of trips and vacations
• Talk and write about favorite and imaginary trips
• Exchange information while describing your best vacation

Culture

You will also be able to:
• Explain the tradition of the *ojo de Dios* and compare it to crafts in the United States
• Identify places of geographical and historical importance in Spanish-speaking countries, and compare them to places in the United States

You will demonstrate what you know and can do:
• Presentación oral, p. 243
• Preparación para el examen, p. 247

You will use:

Vocabulary	Grammar
• Vacation destinations and activities	• The preterite of *-er* and *-ir* verbs
• Modes of transportation	• The preterite of *ir*
• Attractions, parks, and animals	• The personal *a*
• Expressions to talk about a trip or vacation	

Exploración del mundo hispano

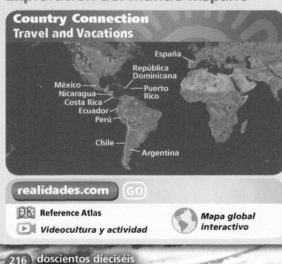

Country Connection
Travel and Vacations

España
República Dominicana
México
Nicaragua — Puerto Rico
Costa Rica
Ecuador
Perú
Chile
Argentina

realidades.com GO

Reference Atlas

▶ Videocultura y actividad

Mapa global interactivo

216 doscientos dieciséis
Tema 8 • Experiencias

ENRICH YOUR TEACHING

Using Backward Design
Have students preview the sample performance tasks on *Preparación para el examen*, p. 247, and connect them to the Chapter Objectives. Explain to students that by completing the sample tasks they can self-assess their learning progress.

Mapa global interactivo
Download the *Mapa global interactivo* files for Chapter 8A and preview the activities. In Activity 1, you visit Valencia, Spain. In Activity 2, you travel to Argentina and in Activity 3 to the Dominican Republic. In Activity 4, you visit Mexico City. In Activity 5, you explore Peru.

Una excursión a las cataratas del río Iguazú, Argentina

Arte y cultura | España

Spanish artist Joaquín Sorolla y Bastida (1863–1923) was famous for his paintings of the sea and coastline. Known as *el pintor de la luz* (the painter of light), Sorolla was a master at capturing the movement and reflection of light and water in sea and sky. He did many portraits of beachgoers along the coast of his native Valencia. The city of Valencia continues to be a destination for Spaniards and international tourists, who visit the beautiful towns and beaches of the Costa Blanca.

• What would you highlight if you were painting your town or city?

"La hora del baño, Valencia" (1909), Joaquín Sorolla y Bastida ▶

La hora del baño, Valencia (1909). O/L-1,50x1,505. Sorolla, Joaquín.

doscientos diecisiete **217**
Capítulo 8A

Chapter Opener
Core Instruction

Resources: Map Transparencies 12–16, 18

Suggestions: Have students predict the types of vocabulary words that might be introduced for talking about vacations. Discuss the kinds of activities they do while on vacation. Inform them that this chapter's *Videohistoria* presents a journey to Sarapiquí, a national park in Costa Rica.

Tell students that upon completion of the chapter, they will be able to talk about events that happened in the past, using the preterite tense of *-er* and *-ir* verbs.

◼ **Videocultura** View *Las vacaciones* with the class to learn about places to visit in Spanish-speaking countries.

Arte y cultura

Standards: 2.2, 3.1

Resources: Fine Art Transparencies p. 18

Mapa global interactivo, Actividad 1 Visit Valencia, Spain, home of the artist Joaquín Sorolla.

Suggestions: Joaquín Sorolla is best known for his landscapes and portraits, and for beach scenes of his native Valencia. Have students notice the relationship between light and shadows in the painting, *La hora del baño* (1909)—the light on the water, and the shadows at the women's feet. Mention that Sorolla was an Impressionist painter, and that this art movement is characterized partly by such attention to light effects.

Answers will vary.

TEACHING WITH ART

Resources: Fine Art Transparencies, p. 18

Suggestions: Have students look at the painting by Sorolla and make a list of 10 words, expressions, or descriptions that come to mind. Have students share their lists.

DIFFERENTIATED INSTRUCTION

Digital resources such as the *Interactive Whiteboard* activity banks, *Videomodelos*, additional *Online Activities*, *Study Plans*, automatically graded *Leveled Workbook*, animated *Grammar Tutorials*, *Flashcards*, and *Vocabulary and Grammar Videos* will help you reach students of different ability levels and learning styles.

STUDENTS NEEDING EXTRA HELP

Guided Practice Activities
• Flashcards, pp. 95–100
• Vocabulary Check, pp. 101–104
• Grammar Support, pp. 105–108

HERITAGE LEARNERS

Realidades para hispanohablantes
• Chapter Opener, pp. 290–291
• A primera vista, p. 292
• Videohistoria, p. 293
• Manos a la obra, pp. 294–301
• ¡Adelante!, pp. 302–307
• Repaso del capítulo, pp. 308–309

ADVANCED/PRE-AP*

Pre-AP* Resource Book,
• pp. 90–93
Communications Workbook
• Integrated Performance Assessment, p. 170

Vocabulario en contexto

Core Instruction

Standards: 1.2, 4.1

Resources: Teacher's Resource Book: Input Script, p. 236, Clip Art, pp. 250–251, Audio Script, p. 237; Voc. and Gram. Transparencies: 143–144; TPR Stories Book: pp. 107–121; Audio Program DVD: Cap. 7B, Tracks 1–2

Focus: Presenting vocabulary for places to visit and things to see and do on vacation; vocabulary to talk about travel; preterite of *-er* and *-ir* verbs; preterite of *ir*

Suggestions: Use the Input Script from the *Teacher's Resource Book* or the story in the *TPR Stories Book* to present this new vocabulary and grammar. You may wish to present the vocabulary in three groups: places to visit, things to do, and ways to travel. Use the audio to introduce the dialogues. Guide the presentation using the transparencies. Cue the idea of "past" by gesturing back over your shoulder. Ask short-answer questions to check comprehension: *¿Vas de vacaciones con tu familia? ¿Adónde vas? ¿Qué te gusta hacer cuando estás de vacaciones? ¿Te gusta más ir al parque de diversiones o al museo?*

BELLRINGER REVIEW

Show Vocabulary and Grammar Transparency 81. Ask volunteers to tell you where they would most likely do each of these activities: *nadar, practicar básquetbol, cenar, ir de compras, caminar, buscar un libro.*

A primera vista | 🔊 | 💬 | **▼ Objectives**

Read, listen to, and understand information about
▸ travel and vacations
▸ vacation activities
▸ past events

Vocabulario en contexto

- el parque de diversiones
- el monumento
- el museo
- el estadio
- el teatro
- la obra de teatro
- el lago
- pasear en bote
- el zoológico
- el oso
- el mono

—**Dime,** ¿adónde **fuiste** el mes pasado?

—**Fui de vacaciones** con mis padres a **un lugar fantástico.**

—¿Qué lugar **visitaste?**

—Fui a Barcelona. Me gusta mucho **viajar** a otros **países como** México, España, Guatemala . . .

—¿Qué **hiciste?**

—Pues, fui al zoológico con mi familia.

—¿Te **gustó?** ¿Qué **viste?**

—Fue fantástico. **Vi** muchos **animales** como osos y monos y también muchas otras **atracciones.** También compré **unos recuerdos:** una camiseta, unos aretes y un llavero.

 doscientos dieciocho
Tema 8 • Experiencias

DIFFERENTIATED INSTRUCTION

Students with Learning Difficulties

Remind students that using what they already know is very important when beginning a new lesson. If they think of all the activities that can be done at each of the places shown, it will be easier for them to understand the vocabulary. Reinforce this by asking general questions about vacation spots and activities as you proceed.

—Y ¿**saliste** de la ciudad?

—¡Por supuesto! **Salí*** muy **temprano** para ir al **mar**. **Durante** el día **aprendí a** bucear. Fue muy divertido. **Regresamos** al **hotel** muy **tarde,** como a las diez de la noche.

*The verb salir has an irregular yo form in the present tense: salgo.

el avión

el barco

el tren

el autobús

—¿Cómo prefieres viajar?

—**En avión.**

▼1 | 🔊 | Escuchar

El viaje de María Luisa

Vas a escuchar a María Luisa describir su viaje. Señala en tu libro cada lugar que ella menciona.

▼2 | 🔊 | Escuchar

¿Qué piensas? ¿Sí o no?

Vas a escuchar diez frases. Si la frase es lógica, haz el gesto del pulgar hacia arriba (*"thumbs-up" sign*). Si es ilógica, haz el gesto del pulgar hacia abajo (*"thumbs-down" sign*).

Más práctica		GO
	realidades.com	print		
Instant Check	✔	
Guided WB pp. 95–100	✔	✔
Core WB pp. 55–56	✔	✔
Comm. WB p. 69	✔	✔
Hispanohablantes WB p. 292		✔

doscientos diecinueve **219**
Capítulo 8A

---

1 Standards: 1.2

Resources: Teacher's Resource Book: Audio Script, p. 237; Audio Program DVD: Cap. 7B, Track 3; Answer Keys: Student Edition, p. 156

Focus: Listening comprehension

Suggestions: Be sure students see that the answers may be on either page.

🔊 **Script and Answers:**

1. Fui al mar a nadar y tomar el sol. *(ocean)*
2. Visité el zoológico y vi muchos animales. *(zoo)*
3. Fui al lago a pasear en bote. *(lake)*
4. Vi una obra de teatro en el Teatro Nacional. *(theater)*
5. El parque de diversiones fue muy divertido. *(amusement park)*
6. Vi un monumento grande en el parque. *(park)*
7. Me gustó mucho ver el partido de fútbol en el estadio. *(stadium)*

2 Standards: 1.2

Resources: Teacher's Resource Book: Audio Script, p. 237; Audio Program DVD: Cap. 7B, Track 4; Answer Keys: Student Edition, p. 157

Focus: Listening comprehension

Suggestions: Give the "thumbs-up" or "thumbs-down" sign, without always being correct, and have students agree or disagree.

🔊 **Script and Answers:**

1. Nado en el mar. *(up)*
2. Hay un parque de diversiones en la cafetería. *(down)*
3. Paseamos en bote en el hotel. *(down)*
4. Voy a un concierto con los monos del zoológico. *(down)*
5. Me gusta tomar el sol cuando voy al lago. *(up)*
6. Hago mi tarea en el parque de diversiones. *(down)*
7. Aprendo a bucear en el museo. *(down)*
8. Saco fotos del monumento. *(up)*
9. Voy a la escuela en avión. *(down)*
10. En el mar viajo en barco. *(up)*

ENRICH YOUR TEACHING

Teacher-to-Teacher

If you have traveled in Spanish-speaking countries, reinforce the new vocabulary by sharing photos, printed materials, or souvenirs from places you have visited. If you have not, request brochures with photos from a travel agent or download pictures from the Internet to print or project for the class.

21st Century Skills

Communication After students have practiced the vocabulary with the eText embedded audio files and have done the auto scored online practice, have them use the flashcards to interview each other about things they do when they go on vacation.

8A Language Input

Videohistoria 🔊

Core Instruction

Standards: 1.2

Resources: Voc. and Gram. Transparencies 145–146; Audio Program DVD: Cap. 7B, Track 5; Answer Keys: Student Edition, p. 157

Focus: Presenting additional contextualized vocabulary

Suggestions:

Pre-reading: Direct students' attention to the *Antes de leer* questions. Have students work in pairs to answer the questions. Remind them that there are four panels on p. 222 that will help them with their pre-reading questions.

Answers:

Strategy: Answers will vary.
1. Answers will vary.
2. birds
3. Answers may include: autobús, parque, kilómetros, mapa, nacional, favorito, animales, tucán, especies, palmas, foto, fantástica, momento, tremenda, impresionante, desastre.

¿Qué te pasó?

¿Qué le pasó a Tomás durante su visita al parque nacional Sarapiquí en Costa Rica?

Costa Rica

Raúl Gloria Tomás

Antes de leer

Strategy **Using visuals to make predictions** Before you read the story, look at the pictures to try to predict what will happen. After you finish reading, see how your predictions compared with what you read.

- What do you think will happen to Raúl, Gloria, and Tomás?

1. Based on what you already know about rain forests, what kinds of things would you expect Raúl, Gloria, and Tomás to see on their visit to *el parque Sarapiquí?*

2. Look at photo 3. What animals do you think they are going to talk about?

3. Skim the *Videohistoria* and make a list of five cognates that will help you understand the story.

 220 doscientos veinte
Tema 8 • Experiencias

DIFFERENTIATED INSTRUCTION

Advanced Learners
Have students research and prepare a report about the Sarapiquí National Park in Costa Rica. Students may use drawings or pictures from the Internet for their presentations.

Students with Learning Difficulties
If a student has low reading comprehension abilities, pair him or her with a skilled reader for pre-reading activities. Ask students to make notes for the *Antes de leer* activities. Collect these notes and use them to monitor students' progress.

Raúl: Aquí están **los boletos** para **el autobús.**

Tomás: ¿Cuánto dura **el viaje?**

Gloria: El parque está a 82 kilómetros de San José. Es un viaje de hora y media.

Gloria: Mira este mapa del **parque nacional.** Es mi parque favorito y lo llamamos "bosque lluvioso".* No hace ni frío ni calor, pero llueve mucho.

Tomás: Aquí hay un libro sobre los animales del parque.

*rain forest

Gloria: ¿Lo ves? Allí en **el árbol.**

Tomás: No, no lo veo. ¿Qué es?

Gloria: Es un **pájaro.** Es un tucán. Hay más de cuatrocientas especies de pájaros en el parque.

Raúl: Tomás, ¿qué te pasó?

Tomás: ¡Hay agua en las palmas! Eh . . . ¡no es nada divertido!

Raúl: Pero, Tomás, es un bosque lluvioso y llueve todo el tiempo. Siempre hay agua en las palmas. Pero sólo es un poco de agua.

Gloria: Estás aprendiendo muchas cosas, ¿verdad?

doscientos veintiuno
Capítulo 8A

Suggestions:
Reading: While volunteers read the roles, have the other students make a list of unfamiliar words. Help students determine the meaning of new words by using visual cues and context. Have a new group reread the text or play the audio.

Post-reading: Have students compare their predictions with what actually happened. Complete *Actividades* 3–5 to check comprehension.

Teacher-to-Teacher

Restatement is a good means of assessing comprehension. Display the transparencies for the *Videohistoria* and have students give summaries in their own words. This will demonstrate their full comprehension, not their ability to repeat the text verbatim.

Pre-AP* Support

- **Learning Objective:** Presentational Speaking
- **Activity:** Prepare large clip art flashcards of the places presented in this chapter. Have pairs of students come to the front of the class and randomly select one of the flashcards from the stack. Then have the pair re-read to the class one of the dialogues presented on pp. 218–219, and make the appropriate substitutions to go along with the flashcard they have drawn.
- **Pre-AP* Resource Book:** Comprehensive guide to Pre-AP* vocabulary skill development, pp. 51–57

ENRICH YOUR TEACHING

Culture Note

The Sarapiquí region is named for the river that drains into the area at the foot of the Cordillera Central mountain range in Costa Rica. Besides being known for its many species of birds, the area also has many banana plantations. If you were to take a trip down the Sarapiquí River, you might be able to spot crocodiles, spider monkeys, sloths, parrots, toucans, and other exotic birds and animals.

Video ▶

Standards: 1.2

Resources: Teacher's Resource Book: Video Script, p. 241; Video Program: Cap. 8A; Video Program Teacher's Guide: Cap. 8A

Focus: Listening comprehension of contextualized vocabulary

Suggestions:

Pre-viewing: Have students recall main ideas of the *Videohistoria.*

Viewing: Show the video once without pausing; then show it again, stopping periodically to check comprehension. Point out that Gloria uses the word **aves** to refer to birds. Do students see the connection to the English word *aviation*?

Post-viewing: Have students complete the Video Activities in the *Communication Workbook.*

3 Standards: 1.2, 1.3

Resources: Answer Keys: Student Edition, p. 158

Focus: Checking comprehension of the *Videohistoria*

Suggestions: Have students identify key words in each statement that will help them to determine if it is true or false. Tell them to use the key words to scan the text again for the answer.

Answers:

1. C
2. C
3. F – Hay más de cuatrocientas especies de pájaros.
4. C
5. F – No hace ni frío ni calor.
6. C

5

Gloria: Va a ser una foto fantástica, Tomás. Un momento . . . un poco más a la izquierda.

Tomás: ¿Aquí?

Gloria: No, un poco más. Uno, dos . . .

Tomás: ¡Ay!

Raúl: Tomás, ¿dónde estás? ¿Estás bien?

6

Gloria: Lo siento, Tomás. ¿Quieres regresar a casa?

Raúl: ¿Quieres **descansar** un poco?

Tomás: No. Estoy bien. ¡Vamos a la catarata* La Paz!

*waterfall

7

Tomás: Quiero una foto de la catarata. ¡Es **tremenda, impresionante!** Uno puede estar muy cerca de ella.

Raúl: No, creo que estar un poco lejos de ella es mejor. Voy a ayudarte, Tomás.

Gloria: Un poco más hacia atrás* y a la derecha . . .

*towards the back

8

Mamá: ¡Tomás! ¿Cómo lo pasaste? ¿Qué te pasó?

Gloria: Pobre* Tomás . . . fue un desastre.

Tomás: No fue tan malo. **Me gustó.** Aprendí mucho y vi muchas cosas nuevas. ¡Pero hay mucha agua en el bosque lluvioso y en la catarata!

*Poor

 222 **doscientos veintidós**
Tema 8 • Experiencias

DIFFERENTIATED INSTRUCTION

Heritage Language Learners

Have students write a journal entry pretending that they are Tomás. Have them recall the trip to Sarapiquí National Park, and summarize the details in their own words. Tell them to add fictional details to their journal entry to explain what Tomás did after returning home from the park.

Advanced Learners

Make copies of each panel to distribute to students. Have students work in groups to write a one-sentence caption in their own words for each picture that they have. Display their summaries in class so that the other students may use them as a reference while completing *Actividades* 3, 4, and 5.

▼3 Leer · Escribir

¿Cierto o falso?

Lee estas frases sobre el bosque lluvioso Sarapiquí. Escribe los números del 1 al 6 en una hoja de papel. Según la información en la *Videohistoria*, escribe *C* (cierto) si la frase es cierta o *F* (falso) si es falsa. Corrige *(Correct)* las frases falsas.

1. El parque Sarapiquí es un parque nacional.

2. El bosque lluvioso está a una hora y media de San José.

3. En el bosque lluvioso hay cuarenta especies de pájaros.

4. El tucán es un pájaro que vive en el bosque lluvioso.

5. Hace muchísimo calor en el bosque lluvioso.

6. Llueve todo el tiempo en el bosque lluvioso.

▼4 Leer · Escribir

¿Tomás, Gloria o Raúl?

Lee estas frases sobre las personas en la *Videohistoria*. Escribe los números del 1 al 6. Para cada frase, escribe el nombre de la persona a quien se refiere *(to whom it refers)*.

Raúl   **Gloria**   **Tomás**

1. Compró los boletos para el autobús.

2. Sacó fotos de los otros.

3. No vio el pájaro.

4. Sarapiquí es su parque favorito.

5. Ayudó a Tomás delante de la catarata La Paz.

6. Decidió no descansar.

▼5 Leer · Escribir

El diario de Tomás

Tomás está escribiendo en su diario sobre todo lo que le pasó en Costa Rica. Pon estas frases en orden según la *Videohistoria*. Escribe las frases en una hoja de papel para crear un párrafo *(paragraph)*.

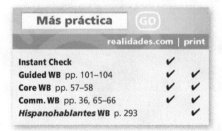

29 de mayo: Hoy fui con Gloria y Raúl y pasé un día fantástico.

1. Hablé con la mamá de Raúl sobre el viaje al parque.

2. Vi un libro sobre los animales del parque.

3. Viajé una hora y media al parque.

4. Yo salí de San José para ir al parque nacional Sarapiquí.

5. Fui a la catarata de La Paz.

6. Me mojé* porque siempre hay agua en las palmas.

*I got wet

Más práctica (GO)

realidades.com | print

Instant Check	✔	
Guided WB pp. 101–104	✔	✔
Core WB pp. 57–58	✔	✔
Comm. WB pp. 36, 65–66	✔	✔
Hispanohablantes **WB** p. 293		✔

doscientos veintitrés 223
Capítulo 8A

4 Standards: 1.2, 1.3

Resources: Answer Keys; Student Edition, p. 158

Focus: Checking comprehension of the *Videohistoria*

Suggestions: Have students make a chart with each character's name and write the number of each sentence in the appropriate space.

Answers:

1.	Raúl	3.	Tomás	5.	Raúl
2.	Gloria	4.	Gloria	6.	Tomás

5 Standards: 1.2, 1.3

Resources: Answer Keys; Student Edition, p. 158

Focus: Reading and sequencing the events of the *Videohistoria*

Suggestions: Cut a sheet of transparency film into six pieces. On each piece, write one of the statements. Have a volunteer put the sentences in order on the projector. Have the rest of the class verify their answers.

Answers:

4, 3, 2, 6, 5, 1

Additional Resources

• Communication Wbk.: Audio Act. 5, p. 66
• Teacher's Resource Book: Audio Script, p. 238
• Audio Program DVD: Cap. 7B, Track 9

ENRICH YOUR TEACHING

Culture Note

Central and South America are destinations for an increasingly popular type of vacation—ecotourism. Ecotourism involves travel to natural areas to study and enjoy the wild plants and animals, as well as the cultural aspects of the areas. Costa Rica has tens of thousands of visitors every year who come there to explore the rich biodiversity of its rain forests, cloud forests, wetlands, and other habitats.

✔ASSESSMENT

Quiz: Vocabulary Recognition
• Prueba 8A-1: pp. 201–202

Objectives

▶ Write and talk about trips and vacation activities
▶ Listen to a description of a trip
▶ Read and write about boating and scuba-diving vacations
▶ Exchange information while comparing favorite trips

INTERACTIVE WHITEBOARD
Vocabulary Activities 8A

BELLRINGER REVIEW

Have students review the vacation vocabulary on pp. 218–219 and say the phrases to a partner.

6 Standards: 1.3

Resources: Answer Keys: Student Edition, p. 159

Focus: Answering questions about places

Suggestions: Tell students that there is only one word in the box to logically correspond to each question. Have students personalize the activity by renaming the words in the box with specific places in the community (for example, *El teatro municipal* instead of *el teatro*). Remind students that they will need to use the contraction *al* before masculine place names.

Answers:

1. Fui al teatro.
2. Fui al museo.
3. Fui al lago.
4. Fui al zoológico.
5. Fui al parque de diversiones.
6. Fui al estadio.

7 Standards: 1.2, 1.3

Resources: Teacher's Resource Book: Audio Script, p. 237; Audio Program DVD: Cap. 7B, Track 6; Answer Keys: Student Edition, p. 160

Focus: Listening and writing about a vacation in Puerto Rico

Suggestions: Play the audio or read the script once without stopping. Then play or read the script a second time, pausing to allow students to write the sentences. Finally, allow students to hear it a third time to check their answers.

🔊 Script and Answers:

1. El verano pasado fui a Puerto Rico con mi familia.
2. Fue mi primer viaje en avión y me gustó mucho.
3. Puerto Rico es un país impresionante y fantástico.
4. Puedes bucear, descansar y tomar el sol en la playa.
5. También puedes visitar El Yunque para ver pájaros, árboles y flores.
6. Quiero regresar a Puerto Rico. Compro mi boleto hoy.

Common Errors: Students may forget to write accent marks. Write the words with accents on the board, using colored chalk to mark the accents.

Vocabulario en uso

▼6 Escribir

Durante las vacaciones

El verano pasado, fuiste a muchos lugares interesantes y tus amigos quieren más información. En una hoja de papel, contesta estas preguntas usando las palabras de la lista.

el teatro	el lago
la ciudad	el estadio
el museo	el parque de diversiones
el zoológico	

Modelo
¿Adónde fuiste para ir a las tiendas y los restaurantes?
Fui a la ciudad.

1. ¿Adónde fuiste para ver esta obra de teatro?
2. ¿Adónde fuiste para ver el arte de Botero y Picasso?
3. ¿Adónde fuiste para nadar y descansar?
4. ¿Adónde fuiste para ver los monos y los osos?
5. ¿Adónde fuiste para ver las atracciones?
6. ¿Adónde fuiste para ver el partido de fútbol americano?

▼7 | 🔊 | Escuchar · Escribir

Escucha y escribe

Vas a escuchar a una persona describir su viaje a Puerto Rico. Uno de los lugares que visitó es El Yunque. En una hoja de papel, escribe los números del 1 al 6 y escribe las frases que escuchas.

Puerto Rico

El Yunque, un parque nacional de Puerto Rico

224 doscientos veinticuatro
Tema 8 • Experiencias

DIFFERENTIATED INSTRUCTION

Heritage Language Learners

Have students research an interesting or important natural area or national park in their heritage country and report on it. Have them write its name, show its location on a map, and tell about distinctive features such as unusual animals, plant life, and scenery.

▼**8** | 🗣️👥 | Escribir · Hablar

Una lista de actividades

① ¿Qué actividades te gusta hacer cuando vas de vacaciones? ¿Qué actividades no te gusta hacer? En una hoja de papel, haz tres columnas y escribe *me gusta mucho, me gusta* y *no me gusta nada.* Debajo de cada expresión, escribe estas actividades en la columna apropiada.

ver . . .

visitar . . .

sacar fotos de . . .

ir a . . .

ir a . . .

comprar . . .

② Usa tu lista de actividades y habla con otro(a) estudiante. Pregunta y contesta según el modelo. Haz por lo menos *(at least)* cuatro preguntas.

▶️ **Modelo**

A —*Cuando vas de vacaciones, ¿qué te gusta más, ver una obra de teatro o ir al zoológico?*
B —*Me gusta más ir al zoológico.*

▼**9** | 🗣️👥 | Hablar

¿Qué te gustaría hacer?

Habla con otro(a) estudiante sobre adónde les gustaría ir de vacaciones.

▶️ **Modelo**

A —*Dime, ¿te gustaría ir de vacaciones a una ciudad?*
B —*Sí, porque en una ciudad puedes ir de compras y comer en restaurantes fantásticos.*
o: *No, me gustaría más ir a un parque nacional porque puedes ir de cámping.*

Estudiante A

1. una ciudad
2. un parque nacional
3. un lago
4. el mar

Estudiante B

¡Respuesta personal!

doscientos veinticinco **225**
Capítulo 8A

BELLRINGER REVIEW

Use the transparencies to review vocabulary for places to eat, things to do in a city, and leisure activities.

▼**8** Standards: 1.3

Focus: Rating and talking about vacation activities

Suggestions: For Step 1, tell students that if they have not done the activity they may simply say *(no) me gustaría.* For Step 2, remind Student A to choose from all ten choices, not only from the items that he or she liked.

Answers will vary.

▼**9** Standards: 1.1

Focus: Talking about vacation preferences

Suggestions: Have students make a four-column chart using the locations in the Student A bubble as the headings. Tell students to brainstorm activities they associate with each location and to write them in the appropriate columns. Practice the *Modelo* with a student volunteer and explain how students can use their notes to communicate with their partners.

Answers will vary.

ENRICH YOUR TEACHING

Teacher-to-Teacher
Have students bring in photographs from magazines or the Internet of vacation destinations in both the United States and in different countries. Have students work in groups of 4 or 5 and ask questions similar to those in *Actividad* 9 about their photos.

21st Century Skills

Social and Cross-Cultural Skills If there are exchange students in your school from Central America or South America, have students interview them about how people in their country feel about the rain forests. Have them compare their findings to attitudes toward such natural resources in the United States.

225

▼10 Standards: 1.2, 1.3

Resources: Answer Keys: Student Edition, p. 160

🌐 **Mapa global interactivo, Actividad 2**
Follow the Paraná River on its course through Argentina.

Focus: Reading for comprehension

Suggestions: Have students begin by reading the article silently, without filling in the blanks. Encourage them to read for meaning, rather than stopping whenever they encounter an unfamiliar word. Have them read again, one paragraph at a time. Point out that the questions at the end are asking them to apply the facts they learned to form an opinion about whether they would like to spend time in this area.

Answers:

1. ciudad
2. lugar
3. tren
4. pasear
5. descansar
6. montar
7. recuerdos
8. pájaros
9. árboles

▼11 Standards: 1.1

Focus: Using vocabulary to talk about different places and modes of transportation

Recycle: *me gustaría; poder*

Suggestions: Refer students to the maps on pp. xv–xxvii. Have them choose two destinations. If students choose a country whose vocabulary is listed in the *También se dice...*, they may wish to use the culturally appropriate word.

Answers will vary.

Pre-AP* Support

- **Learning Objective:** Presentational Writing
- **Activity 10:** Have students write a short paragraph to expand on their answer to the first of the two questions after the reading, defending their choice, and suggesting an alternative, if needed.
- *Pre-AP* Resource Book:* Comprehensive guide to Pre-AP* writing skill development, pp. 27–38

▼10 Leer · Escribir | 🌐

El delta del río¹ Paraná

Lee la descripción del delta del río Paraná, a 30 kilómetros de Buenos Aires, y completa las frases con las palabras apropiadas de la casilla. Después, contesta las preguntas.

El delta del río Paraná, Tigre, Argentina

tren	descansar	recuerdos
ciudad	regresar	lagos
país	pasear	pájaros
lugar	montar	árboles

Al norte de la __1.__ de Buenos Aires, Argentina, está el delta del río Paraná, un laberinto de islas y canales con más de 2,500 kilómetros navegables. Es un __2.__ favorito de los habitantes de Buenos Aires para ir de excursión. Para ir de Buenos Aires al delta, muchas personas viajan en __3.__ hasta² el Tigre, un pueblo³ pequeño.

Aquí las personas pueden __4.__ en bote por los canales, __5.__ y tomar el sol en la orilla,⁴ __6.__ a caballo o practicar el esquí acuático.

También pueden comprar comida y __7.__ turísticos en los mercados.⁵ Las personas siempre tienen sus cámaras en las excursiones al delta porque hay muchos tipos de animales y __8.__ que viven en los __9.__ muy altos.

¹river ²as far as ³town ⁴riverbank ⁵markets

- Para ti, ¿es el delta del río Paraná un buen lugar para ir de vacaciones? ¿Por qué?
- ¿Qué actividades te gustaría hacer en este lugar?

▼11 | 💬👥 | Hablar

Cómo puedes viajar

Mira los mapas en las páginas xii–xxv. Dile a tu compañero(a) que te gustaría viajar de un lugar o país a otro. Tu compañero(a) debe decir cómo puedes viajar entre los dos lugares.

También se dice . . .

el autobús = el camión (*México*); el colectivo, el ómnibus (*Argentina, Bolivia*); la guagua (*Puerto Rico, Cuba*); el micro (*Perú*)

▶️ **Modelo**

A —*Me gustaría viajar de la República Dominicana a Puerto Rico.*

B —*Pues, entonces, puedes viajar en barco o en avión.*

Estudiante A

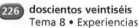

¡Respuesta personal!

Estudiante B

DIFFERENTIATED INSTRUCTION

Students with Special Needs

If students with fine motor skill difficulties cannot make the appropriate gestures for item 2 of *Actividad 12*, have them point to the correct illustration as they tell its meaning.

▼12 | 👥 | Leer · Escribir · Hablar | 🌐

¿Quieres aprender a bucear?

Lee el anuncio y contesta las preguntas.

República Dominicana

Escuela de buceo "Flor del mar"

Puerto Plata, República Dominicana

Cursos de buceo "Flor del mar"

¡Aprende a bucear en sólo tres cursos!
Ve peces impresionantes y otros animales del mar.
Practica un deporte interesante y divertido.
Pasa tiempo con amigos en un lugar fantástico.

Señales de buceo

Hay un lenguaje especial que permite a los buzos comunicarse en el agua con señales. En los cursos de buceo, puedes aprender estas señales. Así no vas a tener ningún problema practicando este deporte. Algunas de las señales más importantes son:

Si quieres información sobre un curso de buceo en la República Dominicana, comunícate al 555-19-19 con la Dra. María Elena Santos o al 555-02-28 con Marcos Morelos.

| Alto | Ir hacia arriba | Ir hacia abajo | Preguntar si estás bien | Contestar OK o sí | Hay un problema | ¡Peligro! |

1. ¿Por qué debes estudiar buceo en la escuela "Flor del mar"?
2. Practica las señales con otro(a) estudiante. ¿Qué puedes comunicar?

▼13 | (Talk!) 👥 | ♻ | Hablar

¿Dónde aprendiste a bucear?

Habla con otro(a) estudiante sobre dónde aprendió a hacer las actividades de la lista.

1. bucear
2. montar a caballo
3. esquiar
4. montar en bicicleta
5. patinar
6. tocar la guitarra

 Modelo

nadar
A —¿Dónde aprendiste a *nadar*?
B —Aprendí a *nadar* en *California*.
o: —No aprendí a *nadar* nunca, pero me gustaría aprender.
o: —No aprendí a *nadar* nunca y no quiero aprender.

doscientos veintisiete 227
Capítulo 8A

▼12 Standards: 1.2

Resources: Voc. and Gram. Transparency 149

🌐 **Mapa global interactivo, Actividad 3** Locate Puerto Plata in the Dominican Republic.

Focus: Reading, writing, and speaking about scuba diving

Suggestions: Point out the two basic themes of the advertisement—reasons why one should take the *Flor del mar* course and important safety signals. Before students do item 2, practice the signals as a class. Have volunteers communicate messages to share with the class and have other students interpret them.

Answers will vary but may include:

1. Porque puedo aprender a bucear con sólo tres cursos, puedo ver peces impresionantes y otros animales del mar, o puedo practicar un deporte interesante y divertido.
2. Answers will vary.

Extension: Have students create an ad for another activity taught in this chapter, such as **montar a caballo, pasear en bote, tomar el sol,** or **ver una obra de teatro.**

▼13 Standards: 1.1

Focus: Communicating about different activities

Recycle: Leisure activities

Suggestions: Have student volunteers read the model various times, so as to include all possible options. Point out the preterite forms **aprendiste** and **aprendí**. Remind students to switch roles.

Answers will vary.

ENRICH YOUR TEACHING

Culture Note

The Paraná River drains a larger land area than any other river system in South America, except the Amazon. It flows southwest from Brazil and travels along part of the border between Argentina and Paraguay. Large ships are able to steam up the Paraná into Argentina.

21st Century Skills

Leadership and Responsibility Have groups of students research on the Internet the current status of one of the rain forests in Central America or South America and suggest a possible long term solution for protecting it. Have each group present its solutions to the class, so that they can select the best plan and post it on the class Web site.

14 Standards: 1.1

Resources: Answer Keys: Student Edition, p. 161

Focus: Communicating about a vacation in Mexico City

Recycle: Question words

Suggestions: Point out that *fui, fuiste,* and *fue* are the first-, second-, and third-person preterite forms of *ir;* and that *vi* and *viste* are the first- and second-person preterite forms of *ver.* Also point out that *a + el* becomes *al.* Before students begin, have them study the pictures and the captions they will use.

Answers:

Student A:
—¿Adónde fuiste?
—¿Qué viste?
—¿Cómo lo pasaste allí? ¿Te gustó?

Student B:
1. —Fui al Museo de Arte de Frida Kahlo.
   —Vi muchos cuadros interesantes.
   —¡Fue fantástico!
2. —Fui al Zoológico del Parque Chapultepec.
   —Vi animales como osos y monos.
   —¡Fue tremendo!
3. —Fui al parque de diversiones en el Parque Chapultepec.
   —Vi muchas atracciones.
   —¡Fue muy divertido!
4. —Fui al Teatro del Auditorio.
   —Vi una obra de teatro.
   —¡Fue fenomenal!
5. —Fui al Estadio.
   —Vi un partido de fútbol.
   —¡Fue genial!

Fondo cultural

Standards: 2.2

Suggestions: Tell students that Mexico City has the largest population of any city in the world. Car owners are limited to specific days they can drive, in an effort to reduce pollution.

Answers will vary but may include the fact that many people in large cities do not own cars, or that people need to commute into and around the central city for work.

🌐 **Mapa global interactivo, Actividad 4**
Visit sites along the Metro in Mexico City.

▼14 | 👥👥 | Hablar

¿Adónde fuiste?

La primavera pasada fuiste de vacaciones a la Ciudad de México. Ahora tienes tus fotos y hablas con otro(a) estudiante. En la Ciudad de México viste estas cosas:

El Paseo de la Reforma con el monumento del Ángel de la Independencia
¡Impresionante!

- un partido de fútbol
- el monumento del Ángel de la Independencia
- muchas atracciones
- animales como osos y monos
- una obra de teatro
- muchos cuadros interesantes

▶ **Modelo**
A —¿Adónde fuiste?
B —Fui *al Paseo de la Reforma.*
A —¿Qué viste?
B —Vi *el monumento del Ángel de la Independencia.*
A —¿Cómo lo pasaste allí? ¿Te gustó?
B —*Fue impresionante. Me gustó mucho.*

1.
Museo de arte de Frida Kahlo
¡Fantástico!

2.
El Zoológico del Parque Chapultepec
¡Tremendo!

3.
El parque de diversiones en el Parque Chapultepec
¡Muy divertido!

4.
El Teatro del Auditorio
¡Fenomenal!

5.
El Estadio Azteca
¡Genial!

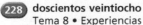

🌐 **Fondo Cultural** | México

Mexico City's *Metro* is one of the most advanced subway systems in the world. It is fast, modern, and very inexpensive. In addition, an extensive bus service crosses the whole city, with even-numbered lines running east-west and odd-numbered lines running north-south. Smaller green and gray minibuses, called *peseros,* also serve passengers along major routes.

- Why do you think Mexico City has such an advanced and varied public transportation system?

La parada *(stop)* de Chapultepec, Ciudad de México

228 doscientos veintiocho
Tema 8 • Experiencias

DIFFERENTIATED INSTRUCTION

Heritage Language Learners

Have students research information on the **Metro** in Mexico City. Have them write a report about its size, the names of different stations, and other facts of importance.

Practice and Communicate **8A**

▼ Pronunciación | 🔊 | 💬

Diphthongs

In Spanish, there are two groups of vowels, "strong" (*a, e,* and *o*) and "weak" (*i* and *u*). The strong vowels are *a, e,* and *o.*

When a weak vowel is combined with any other vowel, the individual vowel sounds become blended to form a single sound called a diphthong (*un diptongo*). Listen to and say these words:

limpiar	cuarto	seis	piensas
fuimos	siete	aire	ciudad
baile	juego	estadio	autobús

When two strong vowels are together, each vowel is pronounced as a separate sound. Listen to and say these words:

teatro	museo	pasear	bucear
cereal	video	leer	zoológico
traer	idea	tarea	cumpleaños

If there is an accent mark over a weak vowel, it causes that letter to be pronounced as though it were a strong vowel. Listen to and say these words:

día	frío	tíos	zapatería
joyería	país	esquío	gustaría

Try it out! Listen to some of the lines of "*Cielito lindo,*" a song from Mexico that is very popular with mariachi bands. Can you identify the diphthongs in the lyrics? Try saying the words and then singing the song.

> De la sierra morena,
> cielito lindo, vienen bajando
> un par de ojitos negros,
> cielito lindo, de contrabando.
> ¡Ay, ay, ay, ay!
> Canta y no llores,
> porque cantando se alegran,
> cielito lindo, los corazones.

▼ 15 | 💬 | Escribir • Hablar

Y tú, ¿qué dices?

1. ¿Adónde te gustaría ir de vacaciones en los Estados Unidos? ¿Cómo quieres viajar? ¿Qué te gustaría hacer?

2. ¿Qué ciudades te gustaría visitar? ¿Qué lugares en esas ciudades quieres ver?

3. Cuando viajas, ¿prefieres salir temprano o tarde?

4. Durante un viaje, ¿descansas mucho o regresas a casa muy cansado(a)?

doscientos veintinueve **229**
Capítulo 8A

Pronunciación
Core Instruction

Standards: 4.1

Resources: Teacher's Resource Book: Audio Script, pp. 237–238; Audio Program DVD: Cap. 7B, Tracks 7–8

Suggestions: Use the audio or read the *Pronunciación* with students. Remind them that the vowel sounds in diphthongs should blend together. Have students practice with each other, first saying the list of words with diphthongs and then the list of words with the vowels pronounced as separate sounds.

Play the recording of "*Cielito lindo*" from the audio. Have students with musical ability record their own version of the song.

▼ 15 Standards: 1.1, 1.3

Focus: Writing and speaking about vacations

Suggestions: You might assign this activity as homework. Suggest that students read all the questions and think about their answers before they write.

Answers will vary.

Additional Resources

- Communication Wbk.: Audio Act. 6, p. 66
- Teacher's Resource Book: Audio Script, p. 238, Communicative Pair Activity BLM, pp. 244–245
- Audio Program DVD: Cap. 7B, Track 10

ENRICH YOUR TEACHING

Culture Note

The Frida Kahlo Museum was the home of the artist Frida Kahlo. She lived there with her husband, the muralist Diego Rivera, who donated the house to the people of Mexico upon Kahlo's death in 1954. The museum gives visitors a glimpse into the lives of these two talented, sometimes controversial, artists.

21st Century Skills

Information Literacy Have students choose two of the destinations pictured in Activity 14 and compare them by finding information about each on the Internet or at the library. Have them decide which would they rather visit, and why.

✓ ASSESSMENT

Prueba 8A-2 with Study Plan (online only)

Quiz: Vocabulary Production
- Prueba 8A-2: pp. 203–204

Gramática

Core Instruction

Standards: 4.1

Resources: Voc. and Gram. Transparency 147; Teacher's Resource Book: Video Script, p. 242; Video Program: Cap. 8A

INTERACTIVE WHITEBOARD

Grammar Activities 8A

Suggestions: Ask students to scan the *Gramática*, and recall where they may have seen any of these verb forms. Use the transparencies and the *GramActiva* Video to reinforce your presentation. Point out the accent marks and stress their importance.

▼16 Standards: 1.3

Resources: Answer Keys: Student Edition, p. 162
Focus: Conjugating **-er** and **-ir** verbs in the preterite in a story context
Recycle: Various **-er** and **-ir** infinitives
Suggestions: Have students identify the story title before beginning. Remind them that their background knowledge of the story can help them determine the meanings of unfamiliar words.

Answers:

1. salieron	7. abrieron
2. vio	8. vieron
3. abrió	9. vio
4. comprendió	10. salió
5. comió	11. Corrió
6. decidió	

Theme Project

Give students copies of the Theme Project outline and rubric from the *Teacher's Resource Book*. Explain the task to them, and have them perform Step 1. (For more information, see p. 216-b.)

Gramática

The preterite of *-er* and *-ir* verbs

Regular *-er* and *-ir* verbs are similar to one another in the preterite. Here are the preterite forms of *aprender* and *salir*. Notice the accent marks on the endings -*í* and -*ió*:

¿Recuerdas?

You have already learned to talk about completed past actions using regular *-ar* verbs.

(yo)	aprendí	(nosotros) (nosotras)	aprendimos
(tú)	aprendiste	(vosotros) (vosotras)	aprendisteis
Ud. (él) (ella)	aprendió	Uds. (ellos) (ellas)	aprendieron

(yo)	salí	(nosotros) (nosotras)	salimos
(tú)	saliste	(vosotros) (vosotras)	salisteis
Ud. (él) (ella)	salió	Uds. (ellos) (ellas)	salieron

The verb *ver* is regular in the preterite but does not have accent marks in any of its forms:

vi viste vio vimos visteis vieron

Más ayuda **realidades.com**

▶ **GramActiva** Video
Animated Verbs
Tutorials: Preterite, Preterite of regular verbs

📝 **GramActiva** Activity

▼16 | ♻ | Leer • Escribir

Ricitos de Oro y los tres osos

Escribe los verbos apropiados en el pretérito para completar cada frase del cuento *Ricitos de Oro y los tres osos*.

Un día los tres osos __1.__ *(salir/beber)* temprano de su casa para caminar. Ricitos de Oro, una chica muy bonita, __2.__ *(comer/ver)* la casa de los tres osos y __3.__ *(recibir/abrir)* la puerta. Ella no __4.__ *(ver/comprender)* que era[1] la casa de los tres osos y __5.__ *(comer/aprender)* toda la comida del oso chiquito. Luego ella __6.__ *(beber/decidir)* dormir un poco. Poco después, los tres osos regresaron a su casa, __7.__ *(abrir/salir)* la puerta y __8.__ *(deber/ver)* a Ricitos de Oro en la cama del osito. Cuando Ricitos de Oro __9.__ *(viajar/ver)* a los osos __10.__ *(abrir/salir)* de la casa rápidamente. __11.__ *(Comer/Correr)* hasta llegar[2] a su propia casa.

[1]it was [2]until she arrived

230 doscientos treinta
Tema 8 • Experiencias

DIFFERENTIATED INSTRUCTION

Advanced Learners/Pre-AP*

Have students use their notes from *Actividades* 17 and 18 to create a short travel journal. They may describe a real trip or an imaginary one. They should tell where they went, with whom they traveled, what they did, and what they saw.

Multiple Intelligences

Visual/Spatial: Students may find that it is easier to organize their information for *Actividades* 17 and 18 if they create a Venn diagram. The first oval should contain information about themselves, and the second should have information about their friend. Have students highlight the sentences that overlap and need to be put in the **nosotros(as)** form.

▼17 | ♻ | **Escribir**

Durante las vacaciones

Escribe seis frases para decir qué hicieron *(did)* estas personas durante las vacaciones. Usa las palabras de la lista.

1. mi familia y yo
2. mis amigos
3. yo
4. mis padres
5. mi hermano(a)
6. mi amigo(a) *(nombre)*

Modelo

Durante las vacaciones, mi hermana y yo corrimos en la playa de Punta Cana.

comer en . . .	aprender a . . .
compartir una casa en . . .	ver . . .
escribir . . .	salir de casa temprano para . . .
correr en . . .	salir con . . .

▼18 | 🗣 | ♻ | **Hablar • Escribir**

Tú y yo

❶ Trabaja con otro(a) estudiante. Lee una frase de la Actividad 17. Tu compañero(a) va a contestar si tiene una idea similar en su hoja de papel.

▶ **Modelo**

A —*Mi hermana y yo corrimos en la playa de Punta Cana.*

B —*Mi amigo y yo también corrimos, pero nosotros corrimos en un estadio.*

o:—*Yo no corrí en las vacaciones. Escribí cuentos todos los días.*

❷ Escribe seis frases para comparar lo que hicieron tú y tu compañero(a) durante las vacaciones.

Modelo

Adela y yo corrimos durante las vacaciones. Ella corrió en un estadio con su amigo. Yo corrí en la playa con mi hermana.

Más práctica	GO
	**realidades.com	print**
Instant Check	✔
Guided WB pp. 105–106	✔ ✔
Core WB p. 59	✔ ✔
Comm. WB pp. 67, 70	✔ ✔
Hispanohablantes WB pp. 294–297	✔

En la playa de Punta Cana, República Dominicana

doscientos treinta y uno **231**
Capítulo 8A

ENRICH YOUR TEACHING

Culture Note

Tourism, along with agriculture and the textile industry, is one of the top generators of revenue for the Dominican Republic. In fact, almost half of the country's revenue comes from tourism. The industry continues to grow, as many visitors from all over the world come to Punta Cana, Puerto Plata, and Santo Domingo.

Teacher-to-Teacher

Encourage small groups of students to act out the events of *Ricitos de Oro y los tres osos* while you or a student volunteer reads the story aloud. You may wish to bring in props for the story, such as a blond wig, bowls, and spoons.

Gramática

Core Instruction

Standards: 4.1

Resources: Voc. and Gram. Transparency 148; Teacher's Resource Book: Video Script, p. 242; Video Program: Cap. 8A

INTERACTIVE WHITEBOARD

Grammar Activities 8A

Suggestions: Have students scan the *Gramática*. Point out that the preterite forms of **ir** do not have accent marks. Use the *Strategy* to discuss the use of memory devices. Play the *GramActiva* Video either as an initial introduction or as a follow-up to your grammar explanation.

19 Standards: 1.3

Resources: Answer Keys: Student Edition, p. 162

Focus: Writing the preterite forms of **ir**

Suggestions: Remind students to invent answers if they do not have the information to answer the question. Suggest that they personalize the activity by providing specific place names in the community.

Answers will vary but will include:

1. Yo fui ...
2. Mi mejor amigo(a) fue ...
3. Mis amigos fueron ...
4. Mis amigos y yo fuimos ...
5. Uno(a) de mis compañeros(as) de clase fue ...

Gramática

The preterite of *ir*

Ir is irregular in the preterite. Notice that the preterite forms of *ir* do not have accent marks:

(yo)	fui	(nosotros) (nosotras)	fuimos
(tú)	fuiste	(vosotros) (vosotras)	fuisteis
Ud. (él) (ella)	fue	Uds. (ellos) (ellas)	fueron

The preterite of *ir* is the same as the preterite of *ser*. The context makes the meaning clear.

José fue a Barcelona. *José went to Barcelona.*
El viaje fue un desastre. *The trip was a disaster.*

Strategy

Using memory devices
Here's a memory tip to help you remember the subjects of *fui* and *fue:*

The "I" form ends in *-i (fui)*.

The "he" and "she" form ends in *-e (fue)*.

Más ayuda **realidades.com**

 GramActiva Video Animated Verbs

 Canción de hip hop: *¿Adónde fuiste?*

GramActiva Activity

▼ **19 Escribir**

Mis amigos y yo fuimos a...

En una hoja de papel, escribe cinco frases para decir adónde fueron tú y tus amigos.

1. yo
2. mi mejor amigo(a)
3. mis amigos
4. mis amigos y yo
5. uno(a) de mis compañeros de clase

¡Respuesta personal!

DIFFERENTIATED INSTRUCTION

Multiple Intelligences

Visual/Spatial: Have students make a vacation photo album, using real photos or illustrations. Have them make a cover using folded sheets of construction paper, pages for at least six pictures, and have them write a Spanish caption for each picture. Display the photo albums so students can share their stories with the class. Include these in the students' portfolios.

Students with Learning Difficulties

Point out that in a question like *¿Cómo fuiste?*, the single preterite form of the verb conveys the idea of "... did you go?" and no other words are necessary.

▼20 | 🗣️ | ♻️ | Hablar

¿Adónde fueron?

Con otro(a) estudiante, di adónde y cómo fueron estas personas a estos lugares.

Óscar y Lourdes

📹 **Modelo**

A —¿Adónde fueron Óscar y Lourdes?
B —Fueron al teatro.
A —¿Cómo fueron?
B —Fueron en coche.

1.

los Sánchez

2.

tus amigos y tú

3.

Liliana

4.

Uds.

5.

Gregorio

6.

¡Respuesta personal!

tú

▼21 | 🗣️ | Hablar

¿Cómo fuiste tú?

El mes pasado fuiste a muchos lugares, unos cerca y otros más lejos. Trabaja con otro(a) estudiante para hablar de cómo fueron Uds. a cada uno de estos lugares.

📹 **Modelo**

A —¿Cómo fuiste de tu casa a tu restaurante favorito?
B —Fui en el coche de mis padres.

Estudiante A

1. de tu casa a tu escuela
2. de tu escuela al centro comercial
3. de tu ciudad a tu lugar favorito
4. de Miami a Puerto Rico
5. de la Ciudad de México a Cancún
6. de Nueva York a la República Dominicana

Estudiante B

doscientos treinta y tres 233
Capítulo 8A

20 Standards: 1.1

Resources: Answer Keys: Student Edition, p. 163
Focus: Communicating about travel using the preterite of *ir*
Recycle: Leisure activities
Suggestions: Point out that some of the pictures are of specific places, while others will require students to use general vocabulary words.

Answers:
1. —¿Adónde fueron los Sánchez?
   —Fueron al parque de diversiones.
   —¿Cómo fueron?
   —Fueron en coche.
2. —¿Adónde fueron tus amigos y tú?
   —Fuimos a la ciudad.
   —¿Cómo fueron?
   —Fuimos en tren.
3. —¿Adónde fue Liliana?
   —Fue a Puerto Rico.
   —¿Cómo fue?
   —Fue en barco.
4. —¿Adónde fueron Uds.?
   —Fuimos a Chile.
   —¿Cómo fueron?
   —Fuimos en avión.
5. —¿Adónde fue Gregorio?
   —Fue al estadio.
   —¿Cómo fue?
   —Fue en autobús.
6. —¿Adónde fuiste tú?
   —Answers will vary.
   —¿Cómo fuiste?
   —Answers will vary.

21 Standards: 1.1

Focus: Speaking about traveling from place to place
Suggestions: Remind students that the first three sentences will be factual, and the second three will most likely rely on speculation. Have students specify where their favorite place is for item 3.
Answers will vary.
Extension: For homework, have students write a sentence saying where they went for each mode of transportation pictured.

ENRICH YOUR TEACHING

Teacher-to-Teacher

Fill your classroom with travel posters, advertisements, banners, souvenirs, ticket stubs, and anything you can find to correspond with the theme of vacation places and activities. Provide students with a library of Spanish-language travel magazines and books to browse through. This linguistically and culturally rich environment will enhance learning.

22 Standards: 1.1, 1.3

Focus: Playing a game to create and revise illogical sentences

Recycle: Places; modes of transportation

Suggestions: Point out that in Step 2, students have to decide which of their sentences is the silliest and then correct it. Have them share suggestions for corrections, as they can change any parts of the sentence to make it correct.

Answers will vary.

23 Standards: 1.3

Focus: Writing about a vacation in the past

Recycle: Places; modes of transportation; leisure activities

Suggestions: Have students make their letters into postcards, including illustrations on the other side. Encourage them to write about Spanish-speaking countries discussed in this lesson. Hang the postcards on a clothesline, going diagonally across the room, so that both sides are visible.

Answers will vary.

24 Standards: 1.1

Resources: Answer Keys: Student Edition, p. 164

Focus: Speaking about a past vacation

Recycle: Places; preterite tense of *-ar* verbs

Suggestions: Remind students to reread their letter from *Actividad* 23 before beginning. Encourage them to speak without reading from the postcard.

Answers:

Student A:	Student B:
—¿Adónde fuiste de vacaciones?	Answers will vary.
—¿Qué hiciste allí?	
—¿Cómo lo pasaste?	

▼22 | Escribir · Hablar · GramActiva

Juego

1 Play in groups of four. Each person cuts a sheet of paper to form a perfect square. Fold that square into four smaller squares. Unfold the paper and label the squares *a, b, c,* and *d.* Follow Step a below for the *a* square. Fold the corner of that little square so it covers what you have written. Pass the paper to the person on your left. Follow Step b for the *b* square on the paper you receive from the person on your right, fold down the corner, and pass it to your left. Continue until all the squares have been filled. Do not look at what is written on the paper you receive. Write all of your answers in Spanish.

a. Write a subject plus the correct preterite form of *ir.*

b. Write a destination or place *(a / al / a la . . .).*

c. Write a mode of transportation.

d. Write a reason *(para* + infinitive) for going somewhere.

2 When you get your original paper back, unfold each square and read the complete sentence to your group. Let the group decide, *¿Cuál es la frase más tonta* (silly)? Read your silliest sentence to the class. Then make changes to the sentence so it makes sense.

▼23 | Escribir

En mis vacaciones . . .

Inventa unas vacaciones fantásticas. En una hoja de papel, escribe una carta en que hablas de dónde fuiste y qué hiciste. Necesitas responder a estas preguntas.

¡Hola amigos!

Durante mis vacaciones . . .

¿Adónde fuiste?

¿Cómo fuiste?

¿Con quién(es) fuiste?

¿Qué son tres cosas que hiciste?

¿Qué son dos cosas que viste?

¡Hasta pronto!

DIFFERENTIATED INSTRUCTION

Multiple Intelligences

Verbal/Linguistic: For *Actividad* 22, have groups of students collect all of the illogical sentences and compile them into a story. Remind them that they may have to adapt some of the sentences to make them fit better, but the goal is to be silly and entertaining. Encourage them to include illustrations and share their writing with the class.

Students with Learning Difficulties

For *Actividad* 23, remind students of the writing process, which they may be familiar with from their language arts classes. Have them brainstorm ideas, write a rough draft, and then rewrite a final copy, incorporating your corrections and suggestions.

▼24 |  | Hablar

Hablando de nuestras experiencias

Con otro(a) estudiante, usa la información en la Actividad 23 para hablar de lo que hiciste en tus vacaciones.

▶ **Modelo**

A —*¿Adónde fuiste de vacaciones?*
B —*Fui a Argentina.*
A —*¿Qué hiciste allí?*
B —*Visité Patagonia y vi mucha nieve.*
A —*¿Cómo lo pasaste?*
B —*¡Fantástico!*

▼25 | | Escribir • Hablar

Las mejores vacaciones

Con tu compañero(a) de la Actividad 24, escribe una comparación *(comparison)* de sus vacaciones. Después, trabaja con otra pareja. Lee su comparación y decide quién en el grupo pasó las mejores vacaciones *(who had the best vacation)*.

Modelo

Yo fui a la Argentina y Pedro fue a San Antonio. Él fue a unos restaurantes mexicanos, y vio muchos monumentos, y yo vi mucha nieve. Pedro y yo aprendimos mucho en nuestras vacaciones ...

▼ **Fondo Cultural** | Argentina | Chile

Patagonia is a vast, windy region of diverse climates and terrains at the southern tip of South America. It lies east of the Andes and spans parts of Chile and nearly a quarter of Argentina. A sparsely populated area, it is home to many species, including a large colony (325,000 breeding pairs) of Magellanic penguins, whose breeding grounds are the eastern and western coasts of Chile and Argentina, as well as offshore islands.

• What regions of the United States can be compared to Patagonia? What types of animals live in those regions?

Más práctica GO realidades.com | print

Instant Check	✔	
Guided WB p. 107	✔	✔
Core WB p. 60	✔	✔
Comm. WB pp. 67, 71, 168	✔	✔
Hispanohablantes WB p. 298		✔

doscientos treinta y cinco **235**
Capítulo 8A

---

25 Standards: 1.1, 1.3

Focus: Comparing and writing about past vacations

Recycle: Places; preterite tense of **-ar** verbs

Suggestions: Have students make a chart, use one column per classmate, and highlight the items they have in common.

Answers will vary.

Pre-AP* Support

• **Learning Objective:** Interpersonal Speaking

• **Activity 24:** Students practice informal speaking as they describe imaginary vacations to one another.

Fondo cultural

Standards: 2.2

Suggestions: Help students locate Patagonia on a map. Explain that winter temperatures go to –27° F, and summer temperatures often exceed 100° F.

Answers will vary but may include references to Arizona, Nevada, or Alaska and to animals such as coyotes or reptiles.

Additional Resources

• Communication Wbk.: Audio Act. 8, p. 67
• Teacher's Resource Book: Audio Script, p. 239
• Audio Program DVD: Cap. 7B, Track 12

ENRICH YOUR TEACHING

Teacher-to-Teacher

Play the Silly-Souvenir Game with students. Bring in a box of anything you can find around the house—knickknacks, pictures, T-shirts, or jewelry, for example. With their eyes closed, students will pick an item out of the box. Have pairs of students prepare a story about an imaginary vacation that they went on, during which they bought the souvenir. Once students have shared their stories with the class, vote on the best story. Reward the most creative pair by giving them each a souvenir of their choice.

✓ ASSESSMENT

Prueba 8A-4 with Study Plan (online only)

Quiz: The preterite of *ir*
• Prueba 8A-4: p. 206

Gramática

Core Instruction

Standards: 4.1

Resources: Teacher's Resource Book: Video Script, p. 242; Video Program: Cap. 8A

INTERACTIVE WHITEBOARD
Grammar Activities 8A

Suggestions: On the board, write a sentence in Spanish that has a *subject + verb + direct object* structure. Have students identify the direct object. Write another sentence in which the direct object is a person. Once students have identified the direct object in the second example, proceed with the presentation of the use of the personal *a* before a person or animal. Use the *GramActiva* Video either as an introduction to the structure or as a follow-up after your own grammar explanation.

26 Standards: 1.2, 1.3

Resources: Answer Keys: Student Edition, p. 164

Focus: Reading, writing, and speaking using the personal *a*

Recycle: Family members

Suggestions: Explain to students that in Step 2, they must change the family member, the form of the possessive adjectives (**mi** and **su**), and the pronouns. Point out the *Nota* to prevent students from overgeneralizing the personal *a* rule. If students ask why there is both a direct object noun (**abuela**) and a pronoun (**la**), explain that when a direct object noun precedes a verb, the pronoun is also used.

Answers:

1. —¿Vio Ud. a mis tíos?
   —A sus tíos no los vi.
2. —¿Vio Ud. a mi hermano?
   —A su hermano no lo vi.
3. —¿Vio Ud. a mis primas?
   —A sus primas no las vi.
4. —¿Vio Ud. a mi hermanita?
   —A su hermanita no la vi.

Extension: Have students write two sentences naming people that they would like to visit and two sentences naming places that they would like to visit.

▶ Read and represent a traditional children's rhyme
▶ Identify geographical features of some Spanish-speaking countries
▶ Write about and discuss whom you saw and what you visited on a trip

Gramática

The personal *a*

You know that the direct object is the person or thing that receives the action of a verb. When the direct object is a person or group of people, you usually use the word *a* before the object. This is called the "personal *a*."

Visité a mi abuela.	*I visited **my grandmother**.*
Vimos a Juan y Gloria.	*We saw **Juan and Gloria**.*

You can also use the personal *a* when the direct object is a pet.

Busco a mi perro, Capitán.

To ask who receives the action of a verb, use *¿A quién?*

¿A quién visitaron Uds.?

Más ayuda **realidades.com**

GramActiva Video
Tutorial: Personal a

▼26 | Leer · Escribir · Hablar

Don Pepito y don José

1 Lee esta rima tradicional.

—Hola, don Pepito.
—Hola, don José.
—¿Pasó* Ud. por mi casa?
—Por su casa no pasé.
—¿Vio Ud. a mi abuela?
—A su abuela no la vi.
—Adiós, don Pepito.
—Adiós, don José.

*Did you stop by

2 Ahora escribe las líneas *¿Vio Ud. a mi abuela?* y *A su abuela no la vi* y sustituye estos miembros de la familia por "abuela". Usa el pronombre *(pronoun)* apropiado.

1. tíos
2. hermano
3. primas
4. hermanita

3 Con otro(a) estudiante, lee la rima. Un(a) estudiante va a ser don Pepito y el/la otro(a), don José. Lean la rima cuatro veces, cada vez con un miembro diferente de la familia.

236 doscientos treinta y seis
Tema 8 • Experiencias

Nota

You have learned the direct object pronouns *lo*, *la*, *los*, and *las*. These direct object pronouns can refer to people as well as to things. Note that the direct object pronouns do not take the personal a.

• ¿Viste **a tus primos** durante tus vacaciones?
• Sí, **los** vi.

En Barcelona, España

DIFFERENTIATED INSTRUCTION

Students with Learning Difficulties

Before beginning *Actividad 27*, have students write the appropriate direct object pronouns in the margin of their paper before each entry. This will make it easier for them to focus on describing whom they visited rather than on grammatical details.

Heritage Language Learners

Have students write a paragraph telling about an experience when their Spanish-language skills helped someone in the community. Or they can write a fictional story. Encourage them to provide details such as whom they helped and why, what they did, and how long ago the event took place. As you read the essay, check for correct use of the personal *a*.

▼**27** | 👥 | ♻ | Escribir • Hablar

De visita el año pasado

❶ ¿Visitaste a muchas personas o muchos lugares el año pasado? Copia esta tabla en una hoja de papel y complétala *(complete it)* con la información apropiada.

❷ Usa la información en tu tabla para hablar con un(a) compañero(a) sobre tus visitas del año pasado.

▶ **Modelo**

A —¿Visitaste a tus abuelos durante las vacaciones?

B —Sí, los visité el verano pasado.

o: —No, no los visité.

A —¿Dónde los visitaste?

B —Los visité en Puerto Rico.

Personas y lugares	¿Cuándo?	¿Dónde?
1. tus abuelos	el verano pasado	en Puerto Rico
2. un(a) amigo(a) que no vive aquí		
3. un parque de diversiones		
4. tus primos		
5. una nueva ciudad		
6. un museo de arte		

El español en la comunidad

POR FAVOR NO LE DE COMIDA A LOS ANIMALES

Your community may have some of the tourist destinations you learned about in this chapter, such as *un museo, un teatro, un zoológico,* or *un parque de diversiones.* Think of different opportunities to use your Spanish at each of the locations. As you learn more Spanish, perhaps you could provide tours to visitors who speak Spanish. You could help write brochures and maps in Spanish to assist Spanish-speaking visitors. Can you think of other opportunities?

• Visit one of these locations in person or online and see what resources are available in Spanish. Bring them to share with the class.

doscientos treinta y siete **237**
Capítulo 8A

---

27 Standards: 1.1, 1.3

Resources: Answer Keys: Student Edition, p. 165

Focus: Asking and answering questions with and without the personal *a*

Recycle: Direct object pronouns; family members

Suggestions: Point out that some of the items are people and others are places, so students will need to decide when to use the personal *a.* Remind students that they will not fill out all of the columns of their chart if they haven't visited each person or place listed.

Answers:
Student A
1. —¿Visitaste a tus abuelos durante las vacaciones?
2. —¿Visitaste a un(a) amigo(a) que no vive aquí ...?
3. —¿Visitaste un parque de diversiones ...?
4. —¿Visitaste a tus primos ...?
5. —¿Visitaste una nueva ciudad ...?
6. —¿Visitaste un museo de arte ...?
Student B
Answers will vary.

El español en la comunidad

Core Instruction

Standards: 5.1

Suggestions: If you live in a small community, encourage students to think about a larger city near you or one that they have visited.

Teacher-to-Teacher

Have students search the Internet for some of the tourist destinations in their town or in a larger town nearby. They should try to find out if any of the tours at these destinations are conducted in Spanish. Also, have them find out if there are any art exhibits, movies, or theater productions that are in Spanish or relate to Spanish or Spanish American cultural themes.

ENRICH YOUR TEACHING

Culture Note
Use of the titles *don* and *doña* in the Spanish-speaking world is a gesture of courtesy today. These titles were originally used to display a high level of respect and formality. The words come from the Latin words *dominus* (male) or *domina* (female), meaning "lord" or "master." In centuries past, only people of high rank and nobility were referred to as *don* or *doña* out of respect for their authority.

Teacher-to-Teacher
Encourage more musically inclined students to put the rhyme about don Pepito and don José to music. Let them play or sing their compositions to the class.

28 Standards: 3.1

Resources: Answer Keys: Student Edition, p. 165

Focus: Reading about geography

Recycle: Countries and geography

Suggestions: Encourage students to refer to the maps on pp. xv–xxvii as they work to identify each country.

Answers:

1. Nicaragua
2. Ecuador
3. México
4. Brasil
5. Colombia

Extension: Have students each write one clue about one of the countries on the list that wasn't used in the activity. As each student reads the clue, the rest of the class will guess which country he or she is talking about.

▼28 ♻ Leer · Pensar

Juego de geografía: Las Américas

¿Conoces[1] bien los países de las Américas? Empareja las descripciones con los países apropiados.

Conexiones | La geografía

1. Este país es el más grande de América Central. En el suroeste hay un lago muy grande que tiene el mismo nombre que el país. El lago está muy cerca de la frontera[2] con Costa Rica. En el este del país está el mar Caribe donde el clima es tropical y llueve mucho.

2. Este país pequeño tiene dos regiones tropicales, en el este y en el oeste, con montañas en el centro. Un cuarto de las personas en el país son de origen indígena y hablan quechua, el idioma[3] de los incas. Su nombre viene de la línea imaginaria que cruza el país.

3. Las ciudades más grandes de este país, como la capital, están en el centro del país donde hay montañas y volcanes. En el norte hay desiertos extensos y en el sur hay selvas[4] tropicales. Este país comparte una frontera con los Estados Unidos.

4. Este país es el más grande de América del Sur, con el río más grande del mundo.[5] Una gran parte del país es selva tropical con miles de especies de plantas, árboles y animales como monos, jaguares y tucanes. No hablan español aquí; hablan portugués.

5. Es el único[6] país de América del Sur que tiene playas en el mar Caribe y el océano Pacífico. Es un país famoso por su café, que viene de los valles fértiles.

México
El Salvador
Nicaragua
Colombia
Brasil
Uruguay
Chile
Bolivia
Ecuador
Cuba

norte
oeste · este
sur

[1]Do you know [2]border [3]language [4]forests [5]world [6]only

DIFFERENTIATED INSTRUCTION

Heritage Language Learners

Have students create clues like those in *Actividad* 28 about their heritage country. To guide them, ask questions about the climate, the land formations, the bodies of water, the capital, and the largest cities. Correct their work and use the clues to further extend the *Actividad*.

▼ Exploración del lenguaje

Nouns that end in *-io* and *-eo*

Latin words for buildings and places have carried into many modern languages, including Spanish. In many place names the Latin ending *-um* (which remains in a number of words in English today) changed to an *-io* or *-eo* in Spanish. You know some of these words: *el estadio, el museo, el gimnasio.*

Try it out! Based on your knowledge of English and what you have learned about Spanish place names from Latin, match the definitions with the Spanish words in the list.

El acuario de Valencia, España

1. where you stand to deliver a speech
2. usually found in a cemetery
3. where you can see all kinds of sea life
4. where you sit when you see school plays or concerts
5. where you go to learn about stars and planets
6. where the ancient Romans went to see sporting events

a. el auditorio
b. el podio
c. el acuario
d. el planetario
e. el coliseo
f. el mausoleo

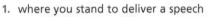

▼**29** | 🔊 | Escribir • Hablar

Y tú, ¿qué dices?

1. ¿Qué puedes visitar en tu comunidad? ¿Hay museos, parques de diversiones o monumentos? ¿Cuál prefieres visitar?

2. El año pasado, ¿fuiste a ver una obra de teatro en tu comunidad o en tu escuela? ¿Te gustó? ¿Por qué?

3. El año pasado, ¿visitaste un museo o un zoológico en tu comunidad? ¿Cómo lo pasaste?

4. ¿Prefieres viajar a otros países o ciudades, o prefieres visitar lugares en tu comunidad?

Más práctica	GO	
realidades.com	print	
Instant Check	✔	
Guided WB p. 108	✔	✔
Core WB p. 61	✔	✔
Comm. WB p. 68	✔	✔
Hispanohablantes WB pp. 299–301		✔

Exploración del lenguaje
Core Instruction
Standards: 4.1

Resources: Answer Keys: Student Edition, p. 165
Suggestions: Before beginning, ask students to brainstorm a list of English words ending in *-um*. Compare their list with the list in *Try it out!*
Answers:
1. b   4. a
2. f   5. d
3. c   6. e

▼**29** Standards: 1.1, 1.2
Focus: Writing and talking about places to visit in your community
Suggestions: Arrange students in small groups to discuss each question. When reviewing answers, be sure you ask a student about others in his or her group.
Answers will vary.

Theme Project
Students can perform Step 2 at this point. Be sure they understand your corrections and suggestions. (For more information, see p. 216-b.)

Additional Resources
• Communication Wbk.: Audio Act. 9, p. 68
• Teacher's Resource Book: Audio Script, p. 239, Communicative Pair Activity BLM, pp. 246–247
• Audio Program DVD: Cap. 7B, Track 13

ENRICH YOUR TEACHING

Teacher-to-Teacher
Have students work in small groups to create a vacation brochure for Spanish speakers who might visit your community. Students should include places to visit, things to see and do, and perhaps the best way to travel. You might submit copies of the best brochures to the local visitor's bureau or Chamber of Commerce.

21st Century Skills
Technology Literacy Remind students of the various digital tools available in **realidades.com** that target various types of learners and will help them learn and practice the grammar points in the chapter: eText with embedded audio, tutorials, Canción de hip-hop, and online grammar practice.

✓ASSESSMENT
Prueba 8A-5 with Study Plan (online only)

Quiz: The personal *a*
• Prueba 8A-5: p. 207

Lectura

Core Instruction

Standards: 1.2, 1.3, 2.1, 2.2, 3.1

Resources: Map Transparency 15

🌐 **Mapa global interactivo, Actividad 5**
Explore ancient and modern-day Perú.

Focus: Reading comprehension of journal entries about a trip to Peru

Suggestions:

Pre-reading: Direct students' attention to the *Strategy* and model how familiar words in a sentence can help determine the meaning of unfamiliar words. Have students write the words from the *Strategy* on a sheet of paper and identify each word as they encounter it in the journal entries.

Reading: Have students read *Álbum de mi viaje al Perú* silently. When they have finished, have student volunteers reread the journal entry aloud. After each entry, ask students to give a brief summary of the day's events.

Post-reading: Ask students to tell what context clues or familiar words they used to determine the meaning of the words from the *Strategy*. Have students identify the main locations in Peru—Cuzco, Lima, Machu Picchu, lago Titicaca, and Nazca. Use the ¿*Comprendes?* questions to check comprehension.

BELLRINGER REVIEW

Show the map of *La América del Sur* to locate these places. *Cuzco, Lima, Machu Picchu, Lago Titicaca, las Líneas de Nazca.*

240

Lectura

Perú

Álbum de mi viaje al Perú

Por Sofía Porrúa

> **Strategy**
>
> **Using context clues**
> If you don't recognize a word, use the other words in the sentence to help you guess its meaning. Use context clues to guess the meaning of words such as *antigua, altura, construyeron,* and *nivel.*

domingo, 25 de julio
Estoy en el Perú con mis amigos Beto y Carmen. Vamos en autobús a Cuzco, antigua capital del imperio inca. Hoy día es una ciudad pequeña y una atracción turística. Beto está sacando muchas fotos con su cámara digital. Carmen está dibujando todo lo que ve. Las montañas son fantásticas.

miércoles, 28 de julio
Hoy es el Día de la Independencia peruana. En esta fecha en 1821, José de San Martín proclamó la independencia del Perú. En Lima, una gran ciudad moderna y capital del país, hay grandes celebraciones.

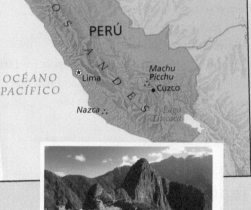

jueves, 29 de julio
Hoy estamos en Machu Picchu, ruinas impresionantes de una ciudad antigua de los incas. A más de 2.000 metros de altura en los Andes, los incas construyeron calles, casas, acueductos, palacios, templos y terrazas para cultivar. Hiram Bingham, un arqueólogo de la Universidad de Yale, descubrió[1] Machu Picchu en 1911.

[1] discovered

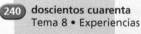
240 doscientos cuarenta
Tema 8 • Experiencias

DIFFERENTIATED INSTRUCTION

Advanced Learners

Have students research a location they would go to if they could only visit one of the places described in the journal. Students should find additional information about the location and write a short description about it. The paragraph could be written in a journal style and might include a drawing or magazine picture as illustration.

Heritage Language Learners

Have students use the graphic organizer on p. 241 to research and write down information about a country of their choice. Then have them write journal entries that include their findings, using the *Lectura* as a model.

sábado, 31 de julio

Estamos paseando en bote por el lago Titicaca, en la frontera del Perú y Bolivia. Es el lago más grande de estos países y el más alto del mundo.[2] ¡Estamos a más de 3.800 metros sobre el nivel del mar!

miércoles, 4 de agosto

Ahora estamos en un avión pequeño. Sobre la tierra[3] podemos ver algo muy misterioso: hay un desierto donde vemos enormes dibujos de animales y figuras geométricas. Estos dibujos se llaman las Líneas de Nazca. Miden[4] más de 300 metros y tienen más de dos mil años. ¿Quiénes los dibujaron, y por qué? Es necesario estar en un avión para verlos. ¿Cómo dibujaron los artistas algo tan[5] grande sin poder verlo?

Mañana regresamos al Cuzco y el domingo salimos de Perú. ¡Un viaje muy interesante! Beto tiene sus fotos y Carmen, sus dibujos. Yo no soy ni fotógrafa ni artista, por eso voy a comprar tarjetas postales[6] como recuerdos.

[2]world [3]ground [4]They measure [5]so [6]postcards

¿Comprendes?

1. ¿Cómo va a recordar Sofía su viaje al Perú? ¿Y Beto y Carmen?

2. Pizarro y los españoles descubrieron muchas de las ciudades de los incas. ¿Por qué piensas que no descubrieron Machu Picchu? ¿Quién lo descubrió?

3. Para muchos turistas que visitan el lago Titicaca es difícil caminar y respirar (to breathe). ¿Por qué piensas que tienen estos problemas?

4. ¿Cuáles son los misterios de las Líneas de Nazca?

5. Copia la tabla en una hoja de papel. Usa la información de la lectura para comparar el Perú con los Estados Unidos.

		Perú	Estados Unidos
a.	Dos lugares históricos y turísticos		
b.	Día de la Independencia		
c.	Año de la proclamación de la independencia		
d.	Capital del país hoy		
e.	Héroe nacional		

Más práctica (GO)

realidades.com | print

Guided WB p. 109	✔	✔
Comm. WB pp. 72, 169	✔	✔
Hispanohablantes WB pp. 302–303		✔
Cultural Reading Activity		✔

doscientos cuarenta y uno **241**
Capítulo 8A

ENRICH YOUR TEACHING

Culture Note

In southwestern Peru, ancient geometric symbols and depictions of animals are etched into the surface of the barren plain in the vicinity of Nazca. Known collectively as the "Nazca Lines," the artwork spans an area of approximately 200 square miles and includes representations of animals such as a hummingbird, monkey, heron, whale, and a spider, some of which span as much as 1,000 feet.

¿Comprendes? Standards: 1.2, 1.3

Resources: Answer Keys: Student Edition, p. 166

Focus: Reading comprehension of facts about Peru and the United States

Suggestions: Suggest that students read the questions first, and then reread the passage to find the correct answer. If necessary, suggest that they use their history books or other reference materials for additional information about the United States.

Answers:

1. Sofía escribe en su álbum. Beto saca fotos. Carmen dibuja.
2. Porque está a más de 2.000 metros de altura. Lo descubrió Hiram Bingham, un arqueólogo de la Universidad de Yale.
3. Porque está a 3.800 metros sobre el nivel del mar.
4. ¿Quiénes las dibujaron y por qué? ¿Cómo dibujaron los artistas algo tan grande sin poder verlo?
5. Answers will vary.

Pre-AP* Support

- **Learning Objective:** Interpersonal Writing
- **Activity:** Have students bring to class a picture of a historical place they have visited or would like to visit. Have them write two diary entries for activities they did or might have done on those days. Then have them summarize one of the two activities in an e-mail to a far-away relative.
- **Pre-AP* Resource Book:** Comprehensive guide to Pre-AP* reading skill development, pp. 19–26

Theme Project

Students can perform Step 3 at this point. (For more information, see p. 216-b.)

Teacher-to-Teacher

Careers: *Capítulo* 8A has focused on travel. Have students work in small groups to talk about a career in the travel business. Ask them to generate a list of words, expressions, and sentences they have learned that would be useful for giving Spanish tours of their community. Ask groups to share their lists.

For Further Reading

Student Resource: *Realidades para hispanohablantes: Lectura 2*, pp. 304–305

La cultura en vivo

Core Instruction

Standards: 2.2, 4.2

Focus: Reading about and creating an *ojo de Dios*

Presentation: Begin a brief discussion about good-luck charms. Point out some common ones, such as rabbits' feet and four-leaf clovers. Tell students that they will learn about and make a kind of good-luck charm that dates back hundreds of years.

Have them read the two paragraphs. Point out that **ojos de Dios** are a form of artwork. Remind them that before machines and electricity existed, people made things by hand. Many of these handmade items have become important forms of artwork that help keep traditions alive. Direct attention to the woman in the photo. She is from one of the indigenous groups of Mexico that still make **ojos de Dios** today. Have students look at the photo of the **ojo de Dios.** Ask why this might be considered an "eye."

Suggestions: Popsicle sticks or cut dowels will work well for this. Make your own **ojo de Dios** in advance so you can estimate the amount of time and yarn needed. Yours can then be used as a model. Also make a partial one, stopping at Step 2, so that students can use it as a guide.

Prior to class, gather enough materials for each student. Have a variety of colors of yarn, and if possible have more than one ball of each color to make sharing easier. Make sure your colors include white for those who wish to represent the white of an eye. Have students read the steps before beginning. Answer any questions. Go through the steps slowly and circulate to give assistance as needed.

You may wish to have students bring in feathers, beads, or tassels for decoration.

Direct attention to *Think about it!* and have students discuss the questions.

Answers will vary.

Additional Resources

Student Resource: Realidades para hispanohablantes, p. 306

¡Adelante!

La cultura en vivo

El ojo de Dios

Traveling in the Spanish-speaking world you will encounter a marvelous variety of artwork and crafts, many of which have their origins in the time before the Spaniards came to the Americas. One form of art that is popular among visitors to parts of Mexico is the *ojo de Dios*.

Mujer tarahumara en San Rafael, México

The *ojo de Dios* is a diamond-shaped weaving. As a gift, it symbolizes good wishes from one person to another. *Ojos de Dios* may have originated in Peru about 300 B.C. The people best known for making these today are the Indians of Mexico's Sierra Madre region. The Cora, Huichol, Tarahumara, and Tepehuane all make and use these weavings in their daily lives.

How to make an ojo de Dios

Materials

- yarn
- scissors
- two sticks of the same size
- optional: feathers, beads, or tassels for finishing touches

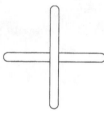

Figure 1

Directions

1 Tie the sticks together to form a cross. *(Fig. 1)*

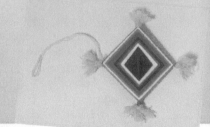

Figure 2

2 Tie the end of the yarn to the center of the cross.

3 Weave the yarn over and around each stick, keeping the yarn pulled tight. *(Fig. 2)* To change color, knot together two ends of different-colored yarn. The knot should fall on the back side. Continue wrapping until the sticks are covered with yarn. Tie a small knot at the back and leave enough yarn to make a loop for hanging.

4 You may want to add feathers, beads, or tassels to the ends of the sticks. Hang your decorative piece for everyone to enjoy.

Think about it! What are some of the traditional handicrafts in the United States? What is the ethnic heritage of these crafts?

Figure 3

DIFFERENTIATED INSTRUCTION

Multiple Intelligences

Visual/Spatial: Students may pick this up quickly. If so, encourage them to add finishing touches to personalize their **ojo de Dios.** They may also be able to help others who are having difficulties with the process.

Students with Special Needs

Students may have difficulties getting the two sticks to stay together as in Figure 1. If so, you may prepare the sticks for them, or ask a more adept student to help out. Some may also have trouble wrapping the yarn. If so, provide a model and demonstrate for them a few times. Students may benefit from working in pairs.

Presentación oral 🗨Talk!

▼ Objectives
▶ Describe a trip you took
▶ Use a word web to organize your ideas

Aplicación

Speaking | 8A

Mi viaje

Task
Tell a friend about a trip you took. It could be a vacation, a visit to family, or an imaginary trip. Use photos or drawings to make your talk more interesting

1 Prepare Use the word web to think about what you did on your trip. Include information and events in each circle. Use photos or pictures to illustrate each part of the trip noted on the word web. Design an appealing illustration of your trip.

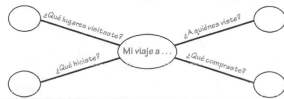

¿Qué lugares visitaste?
¿A quiénes viste?
Mi viaje a . . .
¿Qué hiciste?
¿Qué compraste?

> **Strategy**
>
> **Using graphic organizers**
> Using a graphic organizer such as a word web will help you think through what you want to say in your presentation.

2 Practice Use the information in your word web to tell a partner about your trip. Go through your story several times using the photographs or illustrations. Use your notes in practice, but not when you present. End by saying how you felt about the trip.

Modelo
En marzo, fui a la Florida para visitar a mis primos. Tomamos el sol en la playa y nadamos mucho. Aprendí a bucear y vi animales muy interesantes en el mar. La Florida es un lugar fantástico. El viaje fue muy divertido.

3 Present Talk about your trip to a small group or the whole class. Use your photos or drawings to help you.

4 Evaluation The following rubric will be used to grade your presentation.

Rubric	Score 1	Score 3	Score 5
Amount of information provided	You include two categories from the word web.	You include three categories from the word web.	You include all four categories from the word web.
Use of photographs or visuals	You include only two visuals that clearly connect to trip.	You include three visuals that clearly connect to trip.	You include four visuals that clearly connect to trip.
How easily you are understood	You are extremely difficult to understand. Your teacher could only recognize isolated words and phrases.	You are understandable, but have frequent errors in vocabulary and/or grammar that hinder your comprehensibility.	You are easily understood. Your teacher does not have to "decode" what you are trying to say.

ENRICH YOUR TEACHING

Teacher-to-Teacher
To create the *Mi viaje* presentation, have students use the photos, illustrations, and information they have used in creating other class projects for this chapter, or souvenirs from vacations they have taken. Have them try to think of an illustration for each of the word web questions.

21st Century Skills

Critical Thinking and Problem Solving Have students interview family members to find out what kind of vacation they would like to take in the summer. Have them use a Venn diagram to compare and contrast two vacation sites they have learned about in this chapter. By looking at the similarities and differences, they can make an informed decision about where to go with the family.

Presentación oral

Core Instruction
Standards: 1.1, 1.3

Resources: Voc. and Gram. Transparency 150; Teacher's Resource Book: GramActiva BLM, p. 249

Focus: Communicating about vacations in a personalized context

Suggestions: Review the task and the four-step approach with students. Review the rubric with the class to explain how you will grade the performance task. Emphasize that it is quality, not length, that is most important.

Remind students that success begins with good planning. Students should do word webs and incorporate their visual aids as they speak. Remind students to practice with a partner since they will not be able to use notes when they present.

Portfolio
Make video or audio recordings of student presentations in class, or assign the RealTalk activity so they can record their presentations online. Include the recording in their portfolios.

Pre-AP* Support
- **Learning Objective:** Presentational Speaking
- **Activity:** Remind students to focus on the presentational speaking skills used in this task such as fluency, pronunciation, and comprehensibility.
- *Pre-AP* Resource Book:* Comprehensive guide to Pre-AP* speaking skill development, pp. 39–50

Additional Resources
Student Resources: Realidades para hispanohablantes: p. 307; Guided Practice: Presentación oral, p. 110

✓ASSESSMENT

Presentación oral
- Assessment Program: Rubrics, p. T33
  Go over the descriptions of the different levels of performance. After assessing students, help individuals understand how their performance could be improved.

8A Video

Videomisterio ▶

Core Instruction

Standards: 1.2, 2.1, 5.2

Resources: Teacher's Resource Book: Video Script, pp. 242–243; Video Program: Cap. 8A; Video Program Teacher's Guide: Cap. 8A

Focus: Introducing the episode, scanning, and reading the summary.

Personajes importantes:

Lola Lago, detective
Rosalinda, nurse
Pedro, Doña Gracia's grandson

Synopsis: Rosalinda finds out Julia Romero's address and calls Lola to let her know. Then Pedro and Lola meet at doña Gracia's apartment. There they find a postcard sent to María from Luis Antonio Llamas, a former secretary to doña Gracia's husband. By chance, the name of one of the nurses that cared for Julia in the hospital was Luis Antonio. Next they go to Julia Romero's apartment. They discover that she no longer lives there, but the new tenant has a box of Julia's belongings. In the box they find several letters from Luis Antonio.

Suggestions:

Pre-viewing: Review with students the events of the previous episode. Pedro Requena decides to hire Lola to investigate what caused the incident at his grand-mother's house that sent her to the hospital and who stole doña Gracia's jewels from her apartment. Inspector Gil suspects María, since she has disappeared.

When discussing the *Nota cultural,* ask students how addresses in Spain are different from those in the United States. Provide examples of the *Palabras para comprender* in context and write them on the board. Remind students that these words are only used to help them understand the episode and they are not responsible for that vocabulary.

¿Eres tú, María? Episodio 7

Antes de ver el video

Resumen del episodio

Lola y Pedro visitan el piso elegante de doña Gracia. Entran en la habitación[1] de María. Hay ropa, libros, unas fotos y una tarjeta postal. Lola y Pedro leen algo muy interesante en la tarjeta postal. Después, van al piso de Julia. Allí vive un hombre que no conoce a Julia. Pero antes vivía[2] una chica en el piso. Todavía hay unas cosas de esa chica: ropa, unas cartas y unos papeles. ¿Y qué más?

[1] bedroom   [2] used to live

Nota cultural Addresses in Spain are written differently than in the United States. For example, the name of Julia's street is Calle Norte. The building number is 23. The 1° *(primero)* indicates the apartment is on the first floor (not the ground floor, but what we would call the second floor), and Julia lives in apartment D.

Palabras para comprender

¡Suerte!	Good luck!
No la conozco.	I don't know her.
tenía un secretario	had a secretary
tuvo problemas con él	had problems with him
¡Qué casualidad!	What a coincidence!

"Lola, te llamo porque tengo información sobre la otra chica en el accidente. Tengo la dirección de su piso. Es Calle Norte, 23, 1°, D".

(244) **doscientos cuarenta y cuatro**
Tema 8 • Experiencias

DIFFERENTIATED INSTRUCTION

Advanced Learners

Have advanced learners explain what they think the relationship is between Luis Antonio and Julia. How did Pedro know who Luis Antonio was?

Heritage Language Learners

In this episode, Pedro and Lola speak of several coincidences as *una casualidad,* which is a false cognate. "Casualty" in English is equivalent to *muerto* or *pérdida* in Spanish. Ask students to mention other false cognates they know or have noticed, such as "resume" and *resumen* ("resume" translates as *volver a empezar* or *comenzar de nuevo).*

"¿A quién buscáis? Antes aquí vivía una chica . . .".

"Mira esta tarjeta postal. Interesante, ¿no?"

"¿Sabes, Pedro? En mi profesión la casualidad no existe".

Después de ver el video

¿Comprendes?

Pon las frases en orden según el episodio.

1. Pedro recuerda el nombre de Luis Antonio Llamas, un secretario de su papá.
2. Leen la tarjeta postal de Luis Antonio.
3. Pedro llama a Lola para invitarla a visitar el piso de su abuela.
4. El joven en el piso de Julia no está nada contento.
5. Rosalinda llama a Lola para darle la dirección de Julia.
6. Quieren ver la habitación de María.
7. Deciden visitar el piso de Julia.

Nota gramatical In this episode you will hear a few more examples of the *vosotros* form: *queréis, sois, podéis, buscáis.* Remember that you use *vosotros* or *vosotras* when talking to more than one person whom you would address individually as *tú.*

Más práctica GO

realidades.com | print

Actividades ✔

doscientos cuarenta y cinco 245
Capítulo 8A

Visual scanning: Discuss who is pictured before students read the *Resumen del episodio.* Have them scan the text and find three cognates. *(visitan, fotos, interesante)*

Viewing: If there is time after viewing the full episode, go back and replay some key moments that you wish to highlight, such as the scene in which Lola and Pedro visit doña Gracia's apartment.

Post-viewing: Point out the *Nota gramatical.* Write the vocabulary presented in this episode on the board to help students create sentences for each important scene that adds new information to the plot. Then have students do the *¿Comprendes?* activity.

▼ **¿Comprendes?** Standards: 1.2, 1.3

Resources: Answer Keys: Student Edition, p. 166

Focus: Verifying comprehension; reviewing the plot

Suggestions: Before they put the sentences in the correct order, have students look at the photos and summarize what happened in each one. It may be helpful to have students work in pairs or groups.

Answers: 5, 3, 6, 2, 1, 7, 4

Additional Resources

• *¿Eres tú, María?* Video Workbook, Episode 7
• *¿Eres tú, María?* Teacher's Video Guide: Answer Key

ENRICH YOUR TEACHING

Teacher-to-Teacher

The **vosotros** form, as in **queréis, sois, podéis,** and **buscáis,** presented in the Nota gramatical, is formed by adding the endings **-áis, -éis,** and **-ís** to **-ar, -er,** and **-ir** verbs. It may help to write on the board a few of the verbs presented so far using the corresponding **vosotros** endings.

Remind students that **vosotros** is used to speak to a group of people whom you would address as **tú** individually.

Review Activities

To talk about places to visit and things to see on vacation: Have students work in pairs to quiz each other on the vocabulary. Students can create flashcards, writing the Spanish word on one side of an index card and the English word on the other.

To talk about things to do on vacation: Have students name a location from the previous section, and then ask one another: *¿Qué viste?* or *¿Qué aprendiste?*

To talk about ways to travel: Have one student name a vacation place. The other student will suggest an appropriate way to get there.

To talk about your vacation and to express time: Have students create a cloze passage in which they leave out vocabulary words and expressions. They should provide a word bank and exchange their passages with another student.

Portfolio

Invite students to review the activities they completed in this chapter, including written reports, posters or other visuals, recordings of oral presentations, or other projects. Have them select one or two items that they feel best demonstrate their achievements in Spanish to include in their portfolios. Have them include this with the Chapter Checklist and Self-Assessment Worksheet.

Additional Resources

Student Resources: Realidades para hispanohablantes, p. 308

Teacher Resources:
• Teacher's Resource Book: Situation Cards, p. 248, Clip Art, pp. 250–251
• Assessment Program: Chapter Checklist and Self-Assessment Worksheet, pp. T56–T57

Repaso del capítulo
Vocabulario y gramática

to talk about places to visit on vacation

la ciudad	city
el estadio	stadium
el lago	lake
el lugar	place
el mar	sea
el monumento	monument
el museo	museum
el país	country
el parque de diversiones	amusement park
el parque nacional	national park
el teatro	theater
la obra de teatro	play
el zoológico	zoo

to talk about things to see on vacation

el animal	animal
el árbol	tree
la atracción, *pl.* las atracciones	attraction(s)
el mono	monkey
el oso	bear
el pájaro	bird

to talk about things to do on vacation

aprender (a)	to learn
bucear	to scuba dive / snorkel
(comprar) recuerdos	(to buy) souvenirs
descansar	to rest, to relax
montar a caballo	to ride horseback
pasear en bote	to go boating
tomar el sol	to sunbathe
visitar	to visit

to talk about ways to travel

en	by
el autobús	bus
el avión	airplane
el barco	boat, ship
el tren	train

to talk about your vacation

el boleto	ticket
como	like, as
¿Cómo lo pasaste?	How was it (for you)?
dime	tell me
fantástico, -a	fantastic
Fue un desastre.	It was a disaster.
el hotel	hotel
impresionante	impressive
ir de vacaciones	to go on vacation
Me gustó.	I liked it.
¿Qué hiciste?	What did you do?
¿Qué te pasó?	What happened to you?
regresar	to return
salir	to leave, to go out
¿Te gustó?	Did you like it?
tremendo, -a	tremendous
viajar	to travel
el viaje	trip
vi	I saw
¿Viste . . . ?	Did you see . . . ?

to express time

durante	during
tarde	late
temprano	early

preterite of *-er* and *-ir* verbs

aprendí salí	aprendimos salimos
aprendiste saliste	aprendisteis salisteis
aprendió salió	aprendieron salieron

preterite of *ir*

fui	fuimos
fuiste	fuisteis
fue	fueron

For *Vocabulario adicional*, see pp. 336–337.

 246 doscientos cuarenta y seis
Tema 8 • Experiencias

DIFFERENTIATED INSTRUCTION

Heritage Language Learners

Have students write a ten-sentence paragraph describing a trip. The sentences must use the preterite of *-er* and *-ir* verbs, and of *ir*. Encourage them to use different subject pronouns as they tell the story. Have them check their spelling and verb forms carefully.

Multiple Intelligences

Logical/Mathematical: Give students a blank grid on which to create a word search puzzle. Have them choose fifteen vocabulary words or expressions and write them into the grid. Ask them to fill in the remaining blocks with random letters. Underneath the grid, have students write how many words are hidden in the puzzle. Have them exchange puzzles.

Más repaso GO realidades.com | print

Instant Check	✔	
Puzzles	✔	
Core WB pp. 62–63	✔	✔
Comm. WB pp. 170, 171–174	✔	✔

Preparación para el examen

On the exam you will be asked to . . .	Here are practice tasks similar to those you will find on the exam . . .	For review go to your print or digital textbook . . .
1 Escuchar Listen and understand what people say they did and where they went during their last vacation	As part of a presentation in Spanish class, a student talked about his last vacation. As you listen, see if you can determine: a) where he went; b) one thing he did; c) one thing he saw.	pp. 218–223 *Vocabulario en contexto* p. 219 Actividad 1 p. 224 Actividad 7 p. 225 Actividades 8–9
2 Hablar Tell about your best trip or vacation	Find out where your partner went on his or her best vacation, and what he or she did and saw. As you listen, make a drawing that includes details of the trip. Then your partner will ask you to describe your best vacation. Do your drawings match the descriptions?	p. 226 Actividad 11 p. 228 Actividad 14 p. 233 Actividad 20 p. 237 Actividad 27 p. 243 *Presentación oral*
3 Leer Read and understand a vacation postcard	Read the postcard Javier sent to his friend last summer during his family vacation. Which things does he say he liked? Was there anything he didn't like? ¡Hola! Salí de vacaciones la semana pasada y ahora estamos aquí en Puerto Rico. Visitamos a nuestra tía en San Juan. Ayer fuimos al Viejo San Juan, donde vi muchos monumentos. También vi El Morro, un lugar muy famoso. ¡Fue fabuloso! Hoy fui a la playa de Luquillo y tomé el sol. Los otros bucearon por tres horas, pero a mí no me gusta el mar. Después, comimos arroz con pollo en un restaurante. ¡Uf! ¡Siempre arroz con pollo aquí! Regreso el sábado. ¡Hasta luego! Javier	p. 226 Actividad 10 p. 227 Actividad 12 p. 238 Actividad 28 pp. 240–241 *Lectura*
4 Escribir Write a brief narrative about an imaginary character's trip	A first-grade teacher has asked you to write a story in Spanish for her students. You decide to write about a stuffed bear, *el Oso Teo*, and his trip. Tell where he went, what he did, what he saw, and what he ate. Begin with something like, *"El Oso Teo fue de viaje a su parque favorito . . ."*	p. 225 Actividad 8 p. 231 Actividades 17–18 p. 237 Actividad 27 p. 239 Actividad 29 pp. 240–241 *Lectura*
5 Pensar Demonstrate an understanding of cultural perspectives regarding artwork and crafts.	Think about a gift you might give someone to symbolize good luck and good fortune in our culture. Compare it to a traditional craft from Mexico that is given for the same reason. Describe its significance and history in the Spanish-speaking world.	p. 242 *La cultura en vivo*

doscientos cuarenta y siete **247**
Capítulo 8A

DIFFERENTIATED ASSESSMENT

CORE ASSESSMENT
- **Assessment Program:** Examen del capítulo 8A, pp. 208–214
- **Audio Program DVD:** Cap. 7B, Track 16
- **ExamView:** Chapter Test, Test Banks A and B

ADVANCED/PRE-AP*
- **ExamView: Pre-AP* Test Bank**
- **Pre-AP* Resource Book,** pp. 90–93

STUDENTS NEEDING EXTRA HELP
- **Alternate Assessment Program:** Examen del capítulo 8A
- **Audio Program DVD:** Cap. 7B, Track 16

HERITAGE LEARNERS
- **Assessment Program: Realidades para hispanohablantes:** Examen del capítulo 8A
- **ExamView: Heritage Learner Test Bank**

Performance Tasks

Standards: 1.1, 1.2, 1.3, 2.1, 3.1

Student Resource: Realidades para hispanohablantes: p. 309
Teacher Resources: Teacher's Resource Book: Audio Script, p. 240; Audio Program DVD: Cap. 7B, Track 15; Answer Keys: Student Edition, p. 166

1. Escuchar

Suggestions: Have students create three columns on their paper: Where they went; What they did; What they saw.

Script

Oye. Todo fue tremendo. Fuimos de vacaciones al parque nacional por una semana. Monté a caballo con mis primos y pasé en bote con mi padre. ¡Vi unos árboles más grandes que una casa!

Answers:

a) He went to the national park.
b) He went horseback riding and boating.
c) He saw trees bigger than houses.

2. Hablar

Suggestions: Encourage students to draw quickly while they listen, sketching out the main idea rather than focusing on drawing with a lot of detail.

Answers will vary.

3. Leer

Suggestions: Encourage students to make a list of pros and cons to determine what Javier liked about his trip and what he didn't like.

Answers:

What Javier liked: San Juan, monuments, and El Morro
What Javier didn't like: the sea, arroz con pollo

4. Escribir

Suggestions: Have students organize their thoughts by taking notes to answer these questions: Who? Where? What did he do? What did he see? What did he eat?

5. Pensar

Suggestions: Refer students to the reading on p. 242 to prepare them.

Answers will vary.

AT A GLANCE

Objectives

- Listen to and read about community service
- Talk and write about volunteer activities and recycling
- Exchange information about volunteering
- Compare perspectives about volunteer activities in Spanish-speaking countries to your community
- Compare environmental efforts in Spain, Costa Rica, and other Spanish-speaking countries to programs in your community

Vocabulary

- Recycling
- Places in a community
- Volunteer work

Grammar

- The present tense of *decir*
- Indirect object pronouns
- The preterite of *hacer* and *dar*

Culture

- Peace Corps, p. 249
- Recycling efforts in Spain, p. 257
- The doctors of Interplast, p. 259
- Protected natural areas of Costa Rica, p. 259
- Conservation efforts in Puerto Rico, p. 261
- Blown glass art in Mexico, p. 261
- *El Hospital de la Caridad,* Spain, p. 267
- *las tortugas tinglar,* p. 271
- *Hábitat para la Humanidad,* pp. 272–273
- Cultural perspectives on volunteer work, p. 274

Recycle ♻

- Direct object pronouns *lo, la, los, las*
- Expressions *¿Cómo se dice?* and *Y tú ¿qué dices?*
- *¿Qué hiciste?*
- *tener* idioms
- *poder*
- *me gusta(n), me encanta(n)*
- Adjectives
- *dar*
- *ir a* + infinitive
- Preterite of *-ar,-er,* and *-ir* verbs

RESOURCES

	FOR THE STUDENT	ONLINE	DVD	PRINT	FOR THE TEACHER	ONLINE	PREEXP	DVD	PRINT
Plan					Interactive TE and Resources DVD	•		•	
					Teacher's Resource Book, pp. 268–301	•		•	•
					Pre-AP* Resource Book, pp. 90–93	•		•	•
					Mapa global interactivo	•			
					Lesson Plans	•			•

Introducción PP. 248–249

	FOR THE STUDENT	ONLINE	DVD	PRINT	FOR THE TEACHER	ONLINE	PREEXP	DVD	PRINT
Present	Student Edition, pp. 248–249	•	•	•	Interactive TE and Resources DVD	•		•	
	DK Reference Atlas	•	•		Teacher's Resource Book, pp. 268–269	•		•	•
	Videocultura	•	•		Galería de fotos		•		
	Hispanohablantes WB, pp. 310–311			•	Map Transparencies, 12–15, 18	•	•	•	

Vocabulario en contexto PP. 250–255

	FOR THE STUDENT	ONLINE	DVD	PRINT	FOR THE TEACHER	ONLINE	PREEXP	DVD	PRINT
Present & Practice	Student Edition, pp. 250–255	•	•	•	Interactive TE and Resources DVD	•		•	
	Audio	•	•		Teacher's Resource Book, pp. 271–273, 276, 284–285	•		•	•
	Videohistoria	•	•		Vocabulary Clip Art	•	•	•	
	Flashcards	•	•		Audio Program	•	•	•	
	Instant Check	•			Video Program: Videohistoria	•		•	
	Guided WB, pp. 111–120	•	•	•	Video Program Teacher's Guide: Cap. 8B	•		•	
	Core WB, pp. 64–67	•	•	•	Vocabulary and Grammar Transparencies, 151–154	•	•	•	
	Comm. WB, pp. 73–76, 79	•	•	•	Answer Keys: Student Edition, pp. 167–168	•	•	•	
	Hispanohablantes WB, pp. 312–313			•	TPR Stories, pp. 107–121				
Assess and Remediate					Prueba 8B–1: Assessment Program, pp. 215–216	•		•	•
					Assessment Program para hispanohablantes, pp. 215–216	•		•	•

RESOURCES

FOR THE STUDENT	ONLINE	DVD	PRINT	FOR THE TEACHER	ONLINE	PREEXP	DVD	PRINT
Vocabulario en uso PP. **256–261**								
Present & Practice Student Edition, pp. 256–261	•	•	•	Interactive Whiteboard Vocabulary Activities	•		•	
Instant Check	•			Interactive TE and Resources DVD	•		•	
Comm. WB, p. 76	•	•	•	Teacher's Resource Book, pp. 272–273, 278–279	•		•	•
Hispanohablantes WB, pp. 314–315, 320–321			•	Communicative Pair Activities, pp. 278–279	•		•	•
Communicative Pair Activities	•			Audio Program	•	•	•	
				Videomodelos	•		•	
				Vocabulary and Grammar Transparencies, 158	•	•	•	•
				Answer Keys: Student Edition, pp. 169–171	•	•	•	•
Assess and Remediate				Prueba 8B–2 with Study Plan	•			
				Prueba 8B–2: Assessment Program, pp. 217–218	•		•	•
				Assessment Program para hispanohablantes, pp. 217–218	•		•	•
Gramática PP. **262–271**								
Present & Practice Student Edition, pp. 262–271	•	•	•	Interactive Whiteboard Grammar Activities	•		•	
Instant Check	•			Interactive TE and Resources DVD	•		•	
Animated Verbs	•			Teacher's Resource Book, pp. 273–275, 276–277, 280–281, 283	•		•	•
Tutorial Video: Grammar	•			Communicative Pair Activities, pp. 280–281	•		•	•
Canción de hip hop	•			Audio Program	•	•	•	
Guided WB, pp. 121–124	•	•	•	Videomodelos	•		•	
Core WB, pp. 68–70	•	•	•	Video Program: GramActiva	•		•	•
Comm. WB, pp. 77–78, 80–81, 175	•	•	•	Vocabulary and Grammar Transparencies, 155–157	•	•	•	•
Hispanohablantes WB, pp. 316–321			•	Answer Keys: Student Edition, pp. 171–173	•	•	•	
Communicative Pair Activities	•							
Assess and Remediate				Pruebas 8B–3, 8B–4, and 8B–5 with Study Plans	•			
				Pruebas 8B–3, 8B–4, 8B–5: Assessment Program, pp. 219–221	•		•	•
				Assessment Program para hispanohablantes, pp. 219–221	•		•	•
¡Adelante! PP. **272–277**								
Application Student Edition, pp. 272–277	•	•	•	Interactive TE and Resources DVD	•		•	
Online Cultural Reading	•			Teacher's Resource Book, p. 277	•		•	•
Guided WB, pp. 125–126	•	•	•	Video Program: Videomisterio ¿Eres tú, María?	•		•	
Comm. WB, pp. 82, 176	•	•	•	Video Program Teacher's Guide: Cap. 8B	•		•	
Hispanohablantes WB, pp. 322–327			•	Videomisterio Quiz		•		
¿Eres tú, María? Video WB, pp. 58–66	•	•	•	Answer Keys: Student Edition, pp. 173–174	•	•	•	
Repaso del capítulo PP. **278–279**								
Review Student Edition, pp. 278–279	•	•	•	Interactive TE and Resources DVD	•		•	
Online Puzzles and Games	•			Teacher's Resource Book, pp. 275, 282, 284–285	•		•	•
Core WB, pp. 71–72	•	•	•	Audio Program	•	•	•	
Comm. WB, pp. 177–180	•	•	•	Answer Keys: Student Edition, p. 174	•	•	•	
Hispanohablantes WB, pp. 328–329			•					
Instant Check	•							
Chapter Assessment								
Assess				Examen del capítulo 8B	•		•	•
				Assessment Program, pp. 222–228	•		•	•
				Alternate Assessment Program, pp. 95–99	•		•	•
				Assessment Program para hispanohablantes, pp. 222–228	•		•	•
				Audio Program, Cap. 8B, Examen	•		•	
				ExamView: Test Banks A and B questions only online	•		•	
				Heritage Learner Test Bank	•		•	
				Pre-AP* Test Bank	•		•	

REGULAR SCHEDULE (50 MINUTES)

DAY	Warm-up / Assess	Preview / Present / Practice / Communicate	Wrap-up / Homework Options
1	Return Examen del capítulo (10 min.)	Vocabulario en contexto (35 min.) • Objectives • Presentation: *Vocabulario y gramática en contexto* • *Actividades* 1, 2 • Arte y cultura • Videocultura: *Las vacaciones*	Wrap-up and Homework Options (5 min.) • Core Practice • Vocabulary Clip Art
2	Warm-up (5 min.) • Homework check	Vocabulario en contexto (40 min.) • Review: *Vocabulario en contexto* • Presentation: *Videohistoria Cómo ayudamos a los demás* • View: Video *Cómo ayudamos a los demás* • Video Activities • *Actividades* 3, 4, 5	Wrap-up and Homework Options (5 min.) • *Prueba* 8B-1: Vocabulary recognition • Core Practice
3	Warm-up (5 min.) • Homework check ✔Formative Assessment (10 min.) • *Prueba* 8B-1: Vocabulary recognition	Vocabulario en uso (30 min.) • Objectives • *Actividades* 6, 7, 9 • *Fondo cultural* • Communicative Pair Activities	Wrap-up and Homework Options (5 min.) • *Actividad* 8
4	Warm-up (5 min.) • Homework check • Return *Prueba* 8B-1: Vocabulary recognition	Vocabulario en uso (40 min.) • *Actividades* 10, 11 • Interactive Whiteboard Vocabulary Activities • *Exploración del lenguaje* • *Fondo cultural*	Wrap-up and Homework Options (5 min.) • *Actividad* 12
5	Warm-up (5 min.) • Homework check	Vocabulario en uso (40 min.) • *Conexiones: Actividad* 13 • *Fondo cultural* • *Actividad* 14	Wrap-up and Homework Options (5 min.) • *Actividad* 14
6	Warm-up (5 min.) • Homework check	Gramática y vocabulario en uso (40 min.) • Presentation: The present tense of *decir* • *GramActiva* Video • Interactive Whiteboard Grammar Activities • *Actividades* 15, 16, 17 • Communicative Pair Activities	Wrap-up and Homework Options (5 min.) • Core Practice • *Prueba* 8B-3 with Study Plan: The present tense of *decir*
7	Warm-up (5 min.) • Homework check ✔Formative Assessment (10 min.) • *Prueba* 8B-3 with Study Plan: The present tense of *decir*	Gramática y vocabulario en uso (30 min.) • Presentation: Indirect object pronouns • *GramActiva* Video • Interactive Whiteboard Grammar Activities • *Actividades* 18, 20, 21 • *Juego: Actividad* 19	Wrap-up and Homework Options (5 min.) • Core Practice
8	Warm-up (5 min.) • Homework check • Return *Prueba* 8B-3 with Study Plan: The present tense of *decir*	Gramática y vocabulario en uso (40 min.) • Presentation: The preterite of *hacer* and *dar* • *GramActiva* Video • Interactive Whiteboard Grammar Activities • *Actividades* 22, 24 • *Fondo cultural*	Wrap-up and Homework Options (5 min.) • *Actividad* 23 • *Prueba* 8B-2 with Study Plan: Vocabulary production

REGULAR SCHEDULE (50 MINUTES)

DAY	Warm-up / Assess	Preview / Present / Practice / Communicate	Wrap-up / Homework Options
9	**Warm-up (5 min.)** • Homework check ✔**Formative Assessment (10 min.)** • *Prueba* 8B-2 with Study Plan: Vocabulary production	**Gramática y vocabulario en uso (30 min.)** • *Actividades* 26, 27 • *Juego: Actividad* 28	**Wrap-up and Homework Options (5 min.)** • *Actividad* 25 • *Pruebas* 8B-4, 8B-5 with Study Plans: Indirect object pronouns; the preterite of *hacer* and *dar*
10	**Warm-up (5 min.)** • Homework check • Return *Prueba* 8B-2: Vocabulary production ✔**Formative Assessment (10 min.)** • *Pruebas* 8B-4, 8B-5 with Study Plans: Indirect object pronouns; the preterite of *hacer* and *dar*	**Gramática y vocabulario en uso (30 min.)** • *Pronunciación* • *Actividades* 29, 30 • *El español en el mundo del trabajo*	**Wrap-up and Homework Options (5 min.)** • Core Practice
11	**Warm-up (5 min.)** • Homework check • Return *Pruebas* 8B-4, 8B-5 with Study Plans: Indirect object pronouns; the preterite of *hacer* and *dar*	**¡Adelante! (40 min.)** • *Presentación escrita:* Prewrite • *Lectura* • *Fondo cultural*	**Wrap-up and Homework Options (5 min.)** • *Presentación escrita:* Prewrite
12	**Warm-up (5 min.)** • Homework check	**¡Adelante! (40 min.)** • *Presentación escrita:* Draft, revise • *Perspectivas del mundo hispano*	**Wrap-up and Homework Options (5 min.)** • *Presentación escrita:* Publish
13	**Warm-up (5 min.)** • Homework check	**¡Adelante! (40 min.)** • *Presentación escrita:* Present	**Wrap-up and Homework Options (5 min.)** • Writing Activities • Core Practice Organizer
14	**Warm-up (5 min.)** • Homework check • Core Practice Organizer	**¡Adelante! (20 min.)** • *Videomisterio* **Repaso (20 min.)** • *Vocabulario y gramática* • *Preparación para el examen*	**Wrap-up and Homework Options (5 min.)** • Instant Check • *Examen del capítulo*
15	**Warm-up (5 min.)** • Answer questions ✔**Summative Assessment (45 min.)** • *Examen del capítulo*		

Standards for *Capítulo* 8B

• To achieve the goals of the Standards, students will:

Communication

1.1 Interpersonal

• Talk about: volunteer work; community service; recycling and conservation; gifts and gift-giving; past activities in which people engaged; prestigious awards people have received

1.2 Interpretive

• Read and listen to information about: volunteer work; community service; recycling
• Read a picture-based story
• Listen to and watch a video about recycling and volunteer work
• Read about: protected areas of Costa Rica; Habitat for Humanity in Guatemala
• Read a public service announcement about recycling
• Listen to information about tinglar tortoise protection
• View a video mystery series

1.3 Presentational

• Present information about: recycling; volunteer work; donations and charity
• Write about: past activities in which people engaged; prestigious awards people have received
• Present information about tinglar tortoise protection

Culture

2.1 Practices and Perspectives

• Learn about: recycling in Spain; *la Asociación conservacionista de Monteverde* in Costa Rica; *el Hospital de la Caridad* in Seville
• Understand student volunteerism in Spanish-speaking countries

2.2 Products and Perspectives

• Learn about Mexico's glass art made from recyclables

Connections

3.1 Cross-curricular

• Read about protected areas of Costa Rica
• Reinforce math skills
• Learn about: recycling and environmental issues; Americorps

Comparisons

4.1 Language

• Learn: vocabulary through the recognition of cognates; about nouns endings *-dad, -tad, -ción,* and *-sión;* the present tense of the verb *decir;* the pronunciation of *gue, gui, que,* and *qui;* the preterite of the verbs *hacer* and *dar;* the pronunciation of the letter *x*
• Understand indirect object pronouns

4.2 Culture

• Compare: Spain's recycling program to local programs; reuse of recyclable materials in other products; involvement in volunteerism projects; local programs in place to help the needy

Communities

5.1 Beyond the School

• Identify: ways to apply Spanish to volunteerism; opportunities for Spanish-speakers in the non-profit sector

5.2 Lifelong Learner

• View a video mystery series

▼ Chapter Objectives

Communication

By the end of this chapter you will be able to:

• Listen to and read about community service
• Talk and write about volunteer activities and recycling
• Exchange information about volunteering

Culture

You will also be able to:

• Compare perspectives about volunteer activities in Spanish-speaking countries to your community
• Compare environmental efforts in Spain, Costa Rica, and other Spanish-speaking countries to programs in your community

You will demonstrate what you know and can do:

• Presentación escrita, p. 275
• Preparación para el examen, p. 279

You will use:

Vocabulary	Grammar
• Recycling	• The present tense of *decir*
• Places in a community	• Indirect object pronouns
• Volunteer work	• The preterite of *hacer* and *dar*

Exploración del mundo hispano

Country Connection
Helping in Your Community

Florida
España
República Dominicana
México
Guatemala
El Salvador — Puerto Rico
Costa Rica
Ecuador

realidades.com GO

📖 Reference Atlas
▶ Videocultura y actividad

🌐 Mapa global interactivo

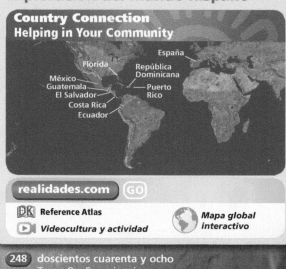

Una joven ayuda con un proyecto de voluntarios en Miami, Florida.

ENRICH YOUR TEACHING

Using Backward Design

Have students preview the sample performance tasks on *Preparación para el examen*, p. 279, and connect them to the Chapter Objectives. Explain to students that by completing the sample tasks they can self-assess their learning progress.

Mapa global interactivo

Download the *Mapa global interactivo* files for Chapter 8B and preview the activities. Activity 1 looks at Peace Corps projects in Latin America. Activity 2 visits the Cloud Forest of Costa Rica, and Activity 3 looks at tortoise habitats in the Dominican Republic, Puerto Rico, and Costa Rica.

Preview 8B

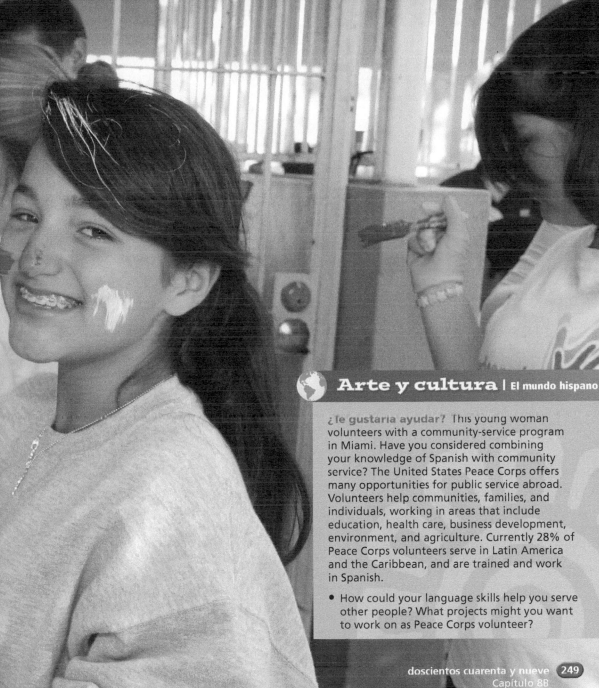

Tema 8 • Experiencias

Arte y cultura | El mundo hispano

¿Te gustaría ayudar? This young woman volunteers with a community-service program in Miami. Have you considered combining your knowledge of Spanish with community service? The United States Peace Corps offers many opportunities for public service abroad. Volunteers help communities, families, and individuals, working in areas that include education, health care, business development, environment, and agriculture. Currently 28% of Peace Corps volunteers serve in Latin America and the Caribbean, and are trained and work in Spanish.

• How could your language skills help you serve other people? What projects might you want to work on as Peace Corps volunteer?

doscientos cuarenta y nueve **249**
Capítulo 8B

Chapter Opener

Core Instruction

Resources: Map Transparencies 12–15, 18

Suggestions: Have students tell you what activities they participate in that help the community. Ask them to name volunteer organizations at your school. Tell students that the *Videohistoria* for this chapter deals with the various volunteer projects being done by students. Remind students that they will continue to work with the past tense of verbs as they discuss how people helped others. Students will also learn about volunteer organizations. Discuss which organizations they are familiar with and tell what the aim of each group is.

▶ **Videocultura** View *Las vacaciones* with the class to learn about places to visit in Spanish-speaking countries.

Arte y cultura

Standards: 5.1

Suggestions: Point out to students that volunteer organizations such as the Peace Corps are great launching places for careers in medicine, education, health care, and engineering. Volunteers travel and experience new cultures while making a contribution to humanity. Discuss whether or not they would be interested in joining the Peace Corps or a similar organization.

Answers will vary.

Mapa global interactivo, Actividad 1 Explore Peace Corps projects in Latin America.

Teaching with Photos

Suggestions: What is the mood of the photo? (Light and happy.) These people seem to be having a good time while performing a valuable service for their community. How might working side by side with others help a language learner improve their second language skills?

DIFFERENTIATED INSTRUCTION

Digital resources such as the *Interactive Whiteboard* activity banks, *Videomodelos*, additional *Online Activities*, *Study Plans*, automatically graded *Leveled Workbook*, animated *Grammar Tutorials*, *Flashcards*, and *Vocabulary and Grammar Videos* will help you reach students of different ability levels and learning styles.

STUDENTS NEEDING EXTRA HELP

Guided Practice Activities
• Flashcards, pp. 111–116
• Vocabulary Check, pp. 117–120
• Grammar Support, pp. 121–124

HERITAGE LEARNERS

Realidades para hispanohablantes
• Chapter Opener, pp. 310–311
• A primera vista, p. 312
• Videohistoria, p. 313
• Manos a la obra, pp. 314–321
• ¡Adelante!, pp. 322–327
• Repaso del capítulo, pp. 328–329

ADVANCED/PRE-AP*

Pre-AP* Resource Book,
• pp. 90–93
Communications Workbook
• Integrated Performance Assessment, p. 177

249

Vocabulario en contexto

Core Instruction

Standards: 1.2

Resources: Teacher's Resource Book: Input Script, p. 271, Clip Art, pp. 284–285, Audio Script, p. 272; Voc. and Gram. Transparencies 151–152; TPR Stories Book: pp. 107–121; Audio Program DVD: Cap. 7B, Tracks 1–2

Focus: Presenting new vocabulary for volunteer work, places in the community, and recycling; the verb *decir;* the preterite of *dar* and *hacer*

Suggestions: Use the transparencies to present the vocabulary in three sections: people and places for volunteer work, recycling vocabulary, and names of places in a community. Use the story in the *TPR Stories Book* to present the new vocabulary and grammar.

Have students scan the text to predict what the students' conversations are about. Then, while volunteers act out the dialogue, have other students make a list of unfamiliar words. Use visual cues or context to help students understand the meanings of the words on their list.

BELLRINGER REVIEW

Show Vocabulary and Grammar Transparency 121. Have students share with the class an activity that they do to help around the house.

A primera vista | ▼ Objectives

Read, listen to, and understand information about
▶ volunteer work
▶ community-service tasks
▶ what people did to help others

Vocabulario en contexto

¿Quieres ayudar a los demás?

¡Trabaja como **voluntario** en tu comunidad!

¡Habla con los Amigos del **barrio** hoy! ¡Tú puedes ser la diferencia!

ayudar en un jardín de verduras

trabajar en un proyecto de construcción

hacer trabajo voluntario **en** una escuela primaria

trabajar en un campamento **de deportes**

—Mira el cartel. Hay **problemas*** en nuestra comunidad. Debemos trabajar como voluntarios.

—Tienes razón. ¿Cómo puedes **decidir** qué hacer? Es la primera **vez** que trabajo como voluntario.

—Quiero enseñarles a **los niños** a leer. **Es necesario** poder leer, ¿no crees?

*Even though *problema* ends in -a, it is a masculine noun: *Tengo un problema.*

(250) **doscientos cincuenta**
Tema 8 • Experiencias

DIFFERENTIATED INSTRUCTION

Multiple Intelligences

Naturalist: Have students work in groups to create recycling bins for the Spanish classes at your school. Give them a box and have them illustrate and label items that should and should not be placed in the box. Leave one recycling bin in your room and share the other with various staff members to display in their classrooms or offices.

Centro de reciclaje

los periódicos las latas las botellas

el plástico el vidrio las cajas

las bolsas el cartón

recoger la basura de la calle

al lado del río

—¿Me ayudas a **reciclar** la basura del río y de las calles? Son cosas que pueden usar **otra vez. Dicen** que tenemos que **separarlas.**

—Bueno, te ayudo. ¿Adónde vamos a **llevarlas?**

—Al centro de reciclaje en la calle Bolívar.

▼**2** | 🔊 | Escuchar _____

¿Qué puedes reciclar?

Estás separando unos artículos en dos cajas: una es para el papel y la otra es para todos los demás artículos. Levanta una mano si debes poner el artículo en la caja para papel. Levanta dos manos si debes ponerlo en la otra caja.

▼**1** | 🔊 | Escuchar _____

El trabajo voluntario

Gloria investiga *(is researching)* los trabajos voluntarios en la comunidad. Señala cada lugar que ella menciona.

Más práctica	GO

	realidades.com	print
Instant Check	✔	
Guided WB pp. 111–116	✔	✔
Core WB pp. 64–65	✔	✔
Comm. WB p. 79	✔	✔
Hispanohablantes WB p. 312		✔

doscientos cincuenta y uno **251**
Capítulo 8B

1 Standards: 1.2

Resources: Teacher's Resource Book: Audio Script, p. 272; Audio Program DVD: Cap. 7B, Track 3; Answer Keys: Student Edition, p. 167

Focus: Listening to identify places to volunteer

Suggestions: Play the audio or read the script. Pause between each sentence to monitor students' answers.

🔊 **Script and Answers:**

1. **Me gustaría trabajar en una escuela primaria.** *(escuela primaria)*
2. **Es importante recoger basura del río.** *(al lado del río)*
3. **Mucha gente ayuda en los proyectos de construcción.** *(proyecto de construcción)*
4. **Puedo ayudar en el centro de reciclaje.** *(centro de reciclaje)*
5. **Me gustan las flores. Puedo ayudar en un jardín.** *(un jardín)*
6. **Es importante recoger basura del lado de la calle.** *(la calle)*

2 Standards: 1.2

Resources: Teacher's Resource Book: Audio Script, p. 272; Audio Program DVD: Cap. 7B, Track 4; Answer Keys: Student Edition, p. 167

Focus: Listening to identify recyclables

Suggestions: Play the audio or read the script. As a variation of this activity, have students draw two bins on a sheet of paper, and label one *papel,* and the other *otro.* Then, have them write in the correct box the vocabulary word that they hear in each sentence. This may be useful in larger classes, where it may be difficult to monitor students' hand-raising.

🔊 **Script and Answers:**

1. **Aquí están los periódicos.** *(una mano)*
2. **¿Dónde pongo la botella?** *(dos manos)*
3. **¿Y las latas?** *(dos manos)*
4. **Tengo unas revistas.** *(una mano)*
5. **¿Y estos papeles?** *(una mano)*
6. **Hay muchos vasos de vidrio aquí.** *(dos manos)*

ENRICH YOUR TEACHING

Culture Note

Over the past 20 years, the United States has increased its recycling rate because many neighborhoods have increased their recycling. Paper is the largest waste product in the United States and represents about 30% of all our garbage. In 2009, for the first time, more than 60% of waste paper in the U.S. was recycled. For each ton of recycled paper, 17 trees and large amounts of energy resources are conserved.

Teacher-to-Teacher

Start a bulletin board display with the title: *¿Quieres ayudar a los demás?* As you go through the chapter, gradually add students' work to the display. Encourage students to look for appropriate materials in Spanish about recycling and volunteering to post on the bulletin board.

8B **Language Input**

Videohistoria 🔊

Core Instruction

Standards: 1.2

Resources: Voc. and Gram. Transparencies 153–154; Audio Program DVD: Cap. 7B, Track 5

Focus: Presenting new vocabulary and grammar in the context of the story; previewing the language video

Suggestions:

Pre-reading: Have students point to pictures of volunteer work that they have done. Then, direct their attention to the *Strategy* in *Antes de leer.* Have them consider the possible volunteer jobs available as they read.

Answers will vary but may include:

1. Reading to and working with the elderly; recycling paper and plastic bottles; reading to and playing with children in hospitals; collecting used clothing and redistributing it to underprivileged neighborhoods.
2. They are recycling paper, plastic, and glass.

Cómo ayudamos a los demás

Gloria, Raúl y Tomás hacen trabajos voluntarios.
¿Por qué les gusta ser voluntarios?

Costa Rica

Raúl   Gloria   Tomás

Antes de leer

 Strategy   **Activating prior knowledge** Before you read the *Videohistoria,* think about what you know about the topic of volunteer work.

• In what ways can someone volunteer in your community? How do you think Gloria, Tomás, and Raúl might help their communities?

1. Look at the photos and make a list of the kinds of volunteer work that you see Gloria, Tomás, and Raúl doing.

2. Look at photo 7. What kinds of things are Raúl, Gloria, and Tomás recycling?

252 **doscientos cincuenta y dos**
Tema 8 • Experiencias

DIFFERENTIATED INSTRUCTION

Multiple Intelligences

Interpersonal/Social: Have students create a flier to promote a canned food drive. Then, copy the fliers to distribute to the entire class and other classes. If possible, have these students set up a table in the cafeteria to collect canned goods for a local food bank. Another option is to have them organize a clothing drive for a community organization.

Gloria: Raúl y yo trabajamos como voluntarios en **el Hospital** Nacional de Niños. ¿Quieres venir con nosotros?

Tomás: Sí. Me encanta el trabajo voluntario. Es **increíble** la satisfacción que **nos** da cuando ayudamos a los demás.

Papá: Un momento. ¿Pueden Uds. reciclar este papel y estas botellas?

Tomás: ¡Por supuesto! Dame la bolsa de plástico.

Tomás: ¿Y qué hacen Uds. en el hospital?

Gloria: Ayudamos con los niños. Leemos libros y cantamos y jugamos con ellos. **A menudo** les traemos **juguetes.**

Gloria: A veces es difícil porque los niños están muy enfermos. Pero es **una experiencia inolvidable.**

Suggestions:

Reading: Play the audio and allow students to follow along in their books. Using the transparencies and pantomime, help students understand the new words in blue type.

Post-reading: Complete *Actividades* 3–5 to check comprehension.

Pre-AP* Support

- **Learning Objective:** Interpretive: Audio
- **Activity:** Working in pairs, have students make a two-column chart by folding a piece of paper in half and printing the vocabulary from the chapter in two columns. One student should list vocabulary to talk about recycling/places in a community, and the other student should list vocabulary to discuss possibilities for volunteer work/other useful expressions. Then have them drill each other Spanish to English and English to Spanish from their prepared lists.
- *Pre-AP* Resource Book:* Comprehensive guide to Pre-AP* vocabulary skill development, pp. 51–57

ENRICH YOUR TEACHING

Culture Note

Amigos de las Américas is an international volunteer organization. All volunteers need to be able to speak Spanish before they travel to one of 15 countries in Central or South America. Volunteers help communities in many ways. Particular areas of emphasis are education and public health.

21st Century Skills

Social and Cross-cultural Skills Ask students which volunteer opportunity they find most interesting of those mentioned—and why. Have them ask a native Spanish speaker what the top three volunteer opportunities are in their city, or do Internet research to find answers.

Video ▶️

Core Instruction

Standards: 1.2

Resources: Teacher's Resource Book: Video Script, p. 276; Video Program: Cap. 8B; Video Program Teacher's Guide: Cap. 8B

Focus: Comprehending new vocabulary and grammar in authentic visual context

Suggestions:

Pre-viewing: Have students quickly scan the panels and captions to identify cognates that will help them understand the video.

Viewing: Remind students that they do not need to understand every word in the video to understand what is happening, but they should consider the context of the video and what they read in the *Videohistoria* reading to guide their comprehension. Show the video once without pausing; then show it again, stopping to check comprehension.

Post-viewing: Complete the Video Activities in the *Communication Workbook*.

Pre-AP* Support

- **Learning Objective:** Presentational Writing and Speaking
- **Activity:** As a post-viewing activity, have students work in small groups to write a short additional scene for the video. Have them imagine they go into the hospital, and meet the Volunteer Services Coordinator. The coordinator will greet them, and ask about any previous volunteer experiences they have had. The students playing Gloria, Tomás and Raúl introduce themselves, and briefly describe their past experiences, according to the information in the video. Have volunteers act out their new scene in front of the class.
- *Pre-AP* Resource Book:* Comprehensive guide to Pre-AP* vocabulary skill development, pp. 51–57

5

Raúl: El año pasado yo trabajé en un centro para **ancianos.** Pasé mucho tiempo con ellos.

6

Tomás: Soy miembro de un club que se llama "Casa Latina". El año pasado recogimos ropa **usada.** ¿Sabes que **hay que** separar la ropa y después lavarla?

Gloria: ¿**Qué más hicieron** Uds.?

Tomás: Luego le **dimos** la ropa a **la gente pobre.**

7

Raúl: Aquí podemos reciclar el papel y las botellas.

Gloria: Mira, para el plástico, el papel y el vidrio.

Tomás: En mi comunidad también reciclamos.

8

Raúl: Mira. Aquí está el hospital. ¿Entramos?

DIFFERENTIATED INSTRUCTION

Multiple Intelligences

Bodily/Kinesthetic: Using the text from the *Videohistoria* as a model, have students work in small groups to prepare a skit about the advantages of different types of volunteering. Suggest that they bring in props. Make a video of their skits to play for the class.

▼**3** Leer • Escribir

¿"Casa Latina" u Hospital Nacional de Niños?

Escribe los números del 1 al 6 en una hoja de papel. Lee cada frase. Si una frase describe una actividad que los jóvenes hacen en el Hospital Nacional de Niños, escribe las letras *HNN*. Si la frase describe una actividad que hacen en el club "Casa Latina", escribe las letras *CL*.

1. Recoge ropa usada de sus compañeros de clase.

2. Lee un libro a María y Juanito.

3. Canta una canción de niños.

4. Trae un traje y dos camisas blancas al Sr. Mendoza.

5. Compra unos juguetes para dos chicas enfermas.

6. Separa la ropa blanca de la ropa de colores.

▼**4** Leer • Escribir

¿Quién es?

¿Quién diría *(would say)* estas frases: Gloria, Tomás o Raúl? Escribe los números del 1 al 6 y escribe el nombre de la persona que diría cada frase. ¡Ojo! Una frase puede ser de más de una persona.

Gloria

Tomás

Raúl

1. Me gusta mucho el trabajo voluntario.

2. Trabajo en un hospital para niños.

3. Ayudar a los demás me da mucha satisfacción.

4. Trabajo con los niños y les traigo juguetes.

5. Me gusta pasar tiempo con los ancianos. Les leo el periódico y hablo con ellos.

6. Recojo* la ropa usada.

*Recoger es un regular *-er* verb with a spelling change in the *yo* form of the present tense: *recojo*.

▼**5** Leer • Escribir

¿Comprendes?

1. Para Gloria, ¿es fácil trabajar en el hospital? ¿Por qué sí o por qué no?

2. ¿Por qué quiere ir Tomás con Raúl y Gloria al hospital?

3. ¿Dónde hace Tomás su trabajo voluntario?

4. ¿Qué hace Tomás antes de dar ropa a la gente pobre?

5. ¿Qué cosas necesita reciclar el papá de Gloria y Raúl?

Más práctica

realidades.com | print

Instant Check	✔	
Guided WB pp. 117–120	✔	✔
Core WB pp. 66–67	✔	✔
Comm. WB pp. 73–75, 76	✔	✔
Hispanohablantes **WB** p. 313		✔

doscientos cincuenta y cinco **255**
Capítulo 8B

▼**3** Standards: 1.2

Resources: Answer Keys: Student Edition, p. 168

Focus: Verifying understanding of the *Videohistoria*

Suggestions: Before beginning, have students read the sentences and list the key words to help them find the answers.

Answers: 1. CL; 2. HNN; 3. HNN; 4. CL; 5. HNN; 6. CL

▼**4** Standards: 1.2

Resources: Answer Keys: Student Edition, p. 168

Focus: Verifying understanding of the *Videohistoria*

Suggestions: Point out to students the *¡Ojo!* note and make sure they understand it. When you call on students, have them read the part of the dialogue that supports their answer.

Answers:

1. Tomás, Gloria y Raúl   4. Gloria y Raúl
2. Raúl y Gloria   5. Raúl
3. Tomás y Gloria   6. Tomás

▼**5** Standards: 1.2, 1.3

Resources: Answer Keys: Student Edition, p. 168

Focus: Demonstrating comprehension of the *Videohistoria*

Suggestions: Discuss the questions in class before students write their answers.

Answers:

1. No es fácil porque los niños están muy enfermos.
2. A Tomás le encanta el trabajo voluntario.
3. Trabaja en la "Casa latina."
4. Él separa la ropa y la lava.
5. Necesita reciclar papel y botellas.

Additional Resources

• Communication Wbk.: Audio Act. 5, p. 76
• Teacher's Resource Book: Audio Script, pp. 272–273
• Audio Program DVD: Cap. 7B, Track 7

ENRICH YOUR TEACHING

Teacher-to-Teacher

If possible, invite representatives from a local volunteer organization or the Peace Corps to talk about volunteer opportunities. Ask the representative to talk about how speaking Spanish or another language other than English can be an advantage for working in almost any profession.

21st Century Skills

Communication Remind students of the various tools available in **realidades.com**, such as eText with embedded audio files and computer corrected activities. Using these tools on a regular basis will help students develop fluency at a faster rate.

✔**ASSESSMENT**

Quiz: Vocabulary Recognition
• Prueba 8B-1: pp. 215–216

▼ Objectives

▶ Listen and write about a recycling program
▶ Talk and write about community service
▶ Discuss recycling in your community
▶ Read about Costa Rican and Spanish conservation efforts and compare them to programs in the United States

INTERACTIVE WHITEBOARD
Vocabulary Activities 8B

▼ 6 Standards: 1.2, 1.3

Resources: Teacher's Resource Book: Audio Script, p. 272; Audio Program DVD: Cap. 7B, Track 6; Answer Keys: Student Edition, p. 169

Focus: Listening to and writing sentences about recycling

Recycle: Colors

Suggestion: Play the audio or read the script aloud. Allow students to listen once before they begin to write.

🔊 **Script and Answers:**

1. Las personas llevan su basura en bolsas de plástico al centro de reciclaje.
2. En el centro hay cuatro cajas diferentes.
3. La primera caja es para la basura regular.
4. Hay que separar el vidrio. Lo ponemos en la caja verde.
5. Es necesario reciclar el papel. Usamos la caja azul para el papel.
6. La caja amarilla es para el plástico y las latas.

▼ 7 Standards: 1.2, 1.3

Resources: Answer Keys: Student Edition, p. 169

Focus: Reading and writing about helping the community

Suggestions: Have students read the flier through once before answering.

Answers:

1. comunidad
2. ancianos
3. escuela primaria
4. voluntario
5. calle
6. separar
7. vidrio
8. problemas

Pre-AP* Support

- **Learning Objective:** Interpretive: Print and Audio
- **Activity:** Alternate assigning one of the two subtitled sections of *Actividad* 7 to pairs of students. They are to copy and complete their section by filling in the blanks. Then, working with their partner, have students read their section to each other as a dictation activity. Have them first read the section without pausing. Then, read it with pauses. Finally, re-read for verification.
- **Pre-AP* Resource Book:** Comprehensive guide to Pre-AP* communication skill development, pp. 10–57

Vocabulario en uso

▼ 6 🔊 Escuchar • Escribir

Escucha y escribe

En la región de Cataluña en España, hay un sistema para reciclar que usan muchas personas. En una hoja de papel, escribe los números del 1 al 6. Escucha la descripción de este sistema y escribe las frases.

> **También se dice . . .**
> la lata = el bote *(España, Puerto Rico)*

España —

En España separan los materiales para reciclarlos.

▼ 7 Leer • Escribir

Lo que podemos hacer todos

Lee el cartel que dice cómo puedes ayudar en la comunidad. En una hoja de papel, escribe los números del 1 al 8 y escribe las palabras apropiadas para completar cada frase.

ancianos	vidrio
calle	separar
escuela primaria	comunidad
problemas	voluntario

Todos queremos:
Una comunidad que ayuda

Para ayudar a la __1.__, tenemos que hacer muchas cosas. Por ejemplo, podemos trabajar en un hospital con los __2.__, o en una __3.__ con los niños. El trabajo __4.__ es muy importante para toda la gente de la comunidad.

Una comunidad limpia

Podemos ayudar cuando recogemos la basura de la __5.__. El reciclaje es importante también. Debemos __6.__ el papel, el plástico y el __7.__ de la basura y traerlos al centro de reciclaje.

 Cuando todos ayudan, tenemos menos __8.__ y más soluciones.

Para aprender más de cómo ayudar en la comunidad, Ud. debe venir al: Centro de la Comunidad este viernes entre las 6:00 P.M. y las 9:00 P.M.

DIFFERENTIATED INSTRUCTION

Multiple Intelligences
Visual/Spatial: Have students create and caption a collage that demonstrates the benefits of recycling or another environmental conservation effort. Students can post their collage in the classroom and give a brief presentation.

Heritage Language Learners
Ask students to use the pictures above to compare the Spanish recycling system to that of their heritage country. How important is recycling in the communities of their heritage countries? If possible, have students compare with the one in your community.

Practice and Communicate **8B**

▼8 Pensar • Escribir

Un cartel para ayudar en la comunidad

En una hoja de papel, escribe tu propio cartel con cuatro o más cosas que uno puede hacer para ayudar a la comunidad. Usa el cartel en la Actividad 7 como modelo.

▼9 | Talk! | Hablar

El reciclaje

Habla con otro(a) estudiante sobre el reciclaje.

> **¿Recuerdas?**
> The direct object pronouns *lo, la, los,* and *las* replace nouns. They have the same gender and number as the nouns they replace.

▶ **Modelo**
A —*En nuestra comunidad, ¿hay que reciclar el papel?*
B —*¡Por supuesto! Lo separamos y lo ponemos en una caja azul.*
o: —*No sé. Nosotros no lo reciclamos.*

1.
2.
3.
4.
5.
6.

▼ Fondo Cultural | España

El reciclaje Spain is one of the leading European countries in recycling. Spain's glass recycling program is called *Ecovidrio,* from the Spanish words for *ecology (ecología)* and *glass (vidrio). Ecovidrio* started in the 1990s and has been very successful. Glass recycling is an excellent way of reducing waste and protecting the environment.

• How do efforts in your community compare to glass recycling in Spain? What other efforts are available in your community?

Reciclaje de vidrio en Andalucía, España ▶

ENRICH YOUR TEACHING

Teacher-to-Teacher
Have students promote recycling and Spanish in school by creating reminders for people to recycle. Post them in the cafeteria, the library, classrooms, and the copy room.

21st Century Skills
Technology Literacy Have students research volunteer opportunities in the school or community that require knowledge of Spanish. Interested students submit a list of their skills and interests, along with a digital photo, so that an electronic volunteer directory can be created.

BELLRINGER REVIEW
Mention places in a community where people volunteer and have students raise their hands if they would like to work there.

▼8 Standards: 1.3
Focus: Writing about helping the community
Suggestions: Before they write, have students brainstorm additional ways to help the community. Write their ideas on the board.
Answers will vary.

▼9 Standards: 1.1
Resources: Answer Keys: Student Edition, p. 170
Focus: Communicating about recycling
Suggestions: Remind students to pay attention to the gender and number of the item pictured so that they can use the correct direct object pronoun.
Answers:
Student A
1. ¿Hay que reciclar las latas?
2. ¿Hay que reciclar el periódico (los periódicos)?
3. ¿Hay que reciclar el vidrio?
4. ¿Hay que reciclar el plástico?
5. ¿Hay que reciclar las cajas?
6. ¿Hay que reciclar las revistas?

Student B answers will vary but direct object pronouns should be: 1. las; 2. lo (los); 3. lo; 4. lo 5. las; 6. las.

Fondo cultural
Standards: 2.1, 4.2
Suggestions: Remind students that when they are answering the second question, they should consider all recyclables, not just glass. Refer them to the picture in *Actividad* 6 to point out the various types of recycling.
Answers will vary.

▼10 Leer • Pensar • Escribir • Hablar

El trabajo voluntario

Según las preferencias de los jóvenes de las fotos, explica dónde debe trabajar cada uno de ellos.

Modelo
Samuel debe trabajar en un hospital.

Teresa: Prefiero los trabajos al aire libre,* como un proyecto de construcción. Me encanta trabajar con las manos.

*outdoors

Rafael: Mi trabajo voluntario favorito es estar con niños en un campamento o una escuela primaria. Para mí es una experiencia inolvidable ver cómo aprenden tanto.

Samuel: Me gusta mucho ayudar a la gente pobre o a las víctimas de los desastres. Sus problemas son muy importantes para mí.

Bárbara: Me gusta mucho pasar tiempo con los ancianos. Son muy interesantes y simpáticos y me enseñan muchas cosas.

1.   2.   3.

4.   5.   6.

▼11 | Talk! | Hablar

¿Dónde quieres hacer el trabajo voluntario?

Escoge dos de los lugares de la Actividad 10 donde te gustaría hacer el trabajo voluntario. Con otro(a) estudiante, explica por qué prefieres estos lugares.

▶ **Modelo**

A —*¿Dónde quieres hacer trabajo voluntario?*
B —*Me gustaría hacer trabajo voluntario en <u>un hospital.</u>*
A —*Y, ¿por qué?*
B —*Porque <u>me gusta trabajar con los ancianos.</u> <u>Siempre ayudo a mis abuelos.</u>*

DIFFERENTIATED INSTRUCTION

Advanced Learners
Have students create profiles, like the ones for *Actividad* 10, giving their opinions on volunteer work. Give them colored paper to write their final copies on, and suggest that they include a photo. Post the profiles in the classroom.

Students with Learning Difficulties
For *Actividad* 11, it may be helpful to list the various volunteering opportunities on the board so that students can better organize their ideas.

Fondo cultural | Costa Rica

La Asociación Conservacionista de Monteverde in Costa Rica helps protect the rain forest around the Monteverde Cloud Forest Preserve. Young people from around the world come to help preserve the natural forest. Volunteers maintain trails and help in preservation projects. They also get the chance to make friends with local families while enjoying one of the most impressive landscapes in the world.

● What programs in your community or state are similar to the program in Costa Rica?

Entrada a la Reserva Bosque Nuboso, Monteverde, Costa Rica

▼12 Escribir

Una experiencia inolvidable

Hay un proyecto voluntario en tu escuela. Los miembros van a viajar a Costa Rica este verano para trabajar en un pueblo en Guanacaste y necesitan voluntarios. Escribe un párrafo de cinco frases para explicar por qué te gustaría ir con ellos y por qué vas a ser un(a) buen(a) voluntario(a). Si nunca haces el trabajo voluntario, puedes inventarlo *(invent it)*.

Modelo

Me gustaría ir a Costa Rica porque me encanta el trabajo voluntario. El año pasado yo trabajé en un hospital y ayudé a los ancianos.

Los médicos *(doctors)* de Interplast, una organización voluntaria, ayudan a la comunidad ecuatoriana de Azogues, en los Andes del Ecuador.

▼ Exploración del lenguaje

Nouns that end in -*dad*, -*tad*, -*ción*, and -*sión*

You know that *actividad* means "activity" and that *comunidad* means "community." In Spanish, nouns that end in -*dad* or -*tad* usually correspond to nouns in English that end in -*ty*. Nouns that end in -*dad* or -*tad* are feminine.

In a similar way, nouns in Spanish that end in -*ción* or -*sión* frequently correspond to nouns in English that end in -*tion* or -*sion*. These nouns are also feminine. You know that *construcción* means "construction" and that *posesión* means "possession."

Try it out! Figure out the meanings of these Spanish words.

la generosidad	la comunicación
la responsabilidad	la comisión
la variedad	la vegetación
la tranquilidad	la información
la libertad	la organización
la universidad	la presentación

doscientos cincuenta y nueve `259`
Capítulo 8B

ENRICH YOUR TEACHING

13 Standards: 1.2, 1.3, 3.1

Resources: Answer Keys: Student Edition, p. 171

Focus: Reading about recycling; understanding the process of recycling

Suggestions: Ask students to use their background knowledge to describe the recycling process. Have them use the pictures to guess the meaning of the captions without looking at the footnotes. Remind them that questions 1–3 are personal, and that they need to refer to the reading to answer questions 4 and 5.

Answers:

1.–3. Answers will vary.
4. Hacen nuevas botellas.
5. Pasos 1 y 7.

Extension: Reproduce the images here, cut them out, and place them in envelopes. Arrange students in groups of three, give each group an envelope, and ask them to determine the recycling chain without using their books.

▼**13** Leer • Escribir

La cadena de reciclaje

Todos estamos de acuerdo en que la protección del medio ambiente *(environment)* es importantísima. Una cosa que hacemos es reciclar el vidrio. Pero, después de poner las botellas y otros objetos de vidrio en los contenedores de reciclaje, ¿qué pasa? Mira esta "Cadena de reciclaje", y contesta las preguntas en una hoja de papel.

Conexiones | Las ciencias

1 Consumidor¹ responsable
¡Eres muy importante! Si no ayudas, es imposible empezar la cadena de reciclaje. Hay que poner las botellas de vidrio en los contenedores de reciclaje.

2 Recoger el vidrio
Recogen el vidrio de los contenedores y lo llevan a una planta de tratamiento².

3 Planta de tratamiento
En la planta de tratamiento limpian las botellas de vidrio y las trituran³.

4 Fábrica⁴ de botellas
Con el vidrio que trituraron, hacen nuevas botellas que son como las botellas originales.

5 Envasador⁵
El envasador pone productos, como refrescos y jugos, en las botellas nuevas.

6 Tiendas
En las tiendas venden productos en botellas que tienen el símbolo:

7 Consumidor
Si compras estos productos, completas la cadena de reciclaje. Ahora, ¡puedes empezar otra vez!

¹consumer ²treatment plant ³crush and grind ⁴factory ⁵bottler

1. ¿Reciclas las botellas de vidrio a menudo? ¿Cuántas veces a la semana?

2. ¿Dónde hay un centro de reciclaje en tu comunidad?

3. ¿Dónde están los contenedores de reciclaje en tu escuela o en tu comunidad?

4. ¿Qué hacen con el vidrio que trituran?

5. ¿En cuáles de los pasos *(steps)* de la "Cadena de reciclaje" puedes participar tú?

DIFFERENTIATED INSTRUCTION

Advanced Learners
Have students make an advertisement like the one on p. 261 to promote recycling. Distribute the fliers to other students in the school.

Students with Learning Difficulties
You may want to provide a simplified, written list of the steps for recycling and have students refer to it as they read *Actividad 13*.

▼14 Leer • Escribir • Hablar

Las 3 Rs

Lee el anuncio que está abajo *(below)*. Habla de Puerto Rico y la importancia de la conservación. Luego contesta las preguntas.

Puerto Rico

¡Tú puedes ser parte de la solución del problema de la basura en nuestra isla!

Recuerda esta guía práctica de las 3Rs

Reduce: Cuando vas de compras, decide no comprar cosas que no son necesarias.

Reusa: Usa un producto, objeto o material varias veces[1]. No debes tirar[2] a la basura las cosas que puedes usar otra vez.

Recicla: Usa los mismos materiales otra vez o usa un proceso natural o industrial para hacer el mismo o nuevos productos.

Lo que compras, comes, cultivas o tiras puede ser la diferencia entre un buen futuro o un futuro de destrucción para Puerto Rico.

Reduce
Reusa
Recicla

| Vidrio |
| Aluminio |
| Papel y periódicos |
| Cartón |
| Plástico |
| Materia orgánica |

[1]several times   [2]throw away

1. ¿Cómo puedes "reducir"? ¿Qué cosas compras o usas a veces que no son necesarias?

2. ¿Cómo puedes reciclar o reusar cosas en casa o en la escuela?

3. Según las frases que escribiste para la Actividad 11, escribe tres recomendaciones para cuidar *(take care of)* más tu comunidad.

▼ Fondo Cultural | México

Arte de vidrio Mexico is known for its production of beautiful glassware. Many of these works of art—including a wonderful variety of drinking glasses, bowls, and vases—are made from recycled bottles or car windshields. The glass is melted and hand-blown into new forms. Artisans also make trays and decorative windows by cutting different pieces of colored glass into a collage, then melting them together into a single piece. Each recycled glass artwork is unique.

• What everyday items or art objects are you familiar with that are made from recycled materials?

doscientos sesenta y uno **261**
Capítulo 8B

---

14 Standards: 1.1, 1.2, 1.3, 4.1

Resources: Voc. and Gram. Transparency 158

Focus: Reading and writing about recycling

Suggestions: Have students recall where they see the recycling symbol in their everyday lives. Brainstorm what kinds of products are commonly labeled with the symbol. Ask students to keep their own recycling habits in mind as they answer the questions.

Point out the cognates before students read. After students finish reading, ask a volunteer to summarize the goal of the advertisement.

Answers will vary but may include:
1. Puedo comprar sólo las cosas que son necesarias.
2. Puedo llevar los productos usados a un centro de reciclaje.
3. Answers will vary.

Fondo cultural

Standards: 2.2, 4.2

Suggestions: Before beginning, discuss how recycled materials can be used in everyday items and art objects.

Answers will vary but may include stationery and other paper products, bottles, and jars.

Additional Resources

• Communication Wbk.: Audio Act. 6, p. 76
• Teacher's Resource Book: Audio Script, p. 273, Communicative Pair Activity BLM, pp. 278–279
• Audio Program DVD: Cap. 7B, Track 8

✓ASSESSMENT

Prueba 8B-2 with Study Plan (online only)

Quiz: Vocabulary Production
• Prueba 8B-2: pp. 217–218

ENRICH YOUR TEACHING

Culture Note

The Purepecha people, from the state of Michoacán in Mexico, are famous for their skill in working with copper. When their copper mines were exhausted, they began to use traditional tools and techniques on copper recycled from wire and cable. Each week they use a great quantity of recycled copper.

21st Century Skills

Media Literacy Have students find out how a local nonprofit gets its message to the public, by paying a visit, making a phone call, searching the Internet, and going to the library. Students should report back, not only what they learned about the nonprofit, but also which media sources were the most useful to them.

Gramática

Core Instruction

Standards: 4.1

Resources: Voc. and Gram. Transparency 155; Teacher's Resource Book: Video Script, p. 276; Video Program: Cap. 8B

INTERACTIVE WHITEBOARD
Grammar Activities 8B

Suggestions: Before beginning, direct students' attention to the *¿Recuerdas?* Point out that all forms of the verb have an **e → i** stem change except for the **nosotros** and **vosotros** forms.

Copy a cartoon from the Sunday paper and white out the text in the speech bubbles. Write in your own dialogue in Spanish, turning the characters in the cartoon into students in your class. Distribute copies of your new cartoon and use it to tell what people say. For example, ask students *¿Qué dice Ángela?* and have them respond using the quotation from the cartoon.

Show the *GramActiva* Video either as an introduction to the structure or as a follow-up after your own grammar explanation.

BELLRINGER REVIEW

Ask students to respond to your questions using *"¿Cómo se dice?"* Focus on recyclable materials. (Ex. *¿Cómo se dice* glass *en español?*)

15 Standards: 1.2, 1.3

Resources: Answer Keys: Student Edition, p. 171
Focus: Conjugating the verb **decir**
Suggestions: Point out the information in the *Nota* for question 2.

Answers:

1. dicen	5. decimos
2. dice	6. digo
3. dicen	7. dices
4. dice	

Common Errors: Some students may apply the stem change to the **nosotros** form. Remind them that stem changes are not used in the **nosotros** and **vosotros** forms. Tell them that only stressed syllables have a stem change.

Manos a la obra

Gramática

The present tense of *decir*

The verb *decir* means "to say" or "to tell." Here are its present-tense forms:

(yo)	digo	(nosotros) (nosotras)	decimos
(tú)	dices	(vosotros) (vosotras)	decís
Ud. (él) (ella)	dice	Uds. (ellos) (ellas)	dicen

The *yo* form is irregular: **digo**.

Notice that the *e* of *decir* changes to *i* in all forms except *nosotros* and *vosotros*.

¿Recuerdas?

You have used forms of *decir* in the questions *¿Cómo se dice?* and *Y tú, ¿qué dices?*

Más ayuda   realidades.com

 GramActiva Video
Tutorial: *Decir*
Animated Verbs

 GramActiva Activity

▼15 Escribir

Hay que reciclar

En una hoja de papel, escribe las formas apropiadas del verbo *decir* para completar las opiniones de diferentes personas sobre cómo tener una comunidad limpia.

1. Mis padres ___ que es necesario recoger la basura en las calles.
2. La gente ___ que es importante llevar los periódicos a un centro de reciclaje.
3. Las personas en mi comunidad ___ que tenemos que separar la basura.
4. Mi profesor de biología ___ que es necesario reciclar el vidrio y el plástico.
5. Nosotros ___ que debemos limpiar nuestro barrio y comunidad.
6. Yo ___ que el reciclaje es muy importante.
7. ¿Qué ___ tú?

Nota

Use the *él/ella* form of the verb with *la gente*.

To tell *what* people say, use **que** after *decir:*

• La gente dice **que**...

DIFFERENTIATED INSTRUCTION

Advanced Learners/Pre-AP*

Have students write a short newspaper article about recycling. Students should use the verb **decir,** quoting what experts and officials say about the topic. As a variation, have students use presentation software to create a slide show to present to the class.

Heritage Language Learners

Have groups of students prepare a news report about recycling in their heritage countries. Have them present it to the class. If possible, make a video of their performances.

▼**16** | Talk! | **Escribir • Hablar** _____

¿Qué dices sobre . . . ?

1 Copia esta tabla en una hoja de papel. En la segunda columna, escribe *muy importante, importante* o *no es importante* para decir tu opinión de cada actividad. En la tercera columna, escribe *a menudo, a veces* o *nunca* para decir con qué frecuencia (*how often*) haces estas actividades para ayudar a tu comunidad.

2 Usa la información en tu tabla para hablar con otro(a) estudiante de lo que haces para ayudar en tu comunidad.

▶ **Modelo**

A —*Yo digo que recoger la basura de las calles y ríos es muy importante y a veces lo hago. Y tú, ¿qué dices?*

B —*Yo digo que es importante pero sólo lo hago a veces.*

Actividad	¿Importante o no?	¿Con qué frecuencia?
recoger la basura de las calles o ríos	muy importante	a veces
separar el vidrio y el plástico de la basura para reciclar		
llevar los periódicos al centro de reciclaje		
ser voluntario(a)		
ayudar a la gente pobre		

▼**17** | Talk! | **Hablar • Escribir** _____

¿Cómo podemos ayudar más?

Con tu compañero(a) de la Actividad 16, trabaja con otro grupo para decidir lo que pueden hacer para ayudar más en la comunidad. En una hoja de papel, escriban sus ideas y luego presenten sus ideas a la clase.

▶ **Modelo**

A —*Yo digo que es muy importante recoger la basura de las calles y ríos. Juan dice que es importante, pero Luisa y Rafael dicen que no es importante. Todos lo hacemos a veces.*

B —*¿Qué más podemos hacer?*

C —*Yo digo que podemos limpiar el barrio dos veces al mes.*

D —*Bueno, también podemos recoger el plástico cerca del río y reciclarlo.*

Más práctica	GO

realidades.com | print

Instant Check	✔	
Guided WB p. 121	✔	✔
Core WB p. 68	✔	✔
Comm. WB pp. 77, 80	✔	✔
Hispanohablantes WB pp. 314–316, 320	✔	

doscientos sesenta y tres **263**
Capítulo 8B

---

16 Standards: 1.1, 1.3

Focus: Writing and talking about helping the community

Suggestions: Model variations of the answers for the *Modelo*. Point out that the expression **lo hago** can help them avoid redundancy in their answers.

Answers will vary.

Common Errors: Students may forget to use **que** after **decir.** Remind them that **que** means "that" and cannot be omitted in Spanish.

BELLRINGER REVIEW

Write these expressions of frequency: *todos los días, a veces, nunca* on the board and ask each student to write one sentence telling how often he completes any one of the recycling activities. Share with the class.

17 Standards: 1.1, 1.2, 1.3, 3.1

Focus: Talking about helping the community

Suggestions: Have students prioritize by presenting the most important activities that they listed. If you are hearing a lot of repetition in students' responses, change the tone of the conversation by asking: *¿Qué no es importante?*

Answers will vary.

Pre-AP* Support

• **Learning Objective:** Interpersonal Writing
• **Activity 16:** Have students turn the group's answers into an e-mail to you, the teacher, summarizing their findings.

Additional Resources

• Communication Wbk.: Audio Act. 7, p. 77
• Teacher's Resource Book: Audio Script, p. 273
• Audio Program DVD: Cap. 7B, Track 9

✓ASSESSMENT

Prueba 8B-3 with Study Plan (online only)

Quiz: The present tense of *decir*
• Prueba 8B-3: p. 219

ENRICH YOUR TEACHING

Teacher-to-Teacher

To hold students accountable for group work, you may want to grade their oral presentations. Provide students with clear expectations by using the rubrics available in the *Presentación oral* section, or by creating a simple rubric of your own. You may also want to have students evaluate one another when they work in groups to help promote participation.

21st Century Skills

Initiative and Self-Direction Have students practice the various forms of *decir* by investigating points of view that people have toward recycling. Encourage students to research and develop a list of pros and cons, difficulties and solutions. Some statements could begin, "El gobierno de la ciudad dice...."

Gramática

Core Instruction

Standards: 4.1

Resources: Voc. and Gram. Transparency 156; Teacher's Resource Book: Video Script, pp. 276–277; Video Program: Cap. 8B

INTERACTIVE WHITEBOARD

Grammar Activities 8B

Suggestions: Have two volunteers role-play one person giving something to another. As they do this, narrate their action using indirect object pronouns. Have students provide sample sentences in English that contain indirect object pronouns. Remind students that, unlike in English, prepositions such as "for" or "to" are not necessary when using indirect object pronouns in Spanish. Use the *GramActiva* Video either as an introduction to the structure or as a follow-up after your own grammar explanation.

▼ 18 Standards: 1.3

Resources: Answer Keys: Student Edition, p. 171
Focus: Using indirect object pronouns
Suggestions: Point out to students that they need to know what the indirect object is before they can choose the correct indirect object pronoun. Point out that the indirect object noun follows the word *a* in each sentence

Answers:

1. Les	3. Les	5. Nos	7. Nos
2. Le	4. Les	6. Me	

Common Errors: Students often confuse direct object pronouns (*lo, los, la, las*) with indirect object pronouns. Remind them that *le* and *les* are the indirect object pronouns, whereas *los, la,* and *las* are identical to the definite articles.

Gramática

▼ Objectives
▶ Write about and discuss what you and others do for people in the community
▶ Play a listening comprehension game with classmates

Indirect object pronouns

An indirect object tells *to whom* or *for whom* an action is performed. Indirect object pronouns are used to replace an indirect object noun.

Les doy dinero.	*I give money to them.*
Te llevo el vidrio y las latas.	*I'll bring you the glass and the cans.*
¿Nos reciclas estas botellas?	*Will you recycle these bottles for us?*

The indirect object pronoun comes right before the conjugated verb. Here are the different indirect object pronouns:

	SINGULAR		PLURAL
me	(to/for) me	nos	(to/for) us
te	(to/for) you	os	(to/for) you
le	(to/for) him, her; you *(formal)*	les	(to/for) them; you *(formal)*

When an infinitive follows a conjugated verb, the indirect object pronoun can be attached to the infinitive or be placed before the conjugated verb.

Quiero darle un juguete al niño.

o: Le quiero dar un juguete al niño.

Because *le* and *les* have more than one meaning, you can make the meaning clear, or show emphasis, by adding *a* + the corresponding name, noun, or pronoun.

Les damos lecciones a Miguel y a Felipe.

Les damos lecciones a los niños.

Les damos lecciones a ellos.

Más ayuda	realidades.com

 GramActiva Video
Tutorials: Indirect object pronouns, Indirect objects

 Canción de hip hop: Experiencia inolvidable

 GramActiva Activity

▼ 18 Leer · Escribir

Las Olimpíadas Especiales

Unos jóvenes ayudan con las Olimpíadas Especiales. En una hoja de papel, escribe *me, te, le, nos* o *les* para completar cada frase.

Modelo

___ ayudan a los padres de los niños.
Les ayudan a los padres de los niños.

1. ___ dan naranjas y jugo a los participantes.
2. ___ hacen una donación a la señora que organizó el evento.
3. ___ traen agua a mis compañeros porque tienen sed.
4. ___ dan lecciones de varios deportes a los participantes.
5. ___ dicen a nosotros que debemos preparar los concursos *(contests)*.
6. ___ traen a mí un sándwich porque tengo hambre.
7. ___ dicen a nosotros que necesitan más ayuda.

Voluntarios y atletas en las Olimpíadas Especiales, Miami

264 doscientos sesenta y cuatro
Tema 8 • Experiencias

DIFFERENTIATED INSTRUCTION

Heritage Language Learners

Have students write a short composition in which they use at least six examples of indirect object pronouns. You might want to give them topics such as a gift exchange, a mix-up, or a family gathering, all of which might easily elicit the use of the pronouns. Once students have written their rough drafts, have them peer-edit the compositions and prepare a final draft.

Students with Learning Difficulties

For *Actividad* 20, you may want to write out each sentence on a strip of paper and cut the words apart or write them on index cards. Have groups of students put the words in order.

▼19 | 👥 | ♻ | Hablar • GramActiva

Juego

❶ Tu profesor(a) va a dividir a los estudiantes en grupos de cinco. Cada grupo forma una fila *(line)*. Las primeras personas de cada fila van al frente de la clase y el/la profesor(a) les dice una frase.

❷ Las personas regresan a sus grupos y le dicen a la primera persona en la fila, *"Me dice que . . ."* y repite la frase del (de la) profesor(a). Luego la primera persona repite la frase a la segunda persona de la fila.

❸ Cada grupo continúa hasta decir la frase a la última *(last)* persona. Esta persona escribe la frase que escucha en una hoja de papel. El grupo más rápido y que dice la frase más correcta gana *(wins)* el juego.

▼20 | ♻ | Escribir

¿Cómo ayuda la gente a los demás?

Escribe frases para decir cómo la gente ayuda a los demás. Usa las palabras de las listas y *a menudo, a veces* o *nunca*.

Modelo
A veces la gente les lleva comida a los ancianos.

dar	dinero	ropa usada	los pobres
enseñar	flores	juguetes	los niños
comprar	cuentos	periódicos	las personas
llevar	comida	revistas	enfermas
leer	una lección de . . .		los ancianos

▼21 | 💬👥 | ♻ | Escribir • Hablar

Regalos

❶ En una hoja de papel, haz dos listas. En la primera, escribe los nombres de cinco personas. En la segunda, describe un regalo que vas a comprar para cada una de estas personas.

❷ Habla con otro(a) estudiante sobre los regalos que vas a comprar.

 Modelo

A —¿Para quién vas a comprar un regalo?
B —*Le voy a comprar un regalo a mi abuela.*
A —¿Qué le vas a comprar?
B —*Le voy a comprar flores.*

Más práctica GO

realidades.com | print

Instant Check	✔	
Guided WB pp. 122–123	✔	✔
Core WB p. 69	✔	✔
Comm. WB pp. 78, 81, 175	✔	✔
***Hispanohablantes* WB** pp. 317–318	✔	

doscientos sesenta y cinco 265
Capítulo 8B

▼19 Standards: 1.2

Focus: Reviewing indirect object pronouns
Recycle: *Decir*
Suggestions: Remind students to use the indirect object pronouns as they pass the message through the line.
Answers will vary.
Extension: Play the game again, letting the winning group choose a leader to come up with a secret sentence with which to begin the game. Encourage students to use vocabulary from previous chapters.

▼20 Standards: 1.3

Focus: Writing about helping others
Recycle: Expressions of frequency
Suggestions: To personalize the activity, have students use themselves, family members, and people in their school as the subjects of their sentences.
Answers will vary.

▼21 Standards: 1.1, 1.3

Focus: Writing and speaking about giving gifts
Recycle: Gift items
Suggestions: Brainstorm a list of possible gifts that students could mention. Remind them to take turns being Student A and Student B, so that each one has the opportunity to ask and answer questions.
Answers will vary.

Additional Resources

• Communication Wbk.: Audio Act. 8, p. 78
• Teacher's Resource Book: Audio Script, pp. 273–274
• Audio Program DVD: Cap. 7B, Track 10

✓ASSESSMENT

Prueba 8B-4 with Study Plan (online only)

Quiz: Indirect Object Pronouns
• Prueba 8B-4: p. 220

ENRICH YOUR TEACHING

Culture Note

Founded in the United States in 1968, the Special Olympics have grown steadily over the years. Now over 150 countries participate in the various tournaments that take place. The most important tournaments are the Special Olympics World Summer and World Winter Games, which are held at alternating four-year intervals. Special Olympics events attract more than one million athletes worldwide. All Spanish-speaking countries are involved with Special Olympics. In Central and South America, there are over 60,000 athletes who participate.

Gramática

Core Instruction

Standards: 4.1

Resources: Voc. and Gram. Transparency 157; Teacher's Resource Book: Video Script, p. 277; Video Program: Cap. 8B

INTERACTIVE WHITEBOARD

Grammar Activities 8B

Suggestions: Tell students to give an object to another student. After they act out the command, ask the rest of the class: *¿Qué hizo Elisa?* Have students respond using the preterite tense of **dar.** You may wish to give various students the same action to elicit various forms of the verbs. Remind students that there are no accent marks on either verb. Use the *GramActiva* Video either as an introduction to the structure or as a follow-up after your own grammar explanation.

▼22 Standards: 1.3

Resources: Answer Keys: Student Edition, p. 172

Focus: Using the preterite tense of **dar**

Recycle: Numbers

Suggestions: Before they write, have students say the number of cans as you call out each name from the chart.

Answers:
1. Él dio 50 latas.
2. Nosotros dimos 70 latas.
3. Yo di 40 latas.
4. Ellas dieron 100 latas.
5. Él dio 20 latas.
6. Nosotros dimos 90 latas.

Theme Project

Students can perform Step 4 at this point. Be sure they understand your corrections and suggestions. (For more information, see p. 216-b.)

▼ Objectives
▶ Listen to a description of disaster-relief efforts
▶ Exchange information and write about what you and others did
▶ Read and write about a program to protect sea turtles

Gramática

The preterite of *hacer* and *dar*

Hacer and *dar* are irregular verbs in the preterite. Notice that these verbs do not have any accent marks in the preterite.

- The preterite stem for *hacer* is *hic-*. In the *Ud./él/ella* form, the *c* changes to a *z* so that it still has an "s" sound: *hizo*.

- The preterite stem for *dar* is *di-*. The same stem is used for all the preterite forms.

¿Recuerdas?

You used the preterite *tú* form of *hacer* when you asked, *¿Qué hiciste?*

(yo)	hice	(nosotros) (nosotras)	hicimos
(tú)	hiciste	(vosotros) (vosotras)	hicisteis
Ud. (él) (ella)	hizo	Uds. (ellos) (ellas)	hicieron

(yo)	di	(nosotros) (nosotras)	dimos
(tú)	diste	(vosotros) (vosotras)	disteis
Ud. (él) (ella)	dio	Uds. (ellos) (ellas)	dieron

Más ayuda — realidades.com

- ▶ *GramActiva* Video
  Animated Verbs
- ✎ *GramActiva* Activity

▼22 ♻ Pensar • Escribir

Ayudando a los pobres

Los estudiantes en tu escuela recogieron latas de comida para los pobres. Lee la gráfica para saber cuántas latas dieron estas personas. Escribe las frases en una hoja de papel.

Modelo

José y David
Ellos dieron 60 latas.

1. Guillermo
2. Lupita y yo
3. yo
4. Marta, Lupita y Raquel
5. José
6. David, Marta y yo

 = 10 latas de comida

DIFFERENTIATED INSTRUCTION

Advanced Learners

Have students prepare a pamphlet that outlines volunteering options in the community. For each organization that they name, have students obtain contact information and write the duties of the volunteers.

Heritage Language Learners

Have students write a mission statement for a real or fictitious community organization. You may wish to provide them with a copy of a sample mission statement, such as the one for your school, as an example.

▼ Fondo Cultural | España

El Hospital de la Caridad, a hospice in Seville, Spain, was founded in the 1600s by the monks of *la Hermandad de la Caridad* (Charity Brotherhood). Today, the brothers still look after people who are old or poor as part of a long tradition of caring for the needy.

• What programs in your community or state provide support for people in need?

El Hospital de la Caridad en Sevilla, España

▼23 | ♻ | Leer · Escribir

En un hospital

Una joven habla de su experiencia como voluntaria en un hospital. Escribe los verbos en el pretérito para completar las frases.

Mis amigos y yo __1.__ *(dar / decidir)* hacer un trabajo voluntario en un hospital. Nosotros __2.__ *(ir / hacer)* dibujos para los ancianos en el hospital. La semana pasada una amiga y yo __3.__ *(llevar / hablar)* los dibujos al hospital. La enfermera[1] nos __4.__ *(dar / decidir)* permiso para entrar en los cuartos de varios ancianos. Nosotros __5.__ *(llevar / visitar)* a los ancianos y les __6.__ *(decidir / dar)* los dibujos. Los ancianos nos __7.__ *(hablar / llevar)* de sus familias y nos __8.__ *(decidir / dar)* abrazos.[2] Ésta fue la primera vez que yo __9.__ *(hacer / llevar)* un trabajo voluntario. Fue una experiencia inolvidable para nosotros. Vamos a regresar al hospital otra vez.

[1] nurse [2] hugs

▼24 | 🔊 | Escuchar · Escribir

Las donaciones

Vas a escuchar cómo varias personas y organizaciones, como la Cruz Roja, ayudaron a las víctimas de un desastre en El Salvador. En una hoja de papel, escribe los números del 1 al 6. Escribe las frases que escuchas.

La Cruz Roja ayuda en El Salvador.

Fondo cultural

Standards: 2.1, 4.2

Suggestions: As students discuss the question, remind them that a person "in need" does not have to be poor or old. They should also consider community programs designed to help youths and adults in social or educational areas.

Answers will vary but may include *Meals on Wheels* and *Big Brother / Big Sister* organizations.

▼23 Standards: 1.2, 1.3

Resources: Answer Keys: Student Edition, p. 172

Focus: Writing in the preterite

Recycle: Preterite of *-ar, -er,* and *-ir* verbs and *ir*

Suggestions: Have students read the paragraph once before trying to fill in the blanks. Reproduce the text on a transparency for review and have volunteers provide the correct answers.

Answers:

1. decidimos	4. dio	7. hablaron
2. hicimos	5. visitamos	8. dieron
3. llevamos	6. dimos	9. hice

▼24 Standards: 1.2, 1.3

Resources: Teacher's Resource Book: Audio Script, p. 274; Audio Program DVD: Cap. 7B, Track 11; Answer Keys: Student Edition, p. 172

Focus: Listening and writing about how people helped others

Suggestions: Play the audio or read the script aloud several times.

🔊 Script and Answers:

1. Los voluntarios hicieron mucho para ayudar a las personas.
2. Muchos estudiantes en los Estados Unidos dieron dinero.
3. Otras personas les dieron ropa y zapatos usados.
4. Nosotros les dimos botellas de agua y comida.
5. La Cruz Roja les dio camas a muchas personas.
6. Una familia de mi comunidad trabajó como voluntaria allí.

ENRICH YOUR TEACHING

Teacher-to-Teacher

To practice the preterite, have students keep a journal. Provide students with two or three questions at the start of each class to respond to in their journals. For more advanced groups, allow students to write to the best of their ability without prompts. When you collect the journals, write back a response to students, and ask them follow-up questions to keep the dialogue going.

25 Standards: 1.2, 1.3

Resources: Answer Keys: Student Edition, p. 173

Focus: Reading and writing about volunteer work

Suggestions: Point out that students will use the phrase *hacer trabajo voluntario* in each sentence.

Answers:

1. **Mis amigos hicieron trabajo voluntario en el hospital.**
2. **Yo hice trabajo voluntario en el centro de reciclaje.**
3. **Un chico hizo trabajo voluntario en el jardín de la comunidad.**
4. **Mi compañero de clase y yo hicimos trabajo voluntario en el barrio.**
5. **Los demás hicieron trabajo voluntario en el centro de la comunidad.**

26 Standards: 1.1

Focus: Using indirect object pronouns and the preterite tense of *dar*

Suggestions: Remind students to choose the form of *dar* according to the person who gave the item, and the indirect object pronoun according to the person who received it.

Answers will vary.

▼25 Leer · Escribir

¿Dónde hicieron trabajo voluntario?

Lee estas frases que describen el trabajo voluntario de varias personas. En una hoja de papel, escribe frases que dicen dónde lo hicieron.

el barrio
el centro de la comunidad
el centro de reciclaje
la escuela primaria
el jardín de la comunidad
el hospital

Modelo

Antonio trabajó con los niños.
Antonio hizo trabajo voluntario en la escuela primaria.

1. Mis amigos pasaron tiempo con los ancianos enfermos.
2. Yo separé las botellas de plástico y las botellas de vidrio de la basura.
3. Un chico en la clase cultivó *(grew)* flores.
4. Mi compañero de clase y yo recogimos basura de la calle.
5. Los demás recogieron ropa usada para los pobres.

▼26 | Hablar

¿Qué les dieron?

Trabaja con otro(a) estudiante para hablar de lo que tú y tus amigos les dieron a las organizaciones voluntarias el año pasado.

▶ **Modelo**

A —*¿Qué le diste tú a una organización voluntaria?*
B —*Yo les di flores a los ancianos en el hospital.*

Estudiante A

tú
tú y tus amigos
tu mejor amigo(a)
tus compañeros de clase
tu profesor(a)

¡Respuesta personal!

Estudiante B

ropa usada   flores
juguetes para   libros
  niños pobres   latas y botellas
comida   para reciclar
regalos   periódicos

¡Respuesta personal!

DIFFERENTIATED INSTRUCTION

Advanced Learners

Have students think of awards that they could present to other students in the class. They should write a short introduction about each award winner that explains why he or she is getting the award. Encourage students to use indirect object pronouns and the verb *dar* in their presentations.

Students with Learning Difficulties

It may be helpful to students if you provide them with a list of additional vocabulary when they see a *¡Respuesta personal!*

▼**27** | Escribir • Hablar

¿Qué hicieron el sábado pasado?

❶ Escribe lo que hicieron estas personas el fin de semana pasado.

tu mejor amigo(a)	tu profesor(a) de . . .
tu madre (padre)	tus amigos(as)
tú y tus amigos	tú

❷ Habla con otro(a) estudiante sobre lo que hicieron las personas.

▶ **Modelo**

tus amigos

A —¿Qué _hicieron_ tus amigos el fin de semana pasado?

B —Mis amigos _fueron al río_. Y tus amigos,
   ¿qué _hicieron ellos_?

A —_Vieron una película en el cine_.

o:—_No sé qué hicieron ellos_.

▼**28** | Escribir • Hablar

Juego

❶ En grupos de cuatro, deben pensar en diferentes
premios (prizes) que reciben las personas: por
ejemplo, el premio Nobel, el Heisman, el Oscar, el
Emmy, el Golden Globe o el Grammy. Cada uno
escribe una pregunta que tu grupo va a hacerle a otro
grupo sobre los premios que dieron el año pasado.

❷ Tu grupo debe leer una de las preguntas a otro grupo,
que tiene 30 segundos para contestarla. Si el grupo
contesta bien la primera vez, recibe tres puntos. Si
contesta bien la segunda vez, recibe un punto. Si
contesta mal, tu grupo debe decirles la respuesta.

▶ **Modelo**

A —¿A quién le dieron el Oscar por ser la
   mejor actriz el año pasado?

B —Le dieron el premio a . . .

Para decir más . . .

la actriz   actress
el actor   actor
el/la cantante   singer
el/la atleta   athlete

Al autor colombiano Gabriel García Márquez
le dieron el premio Nobel de Literatura.

doscientos sesenta y nueve **269**
Capítulo 8B

---

27 Standards: 1.1, 1.3

Focus: Writing and speaking about past activities

Recycle: Leisure activities, sports

Suggestions: Have students brainstorm a list of activities that they, their families, or their friends do over the weekend. Point out to students that, if necessary, it is okay to respond that they don't know what the others did.

Answers will vary.

28 Standards: 1.1, 1.3

Resources: Teacher's Resource Book: GramActiva BLM, p. 283

Focus: Writing questions to use vocabulary and grammar in context

Suggestions: Provide students with copies of popular magazines or have them use the Internet if they cannot name the people from memory.

Answers will vary.

Teacher-to-Teacher

Have students use the results of *Actividad* 28 to have an awards ceremony. In groups of four or five, have students prepare a short skit in which two of them are the hosts of the ceremony, and the others play the roles of celebrities accepting the prizes. Encourage humor and creativity. If possible, have students use costumes for their presentations and videotape them.

ENRICH YOUR TEACHING

Culture Note

Some Nobel prizes awarded to Spanish speakers are: 1995 Chemistry prize to Mario Molina, a Mexican-born scientist; 2010 Literature prize to Mario Vargas Llosa, a Peruvian writer; 1992 Peace prize to Rigoberta Menchú, a Guatemalan social activist; and the 1987 Peace prize to Oscar Arias Sánchez, president of Costa Rica.

21st Century Skills

Initiative and Self-Direction Have students use the many tools available in **realidades.com** to support grammar learning, such as the online text with audio. Have students track the different tools they use and how effective each is, so they can establish over time what type of learners they are. This will help them in all areas of learning.

269

Pronunciación
Core Instruction

Standards: 4.1

Resources: Teacher's Resource Book: Audio Script, p. 274; Audio Program DVD: Cap. 7B, Track 12

Suggestions: After you model the typical pronunciation of the letter **x** for students, point out the exception noted in the right-hand column. Read the picture caption to demonstrate the difference. Remind students that they are not only reading the questions for the *Try it out!* but they should also answer in a way that will practice pronunciation of the letter **x.**

▼ 29 Standards: 1.1, 1.3

Focus: Speaking about past events
Suggestions: You may want to have students write these answers in their notebooks, in the form of a journal entry.
Answers will vary.

Theme Project

Students can perform Step 5 at this point. Record their presentations for inclusion in their portfolios. (For more information, see p. 216-b.)

▼ Pronunciación

The letter x

The letter *x* is pronounced several ways in Spanish. When it is between vowels or at the end of a word, it is pronounced /ks/. Listen to and say these words:

examen	*taxi*	*aproximadamente*
exactamente	*dúplex*	*éxito*

When the *x* is at the beginning of a word, it is usually pronounced /s/. At the end of a syllable, the *x* can be pronounced /s/, /ks/, or /gs/. Listen to and say these words:

xilófono	*explicar*	*experiencia*
exploración	*experimento*	*experto*

Try it out! Work with a partner to ask and answer these questions, paying special attention to how you pronounce the letter *x*.

1. ¿En qué clase son más difíciles los exámenes?
2. ¿Qué clase tienes durante la sexta hora?
3. ¿En qué clase haces experimentos? ¿Qué tipo de experimentos haces?
4. ¿En qué clase hablas o escribes mucho de tus experiencias personales?

In the 1500s, the *x* represented the "h" sound of the Spanish letter *j*. That is why you see some words, like *México, Oaxaca,* and *Texas* written with *x*, even though they are pronounced like the letter *j*. In words from indigenous languages of present-day Mexico and Central America, the *x* has the "sh" sound, as with the Mayan cities of Xel-há and Uxmal.

Una familia en Xochimilco, México

▼ 29 | Escribir • Hablar

Y tú, ¿qué dices?

1. ¿Qué hiciste el viernes pasado? ¿Qué hicieron tus amigos?
2. ¿Qué hizo tu familia el verano pasado?
3. ¿Qué les diste a tus hermanos o a tus amigos para su cumpleaños? ¿Qué te dieron a ti?
4. ¿Qué hizo la gente de tu comunidad el año pasado para ayudar a los pobres o a las víctimas de un desastre?
5. ¿Hizo tu barrio algo para ayudar a los ancianos o a los niños? ¿Qué?

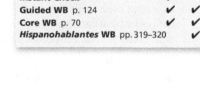

Más práctica	GO

realidades.com | print

Instant Check	✔	
Guided WB p. 124	✔	✔
Core WB p. 70	✔	✔
***Hispanohablantes* WB** pp. 319–320		✔

DIFFERENTIATED INSTRUCTION

Heritage Language Learners

Let pairs or small groups work together to make up tongue twisters that the class can use to practice the pronunciation of words with the letter **x.** Then, have them teach the tongue twisters to the class.

Multiple Intelligences

Naturalist: Have students research another endangered animal from Latin America and create a poster that includes facts about the animal and describes efforts to protect it and its habitat.

▼30 Leer • Escribir • Hablar | 🌐

Las tortugas tinglar

Lee esta información sobre las tortugas tinglar. Luego contesta las preguntas.

¡La tortuga tinglar es enorme! Es la tortuga marina más grande del mundo[1]. Los tinglares adultos pueden ser de hasta siete pies de largo y pesar[2] hasta 1.400 libras[3]. Cada año, entre febrero y julio, esta tortuga sale del mar en la noche y pone sus huevos en playas tropicales, como las de la República Dominicana, Costa Rica o de la isla de Culebra cerca de Puerto Rico. Después regresa a aguas frías.

Desde 1970 el tinglar está en peligro[4] de extinción. Por eso, en la primavera voluntarios de diferentes países van a las playas como las de la isla de Culebra. Llevan trajes de baño, jeans, sudaderas, camisetas, cámaras, binoculares, linternas[5], repelente contra mosquitos y muchas ganas de[6] ayudar a las tortugas. Patrullan[7] las playas buscando las tortugas.

Después de que las tortugas ponen los huevos, los voluntarios los llevan a un nido artificial. Aproximadamente 60 días después, las tortuguitas salen de los huevos. Los voluntarios llevan a las tortuguitas al mar donde nadan continuamente por unas 28 horas. Estos voluntarios son muy importantes para la preservación de la tortuga tinglar.

[1]in the world   [2]weigh   [3]pounds   [4]danger   [5]flashlights   [6]the desire   [7]They patrol

El español en el mundo del trabajo

There may be community service organizations in your neighborhood where knowing Spanish is helpful. These organizations include medical clinics, food kitchens, senior centers, career counseling and job training, and after-school programs. Volunteering your skills for these agencies is the first step to find out if you would be interested in pursuing work in the nonprofit sector.

• Check with local agencies to find out which ones offer services in Spanish (or in other languages). Develop a class list of volunteer opportunities in your community in which you could use your Spanish skills.

1. Para ti, ¿cuáles son los hechos (facts) más increíbles sobre la tortuga tinglar?

2. Escribe una lista, en orden, del trabajo que hacen los voluntarios en la playa.

3. ¿Te gustaría trabajar como voluntario en una de las playas donde están las tortugas tinglar? ¿Por qué?

doscientos setenta y uno 271
Capítulo 8B

ENRICH YOUR TEACHING

Culture Note
Other endangered species found in Spanish-speaking countries are the great harpy eagle, which can be found in Central and South America; the short-tailed chinchilla in Peru, Argentina, Chile, and Bolivia; the yellow-tailed woolly monkey in Peru, and the Bolivian blue-throated macaw.

21st Century Skills

Initiative and Self-Direction Remind students of the tools available for extra reading support in **realidades.com**. Computer-corrected activities use different strategies to help students comprehend the new vocabulary, monitor their learning needs, and progress at their own pace through the reading.

---

30 Standards: 1.2, 1.3, 3.1

Focus: Reading for comprehension

🌐 **Mapa global interactivo, Actividad 3** Look at tortoise nesting sites in the Dominican Republic, Puerto Rico, and Costa Rica.

Suggestions: Have students look at the photos and predict what the text will be about. Ask students to read the article silently and then have a volunteer read aloud. To check comprehension, have volunteers provide summaries of each paragraph. For item 2, have students create a visual such as a flowchart to show the process that the volunteers go through with the newborn turtles.

Answers will vary but may include:

1. Que es la más grande del mundo; pueden ser de hasta siete pies de largo y pesar hasta 1.400 libras.
2. Los voluntarios van a las playas de la Isla de Culebra; Patrullan las playas buscando tortugas; Llevan los huevos a un nido artificial; Llevan las tortuguitas al mar.
3. Answers will vary.

Extension: Read several sentences about the turtles and the volunteers from the article. Leave out the subject of the sentence as you read it: *Llevan las tortuguitas al mar.* Have students listen and write **tortuga** or **voluntario** on their papers.

El español en el mundo del trabajo

Core Instruction

Standards: 5.1

Suggestions: After they read the passage, provide students with local directories of community service organizations to expose them to any agencies that they may not be familiar with.

Additional Resources
• Communication Wbk.: Audio Act. 9, p. 78
• Teacher's Resource Book: Audio Script, pp. 274–275, Communicative Pair Activity BLM, pp. 280–281
• Audio Program DVD: Cap. 7B, Track 13

✓**ASSESSMENT**

Prueba 8B-5 with Study Plan (online only)

Quiz: The preterite of *hacer* and *dar*
• Prueba 8B-5: p. 221

Lectura

Focus: Reading an article about an international volunteer organization

Suggestions:

Pre-reading: Ask students if they are familiar with Habitat for Humanity. If so, ask volunteers to provide whatever background information they have about the organization.

Reading: Have students read the article silently all the way through and make a list of cognates they encounter while they read. Then have volunteers read the selection aloud or listen to the audio. Stop after each paragraph and ask students to summarize the main idea.

Post-reading: Have students complete the *¿Comprendes?* questions or give a summary of the text to check comprehension.

BELLRINGER REVIEW

Start this activity by mentioning an important year in recent history. Then review numbers by asking students to tell the class in what year they were born.

Pre-AP* Support

• **Learning Objective:** Interpretive: Print and Audio

• **Activity:** Divide the reading of the selection in this way:

1. For the first paragraph, have students read silently one sentence at a time, looking up after each sentence. Ask a quick, one-word-answer question about that sentence.

2. Have students read the second paragraph silently. Then read several true/false statements to the class for response.

3. Working in pairs, have one student read aloud the final section to his or her partner. Then have the partner write a one-sentence summary to share with the class.

• **Pre-AP* Resource Book:** Comprehensive guide to Pre-AP* reading skill development, pp. 19–26

Lectura

Lee este artículo sobre una organización que hace proyectos de construcción en muchos países del mundo.

Strategy

Recognizing cognates
Recognizing cognates in the following article can help improve your understanding of the reading.

Hábitat para la Humanidad Internacional

Hábitat es una organización internacional que ayuda a la gente pobre a tener casa. Su objetivo es construir casas seguras[1] que no cuestan mucho para las personas que no tienen mucho dinero. Hábitat trabaja con las familias pobres, con los grupos de voluntarios y con las personas que les dan dinero. Esta organización tiene más de 2.500 proyectos en muchas comunidades de los Estados Unidos y otros 1.600 proyectos en más de 83 países diferentes. Hábitat ha construido[2] unas 250.000 casas en todo el mundo.

Guatemala tiene quince afiliados de Hábitat. Cada afiliado tiene su propio dinero y hace su plan de construcción y sus proyectos. Los afiliados de Guatemala tienen mucho éxito.[3] Han construido más de 10.000 casas y tienen planes para construir 15.000 más en los años que vienen. Según Hábitat, las personas pobres tienen que ayudar a construir sus casas. Es una manera positiva de ayudar a los demás. Hábitat les da los materiales de construcción y los trabajadores voluntarios. Cuando la casa está construida, el nuevo propietario[4] paga una pequeña hipoteca[5] cada mes. Después, los nuevos propietarios tienen que ayudar a otros futuros propietarios a construir sus casas.

[1] safe [2] has built [3] success [4] owner [5] mortgage

Un proyecto de Hábitat para la Humanidad Internacional

DIFFERENTIATED INSTRUCTION

Heritage Language Learners

Have students research other Spanish-speaking countries in which Habitat for Humanity has assisted in building homes. Have students write a brief newspaper article about a specific project.

Para todos, es una experiencia increíble.

Trabajadores de Hábitat para la Humanidad Internacional

—Ayer fue mi cumpleaños y recibí el mejor regalo de mi vida, mi propia casa —dijo una señora de la comunidad de Baja Verapaz.

La mayoría[6] del dinero viene de donaciones privadas y del trabajo voluntario de muchísimas personas.

¿Sabes que el ex-presidente Jimmy Carter y su esposa Rosalynn son dos de los primeros miembros voluntarios de Hábitat? Los grupos de voluntarios son una parte fundamental del éxito de la organización.

—Es una experiencia inolvidable para ayudar a los demás —dijo un voluntario en Guatemala.

[6] the majority

¿Comprendes?

1. ¿Qué hace Hábitat?
2. ¿Con quiénes trabaja Hábitat?
3. ¿En cuántos países está Hábitat?
4. ¿Cuántas casas construyeron los afiliados de Guatemala?
5. ¿Qué tienen que pagar los nuevos propietarios?
6. ¿Qué tienen que hacer los nuevos propietarios?
7. ¿De dónde viene el dinero para construir las casas?
8. Y a ti, ¿te gustaría trabajar con Hábitat? ¿Por qué?

Más práctica	GO		
realidades.com | print			
Guided WB p. 125		✔	✔
Comm. WB pp. 82, 176		✔	✔
Hispanohablantes WB pp. 322–323			✔
Cultural Reading Activity			✔

▼ Fondo Cultural | Estados Unidos

El trabajo voluntario AmeriCorps is an organization of volunteers who work in urban and rural communities throughout the United States. They teach children to read, assist victims of natural disasters, and participate in other activities that benefit needy people.

One of the advantages of serving as an AmeriCorps volunteer is learning skills that can be used later in the workplace.

• What are some of the skills a volunteer might learn? Why are they important?

Doctores de las Naciones Unidas en Santa Cruz, Perú

doscientos setenta y tres **273**
Capítulo 8B

Perspectivas del mundo hispano

Perspectivas del mundo hispano

¿Trabajas como voluntario?

Core Instruction

Standards: 2.1

Focus: Reading about volunteer organizations and activities

Presentation: Discuss opportunities for volunteering. Help students see that both the volunteer and the community benefit. It is a good way to gain hands-on experience, and sometimes volunteers discover that they want to pursue a career in that field. Have students read the text. Discuss the different types of volunteer work students in Spanish-speaking countries do. Have students complete the *Check it out!* section.

Suggestions: Discuss different types of volunteer work. Using the examples cited in the text, ask students if the same types of work could be done in their community. What other types of volunteer work might be available? Help students understand that communities always have a need for volunteers, but that some positions may be needed more than others.

Direct attention to the *Think about it!* section and have students discuss the question.

Answers will vary.

Teacher-to-Teacher

Have students display the posters they made for the *Presentación escrita* around the school for other students to read.

Pre-AP* Support

- **Learning Objective:** Presentational Speaking (Cultural Comparisons)
- **Background:** This task prepares students for the Spoken Presentational Communication tasks that focus on cultural comparisons in the exam.
- **Activity:** After reviewing this reading, have students interview their peers and/or use the Internet to develop a two-minute (maximum) presentation on attitudes toward volunteer activities among teenagers in different cultures. Have students summarize, compare, and explain similarities and differences.
- *Pre-AP* Resource Book:* Comprehensive guide to Pre-AP* speaking skill development, pp. 39–50

Additional Resources

Student Resource: Realidades para hispanohablantes, p. 326

Throughout the Spanish-speaking world students are involved in volunteer activities and organizations. In many private schools students are encouraged to serve their community for two to three hours per week to help them learn responsibilities that will make them good citizens. Community service also provides a good occasion to explore different professions such as education, medicine, or social work. For example, many young people work with local branches of the *Cruz Roja* (Red Cross) and learn how to respond in times of emergency. Courses are offered by the organization, and some students even study for a degree in health services.

In many Spanish-speaking countries, students are involved in causes dealing with the environment. In many countries, the natural beauty of the land is not only a source of national pride, it is also an economic resource and important to the well-being of the country. Students work at recycling centers collecting paper, glass, and plastic and collect trash along roadsides and in parks.

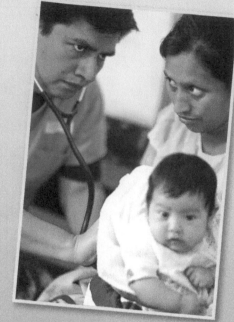

Un médico voluntario en una clínica de Guatemala

Check it out! Survey the students in your class. Who does volunteer work? What kind of work do they do? How often are they involved in community service activities?

Think about it! How does the involvement in volunteerism among teenagers in many Spanish-speaking countries compare with the involvement in your community?

En la Reserva Ecológica El Ángel, en el Ecuador

DIFFERENTIATED INSTRUCTION

Heritage Language Learners

Have students learn about the **Cruz Roja** or another community-based organization in a Spanish-speaking country of their choice. Ask them to prepare a short report on what the organization does.

Presentación escrita

¿Puedes ayudarnos?

Task
Your school wants to organize a clean-up campaign for a park, recreation center, playground, or other place in your community. Make a poster announcing the project and inviting students to participate.

1 **Prewrite** Answer the following questions about your project.
- ¿Qué van a limpiar y qué tienen que hacer?
- ¿Dónde está el lugar?
- ¿Cuándo y cuántas horas van a trabajar?
- ¿Quién(es) puede(n) participar?

2 **Draft** Use the answers to the questions to prepare a first draft. Organize the information logically. Remember that you want students to stop and read the poster.

3 **Revise** Check your draft for spelling, accent marks, punctuation, and vocabulary usage. Share your work with a partner, who will check the following:
- Is the information presented clearly and arranged logically?
- Is there anything that you should add or change?
- Are there any errors?

4 **Publish** Prepare a final version, making any necessary changes. Add visuals to make the poster appealing. Display it in the classroom, cafeteria, or school library, or add it to your portfolio.

5 **Evaluation** The following rubric will be used to grade your presentation.

> **Strategy**
>
> **Using key questions**
> Answering key questions can help you think of ideas for writing.

Rubric	Score 1	Score 3	Score 5
Completeness of information	You provide only the name of your project.	You provide the name and location of your project.	You provide your project name, location, plus when, for how long, and who.
Accuracy of language	You use little variation of vocabulary with many grammar errors.	You use limited vocabulary with some grammar errors.	You use a variety of vocabulary with very few grammar errors.
Visual presentation	Your only visual on the poster is the title.	You provide the title and one visual on your poster, in color.	You provide the title and two or more visuals on your poster, in color.

Writing   8B

Presentación escrita

Persuasive

Standards: 1.3, 1.2

Focus: Communicating about a community-service project in a personalized context

Suggestions: Bring in a sample poster from a local organization. Point out that the key parts of a successful poster are the answers to the questions listed in Step 1. Encourage students to make their posters visually appealing as well as persuasive.

Portfolio

Include the final poster in students' portfolios.

Pre-AP* Support

- **Learning Objective:** Presentational Writing
- **Activity:** You've announced a worthwhile community event and invited people to attend. Now, write a brief, persuasive paragraph defending community service in general. Who benefits from these activities? Why should every student participate?
- *Pre-AP* Resource Book:* Comprehensive guide to Pre-AP* writing skill development, pp. 27–38

Additional Resources

Student Resources: Realidades para hispanohablantes, p. 327; Guided Practice: Presentación escrita, p. 126

ENRICH YOUR TEACHING

Teacher-to-Teacher
Careers: *Capítulo* 8B has focused on volunteerism. Have students work in small groups to talk about a career in community service. Ask them to write a list of words, expressions, and sentences they have learned that would be helpful in creating promotional materials in Spanish to recruit volunteers for a food bank. Ask groups to share their lists.

21st Century Skills
Technology Literacy Have students participate in a real event in the community and make an electronic poster advertising the event, combining print, video, audio, and digital images. Have them get permission to show the poster to other Spanish classes or even in the community, at places where Spanish is spoken.

✓ ASSESSMENT
Presentación escrita
- Assessment Program: Rubrics, p. T33
Review the rubric with students. Go over the descriptions of the different levels of performance. After assessing students, help individuals understand how their performance could be improved.

275

8B Video

Videomisterio ▶

Core Instruction

Standards: 1.2, 1.3, 5.2

Resources: Teacher's Resource Book: Video Script, p. 277; Video Program: Cap. 8B; Video Program Teacher's Guide: Cap. 8B

Focus: Introducing the events and vocabulary of this episode; scanning and reading the episode summary

Personajes importantes:

Lola Lago, detective
Pedro, Doña Gracia's grandson
Carmela, Lola Lago's friend
Julia Romero, María's friend who died in the hospital
Inspector Gil, police officer

Synopsis: Pedro and Lola discuss the clues they have so far. They do not know where María may be, but now they know that she went to Julia Romero's apartment. Lola sees María in front of doña Gracia's apartment. Lola calls Inspector Gil to let him know that she has seen María.

Suggestions: Review the events of *Episodio* 7: Rosalinda finds out Julia Romero's address and calls Lola to let her know. Then Pedro and Lola meet at doña Gracia's apartment. There they find a postcard sent to María from Luis Antonio Llamas, a former secretary to doña Gracia's husband. By chance, the name of one of the nurses that cared for Julia in the hospital was Luis Antonio. Next they go to Julia Romero's apartment. They discover that she no longer lives there, but the new tenant has a box of Julia's belongings. In the box they find several letters from Luis Antonio.

Point out the *Palabras para comprender*, saying examples in context and writing the sentences on the board. Remind students that these words are only used to help them understand the episode and they are not responsible for knowing that vocabulary.

¿Eres tú, María? Episodio 8

Antes de ver el video

"A ver. Esta foto. Yo conozco a este hombre. Pero no sé de qué. ¡Qué problema!"

Resumen del episodio

Después de visitar el piso de Julia, Lola y Pedro van a un café a tomar unos refrescos. Hablan de las cosas de Julia que el joven acaba de darles:[1] la ropa, las fotos, los papeles. Cuando Lola llega a su piso en la noche, ve que una mujer entra en el edificio número 8. Lola cree que es María. Sale rápidamente de su piso y espera[2] enfrente. Una mujer sale del edificio y Lola le pregunta, "¿Eres tú, María?"

[1] just gave them   [2] waits

Palabras para comprender

María tenía las llaves.	María had the keys.
Ella las perdió.	She lost them.
¡No me sigas!	Don't follow me!
Acabo de ver . . .	I just saw . . .
Acabo de hablar con . . .	I just spoke with . . .

276 doscientos setenta y seis
Tema 8 • Experiencias

DIFFERENTIATED INSTRUCTION

Advanced Learners

Ask students to prepare questions to test the class's comprehension of the reading. Have them work in pairs or small groups to ask *who, what, when, where,* and *why* questions. Provide them with a model.

Heritage Language Learners

Have students write a creative continuation of the episode. Tell them to include information on what happens to each character in the video.

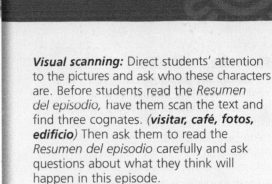

—¿Eres María Requena?
—¿Por qué quieres saberlo?

—Acabo de hablar con María Requena delante del piso de doña Gracia.

—Srta. Lago, esto es cosa de la policía.

Después de ver el video

¿Comprendes?

A. ¿Quién lo dice: Lola, Carmela, Pedro, el Inspector Gil, la camarera o María?

1. ¿Qué desean Uds.?
2. Y yo, un agua mineral.
3. ¿Cómo es que tienes las llaves del piso de Julia?
4. ¿Sabes algo más sobre el caso de doña Gracia?
5. Las diez y media. ¡Por fin!
6. ¿Qué quieres? ¿Quién eres?
7. ¡No me sigas! ¡No me sigas!
8. Acabo de ver a María Requena.

9. Ahora trabajo para Pedro Requena, el nieto de doña Gracia.
10. Hay que decirlo todo a la policía.

B. Escribe dos frases que describan cada foto de esta página.

Más práctica GO
realidades.com | print
Actividades ✔

Video 8B

Visual scanning: Direct students' attention to the pictures and ask who these characters are. Before students read the *Resumen del episodio,* have them scan the text and find three cognates. (*visitar, café, fotos, edificio*) Then ask them to read the *Resumen del episodio* carefully and ask questions about what they think will happen in this episode.

Viewing: Play *Episodio* 8 for the class. If necessary, rewind and replay parts of the video that give important information about the story.

Post-viewing: Complete the *¿Comprendes?* questions in class.

▼ **¿Comprendes?** Standards: 1.2, 1.3
Resources: Answer Keys: Student Edition, p. 174
Focus: Verifying comprehension by answering questions; reviewing the plot
Suggestions: After each item, verify the correct answer by playing the appropriate section of the video. For part B, have students write the sentences in the form of a summarizing paragraph.

Answers:
Part A:
1. Lo dice la camarera.
2. Lo dice Lola.
3. Lo dice Pedro.
4. Lo dice Carmela.
5. Lo dice Lola.
6. Lo dice María.
7. Lo dice María.
8. Lo dice Lola.
9. Lo dice Lola.
10. Lo dice el inspector Gil.
Part B answers will vary.

Additional Resources
• *¿Eres tú, María?* Video Workbook, Episode 8
• *¿Eres tú, María?* Teacher's Video Guide: Answer Key

ENRICH YOUR TEACHING

Teacher-to-Teacher
To help students better understand the stories, have them identify the elements of a plot for the *Videomisterio.* Review the meanings of each element: *el enredo o complicación* ("set up" or "introduction"), *el punto culminante* ("climax"), and *el desenredo* or *resolución* ("outcome").

277

Review Activities

To talk about recycling and places in a community: Have students make a sketch of a recyclable item. Then, line students up in two rows, facing each other. Have each team take turns indentifying the other team's items, in order. Have the students rotate in the line for variation.

To talk about possibilities for volunteer work: Have students work in pairs. Student A tells Student B what his or her interests are and Student B recommends a place in the community where Student A can volunteer his or her time. Have students switch roles.

To practice decir, *the preterite of* dar *and* hacer, *and indirect object pronouns:* Have students write five sentences telling what different people say about recycling and volunteer work. Students should try to include the past tense of *dar* and *hacer* and use indirect object pronouns. Have students review each other's sentences and then read them aloud. Example: *Mi profesora dice que ella le dio ropa a los niños en su comunidad.*

Portfolio

Invite students to review the activities they completed in this chapter, including written reports, posters or other visuals, recordings of oral presentations, or other projects. Have them select one or two items that they feel best demonstrate their achievements in Spanish to include in their portfolios. Have them include this with the Chapter Checklist and Self-Assessment Worksheet.

Additional Resources

Student Resources: Realidades para hispanohablantes, p. 328

Teacher Resources:
- Teacher's Resource Book: Situation Cards, p. 282, Clip Art, pp. 284–285
- Assessment Program: Chapter Checklist and Self-Assessment Worksheet, pp. T56–T57

Repaso del capítulo
Vocabulario y gramática

▶ Review the vocabulary and grammar
▶ Demonstrate you can perform the tasks on p. 279

to talk about recycling

la bolsa	bag, sack
la botella	bottle
la caja	box
el cartón	cardboard
el centro de reciclaje	recycling center
la lata	can
llevar	to take; to carry
el periódico	newspaper
el plástico	plastic
reciclar	to recycle
recoger	to collect; to gather
separar	to separate
usado, -a	used
el vidrio	glass

to talk about places in a community

el barrio	neighborhood
la calle	street, road
la comunidad	community
el jardín	garden, yard
el río	river

to discuss possibilities for volunteer work

los ancianos	older people
el anciano	older man
la anciana	older woman
el campamento	camp
los demás	others
la escuela primaria	primary school
la gente	people
el hospital	hospital
el juguete	toy
los niños	children
el niño	young boy
la niña	young girl
pobre	poor
el problema	problem
el proyecto de construcción	construction project
el trabajo voluntario	volunteer work
el voluntario, la voluntaria	volunteer

other useful words and expressions

a menudo	often
decidir	to decide
Es necesario.	It's necessary.
la experiencia	experience
Hay que . . .	One must . . .
increíble	incredible
inolvidable	unforgettable
¿Qué más?	What else?
la vez, *pl.* las veces	time
otra vez	again

decir *to say, to tell*

digo	decimos
dices	decís
dice	dicen

indirect object pronouns

SINGULAR	PLURAL
me (to/for) me	nos (to/for) us
te (to/for) you	os (to/for) you
le (to/for) him, her; you *(formal)*	les (to/for) them; you *(formal)*

preterite of *dar*

di	dimos
diste	disteis
dio	dieron

preterite of *hacer*

hice	hicimos
hiciste	hicisteis
hizo	hicieron

For *Vocabulario adicional,* see pp. 336–337.

DIFFERENTIATED INSTRUCTION

Heritage Language Learners

Have students write a letter to the editor about a problem in their community. Students should describe the situation and offer a solution to the problem. Remind them to include the preterite forms of *dar* and *hacer,* and indirect object pronouns.

Students with Learning Difficulties

Have students use the Organizer from the *Practice Workbook* to create a study list and to reinforce their knowledge of the chapter's vocabulary and grammar.

0Repaso

Más repaso GO realidades.com | print

Instant Check ✔
Puzzles ✔
Core WB pp. 71–72 ✔ ✔
Comm. WB pp. 177, 178–180 ✔ ✔

Review **8B**

Preparación para el examen

On the exam you will be asked to ...	Here are practice tasks similar to those you will find on the exam ...	For review go to your print or digital textbook ...
1 Escuchar Listen and understand as someone describes what he did in his community	A radio station is sponsoring a contest to encourage people to help in the community. Listen as a teen tells the announcer what he did. Identify whether he: a) helped older people; b) worked on a recycling project; c) contributed money; d) volunteered in a hospital or school.	**pp. 250–255** *Vocabulario en contexto* **p. 251** *Actividades 1–2* **p. 256** *Actividad 6* **p. 267** *Actividad 24*
2 Hablar Ask and answer questions about what you or someone you know did to help others in the past few months	Many organizations offer scholarships to students who help others. With a partner, practice asking and answering the following questions for the scholarship interviews with a local agency that works in the Spanish-speaking community: a) What did you do to help others? b) Why did you decide to do volunteer work?	**p. 257** *Actividad 9* **p. 258** *Actividad 10*
3 Leer Read and understand what people gave as donations to various people or groups	The Spanish Club treasurer's report about contributions to various organizations and individuals in the community is ready for the members. Read one line from the report. Indicate whether the member(s) donated: a) cash; b) lessons for an individual group; c) clothing; d) furniture. For example, you might read: *Scott y Jamie le dieron una cama y una cómoda a una familia pobre.*	**p. 267** *Actividad 23* **p. 271** *Actividad 30* **pp. 272–273** *Lectura*
4 Escribir Write a list of things teenagers can do to help in their communities	To encourage your classmates to participate in *La semana de la comunidad,* make a poster for your classroom with at least five suggestions for activities. For example: *Recicla las botellas. Ayuda a los niños de la escuela primaria.*	**p. 260** *Actividad 13* **p. 261** *Actividad 14* **p. 263** *Actividad 17* **p. 267** *Actividad 23* **p. 275** *Presentación escrita*
5 Pensar Demonstrate an understanding of cultural perspectives regarding volunteer work	Think about the volunteer activities in which you and your friends participate. Based on what you've learned in this chapter, compare these to the type of work teenage volunteers do in Spanish-speaking countries.	**p. 248** *Fondo cultural* **pp. 250–255** *Vocabulario en contexto* **p. 267** *Fondo cultural* **pp. 272–273** *Lectura* **p. 274** *Perspectivas del mundo hispano*

doscientos setenta y nueve **279**
Capítulo 8B

Performance Tasks

Standards: 1.1, 1.2, 1.3, 4.2

Student Resource: Realidades para hispanohablantes: p. 329

Teacher Resources: Teacher's Resource Book: Audio Script, p. 275; Audio Program DVD: Cap. 7B, Track 15; Answer Keys: Student Edition, p. 174

1. Escuchar

Suggestions: Play the audio or read the script aloud.

Script:
Ayer yo fui al hospital para pasar tiempo con los niños de cinco y seis años. Les leí unos cuentos y les traje juguetes y libros. Fue increíble la satisfacción que me dio cuando ayudé a los niños.

Answers:
a) no   b) no   c) no   d) yes

2. Hablar

Suggestions: Assign students fictitious volunteer jobs to describe for the purpose of variation or for students who have not done volunteer work.

Answers will vary.

3. Leer

Suggestions: Point out to students that they are only reading one line from the report, which is included here.

Answers: d

4. Escribir

Suggestions: Have students begin each suggestion with a command—**recicla, ayuda, recoge,** etc. Encourage students to vary their vocabulary words for each of the suggestions.

Answers will vary.

5. Pensar

Suggestions: Have students brainstorm ideas and write them on the board or on an overhead transparency.

Answers will vary.

DIFFERENTIATED ASSESSMENT

CORE ASSESSMENT
- **Assessment Program:** Examen del capítulo 8B, pp. 222–228
- **Audio Program DVD:** Cap. 7B, Track 16
- **ExamView:** Chapter Test, Test Banks A and B

ADVANCED/PRE-AP*
- **ExamView:** Pre-AP* Test Bank
- **Pre-AP* Resource Book,** pp. 90–93

STUDENTS NEEDING EXTRA HELP
- **Alternate Assessment Program:** Examen del capítulo 8B
- **Audio Program DVD:** Cap. 7B, Track 16

HERITAGE LEARNERS
- **Assessment Program: Realidades para hispanohablantes:** Examen del capítulo 8B
- **ExamView: Heritage Learner Test Bank**

9A El cine y la televisión

• **Movies, television, and recent events**

Vocabulary: television shows; movie genres; giving opinions

Grammar: *acabar de* + infinitive; *gustar* and similar verbs

Cultural Perspectives: movies and television; common gestures

9B La tecnología

• **Computers and the Internet**

Vocabulary: computers; communication; computer-related activities

Grammar: the verbs *pedir* and *servir*; *saber* and *conocer*

Cultural Perspectives: the use of technology

THEME SUPPORT

Bulletin Boards

Theme: *Medios de comunicación*

Ask students to cut out, copy, or download photos of movies and television shows from around the world, as well as photos of computers and computer-related items. Cluster photos to reflect the three categories just mentioned.

Hands-on Culture

Art: *Pintar un mural*

Murals decorate many public buildings in Mexico and the Spanish-speaking communities of the United States. They often celebrate the culture of the local community by communicating the history and accomplishments of its residents, thus serving as an important **medio de comunicación.**

Materials: butcher paper, pencils, paint brushes, paint of different colors, tape

1. Divide students into four or five groups. Ask each group to brainstorm a list of important events in the history of their community or state. Have groups then choose one event to depict in their mural.

2. Students discuss what to include, then draw their mural in pencil on two large pieces of butcher paper that have been taped together.

3. Students paint their mural.

4. Display the murals in the classroom. Have each group explain its mural.

Game

Te voy a explicar

This game practices the skill of circumlocution. Play it to review the vocabulary from *Capítulo* 9B.

Players: the whole class, playing in pairs

Materials: index cards, timer or stopwatch

Rules:

1. Divide the class into two teams, A and B. Have students from Team A partner with students from Team B to write all the new verbs and nouns from *Capítulo* 9B on index cards.

2. Ask partners to shuffle their cards and place them face down in two piles, one in front of each student.

3. Set your timer or stopwatch for 30 seconds. When you call **"Empieza,"** one student turns over a card. He or she then describes or explains the word to his or her partner without saying the word itself. If the partner guesses the word before the 30 seconds is up, he or she receives three points.
   Student A: Es una cosa. Sirve para tomar fotos. Después, bajas las fotos en la computadora.
   Student B: La cámara digital

4. Have partners switch roles to repeat Step 3. Students should write on a sheet of paper how many points they received in this round.

5. Have the members of Team A move to work with a different partner from Team B.

6. Repeat Steps 3–5 until all the vocabulary has been practiced. At the end of play, ask each team to tally its cumulative points. Check each team's math. The team with the most points wins.

Variation: Have only one player from each team play each round while the rest of the class watches.

THEME PROJECT

Cápsula de información

Overview: Students create time capsules that would show someone from the future what life is like today. They should include short descriptions accompanied by illustrations of popular movies, television shows, music videos, computer programs and / or Web sites, how people spend their time, and so on. Students then present their time capsules to the class, explaining why they included each time.

Resources: colored pencils or crayons, pens, blank paper, paper-towel tubes, or electronic software and hardware (e.g., thumb drives) to serve as "time capsules"

Sequence: (suggestions for when to do each step are found throughout the chapters)

9A **STEP 1.** Review instructions so students know what is expected of them. Hand out the "Theme 9 Project Instructions and Rubric" from the *Teacher's Resource Book.*

STEP 2. Students submit a list of items / activities and sketches of the illustrations they wish to include in their time capsule. Return the lists and visuals with your suggestions.

STEP 3. Students create layouts for the pages to go in the time capsule. Each page contains a description and an illustration of one of the items from the student's list.

9B **STEP 4.** Students submit a draft of their descriptions for each item on their list. Note your corrections and suggestions, then return drafts to students. Students correct their drafts, then partner to describe their time capsules.

STEP 5. Students present their time capsules to the class, explaining why they chose each item they included.

Options:

1. Students research another time period and create a time capsule for that era.
2. Students create a list of the year's best and worst media: television shows, movies, songs, computer programs, Web sites, etc.

Assessment:

Here is a detailed rubric for assessing this project:
Theme 9 Project: *Cápsula de información*

RUBRIC	Score 1	Score 3	Score 5
Evidence of planning	You didn't submit a list, sketches, or draft.	You submitted the draft and layout but didn't correct them.	You submitted and corrected your draft and layout.
Use of Illustrations	You didn't include any illustrations.	You included Illustrations for most items.	You included Illustrations for all items.
Presentation	You listed items to be included in the capsule, but did not adequately describe them or explain why they were chosen.	You briefly described items to be included in the capsule, but did not adequately explain why they were chosen.	You briefly described items to be included in the time capsule and explained why they were chosen.

21st Century Skills

Look for tips throughout *Tema 9* to enrich your teaching by integrating 21st Century Skills. Suggestions for the Theme Project and Theme Culture follow below.

Theme Project

Modify the Theme Project with one or more of these suggestions:

Develop Technology Literacy

Have students include in the time capsule an electronic representation of their activities as a class, to post on the class Web site. Have different groups of students prepare video explanations of their various activities during the year, including why they organized the events and what they learned from them.

Encourage Collaboration

Have students work in groups to study the individual choices in each category. Working with the handout "Analyze Media Content," each group member should explain their choices; then, the group decides which DVD, Web site, etc. best represents today's world.

Foster Productivity and Accountability

Have students work with the rubric for this assignment and figure out what they need to do to make the best grade possible. Have students evaluate each other's choices, presentations, etc. with the rubric in mind and make suggestions for improvement.

Theme Culture

Support Critical Thinking and Problem Solving

Have students do Internet research on a TV network in two Spanish-speaking countries, then compare the types of programs they find and discuss any similarities and differences. How do the networks compare to those in the United States?

▶ **Videocultura** View *Medios de comunicación* with the class to learn about Spanish media in the United States and the world.

AT A GLANCE

Objectives

- Listen to and read different opinions about television
- Talk and write about TV programs and movies
- Exchange information while sharing opinions about television and film
- Understand and use common gestures and compare them to ones you use
- Compare popular television programs in Spanish-speaking countries with programs in the U.S.

Vocabulary

- Television programs
- Movies
- Words and expressions to give opinions

Grammar

- *Acabar de* + infinitive
- *Gustar* and similar verbs

Culture

- Alfonso Cuarón, p. 281
- Luis Buñuel, Salvador Dalí, p. 281
- *telenovelas,* p. 290
- Average numbers of hours people watch television in different countries, p. 292
- *Sábado gigante,* p. 294
- Influences of Greek and Arabic on Spanish, p. 295
- Spanish-language television networks, p. 297
- TV-watching habits of teens, pp. 300–301
- Gestures, p. 302

Recycle ♻

- Adverbs
- *me gusta(n), me encanta(n)*
- Adjective agreement
- *dar*
- Question words
- Infinitives

RESOURCES

	FOR THE STUDENT	ONLINE	DVD	PRINT	FOR THE TEACHER	ONLINE	PREEXP	DVD	PRINT
Plan					Interactive TE and Resources DVD	•		•	
					Teacher's Resource Book, pp. 304–339	•		•	•
					Pre-AP* Resource Book, 94–97	•	•		
					Mapa global interactivo	•			
					Lesson Plans	•			•
Introducción PP. 280–281									
Present	Student Edition, pp. 280–281	•	•	•	Interactive TE and Resources DVD	•		•	
	DK Reference Atlas	•	•		Teacher's Resource Book, pp. 304–307	•		•	•
	Videocultura	•	•		Galería de fotos		•		
	Hispanohablantes WB, pp. 330–331			•	Fine Art Transparencies, 13	•	•		•
					Map Transparencies, 12, 15–16, 18, 20	•	•		•
Vocabulario en contexto PP. 282–287									
Present & Practice	Student Edition, pp. 282–287	•	•	•	Interactive TE and Resources DVD	•		•	
	Audio	•	•		Teacher's Resource Book, pp. 309–311, 314, 322–323	•		•	•
	Videohistoria	•	•		Vocabulary Clip Art	•	•		
	Flashcards	•	•		Audio Program	•	•	•	
	Instant Check	•			Video Program: Videohistoria	•		•	
	Guided WB, pp. 127–136	•	•	•	Video Program Teacher's Guide: Cap. 9A	•		•	
	Core WB, pp. 73–76	•	•	•	Vocabulary and Grammar Transparencies, 159–162	•	•		•
	Comm. WB, pp. 83–86	•	•	•	Answer Keys: Student Edition, pp. 175–177	•		•	
	Hispanohablantes WB, pp. 332–333			•	TPR Stories, pp. 122–133	•	•		•
Assess and Remediate					Prueba 9A–1: Assessment Program, pp. 229–230	•		•	•
					Assessment Program para hispanohablantes, pp. 229–230	•		•	•

RESOURCES

FOR THE STUDENT	ONLINE	DVD	PRINT	FOR THE TEACHER	ONLINE	PREEXP	DVD	PRINT
Vocabulario en uso PP. **288–293**								
Present & Practice — Student Edition, pp. 288–293	•	•	•	Interactive Whiteboard Vocabulary Activities	•		•	
Instant Check	•			Interactive TE and Resources DVD	•		•	
Comm. WB, p. 86	•	•	•	Teacher's Resource Book, pp. 310–312, 316–317	•		•	•
Hispanohablantes WB, pp. 334–335, 341			•	Communicative Pair Activities, pp. 316–317	•			•
Communicative Pair Activities	•			Audio Program	•	•	•	
				Videomodelos	•		•	
				Vocabulary and Grammar Transparencies, 164	•	•	•	
				Answer Keys: Student Edition, pp. 177–179	•	•	•	
Assess and Remediate				Prueba 9A–2 with Study Plan	•			
				Prueba 9A–2: Assessment Program, pp. 231–232	•		•	•
				Assessment Program para hispanohablantes, pp. 231–232	•		•	•
Gramática PP. **294–299**								
Present & Practice — Student Edition, pp. 294–299	•	•	•	Interactive Whiteboard Grammar Activities	•		•	
Instant Check	•			Interactive TE and Resources DVD	•		•	
Animated Verbs	•			Teacher's Resource Book, pp. 312–315, 318–319	•		•	•
Tutorial Video: Grammar	•			Communicative Pair Activities, pp. 318–319	•			•
Canción de hip hop	•			Audio Program	•	•	•	
Guided WB, pp. 137–140	•	•	•	Videomodelos	•		•	
Core WB, pp. 77–79	•	•	•	Video Program: GramActiva	•		•	
Comm. WB, pp. 87–88, 90–91, 181	•	•	•	Vocabulary and Grammar Transparencies, 2, 163	•	•	•	
Hispanohablantes WB, pp. 336–341			•	Answer Keys: Student Edition, pp. 180–181	•	•	•	
Communicative Pair Activities	•							
Assess and Remediate				Pruebas 9A–3 and 9A–4 with Study Plans	•			
				Prueba 9A–3, 9A–4: Assessment Program, pp. 233, 234	•		•	•
				Assessment Program para hispanohablantes, pp. 233, 234	•		•	•
¡Adelante! PP. **300–305**								
Application — Student Edition, pp. 300–305	•	•	•	Interactive TE and Resources DVD	•		•	
Online Cultural Reading	•			Teacher's Resource Book, pp. 315, 321	•		•	•
Guided WB, pp. 141–142	•	•	•	Video Program: Videomisterio ¿Eres tú, María?	•		•	
Comm. WB, pp. 92, 182	•	•	•	Video Program Teacher's Guide: Cap. 9A	•		•	
Hispanohablantes WB, pp. 342–347			•	Videomisterio Quiz		•		
¿Eres tú, María? Video WB, pp. 67–73	•	•	•	Vocabulary and Grammar Transparencies, 165	•	•	•	
				Answer Keys: Student Edition, p. 181	•		•	
Repaso del capítulo PP. **306–307**								
Review — Student Edition, pp. 306–307	•	•	•	Interactive TE and Resources DVD	•		•	
Online Puzzles and Games	•			Teacher's Resource Book, pp. 313, 320, 322–323	•		•	•
Core WB, pp. 80–81	•	•	•	Audio Program	•	•	•	
Comm. WB, pp. 183–186	•	•	•	Answer Keys: Student Edition, p. 182	•	•	•	
Hispanohablantes WB, pp. 348–349			•					
Instant Check	•							
Chapter Assessment								
Assess				Examen del capítulo 9A	•		•	•
				Assessment Program, pp. 235–240	•		•	•
				Alternate Assessment Program, pp. 101–105	•		•	•
				Assessment Program para hispanohablantes, pp. 235–240	•		•	•
				Audio Program, Cap. 9A, Examen	•		•	
				ExamView: Test Banks A and B questions only online	•			
				Heritage Learner Test Bank	•			
				Pre-AP* Test Bank	•			

REGULAR SCHEDULE (50 MINUTES)

DAY	Warm-up / Assess	Preview / Present / Practice / Communicate	Wrap-up / Homework Options
1	Return Examen del capítulo (10 min.)	Vocabulario en contexto (35 min.) • Objectives • Presentation • *Actividades* 1, 2 • Arte y cultura • Videocultura: *Medios de comunicación*	Wrap-up and Homework Options (5 min.) • Core Practice • Vocabulary Clip Art
2	Warm-up (5 min.) • Homework check	Vocabulario en contexto (40 min.) • Review: *Vocabulario en contexto* • Presentation: *Videohistoria ¿Qué dan en la tele?* • View: Video *¿Qué dan en la tele?* • Video Activities • *Actividades* 3, 4	Wrap-up and Homework Options (5 min.) • *Prueba* 9A-1: Vocabulary recognition • Core Practice
3	Warm-up (5 min.) • Homework check ✔Formative Assessment (10 min.) • *Prueba* 9A-1: Vocabulary recognition	Vocabulario en uso (30 min.) • Objectives • Interactive Whiteboard Vocabulary Activities • *Actividades* 5, 6	Wrap-up and Homework Options (5 min.) • *Actividad* 7
4	Warm-up (5 min.) • Homework check • Return *Prueba* 9A-1: Vocabulary recognition	Vocabulario en uso (40 min.) • Review: *Vocabulario* • *Fondo cultural* • *Actividades* 8, 9, 10 • Communicative Pair Activities	Wrap-up and Homework Options (5 min.)
5	Warm-up (5 min.) • Homework check	Vocabulario en uso (40 min.) • Review: *Vocabulario* • *Actividades* 10, 11, 12	Wrap-up and Homework Options (5 min.)
6	Warm-up (5 min.) • Homework check	Vocabulario en uso (40 min.) • *Conexiones: Actividades* 13, 14 • *Pronunciación*	Wrap-up and Homework Options (5 min.) • *Actividad* 15
7	Warm-up (5 min.) • Homework check	Gramática y vocabulario en uso (40 min.) • Presentation: *acabar de* + infinitive • *GramActiva* Video • *Fondo cultural* • Interactive Whiteboard Grammar Activities • *Actividades* 16, 17 • *Exploración del lenguaje*	Wrap-up and Homework Options (5 min.) • Core Practice • *Prueba* 9A-3 with Study Plan: *acabar de* + infinitive
8	Warm-up (5 min.) • Homework check ✔Formative Assessment (10 min.) • *Prueba* 9A-3 with Study Plan: *acabar de* + infinitive	Gramática y vocabulario en uso (30 min.) • Presentation: *gustar* and similar verbs • *GramActiva* Video • Interactive Whiteboard Grammar Activities • *Actividades* 18, 19 • *Fondo cultural* • Communicative Pair Activities	Wrap-up and Homework Options (5 min.) • *Actividad* 20 • *Prueba* 9A-2 with Study Plan: Vocabulary production

REGULAR SCHEDULE (50 MINUTES)

DAY	Warm-up / Assess	Preview / Present / Practice / Communicate	Wrap-up / Homework Options
9	**Warm-up (5 min.)** • Homework check • Return *Prueba* 9A-3 with Study Plan: *acabar de* + infinitive ✔**Formative Assessment (10 min.)** • *Prueba* 9A-2 with Study Plan: Vocabulary production	**Gramática y vocabulario en uso (30 min.)** • Review: *gustar* and similar verbs • *Juego: Actividad* 21 • *El español en la comunidad*	**Wrap-up and Homework Options (5 min.)** • *Prueba* 9A-4 with Study Plan: *gustar* and similar verbs
10	**Warm-up (5 min.)** • Homework check • Return *Prueba* 9A-2 with Study Plan: Vocabulary production ✔**Formative Assessment (10 min.)** • *Prueba* 9A-4 with Study Plan: *gustar* and similar verbs	**Gramática y vocabulario en uso (30 min.)** • Review: *gustar* and similar verbs • *Actividades* 22, 23	**Wrap-up and Homework Options (5 min.)** • Core Practice
11	**Warm-up (5 min.)** • Homework check • Return *Prueba* 9A-4 with Study Plan: *gustar* and similar verbs	**¡Adelante! (40 min.)** • *Lectura* • *Presentación oral:* Prepare	**Wrap-up and Homework Options (5 min.)** • *Presentación oral:* Prepare
12	**Warm-up (5 min.)** • Homework check	**¡Adelante! (40 min.)** • *La cultura en vivo* • *Presentación oral:* Practice	**Wrap-up and Homework Options (5 min.)**
13	**Warm-up (5 min.)** • Homework check	**¡Adelante! (40 min.)** • *Presentación oral:* Present	**Wrap-up and Homework Options (5 min.)** • Writing Activities • Core Practice Organizer
14	**Warm-up (5 min.)** • Homework check • Core Practice Organizer	**¡Adelante! (20 min.)** • *Videomisterio* **Repaso (20 min.)** • *Vocabulario y gramática* • *Preparación para el examen*	**Wrap-up and Homework Options (5 min.)** • Instant Check • *Examen del capítulo*
15	**Warm-up (5 min.)** • Answer questions ✔**Summative Assessment (45 min.)** • *Examen del capítulo*		

Standards for *Capítulo* 9A

- To achieve the goals of the Standards, students will:

Communication

1.1 Interpersonal
- Talk about movies and television
- Talk about opinions about the media
- Talk about favorite actors
- Talk about likes and dislikes

1.2 Interpretive
- Read and listen to information about movies and television
- Read and listen to opinions about the media
- Read a picture-based story
- Listen to and watch a video about television choices
- View a video mystery series

1.3 Presentational
- Present information about movies and television
- Present information about opinions about the media
- Write about household chores

Culture

2.1 Practices and Perspectives
- Learn about the popularity of *Sábado Gigante*

2.2 Products and Perspectives
- Learn about Mexican-born director Alfonso Cuarón
- Learn about Spanish-born film director Luis Buñuel
- Learn about Salvador Dalí and his painting
- Learn about the popularity and style of ***telenovelas***
- Learn about the variety show *Sábado Gigante*

Connections

3.1 Cross-curricular
- Learn about important artists and their work: Cuarón, Buñel, Dalí
- Reinforce math skills

Comparisons

4.1 Language
- Learn vocabulary through the recognition of cognates
- Learn to use **acabar de** + **infinitive** for recent events
- Understand the influence of Greek, Latin, and Arabic on the Spanish language
- Understand **gustar** and similar verbs
- Learn about linking words
- Learn about and compare communicative gestures

4.2 Culture
- Compare avant garde film makers
- Compare **las telenovelas** to soap operas
- Compare *Sábado Gigante* to other long-running shows

Communities

5.1 Beyond the School
- Identify local Spanish language television programming

5.2 Lifelong Learner
- View Latin American cable or satellite television
- View a video mystery series

Capítulo

9A El cine y la televisión

▼ Chapter Objectives

Communication
By the end of this chapter you will be able to:
- Listen to and read different opinions about television
- Talk and write about television programs and movies
- Exchange information while sharing opinions about television and film

Culture
You will also be able to:
- Understand and use common gestures in Spanish-speaking countries, and compare them to ones you use
- Compare popular television programs in Spanish-speaking countries with programs in the United States

You will demonstrate what you know and can do:
- Presentación oral, p. 331
- Preparación para el examen, p. 335

You will use:

Vocabulary	Grammar
• Television programs	• *Acabar de* + infinitive
• Movies	• *Gustar* and similar verbs
• Words and expressions to give opinions	

Exploración del mundo hispano

Country Connection
Movies and Television

España
Florida
México
Venezuela
Argentina

realidades.com [GO]

Reference Atlas
Videocultura y actividad
Mapa global interactivo

(280) doscientos ochenta
Tema 9 • Medios de comunicación

Alfonso Cuarón, director de cine mexicano, filmando una película

---

ENRICH YOUR TEACHING

Using Backward Design
Have students preview the sample performance tasks on *Preparación para el examen*, p. 307, and connect them to the Chapter Objectives. Explain to students that by completing the sample tasks they can to self-assess their learning progress.

Mapa global interactivo
Download the *Mapa global interactivo* files for Chapter 9A and preview the activity. In this activity, you discover Andalusia and Granada.

Tema 9 • Medios de comunicación

Arte y cultura | España

Luis Buñuel (1900–1983) was a Spanish-born film director. He made films in Spain, the United States, Mexico, and France. His films were often controversial because of their strong imagery and difficult topics. Buñuel made two surrealist films with artist Salvador Dalí (1904–1989), Spain's most famous Surrealist painter. The films mixed reality and dreams. This portrait of Buñuel was painted by Dalí in 1924 when the painter was 20 years old and Buñuel was 24.

• Who are some young directors today whose films are considered to be "cutting edge"?

"Retrato de Luis Buñuel" (1924), Salvador Dalí ▶
Oil on canvas, .70 x .60 m. Coll. Luis Buñuel, Mexico City, D.F., Mexico. © 2004 Salvador Dalí, Gala-Salvador Dalí Foundation/Artists Rights Society (ARS), NY. Photo credit: Bridgeman-Giraudon / Art Resource, NY.

doscientos ochenta y uno **281**
Capítulo 9A

Preview 9A

Chapter Opener

Core Instruction

Resources: Map Transparencies 12, 15–16, 18, 20

Suggestions: Explain that students will learn how to talk about movies and television. Brainstorm a list of different types of movies and television shows. Have students give one example and a short description. The video story is about a group of friends who try to agree on what to watch on television.

▶ **Videocultura** View *Medios de comunicación* with the class to learn about Spanish media in the United States and the world.

Arte y cultura

Standards: 2.2, 4.2

Resources: Fine Art Transparencies, p. 13

Suggestions: Explain the concept of surrealism. Refer students to the painting of Luis Buñuel and ask them if they think this painting exemplifies this artistic movement.

Answers will vary.

Teaching with Photos

By the time Alfonso Cuarón was 12 years old, he already knew a lot about filmmaking. His hobbies were watching films at home or in theaters, and making Super 8 films—using his siblings as actors. Have students imagine that they are behind the camera, directing a film. What subject would they choose? How would they go about making their movie?

Culture Note

Alfonso Cuarón was born in Mexico City, but his success is international, and he has directed films in English and Spanish. His *Harry Potter and the Prisoner of Azkaban* won a BAFTA Award in 2011, for Kid's Vote for Film of the Decade. Cuarón has also directed film adaptations of novels by Frances Hodson and Charles Dickens.

DIFFERENTIATED INSTRUCTION

Digital resources such as the *Interactive Whiteboard* activity banks, *Videomodelos*, additional *Online Activities*, *Study Plans*, automatically graded *Leveled Workbook*, animated *Grammar Tutorials*, *Flashcards*, and *Vocabulary and Grammar Videos* will help you reach students of different ability levels and learning styles.

STUDENTS NEEDING EXTRA HELP

Guided Practice Activities
• Flashcards, pp. 127–132
• Vocabulary Check, pp. 133–136
• Grammar Support, pp. 137–140

HERITAGE LEARNERS

Realidades para hispanohablantes
• Chapter Opener, pp. 330–331
• A primera vista, p. 332
• Videohistoria, p. 333
• Manos a la obra, pp. 334–341
• ¡Adelante!, pp. 342–347
• Repaso del capítulo, pp. 348–349

ADVANCED/PRE-AP*

Pre-AP* Resource Book,
• pp. 94–97
Communications Workbook
• Integrated Performance Assessment, p. 183

281

Vocabulario en contexto

Core Instruction

Standards: 1.2, 4.2

Resources: Teacher's Resource Book: Input Script, p. 309, Clip Art, pp. 322–323, Audio Script, p. 310; Voc. and Gram. Transparencies 159–160; TPR Stories Book, pp. 122–133; Audio Program DVD: Cap. 9A, Tracks 1–2

Focus: Presenting new vocabulary about television shows

Suggestions: Use the story in the *TPR Stories Book* to present the new vocabulary and grammar or use the Input Script from the *Teacher's Resource Book.*

Explain to the students that they will be reading about television shows that can be seen on *Canal* 9. Before they start the reading, have them look at the pictures and guess what kind of shows are offered. Tell them to rely on cognates and words they already know to help them with the reading. After they have finished reading, have them confirm their guesses.

When presenting the different types of movies, use videos or DVDs from the library as examples and have students tell you what kind of films they are. Ask students to describe the movies.

BELLRINGER REVIEW

Have students copy and complete the following sentences from the board to review time:

1) *La clase de inglés empieza a las _____ y termina a las _____.*

2) *El almuerzo empieza a las _____ y termina a las _____.*

3) *Mi mamá sale de la casa a las _____ y vuelve a las _____.*

Answers will vary.

A primera vista | 🔊 | 📖

▼ Objectives

Read, listen to, and understand information about
▶ movies and television programs
▶ opinions on media entertainment

Vocabulario en contexto

¡LE DAMOS EL MUNDO EN EL CANAL 9!

¿Qué le interesa? Un programa...

¿...de entrevistas?

Entre tú y yo
Pablo Ramírez habla con personas fascinantes.

¿...educativo?

Nuestro planeta
Explora el mundo de los animales.

¿...de concursos?

¡Una fortuna para ti!
¡Los participantes pueden recibir mucho dinero!

¿...de noticias?

Las noticias de hoy
Presentamos todo lo que necesita saber del mundo en 30 minutos.

¿...deportivo?

Fútbol hoy
Hay fútbol, fútbol y más fútbol.

¿...una telenovela?

Secretos de amor
¿Qué va a pasar con Rosario y Felipe en este programa **emocionante**?

¿...musical?

Ritmos latinos
Le presenta música de más de 20 países diferentes.

¿...de dibujos animados?

Patito y Paquito
Una presentación cómica para todos los niños.

—¿Qué quieres ver en la tele?

—¿La verdad? **Me aburre** la televisión. No me interesan nada los programas que **dan.**

—No estoy de acuerdo. Pienso que la televisión presenta muchos programas interesantes y divertidos.

282 doscientos ochenta y dos
Tema 9 • Medios de comunicación

DIFFERENTIATED INSTRUCTION

Multiple Intelligences

Visual/Spatial: Have students create their own movie posters. Encourage them to use their imagination when thinking of titles.

Heritage Language Learners

Have students write a short paragraph describing a recent movie. Students should include the name of the movie and the type of movie it is. They should also tell when the movie begins, using the 24-hour clock. Point out that the 24-hour clock is often used when referring to movie schedules.

CINE FLORIDA

una película policíaca
El crimen perfecto
15:15 17:50 20:25 23:00

una comedia
MI TÍO TONTO
16:40 18:50 21:00 23:10

un drama
La tragedia de Laura
11:20 13:50 16:20 18:50 21:20

una película de ciencia ficción
Los extraterrestres atacan
14:00 16:00 18:00 20:00

una película romántica
Antonio y Ana
15:10 16:30 17:50 19:10

una película de horror
EL TERROR EN EL CASTILLO
13:45 16:15 18:45 21:15

—¿Qué dan en el Cine Florida?

—Hay seis películas. Mis amigos dicen que esta película policíaca es muy **violenta.** No quiero verla. Me interesan más las películas románticas como *Antonio y Ana.*

—Yo también quiero verla. ¿A qué hora va a **empezar?**

—**Empieza** a las cuatro y media, y **termina antes de** las seis. **Dura menos de** una hora y **media.**

—¿**De veras?** Son **casi** las cuatro. ¡Vamos ahora!

Más práctica GO

realidades.com | print

Instant Check	✔	
Guided WB pp. 127–132	✔	✔
Core WB pp. 73–74	✔	✔
Comm. WB p. 89	✔	✔
Hispanohablantes WB p. 332		✔

▼1 | | Escuchar

¿Qué dan en la tele hoy?

Vas a escuchar información sobre ocho programas del Canal 9. Señala cada tipo de programa en tu libro.

▼2 | Escuchar

¿Qué película vamos a ver?

Vas a escuchar siete frases sobre las películas que dan en el Cine Florida. Si una frase es lógica, haz el gesto del pulgar hacia arriba. Si no es lógica, haz el gesto del pulgar hacia abajo.

doscientos ochenta y tres **283**
Capítulo 9A

---

1 Standards: 1.2

Resources: Teacher's Resource Book: Audio Script, p. 310; Audio Program DVD: Cap. 9A, Track 3; Answer Keys: Student Edition, p. 175

Focus: Listening comprehension about television shows

Suggestions: Play the audio or read the script aloud. Pause to monitor that students are selecting the correct television program.

🔊 **Script and Answers:**

1. ¡Puede ganar un televisor nuevo si contesta esta pregunta! *(de concursos)*
2. Hoy vamos a hablar sobre diferentes animales que podemos ver en el zoológico. *(educativo)*
3. ¡Qué partido! Fue fantástico. Los Leones ganaron seis a tres. Son los mejores de la liga. *(deportivo)*
4. Hola amigos. Me llamo Pepita Lupita. ¿Quieres cantar conmigo? ¡La-la-la-la! *(de dibujos animados)*
5. —Hoy estoy hablando con el actor principal de la película romántica *Antonio y Ana*. Hola, Pedro. ¿Cómo está Ud.?
   —Bien, gracias. Me encanta estar aquí. *(de entrevistas)*
6. Muy buenas noches. Habla Ramón Montes. Hoy en Washington, el presidente dice que la situación económica está mejor. *(de noticias)*
7. ¡No puede ser! Por favor, María. Te necesito. Te quiero. Eres la más importante para mí. *(una telenovela)*
8. ¡Ahora aquí para cantar con nosotros, el grupo El Mariachi Michoacán! *(musical)*

---

2 Standards: 1.2

Resources: Teacher's Resource Book: Audio Script, p. 310; Audio Program DVD: Cap. 9A, Track 4; Answer Keys: Student Edition, p. 176

Focus: Listening comprehension

Suggestions: Be sure students base their responses on the ad from *Cine Florida.*

🔊 **Script and Answers:**

1. La película policíaca es muy violenta. *(up)*
2. ¡Ay! No dan una película romántica esta semana. *(down)*
3. Dan un drama muy bueno esta tarde. ¿Por qué no vamos a verlo? *(up)*
4. *Antonio y Ana* es una película de ciencia ficción. *(down)*
5. Vamos con mi hermanito a ver *El terror en el castillo*. Es una comedia muy divertida. *(down)*
6. Esta semana dan la película *La tragedia de Laura* en el Cine Florida. *(up)*
7. *Mi tío tonto* es una película de ciencia ficción. Vamos a verla. *(down)*

ENRICH YOUR TEACHING

Teacher-to-Teacher

Have students record movie listings like those you hear on phone recordings for your local theater. Have them invent four movie titles and give the show times as well as a short description of each film. If possible, play some of the recordings for the class and have students tell which movies they would like to see and why.

21st Century Skills

Communication Have students learn and practice the vocabulary using the embedded audio files of the eBook, and the online vocabulary practice. Then have them use the flashcards to quiz each other about TV preferences.

Videohistoria 🔊

Core Instruction

Standards: 1.2

Resources: Voc. and Gram. Transparencies 161–162; Audio Program DVD: Cap. 9A, Track 5; Answer Keys: Student Edition, p. 176

Focus: Presenting additional contextualized vocabulary and grammar; previewing the video

Suggestions:

Pre-reading: Brainstorm a list of words or phrases used to express agreement or disagreement. Have students compare the words and expressions on their lists with the words they find in the *Videohistoria*.

Answers:

Strategy: They disagree about what programs to watch on TV and about what movie to watch. They use expressions that express surprise, boredom, sarcasm, and dissatisfaction.

1. They decide to go see a movie.
2. televisión; distancia; fabuloso; favorita; emocionante; actor; actriz; principales; canal; programa; realista; música; animados; tele; infantiles; educativo; comedia; romántica; ciencia ficción; drama; especialmente

---

Videohistoria | 🔊 | ▶️

¿Qué dan en la tele?

¿Qué programa de televisión van a ver los chicos? Lee la historia.

Antes de leer

Strategy **Scanning** Scanning the text for key concepts is important for reading comprehension. Look over the *Videohistoria* and find at least two instances where people are disagreeing about something.

- What do they disagree about and what are the expressions they use?

1. Elena and her friends are trying to agree on what to watch on television. Look at the captions for photos 7 and 8 to predict what they decide to do.

2. Make a list of the cognates in the *Videohistoria*. Which ones can you use to help you understand the types of movies that Elena and her friends like to watch?

DIFFERENTIATED INSTRUCTION

Students with Learning Difficulties

To help students keep track of what each character from the *Videohistoria* wants to watch, have them create a T-chart. On one side of their paper students should write: *los programas que quieren ver* along with a list of the kinds of television programs that are discussed in the reading. On the other side they should write: *las películas que quieren ver* along with a list of the kinds of movies Elena and her friends talk about. Have students use the chart as they complete *Actividad 4*.

1

Ignacio: ¿Qué dan en la televisión? Elena, ¿dónde está el mando a distancia?*

Elena: Está encima de la mesita, al lado de la lámpara.

Ignacio: ¡Ah, sí! Lo veo. Vamos a ver lo que hay . . .

*remote control

2

Ana: ¡Fabuloso! Mi telenovela favorita.

Elena: Sí, me encanta. Es muy emocionante. **El actor y la actriz principales** son muy guapos.

Ignacio: ¡No! Me aburren las telenovelas. Vamos a ver otro canal.

Ana y Elena: Ignacio, ¡nuestra telenovela, por favor!

3

Elena: ¿Qué más hay? Mmmm. ¿Qué clase de programa es éste?

Ana: Es un programa de la vida real. Es muy realista.

Ignacio: No son realistas. Pienso que son tontos. ¿Verdad, Javier?

Javier: Pues, no sé mucho sobre esta clase de programas.

4

Jorgito: Elena, quiero ver dibujos animados. Ya son las cuatro.

Elena: Jorgito, ¿no ves que estoy con mis amigos? Tú puedes ver la tele más tarde. Mira, puedes escuchar música en mi cuarto.

Jorgito: Está bien, pero sólo hoy.

Todos: Adiós, Jorgito.

doscientos ochenta y cinco **285**
Capítulo 9A

Reading: Read the captions with students or play the audio. Using transparencies and non-verbal clues helps students understand the new words in blue type.

Post-reading: Complete *Actividad* 3 to check comprehension.

ENRICH YOUR TEACHING

Teacher-to-Teacher

Have students find information on the Web about a television program from a Spanish-speaking country. Tell them to get an idea of what type of show it is by looking at images and skimming any text. Ask them to write a short description of the show. List on the board or on a transparency the programs students found. Have students present their descriptions to the class and vote on the show they would most like to watch.

Video

Core Instruction

Standards: 1.2

Resources: Teacher's Resource Book: Video Script, p. 314; Video Program: Cap. 9A; Video Program Teacher's Guide: Cap. 9A

Focus: Understanding a story about deciding which television show to watch

Suggestions:

Pre-viewing: Ask students if it is difficult to decide what to watch on television. Ask them who gets to decide what shows to watch when they watch television with their friends and family.

Viewing: Remind students that body language and facial expressions can help them understand what people are saying. Show the video once without pausing. Show it again, pausing to check for comprehension.

Post-viewing: Complete the Video Activities in the *Communication Workbook*.

Pre-AP* Support

- **Learning Objective:** Interpersonal Speaking
- **Activity:** As a post-viewing activity, have students create a short conversation based on Scene 7 of this video. Ask them to change the types of movies the friends are discussing, and to finish the dialogue by proposing one movie all the characters agree to go see.
- *Pre-AP* Resource Book:* Comprehensive guide to Pre-AP* vocabulary skill development, pp. 51–57

Ignacio: No me gustan estos programas **infantiles**. ¿Qué más hay?

Elena: Un momento . . . este programa de entrevistas es mi favorito. Hablan de todo. Ohhh, ¡acaban de hablar con mi actor favorito!

Ignacio: Sí, y ya terminaron. **Por eso** no tenemos que verlo.

Ignacio: Podemos ver un programa de concursos.

Javier: ¿O un programa educativo? ¿O las noticias?

Todos: ¡Nooo!

Ignacio: ¡Tantos canales y no hay nada que ver!

Ana: ¿Por qué no vamos al cine?

Ana: Quiero ver una comedia.

Elena: Yo prefiero ver una película romántica.

Ignacio: No, son tontas. ¿Qué tal una película de ciencia ficción?

Todos: ¡Nooo!

Javier: Dan un drama nuevo en el Cine Tamayo.

Todos: ¡Nooo!

Jorgito: Ahora puedo ver los dibujos animados, **especialmente** mi favorito, *Rin, ran, run.* ¡Qué bien!

 286 doscientos ochenta y seis
Tema 9 • Medios de comunicación

DIFFERENTIATED INSTRUCTION

Heritage Language Learners

Have students write a persuasive paragraph to convince their classmates that they should watch a particular television show. Give students the option of writing about a Spanish-language program or one they watch in English. Be sure they include a thesis statement, at least two sentences about why someone should watch the show, and a summary statement.

▼**3** Leer

¿Cierto o falso?

Escribe los números del 1 al 6 en una hoja de papel. Lee estas frases. Si una frase es cierta según la *Videohistoria,* escribe *C.* Si es falsa, escribe *F.*

1. El mando a distancia está encima de la mesita.
2. El actor principal en la telenovela favorita de Ana es muy guapo.
3. Jorgito va a ver la tele cuando Elena y sus amigos están en la sala.
4. Jorgito va a escuchar música en el cuarto de Elena.
5. En el Cine Tamayo dan una película de ciencia ficción.
6. Los amigos deciden ver un programa de televisión.

▼**4** Leer

¿En qué canal?

Según las preferencias de Elena y sus amigos, ¿cuál de estos programas les gustaría ver o no les gustaría ver? Lee la lista de programas y en una hoja de papel, escribe el número del canal que mejor completa cada una de estas frases.

1. A Jorgito le gustaría ver el Canal ___ porque es su programa favorito.
2. A Ana y Elena les gustaría mucho ver el Canal ___.
3. A Ignacio no le gustaría nada ver el Canal ___ porque piensa que es tonto.
4. A Elena le gustaría ver el Canal ___ porque hablan con sus actores favoritos.
5. A Javier le gustaría ver el Canal ___ o un programa educativo.
6. A Ignacio le gustaría ver el Canal ___ pero a los otros no.

Canal 5	Noticias Tele-5
Canal 7	La telenovela del amor
Canal 8	Rin, ran, run
Canal 11	¡Dime más! Entrevistas de Hollywood
Canal 13	Ciencia ficción 3000
Canal 15	La vida real: Un invierno en la Antártida

Más práctica GO

realidades.com | print

Instant Check	✔	
Guided WB pp. 133–136	✔	✔
Core WB pp. 75–76	✔	✔
Comm. WB pp. 83–85, 86	✔	✔
Hispanohablantes WB p. 333		✔

▼**3** Standards: 1.2

Resources: Answer Keys: Student Edition, p. 177
Focus: Reading for understanding
Suggestions: To help students find the information more quickly, tell them that the statements in *Actividad* 3 are written in the order that they appear in the *Videohistoria.*
Answers:
1. C	3. F	5. F
2. C	4. C	6. F

▼**4** Standards: 1.2

Resources: Answer Keys: Student Edition, p. 177
Focus: Reading for understanding
Suggestions: Before beginning, have students list the names of the television shows and write what kind of shows they are. Tell them to use their lists to help them with the activity.
Answers:
1. 8	3. 15	5. 5
2. 7	4. 11	6. 13

Additional Resources
- Communication Wbk.: Audio Act. 5, p. 86
- Teacher's Resource Book: Audio Script, p. 311
- Audio Program DVD: Cap. 9A, Track 9

ENRICH YOUR TEACHING

Culture Note
Point out that in the past, Spanish-speaking celebrities were not as well known in the United States as they are today. Ask them if they have heard of Desi Arnaz and explain that he was one of the first actors from a Spanish-speaking country to succeed on American television. Ask them to name Spanish speakers they have seen on television shows or in movies.

21st Century Skills

Critical Thinking and Problem Solving Have students use a graphic organizer (Venn diagram, pie chart, table) to compare soap operas (*telenovelas*) and reality shows: how are they similar and how are they different?

✔**ASSESSMENT**

Quiz: Vocabulary Recognition
- Prueba 9A-1: pp. 229–230

INTERACTIVE WHITEBOARD
Vocabulary Activities 9A

5 Standards: 1.2, 1.3

Resources: Answer Keys: Student Edition, p. 177

Focus: Describing movies and television shows in a personalized context

Suggestions: Tell students to complete the part of the sentence that describes the movie or television show first, and then personalize it. Point out that some of the words in the box are nouns and some are adjectives. Remind them to make the adjectives agree with the nouns they describe.

Answers
Names of friends will vary.
1. policíacas
2. educativos
3. dibujos animados
4. drama
5. tonto
6. deportivos

6 Standards: 1.1, 1.2, 1.3

Resources: Teacher's Resource Book: Audio Script, pp. 310–311; Audio Program DVD: Cap. 9A, Track 6; Answer Keys: Student Edition, p. 178

Focus: Listening comprehension and giving your opinion about television shows

Suggestions: Play the audio or read the script aloud. Before students get together with a partner to do Step 2, have them check their answers to Step 1.

Script and Answers:

Step 1:
1. Siempre vemos los programas educativos porque son realistas. *(educativos / realistas)*
2. ¿Los programas de dibujos animados? ¡No! Son demasiado infantiles. *(los dibujos animados / infantiles)*
3. ¡Uy!, me aburren los programas de entrevistas. Son muy tontos. *(de entrevistas / tontos)*
4. Me encantan las telenovelas. ¡Qué emocionantes son! *(las telenovelas / emocionantes)*
5. No veo los programas de concursos porque generalmente son aburridos. *(de concursos / aburridos)*
6. Me interesan los programas de la vida real. Son fascinantes. *(de la vida real / fascinantes)*

Step 2 answers will vary.

Vocabulario en uso

▼**5** Leer · Escribir

Mis amigos ven . . .

Completa estas frases con el nombre de uno(a) de tus amigos y una de las palabras de la lista. Escribe las frases en una hoja de papel.

tonto	drama
dibujos animados	deportivo
educativo	policíaca

1. Mi amigo(a) ___ prefiere las películas ___. Le encantan los detectives.
2. Mi amigo(a) ___ ve los programas ___ porque siempre le gusta aprender más.
3. Mi amigo(a) ___ ve ___ porque le gustan las cosas infantiles.
4. Mi amigo(a) ___ prefiere ver un programa emocionante como un ___.
5. Mi amigo(a) ___ prefiere ver un programa ___ como una comedia.
6. Mi amigo(a) ___ es muy deportista y le interesan los programas ___.

▼**6** | 🗣️ | 🔊 | Escuchar · Escribir · Hablar

Muchas opiniones

Un programa de radio les pregunta a sus oyentes *(listeners)* qué piensan de los diferentes programas de televisión.

1 En una hoja de papel copia la gráfica y escribe los números del 1 al 6. Vas a escuchar las opiniones de unas personas. Escribe la clase de programa en la primera columna y la descripción en la segunda columna. Luego escribe frases para expresar tu opinión.

Programa de televisión	Descripción
1. las comedias	muy cómicas

Modelo
Me encantan las comedias porque son muy cómicas.

2 Habla con otro(a) estudiante. Di si estás de acuerdo con sus opiniones.

Modelo
Estoy de acuerdo. Las comedias son muy cómicas.
o: *No estoy de acuerdo. Las comedias son muy tontas.*

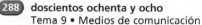

DIFFERENTIATED INSTRUCTION

Students with Special Needs
Using the script for Step 1 in *Actividad 6*, create a cloze passage for hearing-impaired students. Leave out the adjectives and have students choose the correct answer from a word bank.

Students with Learning Difficulties
For *Actividad 7*, assign individual students a specific type of program. Have them read their examples aloud. Create a master list on the board for students to use in *Actividad 8*.

Practice and Communicate 9A

▼**7** Escribir

Buenos ejemplos

Escoge seis de los siguientes programas de televisión. Luego escribe frases para dar un buen ejemplo de los diferentes programas.

Modelo
Pirates of the Caribbean *es una comedia.*

Filmando una película

▼**8** | | | Hablar

¿Te gustaría ver . . . ?

Usa la información que escribiste en la Actividad 7 y habla con otro(a) estudiante sobre qué clase de programas le gustaría ver. Él o ella puede usar las siguientes palabras.

me aburren	tontos, -as	fascinantes
me gustan	emocionantes	cómicos, -as
me interesan	violentos, -as	infantiles
me encantan	realistas	**¡Respuesta personal!**

 Modelo

A —*¿Te gustaría ver una comedia como Pirates of the Caribbean?*
B —*¡Uf! Me aburren las comedias. Son tontas.*
o:—*¡Por supuesto! Me encantan las comedias. Son cómicas.*

Focus: Writing about movies and television shows in a personalized context

Suggestions: Be sure that students understand what type of show each of the pictures represents. Remind students to save their work for *Actividad* 8.

Answers will vary.

BELLRINGER REVIEW

Have students refer to the series of programs illustrated in *Actividad* 7. Have volunteers tell the class the type of program being illustrated.

8 Standards: 1.1

Focus: Using contextualized vocabulary with a model conversation; stating opinions about television programs

Recycle: Likes and dislikes

Suggestions: Use the transparency to quickly review likes and dislikes. Remind Student A to use *¿Te gustaría ver...?* and a specific program from *Actividad* 7. Point out that Student B should use the words and phrases in the box.

Answers will vary.

Common Errors: Forgetting to make the adjective agree in number and gender with the noun. Remind students to make adjectives agree with the nouns they describe.

ENRICH YOUR TEACHING

Teacher-to-Teacher

Use the Internet to search for Spanish titles of recent Hollywood movies. Have students try to guess what the title of the movie is in English. If they get it on the first try, have them explain what kind of movie it is. If they don't get it from the title, give them hints by explaining what type of film it is, who the major actors and actresses are, and so forth. You can also look through the television section in newspapers and magazines from Spanish-speaking countries to get Spanish titles of popular television shows from the United States.

289

▼ Fondo Cultural | Argentina | España | México | Venezuela

Las telenovelas Venezuela, Mexico, Argentina, and Spain produce many soap operas that are popular with people of all ages. Unlike soap operas in the United States that continue for years with the same characters, the *telenovelas* frequently last only a matter of months. They are then replaced with new shows and different characters.

- What are the advantages of stories that continue for years versus stories that are new every several months? Which would you prefer?

Tres actores principales de la telenovela mexicana *Soy tu dueña*

▼9 | ◀)) | Escuchar • Escribir

Escucha y escribe

Escucha y luego escribe en una hoja de papel lo que dice un joven sobre un programa de televisión que ve.

▼10 | 👥 | Escribir • Hablar

¿Qué programa ves tú?

1 Usa la descripción del programa de televisión de la Actividad 9 como modelo y escribe sobre un programa que tú ves. No debes nombrar el programa en la descripción.

2 Lee tu descripción a otros(as) estudiantes de la clase. Ellos deben identificar el programa que describes.

▼11 | 👥 | Escribir • Hablar

Mis actores y actrices favoritos

Haz una lista de tres actores o actrices que te gustan y los nombres de las películas en que trabajaron. Con otro(a) estudiante, habla de los actores y sus películas.

▶ Modelo

A —¿Quién es tu actor favorito?
B —Para mí el mejor actor es Rafael Montenegro. ¿Viste Cuando el amor llega?
A —Sí, creo que es un actor muy talentoso y la película es fascinante.
o: —No me gustan las películas románticas y tampoco me gusta este actor.

290 doscientos noventa
Tema 9 • Medios de comunicación

DIFFERENTIATED INSTRUCTION

Multiple Intelligences
Verbal/Linguistic: Have students write a movie review column for a newspaper. Have them use the questions in *Actividad* 12 to help them begin. If your school has a newspaper, you may want to submit some of the reviews to be published.

Heritage Language Learners
Have students write a movie critique about a film produced in their heritage country or a film featuring their favorite Spanish-speaking actor or actress.

▼12 | 🗣️👥 | ♻️ | Leer · Hablar

¿Qué dicen los críticos?

Lee el artículo de abajo que escribieron los críticos Guillo y Nadia. Luego trabaja con otro(a) estudiante para decidir qué película van a ver. Contesta las preguntas en la casilla.

¿Qué clase de película es?
¿De veras? ¿Cómo es?
¿Sí? ¿Qué pasa en la película?
¿Cuánto tiempo dura?
¿Quiénes son los actores principales?
Pues, ¿quieres verla?

Nota
Use *más/menos de* with numbers.
• más **de** tres horas
• menos **de** diez personas

 Modelo

A —*Acabo de leer un artículo sobre la película....*
¿Te gustaría verla?
B —*¿Qué clase de película es?*

En nuestra opinión

¿Piensas ir al cine este fin de semana? Guillo y Nadia te dan sus impresiones de tres nuevas películas . . .

★★★ recomendable
★★ más o menos
★ no la recomiendo

Guillo

Nadia

Cuando el amor llega Con Cristina Campos y Rafael Montenegro. Una película romántica sobre un joven rico enamorado de una chica pobre. Ante la oposición de sus padres, el amor de los jóvenes es imposible. Esta película, de dos horas y media, es similar a las viejas fórmulas de las telenovelas—un poco tonta y aburrida. Los protagonistas son buenos, pero los actores secundarios son demasiado dramáticos. Recomendable para personas que no tienen nada que hacer.(★)

Mis padres son de otro planeta Unos chicos descubren que sus padres son originarios de otra galaxia y que están en este planeta para explorar y planear una invasión. Una producción para toda la familia que combina elementos de comedia y ciencia ficción. Es tan fascinante y cómica que no puedes creer que estás en el cine por más de tres horas. Los actores principales, Javier Zaragoza y Miguel Vilar, son fantásticos. (★★★)

Mi perro es mi héroe Un drama para toda la familia—no es violenta y es bastante realista. Un poco infantil, pero con mucha acción y emoción. El mejor amigo del hombre, el perro, con inteligencia y valor, le salva la vida* a toda la familia. La película es divertida pero un poco corta (menos de dos horas). Tiene muy buenos actores, como Ana Jiménez y Antonio Barrera. Es una buena película. (★★★)

*saves the life

doscientos noventa y uno **291**
Capítulo 9A

Practice and Communicate 9A

▼12 Standards: 1.1, 1.2

Resources: Voc. and Gram. Transparency 164; Answer Keys: Student Edition, p. 179

Focus: Reading comprehension of movie reviews; asking questions in a personalized context

Recycle: Asking questions

Suggestions: Review question words with students. Remind them that all question words have accent marks. Point out that in questions, the subject often comes after the verb. You may want to use the transparency. Begin by asking students to predict what the article is about by reading the title and opening question. Direct students' attention to the ratings key. What do the stars indicate? Have students scan the article and tell you how many movies are reviewed and which one received the worst rating.

Students should take turns being Student A and Student B, switching roles after each movie. After talking about all three films, students should decide which movie they want to see.

Answers will vary but should include:

Cuando el amor llega: Es una película romántica; es sobre un joven rico enamorado de una chica pobre; el amor de los jóvenes es imposible; dura dos horas y media; los actores principales son Cristina Campos y Rafael Montenegro.

Mis padres son de otro planeta: Es una película de comedia y ciencia ficción; es fascinante y cómica; unos chicos descubren que sus padres son originarios de otro planeta; dura más de tres horas; los actores principales son Javier Zaragoza y Miguel Vilar.

Mi perro es mi héroe: Es un drama; no es violenta, es realista y divertida; el perro le salva la vida a toda la familia; dura menos de dos horas; los actores principales son Ana Jiménez y Antonio Barrera.

Pre-AP* Support

• **Learning Objective:** Interpersonal Writing
• **Activity 12:** Have students choose one of the three movies reviewed in the activity and, based on the information, draft an e-mail inviting a friend to watch it and describing it briefly. Conversely, have them use the information to write the e-mail to a friend describing how good (or bad!) the movie, which they have just seen, was.
• **Pre-AP* Resource Book:** Comprehensive guide to Pre-AP* writing skill development, pp. 27–38

ENRICH YOUR TEACHING

Culture Note

Argentina is known for producing several youth-oriented *telenovelas*, including *Chiquititas* ("Tiny Angels"), *Rebelde Way* ("Rebel's Way"), and *Patito Feo* ("Ugly Duckling"). All gained an international following. An interesting exercise for students might be to see if they can find video clips online by searching for "Chiquititas Episodes" or "Patito Feo." Have them choose a video they like and summarize it for the class. Were they able to guess what was happening in the episode they watched? Could they understand the Spanish? What words and phrases could they pick out?

13 Standards: 1.1, 1.3, 3.1

Focus: Using mathematics

Recycle: Numbers

Suggestions: Write an example of how to calculate an average. Remind students to save this information for *Actividad 14.*

Answers will vary.

Common Errors: Using the incorrect preterite forms of **ver.** Review the preterite of **ver** before beginning the *Actividad.*

14 Standards: 1.1, 1.2, 1.3, 3.1

Focus: Comparing, analyzing, and discussing information about average television-viewing habits

Suggestions: Before beginning the activity, direct students' attention to the transparency or the graph in the book. Tell students to look for cognates to understand words they don't know.

Write the formulas on the board and provide help as needed.

Answers will vary.

Extension: Ask students to calculate the percentage of time they spend watching specific types of television shows.

▼**13** | (Talk!) 👥 | ♻ | Pensar • Hablar • Escribir

¿Cuántas horas de tele?

Vas a calcular el promedio *(average)* de horas que tus compañeros ven la tele.

Conexiones | Las matemáticas

❶ Escribe el número de horas que viste la tele cada día de la semana pasada. Suma *(Add up)* estas horas. Calcula el promedio de horas para cada día.

_____ *(total de horas)* dividido por 7

❷ Trabaja con un grupo de cuatro personas. Pregunta a tus compañeros(as) el tiempo promedio que vieron la televisión cada día. Escribe la información que recibes de tu grupo.

▶ **Modelo**

A —*Como promedio, ¿cuántas horas viste la tele cada día?*

B —*La vi casi dos horas y media cada día.*

❸ Calcula el promedio de horas que tu grupo vio la tele cada día la semana pasada. Escribe una frase para presentar la información a la clase.

▼**14** | 👥 | Pensar • Leer • Hablar

La tele en tu vida

En un estudio reciente, se dio a conocer que, como promedio, las personas de los Estados Unidos ven ocho horas de tele al día. ¡La suma de estas horas equivale a casi cuatro meses al año frente a la televisión!

❶ Usa el promedio de horas de tu grupo de la Actividad 13 y calcula el número total de horas que vieron la tele en un año.

• 365 días al año por *(promedio de horas)* son *(total de horas)* al año.

❷ Usa el total de horas al año para contestar estas preguntas. *(Nota: Hay aproximadamente 720 horas en un mes.)*

Los principales países adictos a la pantalla chica

	2 h	4 h	6 h	8 h
Estados Unidos	8 horas y 11 minutos			
Turquía	5 horas y 1 minuto			
Italia	4 horas y 6 minutos			
Japón	3 horas y 43 minutos			
España	3 horas y 37 minutos			

Los cinco países que ven más televisión al día

Source: Organisation for Economic Co-Operation and Development

1. ¿Tu grupo ve la tele más de un mes al año o menos?

2. ¿La ven Uds. más que el promedio de personas en los Estados Unidos o menos? ¿Y de las personas en los otros países de la gráfica?

3. ¿Crees que las personas en los países de la gráfica ven demasiada tele? ¿Por qué?

DIFFERENTIATED INSTRUCTION

Heritage Language Learners

Have students listen to *Try it out!* and write the sentences they hear without looking at the book. Point out any spelling errors such as leaving out the initial **h** in a word.

Students with Learning Difficulties

To help students calculate averages for *Actividad* 13, create a worksheet for them. Be sure to include the formula and blank spaces for their personal responses. Allow students to use a calculator.

▼ Pronunciación 🔊 💬

Linking words

In Spanish just as in English, you don't pronounce a sentence as completely separate words. Instead, the words flow together in phrases. That is why it often seems that phrases or sentences sound as if they are one long word.

How the words flow together depends on the last sound of a word and the beginning sound of the following word. The flow of sounds is usually created by two of the same vowels, two different vowels, or a consonant followed by a vowel. Listen to and say these word combinations:

Me‿encanta	de‿entrevistas	le‿aburre
nos‿interesa	dibujos‿animados	de‿horror

Try it out! Listen to and say these sentences. Be careful not to break the flow of sound where you see "‿".

Me‿interesa‿ese programa de‿entrevistas.

A‿Ana le‿aburre‿ese programa‿educativo.

La película de‿horror dura‿una‿hora‿y media.

Vamos‿a ver lo que‿hay‿en la tele.

Me‿encanta‿el‿actor de‿esa telenovela.

▼ 15 💬 | Escribir • Hablar

Y tú, ¿qué dices?

1. ¿Qué piensas de los programas de entrevistas? ¿Y de los programas de la vida real?

2. En tu opinión, ¿cómo son los programas policíacos que dan en la televisión? ¿Cómo son las telenovelas?

3. ¿Te interesan o te aburren las películas románticas? ¿Y las películas de ciencia ficción? ¿Por qué?

4. ¿Qué dicen tus amigos y tú sobre las películas de horror? ¿Las ven Uds. a menudo?

doscientos noventa y tres **293**
Capítulo 9A

Pronunciación
Core Instruction

Standards: 4.1

Resources: Teacher's Resource Book: Audio Script, p. 311; Audio Program DVD: Cap. 9A, Track 8

Suggestions: Have students provide examples in English in which their words flow together. Remind students that the **h** in Spanish is silent. Have students practice reading the sentences and tape their final version.

▼ 15 Standards: 1.1, 1.3

Focus: Writing and talking about movies and television shows in a personalized context

Suggestions: Have students work in pairs and interview each other using the questions.

Extension: Use these questions as a starting point for a class survey on which movies and television shows are popular among students.

Answers will vary.

Additional Resources
- Communication Wbk.: Audio Act. 6, p. 86
- Teacher's Resource Book: Audio Script, pp. 311–312, Communicative Pair Activity BLM, pp. 316–317
- Audio Program DVD: Cap. 9A, Track 10

ENRICH YOUR TEACHING

Teacher-to-Teacher

Have the class create a bar graph. Tell them to number one axis from 1 to 24 and to write activities such as **hacer la tarea, comer la cena, practicar deportes,** and **dormir** on the other axis. Have students complete the graph to show how many hours a day they do each activity.

Ask students to compare the time they spend watching television with the time they spend on other activities. When students have completed their graphs, have them calculate the class average.

✓ASSESSMENT

Prueba 9A-2 with Study Plan (online only)

Quiz: Vocabulary Production
- Prueba 9A-2: pp. 231–232

Gramática

Core Instruction

Standards: 1.3

Resources: Teacher's Resource Book: Video Script, p. 314; Video Program: Cap. 9A

INTERACTIVE WHITEBOARD
Grammar Activities 9A

Suggestions: Point out that just as students used the present tense of *ir + a + infinitive* to indicate an action taking place in the future, they can use the present tense of *acabar de + infinitive* to indicate an action that recently took place. You may want to use the *GramActiva* Video to introduce the structure or as a follow-up to your presentation.

16 Standards: 1.3

Resources: Answer Keys: Student Edition, p. 180

Focus: Writing sentences about recently performed activities

Recycle: Household chores and leisure activities

Suggestions: Remind students that in order to write a complete sentence they need to capitalize the first word of the sentence and provide punctuation.

Answers:
1. Mamá acaba de preparar el desayuno para sus hijos.
2. Carlitos acaba de comer el desayuno.
3. Mariel acaba de limpiar su dormitorio.
4. Ezequiel acaba de sacar la basura.
5. Ezequiel, Carlitos y Mariel acaban de terminar su tarea.
6. Papá acaba de pasar la aspiradora en la sala.
7. Elena acaba de dar de comer al gato.
8. Todos acaban de buscar sus abrigos.

Fondo cultural

Standards: 2.1, 2.2

Suggestions: Point out that *Sábado Gigante* incorporates a variety of different programming in one show. Ask students to name the different kinds of programming included in the show and have them give examples of other variety shows in the United States. Explain that *Sábado Gigante* has aired on *Univisión* since 1986.

Answers will vary.

294

Gramática

Acabar de + infinitive

When you want to say that something just happened, use the present tense of *acabar de* + infinitive.

Acabo de ver un programa musical.	*I just saw a music program.*
Mis padres **acaban de ir** al cine.	*My parents just went to the movies.*
Acabamos de hablar de esa película.	*We just talked about that movie.*

Although the action took place in the past, the present-tense forms of *acabar* are used.

Más ayuda	**realidades.com**

 GramActiva Video Tutorial: *Acabar de + infinitive*

GramActiva Activity

▼16 | ♻ | Escribir

¡Acaban de hacer muchas cosas!

La familia Martínez acaba de hacer muchas cosas esta mañana antes de ir a estudiar y trabajar. Lee la lista y escribe quién acaba de hacer qué cosa.

Modelo
mamá/preparar el desayuno para sus hijos
Mamá <u>acaba de preparar</u> el desayuno para sus hijos.

Quehaceres ...

1. mamá/ preparar el desayuno de sus hijos ✓
2. Carlitos / comer el desayuno ✓
3. Mariel / limpiar su dormitorio ✓
4. Ezequiel / sacar la basura ✓
5. Ezequiel, Carlitos y Mariel / terminar su tarea ✓
6. papá/ pasar la aspiradora en la sala ✓
7. Elena / dar de comer al gato ✓
8. todos / buscar sus abrigos ✓

▼ **Fondo Cultural** | El mundo hispano

Sábado Gigante is one of the longest-running shows in television history. Its host, Don Francisco, started the variety program in Chile in 1962. It now airs from Miami every Saturday night and brings comedy, celebrity guests, musical performances, games, and contests to more than 100 million viewers in 42 countries. In the past decade, the program has celebrated its 1000th episode and 20th anniversary on the Miami-based Univisión network.

El famosísimo Don Francisco

DIFFERENTIATED INSTRUCTION

Multiple Intelligences

Verbal/Linguistic: Ask students to write three sentences about what they just did in their last class. Have them read their sentences aloud while other students try to guess which class is being described.

Heritage Language Learners

Ask students if they, or anyone they know, watches *Sábado Gigante*. What is their opinion of the show? If Spanish-language programming is available in your area, ask students to watch *Sábado Gigante* or a similar program in Spanish and write a short description of the show.

▾17 | 👥 | ♻ | Escribir · Hablar

Acabo de ver...

1 Copia la gráfica en una hoja de papel. Escribe los títulos de tres programas de televisión, obras de teatro o películas que acabas de ver. Da el nombre y haz una descripción.

¿Recuerdas?
Some adverbs you can use in descriptions are:
bastante   muy
demasiado   un poco

Acabo de ver...	Nombre	Descripción
una película romántica	¡No puedo vivir sin ti!	demasiado triste

2 Trabaja con otro(a) estudiante para hablar sobre lo que acaban de ver.

▶ Modelo
A —Acabo de ver *una película romántica*.
B —¿De veras? ¿Cómo se llama?
A —¡No puedo vivir sin ti!
B —¿Te gustó?
A —No, no me gustó porque es *demasiado triste*.

Más práctica GO

realidades.com | print

Instant Check	✔	
Guided WB pp. 137–138	✔	✔
Core WB p. 77	✔	✔
Comm. WB pp. 87, 90	✔	✔
Hispanohablantes WB pp. 334–337, 341	✔	

🌎 Exploración del lenguaje

Words of Greek and Arabic origin

Languages change when regions and nations interact with, or are conquered or colonized by, people who speak a different language. Long before the Romans brought Latin to Spain, certain Greek words had entered the Latin language. Words such as *el problema, el programa,* and *el drama* originally were masculine nouns in Greek. When they came into Latin and then Spanish, they kept their masculine gender even though they end in *a*.

Try it out! Which of these new words would you use in the following sentences?

el clima   el sistema   el poema

1. No comprendo ____ de clasificación de películas en ese país.
2. Me gustaría visitar Panamá porque ____ allí es tropical.
3. Me gusta ____ que acabo de leer.

España   Italia   Grecia
DRAMA   AZÚCAR   DRAMA

Arabic also had a large influence on Spanish. Around A.D. 700, the Arabic-speaking Moors invaded Spain from northern Africa. They ruled for 800 years and played a major role in the development of the Spanish language and culture. Words that came from Arabic often begin with the letters *al-*. Many words in Spanish that have a *z* or a *j* in them are also of Arabic origin. You know these words that came from Arabic: *alfombra, azúcar, naranja.*

Try it out! You also know these words that are from Arabic. On your paper, fill in the missing letters.

a__ul   ___macén   ___anahoria

doscientos noventa y cinco **295**
Capítulo 9A

ENRICH YOUR TEACHING

Culture Note
Spanish has also been influenced by indigenous cultures in North America, South America, Central America, and the Caribbean. For example, the words **chocolate, aguacate,** and **tomate** come from Náhuatl while **papa** is from Quechua. The word **huracán** is borrowed from Taino.

Teacher-to-Teacher
Have students look up Spanish-language television stations in their area, and list and describe the programs. Ask if the station carries *Sábado Gigante.*

BELLRINGER REVIEW
Give students two words and have them tell you the type of movie or television show you are describing. For example you say: *triste/novios* and the students respond: *una película romántica.*

▾17 Standards: 1.1, 1.3
Focus: Describing movies and television shows; using *acabar de* + infinitive
Recycle: Adverbs
Suggestions: Direct students' attention to the ¿*Recuerdas?*. Explain that adverbs describe verbs or adjectives and therefore do not agree in number or gender.
Answers will vary.

Exploración del lenguaje
Core Instruction
Standards: 4.1
Resources: Answer Keys: Student Edition, p. 180
🌎 **Mapa global interactivo, Actividad** Discover Andalusia and Granada.
Suggestions: Refer students to an atlas so they can identify Spain, Italy, and Greece. Point out that modern-day maps do not reflect the time periods in the reading.
Answers: 1. el sistema 2. el clima 3. el poema azul; almacén; zanahoria

Theme Project
Give students copies of the Theme Project outline and rubric from the *Teacher's Resource Book.* Have them perform Step 1. (For more information, see p. 280-b.)

Additional Resources
• Communication Wbk.: Audio Act. 7, p. 87
• Teacher's Resource Book: Audio Script, p. 312
• Audio Program DVD: Cap. 9A, Track 11

✔ASSESSMENT
Prueba 9A-3 with Study Plan (online only)
Quiz: *Acabar de* + Infinitive
• Prueba 9A-3: p. 233

Gramática

Core Instruction

Standards: 4.1

Resources: Teacher's Resource Book: Video Script, pp. 314–315; Video Program: Cap. 9A

INTERACTIVE WHITEBOARD
Grammar Activities 9A

Suggestions: Review the indirect object pronouns and objects of prepositions with students. Point out that **mí** and **ti** follow a preposition, not **yo** and **tú.** Play the *GramActiva* Video as reinforcement.

BELLRINGER REVIEW

Show Voc. and Gram. Transparency 160. As you point to different types of movies, ask students to respond to whether they like or don't like each type.

▼18 Standards: 1.2, 1.3

Resources: Teacher's Resource Book: Audio Script, p. 312; Audio Program DVD: Cap. 9A, Track 12; Answer Keys: Student Edition, p. 181

Focus: Listening to opinions; writing with accuracy

Suggestions: Ask students what programs their family members typically like to watch. Play the audio or read the script aloud.

◀))) Script and Answers:

1. A mi hermana le encantan las telenovelas.
2. A mis padres no les gustan nada los programas de la vida real.
3. A nosotros nos interesan mucho los programas deportivos.
4. A mí me aburren los programas de entrevistas.
5. A mi hermanito le interesan los programas educativos sobre los animales.
6. A ti te gustan los programas musicales, ¿no?

Teacher-to-Teacher

Ask your local library to set aside for you magazines it no longer needs. You can use them to illustrate vocabulary, elicit descriptions, and encourage conversation. For example, have students work in groups and look through magazines to find three photos they could write captions for, using **doler, faltar,** and **quedar.**

296

Manos a la obra

Gramática Repaso

▼ Objectives

▶ Listen to a family's comments about programs
▶ Discuss and write opinions about television and movies
▶ Create an ideal television programming schedule

Gustar and similar verbs

Even though we usually translate the verb *gustar* as "to like," it literally means "to please." So when you say, *Me gustan los programas deportivos,* you're actually saying, "Sports programs are pleasing to me." *Programas deportivos* is the subject of the sentence, and *me* is the indirect object. Here's the pattern:

indirect object + form of *gustar* + subject

The subject in a sentence with *gustar* usually follows the verb. You need to know if the subject is singular or plural to know which form of *gustar* to use. If the subject is singular, use *gusta.* If it's plural, use *gustan.* If it's an infinitive, use *gusta.*

Me gusta **el actor** en la telenovela pero no me gustan **las actrices.**

A mis amigos les gusta **ver** películas.

To emphasize or clarify *who* is pleased, you can use an additional *a* + pronoun:

A mí me gustan los dibujos animados, pero a él no le gustan.

Here are the other verbs you know that are similar to *gustar:*

aburrir	A mí **me aburren** las películas románticas.
doler *(o→ue)*	A Fernando **le duelen** los pies.
encantar	A mis padres **les encanta** el teatro.
faltar	**Me faltan** un cuchillo y un tenedor.
interesar	**Nos interesan** mucho los programas musicales.
quedar	¿No te queda bien el vestido?

> **¿Recuerdas?**
>
> You have used *me gusta(n), te gusta(n),* and *le gusta(n)* to talk about what a person likes.
>
> • A mí **me gusta** el cine pero a mi hermano **le gusta** más la televisión.

> **Más ayuda** | **realidades.com**
>
> ▶ *GramActiva* Video **Tutorial:** *Gustar* and similar verbs
>
> ◀))) *Canción de hip hop:* ¿Qué te interesa?
>
> ✎ *GramActiva* Activity

▼18 | ◀))) | Escuchar • Escribir

Escucha y escribe

Escucha las opiniones de la familia Linares sobre los programas que dan en la televisión. En una hoja de papel, escribe los números del 1 al 6 y escribe las frases que escuchas.

Nos gustan las películas cómicas.

296 **doscientos noventa y seis**
Tema 9 • Medios de comunicación

DIFFERENTIATED INSTRUCTION

Heritage Language Learners

Ask students if they have a favorite soccer team from their heritage country. Have them write a short paragraph expressing their opinions about soccer and the World Cup. Encourage them to use the phrases **me aburre, me interesa, me gusta,** and **me encanta.**

▼**19** | 🔊👥 | Escribir · Hablar

A mí y a ti

❶ Trabaja con otro(a) estudiante. Copia el diagrama Venn en una hoja de papel. Escribe el nombre de tu compañero(a) encima del óvalo a la derecha. En el óvalo indicado con *A mí* escribe cinco clases de películas o programas de televisión que te gustan.

❷ Pregunta a tu compañero(a) si le gustan las clases de programas y películas que tú escribiste. Si a él o a ella le gusta la clase de programa o película, escribe el nombre en el óvalo de la derecha. (Vas a usar el diagrama Venn en la Actividad 20.)

Modelo

A mí   A nosotros   A Rosa

los programas policíacos

las películas de horror

las películas de horror

▶️ **Modelo**

A —*¿Te gustan los programas policíacos?*
B —*A ver . . . no, no me gustan mucho.*
A —*Pues, ¿te gustan las películas de horror?*
B —*Sí, me gustan mucho.*

▼**20** Escribir

A nosotros nos gusta . . .

Compara los dos lados de tu diagrama. Escribe las clases de programas y películas que a los dos les gustan en el centro de ese diagrama. Escribe al menos cinco frases completas para describir qué les gusta a Uds.

Modelo

A nosotros nos gustan las películas de horror.
A mí me gustan los programas policíacos pero a Rosa no le gustan.

Modelo

A mí   A nosotros   A Rosa

los programas policíacos

las películas de horror

las películas de horror

las películas de horror

▼ **Fondo Cultural** | El mundo hispano

La televisión The cable and satellite television industry in Latin America has grown tremendously. Hundreds of channels are available to viewers. Some cable channels specialize in news or sports, and offer their programming to other countries as well. Among the sports, soccer is the one that attracts the most viewers. The World Cup is enormously popular in Latin America and around the world.

• What Latin American programs can you find in your local cable or satellite listings? Watch some of them to see what countries the shows are produced in.

doscientos noventa y siete **297**
Capítulo 9A

21
Standards: 1.1, 1.3

Focus: Practicing with verbs similar to *gustar*

Recycle: Leisure activities

Suggestions: Before beginning the activity, brainstorm examples of things that might interest or bore students. Encourage students to use vocabulary from previous chapters as well as from this chapter.

Answers will vary.

El español en la comunidad

Core Instruction

Standards: 5.1

Suggestions: Arrange for students to view a portion of a Spanish-language television show in class. Point out to students that some Spanish speakers may be easier to understand than others. Ask students if they know anyone who speaks English so quickly that it is hard to understand them.

Answers will vary.

Extension: Have students write a short description of a show they watch on Spanish-language television.

Theme Project
Students can perform Step 2 at this point. Be sure students understand your corrections and suggestions. (For more information, see p. 280-b.)

▼ 21 | 👥 | ♻ | **Escribir • Hablar • GramActiva**

Juego

1 Copia esta tabla en una hoja de papel. Escribe siete cosas que te interesan y siete cosas que te aburren. Puedes escribir los nombres de actores, películas, música, programas de televisión, actividades, etc.

2 Con tu lista en la mano, pregúntales a tus compañeros de clase si les interesan o les aburren las mismas que a ti. Si un(a) estudiante responde *sí*, escribe su nombre a lado de esa cosa en tu lista, si responde *no*, tienes que preguntarle a otro(a) estudiante. La primera persona que tiene un nombre diferente al lado de cada cosa en su lista gana *(wins)*.

Cosas que me interesan	Cosas que me aburren
1. los programas de concursos Jaime	1. las telenovelas Ana
2.	2.
3.	3.
4.	4.
5.	5.

El español en la comunidad

While many television networks are losing viewers, the number of viewers watching Spanish-language networks is growing. Choose a Spanish-language network such as *Univisión, Telemundo, Azteca América,* or *Telefutura* and look online at their program listings. Find the name of a program for each kind of show on p. 282. Watch a few minutes of one of the programs. Although you might find it difficult to understand, tune in from time to time. You'll be amazed at how much you'll learn!

• How are the listings similar to or different from those for the networks you usually watch? Write your impressions of the television show you watched.

DIFFERENTIATED INSTRUCTION

Advanced Learners
If your students have access to ePals in Spanish-speaking countries, have them do a variation of *Actividad* 21, asking their ePals to list the type of television programs they like and don't like. If possible, have them interview three ePals from three different countries. Have students make posters to present their results to the class.

▼22 | 👥 | ♻ | Escribir • Hablar

¿Qué hay en la tele?

A veces decimos, "¡Hay tantos canales y programas en la tele pero no hay nada interesante!" Ahora tienes la oportunidad de planear seis horas de televisión para el sábado, desde las 17.00 horas hasta las 23.00 horas, para un concurso que se llama "Tus propias seis horas en la tele".

1 Trabaja con un grupo de tres. Escriban una lista de programas o películas que les gustaría incluir *(to include)* en las seis horas. Den esta información para cada programa o película:

- la clase de programa
- cuánto tiempo dura
- el nombre
- para quiénes es recomendable
- cómo es
- por qué le va a interesar al público

2 Preparen una presentación para la clase. Pueden hacer algo visual para acompañar su presentación.

3 Después de escuchar a los diferentes grupos, cada grupo va a votar por la mejor presentación. ¡No pueden votar por la suya *(your own)*! Los grupos tienen que escribir cuatro frases para explicar su decisión. El grupo que recibe más votos gana *(wins)* el concurso.

Modelo

Nosotros votamos por la presentación del grupo de Ana, David y Laura. Tienen muchos programas que nos interesan a nosotros.

▼23 | 💬 | Escribir • Hablar

Y tú, ¿qué dices?

1. En tu familia, ¿a quién le interesan más las películas de horror? ¿Los dramas? ¿Las comedias?

2. ¿Qué programas de televisión te aburren? ¿Por qué?

3. ¿Qué programas de televisión te encantan? ¿Por qué?

4. ¿A cuáles de tus amigos les gusta ir al cine? ¿Qué tipo de películas les gusta ver?

5. ¿A cuáles de tus amigos no les gusta nada ir al cine? ¿Por qué?

Más práctica	GO
realidades.com | print	

Instant Check	✔	
Guided WB pp. 139–140	✔	✔
Core WB pp. 78–79	✔	✔
Comm. WB pp. 87–88, 91, 181	✔	✔
Hispanohablantes WB pp. 338–341		✔

doscientos noventa y nueve **299**
Capítulo 9A

---

22 Standards: 1.1, 1.2, 1.3

Focus: Describing television shows and movies as a group project

Recycle: Adverbs and adjectives

Suggestions: Have students prepare Step 1 in class. Tell them to decide who will present each television show and have them prepare their presentations for homework. Set aside time before beginning the presentations for students to finalize their projects as a group.

After each presentation, give students the opportunity to ask questions.

Answers will vary.

Pre-AP* Support

- **Learning Objective:** Presentational Writing
- **Activity 22:** Have students write a brief paragraph defending their choice of programming for *"Tus propias seis horas en la tele."* Where did group members agree? Where was there lack of agreement?
- *Pre-AP* Resource Book:* Comprehensive guide to Pre-AP* writing skill development, pp. 27–38

23 Standards: 1.1, 1.3

Focus: Writing and talking about television shows and movies in a personalized context

Suggestions: Point out to students that just as they use *a* + pronoun with *gustar* to clarify who is pleased, *a* is used with the question words *quién* and *cuál(es)* when asking a question using *gustar*.

Answers will vary.

Additional Resources

- Communication Wbk.: Audio Act. 8–9, pp. 87–88
- Teacher's Resource Book: Audio Script, pp. 312–313, Communicative Pair Activity BLM, pp. 318–319
- Audio Program DVD: Cap. 9A, Tracks 13–14

✔ASSESSMENT

Prueba 9A-4 with Study Plan (online only)

Quiz: *Gustar* and similar verbs
- Prueba 9A-4: p. 234

ENRICH YOUR TEACHING

Culture Note

Spanish-speaking countries often consider it important to have a mixture of local and foreign television programming. This allows each country's citizens to experience things such as foreign films while preserving their country's national and cultural identity. Ask students if they think this is a good idea. Also ask how they feel television can influence a culture.

Advanced Learners/Pre-AP*

Have students make crossword puzzles using media-related vocabulary. Have them give the clues using the vocabulary from this chapter. Tell them to use *horizontal* and *vertical* for "across" and "down." Make copies of students' crossword puzzles and distribute them as a vocabulary review.

Lectura

Core Instruction

Standards: 1.2, 1.3

Focus: Reading for comprehension and cultural perspectives

Suggestions:

Pre-reading: Direct students' attention to the *Strategy*. Remind them that they use this strategy when they read in English. Have them look at the title and the photos and predict what the reading is about.

Reading: Have students read the text without stopping and ask them to write a short summary of the reading. After they finish the summary, have them read the text a second time and tell them to make a list of the words that they do not know. Have them use a Spanish-English dictionary to figure out the meaning of the words. Tell students to read the *Lectura* a third time, using their list of defined words, and have them check the accuracy of their summary.

Post-reading: Have students write a list of reasons why watching too much television is not healthy. Tell them to base their list on the *Lectura*. Ask them to tell whether they agree or disagree.

BELLRINGER REVIEW

Have students work in pairs to brainstorm and write three activities that are good for your health that they would be able to do outside. Share with the class.

Pre-AP* Support

• **Learning Objective:** Interpretive: Print and Audio
• **Activity:** As a pre-reading activity, divide the article into two parts—the first two paragraphs and the last three paragraphs. Divide the class in half and give each group one of the reading sections. Have them read their section and then write two multiple-choice questions for the segment they were assigned. Collect the questions and redistribute them to the opposite group of students. Ask them to read the questions that they received. Next, read aloud each segment. The students with the multiple-choice questions listen for the correct answers, while the students who wrote the questions follow along with the article as it is being read.
• **Pre-AP* Resource Book:** Comprehensive guide to Pre-AP* reading skill development, pp. 19–26

▼ Objectives
▶ Read about TV-watching habits of teens
▶ Read without stopping to understand unknown words

Lectura

Una semana sin televisión

Strategy

Reading for comprehension
You don't need to understand every word in a reading to comprehend the key information. Try reading without stopping at unknown words. Then go back and decide if the words are important to the reading, and see if you can guess their meanings.

¿Sabes que los niños estadounidenses pasan más horas al año pegados a la pantalla de su televisión que haciendo cualquier otra cosa, a excepción de dormir?

Hay estudios que dicen que ver demasiado la televisión puede causar malos hábitos de comida, falta de ejercicio y obesidad. En cuatro horas de dibujos animados el sábado por la mañana los niños pueden ver 202 anuncios sobre refrescos, dulces y cereales azucarados. Esta comida combinada con las horas frente a la pantalla resulta en que uno de cada seis niños estadounidenses tenga exceso de peso.

También hay estudios que dan nuevas pruebas de la relación entre la televisión y la violencia. Uno de estos estudios indica que niños que ven más de una hora de televisión al día tienen más probabilidad de ser violentos y agresivos de adultos.

Used with permission from TIME FOR KIDS magazine.

(300) trescientos
Tema 9 • Medios de comunicación

DIFFERENTIATED INSTRUCTION

Multiple Intelligences

Interpersonal/Social: Have students create a flier for a *semana sin televisión* campaign. Ask them to try to convince students in Spanish classes at your school to pledge to refrain from television for a week. Ask students who make the pledge to keep a journal of the activities that they do to replace watching television.

Heritage Language Learners

Have students interview family members or friends who speak Spanish and ask them what interesting activities they can do to replace watching television. Ask them to write a report quoting each person they interviewed.

¿Quieres participar en una solución? Durante el mes de abril millones de personas en más de treinta países apagan la tele por una semana. En vez de ver la tele los participantes van con sus familias o con amigos al campo, o a caminar, montar en bicicleta o visitar un parque.

¿Y qué pasa después de unos días sin televisión? Una niña de diez años dice: —¿Para qué necesito la tele? Hay muchas cosas más interesantes que puedo hacer.

¿Comprendes?

Prepara información para un debate sobre la cuestión: ¿Es bueno o malo ver la televisión?

1. Escribe una lista de cuatro razones *(reasons)* a favor de no ver la tele. Usa información que leíste en el artículo.

2. Escribe una lista de cuatro razones a favor de ver la tele.

Y tú, ¿qué dices?

1. Usa la información en tu lista para expresar tu opinión: ¿Es bueno o malo ver la televisión? ¿Por qué?

2. Para ti, ¿va a ser fácil o difícil pasar una semana sin ver la televisión? ¿Por qué?

3. En Chile, a una persona que ve mucha televisión se le llama "un(a) tevito(a)". ¿Qué puedes decirle a un(a) tevito(a) para persuadirlo(a) a hacer otras cosas que son mejores para la salud?

Más práctica GO

realidades.com | print

Guided WB p. 141	✔	✔
Comm. WB pp. 92, 182	✔	✔
***Hispanohablantes* WB** pp. 342–343		✔
Cultural Reading Activity		✔

trescientos uno **301**
Capítulo 9A

▼ **¿Comprendes?** Standards: 1.2, 1.3
Focus: Demonstrating reading comprehension
Suggestions: Before students answer the questions, brainstorm a list of reasons for and against watching television.
Answers will vary but may include:
1. Puede causar malos hábitos de comida, falta de ejercicio, obesidad y violencia. Uno puede hacer muchas cosas más interesantes.
2. Answers will vary.
Y tú, ¿qué dices?: Answers will vary.
Extension: Arrange desks in a way that facilitates holding a debate. Divide students into two groups: those who support watching television and those who are against it. Have students use information from the reading and their notes to defend their positions.

For Further Reading
Student Resource: Realidades para hispanohablantes: Lectura 2, pp. 344–345

ENRICH YOUR TEACHING

Teacher-to-Teacher
Ask students to verify the information in the reading by watching an hour of cartoons on television and reporting on the commercials that are shown. Tell them to write the names of the cartoon(s) and to keep a log of the advertisements. Have them include the name of each product, the kind of product being advertised, for example, **cereales, juguetes, dulces,** and so forth, and the length of each commercial. Ask them to write their opinion about whether or not the ads could cause bad habits among or otherwise negatively influence young viewers.

La cultura en vivo

Standards: 4.1

Focus: Reading about using gestures to communicate

Suggestions: Before beginning the activity, talk about body language and gestures to make sure students know what they are. Demonstrate some simple gestures, such as nodding your head, shaking your head, and waving your hand; ask students to say what they mean. Explain that all cultures use gestures, but that all gestures do not mean the same thing in every culture. It is important to find out what gestures mean in other cultures before doing them. They could have rude meanings.

Direct students' attention to the photos. Ask which, if any, of the gestures mean the same as in the United States.

Have students work in pairs to practice the gestures. Keep the focus on positive, pleasant gestures. Ask pairs of students to present their skits to the class.

Direct attention to the *Think about it!* and have students discuss the questions.

Answers will vary.

Additional Resources

Student Resource: Realidades para hispanohablantes, p. 346

¡Adelante!

La cultura en vivo

Comunicación sin palabras

Every culture has gestures that communicate a message. You've already seen gestures for *¡ojo!* and *más o menos*. Here are a few more gestures used in many Spanish-speaking countries to communicate a message.

¡Hay mucha gente en la fiesta!

(Place your fingertips together, then open your hand. Repeat this motion in a rhythmic gesture.)

mucha gente

Por favor, un poquito de postre.

un poco

¡Vamos a comer!

(With your fingertips bunched, bring your hand up close to your mouth, then extend it forward, bending your arm at the elbow. Repeat the motion two or three times.)

¡a comer!

¡Este plato está muy rico!

(Kiss the bunched fingertips of one hand, then quickly pull your hand away, extending your fingers.)

¡qué rico!

No sé dónde está el libro.

no sé

No tengo nada.

nada

Try it out! Work with a partner and create a short skit in which you use one of these gestures. Present it for the class.

Think about it! What gestures do you use most often? Do you ever use gestures that are the same as or similar to the ones shown on this page? Do you think you would understand some of the gestures on this page even without explanation?

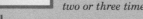

DIFFERENTIATED INSTRUCTION

Advanced Learners
Students may pick these gestures up quickly. If so, have them research additional gestures used in a Spanish-speaking country of their choice. Gestures may be found on the Internet under the category of "body language."

Heritage Language Learners
Ask students if they are familiar with these gestures. Allow them to present a short skit to the class using a socially acceptable gesture from their heritage countries that is not included in *La cultura en vivo*. Be sure to pre-approve the gestures.

Presentación oral

¿Qué dan esta semana?

Task
You are reviewing a movie or television show you have just seen for your school's closed-circuit TV system. Prepare a summary of the movie or show.

① **Prepare** Choose a movie or TV show, then download or cut out ads or photos about it. Copy the chart below and provide the information for the movie or show you have chosen.

Nombre		Cómo es	
Clase de película o programa		Cuánto tiempo dura	
Actor/actores		Para quiénes es	
Actriz/actrices		Tus impresiones	

Strategy

Using charts
Create a chart to help you think through the key information you will want to talk about. This will help you speak more effectively.

② **Practice** Use your notes from the chart for your presentation. Create a poster with the visuals you have collected. Go through your presentation several times. You may use your notes in practice, but not when you present. Try to:

• provide all key information about the film or show
• use complete sentences in your presentation
• speak clearly

③ **Present** Present your chosen movie or television show to a small group or the class. Use your poster to help guide you.

④ **Evaluation** The following rubric will be used to grade your presentation.

Rubric	Score 1	Score 3	Score 5
Completeness of presentation	Your only visual on the poster is the title.	You included the title and one visual on the poster, in color.	You include the title plus two or more visuals on the poster, in color.
Amount of information you communicate	You only include the movie or TV show and actors.	You provide descriptions of the movie or TV show plus actors.	You provide elements shown to the left, plus personal impressions.
How easily you are understood	You are extremely difficult to understand. Your teacher could only recognize isolated words and phrases.	You are understandable, but with frequent errors in vocabulary and/or grammar that hinder your comprehensibility.	You are easily understood. Your teacher does not have to "decode" what you are trying to say.

trescientos tres **303**
Capítulo 9A

Presentación oral

Core Instruction
Standards: 1.3

Resources: Voc. and Gram. Transparency 165; Teacher's Resource Book: GramActiva BLM, p. 321

Focus: Presenting a review of a movie or television show

Suggestions: Review the task and steps with students. After reading the *Strategy*, point out the chart in Step 1 and explain to students how to use it to organize information. Help students understand the chart by choosing a movie or television show that they are familiar with and brainstorm answers for each category. Review the rubric with the class to explain how you will grade the performance task.

Pre-AP* Support

• **Learning Objective:** Presentational Speaking
• **Activity:** Remind students to focus on the presentational speaking skills used in this task such as fluency, pronunciation, and comprehensibility.
• *Pre-AP* Resource Book:* Comprehensive guide to Pre-AP* speaking skill development, pp. 39–50

Portfolio
Make video or audio recordings of student presentations in class, or assign the RealTalk activity so they can record their presentations online. Include the recording in their portfolios.

Additional Resources
Student Resources: Realidades para hispanohablantes, p. 347; Guided Practice: Presentación oral, p. 142

ENRICH YOUR TEACHING

Teacher-to-Teacher
e-amigos: Ask students to write their *e-amigos* about their favorite television show. Have them base their exchanges on their *Presentación oral* summaries. Have them print out or e-mail you their questions and answers.

21st Century Skills

Creativity and Innovation Have students play the role of an agent, pitching the show to a group of investors. They can make a traditional or an electronic presentation of the show, using either print, or digital materials. Part of the presentation should be to explain why the show is so good and why the investors should choose it.

✓ ASSESSMENT

Presentación oral
• Assessment Program: Rubrics, p. T33
Go over the descriptions of the different levels of performance. After assessing students, help individuals understand how their performance could be improved.

Videomisterio ▷◀

Core Instruction

Standards: 1.2, 4.1, 5.2

Resources: Teacher's Resource Book: Video Script, p. 315; Video Program: Cap. 9A; Video Program Teacher's Guide: Cap. 9A

Focus: Introducing the events and characters of this episode

Personajes importantes:

Lola Lago, detective
Paco, Lola Lago's colleague
Margarita, Lola Lago's secretary
Julia Romero, María's friend
Inspector Gil, police officer

Synopsis: Lola calls her office to ask Margarita and Paco to help her follow two people. Margarita overhears that the person Lola thinks is María is really Julia. When the two strangers leave, Paco follows them to the train station. Then, Lola calls Inspector Gil to to ask him to meet her at the train station right away.

Suggestions:

Pre-viewing: Review with students the events of the previous episode. Pedro and Lola discuss the clues that they have so far. They do not know where María may be, but now they know that she went to Julia Romero's apartment. Lola sees María in front of doña Gracia's apartment. Lola calls Inspector Gil to let him know that she has seen María.

Point out the *Nota gramatical.* Direct students' attention to *Palabras para comprender* and give them examples in context. Remind students to use these words to help them understand the episode.

Visual scanning: Direct students' attention to the picture and ask who each of the characters is. Before students read the *Resumen del episodio,* have them scan the text and find three cognates. For example, *café, talentos, detective, evidente,* and *misterioso.*

Extension: Ask students to prepare questions about the reading. Have them work in pairs and ask the questions in a trivia game show format. Have them ask *who, what, when, where,* and *why* questions.

¿Eres tú, María?

Episodio 9

Antes de ver el video

"Paco, te digo que te necesito ahora mismo. Por favor, rápido. Y a Margarita, también."

Nota gramatical What's a good mystery without an expression like "Follow her!"? In this episode you'll hear several uses of the verb *seguir* ("to follow," "to continue").

sigo	seguimos
sigues	seguís
sigue	siguen

Resumen del episodio

Al día siguiente Lola va a su trabajo, cuando ve a María. ¡Qué suerte! Lola la sigue y llama a Paco y a Margarita. Ella necesita a los dos ahora mismo para ayudarla. Vigilan[1] a María y a un hombre en el café, y Margarita muestra[2] sus talentos de detective. Es evidente que María y el hombre no están nada contentos. Pero, ¿quién es este hombre misterioso y por qué quiere irse de Madrid?

[1] They watch   [2] shows

Palabras para comprender

¡Venid!	Come!
ve a sentarte	go sit
aparece	appears
quiere irse	wants to go away
vengan en seguida	come right away
sigue vigilando	continue watching

DIFFERENTIATED INSTRUCTION

Advanced Learners

Have students read the captions under each of the photos and continue the conversations based on what they know so far about the *Videomisterio.* Have students work in pairs to practice their dialogues. Call on volunteers to present their dialogues to the class.

Heritage Language Learners

Point out the *vosotros(as)* command forms of the verb *venir.* Explain that these are used when talking to a group of people whom individually you would address as *tú.* Ask students to compare the *vosotros(as)* command forms with what is used in their heritage countries.

—¡Ay de mí!
—Cálmate, Lola.

"Lola, ¿quién es ese hombre? ¿De qué están hablando?"

★ Madrid   • Barcelona

"Ahora lo comprendo todo. Voy a llamar al Inspector Gil."

Después de ver el video

¿Comprendes?

A. Contesta las preguntas.

1. ¿Quiénes ayudan a Lola con la investigación?

2. ¿Quién va al café para escuchar a María y al hombre?

3. ¿Está Lola tranquila o nerviosa? ¿Por qué?

4. Según Lola, ¿quién es el hombre en el café?

5. Según Margarita, ¿quién es la chica en el café?

6. Según Margarita, ¿el hombre quiere quedarse (stay) en Madrid o quiere irse?

B. Lola dice: "Ahora lo comprendo todo". En tu opinion, ¿qué comprende Lola? ¿Cuál es la solución del misterio?

Más práctica   GO

realidades.com | print

Actividades   ✔

ENRICH YOUR TEACHING

Culture Note

There are two main train stations that service Madrid: Chamartín and Atocha. The Atocha train station, a nineteenth-century-style building, was renovated to include an indoor park with plants and cafés. *RENFE (Red Nacional de los Ferrocarriles Españoles)* is part of the *Ministerio de Fomento* and is the agency in charge of running trains in Spain. Trains to Barcelona generally leave from Chamartín.

Viewing: Play *Episodio* 9 to the class. If there is time after viewing the full episode, select some key moments that you wish to highlight, such as the scene in which Margarita reports to Lola on what she heard in the conversation between the two strangers.

Post-viewing: Have students look at the pictures and the captions at the top of the page and use them to summarize the scenes in this episode. Brainstorm a list of vocabulary in this episode that is used to add new information to the plot. Direct students' attention to the *¿Comprendes?* section.

▼ **¿Comprendes?** Standards: 1.2, 1.3

Resources: Map Transparency 18; Answer Keys: Student Edition, p. 181

Focus: Verifying comprehension by answering questions; reviewing the plot.

Suggestions: For part B, have students write a short paragraph about what Lola really knows and what they think is the answer to the mystery. Have them present their ideas to the class and ask the other students to say why they agree or disagree.

Answers:
Part A:
1. Paco y Margarita ayudan a Lola con la investigación.
2. Margarita va al café para escuchar la conversación.
3. Lola está nerviosa porque no quiere ser descubierta.
4. Según Lola, el hombre en el café es Luis Antonio Llamas, un hombre de Barcelona.
5. Según Margarita, la chica en el café no es María; es Julia.
6. Según Margarita, el hombre quiere irse.

Part B: Answers will vary.

Theme Project

Students can perform Step 3 at this point. (For more information, see p. 280-b.)

Additional Resources

• *¿Eres tú, María?* Video Workbook, Episode 9
• *¿Eres tú, María?* Teacher's Video Guide: Answer Key

▼ Objectives

▶ Review the vocabulary and grammar

▶ Demonstrate you can perform the tasks on p. 307

Repaso del capítulo

Vocabulario y gramática

Review Activities

To talk about television shows: Play a version of charades. Divide students into four or five teams. Have volunteers from one team pantomime a television show. Give team members a point if they correctly guess the kind of show and the name of the program.

To talk about movies: Continue the game of charades, changing the topic to movies.

To give an opinion of a movie or a program: Divide students into pairs. Ask students to brainstorm a list of seven movie titles. While one student reads the titles, the other says an adjective that describes each movie. Have students switch roles.

To ask and tell about movies or programs: Ask students to describe the last movie they saw. Tell them to say the title, what kind of movie it was, the main actor and actress, where they saw the film, when it started, and how long it lasted.

Verbs similar to gustar: On twelve index cards, have students write *-n, me, te, le, nos, les, aburre, duele, encanta, falta, interesa,* and *queda.* Write **a +** prepositional pronoun along with a noun and have students complete the sentence. For example: ***a mí / las películas cómicas.*** Remind them to use ***-n*** for plural subjects.

Portfolio

Invite students to review the activities they completed in this chapter, including written reports, posters or other visuals, videos of oral presentations, or other projects. Have them select one or two items that they feel best demonstrate their achievements in Spanish to include in their portfolios.

Additional Resources

Student Resources: Realidades para hispanohablantes, p. 348

Teacher Resources:
• Teacher's Resource Book: Situation Cards, p. 320, Clip Art, pp. 322–323
• Assessment Program: Chapter Checklist and Self-Assessment Worksheet, pp. T56–T57

to talk about television shows

el canal	channel
el programa de concursos	game show
el programa deportivo	sports show
el programa de dibujos animados	cartoon show
el programa de entrevistas	interview program
el programa de la vida real	reality program
el programa de noticias	news program
el programa educativo	educational program
el programa musical	musical program
la telenovela	soap opera

to talk about movies

la comedia	comedy
el drama	drama
la película de ciencia ficción	science fiction movie
la película de horror	horror movie
la película policíaca	crime movie, mystery
la película romántica	romantic movie

to give your opinion of a movie or program

cómico, -a	funny
emocionante	touching
fascinante	fascinating
infantil	for children; childish
realista	realistic
tonto, -a	silly, stupid
violento, -a	violent
me aburre(n)	it bores me (they bore me)
me interesa(n)	it interests me (they interest me)

to ask and tell about movies or programs

el actor	actor
la actriz	actress
dar	to show
durar	to last
empezar *(e→ie)*	to begin
terminar	to end
más / menos de	more / less than
medio, -a	half
¿Qué clase de...?	What kind of...?

to talk about what has just happened

acabar de + *infinitive*	to have just...

verbs similar to *gustar*

aburrir	to bore
doler *(o→ue)*	to hurt, to ache
encantar	to please very much, to love
faltar	to be missing
interesar	to interest
quedar	to fit

other useful words and expressions

antes de	before
casi	almost
¿De veras?	Really?
especialmente	especially
por eso	therefore, for that reason
sobre	about
ya	already

For *Vocabulario adicional,* see pp. 336–337.

DIFFERENTIATED INSTRUCTION

Students with Learning Difficulties

Have students review the *Repaso del capítulo* and create flashcards for any words that they do not know. Pair them with a student who is more confident with the vocabulary to practice. Before the test, provide students with a practice test, so they can become comfortable with the format.

Heritage Language Learners

Have students write a few paragraphs telling about their perfect birthday celebration: Where are they going to have it? Whom are they going to invite? What food are they going to eat? What kind of music are they going to play? Encourage them to use as many vocabulary words from this chapter as they can.

Instant Check	✔	
Puzzles	✔	
Core WB pp. 80–81		✔
Comm. WB pp. 183, 184–186	✔	✔

Preparación para el examen

On the exam you will be asked to . . . | **Here are practice tasks similar to those you will find on the exam . . .** | **For review go to your print or digital textbook . . .**

1 Escuchar Listen and understand as people express opinions about movies and TV programs

Listen as you hear a phone pollster ask people about TV programs they have watched on the new Spanish-language cable station. For each viewer, decide if the show(s): a) was (were) boring; b) was (were) interesting; c) was (were) too violent; d) was (were) too childish or silly.

pp. 282–287 *Vocabulario en contexto*
p. 288 Actividad 6
p. 289 Actividad 8
p. 290 Actividad 9
p. 295 Actividad 17

2 Hablar Ask and answer questions about the types of movies and TV programs people prefer

Tell your partner about a movie or TV program you just saw and express your opinion about it. Ask if your partner saw the same thing and what he or she thought of it. If your partner didn't see it, ask him or her to tell about something he or she just saw. You might say: *Acabo de ver una película fantástica con Tom Cruise . . .*

pp. 282–287 *Vocabulario en contexto*
p. 288 Actividad 6
p. 289 Actividad 8
p. 291 Actividad 12
p. 295 Actividad 17
p. 297 Actividad 19
p. 303 *Presentación oral*

3 Leer Read and understand what an entertainment critic writes about a new TV program

Before class begins, you grab a Spanish-language magazine and turn to the entertainment section. After reading part of the entertainment critic's review, see if you can determine his opinion of a new soap opera series, *Mi secreto.* Does he like it? Why or why not?

En el primer episodio de *Mi secreto,* nos aburren con una historia infantil y con actores sin talento que quieren ser emocionantes pero no pueden. ¡Pienso que este programa es para las personas que no tienen nada que hacer!

pp. 282–287 *Vocabulario en contexto*
p. 291 Actividad 12

4 Escribir Write about a movie you recently saw

You are keeping a journal to practice writing in Spanish. Today you are going to write about a movie you saw recently. Mention the name of the movie, the type of movie it is, and what you liked or disliked about it.

p. 290 Actividad 10
p. 295 Actividad 17
p. 297 Actividades 19–20
p. 303 *Presentación oral*

5 Pensar Demonstrate an understanding of common gestures

You learned that almost all cultures can communicate without words. With a partner, try making the gestures shown in this chapter from the Spanish-speaking world. Are these similar to those in our culture?

p. 302 *La cultura en vivo*

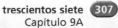
trescientos siete **307**
Capítulo 9A

DIFFERENTIATED ASSESSMENT

CORE ASSESSMENT
- **Assessment Program:** Examen del capítulo 9A, pp. 235–240
- **Audio Program DVD:** Cap. 9A, Track 17
- **ExamView:** Chapter Test, Test Banks A and B

ADVANCED/PRE-AP*
- **ExamView: Pre-AP* Test Bank**
- **Pre-AP* Resource Book,** pp. 94–97

STUDENTS NEEDING EXTRA HELP
- **Alternate Assessment Program:** Examen del capítulo 9A
- **Audio Program DVD:** Cap. 9A, Track 17

HERITAGE LEARNERS
- **Assessment Program: Realidades para hispanohablantes:** Examen del capítulo 9A
- **ExamView: Heritage Learner Test Bank**

Performance Tasks

Standards: 1.1, 1.2, 1.3, 4.1

Student Resource: Realidades para hispanohablantes, p. 349

Teacher Resources: Teacher's Resource Book: Audio Script, p. 313; Audio Program DVD: Cap. 9A, Track 16; Answer Keys: Student Edition, p. 182

Focus: Preparing for the exam

1. Escuchar

Suggestions: Play the audio or read the script.

Script and Answers:

1. A nosotros no nos gusta el programa *Paco Payaso.* Debe ser un programa educativo para niños, pero es demasiado infantil. Mi hijo tiene ocho años y a él no le gusta cantar una canción del alfabeto. *(too childish)*
2. Pienso que los programas de la vida real son ridículos. Me aburren mucho. No me importan ni me interesan. *(boring)*
3. Me gustan mucho los programas de entrevistas. Me encanta el programa *Miguel.* Él es muy cómico y tiene entrevistas muy interesantes. *(interesting)*

2. Hablar

Suggestions: Have students create a chart like the one on p. 303.
Answers will vary.

3. Leer

Suggestions: Before beginning the reading have students discuss their opinions of soap operas.
Answers will vary but may include:
No le gusta nada el programa. Es infantil y aburrido.

4. Escribir

Suggestions: Have students write an entry about the television shows they watch that night.
Answers will vary.

5. Pensar

Suggestions: Monitor students for appropriate gestures.
Answers will vary.

AT A GLANCE

Objectives
- Listen to and read conversations about computers
- Talk about the Internet and write a Web profile
- Exchange information about Internet use and the benefits of computers
- Identify the impact of the Internet on the Spanish language
- Compare computer use in Spanish-speaking countries with your own use of technology

Vocabulary
- Communication
- Computer-related activities
- Internet and digital products

Grammar
- The present tense of *pedir* and *servir*
- *saber* and *conocer*

Culture
- Pablo Picasso, p. 309
- *La Real Academia Española,* p. 316
- Internet use in Spain, p. 318
- Inventions, p. 327
- Impact of the Internet on the Spanish Language, pp. 328–329
- Cultural perspectives on computer use, p. 330

Recycle ♻
- Greetings
- Preterite of *hacer*
- *ir a* + infinitive
- Indirect object pronouns
- *tener*
- *sé, sabes*
- Direct object pronouns
- Personal *a*

RESOURCES

	FOR THE STUDENT	ONLINE	DVD	PRINT	FOR THE TEACHER	ONLINE	PREEXP	DVD	PRINT
Plan					Interactive TE and Resources DVD	•		•	
					Teacher's Resource Book, pp. 340–371	•		•	•
					Pre-AP* Resource Book, pp. 94–97	•		•	•
					Mapa global interactivo	•			
					Lesson Plans	•			•
Introducción PP. 308–309									
Present	Student Edition, pp. 308–309	•	•	•	Interactive TE and Resources DVD	•		•	
	DK Reference Atlas	•	•		Teacher's Resource Book, pp. 340–341	•		•	•
	Videocultura	•	•		Galería de fotos		•		
	Hispanohablantes WB, pp. 350–351			•	Fine Art Transparencies, 45	•	•	•	
					Map Transparencies, 12, 18–20	•	•	•	
Vocabulario en contexto PP. 310–315									
Present & Practice	Student Edition, pp. 310–315	•	•	•	Interactive TE and Resources DVD	•		•	
	Audio	•	•		Teacher's Resource Book, pp. 342–344, 347, 356–357	•		•	•
	Videohistoria	•	•		Vocabulary Clip Art	•	•	•	
	Flashcards	•	•		Audio Program	•	•	•	
	Instant Check	•			Video Program: Videohistoria	•		•	
	Guided WB, pp. 143–150	•	•	•	Video Program Teacher's Guide: Cap. 9B	•		•	•
	Core WB, pp. 82–85	•	•	•	Vocabulary and Grammar Transparencies, 166–169	•	•	•	
	Comm. WB, pp. 93–96, 98	•	•	•	Answer Keys: Student Edition, pp. 183–185	•			
	Hispanohablantes WB, pp. 352–353			•	TPR Stories, pp. 122–123	•	•	•	•
Assess and Remediate					Prueba 9B–1: Assessment Program, pp. 241–242	•		•	•
					Assessment Program para hispanohablantes, pp. 241–242	•		•	•

RESOURCES

FOR THE STUDENT	ONLINE	DVD	PRINT	FOR THE TEACHER	ONLINE	PREEXP	DVD	PRINT
Vocabulario en uso PP. 316–319								
Present & Practice								
Student Edition, pp. 316–319	●	●	●	Interactive Whiteboard Vocabulary Activities	●		●	
Instant Check	●			Interactive TE and Resources DVD	●		●	
Comm. WB, p. 96	●	●	●	Teacher's Resource Book, pp. 343–344, 350–351, 355	●		●	●
Hispanohablantes WB, pp. 354–355, 360			●	Communicative Pair Activities, pp. 350–351	●		●	
Communicative Pair Activities	●			Audio Program	●	●	●	
				Videomodelos	●		●	
				Vocabulary and Grammar Transparencies, 172	●		●	●
				Answer Keys: Student Edition, pp. 185–187	●		●	●
Assess and Remediate				Prueba 9B–2 with Study Plan	●			
				Prueba 9B–2: Assessment Program, pp. 243–244	●		●	●
				Assessment Program para hispanohablantes, pp. 243–244	●		●	●
Gramática PP. 320–327								
Present & Practice								
Student Edition, pp. 320–327	●	●	●	Interactive Whiteboard Grammar Activities	●		●	
Instant Check	●			Interactive TE and Resources DVD	●		●	
Animated Verbs	●			Teacher's Resource Book, pp. 344–345, 347–348, 352–353	●		●	●
Tutorial Video: Grammar	●			Communicative Pair Activities, pp. 352–353	●		●	
Canción de hip hop	●			Audio Program	●	●	●	
Guided WB, pp. 151–154	●	●	●	Videomodelos	●		●	
Core WB, pp. 86–88	●	●	●	Video Program: GramActiva	●		●	
Comm. WB, pp. 96–97, 99–100, 187	●	●	●	Vocabulary and Grammar Transparencies, 170–171	●		●	●
Hispanohablantes WB, pp. 356–361			●	Answer Keys: Student Edition, pp. 187–189	●		●	
Communicative Pair Activities	●							
Assess and Remediate				Pruebas 9B–3 and 9B–4 with Study Plans	●			
				Pruebas 9B–3, 9B–4: Assessment Program, pp. 245, 246	●		●	●
				Assessment Program para hispanohablantes, pp. 245, 246	●		●	●
¡Adelante! PP. 328–333								
Application								
Student Edition, pp. 328–333	●	●	●	Interactive TE and Resources DVD	●		●	
Online Cultural Reading	●			Teacher's Resource Book, pp. 348–349	●		●	
Guided WB, pp. 155–156	●	●	●	Video Program: Videomisterio ¿Eres tú, María?	●		●	
Comm. WB, pp. 101, 188	●	●	●	Video Program Teacher's Guide: Cap. 9B	●		●	
Hispanohablantes WB, pp. 362–367			●	Videomisterio Quiz		●		
¿Eres tú, María? Video WB, pp. 74–81	●	●	●	Answer Keys: Student Edition, p. 190	●		●	
Repaso del capítulo PP. 334–335								
Review								
Student Edition, pp. 334–335	●	●	●	Interactive TE and Resources DVD	●		●	
Online Puzzles and Games	●			Teacher's Resource Book, pp. 346, 354, 356–357	●		●	●
Core WB, pp. 89–90	●	●	●	Audio Program	●	●	●	
Comm. WB, pp. 189–192	●	●	●	Answer Keys: Student Edition, p. 191	●		●	
Hispanohablantes WB, pp. 368–369			●					
Instant Check	●							
Chapter Assessment								
Assess				Examen del capítulo 9B	●		●	●
				Assessment Program, pp. 247–253	●		●	●
				Alternate Assessment Program, pp. 106–110	●		●	●
				Assessment Program para hispanohablantes, pp. 247–253	●		●	●
				Audio Program, Cap. 9B, Examen	●		●	
				ExamView: Test Banks A and B questions only online	●	●		
				Heritage Learner Test Bank	●	●		
				Pre-AP* Test Bank	●			

REGULAR SCHEDULE (50 MINUTES)

DAY	Warm-up / Assess	Preview / Present / Practice / Communicate	Wrap-up / Homework Options
1	Return Examen del capítulo (10 min.)	Vocabulario en contexto (35 min.) • Objectives • Presentation • *Actividades* 1, 2 • Arte y cultura • Videocultura: *Medios de comunicación*	Wrap-up and Homework Options (5 min.) • Core Practice • Vocabulary Clip Art
2	Warm-up (5 min.) • Homework check	Vocabulario en contexto (40 min.) • Review: *Vocabulario en contexto* • Presentation: *Videohistoria ¿Cómo se comunica?* • View: Video *¿Cómo se comunica?* • Video Activities • *Actividades* 3, 4, 5	Wrap-up and Homework Options (5 min.) • *Prueba* 9B-1: Vocabulary recognition • Core Practice
3	Warm-up (5 min.) • Homework check ✔Formative Assessment (10 min.) • *Prueba* 9B-1: Vocabulary recognition	Vocabulario en uso (30 min.) • Objectives • Interactive Whiteboard Vocabulary Activities • *Actividades* 7, 8 • *Fondo cultural*	Wrap-up and Homework Options (5 min.) • *Actividad* 6
4	Warm-up (5 min.) • Homework check • Return *Prueba* 9B-1: Vocabulary recognition	Vocabulario en uso (40 min.) • *Actividades* 9, 10, 11 • Communicative Pair Activities • *Fondo cultural* • *Exploración del lenguaje*	Wrap-up and Homework Options (5 min.) • *Exploración del lenguaje:* Try it out!
5	Warm-up (5 min.) • Homework check	Gramática y vocabulario en uso (40 min.) • Presentation: The present tense of *pedir* and *servir* • *GramActiva* Video • Interactive Whiteboard Grammar Activities • *Actividades* 12, 14	Wrap-up and Homework Options (5 min.) • *Actividad* 13
6	Warm-up (5 min.) • Homework check	Gramática y vocabulario en uso (40 min.) • Review: The present tense of *pedir* and *servir* • *Actividades* 15, 17 • *Pronunciación* • *Juego: Actividad* 16 • Communicative Pair Activities	Wrap-up and Homework Options (5 min.) • Core Practice • *Prueba* 9B-3 with Study Plan: The present tense of *pedir* and *servir*
7	Warm-up (5 min.) • Homework check ✔Formative Assessment (10 min.) • *Prueba* 9B-3 with Study Plan: The present tense of *pedir* and *servir*	Gramática y vocabulario en uso (30 min.) • Presentation: *saber* and *conocer* • *GramActiva* Video • Interactive Whiteboard Grammar Activities • *Actividades* 19, 20	Wrap-up and Homework Options (5 min.) • *Actividad* 18 • *Prueba* 9B-2 with Study Plan: Vocabulary production
8	Warm-up (5 min.) • Homework check • Return *Prueba* 9B-3 with Study Plan: The present tense of *pedir* and *servir* ✔Formative Assessment (10 min.) • *Prueba* 9B-2 with Study Plan: Voc. production	Gramática y vocabulario en uso (30 min.) • Review: *saber* and *conocer* • *Actividades* 21, 22 • *Conexiones: Actividad* 23 • *El español en el mundo del trabajo*	Wrap-up and Homework Options (5 min.) • Core Practice • *Prueba* 9B-4 with Study Plan: *saber* and *conocer*

REGULAR SCHEDULE (50 MINUTES)

DAY	Warm-up / Assess	Preview / Present / Practice / Communicate	Wrap-up / Homework Options
9	**Warm-up (5 min.)** • Homework check • Return *Prueba* 9B-2 with Study Plan: Vocabulary production ✔**Formative Assessment (10 min.)** • *Prueba* 9B-4 with Study Plan: *saber* and *conocer*	**Gramática y vocabulario en uso (10 min.)** • *El español en el mundo del trabajo* **¡Adelante! (20 min.)** • *Lectura*	**Wrap-up and Homework Options (5 min.)** • Core Practice
10	**Warm-up (5 min.)** • Homework check • Return *Prueba* 9B-4 with Study Plan: *saber* and *conocer*	**¡Adelante! (40 min.)** • *Lectura* • *Perspectivas del mundo hispano*	**Wrap-up and Homework Options (5 min.)** • *¿Comprendes?*
11	**Warm-up (5 min.)** • Homework check	**¡Adelante! (40 min.)** • *Presentación escrita:* Prewrite	**Wrap-up and Homework Options (5 min.)**
12	**Warm-up (5 min.)** • Homework check	**¡Adelante! (40 min.)** • *Presentación escrita:* Draft, revise • *Videomisterio*	**Wrap-up and Homework Options (5 min.)** • *Presentación escrita:* Publish
13	**Warm-up (5 min.)** • Homework check	**¡Adelante! (40 min.)** • *Presentación escrita:* Present	**Wrap-up and Homework Options (5 min.)** • Writing Activities • Core Practice Organizer
14	**Warm-up (5 min.)** • Homework check • Core Practice Organizer	**Repaso (40 min.)** • *Vocabulario y gramática* • *Preparación para el examen*	**Wrap-up and Homework Options (5 min.)** • Instant Check • *Examen del capítulo*
15	**Warm-up (5 min.)** • Answer questions ✔**Summative Assessment (45 min.)** • *Examen del capítulo*		

Capítulo 9B La tecnología

Standards for *Capítulo* 9B

- To achieve the goals of the Standards, students will:

Communication

1.1 Interpersonal
- Talk about: computers and technology; asking for and describing things; ordering at restaurants; what activities different people can do; knowledge of mutual acquaintances

1.2 Interpretive
- Read and listen: to information and opinions about computers and technology; to information about communication
- Read: a picture-based story; an advertisement for a *cibercafé;* a survey about computer use, skills, and attitudes
- Listen to and watch a video about communications technology
- View a video mystery series

1.3 Presentational
- Present information about: computers and the Internet; communication; technology; knowledge of people and places
- Write about ordering at restaurants
- Write descriptions of objects
- Perform a scene from a video mystery series

Culture

2.1 Practices and Perspectives
- Learn about: **La Real Academia de la Lengua Española;** the rise in use of *cibercafés*
- Understand how technology is altering user's adherence to pure Spanish

2.2 Products and Perspectives
- Learn about Pablo Picasso and his painting

Connections

3.1 Cross-curricular
- Learn about: Pablo Picasso; the evolution of communications technology
- Read about *las cuevas de Altamira*

Comparisons

4.1 Language
- Learn: vocabulary through the recognition of cognates; about the verbs **pedir** and **servir;** to pronounce words by dividing them into syllables
- Understand: how to use **-mente** to form an adverb; how and when to use **saber** and **conocer**
- Learn about la **invasión del ciberspanglish**

4.2 Culture
- Compare frequency of Internet usage
- Identify ways Spanish is valuable in the communications industry

Communities

5.1 Beyond the School
- Identify ways Spanish-speaking ability is valuable in the communications industry

5.2 Lifelong Learner
- Investigate use of Spanish-language Internet for study and pleasure
- View a video mystery series

Chapter Objectives

Communication

By the end of this chapter you will be able to:

- Listen to and read conversations about computers
- Talk about the Internet and write a Web profile
- Exchange information about Internet use and the benefits of computers

Culture

You will also be able to:

- Identify the impact of the Internet on the Spanish language
- Compare computer use in Spanish-speaking countries with your own use of technology

You will demonstrate what you know and can do:

- Presentación escrita, p. 331
- Preparación para el examen, p. 335

You will use:

Vocabulary	Grammar
• Communication	• The present tense of **pedir** and **servir**
• Computer-related activities	• **Saber** and **conocer**
• Internet and digital products	

Exploración del mundo hispano

Country Connection
Technology and Communication

España
México
Nicaragua

 realidades.com [GO]

DK Reference Atlas

▶ Videocultura y actividad

🌎 Mapa global interactivo

Estudiantes nicaragüenses con sus computadoras nuevas, Tipitapa, Nicaragua

ENRICH YOUR TEACHING

Using Backward Design
Have students preview the sample performance tasks on *Preparación para el examen,* p. 335, and connect them to the Chapter Objectives. Explain to students that by completing the sample tasks they can self-assess their learning progress.

Mapa global interactivo
Download the *Mapa global interactivo* files for Chapter 9B and preview the activity. The activity takes you to the prehistoric caves of Altamira in Spain.

Arte y cultura | España

Reading the Letter is from Picasso's Neo-Classical period, when he was influenced by Roman sculpture. The heavy lines and statue-like shapes highlight the seriousness of the moment shown. In 1921, mail was the main form of communication, and telephone use was limited. Today initiatives such as One Laptop per Child, shown in the photo, help students in developing countries connect with the global community.

• How do you and your friends communicate? How can equal access to technology change communication worldwide?

"Reading the Letter" (1921), Pablo Picasso ►
Oil on canvas, 184 x 105 cm. Photo: J.G. Berizzi. Musée Picasso, Paris, France.
© 2004 Estate of Pablo Picasso/Artists Rights Society ARS, New York.
Photo credit: Réunion des Musées Nationaux/Art Resource, NY.

trescientos nueve **309**
Capítulo 9B

Chapter Opener

Core Instruction

Resources: Map Transparencies 12, 18, 20

Suggestions: Introduce students to the chapter theme and review the objectives. Point out that they will learn technical terms related to computers. The video for *A primera vista* will include a story about teenagers helping one another learn to communicate by computer.

▶️ **Videocultura** View *Medios de comunicación* with the class to learn about Spanish media in the United States and the world.

Arte y cultura

Standards: 2.2, 3.1

Resources: Fine Art Transparencies, p. 45

Suggestions: Ask students to study the painting carefully, including the subjects and their relationship to each other. Can they see clues, such as the posture, hands, and facial expressions, that help inform viewers of the contents of the letter? Ask students if they think the letter contains good news or bad news. Show other examples of Picasso's work from his Neo-Classical period.

Answers will vary.

Culture Note

Tell students that by 2010, the One Laptop per Child Organization (OLPC) had provided 17,000 laptops to public school students and suburban neighborhoods throughout Nicaragua. The students pictured are from the Miguel Larreynaga School, in Tipitapa, a town 27 km north of Managua. Point out that some features of these laptops make them especially useful: They are portable, wireless, and durable.

DIFFERENTIATED INSTRUCTION

Digital resources such as the *Interactive Whiteboard* activity banks, *Videomodelos*, additional *Online Activities*, *Study Plans*, automatically graded *Leveled Workbook*, animated *Grammar Tutorials*, *Flashcards*, and *Vocabulary and Grammar Videos* will help you reach students of different ability levels and learning styles.

STUDENTS NEEDING EXTRA HELP

Guided Practice Activities
• Flashcards, pp. 143–146
• Vocabulary Check, pp. 147–150
• Grammar Support, pp. 151–154

HERITAGE LEARNERS

Realidades para hispanohablantes
• Chapter Opener, pp. 350–351
• A primera vista, p. 352
• Videohistoria, p. 353
• Manos a la obra, pp. 354–361
• ¡Adelante!, pp. 362–367
• Repaso del capítulo, pp. 368–369

ADVANCED/PRE-AP*

Pre-AP* Resource Book,
• pp. 94–97

Communications Workbook
• Integrated Performance Assessment, p. 189

9B Language Input

A primera vista 🔊 📖

| ▼ Objectives

Read, listen to, and understand information about
▶ computers and computer use
▶ ways to communicate

Vocabulario en contexto

Core Instruction

Standards: 1.2

Resources: Teacher's Resource Book: Input Script, p. 342, Clip Art, pp. 356–357, Audio Script, p. 343; Voc. and Gram. Transparencies: 166–167; TPR Stories Book, pp. 122–133; Audio Program DVD: Cap. 9B, Tracks 1–2

Focus: Introducing new vocabulary; using visualized vocabulary and cognates about computer uses and ways to communicate

Suggestions: Use the story in the *TPR Stories Book* to present the new vocabulary and grammar or use the Input Script from the *Teacher's Resource Book*.

Present the vocabulary in three sets: words to talk about communication, computer-related activities, (including *pedir, servir, saber,* and *conocer*) and computer-generated products. With their books closed, tell students that you are going to name various computer functions. They should guess what the function is and picture how they might do that function. Then show the transparencies and have students look at the visualized vocabulary in the book.

BELLRINGER REVIEW

Have students unscramble the words and conjugate the verb to make logical sentences.

1) *usar/la computadora/Mario y Graciela/en el laboratorio*

2) *Paula/en la clase de arte/dibujar*

3) *escribir/una composición/nosotros/en la clase de inglés*

(**Answers:** usan; dibuja; escribimos)

Vocabulario en contexto

En _____ en nuestra escuela, los estudiantes _____ usar las computadoras para hacer muchas cosas. A muchos estudiantes les gusta . . .

. . . **crear documentos** o **escribir una composición,**

. . . hacer **gráficos,**

la diapositiva **la computadora portátil**

. . . y preparar **presentaciones** con diapositivas.

Otros estudiantes **están en línea** para **navegar en la Red.** Pueden **buscar un sitio Web** o **bajar información** para **un informe.**

una canción

Para bailar la bamba

A otros les interesa **grabar un disco compacto.** Esta chica **graba canciones** "

310 trescientos diez
Tema 9 • Medios de comunicación

DIFFERENTIATED INSTRUCTION

Advanced Learners

Using the new vocabulary and phrases, have students develop a survey about computer use. Invite them to create the survey on a computer and insert clip art beside each question. After they write six *sí/no* questions, have them read the questions to a small group and put a check mark beside the things students say they can do.

Heritage Language Learners

Have students work in pairs or small groups to discuss which tasks mentioned on pp. 310–311 they know how to do. Students should also ask each other how they prefer to communicate with friends and family members.

—Nunca me comunico con el correo **electrónico**. ¿Es **complicado**? ¿Debo **tomar un curso** para aprender?

—No, abuelito, puedes aprender fácilmente. No debes **tener miedo de** usar la computadora. Y siempre me puedes **pedir** ayuda. ¿Cómo **te comunicas** con tus amigos que no viven cerca?

—Prefiero **enviarles** una carta o una tarjeta o puedo visitarlos para hablar cara a cara. Es mucho más personal.

hablar

▼1 | ◀)) | Escuchar

¿Sí o no?

Vas a escuchar siete frases. Si la frase es cierta, haz el gesto del pulgar hacia arriba. Si una frase es falsa, haz el gesto del pulgar hacia abajo.

Más práctica (GO)		
realidades.com | print		
Instant Check	✔	
Guided WB pp. 143–146	✔	✔
Core WB pp. 82–83	✔	✔
Comm. WB p. 98	✔	✔
Hispanohablantes WB p. 352		✔

▼2 | ◀)) | Escuchar

¿Es lógico?

Primero lee las respuestas. Luego escucha cada conversación y escoge el comentario más lógico.

1. **a.** Al papá le gusta usar la Red.

   b. El papá no sabe usar la Red.

2. **a.** El estudiante quiere grabar un disco compacto.

   b. El estudiante quiere bajar información.

3. **a.** Va a enviarle una carta.

   b. Va a enviarle una tarjeta.

trescientos once **311**
Capítulo 9B

1 Standards: 1.2

Resources: Teacher's Resource Book: Audio Script, p. 343; Audio Program DVD: Cap. 9B, Track 3; Answer Keys: Student Edition, p. 183

Focus: Listening comprehension; identifying new vocabulary

Suggestions: Play the audio or read the script. Allow students to listen more than once. Pause to monitor students. Give them several chances to listen and give a "thumbs-up" or "thumbs-down" sign.

◀)) **Script and Answers:**

1. **Necesito una computadora para comunicarme cara a cara con mis amigos.** *(down)*
2. **Para navegar en la Red necesito estar en línea.** *(up)*
3. **No es posible jugar juegos en la Red.** *(down)*
4. **No podemos preparar una presentación con diapositivas en una computadora portátil.** *(down)*
5. **Tengo que estar en la Red para crear gráficos y documentos.** *(down)*
6. **Es posible enviar una foto por correo electrónico.** *(up)*
7. **No es posible enviar una tarjeta por correo electrónico.** *(down)*

2 Standards: 1.2

Resources: Teacher's Resource Book: Audio Script, p. 343; Audio Program DVD: Cap. 9B, Track 4; Answer Keys: Student Edition, p. 183

Focus: Listening comprehension

Suggestions: Have students read the sentences carefully and note the differences. In item 2, **grabar** and **bajar** sound very similar. Make sure students can differentiate.

◀)) **Script and Answers:**

1. —Hijo, no me gusta nada navegar en la Red.
   —Pero, papá, no es complicado.
2. —Necesito bajar información de la Red para un informe.
   —Muy bien. Tienes que estar en línea.
3. —Tu tía va a celebrar su cumpleaños en una semana.
   —¿Por qué no le envías una tarjeta?

Answers:
1. b; 2. b; 3. b

ENRICH YOUR TEACHING

Teacher-to-Teacher

Play a form of *Pictionary*, using the words and phrases from pp. 310–311. Divide students into teams and give each team a large piece of paper. Ask a member from each group to come to you for a word to draw for his or her group.

Write it down and make sure that the student does not say it aloud. Have the student go back to the group and silently draw the word until someone guesses it. The group must spell it correctly in order to gain points.

Videohistoria 🔊

Core Instruction

Standards: 1.2, 4.1

Resources: Voc. and Gram. Transparencies 168–169; Audio Program DVD: Cap. 9B, Track 5; Answer Keys: Student Edition, p. 184

Focus: Presenting additional vocabulary and grammar in the context of the story; previewing the language video

Suggestions:

Pre-reading: Using the transparencies, go panel by panel and ask students to predict the storyline. Direct students' attention to the *Strategy* and have them skim the reading and list cognates. Ask them what they think the boy might learn to do.

Discuss the *Antes de leer* questions.

Answers:

1. Ana seems more comfortable. She is showing Javier the camera.
2. Answers will vary.

Reading: Read the captions with students or use the audio. Using the transparencies and nonverbal clues, help students understand the new words in blue type. Ask if the list of cognates helped them with comprehension. Remind students that in panel 4, **ordenador** means **computadora.** Ask students the comprehension questions found on the transparencies.

Post-reading: Complete *Actividad* 3 to check comprehension.

¿Cómo se comunica?

Ana sabe usar una cámara digital y una computadora. Ella puede navegar en la Red y tiene su propia página Web. ¿Qué le va a enseñar a Javier?

> **También se dice . . .**
>
> la computadora = el ordenador
> *(España)*

España

Javier Ana

Antes de leer

 Strategy

Recognizing cognates Recognizing cognates when you read can help improve your understanding.

- Skim the *Videohistoria* and make a list of the cognates. Which words on your list help you understand what types of technology Javier and Ana are talking about?

1. Look at what Javier and Ana are holding in photo 1. Who do you think feels more comfortable with new technology? Why?

2. Think about what you know about computers and the Internet. How would you explain to someone why computers are useful?

312 trescientos doce
Tema 9 • Medios de comunicación

DIFFERENTIATED INSTRUCTION

Multiple Intelligences

Bodily/Kinesthetic: After students have read the *Videohistoria* but before they watch the video, have them form groups of three and take the parts of Ana, Javier, and Esteban. After their own reading, have them watch the video to compare their interpretations of the characters with those in the video.

Language Input 9B

1

Javier: Hola, Ana. ¿Cómo estás?

Ana: Muy bien, ¿y tú? Mira. Acabo de comprar esta **cámara digital.** Es fascinante. ¿La **conoces**?

Javier: A ver. No **conozco** ese tipo de cámara. ¡Qué interesante!

2

Ana: ¿Adónde vas?

Javier: Voy a enviar una tarjeta a Esteban, mi amigo en San Antonio. Mira, tengo una foto de él.

Ana: Mmmm. Es muy simpático, ¿no? Si quieres, te acompaño.

3

Ana: Vamos, Javier. Uno, dos, tres. Y mira, aquí estás. **¿Qué te parece?**

Javier: Muy bien. Sacaste las fotos muy **rápidamente.** Veo que no es complicado.

4

Javier: Un momento, voy a enviar mi tarjeta.

Ana: ¿Por qué no te comunicas con Esteban por correo electrónico?

Javier: Porque no tengo ordenador.

Ana: No importa. En Madrid hay muchos cibercafés. Vamos a uno.

Video ▶

Core Instruction

Standards: 1.2, 4.1

Resources: Teacher's Resource Book: Video Script, p. 347; Video Program: Cap. 9B; Video Program Teacher's Guide: Cap. 9B

Focus: Comprehending new vocabulary and grammar in authentic visual context

Suggestions:

Pre-viewing: Review the *Videohistoria* reading and have students make a list of key ideas. Play an excerpt of the video with the sound down and ask students to tell which panel in the *Videohistoria* it corresponds to.

Viewing: Have students pay attention to the intonation of questions and answers. Ask students if Ana is patient with Javier's questions. Is it easy to teach someone how to use a computer? Show the video once without pausing. Then show it again, stopping to check comprehension.

Post-viewing: Complete the Video Activities in the *Communication Workbook*.

Pre-AP* Support

- **Learning Objective:** Interpersonal Writing
- **Activity:** Have students work in pairs to write the whole text of Javier's e-mail to Esteban. Have students imagine Esteban tells his friend about his adventures in Madrid, including details about his experience in the cibercafé in Madrid.
- **Pre-AP* Resource Book:** Comprehensive guide to Pre-AP* vocabulary skill development, pp. 51–57

ENRICH YOUR TEACHING

Culture Note

Madrid's *cibercafés* are very popular with teens, but in 2002 many young people almost lost the chance to visit them. The Madrid city government had proposed a law classifying *cibercafés* as "casinos," which would have meant that minors would no longer have been allowed entrance. Luckily, due to a great deal of protest from Madrid's citizens, that law did not pass.

3 Standards: 1.2

Resources: Answer Keys: Student Edition, p. 184

Focus: Reading comprehension; writing to verify understanding

Suggestions: Ask students to read all six sentences before they begin to write. Have them number their papers 1–6 and write the name of the character who would say each sentence. Then have volunteers read the sentences aloud, first saying: *Soy ___, y diría* (sentence).

Refer students to the *También se dice...* on p. 312. Ask students to use **ordenador** instead of **computadora** in the fifth and sixth sentences of the activity, making the necessary changes to any modifying words.

Answers:

1. Ana
2. Javier
3. Ana
4. Esteban
5. Javier
6. Ana

Extension: Suggest that students write one or two other sentences that each character might say. This could be a homework assignment.

5

Ana: Aquí puedes navegar en la Red o **visitar salones de chat.** Mira, mi **página Web.** Yo la hice.

Javier: ¿Tú la hiciste? ¡Qué bien! Pero . . . ¿**para qué sirve?**

Ana: El Internet **sirve para** mucho. Puedes **escribir por correo electrónico,** buscar información, jugar juegos . . .

6

Ana: Tengo una idea. Tu amigo Esteban tiene **dirección electrónica,** ¿no?

Javier: Creo que sí. ¡Ah! Aquí está en su carta.

7

Javier: Hola, Esteban. Saludos desde un cibercafé en Madrid . . .

Ana: ¡Eso es! Tú vas a escribirle por correo electrónico. Y le vamos a enviar esta foto de nosotros.

8

Javier: . . . y aquí estoy con mi buena amiga, Ana. ¿Qué tal la familia? Y el cumpleaños de Cristina, ¿cómo lo pasaste?

Esteban: Es evidente que Javier está muy contento en Madrid.

314 trescientos catorce
Tema 9 • Medios de comunicación

DIFFERENTIATED INSTRUCTION

Advanced Learners

Consider student input in planning your lessons. Have students write you a message saying what they would like to learn in this chapter. For example: *Me gustaría navegar en la Red.* For each activity that you do, post the suggestion, and say whose idea it was.

Heritage Language Learners

Suggest that students write a message that Esteban could e-mail back to Javier in response to Javier's message at the end of the story.

▼3 Leer

¿Quién es?

Decide cuál de las personas de la *Videohistoria* diría *(would say)* cada frase. Escribe su nombre en una hoja de papel.

1. ¿Por qué no sacamos fotos con mi cámara digital?
2. Tengo su dirección electrónica en esta carta.
3. Yo hice mi propia página Web.
4. Mis amigos me enviaron fotos a mi dirección electrónica.
5. No tengo mi propia computadora.
6. Sé mucho de computadoras.

Javier

Ana

Esteban

▼4 Leer · Pensar · Escribir

Las computadoras sirven para mucho

Ana da muchas razones *(reasons)* de por qué las computadoras sirven para mucho, pero hay otras también. Lee estas frases y escribe en una hoja de papel sólo las razones que da Ana.

1. Una persona puede navegar la Red.
2. Es fácil escribir por correo electrónico.
3. Puedes grabar un disco compacto.
4. Puedes escribir una composición.
5. Una persona puede buscar información.
6. Es posible mandar fotos.
7. Puedes hacer una presentación.
8. Una persona puede jugar juegos.
9. Puedes visitar salones de chat.
10. Es posible hacer una página Web.

▼5 Leer · Escribir

¿Comprendes?

En cada frase hay un error. Lee la frase y después escribe la frase con la información correcta.

1. Ana acaba de comprar una computadora portátil.
2. Javier quiere enviarle a Esteban una carta.
3. Javier no le escribe por correo electrónico porque no le gusta usar las computadoras.
4. Según Ana, la Red no sirve para mucho.
5. Ana le escribe a Esteban por correo electrónico.
6. Javier le pregunta a Esteban sobre el cumpleaños de Angélica.

Más práctica GO	realidades.com | print		
Instant Check		✔	
Guided WB pp. 147–150		✔	✔
Core WB pp. 84–85		✔	✔
Comm. WB pp. 93–95, 96		✔	✔
Hispanohablantes **WB** p. 353			✔

trescientos quince **315**
Capítulo 9B

4 Standards: 1.2, 1.3

Resources: Answer Keys: Student Edition, p. 184

Focus: Verifying understanding of the *Videohistoria*

Suggestions: Have students read all ten sentences first. Ask them to recall which reasons Ana actually stated in the story and to write as many as they can without looking back at the story. When they have finished, they can double-check their responses by reviewing the story.

Answers:

Sentences 1, 2, 5, 6, 8, 9, 10

5 Standards: 1.2, 1.3

Resources: Answer Keys: Student Edition, p. 185

Focus: Reading comprehension; writing to verify understanding

Suggestions: Encourage students to first attempt to correct the sentences without looking back at the story. Ask volunteers to read their corrected sentences aloud.

Answers:

1. **Ana acaba de comprar una cámara digital.**
2. **Javier quiere enviarle a Esteban una tarjeta.**
3. **Javier no le escribe por correo electrónico porque no tiene computadora.**
4. **Según Ana, el Internet (la Red) sirve para mucho.**
5. **Javier le escribe a Esteban por correo electrónico.**
6. **Javier le pregunta a Esteban sobre el cumpleaños de Cristina.**

Additional Resources

• Communication Wbk.: Audio Act. 5, p. 96
• Teacher's Resource Book: Audio Script, pp. 343–344
• Audio Program DVD: Cap. 9B, Track 7

ENRICH YOUR TEACHING

Culture Note

Increasing numbers of Spanish speakers have found that the use of the Internet has enhanced their relationships with others. Not only can they remain in contact with friends and relatives in their heritage country, but many have also found new friendships on the Web.

21st Century Skills

Social and Cross-Cultural Skills Have students interview native speakers or exchange students to find out if the methods friends use to communicate are the same in their country as in the United States. If those students use text messaging, have them find out some typical text message "lingo" and share with the class.

✓ASSESSMENT

Quiz: Vocabulary Recognition
• Prueba 9B-1: pp. 241–242

315

INTERACTIVE WHITEBOARD
Vocabulary Activities 9B

BELLRINGER REVIEW

Create printouts of computer graphics, word-processing documents, Web pages, and presentation software slides. Hold them up and have students identify them using the new vocabulary.

▼6 Standards: 1.2, 1.3

Resources: Answer Keys: Student Edition, p. 185

Focus: Reading definitions of new vocabulary; writing with accuracy

Suggestions: Allow students to work with a partner. Suggest that they first write down as many terms as they can on their own, and then consult the book for help in finding the remaining words and verifying spelling.

Answers:
1. la diapositiva
2. la canción
3. la carta, la tarjeta
4. el sitio Web
5. la computadora portátil
6. el laboratorio
7. la tarjeta
8. el sitio Web, la página Web, los gráficos
9. el informe, el documento

Fondo cultural

Standards: 2.1

Suggestions: Explain that in the United States there is no single authority on proper English that is equivalent to the *Real Academia Española*. Discuss how the English language changes rapidly, especially with new technology terms.

Answers will vary but may include that communication among generations, even those separated by long periods of time, is easier when the quality and purity of a language have been preserved. For example, reading books in the Spanish language written hundreds of years ago is easier when grammatical rules and vocabulary are kept regular over time.

▶ Read and exchange information about how you and others use computers and the Internet
▶ Listen to and express opinions about computers and communication

Vocabulario en uso

▼6 Leer • Escribir

Definiciones

Lee las definiciones y escribe la palabra correspondiente.

1. Es una foto transparente que podemos proyectar durante una presentación.
2. Es una composición musical que podemos cantar.
3. Es una forma de comunicación que usa bolígrafo y papel. *(Hay dos posibilidades)*.
4. Es un lugar en la Red que da información sobre una organización o una persona.
5. Es una computadora pequeña que puedes llevar a diferentes lugares.

Modelo

Es como enviar una carta por computadora.
el correo electrónico

6. Es un lugar en la escuela donde hay muchas computadoras que los estudiantes pueden usar.
7. Es una forma de comunicación bonita o cómica que le envías* a una persona para su cumpleaños.
8. Es algo visual que puedes crear o ver en la computadora.
9. Es algo que escribes sobre un tema para una clase. *(Hay dos posibilidades)*.

*Enviar has an accent mark on the i in all present-tense forms except nosotros and vosotros.

▼ Fondo Cultural | España

La Real Academia Española was founded in Spain in 1713 to preserve the quality, elegance, and purity of the Spanish language. There are now *Academias* in all the Spanish-speaking countries, including the Philippines and the United States. Today the *Academias* ensure that changes in Spanish reflect the needs of all of its more than 360 million native speakers. *La Real Academia Española* publishes the most complete and authoritative dictionary of the Spanish language.

• Why do you think that it's important to preserve the quality and purity of a language?

La Real Academia Española, en Madrid

DIFFERENTIATED INSTRUCTION

Heritage Language Learners

Have students get acquainted with the Web site of the *Real Academia de la Lengua Española* by typing in *Real Academia Española* in a search engine. Tell them to locate and explore the online dictionary and to look up some of the recent vocabulary words they have learned.

Have them research the history of the *Real Academia Española*, and ask them to come up with two or three benefits of having such an organization. Ask them to also think about some of the problems an organization like the RAE might face.

▼7 | 🔊 | Escuchar • Escribir _____

Opiniones diferentes

❶ Vas a escuchar las opiniones de cuatro personas sobre cómo prefieren comunicarse. En una hoja de papel, escribe los números del 1 al 4 y escribe lo que escuchas.

❷ Después de escuchar sus opiniones, indica si crees que las personas que tienen estas opiniones están en la sala de clases o en el laboratorio de computadoras.

▼8 | 💬👥 | Leer • Pensar • Hablar _____

La computadora y tú

❶ Toma esta prueba *(test)* sobre cómo usas la computadora. Determina tu evaluación y lee la recomendación del Centro de Computación.

❷ Pregunta a otro(a) estudiante qué curso debe tomar según los resultados de la prueba. Tiene que darte tres razones *(reasons)* para justificar el curso.

▶ Modelo

A —*¿Qué curso debes tomar?*
B —*Debo tomar un curso avanzado.*
A —*¿Por qué?*
B —*Porque ya navego en la Red y busco sitios Web. Sé crear un sitio Web.*

La computadora y tú

1. ¿Cómo te comunicas más con otras personas?
  a. Les hablo cara a cara.
  b. Les envío cartas o tarjetas.
  c. Les escribo por correo electrónico.
  d. Visito salones de chat.

2. ¿Cómo buscas información cuando escribes informes?
  a. Voy a la biblioteca por un libro.
  b. Les pido ayuda a mis amigos.
  c. Navego en la Red y busco sitios Web.
  d. Bajo documentos que me sirven mucho.

3. ¿Qué sabes hacer en la computadora?
  a. Sé encender* la computadora.
  b. Sé escribir una composición.
  c. Sé crear una presentación usando diapositivas.
  d. Sé crear un sitio Web.

4. ¿Para qué te sirve la computadora?
  a. No me sirve para nada.
  b. Me sirve para jugar juegos.
  c. Me sirve para navegar en la Red.
  d. Me sirve para buscar y bajar información.

5. ¿Cuál es tu opinión de las computadoras?
  a. Tengo miedo de las computadoras.
  b. Las computadoras son demasiado complicadas.
  c. Las computadoras me ayudan a hacer cosas más rápidamente.
  d. Las computadoras son necesarias para la comunicación.

Evaluación
Cada a = 1 punto
Cada b = 3 puntos
Cada c = 4 puntos
Cada d = 6 puntos

El Centro de Computación tiene cursos ideales para ti. Según el resultado de la prueba, debes tomar uno de estos cursos:

Puntos	Tu curso ideal
de 5 a 10	Básico 1
de 11 a 16	Básico 2
de 17 a 23	Intermedio
de 24 a 30	Avanzado

*to turn on

trescientos diecisiete **317**
Capítulo 9B

▼7 Standards: 1.2, 1.3

Resources: Teacher's Resource Book: Audio Script, p. 343; Audio Program DVD: Cap. 9B, Track 6; Answer Keys: Student Edition, p. 186

Focus: Listening comprehension; writing with accuracy; stating an opinion in a personalized context

Suggestions: Play the audio or read the script. Allow students time to write. For Step 2, students will decide which room is more applicable to each individual.

🔊 **Script and Answers:**

1. **Me gusta más hablar cara a cara con mis amigos. No los visito en los salones de chat.** *(en la sala)*
2. **No me gusta ir a la biblioteca por libros. Prefiero estar en línea en casa buscando información.** *(en el laboratorio de computadoras)*
3. **Me interesa más crear una presentación usando gráficos. Es fácil bajar los gráficos y ponerlos en un documento o archivo.** *(en el laboratorio de computadoras)*
4. **No me comunico con mis amigos por correo electrónico. Les hablo por teléfono o les escribo cartas.** *(en la sala)*

▼8 Standards: 1.1, 1.2, 1.3

Resources: Voc. and Gram. Transparency 172; Teacher's Resource Book: GramActiva BLM, p. 355

Focus: Reading, thinking about, and responding to a survey about computer skills

Suggestions: After students read the quiz aloud and review vocabulary, have them read the questions silently and write the letter of each response. Make sure they know how to add up their points. Use yourself as a model by telling them what you scored and what computer course you should take. Practice the *Modelo* with a student volunteer.

Answers will vary.

Common Errors: Students often confuse the *yo* and *tú* verb forms when conversing with a partner. Review the *yo* and *tú* forms of *deber* before you begin Step 2.

Extension: Create a model exercise that students can do in pairs. Student A: *¿Qué aprendiste en la clase básica?* Student B: *Aprendí a crear documentos.*

ENRICH YOUR TEACHING

Culture Note
Since 1780, the *Real Academia de la Lengua Española* in Madrid has been improving and updating a definitive dictionary of the Spanish language. The *Academia Norteamericana de la Lengua Española,* founded in 1973 and located in New York City, is the most recent official Spanish-language *academia.*

Teacher-to-Teacher
Have students copy some of the definitions from *Actividad* 6 onto index cards. Have students draw a card, read the definition, and tell the word being defined.

Review the meanings of the expressions *a menudo, a veces,* and *nunca.*

9 Standards: 1.2, 1.3, 4.2

Resources: Answer Keys: Student Edition, p. 186

Focus: Reading and interpreting statistics; answering questions in writing about Internet use; sharing those answers in small groups

Suggestions: Before reading the ad aloud, have students review the questions to guide their reading. Point out that students will have to use the information given to figure out the answers to item 1. After they write the remaining answers, have them share their work in pairs or small groups.

Answers:
1. los estadounidenses; los groenlandeses
2.–3. Answers will vary.

Exploración del lenguaje
Core Instruction

Standards: 4.1

Suggestions: Begin by discussing the purpose of adverbs. Remind students that knowing and recognizing patterns of language similarities between Spanish and English will help them learn and use new vocabulary quickly. Have partners practice saying the adjectives and adverbs aloud. You could conduct *Try it out!* either as a whole-class activity or a paired activity.

Answers will vary but may include:
1. completamente, totalmente
2. Frecuentemente, normalmente
3. Recientemente
4. totalmente, completamente
5. Normalmente, frecuentemente

Extension: Write on index cards sets of verbs and adverbs ending in **-mente** that can be pantomimed (e.g., *caminar / lentamente, leer / rápidamente*). Have one student appropriately pantomime each action while the remaining students guess the two words on the card.

▼9 Leer • Escribir • Hablar

¿Quiénes están en línea?

Lee el anuncio y luego contesta estas preguntas.

1. ¿Quiénes usan más el Internet: los estadounidenses o los españoles? ¿Los estadounidenses o los groenlandeses?

2. ¿Usas tú el Internet a menudo, a veces o nunca?

3. Entre *(Among)* las personas que conoces, ¿quién usa más el Internet? ¿Para qué lo usa?

¡A sus teclados[1], listos... a navegar!

¿Usas el Internet? En el mundo hay más de mil millones de internautas. El récord lo tienen groenlandeses:[2] nueve de cada diez personas usan la Red. En los Estados Unidos, siete de cada diez estadounidenses[3] la usan. En España, la gente está lejos de esa cifra.[4] Sólo seis de cada diez españoles están conectados al Internet.

[1] keyboards [2] Greenlanders [3] Americans [4] figure

▼ Exploración del lenguaje

Using *-mente* to form an adverb

Adverbs are words that describe verbs. They often tell *how* an action is performed. Many adverbs in English end in the letters *-ly: slowly, frequently, happily,* and so on. To form similar adverbs in Spanish, you add the ending *-mente* to the feminine singular form of an adjective. This *-mente* ending is equivalent to the *-ly* ending in English.

rápida → rápidamente

práctica → prácticamente

fácil → fácilmente

feliz → felizmente

general → generalmente

especial → especialmente

Note that if the adjective has a written accent, as with *rápida, fácil,* and *práctica,* the accent appears in the same place in the adverb form.

Try it out! Give the adverb for each of the adjectives in the list. Then use each adverb in one of the sentences. Some sentences have more than one possible answer.

normal	total	completo
frecuente	reciente	

1. El laboratorio de nuestra escuela es _____ nuevo.

2. _____ les escribo a mis amigos por correo electrónico pero hoy les envío una carta.

3. _____ mis padres nos compraron una nueva computadora.

4. Mi hermano está _____ contento cuando está usando la computadora.

5. _____ grabamos canciones en un disco compacto.

DIFFERENTIATED INSTRUCTION

Heritage Language Learners

Have students brainstorm a short set of questions as a group and individually interview a Spanish-speaking person about the Internet and e-mail, asking him or her about the influence of English words. Make sure they ask about the difficulty of including accent marks in e-mail. Have students report responses to the class.

Advanced Learners

Have students research the Altamira caves on the Internet. Have them create a brief software slide show or print it out. Divide the class into pairs or groups to write a short report on one aspect of the caves.

▼**10** | **Escribir · Hablar** _____

¿Cómo te comunicas?

❶ Mira cada dibujo y escribe qué forma de comunicación es. Luego escribe por qué se usa esta forma de comunicación.

Modelo
hablar por teléfono
Casi todos tienen teléfonos. Es fácil.

1.    2.   3.    4.

❷ Trabaja con un grupo de cinco personas y pregunta a tus compañeros cómo se comunican con otras personas y por qué. Escriban sus respuestas.

❸ Una persona de cada grupo va a escribir en la pizarra la forma preferida de comunicación de su grupo. Según esta información, ¿cuál es la forma de comunicación preferida de la clase?

▼**11** | | **Escribir · Hablar** _____

Y tú, ¿qué dices?

1. ¿Tienes tú, o tiene tu familia o un(a) amigo(a), una computadora portátil? ¿Qué te parece?
2. ¿A veces tienes miedo de las computadoras? ¿Por qué?
3. ¿Tienes tu propia dirección electrónica? Crea una nueva dirección electrónica "inolvidable" para las personas que nunca recuerdan *(remember)* tu dirección.
4. ¿Qué sabes crear en la computadora?
5. ¿Qué sitio Web conoces mejor? ¿Qué te parece?

> **¿Recuerdas?**
> You use the indirect object pronoun *les* to mean "to them" or "for them."

> **Para decir más . . .**
> **eficiente**   efficient
> **íntimo, -a**   personal
> **rápido, -a**   quick, fast

▶ **Modelo**

A —*¿Cómo te comunicas con otras personas?*
B —*Les hablo por teléfono.*
A —*¿Por qué?*
B —*Porque casi todos tienen teléfonos y es fácil.*

Fondo Cultural

Las cuevas de Altamira Long before people were able to write, they drew pictures on cave walls. These are the first record we have of communication. Spectacular paintings of bison, deer, horses, and wild boars were discovered in 1879 in the caves of Altamira in northern Spain. These drawings are more than 14,000 years old.

• Why do you think the cave dwellers drew pictures of animals? What would you draw?

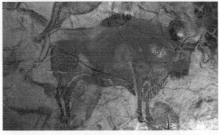

Un bisonte en las cuevas de Altamira

trescientos diecinueve **319**
Capítulo 9B

10 Standards: 1.1, 1.2, 1.3
Resources: Answer Keys: Student Edition, p. 187
Focus: Writing reasons for using various means of communication
Suggestions: Review the ¿Recuerdas? and provide examples of **les** in the context of a few sentences. Tell students that their sentences should tell a fact about the form of communication and state why it is used. Make sure each group keeps a tally of their preferences.
Answers will vary but should include:
1. escribir por correo electrónico   3. escribir tarjetas
2. hablar cara a cara   4. escribir cartas

11 Standards: 1.1, 1.3
Focus: Writing and speaking about computers in a personalized context
Suggestions: After students write their answers, divide them into small groups and have them share their answers.
Answers will vary.

Fondo cultural
Standards: 3.1
Suggestions: Ask why people drew pictures on cave walls. What other unique forms of communication can students think of?
Answers will vary.
🌐 **Mapa global interactivo, Actividad** Explore the prehistoric caves of Altamira in Spain.

Additional Resources
• Communication Wbk.: Audio Act. 6, p. 96
• Teacher's Resource Book: Audio Script, p. 344, Communicative Pair Activity BLM, pp. 350–351
• Audio Program DVD: Cap. 9B, Track 8

✓ASSESSMENT
Prueba 9B-2 with Study Plan (online only)
Quiz: Vocabulary Production
• Prueba 9B-2: pp. 243–244

ENRICH YOUR TEACHING

Culture Note
Ancient civilizations in the Americas also created wall art. Carvings of humans and animals, called petroglyphs, are often found on canyon walls. The Three Rivers Petroglyphs Site in southern New Mexico is a whole park devoted to carvings from 900 to 1400 C.E. Canyon de Chelly in Navajo territory in northeastern Arizona also has some fine examples.

21st Century Skills
Communication Using the Internet, have students find out how technology has influenced Spanish linguistic borrowings. What familiar technology terms have been imported, "as-is," into Spanish? Their lists can be as long as they want, but they should find at least 5 terms. Challenge students by telling them they can't use any of the words or phrases in the *Lectura* on p. 329.

Gramática

Core Instruction

Standards: 4.1

Resources: Voc. and Gram. Transparency 170; Teacher's Resource Book: Video Script, p. 347; Video Program: Cap. 9B

INTERACTIVE WHITEBOARD

Grammar Activities 9B

Suggestions: Ask students to identify any stem-changing verbs that they learned earlier. Then ask them what the rule is for conjugating **pensar, querer,** and **preferir.** Have them compare the charts on p. 182 (in the *Repaso* for *Capítulo* 7A) with the chart here on p. 320 to see how the verbs change **e** to **ie** or **e** to **i.** Show the transparency and the *GramActiva* Video to reinforce your explanation.

▼12 Standards: 1.2, 1.3

Resources: Answer Keys: Student Edition, p. 187
Focus: Reading comprehension; using the present tense of **servir** and **pedir** in context

Suggestions: Ask students to read through the entire description before they begin to write answers. Then have them write the numbers 1–7 on a sheet of paper and write the correct verb form in each blank. Finally, have several volunteers read the paragraph aloud.

Answers:

1. servimos
2. pides
3. sirvo
4. piden
5. sirven
6. sirven
7. pide

Theme Project

Students can perform Step 4 at this point. Be sure they understand your corrections and suggestions. (For more information, see p. 280-b.)

▼ Objectives
▶ Talk and write about asking for help
▶ Discuss what your favorite restaurant serves and give advice about ordering
▶ Discuss an object's use while playing a game

Gramática

The present tense of *pedir* and *servir*

Pedir and *servir* are stem-changing verbs in which the *e* in the stem of the infinitive changes to *i* in all forms except *nosotros* and *vosotros*.

Here are the present-tense forms of *pedir* and *servir*:

(yo)	**pid**o	(nosotros) (nosotras)	**ped**imos
(tú)	**pid**es	(vosotros) (vosotras)	**ped**ís
Ud. (él) (ella)	**pid**e	Uds. (ellos) (ellas)	**pid**en

(yo)	**sirv**o	(nosotros) (nosotras)	**serv**imos
(tú)	**sirv**es	(vosotros) (vosotras)	**serv**ís
Ud. (él) (ella)	**sirv**e	Uds. (ellos) (ellas)	**sirv**en

Pedir means "to ask for."

Juan **pide** la dirección electrónica.

Pedimos más información sobre la Red.

Servir means "to serve" or "to be useful for."

Servimos refrescos después de la clase.

Las computadoras **sirven** para mucho.

Más ayuda	realidades.com

▶ *GramActiva* Video
  Animated Verbs

✎ *GramActiva* Activity

Tecnocapuccino

En el cibercafé Tecnocapuccino no hay sólo computadoras. Nosotros __1.__ café, refrescos y todo tipo de sándwiches. Si tú __2.__ un café con leche yo te __3.__ el mejor café de la ciudad. Cuando nuestros clientes __4.__ un sándwich, nuestros camareros les __5.__ uno de nuestros riquísimos sándwiches con papas fritas y un refresco. Nuestras computadoras te __6.__ para todo: navegar en la Red, escribir por correo electrónico y visitar salones de chat. Si uno __7.__ ayuda, nosotros podemos ayudarle sin problemas.

¡Reserva tu computadora hoy!

▼12 Leer • Escribir

En el cibercafé

Completa esta descripción de un cibercafé con la forma apropiada de *servir* o *pedir*. Escribe los verbos en una hoja de papel.

DIFFERENTIATED INSTRUCTION

Advanced Learners

As a long-term project, have students go online and create a list of Web sites that provide information about Spanish lessons or exchange programs that they might be interested in. Have students preview the sites and rate them. Students can share their results with the class.

▼13 | ♻ | Escribir

Les piden a los profesores

Tú y tus amigos tienen problemas y necesitan pedirles ayuda a los profesores. Usa los nombres de tus amigos y los profesores de tu escuela para decir a quién(es) le(s) piden ayuda. Escribe las frases en una hoja de papel.

Modelo

Mi amigo(a) *(nombre)* no puede bajar los gráficos para hacer su sitio Web.
Mi amiga Lupita le pide ayuda a la Sra. Márquez, la profesora de tecnología.

1. Mi amigo(a) *(nombre)* no puede grabar un disco compacto de música.
2. *(Nombre)* y tú no comprenden por qué hay un error en su tarea de matemáticas.
3. Tú no sabes todas las palabras en una página Web en español.
4. *(Nombre)* y *(nombre)* no pueden abrir un documento sobre un monumento.
5. Yo quiero crear un cuadro de unos árboles.

> **¿Recuerdas?**
>
> The indirect object pronouns *le* and *les* mean "to him, her, you *(pl.)*, them." With *pedir*, they refer to the person whom you ask for something. If you mention that person by name or title, you need to use *a*.
>
> • **Le pido** dinero a mi hermano Juan.

> **Nota**
>
> In English you say that you ask *for* help. In Spanish, "for" is implied in the meaning of *pedir* and a separate word is *not* used.

▼14 | 🗣 | ♻ | Hablar

¿Pides muchas cosas?

Habla con otro(a) estudiante sobre las cosas que les pides a diferentes personas.

 Modelo

dinero
A —¿A quién le pides *dinero*?
B —*Le pido dinero a mi mejor amiga, Luisa.*
o:—*Les pido dinero a mis padres.*

1. ropa nueva
2. tiempo libre sin tarea
3. ayuda con . . .
4. tu propio(a) . . .
5. tiempo libre sin quehaceres
6. **¡Respuesta personal!**

trescientos veintiuno **321**
Capítulo 9B

▼13 Standards: 1.3

Focus: Using correct forms of **pedir** to write sentences asking for help with problems

Recycle: Present tense of **poder**

Suggestions: Review the material in the *¿Recuerdas?* and *Nota* with students. Have volunteers read the *Modelo* aloud, substituting names of people they know. As they write their sentences, remind students to use different people. They may use names or general nouns such as ***hermano, abuelos,*** and ***profesora.*** Have students share their sentences with the whole class or in groups.

Answers will vary.

Common Errors: Students may forget to include the word **a** when mentioning a person by name. Review indirect objects and the use of **a** with indirect object nouns before you begin the activity.

▼14 Standards: 1.1

Focus: Practicing the present tense of **pedir** in pairs

Recycle: Vocabulary from previous chapters

Suggestions: Briefly discuss the drawing and ask what the girl is doing. Go over the *Modelo* with students and make sure they understand that they should begin each question with *¿A quién le pides...?*

Answers will vary.

Common Errors: Students often use direct object pronouns instead of indirect object pronouns. Remind them to use **le** and **les** in this activity.

Extension: Suggest that students write one or more of their oral responses as a homework assignment.

ENRICH YOUR TEACHING

Teacher-to-Teacher

Have students create a class Web page together. Work with the media specialist at your school and assign different tasks to different groups. Get ideas for content and layout from the class as a whole before giving specific assignments to small groups. Ask students who have already made a page to help the others. Develop the content, such as Spanish projects, in your class. One of the many advantages of having a class Web page is that you can publish student writing online for others to read and post information or assignments for the class.

15 Standards: 1.1, 1.3

Focus: Using *pedir* to talk and write about restaurants and ordering food

Recycle: Food vocabulary

Suggestions: For Step 1, have partners brainstorm a list of restaurants and the food they like to eat there. Practice the *Modelo* with a student volunteer. For Step 2, point out the plural forms that are used.

Answers will vary.

Common Errors: Students may forget to make the adjective agree with the food name. Remind students to make adjectives agree with the nouns they describe.

Extension: Based on class recommendations, have students make a poster rating restaurants and describing the best meals.

Pre-AP* Support

• **Learning Objective:** Presentational Speaking
• **Activity 15:** Students practice formal speaking as they present information about restaurants and meals. In addition, have students do a cross-cultural comparison, asking, *"¿Hay restaurantes aquí en nuestra ciudad que sirven la comida del mundo hispanohablante?"*
• *Pre-AP* Resource Book:* Comprehensive guide to Pre-AP* speaking skill development, pp. 39–50

BELLRINGER REVIEW

Ask students to explain the phrase *¿Para qué sirve?,* which they will need to remember to play the game.

16 Standards: 1.1, 1.3

Focus: Writing and saying descriptions of objects

Recycle: Vocabulary from previous chapters; present tense of *servir*

Suggestions: Circulate among students, correcting their descriptions as they write them. If the pair trying to identify the object is having trouble, suggest that the other pair give three possible answers, one of which is correct.

Answers will vary.

▼15 | 👥 | ♻ | Hablar · Escribir

Los mejores restaurantes

❶ Piensa en los restaurantes que conoces. ¿Qué sirven allí que te gusta? Con otro(a) estudiante, habla sobre los restaurantes y la comida que sirven.

▶ Modelo

A —¿En qué restaurante comes?
B —Como en el restaurante.... A menudo pido... allí. Es muy.... Lo sirven con....

❷ Ahora hablen con otra pareja de los restaurantes donde Uds. comen, lo que piden y con qué sirven las comidas. Preparen tres o más recomendaciones de restaurantes para presentar a la clase.

Modelo

Si Uds. quieren comer bien, recomendamos el restaurante Las Palmeras. Siempre pedimos el pescado... ¡es delicioso! Lo sirven con arroz....

Sirven comida muy rica en este restaurante de la Ciudad de México.

▼16 | 👥 | ♻ | Escribir · Hablar

Juego

Con otro(a) estudiante, escriban descripciones de tres cosas y expliquen para qué sirven. Lean las frases a otra pareja para ver si ellos pueden identificar las cosas.

▶ Modelo

A —*Es una cosa bastante pequeña. Puede estar en tu mochila o pupitre. No cuesta mucho dinero.*
B —*¿Para qué sirve?*
A —*Sirve para escribir cartas o composiciones.*
B —*Es un bolígrafo.*

322 trescientos veintidós
Tema 9 • Medios de comunicación

DIFFERENTIATED INSTRUCTION

Multiple Intelligences

Kinesthetic: Have students write a skit about going to a restaurant and ordering a meal. Have them bring in some props and perform the skit for the class or, if possible, record it on video and show it to the class.

Heritage Language Learners

To extend *Actividad* 15, encourage students to describe dishes from their heritage countries that visitors would enjoy ordering in a restaurant in that country. Have students consult their relatives and compile a cookbook with a recipe from each of their families.

▼ Pronunciación | 🔊 | 💬

Dividing words into syllables

Knowing how to divide words into syllables will help you sound out a new word. Just as in English, all syllables in Spanish include a vowel. When there is a consonant between two vowels, you divide the word into syllables before the consonant. The letter combinations *ch*, *ll*, and *rr* are never divided in Spanish. Listen to and say these words:

ju-gar pá-gi-na la-bo-ra-to-rio na-ve-gar
ca-lle no-ti-cias co-mu-ni-dad a-bu-rri-do

When there are two consonants between vowels, you divide the word between the consonants. Exceptions are the blends *pr*, *pl*, *br*, *bl*, *fr*, *fl*, *tr*, *dr*, *cr*, *cl*, *gr*, and *gl*. These blends are never divided and go with the following vowel: *pro-ble-ma*. Listen to and say these words:

car-ta in-fan-til con-cur-sos jar-dín
par-que a-bri-go des-can-sar pa-dres

When there are three or more consonants between vowel sounds, the first two go with the vowel that precedes them and the third goes with the vowel that follows them: *trans-por-te*. When the second and third consonants form a blend, however, the first consonant goes with the vowel before it and the other consonants go with the vowel that follows them: *en-tre*. Listen to and say these words:

es-cri-to-rio com-pli-ca-do
en-tre-vis-tas com-pras-te

Try it out! See if you can separate the following words into the correct syllables.

1. emocionante
2. rápidamente
3. computadora
4. problema
5. electrónico
6. comunicamos

▼17 | 💬 | Escribir • Hablar

Y tú, ¿qué dices?

1. ¿A quién le pides ayuda con la computadora? ¿Le pides ayuda a menudo o sólo a veces?

2. ¿Qué haces cuando tus amigos te piden ayuda con la computadora? ¿Para qué cosas te piden ayuda?

3. ¿Para qué sirve una clase de tecnología? ¿Qué te gustaría aprender en una clase de tecnología?

4. ¿Para qué sirve una computadora portátil? ¿Te gustaría tener una computadora portátil? ¿Por qué sí o por qué no?

Más práctica GO

realidades.com | print

Instant Check	✔	
Guided WB pp. 151–152	✔	✔
Core WB p. 86	✔	✔
Comm. WB pp. 96, 99	✔	✔
Hispanohablantes WB pp. 354–357, 360	✔	

ENRICH YOUR TEACHING

Culture Note

If students were eating in a restaurant in Bolivia, they might want to try *salteñas*, a famous Bolivian "fast food" made of pastry filled with meat, vegetables, and spices. Somewhat similar to Cornish pasties, *salteñas* resemble North American footballs and are eaten as mid-morning snacks throughout Bolivia.

Teacher-to-Teacher

Have students play a different version of the game in *Actividad* 16. Ask them to write descriptions of local restaurants instead of objects. Encourage them to include in their descriptions what they order and what is served at the restaurant. The other pair will try to identify the restaurant.

Pronunciación
Core Instruction

Standards: 4.1

Resources: Teacher's Resource Book: Audio Script, pp. 344–345; Audio Program DVD: Cap. 9B, Track 9; Answer Keys: Student Edition, p. 187

Suggestions: Have students divide the English word *collar* into syllables (*col-lar*). Then outline on the board the rules presented on this page and write examples for each one. To reinforce your teaching, play the audio.

Have students work in pairs to complete the *Try it out!* activity. Ask them to write their answers on the board and to pronounce each word.

Answers:

1. e-mo-cio-nan-te
2. rá-pi-da-men-te
3. com-pu-ta-do-ra
4. a-na-ran-ja-do
5. e-lec-tró-ni-co
6. co-mu-ni-ca-mos

Extension: On the board, write a few words. Have students quietly clap as they say each syllable. Have volunteers divide the words into syllables.

▼17 Standards: 1.1, 1.3

Focus: Writing and answering questions using *pedir*

Suggestions: Make sure that students understand the questions. Divide the class into pairs to answer the questions in writing. Have students share their answers with the class.

Answers will vary.

Extension: Have students take two or more sentences they wrote and divide appropriate words into syllables.

Additional Resources

• Communication Wbk.: Audio Act. 7, p. 96
• Teacher's Resource Book: Audio Script, p. 345
• Audio Program DVD: Cap. 9B, Track 10

✓ASSESSMENT

Prueba 9B-3 with Study Plan (online only)

Quiz: The present tense of *pedir* and *servir*

• Prueba 9B-3: p. 245

Gramática

Core Instruction

Standards: 4.1

Resources: Voc. and Gram. Transparency 171; Teacher's Resource Book: Video Script, pp. 347–348; Video Program: Cap. 9B

INTERACTIVE WHITEBOARD

Grammar Activities 9B

Suggestions: Make sure students can differentiate between **saber** and **conocer**. Remind students that **saber** is used to talk about knowing facts or information, or knowing how to do something. Although **conocer** is primarily used to talk about people and places, it can be used with objects when discussing familiarity. Use the *GramActiva* Video to reinforce the difference between the two verbs.

BELLRINGER REVIEW

You may want to refer students back to the vocabulary for places to visit in the *Repaso* for *Capítulo* 8A.

18 Standards: 1.3

Focus: Completing sentences with **conocer** in a personalized context; comparing experiences

Recycle: Places and classroom vocabulary

Suggestions: Remind students to write complete sentences. Work with students on the first item, modeling how they must supply their own words. Remind students to keep their answers for *Actividad* 19.

Answers:
People and place names will vary.
1. conozco
2. conocemos
3. conoce
4. conocen
5. conozco
6. conoce

Extension: Ask students to describe interesting places in their community for tourists to visit (Example: *Conozco un parque bonito cerca de mi casa.*)

Gramática

Saber and conocer

Sé and *sabes* come from the verb *saber,* "to know." There is another verb in Spanish that also means "to know": *conocer.* Use *conocer* to talk about people, places, and things that you are familiar with.

Here are the present-tense forms of *saber* and *conocer.* Except for the *yo* forms, they are regular in the present tense.

¿Recuerdas?

You have used *(yo) sé* and *(tú) sabes* to talk about knowing a fact and to say what you know how to do.

• ¿**Sabes** dónde está la biblioteca?

• Yo **sé** esquiar bastante bien.

(yo)	sé	(nosotros) (nosotras)	sabemos
(tú)	sabes	(vosotros) (vosotras)	sabéis
Ud. (él) (ella)	sabe	Uds. (ellos) (ellas)	saben

(yo)	conozco	(nosotros) (nosotras)	conocemos
(tú)	conoces	(vosotros) (vosotras)	conocéis
Ud. (él) (ella)	conoce	Uds. (ellos) (ellas)	conocen

Conocer is followed by the personal *a* when the direct object is a person. Direct object pronouns can also be used with *conocer.*

¿Conocen Uds. a la señora que trabaja en el laboratorio?

Sí, la conocemos bien. ¿Quieres conocerla?

Más ayuda **realidades.com**

 GramActiva Video
Tutorials: Adverbs, Adverbial clauses
Animated Verbs

 Canción de hip hop: Tecnología

 GramActiva Activity

▼18 | | Escribir

¿Qué lugares y a qué personas conoces?

Si una persona visita tu comunidad y tu escuela, ¿puedes ayudarla a conocer a diferentes personas y lugares? Escribe la forma apropiada del verbo *conocer* y la información apropiada para cada frase. Escribe las frases en una hoja de papel.

1. (Yo) ___ a muchos de los estudiantes en la clase de ___ .

2. Mis amigos y yo ___ al (a la) secretario(a) de la escuela. Es el (la) Sr. (Sra.) ___ .

3. Mi hermano(a)/amigo(a) ___ bastante bien al (a la) profesor(a) de ___ .

4. Mis amigos ___ bien el parque de diversiones ___ .

5. (Yo) ___ la tienda ___ donde me gusta comprar ___ .

6. Mi padre (madre) ___ bien el monumento de ___ .

DIFFERENTIATED INSTRUCTION

Heritage Language Learners

Have students write five sentences about what their family members know how to do *(saber)* and five sentences about people and places that they know *(conocer)*. Have these students read what they wrote to small groups.

Multiple Intelligences

Visual/Spatial: Have students develop ideas for a virtual tour of their community or school. Have them take photos of places and of people working, and insert the photos into a presentation software program. Students can add captions that explain each photo.

▼19 | Hablar

¿Conocemos a las mismas personas y los mismos lugares?

Trabaja con otro(a) estudiante y lee tus frases de la Actividad 18. Habla de las personas y los lugares que Uds. conocen.

▶ **Modelo**

A —*Conozco a Jaime, que está en mi clase de matemáticas.*

B —*Yo también lo conozco. Está en mi clase de historia.*

o:—*No lo conozco. ¿Cómo es?*

¿Conoces la Plaza de España en Sevilla?

España

▼20 | Hablar

Lo que sabemos hacer

Habla con otro(a) estudiante sobre quiénes saben hacer las diferentes actividades en los dibujos.

▶ **Modelo**

A —*¿Quién sabe grabar un disco compacto?*

B —*Mi hermano Mario sabe grabar un disco compacto. Lo hace a menudo.*

o:—*No sé quién sabe grabar un disco compacto.*

¿Recuerdas?

When you say that you know how to do something, you don't need a separate word for "how."

• **Sabemos crear** presentaciones con diapositivas.

1.

2.

3.

4.

5.

6.

Practice and Communicate 9B

▼19 Standards: 1.1

Focus: Speaking of knowing people and places

Suggestions: Have students form pairs and ask them first to read their written sentences from *Actividad* 18 to each other. Then have one partner begin the conversation with a sentence about knowing a specific person or place, as in the *Modelo*. Make an audio recording of the students' conversations and include a copy in each of their portfolios.

Answers will vary.

Common Errors: Students often forget to include the personal **a.** Before you begin, remind them to use it when they are talking about a person they know.

BELLRINGER REVIEW

Work with students to name the activity shown in each image.

▼20 Standards: 1.1

Resources: Answer Keys: Student Edition, p. 188

Focus: Using *saber* to talk about what people know how to do

Recycle: Leisure activities

Suggestions: Practice the *Modelo* with a student volunteer. Remind students to include a phrase telling how often the person does the activity (e.g., ***todos los días, después de las clases, a veces, los fines de semana***).

Answers:

Student A:

1. —¿Quién sabe jugar al tenis?
2. —¿...sabe esquiar?
3. —¿...sabe tocar la guitarra?
4. —¿...sabe usar la computadora (crear documentos)?
5. —¿ ... sabe hacer gráficos (preparar presentaciones con diapositivas)?
6. —¿...sabe tocar música en la computadora?

Student B

Answers will vary.

Common Errors: Students often insert *cómo* between the conjugated form of *saber* and the infinitive. Remind them that *how* is included in the meaning of *saber* so there is no need for the word *cómo.*

ENRICH YOUR TEACHING

Culture Note

Have students make a virtual visit to the *Plaza de España* in Seville by going to a search engine and typing in its name and the city name. Ask them to compare the plaza in Seville to plazas or squares they have seen in Spanish-speaking countries or in other countries, including the United States.

Teacher-to-Teacher

Create a list of questions for an Internet scavenger hunt. Select a Web site for students to investigate or make sure they know how to use a search engine. Have them use *inventions museum* as a search term. Have them work in pairs to answer questions such as: *¿Quién inventó…?* or *¿Para qué sirve el (la)…?*

21
Standards: 1.1

Resources: Answer Keys: Student Edition, p. 189
Focus: Expressing familiarity with and knowledge of people, places, things, and activities

Suggestions: Practice both models with students, then divide the class into pairs. Have students decide whether to use *saber* or *conocer* to ask the question. Circulate to make sure they are selecting the correct verb.

Answers:
Student A:
1. —¿Conoces a la hermana de...?
2. —¿Sabes bajar información de la Red?
3. —¿Sabes el nombre de una canción en español?
4. —¿Conoces las cámaras digitales?
5. —¿Conoces España o México?
6. —¿Sabes la dirección electrónica de...?
7. —¿Conoces un sitio Web interesante?
8. —¿Sabes enviar fotos por la Red?
Student B: Answers will vary.

22
Standards: 1.2, 1.3

Focus: Reading an advertisement for a telephone caller ID option and writing opinions about the issue

Suggestions: Have the class note the title of the activity, read the ad, and discuss the humor of including a picture of the "Three Little Pigs" and the "Big Bad Wolf." Ask students if they think the ad is effective and if they feel that the product is worthwhile. After students write down their answers, encourage partners to help each other with spelling and grammar. When students have revised their writing, tell them to include this work in their portfolios.

Answers will vary but may include:
1. Sí, lo conocen y saben lo que quiere.
2. –4. Answers will vary.

Extension: Invite pairs of students to use another fairy tale to advertise a different, fictional product.

Theme Project
Students can perform Step 5 at this point. Record their presentations for inclusion in their portfolio. (For more information, see p. 280-b.)

---

21 | Hablar

¿Saber o conocer?
Trabaja con otro(a) estudiante para ver lo que sabe y conoce.

1. la hermana de . . .
2. bajar información de la Red
3. el nombre de una canción en español
4. las cámaras digitales
5. España o México
6. la dirección electrónica de . . .
7. un sitio Web interesante
8. enviar fotos por la Red

▶ Modelo

la persona que trabaja en la biblioteca de la escuela

A —¿Conoces a la persona que trabaja en la biblioteca de la escuela?
B —Sí, la conozco. Es muy simpática. Es la Sra. Wilton.
o:—No, no la conozco.

bailar salsa

A —¿Sabes bailar salsa?
B —Sí, sé bailar salsa. Me encanta.
o:—No, no sé bailar salsa.

22 Leer · Escribir

Los tres cerditos
Lee el anuncio y contesta las preguntas.

1. ¿Conocen los cerditos a la "persona" que está en la puerta? ¿Saben ellos lo que quiere?
2. ¿Tiene tu familia un servicio de identificación de llamadas en su teléfono? ¿Te gusta este servicio, o te gustaría tener este servicio? ¿Por qué?
3. ¿Te parece bien saber quién llama por teléfono? ¿Por qué?
4. ¿Te gusta hablar por teléfono? ¿Con quién te gusta hablar más?

¿Sabes quién es?
Pide el servicio de identificación de llamadas.
Si eres cliente de Teléfonos Caribe, es completamente gratis.

Así, siempre vas a saber quién está llamando.
¡Pídelo hoy! Llama al teléfono 20-05-617.

DIFFERENTIATED INSTRUCTION

Advanced Learners/Pre-AP*
Have students make dioramas showing *lo que hay que saber o conocer* to perform certain jobs. Tell them to include labels explaining what the characters in the diorama know how to do or the people whom they know. Suggest that students first choose a workplace that includes a variety of people.

Heritage Language Learners
Have students speak to relatives about technology use in their heritage country. Ask them to write down one form of communication per index card. On the back, students write who uses the form of communication more (*La gente de los Estados Unidos usa los teléfonos celulares más que la gente de...*).

▼**23** Leer • Pensar • Escribir • Dibujar

¿Qué inventos conoces?

Mucho antes de la invención de la computadora, había *(there were)* otros inventos que nos ayudaron a comunicarnos y que seguimos *(keep)* usando. Mira la línea cronológica y lee la lista de inventos. Luego contesta las preguntas.

Conexiones

La tecnología

| 1829 | 1839 | 1868 | 1910 | 1939 | 1980 | 1989 | 2007 |

1850   1900   1950   2000

| 1837 | 1840 | 1878 | 1884 | 1926 | 1953 | 1999 |

la máquina de escribir
el teléfono celular
el alfabeto Braille
el televisor de color

el lector de libro
  electrónico
la pluma
el reproductor MP3¹

la primera película
  con sonido
el telégrafo
el sello

el código Morse
el teléfono
el walkie-talkie
la Red (World Wide Web)

¹MP3 player

1. Identifica cada invento según el año en que se inventó y explica qué impacto tiene sobre la comunicación.

2. Busca información en la Red o en la biblioteca para identificar los inventores de cada invento de la lista.

3. ¿Cuál de estos inventos te parece el más importante? ¿Por qué?

4. Piensa en un invento que quieres hacer. ¿Para qué sirve? Escribe un párrafo y haz un dibujo para explicar tu invento.

El español en el mundo del trabajo

The ability to share information is crucial in the twenty-first century. Innovations from medicine, science, technology, engineering, manufacturing, and social services need to be communicated across the globe. With a partner, make a list of six ways in which information can be spread. For each, tell how knowing Spanish would be beneficial. Share your ideas with the class.

Más práctica GO

realidades.com | print

Instant Check	✔	
Guided WB pp. 153–154	✔	✔
Core WB pp. 87–88	✔	✔
Comm. WB pp. 97, 100, 187	✔	✔
Hispanohablantes WB pp. 358–361		✔

trescientos veintisiete **327**
Capítulo 9B

ENRICH YOUR TEACHING

Teacher-to-Teacher

Play a version of the game Telephone. Create several teams whose average language ability is similar. Show one member of each team the same sentence, which he or she should silently read. Have those students return to their seats, write the sentence from memory, and then briefly show what they wrote to the next person on the team, who writes the sentence

from memory, and so on. The team that finishes first gets a point. The team that ends up with a sentence that is closest to the original (determined by the teacher) gets one point also. After they have played a few rounds, you might have them play the original Telephone game by whispering sentences.

---

23 Standards: 1.2, 1.3, 3.1

Resources: Answer Keys: Student Edition, p. 189

Focus: Reading a timeline about inventions; evaluating and writing about those inventions; developing and writing an idea for an invention

Suggestions: Direct students' attention to the timeline and discuss the inventions. Read the steps, making sure they understand what to do. This activity will take some time and effort, and you may want students to work together in pairs or small groups. Schedule time for students to research answers in the library as well as online. Students may present their own inventions to the class. Remind students that *servir* also means "to be useful for." Point out that in this activity they will use the phrase *sirve para ....*

Answers:

1. la máquina de escribir—1868; el teléfono celular—1980; el alfabeto Braille—1829; el televisor—1926; el televisor de color—1953; la pluma—1884; el reproductor MP3—1999; la primera película con sonido—1910; el telégrafo—1837; el sello—1840; el código Morse—1839; el teléfono—1878; el walkie-talkie—1939; la Red—1989

2.–4. Answers will vary.

El español en el mundo del trabajo

Core Instruction

Standards: 5.1

Suggestions: Before students read the assignment, ask them how knowing Spanish would be beneficial in the business world. Write a model on the board.

Additional Resources

• Communication Wbk.: Audio Act. 8–9, p. 97
• Teacher's Resource Book: Audio Script, p. 345, Communicative Pair Activity BLM, pp. 352–353
• Audio Program DVD: Cap. 9B, Tracks 11–12

✔ ASSESSMENT

Prueba 9B-4 with Study Plan (online only)

Quiz: *Saber and conocer*
• Prueba 9B-4: p. 246

Lectura

Standards: 1.2, 1.3, 2.1, 4.1

Focus: Reading for comprehension; understanding cultural perspectives

Suggestions:

Pre-reading: Read aloud the *Strategy* and have students write a list of five things they know about the Internet. Make sure they keep this list to use later. Direct them to the title and ask them what they think it means. Ask students to skim the *Lectura* to get a general idea of what it is about.

Reading: As students read the selection, have them focus on information about how the Internet impacts the Spanish language. Have them also look for advantages and disadvantages of the Internet.

Post-reading: Ask students the following questions: Do you think the idea expressed in the title is true or not? In what ways has technology affected the Spanish language? Why do you think many terms are in English? What advantages or disadvantages does the Internet have for Spanish speakers and Spanish-language learners?

Pre-AP* Support

- **Learning Objective:** Interpretive: Print and Audio
- **Activity:** Prepare a crossword puzzle using vocabulary words from the *Términos de ciberspanglish* column. Write the equivalent *Términos en español* for each puzzle entry on a separate index card (numbered to correspond with the puzzle.) Then create a set of these cards for each group. Divide students into groups, giving each group a blank puzzle and a set of equivalents. Distribute the equivalents among the group members.

  Students must explain their words to the rest of the group without using the words themselves. The others must determine the word described and write it in the appropriate space on the puzzle. Allow students to use circumlocution if needed.

- *Pre-AP* Resource Book:* Comprehensive guide to reading skill development, pp. 19–26

¡Adelante!

▶ Read about the impact of the Internet on the Spanish language

▶ Use prior knowledge to understand what you read

Lectura

La invasión del ciberspanglish

Lee este artículo sobre el Internet. El Internet sirve para muchas cosas aquí en los Estados Unidos y también en los otros países donde hablan español. Pero no es siempre fácil traducir¹ los términos técnicos.

Strategy

Using prior knowledge
Use what you know about a topic to help you understand what you read. This article is on the Internet and its impact on the Spanish language. List five things you know about the Internet that might help you with this reading.

La invasión del ciberspanglish

¿Te gusta usar el Internet? Actualmente² hay gente en todos los países del mundo que usa el Internet. Sirve para muchas cosas: para hacer compras, divertirse, educarse, trabajar, buscar información, hacer planes para un viaje y mucho más. Hoy en día uno no puede pensar en una vida sin computadoras o el Internet.

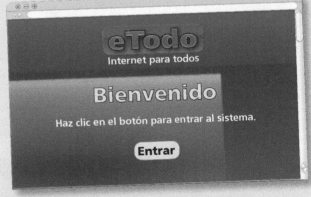

eTodo
Internet para todos

Bienvenido

Haz clic en el botón para entrar al sistema.

Entrar

Si quieres explorar el Internet en español, hay una explosión de portales (sitios que sirven como puerta al Internet) en los Estados Unidos, España y América Latina. Como puedes imaginar, hay una rivalidad³ grande entre estos portales para atraer⁴ a los hispanohablantes. Algunos portales dan la misma información en inglés y español; sólo tienes que hacer clic para cambiarla.

¹to translate ²Nowadays
³rivalry ⁴to attract

328 trescientos veintiocho
Tema 9 • Medios de comunicación

DIFFERENTIATED INSTRUCTION

Heritage Language Learners

Have students read the list of words on p. 329. Have them make posters with helpful phrases related to technology that students might use in the computer lab. Before students make their posters, ask them to make a draft of the phrases they will display so that you can first review them for accuracy.

Students with Learning Difficulties

Provide students with the opportunity to see an authentic Spanish-language Web site. Have students use the visual cues on the site, prior knowledge, and cognates to identify the purpose of the site. Help students to apply what they see in an authentic site to understanding the meaning of the text above.

Juntos,[5] el inglés y el español en el Internet dieron origen al "ciberspanglish". A algunas personas no les gusta nada este nuevo "idioma"[6]. Piensan que el español es suficientemente rico para poder traducir los términos del inglés. Hay otros que dicen que no hay problema con mezclar[7] los idiomas para comunicarse mejor. Piensan que el "ciberspanglish" es más fácil y lógico porque los términos técnicos vienen del inglés y expresarlos en español es bastante complicado.

Éste es un debate que va a durar[8] mucho tiempo, y no presenta grises.

Términos de ciberspanglish	Términos en español
emailear	mandar por correo electrónico
espam	mandar por un bombardeo de grandes cantidades de correo
chatear	conversar
hacer clic	picar con el ratón
hacer doble clic	picar dos veces con el ratón
rebootear	rearrancar
linkear	enlazar con una página en Internet
crashear	quebrar o chocar
formatear	hacer un formato
programar	escribir un programa
escanear	rastrear o digitalizar
surfear	explorar o navegar
hacer un upgrade	actualizar o subir un grado
el clipart	dibujos artísticos
hacer un exit	salir
printear	imprimir

[5]together [6]language [7]mixing [8]to last

¿Comprendes?

1. Look at the list you created for the Strategy "Using prior knowledge." Place a check mark next to any pieces of information mentioned in the article.

2. According to the article, how could the Internet help you learn more Spanish?

3. Summarize briefly the two sides of the argument related to *ciberspanglish*.

4. What do you think the statement *Éste es un debate que . . . no presenta grises* means? Why is it appropriate as the closing statement for this article?

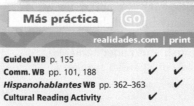

| **Más práctica** | (GO) |

realidades.com | print

Guided WB p. 155	✔	✔
Comm. WB pp. 101, 188	✔	✔
Hispanohablantes **WB** pp. 362–363		✔
Cultural Reading Activity		✔

trescientos veintinueve (329)
Capítulo 9B

ENRICH YOUR TEACHING

Culture Note
Technology and the Internet have created so many new terms in English that new Spanish technology dictionaries are being created. These dictionaries promote the use of vocabulary that reflects the linguistic and cultural sensibilities of Spanish speakers.

21st Century Skills

Communication Have students debate the issue of "ciberspanglish" and the role it plays for Spanish speakers in communication. If possible, have students gather information and opinions from native speakers and exchange students from Spanish-speaking countries to help support their side of the debate. Students should also give examples to illustrate their points.

BELLRINGER REVIEW

Have students unscramble these words for projects that can be completed on a computer: *sacubr minicorofan/bragar nu cisod poctacom/careh cágrofis*

(**Answers:** *buscar información/grabar un disco compacto/hacer gráficos*)

▼¿Comprendes? Standards: 1.3

Focus: Demonstrating reading comprehension

Suggestions: Have students check the lists they made before reading to see which of their ideas were mentioned in the article. Then discuss the remaining questions with students. If they need help with the fourth question, ask students what is meant by the following phrases: *Things are not just black and white. There are shades of gray.*

Answers will vary but may include:
1. Answers will vary.
2. One can find a lot of resources in Spanish, or in both English and Spanish, on the Internet.
3. Some people say it's easier to use "ciberspanglish" because technical terms come from English; others say that Spanish is rich enough for all definitions.
4. It means that it is a heated debate with two definite sides to the argument.

Portfolio
Students might find it helpful to copy into their portfolios "ciberspanglish" terms that they think will be especially useful to remember.

Teacher-to-Teacher
Carefully evaluate a Spanish chat line that would be appropriate for your class. There are options such as bilingual, for those learning Spanish, and voice chat. You can also set up a chat or e-mail exchange with another class in your school or one in another country. Discuss guidelines to follow when using chat, such as not sharing personal information. Start by having students only read the exchanges on the chat line. Then, have students collectively tell you what you should write. Finally, have them fully participate on the chat line, carefully monitoring the questions they receive from others.

For Further Reading
Student Resource: Realidades para hispanohablantes: Lectura 2, pp. 364–365

329

Perspectivas del mundo hispano

Core Instruction

Standards: 2.1, 4.2

Focus: Reading about computer usage

Suggestions: Discuss how computers are used. Point out that today they are found in private homes, libraries, offices, hospitals, schools—just about everywhere. Not long ago they were only used in businesses and the Internet didn't exist. Mention that in most Latin American countries, computers are not as widespread as in the United States. Have students read the text and discuss the reasons why this is true. Talk about what people use the computer for. How does that compare to usage here? Discuss **cibercafés** and how young people from Spanish-speaking countries use them. Have students complete the *Check it out!* section and discuss the question in class.

For many students, the primary use of computers is Internet access. Discuss how they use the Internet. Guide students to see that in Spanish-speaking countries **cibercafés** are a modern way to socialize.

Direct attention to the *Think about it!* section and have students discuss it.

Answers will vary.

Additional Resources

Student Resource: Realidades para hispanohablantes, p. 366

Perspectivas del mundo hispano

¿Para qué usas una computadora?

In many Spanish-speaking countries, the use of computers and access to the Internet are often not as widespread as in the United States. Many homes don't have telephones, computers cost more money, and in many cases, the Internet is not as accessible. Schools and libraries may not have the computers and access to the Internet as they do in most communities in the United States. For these reasons, many cybercafés *(los cibercafés)* have opened. Cybercafés are nice places for students to meet after school and work on assignments, do research, or e-mail friends. They offer very inexpensive access to the Internet.

In recent years, the number of *portales* (portals) that serve as access points to the Internet has increased and many of these are offered in Spanish as well as English. The number of *buscadores* (search engines) has also increased, making it easier for Spanish speakers to search for information or just surf the Internet.

Usando computadoras para estudiar, México

Check it out! Survey your friends. Over the course of one week, how much time do they spend using a computer and for what reasons?

Think about it! Name three ways that you think Spanish-language Internet sites could help you learn more Spanish and understand the perspectives of Spanish speakers.

330 trescientos treinta
Tema 9 • Medios de comunicación

Haciendo la tarea en la computadora

DIFFERENTIATED INSTRUCTION

Advanced Learners

Have students use a Spanish-language Web site of their choice to answer the *Think about it!* section. Have them present their findings to the class.

Heritage Language Learners

Have students use a Spanish-language Web site of their choice to find out about computer usage in their heritage country or in another Spanish-speaking country.

Presentación escrita

La computadora en mi vida

Task
Your parents think you spend too much time on the computer. You disagree. Send an e-mail to your best friend in Mexico explaining your position and how you plan to defend your computer use.

① **Prewrite** In a chart, list at least three ways you use computers and the benefit *(la ventaja)* to you.

Cómo uso la computadora	La ventaja
Busco información para mis clases en Internet.	Aprendo mucho y es muy interesante.

② **Draft** Use the information from the chart to write the first draft of your e-mail. Here are some expressions you might include:

pienso que . . .   tengo que . . .
creo que . . .   primero, segundo, tercero, . . .

③ **Revise** Check for spelling, accent marks, verb forms, pronouns, and vocabulary use. Share the e-mail with a partner. Your partner should check the following:

- Is the paragraph easy to read and understand?
- Does it provide good support for your position?
- What could you add to give more information, or change to make it more understandable?
- Are there any errors?

④ **Publish** Rewrite the e-mail, making necessary changes. Share it with your teacher and add it to your portfolio.

⑤ **Evaluation** The following rubric will be used to grade your e-mail.

Rubric	Score 1	Score 3	Score 5
Amount of information you provided	You list one way and benefit.	You list two ways and benefits.	Your list of ways and benefits is complete.
Presentation of reason and benefit	Your reason and support for your position lack clarity.	Your reasons and support for your position are clear, but not forceful.	You are clear and persuasive in your reasons and support for your position.
Vocabulary, spelling, grammar	Your vocabulary use is limited with several errors in spelling and grammar.	Your vocabulary use is somewhat extensive, but you have many errors in spelling and grammar.	You have very few errors in spelling and grammar and use varied vocabulary.

Strategy

Using supporting examples
When preparing a persuasive argument, you should first clearly state your position and then provide examples to support it. Making a list of your arguments will help you make a strong statement.

trescientos treinta y uno **331**
Capítulo 9B

Presentación escrita
Persuasive

Standards: 1.3

Focus: Writing a defense of frequent use of the computer

Suggestions: Review the task and the five-step approach with students. After reading the *Strategy* with them, have students write a position statement and list three reasons to support it. They can write these statements in a chart or use some other graphic organizer. Review the rubric with the class to explain how you will grade the performance task. Have students work through each step of the writing process.

Pre-AP* Support

- **Learning Objective:** Presentational Writing
- **Activity:** Let's hear the other side of the story. Based on the e-mail you wrote to your friend in Mexico, take the side of your parents. Why do you think they are trying to restrict your access to the Internet? Write a brief paragraph, to "you," from your folks, explaining the parental positions.
- *Pre-AP* Resource Book:* Comprehensive guide to Pre-AP* writing skill development, pp. 27–38

Portfolio
Have students save their finished work for inclusion in their portfolios.

Additional Resources
Student Resources: Realidades para hispanohablantes, p. 367; Guided Practice: Presentación escrita, p. 156

ENRICH YOUR TEACHING

Teacher-to-Teacher
Careers: *Tema* 9 has focused on technology. Have students work in small groups to talk about a career in technology support and services. Ask them to write a list of words and expressions they have learned that would be helpful in training people to use technology. Ask groups to share their lists.

21st Century Skills

Media Literacy In order to make their case to their parents, have students examine appropriate Web sites that contain information about the importance of computers in today's world, so that their argument to their parents is as strong as possible. In order to make their case, have students create an interesting and informative presentation that combines print, video, audio, and images.

✓ASSESSMENT

Presentación escrita
- Assessment Program: Rubrics, p. T34
  Go over the descriptions of the different levels of performance. After assessing students, help individuals understand how their performance could be improved.

9B Video

Videomisterio | ▶️

Videomisterio ▶️

Core Instruction

Standards: 1.3, 3.2, 5.2

Resources: Teacher's Resource Book: Video Script, pp. 348–349; Video Program: Cap. 9B; Video Program Teacher's Guide: Cap. 9B

Focus: Introducing the events and vocabulary of this episode; scanning and reading the episode summary

Personajes importantes:

Lola Lago, detective
Paco, Lola Lago's colleague
Margarita, Lola Lago's secretary
Julia Romero, María's friend
Inspector Gil, police officer
Luis Antonio Llamas, Julia's boyfriend
Pedro, Doña Gracia's grandson
Doña Gracia, Pedro's grandmother

Synopsis: The police arrive at the train station and they arrest the person Lola thought was María. It is really Julia. Then the police arrest Luis Antonio and they find doña Gracia's jewels in his suitcase. Inspector Gil and Lola figure out how Luis Antonio convinced Julia to steal María's identity when María died in the hospital. It was a coincidence that Luis Antonio was a nurse in the same hospital after María's car accident. In the end, Pedro meets his grandmother, who is happy to meet him.

Suggestions:

Pre-viewing: Pre-viewing: Review the events of the previous episode. Lola calls her office to ask Margarita and Paco to help her follow two people. Margarita overhears that the person Lola thought to be María is really Julia. When the two strangers leave, Paco follows them to the train station. Lola calls Inspector Gil to ask him to meet her at the train station right away.

Point out the *Palabras para comprender,* saying examples in context and writing the sentences on the board. Remind students that these words are only used to help them understand the episode and they are not active vocabulary.

¿Eres tú, María? Episodio 10

Antes de ver el video

Resumen del episodio

Es el último episodio y Lola y el Inspector Gil van a solucionarlo todo. En realidad, ¿quién es María? ¿Qué importancia tiene Luis Antonio? ¿Quién tiene las joyas? ¿Cómo y por qué ocurrió el crimen? ¿Quién va a la cárcel? ¿Quién va a necesitar un buen abogado? ¿Qué pasa cuando Pedro ve a su abuela por primera vez?

Palabras para comprender

Deténgala.	Arrest her.
No quería.	I didn't want to.
las reconoció	recognized them
los novios	boyfriend and girlfriend
tomó	took
mucha suerte	a lot of luck
robarlas	to steal them
no quería esperar	didn't want to wait
Parece que . . .	It seems like . . .
la cárcel	jail
un abogado	lawyer

DIFFERENTIATED INSTRUCTION

Students with Learning Difficulties

It may be helpful to visual learners if you provide them with a flowchart to fill in while they watch the *Videomisterio.* Preview the video and decide on the number of key elements that you want to include in the flowchart. Then create and photocopy a chart, including two or three details in the middle so that students have a guide. Ask students to write down important events in the order in which they occur, keeping in mind the events you have already included. Remind students to keep their flowcharts to help them with the *¿Comprendes?* section.

Y tú, ¿qué piensas?

¿Sabes lo que va a pasar en este episodio? Escribe tus respuestas a las preguntas en el *Resumen del episodio*. Ahora, mira el episodio y compara tus respuestas con lo que pasó. ¿Tenías razón?

Visual scanning: Direct students' attention to the photos and ask who these characters are. Before students read the *Resumen del episodio*, have them scan the text and find three cognates (*episodio, inspector, solucionar, importancia, crimen*). Then ask them to read the *Resumen del episodio* carefully and ask questions about what will happen in this episode. Note that the *Resumen* asks several questions about the episode because it is the last one. Point this out to students and ask them to look for the answers as they view this episode.

Post-viewing: Have students look at the photo and tell or guess what happened or will happen in the last scenes of this episode. Write the vocabulary presented in this episode on the board to help students create sentences for each important scene that adds new information to the plot.

Después de ver el video

¿Comprendes?

A. ¿A quién(es) describe cada frase: Lola, María, Julia, Luis Antonio, Pedro o doña Gracia?

1. Pues, señorita, es evidente que Ud. sabe mucho.
2. Las reconoció en el hospital.
3. Es evidente en la foto que son novios.
4. Murió en el hospital.
5. No puede ver muy bien.
6. Viene a Madrid para vivir con ella.
7. Tiene ochenta y cinco años y está de buena salud.
8. Entra en el piso y ataca a la señora.
9. Ud. no va a París, señor. Ud. va a la cárcel.
10. La mejor detective de Madrid.

B. Con un grupo de tres o cuatro estudiantes, escoge una escena del video. Tu profesor(a) les va a dar el guión *(script)* de la escena. Representen la escena para la clase. Hay que aprender de memoria el papel *(the part)*, llevar la ropa del personaje y representar la escena de una manera bien profesional.

Más práctica (GO)

realidades.com | print

Actividades ✔

¿Comprendes? Standards: 1.1, 1.2, 1.3

Resources: Answer Keys: Student Edition, p. 190

Focus: Verifying comprehension by answering questions; reviewing the plot

Suggestions: For part B, have students write two to five sentences about what Lola understands now and about the solution to the mystery. Ask them to use the vocabulary presented in this episode.

Answers:
Part A
1. Lola
2. Luis Antonio
3. Luis Antonio y Julia
4. María
5. doña Gracia
6. Julia
7. doña Gracia
8. Luis Antonio
9. Luis Antonio
10. Lola
Part B
Answers will vary.

Additional Resources
• *¿Eres tú, María?* Video Workbook, Episode 10
• *¿Eres tú, María?* Teacher's Video Guide: Answer Key

ENRICH YOUR TEACHING

Teacher-to-Teacher

Help students review the events of the *Videomisterio* with a concentration game. Photocopy the images of the characters on p. 332 and paste them onto index cards. Then copy or write one of the sentences from the *¿Comprendes?* (or from the Video Script)

on another card. Have students place the cards face down on a desk and take turns matching the picture of the person with the sentence referring to him or her. The student with the most matches wins the game.

Repaso del capítulo
Vocabulario y gramática

Review Activities

To talk about communication: Write *¿Cómo te comunicas?* on the board. Ask students to answer the question orally using vocabulary from the section.

To talk about computer-related activities: On the board, create a chart with three columns with these headings: *los documentos, la Red,* and *los gráficos.* Ask students to write each word under the heading to which it best relates. In cases in which an item could go under more than one heading, have students decide which heading is most appropriate.

Other useful expressions: Use items from this section to create a list of questions and a separate list of responses. Have students work in pairs. Student A selects a question. Student B selects an appropriate answer from the response list.

Portfolio

Invite students to review the activities they completed in this chapter, including written reports, posters or other visuals, and recordings of oral presentations, or other projects. Have them select one or two items to include in their portfolios.

Additional Resources

Student Resources: Realidades para hispanohablantes, p. 368

Teacher Resources:

• Teacher's Resource Book: Situation Cards, p. 354, Clip Art, pp. 356–357

• Assessment Program: Chapter Checklist and Self-Assessment Worksheet, pp. T56–T57

---

to talk about communication

cara a cara	face-to-face
la carta	letter
comunicarse	to communicate
(yo) me comunico	(with)
(tú) te comunicas	
enviar	to send
la tarjeta	card

to talk about computer-related activities

bajar	to download
buscar	to search (for)
la cámara digital	digital camera
la canción,	song
pl. las canciones	
la composición,	composition
pl. las composiciones	
la computadora portátil	laptop computer
crear	to create
el curso	course
tomar un curso	to take a course
la diapositiva	slide
la dirección electrónica	e-mail address
el documento	document
escribir por correo	to send an e-mail
electrónico	message
estar en línea	to be online
grabar un disco	to burn a CD
compacto	
los gráficos	graphics
la información	information
el informe	report
el laboratorio	laboratory
navegar en la Red	to surf the Web
la página Web	Web page
la presentación,	presentation
pl. las presentaciones	
el sitio Web	Web site
visitar salones de chat	to visit chat rooms

For *Vocabulario adicional,* see pp. 336–337.

other useful words and expressions

complicado, -a	complicated
¿Para qué sirve?	What's it (used) for?
¿Qué te parece?	What do you think?
rápidamente	quickly
Sirve para . . .	It's used for . . .
tener miedo (de)	to be afraid (of)

pedir *(e → i) to ask for*

pido	pedimos
pides	pedís
pide	piden

servir *(e → i) to serve, to be useful*

sirvo	servimos
sirves	servís
sirve	sirven

saber *to know (how)*

sé	sabemos
sabes	sabéis
sabe	saben

conocer *to know, to be acquainted with*

conozco	conocemos
conoces	conocéis
conoce	conocen

DIFFERENTIATED INSTRUCTION

Students with Learning Difficulties

Have students review the *Repaso del capítulo* and create flashcards for any words that they do not know. Pair them with a student who is more confident with the vocabulary to practice. Before the test, provide students with a practice test, so they can become comfortable with the format.

Heritage Language Learners

Have students write a few paragraphs telling about their perfect birthday celebration: Where are they going to have it? Whom are they going to invite? What food are they going to eat? What kind of music are they going to play? Encourage them to use as many vocabulary words from this chapter as they can.

Más repaso GO realidades.com | print

Instant Check	✔
Puzzles	✔
Core WB pp. 89–90	✔ ✔
Comm. WB pp. 189, 190–192	✔ ✔

Preparación para el examen

On the exam you will be asked to . . .	Here are practice tasks similar to those you will find on the exam . . .	For review go to your print or digital textbook . . .
1 Escuchar Listen and understand as people talk about how they use computers	You overhear some people expressing their opinions about computers. Tell whether each person likes or dislikes using computers.	**pp. 310–315** *Vocabulario en contexto* **p. 311** Actividades 1–2 **p. 317** Actividad 7
2 Hablar Ask and answer questions about what you know about computers and the Internet	A local Internet company wants to interview you to work as a telephone tech support assistant. To prepare, you and your partner take turns interviewing each other. Ask if your partner: a) knows how to surf the Web; b) is familiar with Web sites for teens; c) knows how to use the computer to create music; d) knows how to make graphics. Then switch roles.	**pp. 310–315** *Vocabulario en contexto* **p. 317** Actividad 8 **p. 319** Actividad 11 **p. 323** Actividad 17 **p. 325** Actividad 20 **p. 326** Actividad 21
3 Leer Read and understand part of an online conversation in a chat room	A teen in the chat room *Mis padres y yo* is upset. According to the teenager, what do his parents not understand? What is his parents' opinion? *¡Yo soy muy impaciente! Para hacer la tarea, me gusta tener la información que necesito rápidamente. Mis padres dicen que puedo ir a la biblioteca y buscar libros allí para hacer mi tarea, pero me gustaría tener mi propia computadora. Ellos piensan que las computadoras sólo sirven para jugar juegos. ¿Qué hago?*	**pp. 310–315** *Vocabulario en contexto* **p. 316** Actividad 6 **p. 317** Actividad 8 **p. 318** Actividad 9 **pp. 328–329** *Lectura*
4 Escribir Write your personal profile (*perfil*) for a Web survey	You are completing a Web survey online for *MundoChat*. Provide answers to the following: a) what you like to do; b) your favorite Web site; c) how often you visit chat rooms; d) how much time you spend online each day.	**p. 321** Actividad 13 **p. 323** Actividad 17 **p. 324** Actividad 18 **p. 331** *Presentación escrita*
5 Pensar Demonstrate an understanding of cultural perspectives regarding technology	Explain why cybercafés are so popular in many Spanish-speaking countries. Compare how you use computers to the way in which teenagers might use them in these countries. If you lived in one of these countries, how might you approach homework differently?	**p. 330** *Perspectivas del mundo hispano*

trescientos treinta y cinco **335**
Capítulo 9B

DIFFERENTIATED ASSESSMENT

CORE ASSESSMENT
- **Assessment Program:** Examen del capítulo 9B, pp. 247–253
- **Audio Program DVD:** Cap. 9B, Track 15
- **ExamView:** Chapter Test, Test Banks A and B

ADVANCED/PRE-AP*
- **ExamView: Pre-AP* Test Bank**
- **Pre-AP* Resource Book,** pp. 94–97

STUDENTS NEEDING EXTRA HELP
- **Alternate Assessment Program:** Examen del capítulo 9B
- **Audio Program DVD:** Cap. 9B, Track 15

HERITAGE LEARNERS
- **Assessment Program: Realidades para hispanohablantes:** Examen del capítulo 9B
- **ExamView: Heritage Learner Test Bank**

Performance Tasks

Standards: 1.1, 1.2, 1.3, 4.2

Student Resource: Realidades para hispanohablantes, p. 369

Teacher Resources: Teacher's Resource Book: Audio Script, p. 346; Audio Program DVD: Cap. 9B, Track 14; Answer Keys: Student Edition, p. 191

1. Escuchar

Suggestions: You may wish to play or read the entire script aloud first, and then start over again, stopping after each person's statement.

Script and Answers:

1. A mí me gusta más hablar cara a cara con mis amigos. Así, puedo ver si están aburridos, interesados o impacientes. No puedo verlos si uso la computadora. *(dislikes using computers)*
2. Prefiero usar mi computadora para escribir correos electrónicos a mis amigas. Es más rápido y económico. *(likes using computers)*
3. Con las computadoras puedo buscar información para mis presentaciones en clase. Es más práctico que ir a la biblioteca. *(likes using computers)*
4. A veces las computadoras no funcionan bien o hay muchas personas en el laboratorio. Me gusta más escribir las composiciones en mi cuaderno. *(dislikes using computers)*

2. Hablar

Suggestions: If students have difficulty expressing their opinions orally, they can write them first, using model phrases from the chapter.

Answers will vary.

3. Leer

Suggestions: Remind students that cognates can help them understand unfamiliar words.

Answers will vary but may include:

His parents don't understand that computers can be used for doing research. They think computers are just for entertainment.

4. Escribir

Suggestions: Have students first try this activity without consulting the vocabulary list, notes, or completed activities.

Answers will vary.

5. Pensar

Suggestions: Have students reread the *Perspectivas del mundo hispano* and look at the photos throughout the chapter. Reflect with them on the questions asked.

Answers will vary.

Vocabulario adicional

realidades.com GO

 Bilingual Visual Dictionary

Tema 5

Los animales
el **conejillo de Indias** guinea pig

el **conejo** rabbit

el **gerbo** gerbil

el **hámster**, *pl.* **los hámsters** hamster

el **hurón**, *pl.* **los hurones** ferret

el **loro** parrot

el **pez**, *pl.* **los peces** fish

la **serpiente** snake

la **tortuga** turtle

Los miembros de la familia
el **bisabuelo, la bisabuela** great-grandfather, great-grandmother

el **nieto, la nieta** grandson, granddaughter

el **sobrino, la sobrina** nephew, niece

Las descripciones de personas
llevar anteojos to wear glasses

ser

    calvo, -a bald

    delgado, -a thin

    gordo, -a fat

tener

    la **barba** beard

    el **bigote** moustache

    las **pecas** freckles

    el **pelo lacio** straight hair

    el **pelo rizado** curly hair

    las **trenzas** braids

Tema 6

Las partes de la casa y cosas en la casa
el **balcón**, *pl.* **los balcones** balcony

la **estufa** stove

el **jardín**, *pl.* **los jardines** garden

el **lavadero** laundry room

la **lavadora** washing machine

el **lavaplatos**, *pl.* **los lavaplatos** dishwasher

el **microondas**, *pl.* **los microondas** microwave oven

los **muebles** furniture

el **patio** patio

el **refrigerador** refrigerator

la **secadora** clothes dryer

el **sillón**, *pl.* **los sillones** armchair

el **sofá** sofa

el **tocador** dressing table

Los quehaceres
quitar

    la **nieve con la pala** to shovel snow

    los **platos de la mesa** to clear the table

rastrillar las hojas to rake leaves

Los colores
(azul) claro light (blue)

(azul) marino navy (blue)

(azul) oscuro dark (blue)

Tema 7

Las expresiones para las compras
ahorrar to save

el **dinero en efectivo** cash

gastar to spend

la(s) rebaja(s) sale(s)

regatear to bargain

se vende for sale

La ropa
la **bata** bathrobe

el **chaleco** vest

las **pantimedias** pantyhose

el **paraguas**, *pl.* **los paraguas** umbrella

el **pijama** pajamas

la **ropa interior** underwear

el **saco** loose-fitting jacket

los **tenis** tennis shoes

las **zapatillas** slippers

los **zapatos atléticos** athletic shoes

los **zapatos de tacón alto** high-heeled shoes

Tema 8

Las expresiones para los viajes

el aeropuerto airport

la agencia de viajes travel agency

los cheques de viajero travelers' checks

el equipaje luggage

hacer una reservación to make a reservation

el lugar de interés place of interest

el pasaporte passport

volar *(o → ue)* to fly

Los animales del zoológico

el ave *(f.), pl.* **las aves** bird

el canguro kangaroo

la cebra zebra

el cocodrilo crocodile

el delfín, *pl.* **los delfines** dolphins

el elefante elephant

la foca seal

el gorila gorilla

el hipopótamo hippopotamus

la jirafa giraffe

el león, *pl.* **los leones** lion

el oso bear

el oso blanco polar bear

el pingüino penguin

el tigre tiger

Tema 9

Las expresiones para las computadoras

la búsqueda search

comenzar *(e → ie)* **la sesión** to log on

el disco duro hard disk

la impresora printer

imprimir to print

el marcapáginas, *pl.* **los marcapáginas** bookmark

multimedia multimedia

la página inicial home page

la tecla de borrar delete key

la tecla de intro enter key

Resumen de gramática
Grammar Terms

Adjectives describe nouns: *a **red** car*.

Adverbs usually describe verbs; they tell when, where, or how an action happens: *He read it **quickly.*** Adverbs can also describe adjectives or other adverbs: ***very** tall, **quite well.***

Articles are words in Spanish that can tell you whether a noun is masculine, feminine, singular, or plural. In English, the articles are ***the, a,*** and ***an.***

Commands are verb forms that tell people to do something: ***Study!, Work!***

Comparatives compare people or things.

Conjugations are verb forms that add endings to the stem in order to tell who the subject is and what tense is being used: *escrib**o**, escrib**iste.***

Conjunctions join words or groups of words. The most common ones are ***and, but,*** and ***or.***

Direct objects are nouns or pronouns that receive the action of a verb: *I read **the book.** I read **it.***

Gender in Spanish tells you whether a noun, pronoun, or article is masculine or feminine.

Indirect objects are nouns or pronouns that tell you to whom / what or for whom / what something is done: *I gave **him** the book.*

Infinitives are the basic forms of verbs. In English, infinitives have the word "to" in front of them: ***to walk.***

Interrogatives are words that ask questions: ***What** is that? **Who** are you?*

Nouns name people, places, or things: ***students, Mexico City, books.***

Number tells you if a noun, pronoun, article, or verb is **singular** or **plural.**

Prepositions show the relationship between the object and another word in the sentence: *He is **in** the classroom.*

Present tense is used to talk about actions that always take place, or that are happening now: *I always **take** the bus; I **study** Spanish.*

Present progressive tense is used to emphasize that an action is happening *right now: I **am doing** my homework; he **is finishing** dinner.*

Preterite tense is used to talk about actions that were completed in the past: *I **took** the train yesterday; I **studied** for the test.*

Pronouns are words that take the place of nouns: ***She** is my friend.*

Subjects are the nouns or pronouns that perform the action in a sentence: ***John** sings.*

Superlatives describe which things have the most or least of a given quality: *She is the **best** student.*

Verbs show action or link the subject with a word or words in the predicate (what the subject does or is): *Ana **writes;** Ana **is** my sister.*

Nouns, Number, and Gender

Nouns refer to people, animals, places, things, and ideas. Nouns are singular or plural. In Spanish, nouns have gender, which means that they are either masculine or feminine.

Singular Nouns		Plural Nouns	
Masculine	**Feminine**	**Masculine**	**Feminine**
libro	carpeta	libros	carpetas
pupitre	casa	pupitres	casas
profesor	noche	profesores	noches
lápiz	ciudad	lápices	ciudades

Definite Articles

El, la, los, and *las* are definite articles and are the equivalent of "the" in English. *El* is used with masculine singular nouns; *los* with masculine plural nouns. *La* is used with feminine singular nouns; *las* with feminine plural nouns. When you use the words *a* or *de* before *el*, you form the contractions *al* and *del*: *Voy al centro*; *Es el libro del profesor.*

Masculine	
Singular	Plural
el libro	los libros
el pupitre	los pupitres
el profesor	los profesores
el lápiz	los lápices

Feminine	
Singular	Plural
la carpeta	las carpetas
la casa	las casas
la noche	las noches
la ciudad	las ciudades

Indefinite Articles

Un and *una* are indefinite articles and are the equivalent of "a" and "an" in English. *Un* is used with singular masculine nouns; *una* is used with singular feminine nouns. The plural indefinite articles are *unos* and *unas.*

Masculine	
Singular	Plural
un libro	unos libros
un escritorio	unos escritorios
un baile	unos bailes

Feminine	
Singular	Plural
una revista	unas revistas
una mochila	unas mochilas
una bandera	unas banderas

Pronouns

Subject pronouns tell who is doing the action. They replace nouns or names in a sentence. Subject pronouns are often used for emphasis or clarification:
Gregorio escucha música.
Él escucha música.

A *direct object* tells who or what receives the action of the verb. To avoid repeating a direct object noun, you can replace it with a *direct object pronoun*. Direct object pronouns have the same gender and number as the nouns they replace: *¿Cuándo compraste el libro? Lo compré ayer.*

An *indirect object* tells to whom or for whom an action is performed. *Indirect object pronouns* are used to replace an indirect object noun: *Les doy dinero. (I give money to them.)* Because *le* and *les* have more than one meaning, you can make the meaning clear, or show emphasis, by adding *a* + the corresponding name, noun, or pronoun: *Les doy el dinero a ellos.*

After most prepositions, you use *mí* and *ti* for "me" and "you." The forms change with the preposition *con: conmigo, contigo.* For all other persons, you use subject pronouns after prepositions.

The personal a

When the direct object is a person, a group of people, or a pet, use the word *a* before the object. This is called the "personal *a*": *Visité a mi abuela. Busco a mi perro, Capitán.*

Subject Pronouns		Direct Object Pronouns		Indirect Object Pronouns		Objects of Prepositions	
Singular	Plural	Singular	Plural	Singular	Plural	Singular	Plural
yo	nosotros, nosotras	me	nos	me	nos	(para) mí, conmigo	nosotros, nosotras
tú	vosotros, vosotras	te	os	te	os	(para) ti, contigo	vosotros, vosotras
usted (Ud.)	ustedes (Uds.)	lo, la	los, las	le	les	Ud.	Uds.
él, ella	ellos, ellas					él, ella	ellos, ellas

Adjectives

Words that describe people and things are called adjectives. In Spanish, most adjectives have both masculine and feminine forms, as well as singular and plural forms. Adjectives must agree with the noun they describe in both gender and number. When an adjective describes a group including both masculine and feminine nouns, use the masculine plural form.

Masculine		Feminine	
Singular	**Plural**	**Singular**	**Plural**
alto	altos	alta	altas
inteligente	inteligentes	inteligente	inteligentes
trabajador	trabajadores	trabajadora	trabajadoras
fácil	fáciles	fácil	fáciles

Shortened Forms of Adjectives

When placed before masculine singular nouns, some adjectives change into a shortened form.

bueno	buen chico
malo	mal día
primero	primer trabajo
tercero	tercer plato
grande	gran señor

One adjective, **grande,** changes to a shortened form before any singular noun: *una gran señora, un gran libro.*

Possessive Adjectives

Possessive adjectives are used to tell what belongs to someone or to show relationships. Like other adjectives, possessive adjectives agree in number with the nouns that follow them.

Only *nuestro* and *vuestro* have different masculine and feminine endings. *Su* and *sus* can have many different meanings: *his, her, its, your,* or *their.*

Singular	Plural
mi	mis
tu	tus
su	sus
nuestro, -a	nuestros, -as
vuestro, -a	vuestros, -as
su	sus

Demonstrative Adjectives

Like other adjectives, demonstrative adjectives agree in gender and number with the nouns that follow them. Use *este, esta, estos, estas* ("this" / "these") before nouns that name people or things that are close to you. Use *ese, esa, esos, esas* ("that" / "those") before nouns that name people or things that are at some distance from you.

Singular	Plural	Singular	Plural
este libro	estos libros	ese niño	esos niños
esta casa	estas casas	esa manzana	esas manzanas

Interrogative Words

You use interrogative words to ask questions. When you ask a question with an interrogative word, you put the verb before the subject. All interrogative words have a written accent mark.

¿Adónde?	¿Cuándo?	¿Dónde?
¿Cómo?	¿Cuánto, -a?	¿Por qué?
¿Con quién?	¿Cuántos, -as?	¿Qué?
¿Cuál?	¿De dónde?	¿Quién?

Comparatives and Superlatives

Comparatives Use *más . . . que* or *menos . . . que* to compare people or things: *más interesante que . . . , menos alta que . . .*

When talking about number, use *de* instead of *que: Tengo **más de** cien monedas en mi colección.*

Superlatives Use this pattern to express the idea of "most" or "least."

el
la
los   + *noun* + más / menos + *adjective*
las

*Es la chica **más seria de** la clase.*
*Son los perritos **más pequeños.***

Several adjectives are irregular when used with comparisons and superlatives.

mayor	older
menor	younger
mejor	better
peor	worse

Affirmative and Negative Words

To make a sentence negative in Spanish, *no* usually goes in front of the verb or expression. To show that you do not like either of two choices, use *ni . . . ni.*

Alguno, alguna, algunos, algunas and *ninguno, ninguna* match the number and gender of the noun to which they refer. *Ningunos* and *ningunas* are rarely used. When *alguno* and *ninguno* come before a masculine singular noun, they change to *algún* and *ningún.*

Affirmative	Negative
algo	nada
alguien	nadie
algún	ningún
alguno, -a, -os, -as	ninguno, -a, -os, -as
siempre	nunca
también	tampoco

Adverbs

To form an adverb in Spanish, *-mente* is added to the feminine singular form of an adjective. This *-mente* ending is equivalent to the "-ly" ending in English. If the adjective has a written accent, such as *rápida, fácil,* and *práctica,* the accent appears in the same place in the adverb form.

general → generalmente
especial → especialmente
fácil → fácilmente
feliz → felizmente
rápida → rápidamente
práctica → prácticamente

Verbos

Regular Present and Preterite Tenses

Here are the conjugations for regular -ar, -er, and -ir verbs in the present and preterite tense.

Infinitive	Present		Preterite	
estudiar	estudio	estudiamos	estudié	estudiamos
	estudias	estudiáis	estudiaste	estudiasteis
	estudia	estudian	estudió	estudiaron
correr	corro	corremos	corrí	corrimos
	corres	corréis	corriste	corristeis
	corre	corren	corrió	corrieron
escribir	escribo	escribimos	escribí	escribimos
	escribes	escribís	escribiste	escribisteis
	escribe	escriben	escribió	escribieron

Present Progressive

When you want to emphasize that an action is happening *right now,* you use the present progressive tense.

estudiar	estoy estudiando	estamos estudiando
	estás estudiando	estáis estudiando
	está estudiando	están estudiando
correr	estoy corriendo	estamos corriendo
	estás corriendo	estáis corriendo
	está corriendo	están corriendo
escribir	estoy escribiendo	estamos escribiendo
	estás escribiendo	estáis escribiendo
	está escribiendo	están escribiendo

Affirmative tú Commands

When telling a friend, a family member, or a young person to do something, use an affirmative *tú* command. To give these commands for most verbs, use the same present-tense forms that are used for *Ud., él, ella.* Some verbs have an irregular affirmative *tú* command.

Regular	Irregular	
Estudia	decir	di
Corre	hacer	haz
Escribe	ir	ve
	poner	pon
	salir	sal
	ser	sé
	tener	ten
	venir	ven

Stem-changing Verbs

Here is an alphabetical list of the stem-changing verbs. You will learn the verb forms that are in italic type next year.

Infinitive and Present Participle	Present		Preterite	
costar (o → ue) costando	cuesta	cuestan	costó	costaron
doler (o → ue) doliendo	duele	duelen	dolió	dolieron
dormir (o → ue) *durmiendo*	duermo duermes duerme	dormimos dormís duermen	dormí dormiste *durmió*	dormimos dormisteis *durmieron*
empezar (e → ie) empezando	empiezo empiezas empieza	empezamos empezáis empiezan	*empecé* empezaste empezó	empezamos empezasteis empezaron
jugar (u → ue) jugando	juego juegas juega	jugamos jugáis juegan	jugué jugaste jugó	jugamos jugasteis jugaron
llover (o → ue) lloviendo	llueve		llovió	
nevar (e → ie) nevando	nieva		nevó	
pedir (e → i) *pidiendo*	pido pides pide	pedimos pedís piden	pedí pediste *pidió*	pedimos pedisteis *pidieron*
pensar (e → ie) pensando	pienso piensas piensa	pensamos pensáis piensan	pensé pensaste pensó	pensamos pensasteis pensaron
preferir (e → ie) *prefiriendo*	prefiero prefieres prefiere	preferimos preferís prefieren	preferí preferiste *prefirió*	preferimos preferisteis *prefirieron*
sentir (e → ie) *sintiendo*	*See* preferir			
servir (e → i) *sirviendo*	*See* pedir			

Spelling-changing Verbs

These verbs have spelling changes in different tenses. The spelling changes are indicated in black.

You will learn the verb forms that are in italic type next year.

Infinitive and Present Participle	Present		Preterite	
buscar (c → qu) buscando	*See regular verbs*		**busqué** buscaste buscó	buscamos buscasteis buscaron
comunicarse (c → qu) *comunicándose*	*See reflexive verbs*		*See reflexive verbs and* **buscar**	
conocer (c → zc) conociendo	**conozco** conoces conoce	conocemos conocéis conocen	*See regular verbs*	
creer (i → y) *creyendo*	*See regular verbs*		creí creíste *creyó*	creímos creísteis *creyeron*
empezar (z → c) empezando	*See stem-changing verbs*		**empecé** empezaste empezó	empezamos empezasteis empezaron
enviar (i → í) enviando	**envío** **envías** **envía**	enviamos enviáis **envían**	*See regular verbs*	
esquiar (i → í) esquiando	*See* **enviar**		*See regular verbs*	
jugar (g → gu) jugando	*See stem-changing verbs*		**jugué** jugaste jugó	jugamos jugasteis jugaron
leer (i → y) leyendo	*See regular verbs*		*See* **creer**	
pagar (g → gu) pagando	*See regular verbs*		*See* **jugar**	
parecer (c → zc) pareciendo	*See* **conocer**		*See regular verbs*	
practicar (c → qu) practicando	*See regular verbs*		*See* **buscar**	
recoger (g → j) recogiendo	**recojo** recoges recoge	recogemos recogéis recogen	*See regular verbs*	
sacar (c → qu) sacando	*See regular verbs*		*See* **buscar**	
tocar (c → qu) tocando	*See regular verbs*		*See* **buscar**	

Irregular Verbs

These verbs have irregular patterns. You will learn the verb forms that are in italic type next year.

Infinitive and Present Participle	Present		Preterite	
dar dando	doy das da	damos dais dan	di diste dio	dimos disteis dieron
decir *diciendo*	digo dices dice	decimos decís dicen	*dije* *dijiste* *dijo*	*dijimos* *dijisteis* *dijeron*
estar estando	estoy estás está	estamos estáis están	*estuve* *estuviste* *estuvo*	*estuvimos* *estuvisteis* *estuvieron*
hacer haciendo	hago haces hace	hacemos hacéis hacen	hice hiciste hizo	hicimos hicisteis hicieron
ir *yendo*	voy vas va	vamos vais van	fui fuiste fue	fuimos fuisteis fueron
poder *pudiendo*	puedo puedes puede	podemos podéis pueden	*pude* *pudiste* *pudo*	*pudimos* *pudisteis* *pudieron*
poner poniendo	pongo pones pone	ponemos ponéis ponen	*puse* *pusiste* *puso*	*pusimos* *pusisteis* *pusieron*
querer queriendo	quiero quieres quiere	queremos queréis quieren	*quise* *quisiste* *quiso*	*quisimos* *quisisteis* *quisieron*
saber sabiendo	sé sabes sabe	sabemos sabéis saben	*supe* *supiste* *supo*	*supimos* *supisteis* *supieron*
salir saliendo	salgo sales sale	salimos salís salen	salí saliste salió	salimos salisteis salieron
ser siendo	soy eres es	somos sois son	fui fuiste fue	fuimos fuisteis fueron
tener teniendo	tengo tienes tiene	tenemos tenéis tienen	*tuve* *tuviste* *tuvo*	*tuvimos* *tuvisteis* *tuvieron*

Irregular Verbs (continued) You will learn the verb forms that are in italic type next year.

Infinitive and Present Participle	Present		Preterite	
traer *trayendo*	traigo traes trae	traemos traéis traen	*traje* *trajiste* *trajo*	*trajimos* *trajisteis* *trajeron*
venir *viniendo*	vengo vienes viene	venimos venís vienen	*vine* *viniste* *vino*	*vinimos* *vinisteis* *vinieron*
ver viendo	veo ves ve	vemos veis ven	vi viste vio	vimos visteis vieron

Reflexive Verbs You will learn the verb forms that are in italic type next year.

Infinitive and Present Participle	Present	
comunicarse *comunicándose*	me comunico te comunicas *se comunica*	*nos comunicamos* *os comunicáis* *se comunican*
Affirmative Familiar (*tú*) Command	Preterite	
comunícate	me comuniqué te comunicaste *se comunicó*	*nos comunicamos* *os comunicasteis* *se comunicaron*

Expresiones útiles para conversar

The following are expressions that you can use when you find yourself in a specific situation and need help to begin, continue, or end a conversation.

Greeting Someone

Buenos días. Good morning.

Buenas tardes. Good afternoon.

Buenas noches. Good evening. Good night.

Making Introductions

Me llamo . . . My name is . . .

Soy . . . I'm . . .

¿Cómo te llamas? What's your name?

Éste es mi amigo *m.* **. . .** This is my friend . . .

Ésta es mi amiga *f.* **. . .** This is my friend . . .

Se llama . . . His / Her name is . . .

¡Mucho gusto! It's a pleasure!

Encantado, -a. Delighted.

Igualmente. Likewise.

Asking How Someone Is

¿Cómo estás? How are you?

¿Cómo andas? How's it going?

¿Cómo te sientes? How do you feel?

¿Qué tal? How's it going?

Estoy bien, gracias. I'm fine, thank you.

Muy bien. ¿Y tú? Very well. And you?

Regular. Okay. All right.

Más o menos. More or less.

(Muy) mal. (Very) bad.

¡Horrible! Awful!

¡Excelente! Great!

Talking on the Phone

Aló. Hello.

Diga. Hello.

Bueno. Hello.

¿Quién habla? Who's calling?

Habla . . . It's [name of person calling].

¿Está . . . , por favor? Is . . . there, please?

¿De parte de quién? Who is calling?

¿Puedo dejar un recado? May I leave a message?

Un momento. Just a moment.

Llamo más tarde. I'll call later.

¿Cómo? No le oigo. What? I can't hear you.

Making Plans

¿Adónde vas? Where are you going?

Voy a . . . I'm going to . . .

¿Estás listo, -a? Are you ready?

Tengo prisa. I'm in a hurry.

¡Date prisa! Hurry up!

Sí, ahora voy. OK, I'm coming.

Todavía necesito . . . I still need . . .

¿Te gustaría . . . ? Would you like to . . . ?

Sí, me gustaría . . . Yes, I'd like to . . .

¡Claro que sí (no)! Of course (not)!

¿Quieres . . . ? Do you want to . . . ?

Quiero . . . I want to . . .

¿Qué quieres hacer hoy? What do you want to do today?

¿Qué haces después de las clases? What do you do after school (class)?

¿Qué estás haciendo? What are you doing?

Te invito. It's my treat.

¿Qué tal si . . . ? What about . . . ?

Primero . . . First . . .

Después . . . Later . . .

Luego . . . Then . . .

Making an Excuse

Estoy ocupado, -a. I'm busy.

Lo siento, pero no puedo. I'm sorry, but I can't.

¡Qué lástima! What a shame!

Ya tengo planes. I already have plans.

Tal vez otro día. Maybe another day.

Being Polite

Con mucho gusto. With great pleasure.

De nada. You're welcome.

Disculpe. Excuse me.

Lo siento. I'm sorry.

Muchísimas gracias. Thank you very much.

Te (Se) lo agradezco mucho. I appreciate it a lot.

Muy amable. That's very kind of you.

Perdón. Pardon me.

¿Puede Ud. repetirlo? Can you repeat that?

¿Puede Ud. hablar más despacio? Can you speak more slowly?

Keeping a Conversation Going

¿De veras? Really?

¿Verdad? Isn't that so? Right?

¿En serio? Seriously?

¡No lo puedo creer! I don't believe it!

¡No me digas! You don't say!

Y entonces, ¿qué? And then what?

¿Qué hiciste? What did you do?

¿Qué dijiste? What did you say?

¿Crees que . . . ? Do you think that . . . ?

Me parece bien. It seems all right.

Perfecto. Perfect.

¡Qué buena idea! What a good idea!

¡Cómo no! Of course!

De acuerdo. Agreed.

Está bien. It's all right.

Giving a Description When You Don't Know the Name of Someone or Something

Se usa para . . . It's used to / for . . .

Es la palabra que significa . . . It's the word that means . . .

Es la persona que . . . It's the person who . . .

Ending a Conversation

Bueno, tengo que irme. Well, I have to go.

Chao. (Chau.) Bye.

Hasta pronto. See you soon.

Hasta mañana. See you tomorrow.

Vocabulario español–inglés

The *Vocabulario español-inglés* contains all active vocabulary from the text, including vocabulary presented in the grammar sections.

A dash (—) represents the main entry word. For example, **el — pasado** after **el año** means **el año pasado.**

The number following each entry indicates the chapter in which the word or expression is presented. Remember that Temas 1–4 appeared in Level A. The letter *P* following an entry refers to the *Para empezar* section of Level A.

The following abbreviations are used in this list: *adj.* (adjective), *dir. obj.* (direct object), *f.* (feminine), *fam.* (familiar), *ind. obj.* (indirect object), *inf.* (infinitive), *m.* (masculine), *pl.* (plural), *prep.* (preposition), *pron.* (pronoun), *sing.* (singular).

A

a to *(prep.)* (4A)

   — ... le gusta(n) he / she likes (5A)

   — ... le encanta(n) he / she loves (5A)

   — casa (to) home (4A)

   — la derecha (de) to the right (of) (6A)

   — la izquierda (de) to the left (of) (6A)

   — la una de la tarde at one (o'clock) in the afternoon (4B)

   — las ocho de la mañana at eight (o'clock) in the morning (4B)

   — las ocho de la noche at eight (o'clock) in the evening / at night (4B)

   — menudo often (8B)

   — mí también I do (like to) too (1A)

   — mí tampoco I don't (like to) either (1A)

   ¿— qué hora? (At) what time? (4B)

   — veces sometimes (1B)

   — ver Let's see (2A)

al *(a + el),* **a la,** to the (4A)

   al lado de next to (2B)

el **abrigo** coat (7A)

abril April (P)

abrir to open (5A)

la **abuela, el abuelo** grandmother, grandfather (5A)

los **abuelos** grandparents (5A)

aburrido, -a boring (2A)

me **aburre(n)** it bores me (they bore me) (9A)

aburrir to bore (9A)

acabar de + *inf.* to have just . . . (9A)

el **actor** actor (9A)

la **actriz,** *pl.* **las actrices** actress (9A)

acuerdo:

   Estoy de —. I agree. (3B)

   No estoy de —. I don't agree. (3B)

¡Adiós! Good-bye! (P)

¿Adónde? (To) where? (4A)

agosto August (P)

el **agua** *f.* water (3A)

ahora now (5B)

al *(a + el),* **a la,** to the (4A)

   al lado de next to (2B)

la **alfombra** rug (6A)

algo something (3B)

   ¿— más? Anything else? (5B)

allí there (2B)

el **almacén,** *pl.* **los almacenes** department store (7B)

el **almuerzo** lunch (2A)

   en el — for lunch (3A)

alto, -a tall (5B)

amarillo, -a yellow (6A)

el **amigo** male friend (1B)

la **amiga** female friend (1B)

anaranjado, -a orange (6A)

la **anciana, el anciano** older woman, older man (8B)

los **ancianos** older people (8B)

el **anillo** ring (7B)

el **animal** animal (8A)

anoche last night (7B)

los **anteojos de sol** sunglasses (7B)

antes de before (9A)

el **año** year (P)

   el — pasado last year (7B)

   ¿Cuántos años tiene(n) . . . ? How old is / are . . . ? (5A)

   Tiene(n) . . . años. He / She is / They are . . . (years old). (5A)

el **apartamento** apartment (6B)

aprender (a) to learn (to) (8A)

aquí here (2B)

el **árbol** tree (8A)

los **aretes** earrings (7B)

el **armario** closet (6A)

   arreglar el cuarto to straighten up the room (6B)

el **arroz** rice (3B)

el **arte:**

   la clase de — art class (2A)

   artístico, -a artistic (1B)

asco:

   ¡Qué —! How awful! (3A)

la **atracción,** *pl.* **las atracciones** attraction (8A)

atrevido, -a daring (1B)

el **autobús,** *pl.* **los autobuses** bus (8A)

el **avión,** *pl.* **los aviones** airplane (8A)

   ¡Ay! ¡Qué pena! Oh! What a shame / pity! (4B)

ayer yesterday (7B)

ayudar to help (6B)

el **azúcar** sugar (5B)

azul blue (6A)

B

bailar to dance (1A)

el **baile** dance (4B)

bajar (información) to download (9B)

bajo, -a short *(stature)* (5B)

la **bandera** flag (2B)

el **baño** bathroom (6B)

   el traje de — swimsuit (7A)

barato, -a inexpensive, cheap (7B)

el **barco** boat, ship (8A)

el **barrio** neighborhood (8B)

el **básquetbol: jugar al —** to play basketball (4B)

bastante enough, rather (6B)

beber to drink (3A)

las **bebidas** beverages (3B)

béisbol: jugar al — to play baseball (4B)

la **biblioteca** library (4A)

bien well (P)

el **bistec** beefsteak (3B)

blanco, -a white (6A)

la **blusa** blouse (7A)

la **boca** mouth (P)

el **boleto** ticket (8A)

el **bolígrafo** pen (P)

la **bolsa** bag, sack (8B)

el **bolso** purse (7B)

bonito, -a pretty (6A)

las **botas** boots (7A)

el **bote: pasear en —** to go boating (8A)

la **botella** bottle (8B)

el **brazo** arm (P)

bucear to scuba dive, to snorkel (8A)

bueno (buen), -a good (1B)

Buenas noches. Good evening. (P)

Buenas tardes. Good afternoon. (P)

Buenos días. Good morning. (P)

buscar to look for (7A); to search (for) (9B)

C

el **caballo: montar a —** to ride horseback (8A)

la **cabeza** head (P)

cada día every day (3B)

la **cadena** chain (7B)

el **café** coffee (3A); café (4A)

la **caja** box (8B)

los **calcetines** socks (7A)

la **calculadora** calculator (2A)

la **calle** street, road (8B)

calor:

Hace —. It's hot. (P)

tener — to be warm (5B)

la **cama** bed (6A)

hacer la — to make the bed (6B)

la **cámara** camera (5A)

la — digital digital camera (9A)

el **camarero, la camarera** waiter, waitress (5B)

caminar to walk (3B)

la **camisa** shirt (7A)

la **camiseta** T-shirt (7A)

el **campamento** camp (8B)

el **campo** countryside (4A)

el **canal** (TV) channel (9A)

la **canción,** *pl.* **las canciones** song (9B)

canoso: pelo — gray hair (5B)

cansado, -a tired (4B)

cantar to sing (1A)

cara a cara face-to-face (9B)

la **carne** meat (3B)

caro, -a expensive (7B)

la **carpeta** folder (P)

la — de argollas three-ring binder (2A)

la **carta** letter (9B)

el **cartel** poster (2B)

la **cartera** wallet (7B)

el **cartón** cardboard (8B)

la **casa** home, house (4A)

a — (to) home (4A)

en — at home (4A)

casi almost (9A)

castaño: pelo — brown (chestnut) hair (5B)

catorce fourteen (P)

la **cebolla** onion (3B)

celebrar to celebrate (5A)

la **cena** dinner (3B)

el **centro:**

el — comercial mall (4A)

el — de reciclaje recycling center (8B)

cerca (de) close (to), near (6B)

el **cereal** cereal (3A)

cero zero (P)

la **chaqueta** jacket (7A)

la **chica** girl (1B)

el **chico** boy (1B)

cien one hundred (P)

las **ciencias:**

la clase de — naturales science class (2A)

la clase de — sociales social studies class (2A)

cinco five (P)

cincuenta fifty (P)

el **cine** movie theater (4A)

la **ciudad** city (8A)

la **clase** class (2A)

la sala de clases classroom (P)

¿Qué — de . . . ? What kind of . . . ? (9A)

el **coche** car (6B)

la **cocina** kitchen (6B)

cocinar to cook (6B)

el **collar** necklace (7B)

el **color,** *pl.* **los colores** (6A)

¿De qué — . . . ? What color . . . ? (6A)

la **comedia** comedy (9A)

el **comedor** dining room (6B)

comer to eat (3A)

cómico, -a funny, comical (9A)

la **comida** food, meal (3A)

como like, as (8A)

¿Cómo?:

¿— eres? What are you like? (1B)

¿— es? What is he / she like? (1B)

¿— está Ud.? How are you? *formal* (P)

¿— estás? How are you? *fam.* (P)

¿— lo pasaste? How was it (for you)? (8A)

¿— se dice . . . ? How do you say . . . ? (P)

¿— se escribe . . . ? How is . . . spelled? (P)

¿— se llama? What's his / her name? (1B)

¿— te llamas? What is your name? (P)

¿— me/te queda(n)? How does it (do they) fit (me / you)? (7A)

la cómoda dresser (6A)

compartir to share (3A)

complicado, -a complicated (9B)

la composición, *pl.* **las composiciones** composition (9B)

comprar to buy (7A)

> **comprar recuerdos** to buy souvenirs (8A)

comprender to understand (3A)

la computadora computer (2B)

> **la — portátil** laptop computer (9B)

> **usar la —** to use the computer (1A)

comunicarse to communicate (9B)

> **(tú) te comunicas** you communicate (9B)

> **(yo) me comunico** I communicate (9B)

la comunidad community (8B)

con with (3A)

> **— mis / tus amigos** with my / your friends (4A)

> **¿— quién?** With whom? (4A)

el concierto concert (4B)

conmigo with me (4B)

conocer to know, to be acquainted with (9B)

contento, -a happy (4B)

contigo with you (4B)

la corbata tie (7B)

correr to run (1A)

cortar el césped to cut / to mow the lawn (6B)

las cortinas curtains (6A)

corto, -a short *(length)* (5B)

> **los pantalones cortos** shorts (7A)

la cosa thing (6A)

costar (o → ue) to cost (7A)

> **¿Cuánto cuesta(n) . . . ?** How much does (do) . . . cost? (7A)

crear to create (9B)

creer:

> **Creo que . . .** I think . . . (3B)

> **Creo que no.** I don't think so. (3B)

> **Creo que sí.** I think so. (3B)

el cuaderno notebook (P)

el cuadro painting (6A)

¿Cuál? Which?, What? (3A)

> **¿— es la fecha?** What is the date? (P)

¿Cuándo? When? (4A)

¿Cuánto?: ¿— cuesta(n) . . . ? How much does (do) . . . cost? (7A)

¿Cuántos, -as? How many? (P)

> **¿Cuántos años tiene(n) . . . ?** How old is / are . . . ? (5A)

cuarenta forty (P)

cuarto, -a fourth (2A)

el cuarto room (6B)

> **y —** quarter past *(in telling time)* (P)

> **menos —** *(time)* quarter to (P)

cuatro four (P)

cuatrocientos, -as four hundred (7A)

la cuchara spoon (5B)

el cuchillo knife (5B)

la cuenta bill (5B)

el cumpleaños birthday (5A)

> **¡Feliz —!** Happy birthday! (5A)

el curso: tomar un curso to take a course (9B)

D _____

dar to give (6B)

> **— +** *movie or TV program* to show (9A)

— de comer al perro to feed the dog (6B)

de of (2B); from (4A)

> **¿— dónde eres?** Where are you from? (4A)

> **— la mañana / la tarde / la noche** in the morning / afternoon / evening (4B)

> **— nada.** You're welcome. (5B)

> **— plato principal** as a main dish (5B)

> **— postre** for dessert (5B)

> **¿— qué color . . . ?** What color . . . ? (6A)

> **¿— veras?** Really? (9A)

debajo de underneath (2B)

deber should, must (3B)

decidir to decide (8B)

décimo, -a tenth (2A)

decir to say, to tell (8B)

> **¿Cómo se dice . . . ?** How do you say . . . ? (P)

> **dime** tell me (8A)

> **¡No me digas!** You don't say! (4A)

> **¿Qué quiere — . . . ?** What does . . . mean? (P)

> **Quiere — . . .** It means . . . (P)

> **Se dice . . .** You say . . . (P)

las decoraciones decorations (5A)

decorar to decorate (5A)

el dedo finger (P)

delante de in front of (2B)

delicioso, -a delicious (5B)

los demás, las demás others (8B)

demasiado too (4B)

el dependiente, la dependienta salesperson (7A)

deportista athletic, sports-minded (1B)

derecha: a la — (de) to the right (of) (6A)

el desayuno breakfast (3A)

> **en el —** for breakfast (3A)

descansar to rest, to relax (8A)

los descuentos: la tienda de — discount store (7B)

desear to wish (5B)

¿Qué desean (Uds.)? What would you like? (5B)

desordenado, -a messy (1B)

el **despacho** office (home) (6B)

el **despertador** alarm clock (6A)

después (de) after (4A)

después afterwards (4A)

detrás de behind (2B)

el **día** day (P)

    Buenos —s. Good morning. (P)

    cada — every day (3B)

    ¿Qué — es hoy? What day is today? (P)

    todos los —s every day (3A)

la **diapositiva** slide (9B)

dibujar to draw (1A)

el **diccionario** dictionary (2A)

diciembre December (P)

diecinueve nineteen (P)

dieciocho eighteen (P)

dieciséis sixteen (P)

diecisiete seventeen (P)

diez ten (P)

difícil difficult (2A)

digital: la cámara — digital camera (9B)

dime tell me (8A)

el **dinero** money (6B)

la **dirección electrónica** e-mail address (9B)

el **disco compacto** compact disc (6A)

    grabar un disco compacto to burn a CD (9B)

divertido, -a amusing, fun (2A)

doce twelve (P)

el **documento** document (9B)

doler (o → ue) to hurt (9A)

domingo Sunday (P)

dónde:

    ¿—? Where? (2B)

    ¿De — eres? Where are you from? (4A)

dormir (o → ue) to sleep (6A)

el **dormitorio** bedroom (6A)

dos two (P)

    los / las dos both (7A)

doscientos, -as two hundred (7A)

el **drama** drama (9A)

los **dulces** candy (5A)

durante during (8A)

durar to last (9A)

E _____

educación física: la clase de — physical education class (2A)

el **ejercicio: hacer —** to exercise (3B)

el **el** the *m. sing.* (1B)

él he (1B)

los **electrodomésticos: la tienda de —** household appliance store (7B)

electrónico, -a: la dirección — e-mail address (9B)

ella she (1B)

ellas they *f. pl.* (2A)

ellos they *m. pl.* (2A)

emocionante touching (9A)

empezar (e → ie) to begin, to start (9A)

en in, on (2B)

    — + *vehicle* by, in, on (8A)

    — casa at home (4A)

    — la . . . hora in the . . . hour (class period) (2A)

    — la Red online (7B)

    ¿— qué puedo servirle? How can I help you? (7A)

encantado, -a delighted (P)

encantar to please very much, to love (9A)

    a él / ella le encanta(n) he / she loves (5A)

    me / te encanta(n) . . . I / you love . . . (3A)

encima de on top of (2B)

enero January (P)

enfermo, -a sick (4B)

la **ensalada** salad (3A)

    la — de frutas fruit salad (3A)

enseñar to teach (2A)

entonces then (4B)

entrar to enter (7A)

enviar (i → í) to send (9B)

el **equipo de sonido** sound (stereo) system (6A)

¿Eres . . . ? Are you . . . ? (1B)

es is (P); (he / she / it) is (1B)

    — el *(number)* **de** *(month)* it is the . . . of . . . *(in telling the date)* (P)

    — el primero de *(month)*. It is the first of . . . (P)

    — la una. It is one o'clock. (P)

    — necesario. It's necessary. (8B)

    — un(a) . . . it's a . . . (2B)

la **escalera** stairs, stairway (6B)

escribir:

    ¿Cómo se escribe . . . ? How is . . . spelled? (P)

    — cuentos to write stories (1A)

    — por correo electrónico to write e-mail (9B)

    Se escribe . . . It's spelled . . . (P)

el **escritorio** desk (2B)

escuchar música to listen to music (1A)

la **escuela primaria** primary school (8B)

ese, esa that (7A)

eso: por — that's why, therefore (9A)

esos, esas those (7A)

los **espaguetis** spaghetti (3B)

el **español: la clase de —** Spanish class (2A)

especialmente especially (9A)

el **espejo** mirror (6A)

la **esposa** wife (5A)

el **esposo** husband (5A)

esquiar (i → í) to ski (1A)

la **estación,** *pl.* **las estaciones** season (P)

el **estadio** stadium (8A)

el **estante** shelf, bookshelf (6A)

estar to be (2B)

¿Cómo está Ud.? How are you? *formal* (P)

¿Cómo estás? How are you? *fam.* (P)

— + *present participle* to be + *present participle* (6B)

— en línea to be online (9B)

Estoy de acuerdo. I agree. (3B)

No estoy de acuerdo. I don't agree. (3B)

este, esta this (7A)

esta noche this evening (4B)

esta tarde this afternoon (4B)

este fin de semana this weekend (4B)

el **estómago** stomach (P)

estos, estas these (7A)

¿Qué es esto? What is this? (2B)

Estoy de acuerdo. I agree. (3B)

el/la **estudiante** student (P)

estudiar to study (2A)

estudioso, -a studious (1B)

la **experiencia** experience (8B)

F _____

fácil easy (2A)

la **falda** skirt (7A)

faltar to be missing (9A)

fantástico, -a fantastic (8A)

fascinante fascinating (9A)

favorito, -a favorite (2A)

febrero February (P)

la **fecha: ¿Cuál es la —?** What is the date? (P)

¡Feliz cumpleaños! Happy birthday! (5A)

feo, -a ugly (6A)

la **fiesta** party (4B)

el **fin de semana:**

este — this weekend (4B)

los fines de semana on weekends (4A)

la **flor,** *pl.* **las flores** flower (5A)

la **foto** photo (5A)

las **fresas** strawberries (3A)

frío:

Hace —. It's cold. (P)

tener — to be cold (5B)

fue it was (8A)

— un desastre. It was a disaster. (8A)

el **fútbol: jugar al —** to play soccer (4B)

el **fútbol americano: jugar al —** to play football (4B)

G _____

la **galleta** cookie (3A)

el **garaje** garage (6B)

el **gato** cat (5A)

generalmente generally (4A)

¡Genial! Great! (4B)

la **gente** people (8B)

el **gimnasio** gym (4A)

el **globo** balloon (5A)

el **golf: jugar al —** to play golf (4B)

la **gorra** cap (7A)

grabar un disco compacto to burn a CD (9B)

gracias thank you (P)

gracioso, -a funny (1B)

los **gráficos** computer graphics (9B)

grande large (6A)

gris gray (6A)

los **guantes** gloves (7B)

guapo, -a good-looking (5B)

los **guisantes** peas (3B)

gustar:

a él / ella le gusta(n) he / she likes (5A)

(A mí) me gusta . . . I like to . . . (1A)

(A mí) me gusta más . . . I like to . . . better (I prefer to . . .) (1A)

(A mí) me gusta mucho . . . I like to . . . a lot (1A)

(A mí) no me gusta . . . I don't like to . . . (1A)

(A mí) no me gusta nada . . . I don't like to . . . at all. (1A)

Le gusta . . . He / She likes . . (1B)

Me gusta . . . I like . . . (3A)

Me gustaría . . . I would like . . . (4B)

Me gustó. I liked it. (8A)

No le gusta . . . He / She doesn't like . . . (1B)

¿Qué te gusta hacer? What do you like to do? (1A)

¿Qué te gusta hacer más? What do you like better (prefer) to do? (1A)

Te gusta . . . You like . . . (3A)

¿Te gusta . . . ? Do you like to . . . ? (1A)

¿Te gustaría . . . ? Would you like . . . ? (4B)

¿Te gustó? Did you like it? (8A)

H _____

hablar to talk (2A)

— por teléfono to talk on the phone (1A)

hacer to do (3B)

hace + *time expression* ago (7B)

Hace calor. It's hot. (P)

Hace frío. It's cold. (P)

Hace sol. It's sunny. (P)

— ejercicio to exercise (3B)

— la cama to make the bed (6B)

— un video to videotape (5A)

haz *(command)* do, make (6B)

¿Qué estás haciendo? What are you doing? (5B)

¿Qué hiciste? What did you do? (8A)

¿Qué tiempo hace? What's the weather like? (P)

(yo) hago I do (3B)

(tú) haces you do (3B)

hambre: Tengo —. I'm hungry. (3B)

la **hamburguesa** hamburger (3A)

hasta:

— luego. See you later. (P)

— mañana. See you tomorrow. (P)

Hay There is, There are (2B)

— que one must (8B)

el **helado** ice cream (3B)

el **hermano, la hermana** brother, sister (5A)

el **hermanastro, la hermanastra** stepbrother, stepsister (5A)

los **hermanos** brothers; brother(s) and sister(s) (5A)

el **hijo, la hija** son, daughter (5A)

los **hijos** children; sons (5A)

la **hoja de papel** sheet of paper (P)

¡Hola! Hello! (P)

el **hombre** man (5B)

la **hora:**

en la . . . — in the . . . hour (class period) (2A)

¿A qué —? (At) what time? (4B)

el **horario** schedule (2A)

horrible horrible (3B)

el **horror: la película de —** horror movie (9A)

el **hospital** hospital (8B)

el **hotel** hotel (8A)

hoy today (P)

los **huevos** eggs (3A)

I

la **iglesia** church (4A)

igualmente likewise (P)

impaciente impatient (1B)

importante important (6A)

impresionante impressive (8A)

increíble incredible (8B)

infantil childish (9A)

la **información** information (9B)

el **informe** report (9B)

el **inglés: la clase de —** English class (2A)

inolvidable unforgettable (8B)

inteligente intelligent (1B)

interesante interesting (2A)

interesar to interest (9A)

me interesa(n) it interests me (they interest me) (9A)

el **invierno** winter (P)

ir to go (4A)

— a + *inf.* to be going to + *verb* (4B)

— a la escuela to go to school (1A)

— de cámping to go camping (4B)

— de compras to go shopping (4A)

— de pesca to go fishing (4B)

— de vacaciones to go on vacation (8A)

¡Vamos! Let's go! (7A)

izquierda: a la — (de) to the left (of) (6A)

J

el **jardín,** *pl.* **los jardines** garden, yard (8B)

los **jeans** jeans (7A)

el **joven, la joven** young man, young woman (5B)

joven *adj.* young (5B)

la **joyería** jewelry store (7B)

las **judías verdes** green beans (3B)

jueves Thursday (P)

jugar (a) (u → ue) to play *(games, sports)* (4B)

— al básquetbol to play basketball (4B)

— al béisbol to play baseball (4B)

— al fútbol to play soccer (4B)

— al fútbol americano to play football (4B)

— al golf to play golf (4B)

— al tenis to play tennis (4B)

— al vóleibol to play volleyball (4B)

— videojuegos to play video games (1A)

el **jugo:**

— de manzana apple juice (3A)

— de naranja orange juice (3A)

el **juguete** toy (8B)

julio July (P)

junio June (P)

L

la the *f. sing.* (1B); it, her *f. dir. obj. pron.* (7B)

el **laboratorio** laboratory (9B)

lado: al — de next to, besides (2B)

el **lago** lake (8A)

la **lámpara** lamp (6A)

el **lápiz,** *pl.* **los lápices** pencil (P)

largo, -a long (5B)

las the *f. pl.* (2B); them *f. dir. obj. pron.* (7B)

— dos, los dos both (7A)

la **lata** can (8B)

lavar to wash (6B)

— el coche to wash the car (6B)

— la ropa to wash the clothes (6B)

— los platos to wash the dishes (6B)

le (to / for) him, her, *(formal)* you *sing. ind. obj. pron.* (8B)

— gusta . . . He / She likes . . . (1B)

— traigo . . . I will bring you . . . (5B)

No — gusta . . . He / She doesn't like . . . (1B)

la **lección,** *pl.* **las lecciones de piano** piano lesson (class) (4A)

la **leche** milk (3A)

la **lechuga** lettuce (3B)

el **lector DVD** DVD player (6A)

leer revistas to read magazines (1A)

lejos (de) far (from) (6B)

les (to / for) them, *(formal)* you *pl. ind. obj. pron.* (8B)

levantar pesas to lift weights (3B)

la **librería** bookstore (7B)

el **libro** book (P)

la **limonada** lemonade (3A)

limpiar el baño to clean the bathroom (6B)

limpio, -a clean (6B)

línea: estar en — to be online (9B)

llamar:

    ¿Cómo se llama? What's his / her name? (1B)

    ¿Cómo te llamas? What is your name? (P)

    Me llamo . . . My name is . . . (P)

el **llavero** key chain (7B)

llevar to wear (7A); to take, to carry, to bring (8B)

llover (o → ue): Llueve. It's raining. (P)

lo it, him *m. dir. obj. pron.* (7B)

    — siento. I'm sorry. (4B)

los the *m. pl.* (2B); them *m. dir. obj. pron* (7B)

    — dos, las dos both (7A)

    — fines de semana on weekends (4A)

    — lunes, los martes . . . on Mondays, on Tuesdays . . . (4A)

el **lugar** place (8A)

lunes Monday (P)

    los lunes on Mondays (4A)

la **luz,** *pl.* **las luces** light (5A)

M

la **madrastra** stepmother (5A)

la **madre (mamá)** mother (5A)

mal bad, badly (4B)

malo, -a bad (3B)

la **mano** hand (P)

mantener: para — la salud to maintain one's health (3B)

la **mantequilla** butter (3B)

la **manzana** apple (3A)

    el jugo de — apple juice (3A)

mañana tomorrow (P)

la **mañana:**

a las ocho de la — at eight (o'clock) in the morning (4B)

de la — in the morning (4B)

el **mar** sea (8A)

marrón, *pl.* **marrones** brown (6A)

martes Tuesday (P)

    los martes on Tuesdays (4A)

marzo March (P)

más:

    ¿Qué —? What else? (8B)

    — . . . que more . . . than (2A)

    — de more than (9A)

    — o menos more or less (3A)

las **matemáticas: la clase de —** mathematics class (2A)

mayo May (P)

mayor older (5A)

me (to / for) me *ind. obj. pron.* (8B)

    — aburre(n) it / they bore(s) me (9A)

    — falta(n) . . . I need . . . (5B)

    — gustaría I would like (4B)

    — gustó. I liked it. (8A)

    — interesa(n) it / they interest(s) me (9A)

    — llamo . . . My name is . . . (P)

    — queda(n) bien / mal. It / They fit(s) me well / poorly. (7A)

    — quedo en casa. I stay at home. (4A)

    ¿— trae . . . ? Will you bring me . . . ? (5B)

media, -o half (P)

    y — thirty, half past *(in telling time)* (P)

mejor:

    el / la —, los / las —es the best (6A)

    —(es) que better than (6A)

menor younger (5A)

menos:

    más o — more or less (3A)

    — . . . que less / fewer . . . than (6A)

— de less / fewer than (9A)

el **menú** menu (5B)

menudo: a — often (8B)

el **mes** month (P)

la **mesa** table (2B)

    poner la — to set the table (6B)

la **mesita** night table (6A)

la **mezquita** mosque (4A)

mi, mis my (2B, 5A)

mí:

    a — también I do (like to) too (1A)

    a — tampoco I don't (like to) either (1A)

    para — in my opinion, for me (6A)

miedo: tener — (de) to be scared (of), to be afraid (of) (9B)

miércoles Wednesday (P)

mil a thousand (7A)

mirar to look (at) (7B)

mismo, -a same (6A)

la **mochila** bookbag, backpack (2B)

el **momento: un —** a moment (6B)

el **mono** monkey (8A)

las **montañas** mountains (4A)

montar:

    — a caballo to ride horseback (8A)

    — en bicicleta to ride a bicycle (1A)

    — en monopatín to skateboard (1A)

el **monumento** monument (8A)

morado, -a purple (6A)

mucho a lot (2A)

    — gusto pleased to meet you (P)

muchos, -as many (3B)

la **mujer** woman (5B)

el **museo** museum (8A)

muy very (1B)

    — bien very well (P)

N

nada nothing (P)

(A mí) no me gusta — ... I don't like to . . . at all. (1A)

De —. You're welcome. (5B)

nadar to swim (1A)

la **naranja: el jugo de —** orange juice (3A)

la **nariz**, *pl.* **las narices** nose (P)

navegar en la Red to surf the Web (9B)

necesario: Es —. It's necessary. (8B)

necesitar:

   (yo) necesito I need (2A)

   (tú) necesitas you need (2A)

negro, -a black (6A)

   el pelo — black hair (5B)

nevar (e → ie) Nieva. It's snowing. (P)

ni . . . ni neither . . . nor, not . . . or (1A)

el **niño, la niña** young boy, young girl (8B)

los **niños** children (8B)

No estoy de acuerdo. I don't agree. (3B)

¡No me digas! You don't say! (4A)

noche:

   a las ocho de la — at eight (o'clock) in the evening, at night (4B)

   Buenas —s. Good evening. (P)

   de la — in the evening, at night (4B)

   esta — this evening (4B)

nos (to / for) us *ind. obj. pron.* (8B)

   ¡— vemos! See you later! (P)

nosotros, -as we (2A)

novecientos, -as nine hundred (7A)

noveno, -a ninth (2A)

noventa ninety (P)

noviembre November (P)

el **novio, la novia** boyfriend, girlfriend (7B)

nuestro(s), -a(s) our (5A)

nueve nine (P)

nuevo, -a new (7A)

nunca never (3A)

O ————————

o or (1A)

la **obra de teatro** play (8A)

ochenta eighty (P)

ocho eight (P)

ochocientos, -as eight hundred (7A)

octavo, -a eighth (2A)

octubre October (P)

ocupado, -a busy (4B)

el **ojo** eye (P)

once eleven (P)

ordenado, -a neat (1B)

os (to / for) you *pl. fam. ind. obj. pron.* (8B)

el **oso** bear (8A)

el **otoño** fall, autumn (P)

otro, -a other, another (5B)

   otra vez again (8B)

¡Oye! Hey! (4B)

P ————————

paciente patient (1B)

el **padrastro** stepfather (5A)

el **padre (papá)** father (5A)

los **padres** parents (5A)

pagar (por) to pay (for) (7B)

la **página Web** Web page (9B)

el **país** country (8A)

el **pájaro** bird (8A)

el **pan** bread (3A)

   el — tostado toast (3A)

la **pantalla** (computer) screen (2B)

los **pantalones** pants (7A)

   los — cortos shorts (7A)

las **papas** potatoes (3B)

   las — fritas French fries (3A)

el **papel picado** cut-paper decorations (5A)

la **papelera** wastepaper basket (2B)

para for (2A)

   — + *inf.* in order to + *inf.* (4A)

   — la salud for one's health (3B)

   — mantener la salud to maintain one's health (3B)

   — mí in my opinion, for me (6A)

   ¿— qué sirve? What's it (used) for? (9B)

   — ti in your opinion, for you (6A)

la **pared** wall (6A)

el **parque** park (4A)

   el — de diversiones amusement park (8A)

   el — nacional national park (8A)

el **partido** game, match (4B)

pasar:

   ¿Cómo lo pasaste? How was it (for you)? (8A)

   — la aspiradora to vacuum (6B)

   — tiempo con amigos to spend time with friends (1A)

   ¿Qué pasa? What's happening? (P)

   ¿Qué te pasó? What happened to you? (8A)

pasear en bote to go boating (8A)

el **pastel** cake (5A)

los **pasteles** pastries (3B)

patinar to skate (1A)

pedir (e → i) to order (5B); to ask for (9B)

la **película: film,** movie (9A)

   la — de ciencia ficción science fiction movie (9A)

   la — de horror horror movie (9A)

   la — policíaca crime movie, mystery (9A)

   la — romántica romantic movie (9A)

   ver una — to see a movie (4A)

pelirrojo, -a red-haired (5B)

el **pelo** hair (5B)

   el — canoso gray hair (5B)

   el — castaño brown (chestnut) hair (5B)

el — **negro** black hair (5B)

el — **rubio** blond hair (5B)

pensar (e → ie) to plan, to think (7A)

peor:

   el / la —, los / las —es the worst (6A)

   —(es) que worse than (6A)

pequeño, -a small (6A)

Perdón. Excuse me. (7A)

perezoso, -a lazy (1B)

el **perfume** perfume (7B)

el **periódico** newspaper (8B)

pero but (1B)

el **perrito caliente** hot dog (3A)

el **perro** dog (5A)

la **persona** person (5A)

pesas: levantar — to lift weights (3B)

el **pescado** fish (3B)

el **pie** foot (P)

la **pierna** leg (P)

la **pimienta** pepper (5B)

la **piñata** piñata (5A)

la **piscina** pool (4A)

el **piso** story, floor (6B)

   primer — second floor (6B)

   segundo — third floor (6B)

la **pizza** pizza (3A)

la **planta baja** ground floor (6B)

el **plástico** plastic (8B)

el **plátano** banana (3A)

el **plato** plate, dish (5B)

   de — principal as a main dish (5B)

   el — principal main dish (5B)

la **playa** beach (4A)

pobre poor (8B)

poco: un — (de) a little (4B)

poder (o → ue) to be able (6A)

   (yo) puedo I can (4B)

   (tú) puedes you can (4B)

policíaca: la película — crime movie, mystery (9A)

el **pollo** chicken (3B)

poner to put, to place (6B)

   pon *(command)* put, place (6B)

   — la mesa to set the table (6B)

   (yo) pongo I put (6B)

   (tú) pones you put (6B)

por:

   — eso for that reason, therefore (9A)

   — favor please (P)

   ¿— qué? Why? (3B)

   — supuesto of course (3A)

porque because (3B)

la **posesión,** *pl.* **las posesiones** possession (6A)

el **postre** dessert (5B)

   de — for dessert (5B)

practicar deportes to play sports (1A)

práctico, -a practical (2A)

el **precio** price (7A)

preferir (e → ie) to prefer (7A)

   (yo) prefiero I prefer (3B)

   (tú) prefieres you prefer (3B)

preparar to prepare (5A)

la **presentación,** *pl.* **las presentaciones** presentation (9B)

la **primavera** spring (P)

primer (primero), -a first (2A)

   — piso second floor (6B)

el **primo, la prima** cousin (5A)

los **primos** cousins (5A)

el **problema** problem (8B)

el **profesor, la profesora** teacher (P)

el **programa** program, show (9A)

   el — de concursos game show (9A)

   el — de dibujos animados cartoon (9A)

   el — de entrevistas interview program (9A)

   el — de la vida real reality program (9A)

   el — de noticias news program (9A)

   el — deportivo sports program (9A)

   el — educativo educational program (9A)

   el — musical musical program (9A)

propio, -a own (6A)

el **proyecto de construcción** construction project (8B)

puedes: (tú) — you can (4B)

puedo: (yo) — I can (4B)

la **puerta** door (2B)

pues well *(to indicate pause)* (1A)

la **pulsera** bracelet (7B)

   el reloj — watch (7B)

el **pupitre** student desk (P)

Q

que who, that (5A)

qué:

   ¿Para — sirve? What's it (used) for? (9B)

   ¡— + *adj.***!** How . . . ! (5B)

   ¡— asco! How awful! (3A)

   ¡— buena idea! What a good / nice idea! (4B)

   ¿— clase de . . . ? What kind of . . . ? (9A)

   ¿— desean (Uds.)? What would you like? (5B)

   ¿— día es hoy? What day is today? (P)

   ¿— es esto? What is this? (2B)

   ¿— hiciste? What did you do? (8A)

   ¿— hora es? What time is it? (P)

   ¿— más? What else? (8B)

   ¿— pasa? What's happening? (P)

   ¡— pena! What a shame / pity! (4B)

   ¿— quiere decir . . . ? What does . . . mean? (P)

   ¿— tal? How are you? (P)

   ¿— te gusta hacer? What do you like to do? (1A)

¿— te gusta hacer más? What do you like better (prefer) to do? (1A)

¿— te parece? What do you think (about it)? (9B)

¿— te pasó? What happened to you? (8A)

¿— tiempo hace? What's the weather like? (P)

quedar to fit (9A)

los quehaceres (de la casa) (household) chores (6B)

querer (e → ie) to want (7A)

¿Qué quiere decir . . . ? What does . . . mean? (P)

Quiere decir . . . It means . . . (P)

quisiera I would like (5B)

(yo) quiero I want (4B)

(tú) quieres you want (4B)

¿Quién? Who? (2A)

quince fifteen (P)

quinientos, -as five hundred (7A)

quinto, -a fifth (2A)

quisiera I would like (5B)

quitar el polvo to dust (6B)

quizás maybe (7A)

R

rápidamente quickly (9B)

el ratón, pl. los ratones (computer) mouse (2B)

razón: tener — to be correct (7A)

realista realistic (9A)

recibir to receive (6B)

reciclar to recycle (8B)

recoger (g → j) to collect, to gather (8B)

los recuerdos souvenirs (8A)

comprar — to buy souvenirs (8A)

la Red:

en la — online (7B)

navegar en la — to surf the Web (9B)

el refresco soft drink (3A)

el regalo gift, present (5A)

regresar to return (8A)

regular okay, so-so (P)

el reloj clock (2B)

el — pulsera watch (7B)

reservado, -a reserved, shy (1B)

el restaurante restaurant (4A)

rico, -a rich, tasty (5B)

el río river (8B)

rojo, -a red (6A)

romántico, -a: la película — romantic movie (9A)

romper to break (5A)

la ropa: la tienda de — clothing store (7B)

rosado, -a pink (6A)

rubio, -a blond (5B)

S

sábado Saturday (P)

saber to know (how) (9B)

(yo) sé I know (how to) (4B)

(tú) sabes you know (how to) (4B)

sabroso, -a tasty, flavorful (3B)

el sacapuntas, pl. los sacapuntas pencil sharpener (2B)

sacar:

— fotos to take photos (5A)

— la basura to take out the trash (6B)

la sal salt (5B)

la sala living room (6B)

la sala de clases classroom (P)

la salchicha sausage (3A)

salir to leave, to go out (8A)

la salud:

para la — for one's health (3B)

para mantener la — to maintain one's health (3B)

el sándwich de jamón y queso ham and cheese sandwich (3A)

sé: (yo) — I know (how to) (1B)

sed: Tengo —. I'm thirsty. (3B)

según according to (1B)

— mi familia according to my family (1B)

segundo, -a second (2A)

— piso third floor (6B)

seis six (P)

seiscientos, -as six hundred (7A)

la semana week (P)

este fin de — this weekend (4B)

la — pasada last week (7B)

los fines de — on weekends (4A)

señor (Sr.) sir, Mr. (P)

señora (Sra.) madam, Mrs. (P)

señorita (Srta.) miss, Miss (P)

separar to separate (8B)

septiembre September (P)

séptimo, -a seventh (2A)

ser to be (3B)

¿Eres . . . ? Are you . . . ? (1B)

es he / she is (1B)

fue it was (8A)

no soy I am not (1B)

soy I am (1B)

serio, -a serious (1B)

la servilleta napkin (5B)

servir (e → i) to serve, to be useful (9B)

¿En qué puedo servirle? How can I help you? (7A)

¿Para qué sirve? What's it (used) for? (9B)

Sirve para . . . It's used for . . . (9B)

sesenta sixty (P)

setecientos, -as seven hundred (7A)

setenta seventy (P)

sexto, -a sixth (2A)

si if, whether (6B)

sí yes (1A)

siempre always (3A)

siento: lo — I'm sorry (4B)

siete seven (P)

la silla chair (2B)

simpático, -a nice, friendly (1B)

sin without (3A)

la **sinagoga** synagogue (4A)

el **sitio Web** Web site (9B)

sobre about (9A)

sociable sociable (1B)

el **software** software (7B)

el **sol:**

   Hace —. It's sunny. (P)

   los anteojos de — sunglasses (7B)

   tomar el — to sunbathe (8A)

sólo only (5A)

solo, -a alone (4A)

Son las . . . It's . . . *(time)* (P)

la **sopa de verduras** vegetable soup (3A)

el **sótano** basement (6B)

soy I am (1B)

su, sus his, her, your *formal,* their (5A)

sucio, -a dirty (6B)

la **sudadera** sweatshirt (7A)

sueño: tener — to be sleepy (5B)

el **suéter** sweater (7A)

supuesto: por — of course (3A)

T ————————————

tal: ¿Qué — ? How are you? (P)

talentoso, -a talented (1B)

también also, too (1A)

   a mí — I do (like to) too (1A)

tampoco: a mí — I don't (like to) either (1A)

tanto so much (7A)

tarde late (8A); afternoon (4B)

   a la una de la — at one (o'clock) in the afternoon (4B)

   Buenas —s. Good afternoon. (P)

   de la — in the afternoon (4B)

   esta — this afternoon (4B)

la **tarea** homework (2A)

la **tarjeta** card (9B)

la **taza** cup (5B)

te (to / for) you *sing. ind. obj. pron.* (8B)

   ¿— gusta . . . ? Do you like to . . . ? (1A)

   ¿— gustaría . . . ? Would you like . . . ? (4B)

   ¿— gustó? Did you like it? (8A)

el **té** tea (3A)

   el — helado iced tea (3A)

el **teatro** theater (8A)

el **teclado** (computer) keyboard (2B)

la **tecnología** technology / computers (2A)

   la clase de — technology / computer class (2A)

la **telenovela** soap opera (9A)

el **televisor** television set (6A)

el **templo** temple; Protestant church (4A)

temprano early (8A)

el **tenedor** fork (5B)

tener to have (5A)

   (yo) tengo I have (2A)

   (tú) tienes you have (2A)

   ¿Cuántos años tiene(n) . . . ? How old is / are . . . ? (5A)

   — calor to be warm (5B)

   — frío to be cold (5B)

   — miedo (de) to be scared (of), to be afraid (of) (9B)

   — razón to be correct (7A)

   — sueño to be sleepy (5B)

   Tengo hambre. I'm hungry. (3B)

   Tengo que . . . I have to . . . (4B)

   Tengo sed. I'm thirsty. (3B)

   Tiene(n) . . . años. He / She is / They are . . . years old. (5A)

el **tenis: jugar al —** to play tennis (4B)

tercer (tercero), -a third (2A)

terminar to finish, to end (9A)

ti you *fam. after prep.*

¿Y a —? And you? (1A)

para — in your opinion, for you (6A)

el **tiempo:**

   el — libre free time (4A)

   pasar — con amigos to spend time with friends (1A)

   ¿Qué — hace? What's the weather like? (P)

la **tienda** store (7A)

   la — de descuentos discount store (7B)

   la — de electrodomésticos household appliance store (7B)

   la — de ropa clothing store (7A)

Tiene(n) . . . años. He / She is / They are . . . years old. (5A)

el **tío, la tía** uncle, aunt (5A)

los **tíos** uncles; aunt(s) and uncle(s) (5A)

tocar la guitarra to play the guitar (1A)

el **tocino** bacon (3A)

todos, -as all (3B)

   — los días every day (3A)

tomar:

   — el sol to sunbathe (8A)

   — un curso to take a course (9B)

los **tomates** tomatoes (3B)

tonto, -a silly, stupid (9A)

trabajador, -a hardworking (1B)

trabajar to work (1A)

el **trabajo** work, job (4A)

   el — voluntario volunteer work (8B)

traer:

   Le traigo . . . I will bring you . . . (5B)

   ¿Me trae . . . ? Will you bring me . . . ? (5B)

el **traje** suit (7A)

   el — de baño swimsuit (7A)

trece thirteen (P)

treinta thirty (P)

treinta y uno thirty-one (P)

tremendo, -a tremendous (8A)

el **tren** train (8A)

tres three (P)

trescientos, as three hundred (7A)

triste sad (4B)

tu, tus your (2B, 5A)

tú you *fam.* (2A)

U _____

Ud. (usted) you *formal sing.* (2A)

Uds. (ustedes) you *formal pl.* (2A)

¡Uf! Ugh!, Yuck! (7B)

un, una a, an (1B)

un poco (de) a little (4B)

la **una: a la —** at one o'clock (4B)

uno one (P)

unos, -as some (2B)

usado, -a used (8B)

usar la computadora to use the computer (1A)

usted (Ud.) you *formal sing.* (2A)

ustedes (Uds.) you *formal pl.* (2A)

las **uvas** grapes (3B)

V _____

las **vacaciones: ir de —** to go on vacation (8A)

¡Vamos! Let's go! (7A)

el **vaso** glass (5B)

veinte twenty (P)

veintiuno (veintiún) twenty-one (P)

vender to sell (7B)

venir to come (5B)

la **ventana** window (2B)

ver to see (8A)

a — . . . Let's see (2A)

¡Nos vemos! See you later! (P)

— la tele to watch television (1A)

— una película to see a movie (4A)

vi I saw (8A)

¿Viste? Did you see? (8A)

el **verano** summer (P)

veras: ¿De —? Right? (9A)

¿Verdad? Right? (3A)

verde green (6A)

el **vestido** dress (7A)

la **vez,** *pl.* **las veces:**

a veces sometimes (1B)

otra — again (8B)

viajar to travel (8A)

el **viaje** trip (8A)

el **video** video (5A)

los **videojuegos: jugar —** to play video games (1A)

el **vidrio** glass (8B)

viejo, -a old (5B)

viernes Friday (P)

violento, -a violent (9A)

visitar to visit (8A)

— salones de chat to visit chat rooms (9B)

vivir to live (6B)

el **vóleibol: jugar al —** to play volleyball (4B)

el **voluntario, la voluntaria** volunteer (8B)

vosotros, -as you *pl.* (2A)

vuestro(s), -a(s) your (5A)

Y _____

y and (1A)

¿— a ti? And you? (1A)

— cuarto quarter past *(in telling time)* (P)

— media thirty, half past *(in telling time)* (P)

¿— tú? And you? *fam.* (P)

¿— usted (Ud.)? And you? *formal* (P)

ya already (9A)

yo I (1B)

el **yogur** yogurt (3A)

Z _____

las **zanahorias** carrots (3B)

la **zapatería** shoe store (7B)

los **zapatos** shoes (7A)

el **zoológico** zoo (8A)

English–Spanish Vocabulary

The *English-Spanish Vocabulary* contains all active vocabulary from the text, including vocabulary presented in the grammar sections.

A dash (—) represents the main entry word. For example, **to play —** after **baseball** means **to play baseball.**

The number following each entry indicates the chapter in which the word or expression is presented. Remember that Temas 1–4 appeared in Level A. The letter *P* following an entry refers to the *Para empezar* section of Level A.

The following abbreviations are used in this list: *adj.* (adjective), *dir. obj.* (direct object), *f.* (feminine), *fam.*(familiar), *ind. obj.* (indirect object), *inf.* (infinitive), *m.* (masculine), *pl.* (plural), *prep.* (preposition), *pron.* (pronoun), *sing.* (singular).

A

a, an un, una (1B)

  a little un poco (de) (4B)

  a lot mucho, -a (2A)

  a thousand mil (7A)

able: to be — poder (o → ue) (6A)

about sobre (9A)

according to según (1B)

  — my family según mi familia (1B)

acquainted: to be — with conocer (9B)

actor el actor (9A)

actress la actriz, *pl.* las actrices (9A)

address: e-mail — la dirección electrónica (9B)

afraid: to be — (of) tener miedo (de) (9B)

after después (de) (4A)

afternoon:

  at one (o'clock) in the afternoon a la una de la tarde (4B)

  Good —. Buenas tardes. (P)

  in the — de la tarde (4B)

  this — esta tarde (4B)

afterwards después (4A)

again otra vez (8B)

ago hace + *time expression* (7B)

agree:

  I —. Estoy de acuerdo. (3B)

  I don't —. No estoy de acuerdo. (3B)

airplane el avión, *pl.* los aviones (8A)

alarm clock el despertador (6A)

all todos, -as (3B)

almost casi (9A)

alone solo, -a (4A)

already ya (9A)

also también (1A)

always siempre (3A)

am:

  I — (yo) soy (1B)

  I — not (yo) no soy (1B)

amusement park el parque de diversiones (8A)

amusing divertido, -a (2A)

and y (1A)

  ¿— you? ¿Y a ti? *fam.* (1A); ¿Y tú? *fam.* (P); ¿Y usted (Ud.)? *formal* (P)

animal el animal (8A)

another otro, -a (5B)

Anything else? ¿Algo más? (5B)

apartment el apartamento (6B)

apple la manzana (3A)

  — juice el jugo de manzana (3A)

April abril (P)

Are you . . . ? ¿Eres . . . ? (1B)

arm el brazo (P)

art class la clase de arte (2A)

artistic artístico, -a (1B)

as como (8A)

  — a main dish de plato principal (5B)

to **ask for** pedir (e → i) (9B)

at:

  — eight (o'clock) a las ocho (4B)

  — eight (o'clock) at night a las ocho de la noche (4B)

  — eight (o'clock) in the evening a las ocho de la noche (4B)

  — eight (o'clock) in the morning a las ocho de la mañana (4B)

  — home en casa (4A)

  — one (o'clock) a la una (4B)

  — one (o'clock) in the afternoon a la una de la tarde (4B)

  — what time? ¿A qué hora? (4B)

athletic deportista (1B)

attraction(s) la atracción, *pl.* las atracciones (8A)

August agosto (P)

aunt la tía (5A)

aunt(s) and uncle(s) los tíos (5A)

autumn el otoño (P)

B

backpack la mochila (2B)

bacon el tocino (3A)

bad malo, -a (3B); mal (4B)

badly mal (4B)

bag la bolsa (8B)

balloon el globo (5A)

banana el plátano (3A)

baseball: to play — jugar al béisbol (4B)

basement el sótano (6B)

basketball: to play — jugar al básquetbol (4B)

bathroom el baño (6B)

to **be** ser (3B); estar (2B)

  He / She is / They are . . . years old. Tiene(n) . . . años. (5A)

  How old is / are . . . ? ¿Cuántos años tiene(n) . . . ? (5A)

  to — + present participle estar + *present participle* (6B)

  to — able poder (o → ue) (6A)

  to — acquainted with conocer (9B)

  to — afraid (of) tener miedo (de) (9B)

  to — cold tener frío (5B)

  to — correct tener razón (7A)

to — **going to** + *verb* ir a + *inf.* (4B)

to — **online** estar en línea (9B)

to — **scared (of)** tener miedo (de) (9B)

to — **sleepy** tener sueño (5B)

to — **useful** servir (e → i) (9B)

to — **warm** tener calor (5B)

beach la playa (4A)

bear el oso (8A)

because porque (3B)

bed la cama (6A)

    to make the — hacer la cama (6B)

bedroom el dormitorio (6A)

beefsteak el bistec (3B)

before antes de (9A)

to **begin** empezar (e → ie) (9A)

behind detrás de (2B)

best: the — el / la mejor, los / las mejores (6A)

better than mejor(es) que (6A)

beverages las bebidas (3B)

bicycle: to ride a — montar en bicicleta (1A)

bill la cuenta (5B)

binder: three-ring — la carpeta de argollas (2A)

bird el pájaro (8A)

birthday el cumpleaños (5A)

    Happy —! ¡Feliz cumpleaños! (5A)

black hair el pelo negro (5B)

blond hair el pelo rubio (5B)

blouse la blusa (7A)

blue azul (6A)

boat el barco (8A)

boating: to go — pasear en bote (8A)

book el libro (P)

bookbag la mochila (2B)

bookshelf el estante (6A)

bookstore la librería (7B)

boots las botas (7A)

to **bore** aburrir (9A)

    it / they —(s) me me aburre(n) (9A)

boring aburrido, -a (2A)

both los dos, las dos (7A)

bottle la botella (8B)

box la caja (8B)

boy el chico (1B)

    —friend el novio (7B)

    young — el niño (8B)

bracelet la pulsera (7B)

bread el pan (3A)

to **break** romper (5A)

breakfast el desayuno (3A)

    for — en el desayuno (3A)

to **bring** traer (5B); llevar (8B)

    I will — you . . . Le traigo . . . (5B)

    Will you — me . . . ? ¿Me trae . . . ? (5B)

brother el hermano (5A)

brothers; brother(s) and sister(s) los hermanos (5A)

brown marrón, *pl.* marrones (6A)

    — (chestnut) hair el pelo castaño (5B)

to **burn a CD** grabar un disco compacto (9B)

bus el autobús, *pl.* los autobuses (8A)

busy ocupado, -a (4B)

but pero (1B)

butter la mantequilla (3B)

to **buy** comprar (7A)

    to — souvenirs comprar recuerdos (8A)

by + *vehicle* en + *vehicle* (8A)

C

café el café (4A)

cake el pastel (5A)

calculator la calculadora (2A)

camera la cámara (5A)

    digital — la cámara digital (9B)

camp el campamento (8B)

can la lata (8B)

can:

    I — (yo) puedo (4B)

    you — (tú) puedes (4B)

candy los dulces (5A)

cap la gorra (7A)

car el coche (6B)

card la tarjeta (9B)

cardboard el cartón (8B)

carrots las zanahorias (3B)

to **carry** llevar (8B)

cartoon el programa de dibujos animados (9A)

cat el gato (5A)

CD: to burn a — grabar un disco compacto (9B)

to **celebrate** celebrar (5A)

cereal el cereal (3A)

chain la cadena (7B)

chair la silla (2B)

channel (TV) el canal (9A)

cheap barato, -a (7B)

chicken el pollo (3B)

childish infantil (9A)

children los hijos (5A); los niños (8B)

chores: household — los quehaceres (de la casa) (6B)

church la iglesia (4A)

    Protestant — el templo (4A)

city la ciudad (8A)

class la clase (2A)

classroom la sala de clases (P)

clean limpio, -a (6B)

to **clean the bathroom** limpiar el baño (6B)

clock el reloj (2B)

close (to) cerca (de) (6B)

closet el armario (6A)

clothing store la tienda de ropa (7A)

coat el abrigo (7A)

coffee el café (3A)

cold:

    It's —. Hace frío. (P)

    to be — tener frío (5B)

to **collect** recoger (g → j) (8B)

color:

    What — . . . ? ¿De qué color . . . ? (6A)

    —s los colores (6A)

to **come** venir (5B)

comedy la comedia (9A)

comical cómico, -a (9A)

to **communicate** comunicarse (9B)

    I — (yo) me comunico (9B)

    you — (tú) te comunicas (9B)

community la comunidad (8B)

compact disc el disco compacto (6A)

    to burn a — grabar un disco compacto (9B)

complicated complicado, -a (9B)

composition la composición, *pl.* las composiciones (9B)

computer la computadora (2B)

    — graphics los gráficos (9B)

    — keyboard el teclado (2B)

    — mouse el ratón (2B)

    — screen la pantalla (2B)

    —s / technology la tecnología (2B)

    laptop — la computadora portátil (9B)

    to use the — usar la computadora (1A)

concert el concierto (4B)

construction project el proyecto de construcción (8B)

to **cook** cocinar (6B)

cookie la galleta (3A)

correct: to be — tener razón (7A)

to **cost** costar (o → ue) (7A)

    How much does (do) . . . —? ¿Cuánto cuesta(n)? (7A)

country el país (8A)

countryside el campo (4A)

course: to take a course tomar un curso (9B)

cousin el primo, la prima (5A)

    —s los primos (5A)

to **create** crear (9B)

crime movie la película policíaca (9A)

cup la taza (5B)

curtains las cortinas (6A)

to **cut the lawn** cortar el césped (6B)

cut-paper decorations el papel picado (5A)

D _____

dance el baile (4B)

to **dance** bailar (1A)

daring atrevido, -a (1B)

date: What is the —? ¿Cuál es la fecha? (P)

daughter la hija (5A)

day el día (P)

    every — todos los días (3A); cada día (3B)

    What — is today? ¿Qué día es hoy? (P)

December diciembre (P)

to **decide** decidir (8B)

to **decorate** decorar (5A)

decorations las decoraciones (5A)

delicious delicioso, -a (5B)

delighted encantado, -a (P)

department store el almacén, *pl.* los almacenes (7B)

desk el pupitre (P); el escritorio (2B)

dessert el postre (5B)

    for — de postre (5B)

dictionary el diccionario (2A)

Did you like it? ¿Te gustó? (8A)

difficult difícil (2A)

digital camera la cámara digital (9B)

dining room el comedor (6B)

dinner la cena (3B)

dirty sucio, -a (6B)

disaster: It was a —. Fue un desastre. (8A)

discount store la tienda de descuentos (7B)

dish el plato (5B)

    as a main — de plato principal (5B)

    main — el plato principal (5B)

to **do** hacer (3B)

    — (command) haz (6B)

    — you like to . . . ? ¿Te gusta . . . ? (1A)

    I — (yo) hago (3B)

    What are you doing? ¿Qué estás haciendo? (6B)

    What did you —? ¿Qué hiciste? (8A)

    you — (tú) haces (3B)

document el documento (9B)

dog el perro (5A)

    to feed the — dar de comer al perro (6B)

door la puerta (2B)

to **download** bajar (información) (9B)

drama el drama (9A)

to **draw** dibujar (1A)

dress el vestido (7A)

dresser la cómoda (6A)

to **drink** beber (3A)

during durante (8A)

to **dust** quitar el polvo (6B)

DVD player el lector DVD (6A)

E _____

e-mail:

    — address la dirección electrónica (9B)

    to write an — message escribir por correo electrónico (9B)

early temprano (8A)

earrings los aretes (7B)

easy fácil (2A)

to **eat** comer (3A)

educational program el programa educativo (9A)

eggs los huevos (3A)

eight ocho (P)

eight hundred ochocientos, -as (7A)

eighteen dieciocho (P)

eighth octavo, -a (2A)

eighty ochenta (P)

either tampoco (1A)

    I don't (like to) — a mí tampoco (1A)

eleven once (P)

else:

    Anything —? ¿Algo más? (5B)

    What —? ¿Qué más? (8B)

to **end** terminar (9A)

English class la clase de inglés (2A)

enough bastante (6B)

to enter entrar (7A)

especially especialmente (9A)

evening:

    Good —. Buenas noches. (P)

    in the — de la noche (4B)

    this — esta noche (4B)

every day cada día (3B); todos los días (3A)

Excuse me. Perdón. (7A)

to exercise hacer ejercicio (3B)

expensive caro, -a (7B)

experience la experiencia (8B)

eye el ojo (P)

F

face-to-face cara a cara (9B)

fall el otoño (P)

fantastic fantástico, -a (8A)

far (from) lejos (de) (6B)

fascinating fascinante (9A)

fast rápidamente (9B)

father el padre (papá) (5A)

favorite favorito, -a (2A)

February febrero (P)

to feed the dog dar de comer al perro (6B)

fewer:

    — . . . than menos . . . que (6A)

    — than . . . menos de . . . (9A)

fifteen quince (P)

fifth quinto, -a (2A)

fifty cincuenta (P)

film la película (9A)

finger el dedo (P)

to finish terminar (9A)

first primer (primero), -a (2A)

fish el pescado (3B)

    to go —ing ir de pesca (4B)

to fit: It / They —(s) me well / poorly. Me queda(n) bien / mal. (7A)

five cinco (P)

five hundred quinientos, -as (7A)

flag la bandera (2B)

flavorful sabroso, -a (3B)

floor el piso (6B)

ground — la planta baja (6B)

    second — el primer piso (6B)

    third — el segundo piso (6B)

flower la flor, pl. las flores (5A)

folder la carpeta (P)

food la comida (3A)

foot el pie (P)

football: to play — jugar al fútbol americano (4B)

for para (2A)

    — breakfast en el desayuno (3A)

    — lunch en el almuerzo (3A)

    — me para mí (6A)

    — that reason por eso (9A)

    — you para ti (6A)

fork el tenedor (5B)

forty cuarenta (P)

four cuatro (P)

four hundred cuatrocientos, -as (7A)

fourteen catorce (P)

fourth cuarto, -a (2A)

free time el tiempo libre (4A)

French fries las papas fritas (3A)

Friday viernes (P)

friend el amigo, la amiga (1B)

friendly simpático, -a (1B)

from de (4A)

    Where are you —? ¿De dónde eres? (4A)

fruit salad la ensalada de frutas (3A)

fun divertido, -a (2A)

funny gracioso, -a (1B); cómico, -a (9A)

G

game el partido (4B)

    — show el programa de concursos (9A)

garage el garaje (6B)

garden el jardín, pl. los jardines (8B)

to gather recoger (g → j) (8B)

generally generalmente (4A)

gift el regalo (5A)

girl la chica (1B)

—friend la novia (7B)

    young — la niña (8B)

to give dar (6B)

glass el vaso (5B); el vidrio (8B)

gloves los guantes (7B)

to go ir (4A)

    Let's —! ¡Vamos! (7A)

    to be —ing to + verb ir a + inf. (4B)

    to — boating pasear en bote (8A)

    to — camping ir de cámping (4B)

    to — fishing ir de pesca (4B)

    to — on vacation ir de vacaciones (8A)

    to — shopping ir de compras (4A)

    to — to school ir a la escuela (1A)

    to — out salir (8A)

golf: to play — jugar al golf (4B)

good bueno (buen), -a (1B)

    — afternoon. Buenas tardes. (P)

    — evening. Buenas noches. (P)

    — morning. Buenos días. (P)

Good-bye! ¡Adiós! (P)

good-looking guapo, -a (5B)

grandfather el abuelo (5A)

grandmother la abuela (5A)

grandparents los abuelos (5A)

grapes las uvas (3B)

gray gris (6A)

    — hair el pelo canoso (5B)

Great! ¡Genial! (4B)

green verde (6A)

    — beans las judías verdes (3B)

ground floor la planta baja (6B)

guitar: to play the — tocar la guitarra (1A)

gym el gimnasio (4A)

H

hair el pelo (5B)

    black — el pelo negro (5B)

    blond — el pelo rubio (5B)

brown (chestnut) — el pelo castaño (5B)

gray — el pelo canoso (5B)

half media, -o (P)

— past y media (in telling time) (P)

ham and cheese sandwich el sándwich de jamón y queso (3A)

hamburger la hamburguesa (3A)

hand la mano (P)

happy contento, -a (4B)

— birthday! ¡Feliz cumpleaños! (5A)

hardworking trabajador, -a (1B)

to have tener (5A)

to — just . . . acabar de + inf. (9A)

I — to . . . tengo que + inf. (4B)

he él (1B)

he / she is es (1B)

He / She is / They are . . . years old. Tiene(n) . . . años. (5A)

head la cabeza (P)

health:

for one's — para la salud (3B)

to maintain one's — para mantener la salud (3B)

Hello! ¡Hola! (P)

to help ayudar (6B)

How can I — you? ¿En qué puedo servirle? (7A)

her su, sus possessive adj. (5A); la dir. obj. pron. (7B); le ind. obj. pron. (8B)

here aquí (2B)

Hey! ¡Oye! (4B)

him lo dir. obj. pron. (7B); le ind. obj. pron. (8B)

his su, sus (5A)

home la casa (4A)

at — en casa (4A)

— office el despacho (6B)

(to) — a casa (4A)

homework la tarea (2A)

horrible horrible (3B)

horror movie la película de horror (9A)

horseback: to ride — montar a caballo (8A)

hospital el hospital (8B)

hot:

— dog el perrito caliente (3A)

It's —. Hace calor. (P)

hotel el hotel (8A)

hour: in the . . . — en la . . . hora (class period) (2A)

house la casa (4A)

household:

— chores los quehaceres (de la casa) (6B)

— appliance store la tienda de electrodomésticos (7B)

how:

— + adj.! ¡Qué + adj.! (5B)

— awful! ¡Qué asco! (3A)

How? ¿Cómo? (P)

— are you? ¿Cómo está Ud.? formal (P); ¿Cómo estás? fam. (P); ¿Qué tal? fam. (P)

— can I help you? ¿En qué puedo servirle? (7A)

— do you say . . . ? ¿Cómo se dice . . . ? (P)

— does it (do they) fit (you)? ¿Cómo te queda(n)? (7A)

— is . . . spelled? ¿Cómo se escribe . . . ? (P)

— many? ¿cuántos, -as? (P)

— much does (do) . . . cost? ¿Cuánto cuesta(n) . . . ? (7A)

— old is / are . . . ? ¿Cuántos años tiene(n) . . . ? (5A)

— was it (for you)? ¿Cómo lo pasaste? (8A)

hundred: one — cien (P)

hungry: I'm —. Tengo hambre. (3B)

to hurt doler (o → ue) (9A)

husband el esposo (5A)

I yo (1B)

— am soy (1B)

— am not no soy (1B)

— don't think so. Creo que no. (3B)

— stay at home. Me quedo en casa. (4A)

— think . . . Creo que . . . (3B)

— think so. Creo que sí. (3B)

— will bring you . . . Le traigo . . . (5B)

—'m hungry. Tengo hambre. (3B)

—'m sorry. Lo siento. (4B)

—'m thirsty. Tengo sed. (3B)

I do too a mí también (1A)

I don't either a mí tampoco (1A)

I forgot se me olvidó (3A)

I would like Me gustaría (4B); (yo) quisiera (5B)

ice cream el helado (3B)

iced tea el té helado (3A)

if si (6B)

impatient impaciente (1B)

important importante (6A)

impressive impresionante (8A)

in en (2B)

— front of delante de (2B)

— my opinion para mí (6A)

— order to para + inf. (4A)

— the . . . hour en la . . . hora (class period) (2A)

— your opinion para ti (6A)

incredible increíble (8B)

inexpensive barato, -a (7B)

information la información (9B)

intelligent inteligente (1B)

to interest interesar (9A)

it / they interest(s) me me interesa(n) (9A)

interesting interesante (2A)

interview program el programa de entrevistas (9A)

is es (P)

he / she — es (1B)

it la, lo dir. obj. pron. (7B)

— fits (they fit) me well / poorly. Me queda(n) bien / mal. (7A)

— is . . . Son las (in telling time) (P)

— is one o'clock. Es la una. (P)

— is the . . . of . . . Es el *(number)* de *(month) (in telling the date)* (P)

— is the first of . . . Es el primero de *(month).* (P)

— was fue (8A)

— was a disaster. Fue un desastre. (8A)

—'s a . . . es un / una . . . (2B)

—'s cold. Hace frío. (P)

—'s hot. Hace calor. (P)

—'s necessary. Es necesario. (8B)

—'s raining. Llueve. (P)

—'s snowing. Nieva. (P)

—'s sunny. Hace sol. (P)

J

jacket la chaqueta (7A)

January enero (P)

jeans los jeans (7A)

jewelry store la joyería (7B)

job el trabajo (4A)

juice:

    apple — el jugo de manzana (3A)

    orange — el jugo de naranja (3A)

July julio (P)

June junio (P)

just: to have — *(done something)* acabar de + *inf.* (9A)

K

key chain el llavero (7B)

keyboard (computer) el teclado (2B)

kind: What — of . . . ? ¿Qué clase de . . . ? (9A)

kitchen la cocina (6B)

knife el cuchillo (5B)

to **know** saber (4B, 9B); conocer (9B)

    I — (yo) conozco (9B)

    I — (how to) (yo) sé (4B)

    you — (tú) conoces (9B)

    you — (how to) (tú) sabes (4B)

L

laboratory el laboratorio (9B)

lake el lago (8A)

lamp la lámpara (6A)

laptop computer la computadora portátil (9B)

large grande (6A)

last:

    — night anoche (7B)

    — week la semana pasada (7B)

    — year el año pasado (7B)

to **last** durar (9A)

late tarde (8A)

later: See you —! ¡Hasta luego!, ¡Nos vemos! (P)

lazy perezoso, -a (1B)

to **learn** aprender (a) (8A)

to **leave** salir (8A)

left: to the — (of) a la izquierda (de) (6A)

leg la pierna (P)

lemonade la limonada (3A)

less:

    — . . . than menos . . . que (6A)

    — than menos de (9A)

Let's go! ¡Vamos! (7A)

Let's see A ver . . . (2A)

letter la carta (9B)

lettuce la lechuga (3B)

library la biblioteca (4A)

to **lift weights** levantar pesas (3B)

light la luz, *pl.* las luces (5A)

like como (8A)

to **like:**

    Did you — it? ¿Te gustó? (8A)

    Do you — to . . . ? ¿Te gusta . . . ? (1A)

    He / She doesn't — . . . No le gusta . . . (1B)

    He / She —s . . . Le gusta . . . (1B); A él / ella le gusta(n) . . .(5A)

    I don't — to . . . (A mí) no me gusta . . . (1A)

    I don't — to . . . at all. (A mí) no me gusta nada . . . (1A)

    I — . . . Me gusta . . . (3A)

    I — to . . . (A mí) me gusta . . . (1A)

    I — to . . . a lot (A mí) me gusta mucho . . . (1A)

    I — to . . . better (A mí) me gusta más . . . (1A)

    I —d it. Me gustó. (8A)

    I would — Me gustaría (4B); quisiera (5B)

    What do you — better (prefer) to do? ¿Qué te gusta hacer más? (1A)

    What do you — to do? ¿Qué te gusta hacer? (1A)

    What would you —? ¿Qué desean (Uds.)? (5B)

    Would you —? ¿Te gustaría? (4B)

    You — . . . Te gusta . . . (3A)

likewise igualmente (P)

to **listen to music** escuchar música (1A)

little: a — un poco (de) (4B)

to **live** vivir (6B)

living room la sala (6B)

long largo, -a (5B)

to **look:**

    to — (at) mirar (7B)

    to — for buscar (7A)

lot: a — mucho, -a (2A)

to **love** encantar (9A)

    He / She —s . . . A él / ella le encanta(n) . . . (5A)

    I / You — . . . Me / Te encanta(n) . . . (3A)

lunch el almuerzo (2A)

    for — en el almuerzo (3A)

M

madam (la) señora (Sra.) (P)

main dish el plato principal (5B)

    as a — de plato principal (5B)

to **maintain one's health** para mantener la salud (3B)

make *(command)* haz (6B)

to **make the bed** hacer la cama (6B)

mall el centro comercial (4A)

man el hombre (5B)

    older — el anciano (8B)

many muchos, -as (3B)

    how — ¿cuántos, -as? (P)

March marzo (P)

match el partido (4B)

mathematics class la clase de matemáticas (2A)

May mayo (P)

maybe quizás (7A)

me me *ind. obj. pron* (8B)

    for — para mí (6A), me (8B)

    — too a mí también (1A)

    to — me (8B)

    with — conmigo (4B)

meal la comida (3A)

to **mean:**

    It —s . . . Quiere decir . . . (P)

    What does . . . — ? ¿Qué quiere decir . . . ? (P)

meat la carne (3B)

menu el menú (5B)

messy desordenado, -a (1B)

milk la leche (3A)

mirror el espejo (6A)

miss, Miss (la) señorita (Srta.) (P)

missing: to be — faltar (9A)

moment: a — un momento (6B)

Monday lunes (P)

    on Mondays los lunes (4A)

money el dinero (6B)

monkey el mono (8A)

month el mes (P)

monument el monumento (8A)

more:

    — . . . than más . . . que (2A)

    — or less más o menos (3A)

    — than más de (9A)

morning:

    Good —. Buenos días. (P)

    in the — de la mañana (4B)

mosque la mezquita (4A)

mother la madre (mamá) (5A)

mountains las montañas (4A)

mouse (computer) el ratón (2B)

mouth la boca (P)

movie la película (9A)

    to see a — ver una película (4A)

    — theater el cine (4A)

to **mow the lawn** cortar el césped (6B)

Mr. (el) señor (Sr.) (P)

Mrs. (la) señora (Sra.) (P)

much: so — tanto (7A)

museum el museo (8A)

music:

    to listen to — escuchar música (1A)

    —al program el programa musical (9A)

must deber (3B)

    one — hay que (8B)

my mi (2B); mis (5A)

    — name is . . . Me llamo . . . (P)

mystery la película policíaca (9A)

N

name:

    My — is . . . Me llamo . . . (P)

    What is your —? ¿Cómo te llamas? (P)

    What's his / her —? ¿Cómo se llama? (1B)

napkin la servilleta (5B)

national park el parque nacional (8A)

near cerca (de) (6B)

neat ordenado, -a (1B)

necessary: It's —. Es necesario. (8B)

necklace el collar (7B)

to **need**

    I — necesito (2A)

    I — . . . Me falta(n) . . . (5B)

    you — necesitas (2A)

neighborhood el barrio (8B)

neither . . . nor ni . . . ni (1A)

never nunca (3A)

new nuevo, -a (7A)

news program el programa de noticias (9A)

newspaper el periódico (8B)

next to al lado de (2B)

nice simpático, -a (1B)

night:

    at — de la noche (4B)

    last — anoche (7B)

night table la mesita (6A)

nine nueve (P)

nine hundred novecientos, -as (7A)

nineteen diecinueve (P)

ninety noventa (P)

ninth noveno, -a (2A)

nose la nariz, *pl.* las narices (P)

not . . . or ni . . . ni (1A)

notebook el cuaderno (P)

nothing nada (P)

November noviembre (P)

now ahora (5B)

O

o'clock:

    at eight — a las ocho (4B)

    at one — a la una (4B)

October octubre (P)

of de (2B)

    — course por supuesto (3A)

office (home) el despacho (6B)

often a menudo (8B)

Oh! What a shame / pity! ¡Ay! ¡Qué pena! (4B)

okay regular (P)

old viejo, -a (5B)

    He / She is / They are . . . years —. Tiene(n) . . . años. (5A)

    How — is / are . . . ? ¿Cuántos años tiene(n) . . . ? (5A)

    —er mayor (5A)

    —er man el anciano (8B)

    —er people los ancianos (8B)

    —er woman la anciana (8B)

on en (2B)

    — Mondays, on Tuesdays . . . los lunes, los martes . . . (4A)

— top of encima de (2B)

— weekends los fines de semana (4A)

one uno (un), -a (P)

    at — (o'clock) a la una (4B)

one hundred cien (P)

one must hay que (8B)

onion la cebolla (3B)

online en la Red (7B)

    to be — estar en línea (9B)

only sólo (5A)

to **open** abrir (5A)

opinion:

    in my — para mí (6A)

    in your — para ti (6A)

or o (1A)

orange anaranjado, -a (6A)

    — juice el jugo de naranja (3A)

to **order** pedir (e → i) (5B)

other otro, -a (5B)

others los / las demás (8B)

our nuestro(s), -a(s) (5A)

own propio, -a (6A)

P _____

painting el cuadro (6A)

pants los pantalones (7A)

paper: sheet of — la hoja de papel (P)

parents los padres (5A)

park el parque (4A)

    amusement — el parque de diversiones (8A)

    national — el parque nacional (8A)

party la fiesta (4B)

pastries los pasteles (3B)

patient paciente (1B)

to **pay (for)** pagar (por) (7B)

peas los guisantes (3B)

pen el bolígrafo (P)

pencil el lápiz, *pl.* los lápices (P)

    — sharpener el sacapuntas, *pl.* los sacapuntas (2B)

people la gente (8B)

    older — los ancianos (8B)

---

pepper la pimienta (5B)

perfume el perfume (7B)

person la persona (5A)

phone: to talk on the — hablar por teléfono (1A)

photo la foto (5A)

    to take —s sacar fotos (5A)

physical education class la clase de educación física (2A)

piano lesson (class) la lección, *pl.* las lecciones de piano (4A)

pink rosado, -a (6A)

piñata la piñata (5A)

pizza la pizza (3A)

place el lugar (8A)

to **place** poner (6B)

to **plan** pensar (e → ie) (7A)

plastic el plástico (8B)

plate el plato (5B)

play la obra de teatro (8A)

to **play** jugar (a) (u → ue) *(games, sports)* (4B); tocar *(an instrument)* (1A)

    to — baseball jugar al béisbol (4B)

    to — basketball jugar al básquetbol (4B)

    to — football jugar al fútbol americano (4B)

    to — golf jugar al golf (4B)

    to — soccer jugar al fútbol (4B)

    to — sports practicar deportes (1A)

    to — tennis jugar al tenis (4B)

    to — the guitar tocar la guitarra (1A)

    to — video games jugar videojuegos (1A)

    to — volleyball jugar al vóleibol (4B)

please por favor (P)

to **please very much** encantar (9A)

pleased to meet you mucho gusto (P)

pool la piscina (4A)

poor pobre (8B)

---

possession la posesión, *pl.* las posesiones (6A)

poster el cartel (2B)

potatoes las papas (3B)

practical práctico, -a (2A)

to **prefer** preferir (e → ie) (7A)

    I — (yo) prefiero (3B)

    I — to . . . (a mí) me gusta más . . . (1A)

    you — (tú) prefieres (3B)

to **prepare** preparar (5A)

present el regalo (5A)

presentation la presentación, *pl.* las presentaciones (9B)

pretty bonito, -a (6A)

price el precio (7A)

primary school la escuela primaria (8B)

problem el problema (8B)

program el programa (9A)

purple morado, -a (6A)

purse el bolso (7B)

to **put** poner (6B)

    I — (yo) pongo (6B)

    — *(command)* pon (6B)

    you — (tú) pones (6B)

Q _____

quarter past y cuarto *(in telling time)* (P)

quickly rápidamente (9B)

R _____

rain: It's —ing. Llueve. (P)

rather bastante (6B)

to **read magazines** leer revistas (1A)

realistic realista (9A)

reality program el programa de la vida real (9A)

Really? ¿De veras? (9A)

to **receive** recibir (6B)

to **recycle** reciclar (8B)

recycling center el centro de reciclaje (8B)

red rojo, -a (6A)

    —-haired pelirrojo, -a (5B)

to **relax** descansar (8A)

report el informe (9B)

reserved reservado, -a (1B)

to **rest** descansar (8A)

restaurant el restaurante (4A)

to **return** regresar (8A)

rice el arroz (3B)

rich rico, -a (5B)

to **ride:**

　　to — a bicycle montar en bicicleta (1A)

　　to — horseback montar a caballo (8A)

right: to the — (of) a la derecha (de) (6A)

Right? ¿Verdad? (3A)

ring el anillo (7B)

river el río (8B)

road la calle (8B)

romantic movie la película romántica (9A)

room el cuarto (6B)

　　to straighten up the — arreglar el cuarto (6B)

rug la alfombra (6A)

to **run** correr (1A)

s

sack la bolsa (8B)

sad triste (4B)

salad la ensalada (3A)

　　fruit — la ensalada de frutas (3A)

salesperson el dependiente, la dependienta (7A)

salt la sal (5B)

same mismo, -a (6A)

sandwich: ham and cheese — el sándwich de jamón y queso (3A)

Saturday sábado (P)

sausage la salchicha (3A)

to **say** decir (8B)

　　How do you —? ¿Cómo se dice? (P)

　　You — . . . Se dice . . . (P)

　　You don't —! ¡No me digas! (4A)

scared: to be — (of) tener miedo (de) (9B)

schedule el horario (2A)

science:

　　— class la clase de ciencias naturales (2A)

　　— fiction movie la película de ciencia ficción (9A)

screen: computer — la pantalla (2B)

to **scuba dive** bucear (8A)

sea el mar (8A)

to **search (for)** buscar (9B)

season la estación, *pl.* las estaciones (P)

second segundo, -a (2A)

　　— floor el primer piso (6B)

to **see** ver (8A)

　　Let's — A ver . . . (2A)

　　— you later! ¡Nos vemos!, Hasta luego. (P)

　　— you tomorrow. Hasta mañana. (P)

　　to — a movie ver una película (4A)

to **sell** vender (7B)

to **send** enviar (i → í) (9B)

to **separate** separar (8B)

September septiembre (P)

serious serio, -a (1B)

to **serve** servir (e → i) (9B)

to **set the table** poner la mesa (6B)

seven siete (P)

seven hundred setecientos, -as (7A)

seventeen diecisiete (P)

seventh séptimo, -a (2A)

seventy setenta (P)

to **share** compartir (3A)

she ella (1B)

sheet of paper la hoja de papel (P)

shelf el estante (6A)

ship el barco (8A)

shirt la camisa (7A)

　　T- — la camiseta (7A)

shoe store la zapatería (7B)

shoes los zapatos (7A)

short bajo, -a *(stature)*; corto, -a *(length)* (5B)

shorts los pantalones cortos (7A)

should deber (3B)

show el programa (9A)

to **show** + *movie or TV program* dar (9A)

shy reservado, -a (1B)

sick enfermo, -a (4B)

silly tonto, -a (9A)

to **sing** cantar (1A)

sir (el) señor (Sr.) (P)

sister la hermana (5A)

site: Web — el sitio Web (9B)

six seis (P)

six hundred seiscientos, -as (7A)

sixteen dieciséis (P)

sixth sexto, -a (2A)

sixty sesenta (P)

to **skate** patinar (1A)

to **skateboard** montar en monopatín (1A)

to **ski** esquiar (i → í) (1A)

skirt la falda (7A)

to **sleep** dormir (o → ue) (6A)

sleepy: to be — tener sueño (5B)

slide la diapositiva (9B)

small pequeño, -a (6A)

to **snorkel** bucear (8A)

snow: It's —ing. Nieva. (P)

so much tanto (7A)

so-so regular (P)

soap opera la telenovela (9A)

soccer: to play — jugar al fútbol (4B)

sociable sociable (1B)

social studies class la clase de ciencias sociales (2A)

socks los calcetines (7A)

soft drink el refresco (3A)

software el software (7B)

some unos, -as (2B)

something algo (3B)

sometimes a veces (1B)

son el hijo (5A)

　　—s; —(s) and daughter(s) los hijos (5A)

song la canción, *pl.* las canciones (9B)

sorry: I'm —. Lo siento. (4B)

sound (stereo) system el equipo de sonido (6A)

soup: vegetable — la sopa de verduras (3A)

souvenirs los recuerdos (8A)

   to buy — comprar recuerdos (8A)

spaghetti los espaguetis (3B)

Spanish class la clase de español (2A)

to **spell:**

   How is . . . spelled? ¿Cómo se escribe . . . ? (P)

   It's spelled . . . Se escribe . . . (P)

to **spend time with friends** pasar tiempo con amigos (1A)

spoon la cuchara (5B)

sports:

   to play — practicar deportes (1A)

   —-minded deportista (1B)

   — program el programa deportivo (9A)

spring la primavera (P)

stadium el estadio (8A)

stairs, stairway la escalera (6B)

to **start** empezar (e → ie) (9A)

to **stay: I — at home.** Me quedo en casa. (4A)

stepbrother el hermanastro (5A)

stepfather el padrastro (5A)

stepmother la madrastra (5A)

stepsister la hermanastra (5A)

stereo system el equipo de sonido (6A)

stomach el estómago (P)

store la tienda (7A)

   book— la librería (7B)

   clothing — la tienda de ropa (7A)

   department — el almacén, *pl.* los almacenes (7B)

   discount — la tienda de descuentos (7B)

   household appliance — la tienda de electrodomésticos (7B)

jewelry — la joyería (7B)

shoe — la zapatería (7B)

story el piso (6B)

stories: to write — escribir cuentos (1A)

to **straighten up the room** arreglar el cuarto (6B)

strawberries las fresas (3A)

street la calle (8B)

student el / la estudiante (P)

studious estudioso, -a (1B)

to **study** estudiar (2A)

stupid tonto, -a (9A)

sugar el azúcar (5B)

suit el traje (7A)

summer el verano (P)

to **sunbathe** tomar el sol (8A)

Sunday domingo (P)

sunglasses los anteojos de sol (7B)

sunny: It's —. Hace sol. (P)

to **surf the Web** navegar en la Red (9B)

sweater el suéter (7A)

sweatshirt la sudadera (7A)

to **swim** nadar (1A)

swimsuit el traje de baño (7A)

synagogue la sinagoga (4A)

T _____

T-shirt la camiseta (7A)

table la mesa (2B)

   to set the — poner la mesa (6B)

to **take** llevar (8B)

   to — a course tomar un curso (9B)

   to — out the trash sacar la basura (6B)

   to — photos sacar fotos (5A)

talented talentoso, -a (1B)

to **talk** hablar (2A)

   to — on the phone hablar por teléfono (1A)

tall alto, -a (5B)

tasty sabroso, -a (3B); rico, -a (5B)

tea el té (3A)

   iced — el té helado (3A)

to **teach** enseñar (2A)

teacher el profesor, la profesora (P)

technology / computers la tecnología (2A)

technology / computer class la clase de tecnología (2A)

television: to watch — ver la tele (1A)

television set el televisor (6A)

to **tell** decir (8B)

   — me *(command)* dime (8A)

temple el templo (4A)

ten diez (P)

tennis: to play — jugar al tenis (4B)

tenth décimo, -a (2A)

thank you gracias (P)

that que (5A); ese, esa (7A)

   —'s why por eso (9A)

the el, la (1B); los, las (2B)

   — best el / la mejor, los / las mejores (6A)

   — worst el / la peor, los / las peores (6A)

theater el teatro (8A)

   movie — el cine (4A)

their su, sus (5A)

them las, los *dir. obj. pron.* (7B); les *ind. obj. pron.* (8B)

then entonces (4B)

there allí (2B)

   — is / are hay (P, 2B)

therefore por eso (9A)

these estos, estas (7A)

they ellos, ellas (2A)

thing la cosa (6A)

to **think** pensar (e → ie) (7A)

   I don't — so. Creo que no. (3B)

   I — . . . Creo que . . . (3B)

   I — so. Creo que sí. (3B)

   What do you — (about it)? ¿Qué te parece? (9B)

third tercer (tercero), -a (2A)

third floor el segundo piso (6B)

thirsty: I'm —. Tengo sed. (3B)

thirteen trece (P)

thirty treinta (P); y media *(in telling time)* (P)

thirty-one treinta y uno (P)

this este, esta (7A)

  — afternoon esta tarde (4B)

  — evening esta noche (4B)

  — weekend este fin de semana (4B)

  What is —? ¿Qué es esto? (2B)

those esos, esas (7A)

thousand: a — mil (7A)

three tres (P)

three hundred trescientos, -as (7A)

three-ring binder la carpeta de argollas (2A)

Thursday jueves (P)

ticket el boleto (8A)

tie la corbata (7B)

time:

  At what —? ¿A qué hora? (4B)

  free — el tiempo libre (4A)

  to spend — with friends pasar tiempo con amigos (1A)

  What — is it? ¿Qué hora es? (P)

tired cansado, -a (4B)

to a *(prep.)* (4A)

  in order — para + *inf.* (4A)

  — the a la, al (4A)

  — the left (of) a la izquierda (de) (6A)

  — the right (of) a la derecha (de) (6A)

toast el pan tostado (3A)

today hoy (P)

tomatoes los tomates (3B)

tomorrow mañana (P)

  See you —. Hasta mañana. (P)

too también (1A); demasiado (4B)

  I do (like to) — a mí también (1A)

  me — a mí también (1A)

top: on — of encima de (2B)

touching emocionante (9A)

toy el juguete (8B)

train el tren (8A)

to travel viajar (8A)

tree el árbol (8A)

tremendous tremendo, -a (8A)

trip el viaje (8A)

Tuesday martes (P)

  on —s los martes (4A)

TV channel el canal (9A)

twelve doce (P)

twenty veinte (P)

twenty-one veintiuno (veintiún) (P)

two dos (P)

two hundred doscientos, -as (7A)

U

Ugh! ¡Uf! (7B)

ugly feo, -a (6A)

uncle el tío (5A)

uncles; uncle(s) and aunt(s) los tíos (5A)

underneath debajo de (2B)

to understand comprender (3A)

unforgettable inolvidable (8B)

us: (to / for) — nos *ind. obj. pron.* (8B)

to use:

  It's —d for . . . Sirve para . . . (9B)

  to — the computer usar la computadora (1A)

  What's it —d for? ¿Para qué sirve? (9B)

used usado, -a (8B)

useful:

  to be — servir (9B)

  is — for sirve para (9B)

V

vacation: to go on — ir de vacaciones (8A)

to vacuum pasar la aspiradora (6B)

vegetable soup la sopa de verduras (3A)

very muy (1B)

  — well muy bien (P)

video el video (5A)

video games: to play — jugar videojuegos (1A)

to videotape hacer un video (5A)

violent violento, -a (9A)

to visit visitar (8A)

  to — chat rooms visitar salones de chat (9B)

volleyball: to play — jugar al vóleibol (4B)

volunteer el voluntario, la voluntaria (8B)

  — work el trabajo voluntario (8B)

W

waiter, waitress el camarero, la camarera (5B)

to walk caminar (3B)

wall la pared (6A)

wallet la cartera (7B)

to want querer (e → ie) (7A); desear (5B)

  I — (yo) quiero (4B)

  you — (tú) quieres (4B)

warm: to be — tener calor (5B)

was fue (8B)

to wash lavar (6B)

  to — the car lavar el coche (6B)

  to — the clothes lavar la ropa (6B)

  to — the dishes lavar los platos (6B)

wastepaper basket la papelera (2B)

watch el reloj pulsera (7B)

to watch television ver la tele (1A)

water el agua *f.* (3A)

we nosotros, -as (2A)

to wear llevar (7A)

weather: What's the — like? ¿Qué tiempo hace? (P)

Web:

  to surf the — navegar en la Red (9B)

  — page la página Web (9B)

  — site el sitio Web (9B)

Wednesday miércoles (P)

week la semana (P)

  last — la semana pasada (7B)

weekend:

on —s los fines de semana (4A)

this — este fin de semana (4B)

welcome: You're —. De nada. (5B)

well bien (P); pues *(to indicate pause)* (1A)

very — muy bien (P)

What? ¿Qué?, ¿Cuál? (3A)

— **are you doing?** ¿Qué estás haciendo? (6B)

— **are you like?** ¿Cómo eres? (1B)

(At) — time? ¿A qué hora? (4B)

— **color . . . ?** ¿De qué color . . . ? (6A)

— **day is today?** ¿Qué día es hoy? (P)

— **did you do?** ¿Qué hiciste? (8A)

— **do you like better (prefer) to do?** ¿Qué te gusta hacer más? (1A)

— **do you like to do?** ¿Qué te gusta hacer? (1A)

— **do you think (about it)?** ¿Qué te parece? (9B)

— **does . . . mean?** ¿Qué quiere decir . . . ? (P)

— **else?** ¿Qué más? (8B)

— **happened to you?** ¿Qué te pasó? (8A)

— **is she / he like?** ¿Cómo es? (1B)

— **is the date?** ¿Cuál es la fecha? (P)

— **is this?** ¿Qué es esto? (2B)

— **is your name?** ¿Cómo te llamas? (P)

— **kind of . . . ?** ¿Qué clase de . . . ? (9A)

— **time is it?** ¿Qué hora es? (P)

— **would you like?** ¿Qué desean (Uds.)? (5B)

—**'s happening?** ¿Qué pasa? (P)

—**'s his / her name?** ¿Cómo se llama? (1B)

—**'s it (used) for?** ¿Para qué sirve? (9B)

—**'s the weather like?** ¿Qué tiempo hace? (P)

What!:

— **a good / nice idea!** ¡Qué buena idea! (4B)

— **a shame / pity!** ¡Qué pena! (4B)

When? ¿Cuándo? (4A)

Where? ¿Dónde? (2B)

— **are you from?** ¿De dónde eres? (4A)

(To) —? ¿Adónde? (4A)

whether si (6B)

Which? ¿Cuál? (3A)

— **ones?** ¿Cuáles? (6B)

white blanco, -a (6A)

who que (5A)

Who? ¿Quién? (2A)

Why? ¿Por qué? (3B)

wife la esposa (5A)

Will you bring me . . . ? ¿Me trae . . . ? (5B)

window la ventana (2B)

winter el invierno (P)

with con (3A)

— **me** conmigo (4B)

— **my / your friends** con mis / tus amigos (4A)

— **whom?** ¿Con quién? (4A)

— **you** contigo (4B)

without sin (3A)

woman la mujer (5B)

older woman la anciana (8B)

work el trabajo (4A)

volunteer — el trabajo voluntario (8B)

to **work** trabajar (1A)

worse than peor(es) que (6A)

worst: the — el / la peor, los / las peores (6A)

Would you like . . . ? ¿Te gustaría . . . ? (4B)

to **write:**

to — **e-mail** escribir por correo electrónico (9B)

to — **stories** escribir cuentos (1A)

Y ——————————

yard el jardín, *pl.* los jardines (8B)

year el año (P)

He / She is / They are . . . —s old. Tiene(n) . . . años. (5A)

last — el año pasado (7B)

yellow amarillo, -a (6A)

yes sí (1A)

yesterday ayer (7B)

yogurt el yogur (3A)

you *fam. sing.* tú (2A); *formal sing.* usted (Ud.) (2A); *fam. pl.* vosotros, -as (2A); *formal pl.* ustedes (Uds.) (2A); *fam. after prep.* ti (1A); *sing. ind. obj. pron.* te (8B); *pl. fam. ind. obj. pron.* os (8B); *ind. obj. pron.* le, les (8B)

And — ? ¿Y a ti? (1A)

for — para ti (6A)

to / for — *fam. pl.* os (8B)

to / for — *fam. sing.* te (8B)

with — contigo (4B)

—**don't say!** ¡No me digas! (4A)

— **say . . .** Se dice . . . (P)

young joven (5B)

— **boy / girl** el niño, la niña (8B)

— **man** el joven (5B)

— **woman** la joven (5B)

—**er** menor (5A)

your *fam.* tu (2B); *fam.* tus, vuestro(s), -a(s) (5A); *formal* su, sus (5A)

Yuck! ¡Uf! (7B)

Z ——————————

zero cero (P)

zoo el zoológico (8A)

Grammar Index

Structures are most often presented first in *A primera vista*, where they are practiced lexically. They are then explained later in a *Gramática* section or a *Nota*. Lightface numbers refer to the pages where structures are initially presented or, after explanation, where student reminders occur. **Boldface numbers** refer to pages where structures are explained or are otherwise highlighted.

a:
   + indirect object 250, **264**
   personal **236**
   personal, after **conocer 324**
   with **ir** + infinitive 26
aburrir 282, **296**
acabar de 286, **294**
accent marks:
   in preterite **196, 230**
   over weak vowels 229
adjectives:
   agreement and formation 8, 20, 71, 104, 140
   comparative 32, 94–95, **106,** 122
   demonstrative 157, 159–160, **172,** 182
   ending in **-ísimo** 74
   plural. *See* adjectives: agreement and formation
   position of 9
   possessive 35, **48,** 60
   superlative 94, **110,** 122
adverbs **318**
affirmative **tú** commands 130, **138,** 152
age 32, 42, 60
aprender 230
-ar verbs:
   present 13
   preterite 187, **196, 198,** 214
   spelling-changing 187, 189, **198,** 214
articles, definite, with **de** 15

-car and **-gar** verbs, preterite **198,** 214
commands (**tú**) 130, **138,** 152
comparison 94–95, **106,** 122, **291**
conocer 313, **324,** 334

dar 127, 129, **136,** 152
   preterite 254, **266,** 278
dates **200**
de:
   + definite article 15
   possessive 48
decir 251, **262,** 278
derivation of words 239, 295
diminutives **52**
direct object **202.** *See also* pronouns
   with personal **a 236**
doler 296
dormir 98, **112,** 122

encantar 19, 44, **296**
-er verbs:
   present 19
   preterite 219, **230,** 246
estar 14, 80, 193
   use of in present progressive 130, **142,** 152
   vs. **ser 78, 82,** 101
Exploración del lenguaje:
   Adjectives ending in **-ísimo 74**
   Diminutives **52**
   Nonverbal language **166**
   Nouns that end in **-dad, -tad, -ción,** and **-sión 259**
   Nouns that end in **-dor** and **-dora 136**
   Nouns that end in **-ería 195**
   Nouns that end in **-io** and **-eo 239**
   Using **-mente** to form adverbs **318**

Using root words **114**
Words of Greek and Arabic origin **295**

faltar 68, **74, 296**

gender:
   of adjectives agreeing with nouns 48, 104, 140
   of pronouns 202
gustar 7, 18, 44, **296**

hace + time 187, 197
hacer:
   preterite 254, **266,** 278
   tú command form 130, **138,** 152
hay + **que** 254

indirect object **264.** *See also* pronouns
infinitive 7
   + object pronoun **202,** 324
   after **acabar de** 286, **294**
   after **gustar 296**
   after **ir a** 26
   after **pensar / querer / preferir 168**
   after **poder** 113
interesar 282, **296**
interrogative words 25
ir 24
   + **a** + infinitive 26
   preterite 218, **232,** 246
   with future meaning 26
-ir verbs:
   present 19
   preterite 218, **230,** 246

jugar 27
   preterite **198**

Acknowledgments

Maps All maps created by XNR Productions.

Photographs Every effort has been made to secure permission and provide appropriate credit for photographic material. The publisher deeply regrets any omission and pledges to correct errors called to its attention in subsequent editions.

Unless otherwise acknowledged, all photographs are the property of Pearson Education, Inc.

Photo locators denoted as follows: Top (T), Center (C), Bottom (B), Left (L), Right (R), Background (Bkgd)

Cover (L) Tetra Images/Getty Images; **(CL)** Bernardo Galmarini/ Alamy Images; **(CR)** Danita Delimont/Alamy Images; **(R)** SuperStock/Alamy Images

Front Matter v Corbis Flirt/Alamy Images; **vii** (TR) Alamy, (BR, BC) NASA, (BL) StockTrek/SuperStock; **xiv** (Inset) Bettmann/ Corbis, (Bkgd) José Fusta Raga/Corbis; **xv** (Inset) ©Phil Schermeister/ Corbis; **xvi** Danny Lehman/Corbis; **xviii** (Bkgd) ©David Zimmerman/ Corbis, (BL) Exactostock/SuperStock; **xx** Shutterstock; **xxii** Michael Hilton/Alamy Images; **xxiv** (Inset) ©Mark L. Stephenson, (Bkgd) ©Paul Hardy/Corbis; **xxv** (Inset) ©José Fuste Raga/Corbis; **xxvi** (Bkgd) ©Craig Tuttle/Corbis, (Inset) ©Strauss/Curtis/Corbis

1 (BR) ©Ron Watts/Corbis, (BL) Corbis; **2** ©Hisham Ibrahim/PhotoV/ Alamy Images; **12** Todd Wright/Alamy; **26** Corbis; **28** ©Blend Images/ SuperStock, ©imagebroker/Alamy Images; **29** ©dbimages/Alamy Images; **30** ©Blend Images/SuperStock; **31** (Inset) Carmen L. Garza; **37** (TL, BR, BL) Getty Images, (TC) Judith Collins/Alamy Images; **39** Carmen L. Garza, (T) Dick Luria/Taxi/Dick Luria; **40** ©Gardel Bertrand/PhotoLibrary Group, Ltd.; **43** (BL) ©DK Images; **45** eStock Photo, (CR) Jimmy Dorantes/Latin Focus; **46** AFP/Getty Images; **47** Art Resource, NY, Bridgeman Art Library; **52** (T) ©DK Images; **53** ©Felipe Rodríguez/Alamy Images, Felipe Rodríguez/Alamy Images; **54** Joho/Alamy; **55** (BR) Corbis/SuperStock, Collection 67/GlowImages/ Alamy; **56** (T) ©David Seawell/Corbis; **57** (B) SuperStock; **62** ©Gary Latham/Alamy Images; **63** (Inset) Erich Lessing/Art Resource, NY; **72** DDB Stock Photography; **73** (TR) David R. Frazier/PhotoLibrary Group, Inc.; **75** ©Danita Delimont/Alamy Images; **79** michaeljung/Fotolia **81** (T, C) Jimmy Dorantes/Latin Focus, (Inset) NewsCom; **82** (B) Latin Focus; **84** ©Megan Bowers/Latin Focus; **85** (B) Bettmann/Corbis, (T) Danny Lehman/Corbis; **86** (B) NewsCom, (C) Peter Menzel/Peter Menzel/menzelphoto; **87** ©Rob Wilson/Shutterstock; **92** ©William Panzer/Alamy Images; **93** (Inset) Peter Horree/Alamy Images; **103** (T) PhotoLibrary Group, Inc.; **108** ROBYN BECK/AFP/Getty Images/ Newscom; **111** AGE Fotostock; **112** ©Jimmy Dorantes/Latin Focus; **114** ©GoGo Images Corporation/Alamy; **115** Travis Houston/ Shutterstock; **118** SuperStock; **119** ©B2M Productions/Getty Images, (C) Bonnie Kamin/PhotoEdit, Inc.; **135** SuperStock; **144** ©Chad Ehlers/Alamy Images; **148** (BR) ©Mark Boulton/Alamy Images, (TR) SuperStock; **149** (CR) SuperStock; **154** ©John Mitchell/Alamy Images; **155** (BR) Art Resource, NY; **162** Courtesy Marlborough Gallery, NY; **163** Getty Images; **165** (TR) ©Jimmy Dorantes/ Latin Focus, (Inset) JTB Photo Communications, Inc./Alamy Images; **170** Rubberball/Rubberball/Corbis; **175** (CR) NewsCom, (BR) Shutterstock; **176** (BL) ©Alberto Lowe/Reuters/Landov LLC, (TR) ©Dixon Hamby/Alamy, (BR) ©IFA Bilderteam/eStock Photo; **177** (B) ©Stringer/Xinhua/Photoshot/NewsCom, (TL) eStock Photo; **178** Alamy Images; **179** (TR) ©Javier Larrea/AGE Fotostock; **192** Alamy Images; **193** l; **195** (TR) ©Ilene MacDonald/Alamy, (BL) ©Peter Titmuss/Alamy Images, (BR) DDB Stock Photography, (CR) PhotoEdit; **198** Alamy Images; **199** Shutterstock; **201** (TR) ©itsallgood/Fotolia, (TC) ©San Diego Historical Society Photo Collection, (TL) SuperStock; **205** ©age fotostock/Robert Harding World Imagery; **206** Alamy Images; **208** (T, B) PhotoEdit; **209** (TL) ©David Zanzinger/Alamy Images, (TR) ©M. Timothy O'Keefe/Alamy Images; **210** ©John Arnold Images Ltd./Alamy Images; **211** (BR) PhotoEdit; **216** ©Jordi Cami/Alamy Images; **217** (Inset) NewsCom; **224** Bettmann/Corbis; **226** ©David R. Frazier Photolibrary, Inc./Alamy Images; **227** ImageState; **228** (CR) ©Dorothy Alexander/Alamy Images, (B) ©Nina Raingold/Getty Images, (BR) ©Russell Gordon/Danita Delimont, Agent, (C, BC) ©Salatiel Barragan/Latin Focus, (CL) ©Stringer/Mexico/Reuters/Landov LLC, Bettmann/Corbis; **229** DDB Stock Photography; **231** Ian Dagnall/Alamy Images; **235** (B) Shutterstock; **236** ©Bly Photography; **238** Paul Harris/Stone/Getty Images; **239** SuperStock; **240** (CL) ©Kirill Trifonov/Shutterstock, (CL) ©Michele Burgess, (B) Alamy Images; **241** (TR) ©Gavin Hellier/Getty Images, (C) Alamy Images; **242** (T) ©Bly Photography; **243** Corbis; **248** ©Jeff Greenberg/Alamy Images; **256** AGE Fotostock; **257** SuperStock; **258** (CL) ©Michael Newman/PhotoEdit, (R, L) PhotoEdit, (TCR) Rido/Shutterstock; **259** (B) Courtesy of ReSurge International, (TL) SuperStock; **261** (B) ©Jimmy Dorantes/Latin Focus, (T) ©Puerto Rico Conservation Foundation; **264** Alamy Images; **267** (T) ©Fernando Alda/Corbis, (B) National Geographic Image Collection; **269** ©Marcelo Salinas/Latin Focus; **270** SuperStock; **271** (T) Shutterstock; **272** PhotoEdit; **273** (T) ©A. Ramey/PhotoEdit, (B) SuperStock; **274** (T) ©Tina Manley/Alamy Images, (B) Chuck Place Photography; **275** (R) PhotoEdit; **280** ©Universal Pictures/Strike ENT/ Beacon Communications LLC/Album/NewsCom; **281** (Inset) Art Resource, NY; **291** (R, L) PhotoEdit; **294** Bettmann/Corbis; **296** Alamy; **297** epa european pressphoto agency b.v./Alamy; **298** ©Associated Press; **300** (B) ©Michel Bussy/Getty Images, (T) ImageState; **301** ©Andre Jenny/Alamy Images; **303** ©David R. Frazier Photolibrary, Inc./Alamy Images; **308** ©Elmer Martínez/AFP/Getty Images/ NewsCom; **309** (Inset) Art Resource, NY; **316** ©MELBA PHOTO AGENCY/Alamy; **317** (B) ©MELBA PHOTO AGENCY/Alamy; **318** ©Michael Newman/PhotoEdit, Inc.; **322** ©Dorothy Alexander/Alamy Images, Hect/Shutterstock; **327** (CL) ©John Vachon/Corbis, (B) Fancy/ Alamy; **330** (B) ©i love images/Alamy; **331** ©James Davis/ImageState; **336** Corbis; **337** (R) ©i love images/Alamy, (L) Shutterstock

Text

Bayard Presse SA

"A sus teclados, listos…¡a navegar!" Text by Anne-Laure Fournier–Le Ray © Images Doc/Reportero Doc, Bayard Jeunesse, 2002. Reprinted by permission.

La Fundación Puertorriqueña de Conservación

"Reduce—Reusa—Recicla" from LA FUNDACIÓN PUERTORRIQUEÑA DE CONSERVACIÓN & Logo of LA FUNDACIÓN PUERTORRIQUEÑA DE CONSERVACIÓN, Copyright © 2001. Used by permission of La Fundación Puertorriqueña de Conservación.

Muy Interesante

"¿Quién hace las tareas?" by Matilde de la Vara from *Muy Interesante–* Marzo 2002 No. 250. Published by GyJ España Ediciones, S.L. S en C. Used by permission.

PARS International Corporation

"¡Apágala!" from *Time for Kids,* April 12, 2002, Vol. 7, No. 22. Copyright © 2002 Time Inc. Used under license.

Note: Every effort has been made to locate the copyright owner of material reproduced in this component. Omissions brought to our attention will be corrected in subsequent editions.